ENCYCLOPEDIA OF THE GREAT DEPRESSION

EDITORIAL BOARD

ENCYCLOPEDIA OF THE

GREAT DEPRESSION

VOLUME 2: L–Z, INDEX

ROBERT S. McELVAINE
EDITOR IN CHIEF

MACMILLAN
REFERENCE
USA™

THOMSON
————✦————
GALE

New York • Detroit • San Diego • San Francisco • Cleveland • New Haven, Conn. • Waterville, Maine • London • Munich

Encyclopedia of The Great Depression
Robert S. McElvaine, Editor in Chief

LIBRARY OF CONGRESS CATALOGING-IN-PUBLICATION DATA

Encyclopedia of the Great Depression / Robert McElvaine, editor in chief.
  p. cm.
    Includes bibliographical references and index.
    ISBN 0-02-865686-5 (set : hardcover)—ISBN 0-02-865687-3 (v. 1)—
    ISBN 0-02-865688-1 (v. 2)
    1. United States—History—1933–1945—Encyclopedias. 2. United
    States—History—1919–1933—Encyclopedias. 3. United States—
    Economic Conditions—1918–1945—Encyclopedias. 4. Depressions—
    1929—United States—Encyclopedias. 5. New Deal, 1933–1939—
    Encyclopedias. I. McElvaine, Robert S., 1947–

E806.E63 2004
973.91'6'03—dc21
2003010292

This title is also available as an e-book.
ISBN 0-02-865908-2

Contact your Gale sales representative for ordering information.

Printed in the United States of America
10 9 8 7 6 5 4 3 2

LABOR'S NON-PARTISAN LEAGUE

With the approach of the presidential election of 1936, labor unions in the United States offered President Franklin D. Roosevelt their undivided support. Never before in American history had a president been so sympathetic to their needs and so willing to convert that sympathy into protective legislation. The National Industrial Recovery Act of 1933 had provided the country's first minimum wage law, had guaranteed the right of unions to bargain collectively, and had outlawed "yellow-dog" contracts, which required employees to pledge that they would not join a union. The National Labor Relations Act of 1935 went even further, establishing the National Labor Relations Board as an independent federal agency with the power to investigate disputes between labor and management, and enforce legal and judicial regulations regarding labor union rights. The 1935 act also guaranteed majority rule and exclusive representation, outlined unfair practices, and required management to bargain with the labor unions of their employees' choice. William Green, head of the American Federation of Labor (AFL), found the National Labor Relations Act of 1935 so extraordinary that he labeled it the "Magna Carta of the labor movement in the United States."

Not surprisingly, such major labor unions as the AFL and the Committee (later Congress) of Industrial Organizations (CIO) and most of their constituent members considered Roosevelt's reelection critically important to the labor movement. Roosevelt was only too eager to get their support. In April 1936, John L. Lewis, head of the United Mine Workers as well as the CIO, founded Labor's Non-Partisan League. Sidney Hillman of the Amalgamated Clothing Workers union and George L. Berry of the Printing Pressman joined Lewis in the effort. Labor's Non-Partisan League, Lewis bluntly said over and over again, existed for one reason: to secure reelection of the president. To make sure that the League did not appear to be a front organization for the Democratic Party, the term *Non-Partisan* was used, but few were fooled. Labor's Non-Partisan League raised more than $1 million for the president's reelection campaign. On election day, the League provided funds to get Democratic voters to the polls. Finally, the League established the American Labor Party in New York. Many socialists and other left-wing voters wanted Roosevelt reelected, but they were ideologically opposed to supporting the Democratic Party. When the American Labor Party nominated Roosevelt as its presidential candidate, left-wingers could cast a vote for Roosevelt without smudging their virtue.

The effectiveness of Labor's Non-Partisan League will never be accurately measured. Public support for President Roosevelt and the New Deal was already overwhelming. The last thing a substantial majority of Americans wanted in 1936 was to have a Republican back in the White House dismantling the New Deal. When the votes were tabulated, the president won with 27,252,869 popular votes to Landon's 16,674,665; at 523 to 8, the vote in the Electoral College was even more lopsided. William Lemke of the Union Party received 882,479 popular votes and no electoral votes. Labor's Non-Partisan League claimed that their assistance gave the president his margin of victory in Ohio, Illinois, and Indiana. The 1936 election, however, was the high water mark for the League. Leaders quickly fell into ideological squabbling, rendering the League useless in terms of marshaling political support.

John L. Lewis's decision in 1940 to oppose Roosevelt's reelection, and his endorsement of Republican nominee Wendell Willkie, spelled the demise of Labor's Non-Partisan League. In 1944, the CIO formed its own Political Action Committee, spelling the end of the league. Although Labor's Non-Partisan League had a short life span, its legacy—a constituency forming a political action committee to promote its interests—became standard in American politics.

See Also: AMERICAN FEDERATION OF LABOR (AFL); CONGRESS OF INDUSTRIAL ORGANIZATIONS (CIO); ELECTION OF 1936; ORGANIZED LABOR.

BIBLIOGRAPHY

Bernstein, Irving. *Turbulent Years: A History of the American Worker, 1933–1941.* 1970.

JAMES S. OLSON

LA FOLLETTE, PHILIP

Philip Fox ("Phil") La Follette (May 8, 1897–August 18, 1965), three-term governor of Wisconsin (1931–1933, 1935–1939), was one of the most creative and controversial politicians of the Depression era. In appearance, demeanor, and ambition, he resembled his father, Robert M. La Follette, Sr., a former Wisconsin governor and U.S. senator. Phil La Follette was educated in Madison and Washington, D.C., schools and at the University of Wisconsin, where he also obtained a law degree. After engaging in private practice, serving for two years as district attorney of Wisconsin's Dane County, and doing some teaching at the University of Wisconsin law school, La Follette was elected governor on the Republican ticket in 1930. Although he persuaded the legislature to pass the nation's first unemployment compensation law and several other significant measures, he, like many other incumbents that year, lost in his bid for reelection during the desperate economic circumstances of 1932. After spurning offers of a high-level job in Franklin Roosevelt's Democratic administration, he allied himself politically with the president during the early New Deal years. La Follette played the leading role in launching the new Wisconsin Progressive Party in 1934 and recaptured the governorship that fall, while his brother Bob went back to the U.S. Senate on the same ticket.

La Follette's focus during his second term as governor was on a massive public-works program. His cooperative relationship with Roosevelt enabled the state to administer federal relief monies outside the normal bureaucratic channels of the Works Progress Administration. During his third term, with Progressives commanding a tenuous majority in the legislature and amid great acrimony, La Follette rammed through measures for governmental reorganization, a labor relations act, an agricultural authority, and a public power plan that collectively constituted a "Little New Deal" for the state. Meanwhile, political ambition led him to distance himself from the president and launch the National Progressives of America in April 1938. The new party went nowhere and La Follette lost in his run for a fourth term that fall. After service on General Douglas MacArthur's staff during World War II, La Follette practiced law, dabbled in business and politics, and wrote his memoirs.

See Also: ELECTION OF 1930; LA FOLLETTE, ROBERT M., JR.; WISCONSIN PROGRESSIVE PARTY.

BIBLIOGRAPHY

La Follette, Philip F. Papers. State Historical Society of Wisconsin, Madison.

La Follette, Philip F. *Adventure in Politics: The Memoirs of Philip La Follette,* edited by Donald Young. 1970.

McCoy, Donald R. *Angry Voices: Left-of-Center Politics in the New Deal Era.* 1958.

Miller, John E. *Governor Philip F. La Follette, the Wisconsin Progressives, and the New Deal.* 1982.

JOHN E. MILLER

LA FOLLETTE, ROBERT M., JR.

Robert Marion ("Young Bob") La Follette, Jr., (February 6, 1895–February 24, 1953) was a prominent United States senator from Wisconsin. He replaced his illustrious father upon the latter's death in 1925 and was succeeded by another famous political figure, Joseph R. McCarthy, in 1947. During twenty-two years in Congress, La Follette became known as a hardworking legislative craftsman who was devoted to Senate tradition, gaining respect from colleagues and journalists. He and his younger brother, Wisconsin Governor Philip La Follette, carried on the La Follette progressive tradition in Wisconsin and dominated state politics during the 1930s.

La Follette attended the University of Wisconsin for two years, but health problems prevented him from graduating. He served as his father's chief aide in the Senate from 1919 until 1925, when, at the age of thirty, he became the youngest Senator since Henry Clay. Inheriting his father's progressive instincts, he emerged during the late 1920s as a major critic of conservative Republican policies and one of a group of liberal-minded Midwestern politicians referred to as the "sons of the wild jackass." During the Great Depression La Follette became a leading advocate of federal spending for public works and relief for the unemployed and a spokesman for national economic planning.

Though he often cooperated with the Roosevelt administration during the early New Deal, La Follette frequently criticized the president for moving too timidly in addressing the nation's social and economic problems. He played a major role in pass-

ing relief, public works, and tax legislation. In 1934, he somewhat reluctantly went along with the formation of a new state Progressive party, deserting the Republicans, and winning reelection to the Senate that fall. Between 1936 and 1940, as chairman of the La Follette Civil Liberties Committee, he investigated activities of businesses and other groups that were inhibiting labor's right to organize, earning considerable publicity for his efforts. A staunch isolationist before the Japanese attack on Pearl Harbor in December 1941, La Follette backed the war effort once the country entered World War II, becoming an early critic of the country's wartime ally the Soviet Union. Out of politics after 1947, La Follette died of a self-inflicted gunshot wound in 1953.

See Also: LA FOLLETTE, PHILIP; LA FOLLETTE CIVIL LIBERTIES COMMITTEE; MEMORIAL DAY MASSACRE; WISCONSIN PROGRESSIVE PARTY.

BIBLIOGRAPHY

Auerbach, Jerold S. *Labor and Liberty: The La Follette Committee and the New Deal.* 1966.

Johnson, Roger T. *Robert M. La Follette, Jr., and the Decline of the Progressive Party in Wisconsin.* 1964.

La Follette Family Papers. Manuscript Division. Library of Congress, Washington, D.C.

Maney, Patrick J. *"Young Bob" La Follette: A Biography of Robert M. La Follette, Jr., 1895–1953,* 2nd rev. edition. 2002.

JOHN E. MILLER

LA FOLLETTE CIVIL LIBERTIES COMMITTEE

The La Follette Civil Liberties Committee (1936–1940) was a subcommittee of the Senate Committee on Education and Labor set up to investigate the heavy-handed methods employers used to prevent labor unions from organizing and bargaining collectively. Chaired by Senator Robert M. La Follette, Jr., it was the most extensive congressional inquiry ever conducted into civil liberties violations. In the process, it helped galvanize liberals and supporters of organized labor and drew attention to the work of the new National Labor Relations Board.

For years, the American Civil Liberties Union, the American Federation of Labor, various religious organizations, and other groups had urged government probes of civil liberties violations and oppressive labor practices. Senator La Follette, a Progressive from Wisconsin and one of organized labor's staunchest defenders, introduced the Senate resolution that created the investigatory committee in the spring of 1936. Along with La Follette, who became its chairman, the committee consisted of two Democrats—Elbert D. Thomas of Utah and David I. Walsh of Massachusetts (who did not join until 1939, three years after the original appointee died in a car accident).

Although La Follette and Thomas were the most visible representatives of the committee, much of the work of amassing evidence, identifying witnesses, and preparing questions was done by committee staff. In general, staff employees were liberal and pro-labor in orientation and tended to blame business for tensions that existed between labor and management. The Wagner Act (National Labor Relations Act) had been passed the year before, and part of the work of the committee was to ensure that it succeeded. The first phase of the committee's work during the fall of 1936 and the following spring concentrated on four anti-union weapons: the employment of strikebreakers, the use of private police forces, the hiring of private detectives and labor spies, and the stockpiling of munitions, such as tear gas, nauseating agents, billy clubs, and even machine guns.

By May 1937, with the labor situation improving, the Committee for Industrial Organization (later called the Congress of Industrial Organizations) growing in strength, and the Supreme Court having validated the Wagner Act, it appeared that the La Follette Committee might soon complete its task. Then a clash between police and company detectives on one side and striking workers on the other on Memorial Day at the Republic Steel Company's South Chicago plant, which left ten strikers dead and more than one hundred wounded, led to demands for further probes, extending the life of the committee for three more years. During a second round of hearings, attention focused on the Little Steel Strike of 1937, union-busting tactics used by employers' associations, and the violence-ridden farm-labor situation in California. These investigations proved less dramatic and more complex than the earlier ones, and press coverage dwindled. Though failing to generate new legislation, the committee in the end issued seventy-five volumes of transcripts and documents and more than twenty reports, and its work led to a lessening of strong-arm practices by businesses during labor disputes and helped undergird a growing governmental commitment to the cause of civil liberties.

See Also: CIVIL RIGHTS AND CIVIL LIBERTIES; LA FOLLETTE, ROBERT M., JR.

BIBLIOGRAPHY

Auerbach, Jerold S. *Labor and Liberty: The La Follette Committee and the New Deal.* 1966.

Maney, Patrick J. *"Young Bob" La Follette: A Biography of Robert M. La Follette, Jr., 1895–1953.* 1978.

JOHN E. MILLER

LA GUARDIA, FIORELLO H.

Fiorello Henry La Guardia (December 11, 1882–September 20, 1947) was born in New York City to immigrants Achille (Italian) and Irene Coen (Jewish) La Guardia. He grew up in Arizona, where his father was a bandmaster in the U. S. Army. During the Spanish-American War, Achille became seriously ill, probably from eating tainted beef. His health broken, Achille was discharged and returned with his family to Europe.

EARLY CAREER

There, Fiorello obtained a position with the U.S. Consular Service, becoming fluent in five languages, which he used in political campaigns in polyglot New York. In 1906, La Guardia quit his job and returned to the city of his birth. Employed as an interpreter at Ellis Island immigration station by day, La Guardia studied law at night at New York University, gaining admission to the bar in 1910.

The short (5′ 2″), rotund attorney represented primarily poor immigrants and embattled labor unions. He joined the Republican Party because he could not stomach the graft-ridden Tammany Democratic machine and because an Italian-American's chance of political advancement in the Irish-dominated organization was miniscule.

In 1914, La Guardia, running as a Republican for a U.S. House seat from a lower Manhattan district, almost beat his Tammany opponent. Two years later he won. He remained in Congress until 1919, with a brief absence during World War I for army service. That year, he was elected president of New York's board of aldermen and married Thea Almerigotti. He lost this municipal office in 1921. Tragically, that same year, Thea and their infant daughter died of tuberculosis. The grief-stricken La Guardia blamed New York's airless tenements for their deaths.

Winning reelection to congress as a progressive Republican from a mostly working-class Italian and Jewish district in East Harlem, La Guardia joined a small bloc of urban liberals and midwestern and western progressives in bucking the policies of the business-dominated Republican administrations of the 1920s. He denounced prohibition, Secretary of the Treasury Andrew Mellon's tax-cuts for the wealthy, and electric power monopolies. A New Dealer before there was a New Deal, he advocated federal development of public power, child labor laws, old-age pensions, and unemployment insurance. Once the Depression started, he demanded government insurance of savings bank deposits, regulation of the stock market, and federal relief for the destitute. La Guardia's most important legislative achievement was the Norris-La Guardia Act, which curtailed the use of yellow-dog contracts (agreements that employers forced their employees to sign, swearing that they would not join unions or strike) and injunctions against labor unions. In 1929, the crusading congressman made an ill-timed run for mayor against the popular incumbent, James J. Walker and was badly beaten. He also married his devoted secretary, Marie Fisher, with whom he subsequently adopted two children.

Fiorello La Guardia with his wife, Marie, and Eleanor Roosevelt (center) in New York City in May 1934. FRANKLIN DELANO ROOSEVELT LIBRARY

THE DEPRESSION YEARS

Despite his progressive record, La Guardia lost his House seat to Tammany's James Lanzetta in the 1932 Democratic landslide. He decided to run again for mayor in 1933. When La Guardia had charged, in 1929, that the Walker administration was riddled with corruption, New Yorkers, still basking in the afterglow of prosperity, didn't care. By 1933, things were different. The city, with a million jobless, was devastated by the Depression. There had also been three investigations of the municipal government, led by Samuel Seabury, that revealed the truth of La Guardia's accusations. Walker resigned in September 1932, but Tammany continued to run the city under his successor, John P. O'Brien, who proved incapable of handling the economic crises. To stave off bankruptcy, first Walker and then O'Brien had borrowed money from New York bankers, who exacted control over municipal finances as a condition. Whatever relief funds the city had, Tammany dispensed to its loyal supporters. These dire circumstances finally brought together anti-Tammany Democrats, good-government reformers, and Republicans in the Fusion Party. The backing of Seabury and Roosevelt brain-truster Adolf A. Berle, Jr., secured the Fusion nomination for La Guardia, who in a three-way race against O'Brien and Recovery Party candidate Joseph V. Mc Kee, won the election, aided by an outpouring of Italian voters, eager to see one of their own as mayor.

La Guardia took office on January 1, 1934, determined to revitalize his city. The federal government's willingness to spend on pump-priming and employment-creating programs, as well as La Guardia's special relationship with President Roosevelt, provided the opportunity. La Guardia's cooperation with the Roosevelt administration had begun when, as a lame-duck congressman, he had introduced bills for the president-elect. As early as November 1933, Mayor-elect La Guardia helped Federal Emergency Relief Administrator Harry Hopkins plan the Civil Works Administration (CWA) and presented him with a host of carefully drawn projects. As a result, by January 1934 New York's unemployed held 20 percent of all CWA jobs and 4,000 CWA projects were rehabilitating the city's neglected parks, streets, and playgrounds. However, the CWA lasted only four months, and the metropolis needed much more aid. Mayor-elect La Guardia had approached Secretary of the Interior Harold Ickes for Public Works Administration (PWA) funding, only to be told he must first balance his budget. By slashing municipal payrolls through layoffs and salary cuts, and imposing new taxes, the city managed to balance its 1934 budget. This enabled La Guardia to renegotiate earlier loans, reducing the rates of interest and returning control over fiscal policies to elected officials instead of bankers. Ickes then loosened his purse strings. By June 1940, New York had obtained more than $250,000,000 from the PWA. The Mayor fared even better with the freer-spending Hopkins and his Works Progress Administration (WPA), launched in 1935. Anticipating the new program, La Guardia instructed his parks commissioner, Robert Moses, and his engineering committee to prepare blueprints for thousands of projects. Thanks to their quick initiative, by October 1935 the metropolis was receiving more than one-seventh of the WPA's expenditures, and 208,000 New Yorkers were employed.

La Guardia presided over the repair of two thousand miles of streets and highways and construction of fifty miles of expressways, three major bridges, one hundred smaller bridges, and the New York City Municipal Airport-La Guardia Field, which was renamed La Guardia Airport in 1947. Five thousand acres of new parks were developed and seventeen public swimming pools built, as well as ninety-two schools, 255 playgrounds, fifteen clinics, and additions to municipal hospitals that increased bed capacity by eight thousand. Old tenements were razed and thirteen public housing projects, surrounded by landscaped grounds and play areas, provided apartments with bathrooms, heat, and electricity for 17,000 working-class families. While La Guardia captured the lion's share of New Deal largess for his city, he also, as president of the U. S. Conference of Mayors from 1935 to 1945, became the recognized spokesman for more aid and closer ties between Washington and urban America. La Guardia helped convince President Roosevelt that rescuing cities was a federal responsibility.

Besides promoting the federal-urban connection, La Guardia cleaned New York's government. Inefficient and grafting political appointees were driven out and replaced with energetic, capable people. The proportion of city jobs filled through civil service competitive examinations rose from 55 percent in 1933 to 74 percent by 1939. In making appointments not covered by civil service, La Guardia did reward supporters, but rarely compromised his insistence that they must be as dedicated, hardworking, and honest as he was. He also attempted to open municipal employment to minorities, who had been largely ignored by Tammany Hall. The result was a major shift in the ethnic and racial composition of New York's bureaucracy; the previously dominant Irish gave way to Jews, Italians, and blacks. In 1934, the city had three black firemen; by 1941, there were forty-six. After La Guardia took over the subways, African Americans were hired for the first time as conductors, dispatchers, and motormen. There were limits, however, to La Guardia's achievements. The mayor's war on gambling and slot and pinball machines barely fazed organized crime. Continued discrimination against blacks provoked major riots in Harlem in 1935 and 1943. Nor did La Guardia always respect civil liberties. Burlesque theaters and pornography were banned. Cops were encouraged to "mess up" criminals, but not to rough up strikers or demonstrators.

Whatever La Guardia's shortcomings, he was reelected in 1937 and again in 1941. All previous New York Fusion mayors had been kicked out after a single term. La Guardia triumphed because his honest, effective administration continued to recommend him to good-government advocates, while his caring, activist policies won him the gratitude of Jews, Italians, blacks, and union members, many of whom voted for him on the American Labor Party line.

THE LAST TERM AND THE WAR YEARS

La Guardia's last term was his least fruitful. Washington's assistance to cities dwindled after the Japanese attack on Pearl Harbor in 1941. Without federal funds, the building projects halted, and New York found it impossible to maintain its new facilities and continue expanded services without unbalancing its budget. La Guardia increased borrowing rather than impose politically unpopular cutbacks. Further, he was distracted from governing New York by his futile quest for a cabinet post or military commission and by his brief tenure as Director of the Office of Civilian Defense. Still, there were accomplishments: The city passed the earliest laws against housing and employment discrimination in the nation; conceived the first managed health care program, Health Insurance Plan (HIP); and convinced the United Nations to make New York its permanent headquarters.

La Guardia ended his mayoralty in 1946, then briefly directed the United Nations Relief and Rehabilitation Administration. He died of pancreatic cancer on September 29, 1947. During the worst depression in the country's history, La Guardia had forged an unprecedented federal-urban partnership, revitalized New York, and given it the most honest, effective government it had ever known.

See Also: AMERICAN LABOR PARTY; CITIES AND SUBURBS; NORRIS-LA GUARDIA ACT; REPUBLICAN PARTY; TAMMANY HALL.

BIBLIOGRAPHY

Bayor, Ronald H. *Fiorello La Guardia: Ethnicity and Reform.* 1993.

Blumberg, Barbara. *The New Deal and the Unemployed: The View from New York City.* 1979.

Garrett, Charles. *The La Guardia Years: Machine and Reform Politics in New York City.* 1961.

Kessner, Thomas. *Fiorello H. La Guardia and the Making of Modern New York.* 1989.

La Guardia, Fiorello. Papers. La Guardia and the Robert F. Wagner Archives. La Guardia Community College of the City University, Queens, New York.

La Guardia, Fiorello. Papers. New York Municipal Archives, New York.

La Guardia, Fiorello. Papers. New York Public Library, New York.

Lankevich, George J. *American Metropolis: A History of New York City.* 1998.

Mann, Arthur. *La Guardia: A Fighter against His Times, 1882–1933.* 1959.

Mann, Arthur. *La Guardia Comes to Power: The Mayoral Election of 1933.* 1965.

BARBARA BLUMBERG

LAISSEZ-FAIRE

Laissez-faire, literally "leave alone," constituted the core doctrine of classical economics that there should be minimal government intervention in economic affairs. According to this theory, an economy operating under a system of free competition will tend to produce at maximum capacity with the result that labor and other resources of production will be fully utilized. Its adherents also contended that recession was a temporary, self-correcting situation. They reasoned that when unemployment rose, wages and prices fell, with the consequence that the *real* supply of money in the economy grew, which in turn would eventually generate economic expansion.

The political corollary of laissez-faire held that the best government was the one that governed least. This view enjoyed its heyday during the industrial revolution of the late nineteenth century (though it did not preclude protective tariffs). Its last hurrah in the 1920s reflected the view that government had grown too large as a result of progressive regulatory expansion and wartime economic controls. Moreover, big business—once the progressives' whipping boy—had regained popular esteem through its war production success. Getting government off the back of business therefore became a primary goal of the Republican administrations of Warren Harding and Calvin Coolidge.

Though they could not dismantle the progressive state, Harding and Coolidge (just as Ronald Reagan did later) named conservatives unsympathetic to regulation to head the Interstate Commerce Commission, the Federal Reserve Board, and the Federal Trade Commission (FTC). Republican fiscal policy, guided by Secretary of the Treasury Andrew Mellon, also reaffirmed traditional principles. Though federal spending was not reduced to prewar levels, every 1920s budget was balanced, ending a period of regular deficits that stretched from 1894 to 1919. The national debt, which had risen from $1.2 billion in 1916 to $25.5 billion in 1919, was reduced to $16.2 billion by 1930. Finally, convinced that the 1920 to 1921 recession was attributable to the Wilson administration's high taxes, the Republican governments practiced *trickle down economics* to justify tax reductions that principally benefited business and the well-to-do as being necessary for the entire economy's good.

In contrast to other Republican leaders, Herbert Hoover had no truck with what he dubbed "the eighteenth century thesis of laissez-faire." As Secretary of Commerce from 1921 to 1929, Hoover made this hitherto minor agency into the most dynamic federal department in the 1920s by promoting its economic planning and coordination capabilities. When the Depression hit, Hoover's brand of progressive conservatism allowed him to become the first president in American history to exercise federal leadership in such an emergency.

On Hoover's recommendation, Congress reduced personal taxes and increased public works appropriations in 1930 and later enacted measures to underwrite credit to farmers, homebuyers, and

banks. Hoover's most significant initiative in this regard was the creation in January 1932 of the Reconstruction Finance Corporation, which was initially empowered to extend federal loans to banks and other financial institutions and later authorized to loan funds for self-liquidating state and local government public works. Nevertheless, his activism was constrained by concern to preserve the ethos of free enterprise and self-help that he regarded as fundamental to American individualism. Being convinced that there was no major flaw in America's domestic economy—he denied there was maldistribution of wealth and blamed the severity of the downturn on world conditions—Hoover was determined not to spur the irreversible growth of big government. Accordingly he would not use compulsion to restrict business wage-cutting practices and manifested a flinty attitude towards unemployment and farm relief. His anti-Depression programs were largely indirect, involved recoverable outlays (such as loans), and did not entail permanent expansion of the federal budget. As a result they were utterly insufficient to compensate for the catastrophic decline in the private economy.

Hoover's presidential policies represented a pre-modern transitional phase between old-style laissez-faire and New Deal interventionism. His party had little option in the face of Roosevelt's immense first-term popularity but to move further away from its traditional orthodoxy. Some die-hard conservative Republicans and renegade Democrats (including former presidential candidates Alfred E. Smith and John Davis) joined the American Liberty League, created by wealthy businessmen, to demand the restoration of laissez-faire, but its stand hurt the Republican cause in the 1936 elections. By then the bulk of the party recognized the need for some accommodation with the New Deal. The 1936 Republican platform condemned unemployment insurance, old-age pensions, the Wagner Act, and deficit spending, but accepted other Roosevelt policies, including the farm program, federal work relief, and regulation of the financial sector. Even when Roosevelt's popularity declined in the second term, mainstream conservatives did not wholly revert to laissez-faire. The Conservative Manifesto of 1937, a statement of bipartisan congressional conservatism, demanded lower taxes, less spending, and balanced budgets to restore business confidence but accepted unemployment relief (provided it was not politicized and permanent) and government programs that did not harm or compete with private enterprise (the farm program and large scale public works were acceptable, public utility development was not). Business groups like the National Association of Manufacturers and the Chamber of Commerce also railed against New Deal taxes and deficits. Nevertheless, it was evident by the late 1930s that political and economic debate no longer centered on whether government should intervene in the economy but on the extent to which it should do so.

No Western democracy pursued such a wide-ranging program as the New Deal in the face of the 1930s Depression, but none pursued a wholly laissez-faire approach. In the United Kingdom, the national government rejected New Deal-style public works for expenditure retrenchment and tax increases to balance the budget (which it did from 1934 onward). However, old-age pensions, unemployment compensation, and housing assistance programs were already established in Britain. French governments of the 1930s eschewed macroeconomic activism but some intervened in other ways, especially to improve workers' conditions. It was the need for postwar economic reconstruction that compelled the final abandonment of classical economic doctrine in Western Europe.

See Also: CONSERVATIVE COALITION; COOLIDGE, CALVIN; FEDERAL RESERVE SYSTEM; HOOVER, HERBERT; MELLON, ANDREW; MONETARY POLICY.

BIBLIOGRAPHY

Hawley, Ellis W. *The Great War and the Search for a Modern Order: A History of the American People and Their Institutions, 1917–1933.* 1979.

Hoff, Joan. *Herbert Hoover: Forgotten Progressive.* 1975.

Kindleberger, Charles P. *The World in Depression: 1929–1939,* rev. edition. 1986.

Savage, James D. *Balanced Budgets and American Politics,* 1986.

Stein, Herbert. *The Fiscal Revolution in America.* 1969.

IWAN MORGAN

LANDON, ALFRED M.

Alfred Mossman "Alf" Landon (September 7, 1887–October 12, 1987) was the governor of Kansas and Republican presidential candidate in 1936. Landon was born in West Middlesex, Pennsylvania, received a law degree from the University of Kansas in 1908, and became a successful independent oil producer and Republican politician. He was active in Theodore Roosevelt's Bull Moose campaign in 1912, was secretary to Kansas Governor Henry J. Allen in 1922, assisted William Allen White's campaign against the Ku Klux Klan in 1924, and narrowly won the governor's race in Kansas in 1932.

As governor, Landon confronted the effects of the Depression in Kansas and instituted measures to regulate banks, insurance companies, and public utilities. He also moved to protect farmers from bankruptcy, and he developed programs to bring relief to the hard-hit oil industry. Landon's ability to work with the Franklin D. Roosevelt administration resulted in Kansas receiving greater funding from New Deal agencies than did other midwestern states. In 1934, Landon was the only Republican governor in the nation to win reelection. This, together with his moderate conservativism, secured for him the Republican presidential nomination in June 1936, with Chicago publisher Frank Knox as his running mate.

With Roosevelt's popularity at its height, Republicans hoped that Landon's down-home midwestern image as a "liberal Calvin Coolidge" would attract an electorate thought to be weary of the urbane Roosevelt. Landon's campaign initially charted a moderate course, endorsing conservation, farm relief, balanced budgets, efficient administration, business expansion, and fairness to the poor, the unemployed, and organized labor. However, Landon's campaign failed to energize the electorate and was damaged by the vicious attacks launched upon Roosevelt and the New Deal by conservative Republicans and big business. With the election looming, Landon himself made increasingly desperate and immoderate attacks on the president. On November 3, 1936, Roosevelt was reelected in a landslide, receiving 27,751,841 votes compared to Landon's 16,679,491. Roosevelt received 60.8 percent of the popular vote; the plurality (11,072,350) was the largest in presidential election history. Roosevelt won 523 electoral votes to Landon's eight, the biggest margin since James Monroe in 1820. In addition, Roosevelt's coattails brought Democratic majorities in the Senate (75–16) and the House of Representatives (331–88).

Following his election defeat, Landon never again ran for public office, though he remained active in Republican politics for rest of his life. His daughter, Nancy Landon Kassebaum, was elected to the U.S. Senate from Kansas in 1978. Alfred Landon died in 1987, a month after his 100th birthday.

See Also: ELECTION OF 1936; REPUBLICAN PARTY.

BIBLIOGRAPHY

Leuchtenburg, William E. *Franklin D. Roosevelt and the New Deal, 1932–1940.* 1963.

Leuchtenburg, William E. "The Election of 1936." In *The FDR years: On Roosevelt and His Legacy.* 1995.

McCoy, Donald R. *Landon of Kansas.* 1966.

Palmer, Frederick. *This Man Landon: The Record and Career of Governor Alfred M. Landon of Kansas.* 1936.

MICHAEL J. WEBBER

LAND USE PLANNING

Land use planning held the promise of unifying the disparate elements of New Deal agricultural policy. Most agrarian New Dealers thought that poor land use caused "the farm problem." Low farm prices and incomes, poverty and regional underdevelopment, soil erosion and related abuses of the land— these were the central rural problems of the Great Depression, and they all pointed to land use reform. Henry A. Wallace stated in his *Report of the Secretary of Agriculture, 1938*, "There are no separate problems of forestry, of wildlife conservation, of grazing, of soil conservation, and of regional crop adjustment. There is one unified land use problem, of which forestry, grazing, crop adjustment and so forth are merely aspects." Yet with few exceptions, historians have not treated New Deal agricultural policy from this vantage point. Admittedly, the baffling array of alphabet agencies makes it difficult to follow the thread of land use planning policy.

The three main "action agencies" of the New Deal U. S. Department of Agriculture (USDA) changed land use patterns substantially. To raise farm prices, the Agricultural Adjustment Administration (AAA) induced acreage reductions. First the Resettlement Administration, then the Farm Security Administration (FSA), "rehabilitated" poor land as well as poor farmers, and even achieved minor land reform, turning some tenants into owners. The Soil Conservation Service (SCS) demonstrated erosion-control practices and advised farmers on preventing environmental degradation. Further, the SCS acquired a small but important land retirement program that purchased submarginal land, ended crop production, and resettled the residents onto better plots. Most other rural programs (e.g., farm-forestry, flood control, public grazing, wildlife preservation) also required land use adjustments. Wide-ranging alternative policy discussions and experiments pervaded New Deal agricultural circles; stellar examples include two presidential committee reports, *The Future of the Great Plains* (1936) and *Farm Tenancy* (1937), and the remarkable *Farmers in a Changing World: The Yearbook of Agriculture, 1940*. Late in the New Deal, the USDA and the land-grant colleges set up county land use planning committees to localize and coordinate all the new agencies. This participatory planning program represented the intended and long-range unity of agricultural policy.

The county land use planning committees consisted of farmers, local administrators of the new federal agencies (e.g., AAA, SCS, FSA), the extension agent, plus specialists from the state college. Together the citizens, bureaucrats, and scientists sought to unify and adapt all the government programs in the county. The committees began by discussing the philosophy of planning and studying how to subdivide their county for adequate community representation. They investigated each local area by mapping current land uses and then recommended improvements. The committees developed and implemented long-term as well as immediate land use plans, often by modifying the federal programs. By 1941 over two-thirds of all U. S. counties were engaged in this work, which involved 125,000 farm men and women as citizen-planners. The states had similar land use planning committees, and Henry Wallace reorganized the USDA to carry out the program.

Wallace and others believed that the county land use planning program, begun only in 1939, culminated New Deal agricultural policy. They saw it as adding a third major function—planning—to the public agricultural institutions, to complement education and research. It offered the local and programmatic synthesis so obviously lacking at mid-decade. In his final *Report of the Secretary of Agriculture* (1940), Wallace wrote, "Land use planning brings farmers, technicians, and administrators together in broad attacks on wrong land utilization, menacing soil erosion, inefficient farming, anti-social land-tenure relationships, and bad rural living." In an extremely innovative way, the planning program combined adult education, action research (by scientists and farmers), decentralized administration, and participatory policy-making. These features transcended land use planning; they amounted to integrated rural development. Most significantly to the New Dealers, the county planning program extended "grass-roots democracy," engaging meaningful citizen participation far beyond their earlier efforts.

Historians generally disagree with that self-assessment: The farmer-planners almost always came from the local elite, and they did not accomplish either planning or democracy. Actually, most historians argue, the real long-term goal of New Deal land policy was an efficient, rational agriculture. Government support therefore favored modern family-sized and larger operations, and usually ignored the needs of subsistence farmers, tenants, and sharecroppers. These historical judgments are hard to dispute. Still, while emphasizing the aim of modernization, historians underestimate the democratizing aspects of the planning program. Especially compared to the AAA's farmer committees, the land use program broadened the interests represented by local USDA agencies. Conservative enemies of reform—some of the department's own agencies, farm organizations (particularly the Farm Bureau), and anti-New Dealers in Congress—felt threatened enough by the county planning program to destroy it in 1942. Thus America lost the opportunity for a unified agricultural policy that serves more than narrow farm-commodity interests.

See Also: AGRICULTURAL ADJUSTMENT ADMINISTRATION (AAA); FARM POLICY; FARM SECURITY ADMINISTRATION (FSA); SOIL CONSERVATION SERVICE (SCS); WALLACE, HENRY A.

BIBLIOGRAPHY

Badger, Anthony J. *The New Deal: The Depression Years, 1933–40.* 1989.

Daniel, Pete. "A Hundred Years of Dispossession: Southern Farmers and the Forces of Change." In *Outstanding in His Field: Perspectives on American Agriculture in Honor of Wayne D. Rasmussen,* edited by Frederick V. Carstensen, Morton Rothstein, and Joseph A. Swanson. 1993.

Gilbert, Jess. "Democratic Planning in Agricultural Policy: The Federal-County Land-Use Planning Program, 1938–1942." *Agricultural History* 70 (1996): 233–250.

Kirkendall, Richard S. *Social Scientists and Farm Politics in the Age of Roosevelt.* 1966.

Kubo, Fumiaki. "Henry A. Wallace and Radical Politics in the New Deal: Farm Programs and a Vision of the New American Political Economy." *The Japanese Journal of American Studies* 4 (1991): 37–76.

Lehman, Tim. *Public Values, Private Lands: Farmland Preservation Policy, 1933–1985.* 1995.

Summers, Mary. "The New Deal Farm Programs: Looking for Reconstruction in American Agriculture." *Agricultural History* 74 (2000): 241–257.

Tolley, Howard R. *The Farmer Citizen at War.* 1943.

JESS GILBERT

LANGE, DOROTHEA

Dorothea Lange (May 26, 1895–October 11, 1965) was one of the leading documentary photographers of the Depression and arguably the most influential. Some of her pictures were reproduced so repeatedly and widely that they became commonly understood symbols of the human suffering caused by the economic disaster. At the same time, her work functioned to create popular support for New Deal programs.

Born in Hoboken, New Jersey, Lange's life changed when her parents separated and her

A destitute man, photographed by Dorothea Lange in 1935. FRANKLIN DELANO ROOSEVELT LIBRARY

mother went to work. Lange attended school on New York City's lower east side because her mother worked there, and she often entertained herself after school by exploring the city on foot, despite her slight limp as a result of childhood polio. Attracted by photography from her early teen years, Lange created a kind of apprenticeship for herself by persuading studio portrait photographers to hire her as a helper. She went to San Francisco in 1919

and lived the rest of her life in the Bay area. She developed a fashionable and profitable portrait studio there, a success that indicates her remarkable charisma, self-confidence, and drive. Lange's insightful and slightly eccentric portraits made her the favored portraitist of the city's economic elite—the Fleishhackers, Zellerbachs, Strauses, and Kahns—as well as the artistic elite, which included Yehudi Menuhin, Mischa Elman, and Ernst Bloch. Lange

This photograph, shot in 1940 in a migrant camp between Weedpatch and Lamont in California, was one of Lange's many poignant photographs of the children of migrant workers. NATIONAL ARCHIVES AND RECORDS ADMINISTRATION

married the then well-known "western" painter Maynard Dixon, with whom she had two children, and her portrait photography was the family's main source of support until the marriage ended in 1935.

As the Depression hit, Lange's rich clients and her marriage began to seem confining beyond her endurance. She started to move around San Francisco, photographing darker, poorer, more intense scenes. These pictures came to the attention of University of California-Berkeley economist and reformer Paul Schuster Taylor, who hired her to illustrate his exposés of the brutal working and living conditions of migrant farmworkers. Lange fell doubly in love, with Taylor and with the challenges and

rewards of this so-called documentary photography (a phrase she hated). She divorced Dixon and married Taylor, and their marriage was thereafter a collaboration in work as well as life.

Taylor's salary from the university and the federal government's new interest in photographic documentation provided Lange with the economic basis to explore new possibilities in her medium. Between 1935 and 1945, she worked for the Farm Security Administration, the Bureau of Agricultural Economics, the War Relocation Authority, and the Office of War Information. She traveled extensively throughout the United States, often spending months at a time on the road in sweltering southern summers, struggling to keep dust out of her cameras and to develop film in motel bathrooms. Along with Walker Evans, Arthur Rothstein, Ben Shahn, and others, Lange documented the Dust Bowl, agricultural poverty, and, later, wartime defense workers. Among her most powerful work was a series of photographs of the Japanese internment, pictures so critical that many of them were suppressed by the agency that hired her to make them.

Because the pictures taken during this time belonged to the federal government, they were in the public domain and could be reproduced without charge and without permission. Their emotional power touched viewers like no other photographer's work did. Her portrait of a destitute migrant mother with her children has been reproduced thousands of times, sometimes substituting different faces and different situations. Lange believed that her disability gave her a strong connection with those who suffered.

Although Lange was not in any conventional sense a politically oriented person, and her own community was primarily one of artists, she felt not only great sympathy for the victims of injustice, but also intense outrage at the injustices she saw. She was not attracted by the organized Left, but she was in sympathy with some of the Communist-led causes of the period, such as the farmworkers' struggles, the San Francisco general strike of 1934, and the defense of the Scottsboro "boys." She made many insightful and respectful pictures of blacks, Filipinos, Mexicans, and Mexican-Americans, although these were reproduced much less often than her photographs of whites. In her home state she was particularly incensed at the extreme exploitation of farmworkers and the violence directed at those who tried to unionize and improve their conditions by the powerful agribusinesses and their hired thugs.

After 1945, fighting illness for twenty years, Lange slowed her pace considerably, but turned out superb, lasting work. She accompanied Paul Taylor on several of his trips studying land tenure in underdeveloped countries, and she made many beautiful pictures in Vietnam, Egypt, and Indonesia. She also made a series on the work of a public defender in Oakland. This late work continued to reveal her often uncanny eye for human expressiveness and the complexity of the poor, so often stereotyped as simple.

See Also: DUST BOWL; EVANS, WALKER; FARM SECURITY ADMINISTRATION (FSA); PHOTOGRAPHY; ROTHSTEIN, ARTHUR; SHAHN, BEN.

BIBLIOGRAPHY

Daniel, Pete; Merry A. Foresta; Maren Stange; and Sally Stein. *Official Images: New Deal Photography.* 1987.

Davidov, Judith Fryer. *Women's Camera Work: Self/Body/Other in American Visual Culture.* 1998.

Kozol, Wendy. "Madonnas of the Fields: Photography, Gender, and 1930s Farm Relief." *Genders* 2 (summer 1988): 1–23.

Levine, Lawrence W. "The Historian and the Icon: Photography and the History of the American People in the 1930s and 1940s." In *Documenting America, 1935–1943,* edited by Carl Fleischhauer and Beverly W. Brannan. 1988.

McEuen, Melissa A. *Seeing America: Women Photographers between the Wars.* 2000.

Meltzer, Milton. *Dorothea Lange: A Photographer's Life.* 1978.

Partridge, Elizabeth, ed. *Dorothea Lange: A Visual Life.* 1994.

Peeler, David P. *Hope among Us Yet: Social Criticism and Social Solace in Depression America.* 1987.

Wollenberg, Charles. *Photographing the Second Gold Rush: Dorothea Lange and the Bay Area at War, 1941–1945.* 1995.

LINDA GORDON

LATIN AMERICA, GREAT DEPRESSION IN

Although the nations of Latin America had won their political independence during the nineteenth century, they continued to remain subordinate to external economic forces. The reason lay in their adherence to the model of economic development that had begun during the colonial era and which concentrated on the production and export to Europe and North America of large quantities of staple commodities, such as sugar, tobacco, coffee, cotton, grain, wool, meat, fruit, copper, tin, and silver. While the policy of export-led growth could claim considerable success and justification so long as international commerce flourished and the world economy enjoyed prosperity, its inherent defects were displayed at times of adverse economic developments. This was especially the case for Latin America whenever trade and inward investment were affected with the leading economic powers of Great Britain, France, Germany, and the United States. Consequently, the worst international economic crisis of the twentieth century, which began with the stock market crash on Wall Street in October 1929 and subsequently developed into the Great Depression, was extremely damaging to the economies of all the Latin American countries.

ECONOMIC IMPACT

Even before the 1929 crash, Latin America was already experiencing economic difficulties as a result of falling world prices of staple exports, such as Argentine grain, Brazilian coffee, and Cuban sugar. The amount of inward foreign investment had also declined as funds were drawn away to fuel the speculative fever that raged in American and European stock markets in the late 1920s. The economic downturn in 1929 was, therefore, not entirely unexpected. What was surprising was the sheer scale and longevity of the subsequent Depression. Instead of a temporary reduction in external demand for foodstuffs and raw materials, the traditional markets for Latin American goods in Europe and North America severely contracted as the value of world trade fell by more than half within three years. Furthermore, Latin American exports were sharply reduced in terms of both quantity and value and dropped to low levels not seen since World War I. Agriculture and mining were seriously affected throughout the region, ranging from the sugar industry in Cuba to the extraction of tin and copper in Chile. In 1939 the value of these Chilean exports had decreased to one-sixth of the 1929 figure. In addition, the collapse of world commodity prices was so marked that exports fell more in value than imports of capital and manufactured goods so that the terms of trade decisively turned against Latin America. The notable exception was Venezuela, where the production and export of oil continued to be profitable.

GOVERNMENT RESPONSES

The Great Depression caused considerable monetary difficulties for Latin American governments. There was not only a problem in finding sufficient foreign exchange to finance external commerce and particularly to pay for imports, but there were also increasing difficulties in servicing the foreign debt. Taxes on exports and tariff duties on foreign imports had long been a significant item in the revenue of Latin American governments. Declining trade meant, however, a corresponding fall in revenue. The combination of severe balance-of-payments difficulties, budget deficits, and the dwindling of gold reserves to the point of exhaustion led the majority of Latin American governments to suspend payments to foreign bondholders. In some cases, outright default could not be avoided as exemplified by Bolivia in January 1931, followed by Peru in May and Chile in August. Even for those countries that struggled to service their external debt, the fact that the interest rate remained unchanged meant that the debt actually rose in real terms if increased payments could not be made. Indeed, all governments were forced to enter into complex and often protracted negotiations with North American and European governments, bankers, and bondholders to seek a readjustment of their foreign debt and a rescheduling of payments. In contrast to the later debt crisis of the 1980s, however, Latin American indebtedness during the 1930s was not singled out for particular condemnation. Such was the international extent of the debt problem that Latin America was not considered to be any more profligate or financially reckless than other regions of the world.

The effects of the 1929 crash soon brought a severe contraction of economic activity in both agriculture and industry and, consequently, a sharp rise in unemployment and under-employment throughout Latin America. The resulting economic discontent led to political protests directed against the governments in power, which were blamed for economic mismanagement and corruption. A series of successful coups, often involving the military, occurred in 1930. In May, President Hernando Siles was overthrown in Bolivia. In August, President Augusto Leguía resigned in Peru. In September, General José F. Uriburu led a military coup that overthrew President Hipólito Irigoyen in Argentina. In October, Getúlio Vargas assumed power in Brazil. In July 1931 a general strike in Chile forced President Carlos Ibañez to resign and go into exile. Changes of government also took place in several nations of Central America and the Caribbean, including the overthrow of President Gerardo Machado in Cuba in March 1933 in what became known as the 1933 Cuban revolution.

The governments that came into office in Latin America during the early years of the Great Depression found that their economic options were tightly constrained. Even during times of prosperity the political power and influence of entrenched landed oligarchies and business elites made it extremely difficult for central governments to raise income or property taxes. Moreover, the outbreak of the world economic crisis ruled out the customary resort to external borrowing in the form of large foreign loans from European or American bankers. As a result, the newly empowered Latin American governments generally sought to balance their budgets by pursuing orthodox deflationary policies that stressed the reduction of public spending. So great, however, was the scale of economic crisis in the early 1930s that conservative laissez-faire attitudes were gradually abandoned in favor of the state adopting a more active and assertive role in economic policy and planning. This was evident in the establishment of strict exchange controls to alleviate the scarcity of foreign currency caused by the sharp fall in levels of trade. The policy of maintaining the gold standard was also either suspended or abandoned. Local currencies were pegged in value to the pound sterling or the U.S. dollar. In effect, Latin American currencies were allowed to depreciate in value. At the same time the circulation of money was often expanded by reflationary measures that were similar to those undertaken by the New Deal in the United States and the fascist regimes of Benito Mussolini in Italy and Adolf Hitler in Germany. In order to stimulate the domestic economy, a number of Latin American governments resorted to large programs of public spend-

ing, especially in developing economic infrastructure such as roads and highways. However, due to prevailing deflationary conditions resulting from the general lack of world demand, loose monetary policies did not result in rampant inflation.

During the early 1930s the primary objective of governments throughout Latin America was to combat the economic crisis by stimulating exports. This was regarded not only as the best means of generating increased earnings of foreign currency but also as essential to save particular export sectors from what was perceived to be an imminent danger of complete economic collapse. Attempts to improve price levels for staple commodities were not new and had been tried earlier, as in the case of the Brazilian valorization of coffee at the beginning of the twentieth century. Such policies, however, involved an element of manipulating market forces by fixing prices and imposing controls on production. Consequently, they had proved controversial so that their implementation had generally been left to private rather than governmental agencies. To achieve stable price levels during the Great Depression, however, it was necessary for the state to intervene directly in the economy. Central economic planning was adopted to regulate domestic production and prevent overproduction. Surpluses were stored and, where necessary, destroyed. During the decade of the 1930s an estimated sixty million bags of coffee were burned in Brazil, the equivalent of two years of world consumption of coffee.

A similar strategy to improve the balance of payments was import substitution. Known as import-substituting industrialization (ISI), this policy was designed to promote domestic industries by supplying capital investment in the form of government loans and subsidies. In addition, domestic products would be given protection from competing foreign imports, most usually by increases in tariff duties. ISI was initially a series of measures rather than a systematic policy. It was introduced in limited stages and mostly applied to nations with strong manufacturing sectors such as Argentina, Brazil, Mexico, and Chile. At first, the policy was limited to processed food, beverages, and textiles, but it was later extended to a wide range of manufactured goods, chemicals, and pharmaceuticals.

Particular success was achieved in Brazil, where domestic industry accounted for almost 85 percent of the country's supply of manufactured articles in 1938. ISI, however, did not aim to produce self-sufficiency. Foreign imports, especially of capital goods and machinery, were still considered vital for economic growth and could not be readily replaced by domestic production. In fact, during the 1930s Latin American governments placed more importance on export promotion than ISI. Beyond the decade of the 1930s, however, the development of ISI brought significant structural economic change as it influenced the shift of emphasis from agriculture to manufacturing. In the process, Latin American economic growth was made less dependent on foreign trade and inward investment.

POLITICAL CONSEQUENCES

The beginning of the Great Depression in Latin America can be directly associated with the Wall Street crash in 1929. The actual ending is more uncertain, but it is generally accepted that the effects of the Depression lasted throughout the decade of the 1930s and that the next period of significant economic change was started by the outbreak of war in Europe in 1939. In fact, economic recovery was clearly evident in some Latin American nations as early as the 1931 to 1932 period. In 1933 Brazil's trade balance was back in surplus and industrial production had recovered to its 1929 peak. Indeed, economic performance in the region as a whole was superior to that of Europe or the US. With the exceptions of Honduras and Nicaragua, by the end of the 1930s the gross domestic product figures of all the Latin American nations were back to 1929 levels. The actual pace of recovery varied from country to country and was most rapid in Brazil, Chile, Cuba and Mexico and weakest in Panama and Paraguay. Arguably the improvement resulted not so much from particular government policies, such as exchange controls or ISI, but from the pick-up in world economic activity and consequent revival in demand for the staple commodities traditionally produced by Latin America. For example, the recovery of world copper prices meant that Chilean copper production regained its pre-1929 levels in 1937. Similarly, the rise in the price of sugar restored the profits of sugar producers, especially in

Cuba, where the value of exports of sugar doubled between 1932 and 1939. The production of some commodities actually increased in quantity, as well as price, as a result of buoyant world demand. A prominent example was cotton, which was widely and profitably cultivated in Brazil and Peru.

During the 1920s the large majority of Latin American countries exhibited outwardly stable political systems. The shock of the Great Depression, however, brought a general crisis of confidence among the ruling elites of Latin America and contributed to a decade of political turmoil and, on occasion, violent change. This was particularly the case at the beginning of the 1930s when the traditional policy of export-led growth was suddenly brought into serious question. The exploitation of natural resources had greatly benefited the powerful landowning oligarchies and was the basis for their considerable political influence. The sudden collapse of external markets resulted not only in considerable economic loss but also provoked public disaffection with rule by the oligarchies. The political left, including the Communist parties and labor unions, responded by organizing strikes and protests and, in some cases, attempted unsuccessful military coups, as in Cuba in 1933 and Brazil in 1935. The appeal of the left, however, was very limited and was generally confined to the cities and industrial workers. It did not extend to the large masses of population that lived at subsistence level in the countryside and were historically excluded from active participation in the political system. Moreover, the threat of revolutionary upheaval posed by the left and especially the ideology of communism served to unite the urban middle class and the military with the landowning oligarchy. It was a combination of these basically conservative elements, often led by senior military officers, that assumed political power during the period of the Great Depression, which explains the subsequent emphasis of these governments on policies intended to produce stability rather than radical change. In many cases, the result was the establishment of repressive authoritarian regimes in which military figures, such as Augustín Justo in Argentina, Fulgencio Batista in Cuba, Rafael Trujillo in the Dominican Republic, and Jorge Ubico in Guatemala, took a leading role in government.

EXTERNAL ECONOMIC RELATIONS

The political rise of the military notably contributed to the adoption of nationalistic economic policies like ISI. For example, in Brazil the government of Gétulio Vargas was sympathetic to the views held most prominently by junior military officers known as *tenentes* (lieutenants) that industrial growth was essential to reconstruct Brazil into a strong and prosperous modern state. The *tenentes* were also critical of their country's long-standing economic subordination to the world economy. They urged Vargas to assert Brazil's economic independence from external powers by expanding the role of the federal government in regulating foreign owned utilities, such as electricity, telephone, and gas, and by promoting efforts to achieve self-sufficiency in products with natural security implications, notably oil and steel. Similar action was taken in Bolivia in 1937 and Mexico in 1938 to remove foreign control over national oil industries.

While the Great Depression stimulated an increase in antiforeign sentiment among the people of Latin America, it did not promote any marked desire for greater regional economic cooperation or integration. So long as the economies of the Latin America countries were essentially agrarian, there was not a great deal of potential for significant commercial exchange. Consequently, the 1930s saw only a modest increase in trade between Latin American nations. Nor were there any concerted attempts to form cartels to support and manipulate price levels of particular commodities. In fact, the pattern of Latin American trade continued to stress the maintenance of close links with the markets of North America and Europe. In 1933 Argentina negotiated the Roca-Runciman Treaty, a commercial agreement with Great Britain that was designed to make exports of Argentine meat secure. Brazil entered into barter arrangements with Nazi Germany that helped to double Brazilian exports to that country from 1933 to 1939. Indeed, Germany gained from the Great Depression in that the German share of Latin American exports rose from 7 percent in 1930 to more than 10 percent in 1938.

Economic relations between Latin America and the United States followed an ambivalent course during the 1930s. Initially, the United States appeared unsympathetic to the economic plight of Latin American exporters because it maintained a strongly protectionist attitude that was symbolized by the passage of the Hawley-Smoot Tariff in 1930. During the presidency of Franklin D. Roosevelt, however, the United States launched the Good Neighbor Policy in an attempt to improve hemispheric relations. While the policy proclaimed the importance of closer political cooperation, it also stressed closer economic contact to help the American economy recover from the Great Depression. Starting with Cuba in 1934, the Roosevelt administration concluded a series of bilateral trade treaties with eleven Latin American countries by 1939. Although its share of the Latin American export trade actually declined slightly from 33 percent in 1930 to just over 31 percent in 1938, the United States remained the largest single market for Latin American goods. The challenge to the United States of European economic rivals such as Great Britain and especially Germany was substantial but was considerably weakened by the outbreak of World War II in 1939. The resulting wartime economic boom enhanced the preeminent economic role of the United States in the hemisphere and brought an end to the Great Depression in Latin America.

See Also: DICTATORSHIP; GOOD NEIGHBOR POLICY; INTERNATIONAL IMPACT OF THE GREAT DEPRESSION; MEXICO, GREAT DEPRESSION IN.

BIBLIOGRAPHY

Bulmer-Thomas, Victor. *The Economic History of Latin America since Independence.* 1994.

Salvucci, Richard J., ed. *Latin America and the World Economy: Dependency and Beyond.* 1996.

Thorp, Rosemary, ed. *Latin America in the 1930s: The Role of the Periphery in World Crisis.* 1984.

JOSEPH SMITH

LATINO AMERICANS, IMPACT OF THE GREAT DEPRESSION ON

According to the federal census, there were approximately 1.5 million Latinos in the continental Unit-

A Hispanic-American woman weaves rugs as part of a Works Progress Administration Project in 1939 in Costilla, New Mexico.

LIBRARY OF CONGRESS, PRINTS & PHOTOGRAPHS DIVISION, FSA/OWI COLLECTION

ed States in 1930, the vast majority of whom were Mexican or Mexican American. Cubans, Dominicans, Central and South Americans, and Puerto Ricans made up a much smaller portion of the total mainland population. Not included in this enumeration was the population of the island of Puerto Rico, then a protectorate of the United States, which numbered more than one million by 1930.

Although some Latinos predated Anglo-American settlement in what became the United States, many had arrived only recently. Responding to the desperate need for labor during World War I, and often fleeing unrest in their home countries, Latino immigrants transformed American cities not only in the Southwest but in the Midwest and Northeast. Hundreds of thousands arrived between 1900 and 1930. Mexicans, many fleeing the violence of the Mexican Revolution of the 1910s, arrived in the greatest number. Puerto Ricans, made United States citizens by the Jones Act of 1917, increased their migration to the mainland in this period as well, responding in particular to employment opportunities in New York City. Although Cubans, Dominicans, and Central and South Americans would not immigrate to the United States in large numbers until after World War II, small numbers of immigrants from these areas did form communities in the early twentieth century in key U.S. cities, including Chicago, New Orleans, New York, and Tampa.

Latinos were among the hardest hit by the economic downturn of the Great Depression. Al-

Latino ranchers in Chamisal, New Mexico, discuss plans with a representative of the Agricultural Adjustment Administration in 1942. LIBRARY OF CONGRESS, PRINTS & PHOTOGRAPHS DIVISION, FSA/OWI COLLECTION

though more established Latino communities had some upper- and middle-class families, most Latinos in the 1910s and 1920s were working class once they arrived in the United States. They participated in—and oftentimes formed the backbone of—a large range of industries, including mining, agriculture, and textile manufacturing. Despite their vital contributions to the U.S. economy, Latinos often were restricted to the lowest paying jobs, received less pay than their Anglo counterparts, and had highly limited occupational mobility. Their position on the bottom rungs of the economic ladder, combined with the ugly specter of racism, put Latinos at a great disadvantage during the 1930s. As the American economy soured and jobs became

scarce, Latinos—who were perceived by many Anglo Americans as foreigners, regardless of their actual citizenship status—provided an easy scapegoat. In many states, Latinos were the first to be fired, as employers felt obligated to give preference to Anglo workers. In Puerto Rico, where the economy depended heavily on a small number of industries, unemployment rates skyrocketed even faster than in the mainland United States, reaching 36 percent in 1929. Not only were Latinos unable to find work, but they also found the doors of welfare offices and work relief programs closed to them, as increasing numbers of government and charitable organizations adopted a "citizens only" policy. In practice, this policy often meant "whites only."

A Farm Security Administration supervisor checks the tobacco crop of an FSA borrower near Barranquitas in Puerto Rico in 1942.

LIBRARY OF CONGRESS, PRINTS & PHOTOGRAPHS DIVISION, FSA/OWI COLLECTION

MEXICAN REPATRIATION

Latinos of all backgrounds were on the move during the Great Depression. An estimated ten thousand Puerto Ricans returned from the mainland to the island between 1930 and 1934, hoping to find better opportunities at home. In New Mexico and Colorado, workers who had migrated to urban areas in the 1920s returned to rural villages, planning to eke out a living on the land, while in California, unemployed agricultural workers poured into the cities, seeking financial assistance. But by far the largest movement of Latinos during this period occurred among Mexicans and Mexican Americans who returned to Mexico. From 1929 to 1937, more than 450,000 persons of Mexican origin were repatriated. This massive movement of men,

women, and children—representing close to half of the Mexican-origin population in the United States at that time—was triggered by the economic woes of the Depression and exacerbated by a rising tide of xenophobia. Repatriation was sometimes voluntary, other times involuntary, and often somewhere in between. The most notorious cases of involuntary repatriation occurred in the Southwestern states, where self-deputized Anglo citizens took it upon themselves to rid their communities of unwanted populations. These groups rounded up Mexicans and Mexican Americans, without regard for their actual citizenship status, and physically removed them to Mexico.

More common than these vigilante roundups were official repatriation drives, undertaken by city

The members of this Mexican-American family from Texas found work as agricultural laborers in East Grand Forks, Minnesota, in 1937. LIBRARY OF CONGRESS, PRINTS & PHOTOGRAPHS DIVISION, FSA/OWI COLLECTION

and county governments and by the Federal Bureau of Immigration. Local leaders in Los Angeles, shocked by the thousands of new entrants on their relief rolls, saw repatriation as an alternative to providing support for immigrant families. Insisting that paying for a one-way train ticket would be cheaper than providing welfare, county leaders organized train rides back to Mexico and paid for the passage of hundreds of Mexican citizens, and sometimes also for their American-citizen children. Between 1931 and 1934, more than thirteen thousand people rode the Los Angeles county repatriation trains. Similar programs arose in Colorado, Indiana, Minnesota, and Michigan, among other states.

The federal government also participated in efforts to send Mexicans home. Federal repatriation drives focused on all destitute aliens, although those of Mexican origin made up the largest percentage of those actually returned. Federal repatriation drives were largely ineffective: only 9,549 "distressed" immigrants, of all nationalities, were officially repatriated between 1931 and 1940. Tens of thousands of immigrants, however, were deported during this period. Deportation, unlike repatriation, entailed official government proceedings, and a charge of deportability prohibited an alien from legally entering the country again. The Bureau of Immigration capitalized on immigrants' fears of being deported, staging high-profile raids in public spaces and workplaces. In Los Angeles, for example, immigration officials raided a popular park in the middle of the day. Plainclothes officers barred the exits, asking all those there for citizenship documentation. Of the four hundred people stopped and questioned by the officials, only eleven Mexicans were taken into custody. The raid had its intended effect, however, as word of the event spread quickly among immigrant communities and intimidated those who were already facing difficult times. Not content to settle at large-scale deportations, the federal government also attempted to assure that fewer Mexicans would immigrate to the United States during this period by denying visas to any Mexican citizen "likely to become a public charge" or entering to engage in "contract labor." The enforcement of these visa restrictions, combined with the lack of opportunities across the border, effectively cut the official admission of Mexican citizens from 38,980 in 1929 to only 2,627 in 1931.

Some Mexicans and Mexican Americans did travel to Mexico of their own accord, without the aid of government or charitable organizations, but they were no doubt influenced by a variety of factors that made clear that they were no longer welcomed in the United States. Shut out of any gainful means of employment and, in some instances, from any source of charity, many of los repatriados had little choice but to return to their native land, where they hoped to find some support. The first wave of these voluntary repatriates tended to be better off; they left at the beginning of the Depression, able to drive in their own cars with their own belongings in tow. As the Depression worsened, however, the next waves of returnees were far worse off and had to depend on others to assist them in their travels.

Unfortunately, most of those returning found few opportunities south of the border. Anthropologists traveling in Mexico during the 1930s found that the return to Mexico was perhaps hardest for the children among the repatriates, many of whom were born in the United States and had grown accustomed to a different standard of living in the North. Those who returned to the rural areas of their parents had to adjust to new styles of dress, new types of food, and the dominance of a different language. The Mexican government sought to assist the migrants in a variety of ways. In the early years of the Depression, Mexican consulates in the United States cooperated with local governments in

planning the repatriation drives. Inundated with pleas of help from unemployed Mexicans in the United States, the consul offices initially saw repatriation as a chance both to assist their fellow countrymen and to regain the valuable workforce that had been lost during the great migration of the 1910s and 1920s. Mexico paid for the passage of some of its citizens and reduced import taxes for the repatriates so that they could bring their belongings home. The government also established a National Repatriation Committee, which sought to resettle the migrants in colonies along the western coast of Mexico. Living conditions there were hard, however, and most migrants returned to their old hometowns instead. As the economic collapse in the United States turned global, Mexico's economy foundered as well. Frustrated with the government's failure to provide for them, *repatriados* in Mexico City formed their own union, which sought to lobby on behalf of the hundreds of thousands of returnees. The union was largely ineffective, however, and returning migrants had to rely on old support networks instead of the government.

SELF-HELP AND FEDERAL ASSISTANCE

For those Latinos who remained in the United States during the Depression, finding ways to support themselves and their families was a constant challenge. In many parts of the country, even those who were employed had to seek additional help, since wages dropped drastically as the economy worsened. Latino beet workers in Colorado, for example, saw their wages shrink from $27 an acre to $12.37 in just three years. Seeking to supplement the meager family income, Latinas entered the industrial workforce in unprecedented numbers. Teenage daughters were typically the first to go to work, but mothers and grandmothers sometimes followed suit. From pecan shelling factories in San Antonio to garment districts in New York, one could find generations of immigrant women working side by side. Although they struggled with poor working conditions and extremely low pay, women often were able, through their work, to keep their families afloat. Their experiences in the workplace, which allowed them to experience life outside of typical gendered roles, also helped contribute to a nascent Latina women's movement, which would mature after World War II.

When even the multifamily income proved insufficient, many Latinos fell back on ethnic mutual aid societies, or *mutualistas,* for assistance. Self-help in Latino communities ranged from highly organized, structured groups like the *Cruz Azul* (Blue Cross) to informal groups of women banded together to sell tamales at cost to unemployed workers. In cities with long-standing middle-class Latino populations, such as Los Angeles and New York, the *mutualistas* were able to provide some modicum of relief. But in most other towns, the support quickly ran out as benefactors lost their wealth. Latinos then turned to local, state, and federal governments for assistance. Latinos participated in a wide range of federal relief programs under the New Deal. Social security, labor reforms, and housing assistance all benefited Latino families. New Deal welfare relief programs also protected Latinos by insisting that all funds be distributed without discrimination based on citizenship status. Some programs were targeted specifically towards Latino communities, such as the Hispanic arts revival in northern New Mexico, which sought to teach traditional crafts to the local populace as a means of both cultural and financial survival. Other programs retained a majority of Latino workers by default, such as large-scale construction projects that drew on already experienced Latino labor. An estimated 100,000 Mexican nationals alone participated in New Deal work programs in the western states.

As with other racial/ethnic minorities, however, the New Deal left an ambivalent legacy among Latinos. Despite federal efforts to insure that immigrants could find welfare assistance, some state governments continued to turn Latinos away. In 1937 Congress, following a trend already established by the states, declared that all programs of the Works Progress Administration (WPA) would be closed to aliens. The "citizens-only" policy of the WPA extended even to companies that fulfilled government contracts; corporations such as General Motors fired those whom they perceived as foreigners to keep from losing lucrative government business. Southwestern craft programs that sought

to preserve Hispanic villages in reality left many with skills that could not sustain them in an increasingly industrialized nation. In Puerto Rico, the targeted programs of the Puerto Rico Emergency Relief Program provided some aid, but they also paid lesser wages than similar programs in the mainland United States. In sum, Latinos both benefited from and were scarred by their experiences with the New Deal.

POLITICS AND THE GROWTH OF ETHNIC IDENTITY

Desperate times served to politicize many Latinos, both in the workplace and at home. Workers of all backgrounds, united by the trials and tribulations of the Depression, engaged in an unprecedented amount of labor organizing in the 1930s, seeking reforms in wages, hours, and other conditions of employment. In 1934 alone, union membership doubled, and there were more than 1,800 strikes nationwide. As the backbone of the agricultural and manufacturing sectors in some parts of the United States during the 1930s, Latinos provided the union rank and file in many labor disputes, especially in the heavily Hispanic states in the Southwest. Entire families participated in labor activities, helping to staff the picket lines, provide food for strikers and their kin, and lobby local officials. Notably, Latinos also emerged as labor leaders during this period, helping to organize farm workers in California, pecan-shellers in Texas, and steel workers in Illinois, to name just a few.

The scarcity of resources during the Depression did pit some Latinos against each other. Those who were American citizens fought hard to assert their right to all the benefits of citizenship. They sought to differentiate themselves from more recent Latino immigrants who bore the brunt of the "Americans only" policies in this period. On the whole, however, the struggles of the Depression era contributed to a more unified sense of ethnic identity among Latinos. Even relatively conservative Latino groups were forced to recognize that they shared a common fate with the foreigners in their midst. The indiscriminate enforcement of "no aliens" policies, capturing not only undocumented Mexican migrants but also long-standing Latino citizens of the United States, served to raise the consciousness of many Latinos. Second- and third-generation Latino Americans, who had previously argued for restricted immigration and increased deportations, had a change of heart when they themselves suffered harassment and discrimination at the hands of government officials. Those who remained in the United States during these years realized the tenuousness of their membership in the national community, no matter how long they had lived in the country or how much they had given of themselves and their resources.

This new sense of communal identity, born out of repression, led to greater political mobilization. Although a rich variety of local and regional Latino organizations had emerged earlier in the century, it was not until the Depression era that national Latino groups came to prominence. Such groups included the League of Latin American Citizens (LULAC), founded in Texas in 1929, and *El Congreso de Pueblos que Hablan Español* (The National Congress of Spanish Speaking Peoples), established by Guatemalan-American labor leader Luisa Moreno in 1937. Increasingly, Cubans, Puerto Ricans, Mexicans, and other Latinos came together to fight for a range of civil rights, not only in the workplace but also in courts, schools, and places of public accommodation. Although it would take the massive post-1965 immigration to establish a strong pan-ethnic Latino identity, the seeds of this change were planted during the hard times of the 1930s.

See Also: CHAVEZ, DENNIS; LATIN AMERICA, GREAT DEPRESSION IN; MEXICO, GREAT DEPRESSION IN; MIGRATION; MIGRATORY WORKERS; RACE AND ETHNIC RELATIONS.

BIBLIOGRAPHY

Balderrama, Francisco E., and Raymond Rodríguez. *Decade of Betrayal: Mexican Repatriation in the 1930s.* 1995.

Blackwelder, Julia Kirk. *Women of the Depression: Caste and Culture in San Antonio, 1929–1939.* 1984.

Carreras de Velasco, Mercedes. *Los Mexicanos que Devolvió La Crisis, 1929–1932.* 1974.

Forrest, Suzanne. *The Preservation of the Village: New Mexico's Hispanics and the New Deal.* 1989.

Hoffman, Abraham. *Unwanted Mexican Americans in the Great Depression: Repatriation Pressures, 1929–1939.* 1974.

Jaffe, A. J.; Ruth M. Cullen; and Thomas D. Boswell. *The Changing Demography of Spanish Americans.* 1980.

McKay, R. Reynolds. "The Federal Deportation Campaign in Texas: Mexican Deportation from the Lower Rio Grande Valley during the Great Depression." *The Borderlands Journal* 5, no. 1 (1981): 90–120.

Rodríguez-Vásquez, Manuel R. "Power and Development: The Puerto Rican Emergency Relief Administration and the Emergence of a New Colonial Order." Ph.D. diss., Temple University, 2001.

Ruiz, Vicki L. *Cannery Women, Cannery Lives: Mexican Women, Unionization, and the California Food Processing Industry, 1930–1950.* 1987.

Sánchez Korrol, Virginia E. *From Colonia to Community: The History of Puerto Ricans in New York City,* 2nd edition. 1994.

Sánchez, George J. *Becoming Mexican American: Ethnicity, Culture, and Identity in Chicano Los Angeles, 1900–1945.* 1993.

Thatcher, Mary Anne. *Immigrants and the 1930s: Ethnicity and Alienage in Depression and On-Coming War.* 1990.

ALLISON BROWNELL TIRRES

LAW ENFORCEMENT

Law enforcement was especially important during the last years of prohibition and the first half of the Great Depression, a period that saw a wave of violence and well-publicized criminal activity. Homer Cummings, Franklin D. Roosevelt's attorney general from 1933 to 1939, declared that, "We are now engaged in a war that threatens the safety of our country—a war with the organized forces of crime."

The 18th Amendment, which was passed by Congress in 1917 and went into effect in 1920, prohibited the manufacture, sale, and transportation of alcoholic beverages. Prohibition was expected to reduce the consumption of alcohol and thereby reduce crime and poverty, and improve the quality of life. In fact, prohibition led to an explosive growth of crime. The Great Depression compounded the problem as some poor Americans resorted to crime as a way to provide food, clothing, and other necessities.

The crime rate at the end of the 1920s nearly doubled from that of the pre-Prohibition period.

During the Depression police were often called to control disturbances caused by angry strikers. This striker scuffled with a police officer in San Francisco in 1934. FRANKLIN DELANO ROOSEVELT LIBRARY

Serious crimes, such as homicide and assault, increased nearly 13 percent during the Prohibition era. According to Mark Thornton's "Policy Analysis: Alcohol Prohibition was a Failure" (1991) the crime rate increased because prohibition destroyed legal jobs, created black-market violence, diverted resources from enforcement of other laws, and increased the prices people had to pay for prohibited goods. In large cities the homicide rate went from 5.6 percent (per 100,000 population) in the pre-Prohibition period to nearly 10 percent during Prohibition. By 1932, banks were being robbed at a rate of twelve to sixteen each month across the country, and during the earlier two years kidnappings and extortions had increased to what was considered epidemic proportions. Nearly three hundred kidnappings were reported nationally in 1931.

State and local law enforcement officials, who were insufficient in number, poorly trained, and poorly paid and equipped, were unable to deal with the increasing illegal activities that occurred during the Depression years. They were further restricted by laws that prohibited them from chasing suspects across city, county, and state lines, and from inconsistencies in federal and states laws that prevented federal agents from helping local officials track criminals.

Beginning in 1925, the new director of the Bureau of Investigation (the word *Federal* was added in 1935), J. Edgar Hoover, began to reform the problem-plagued agency. He searched for talented, honest men, hired the best of them, and put them through a rigorous orientation program in order to assemble an elite group of specialized in law enforcement agents. The bureau made positive advances at strengthening its crime-fighting capabilities, by, for example, conducting surveys of banks and bank robberies, using laboratories and scientific methods to examine crime evidence, and training police officers in modern investigative methods.

As American citizens grew increasingly alarmed at the epidemic of lawlessness and after local law enforcement officials proved unable to deal with it, the Bureau of Investigation was called to "go to war" against crime. In May 1934 Congress approved an anti-crime package that included the Anti-Racketeering Act, which prohibited extortion through the mail or telephone; the Fugitive Felon Act, which prohibited suspected criminals from crossing state lines to escape prosecution; and the National Firearms Act, which gave the FBI the right to collect taxes on weapons, restrict weapons importation, and require firearms registration. By 1935 Roosevelt had signed seven new crime bills that provided the FBI with comprehensive crime-fighting powers.

During this time, the U.S. attorney general promoted a nationwide public relations campaign to glorify the G-man, or government-man, and to undermine criminal activity. Soon, Americans were reading newspaper articles describing the daring exploits of Hoover's G-men as they battled with gangsters. Children all over the country began wearing tin G-Man badges and playing with toy

Tommy guns. Hollywood even produced a movie called *G-Man* (1935) that starred James Cagney, previously noted for his roles as gangsters, as federal agent James "Brick" Davis. By 1935, federal agents had succeeded in arresting or killing a number of notorious criminals, including John Dillinger, "Baby Face" Nelson (Lester Gillis), George "Machine Gun" Kelly, Bonnie and Clyde (Clyde Barrow and Bonnie Parker), Charles Arthur "Pretty Boy" Floyd, and Al Capone.

See Also: BONNIE AND CLYDE (BONNIE PARKER AND CLYDE BARROW); CAPONE, AL; CRIME; CUMMINGS, HOMER; HOOVER, J. EDGAR; PROHIBITION.

BIBLIOGRAPHY

Breuer, William B. *J. Edgar Hoover and His G-Men.* 1995.

Federal Bureau of Investigation. *History of the FBI.* Available at: www.fbi.gov/libref/historic/history

Powers, Richard Gid. *Secrecy and Power: The Life of J. Edgar Hoover.* 1987.

Thornton, Mark. "Policy Analysis: Alcohol Prohibition Was a Failure." Cato Institute Policy Analysis 57. 1991. Available at: www.cato.org/pubs/pas/pa-157.html

Ungar, Sanford J. *FBI.* 1976.

Watkins, T. H. *The Great Depression: America in the 1930s.* 1993.

WILLIAM ARTHUR ATKINS

LEAGUE FOR INDEPENDENT POLITICAL ACTION

The League for Independent Political Action represented one of the last in a series of attempts to unite workers, farmers, and intellectuals into a viable political organization. In December 1928, Paul H. Douglas, Sherwood Eddy, and Norman Thomas assembled fifty-three activists to form a clearinghouse to coordinate information on existing organizations, while developing a program for a new party. In 1929 a national committee, consisting of numerous well-known progressives, was established, selecting John Dewey, whose political and economic views paralleled the League's own, as chairman,

and Howard Y. Williams as executive secretary. Williams organized some 2,500 members into ninety chapters in thirty-five states. The League emphasized political action as the way to secure a cooperatively-managed, consumer-controlled, planned economy marked by full employment, equal distribution of wealth, and a "Cooperative Commonwealth" based on production for use. The League for Independent Political Action viewed itself as pursuing a pragmatic middle course between the moribund Republican and Democratic parties and the Marxist left.

In 1930, spurred on by the worsening Depression, the League for Independent Political Action endorsed Republican and Democratic candidates only when there were no third-party candidates. Half of these League-supported candidates were elected. The League's second goal, creating a broad-based national party, however, proved more difficult. After the election, Dewey unsuccessfully encouraged Senator George Norris (Republican-Nebraska) to lead Progressive Republicans into a new party. Undaunted, in January 1932 the League issued a "Four Year Presidential Plan" advocating many long-standing reforms, including federal relief and public work programs, more progressive tax rates, old-age pensions, and public ownership of public utilities. The document, which anticipated many New Deal programs, and the League itself attracted only modest support. In July, fewer than one hundred delegates attended a League-sponsored National Progressive Conference. The conference endorsed the Socialist ticket of Norman Thomas and James H. Maurer, a League vice-chairman, and called for another gathering in 1933 to again try to establish a new party. Despite the endorsement, many members of the League, along with many other progressives, eventually supported Franklin D. Roosevelt.

Ultimately the League for Independent Political Action, with a membership under ten thousand, and viewed by some as dominated by an intellectual elite, neither gained broad support nor developed an appealing political vision for radical agrarian and labor groups. Always close to the Minnesota Farmer-Labor Party, the League organized the Farmer-Labor Political Federation in 1933, and two years later created a more broadly based American Commonwealth Political Federation to continue local organizing and build a new party. Unable to differentiate itself from competing groups, and facing internal strife and shifting allegiances, these efforts proved futile. In the wake of Roosevelt's 1936 landslide victory, the League for Independent Political Action and its successor groups disappeared as viable political organizations.

See Also: MINNESOTA FARMER-LABOR PARTY.

BIBLIOGRAPHY

Bicha, Karel Dennis. "Liberalism Frustrated: The League for Independent Political Action, 1928–1933." *Mid-America* 48, no. 1 (1966): 19–28.

Lawson, R. Alan. *The Failure of Independent Liberalism, 1930–1941.* 1971.

McCoy, Donald R. *Angry Voices: Left-of-Center Politics in the New Deal Era.* 1958.

Williams, Howard Y., Jr. Papers. Minnesota Historical Society, Saint Paul, Minnesota.

JOHN SILLITO

LEDBETTER, HUDDIE ("LEADBELLY").
See MUSIC.

LEGAL PROFESSION

The Depression had varying effects on the different segments of the legal profession. Urban lawyers who typically practiced on their own or in association with one or two other lawyers representing individuals suffered severe losses of income. Small-town lawyers struggled to sustain practices based on local businesses and estate planning. Lawyers who represented large corporations found their practices changing from negotiating contracts to negotiating the terms of bankruptcies, but managed to sustain their practices at pre-Depression levels, although large law firms reduced or suspended hiring new lawyers.

The New Deal's regulatory programs also had varying effects. Lawyers had to develop the legal structures for implementing the New Deal's programs and defend those programs against constitutional attack. Substantial numbers of young lawyers joined the administration in Washington, finding in the new regulatory programs legal opportunities they lacked in private practice and hoping to fulfill the professional ideal of public service. Harvard law professor Felix Frankfurter channeled some of his most accomplished students toward government service in Washington. Many Depression-era lawyers became prominent figures in the Roosevelt administration, and later, some, such as Thurman Arnold, the head of the antitrust division at the Department of Justice, helped to found major Washington law firms.

Lawyers representing business interests faced a conflict: Their clients required them to oppose the New Deal's initiatives, and many elite lawyers did. Leaders of the American Bar Association regularly denounced the New Deal in terms that associated the New Deal with tyrannical regimes. The American Liberty League organized a lawyers' committee to provide legal support for constitutional challenges to New Deal programs. John W. Davis, a former solicitor general, 1924 Democratic presidential candidate, and a leader of the elite New York bar, led bar association attacks on Roosevelt's court-packing plan.

The New Deal's regulatory programs generated legal work on the business side because corporations needed advice about how to comply with the new statutes. In that sense, the New Deal created the modern corporate law firm. Corporate lawyers reconciled the conflict between their clients' interests and their own professional interests by developing legal theories that accommodated the new administrative agencies to traditional notions of the rule of law by fitting the agencies into a model based on court procedures. Based on those theories, elite lawyers proposed new statutes to regulate the agencies. Eventually their proposals were reshaped and then adopted in the Administrative Procedure Act of 1946, whose procedural code for administrative agencies encouraged the agencies to act like courts.

In response to attacks on the New Deal by the elite bar, leftist lawyers formed the National Lawyers Guild in 1936 as a vehicle for promoting progressive views within the legal profession. The public interest law movement of the 1960s was foreshadowed between 1931 and 1933 when the National Association for the Advancement of Colored People (NAACP) used a foundation grant to develop a strategic plan for challenging segregation. The plan as proposed was never carried out, but the idea of strategic litigation for social change eventually became an important component of the legal profession's understanding of its social role.

See Also: ARNOLD, THURMAN; FRANKFURTER, FELIX; SUPREME COURT "PACKING" CONTROVERSY.

BIBLIOGRAPHY

Auerbach, Jerold S. *Unequal Justice: Lawyers and Social Change in Modern America.* 1976.

Irons, Peter H. *The New Deal Lawyers.* 1982.

Shamir, Ronen. *Managing Legal Uncertainty: Elite Lawyers in the New Deal.* 1995.

MARK TUSHNET

LEHAND, MARGUERITE (MISSY)

Officially, Marguerite "Missy" LeHand (September 13, 1898–July 31, 1944) was Franklin D. Roosevelt's confidential secretary from 1920 until 1941. Unofficially, she was much more. At a time when personal secretaries were often "office wives," she performed many tasks commonly associated with spouses including handling Roosevelt's finances, overseeing domestic help, and serving as his hostess when Eleanor Roosevelt was away. LeHand's proximity to Franklin D. Roosevelt, coupled with her skill, judgment, and tact, also made her an influential player in his inner circle, particularly after he became president. Beyond this behind-the-scenes influence, she became a public figure in her own right. The *New York Times* reporter Arthur Krock even described her as the president's conscience, a title usually applied to Eleanor. Certainly Franklin D. Roosevelt relied on LeHand's abilities. He also counted on her companionship. Historians have speculated about the exact nature of their rela-

tionship, but most agree that LeHand devoted her life to Roosevelt. Her closeness to him inevitably caused tensions with Eleanor, but for the most part the two women maintained an amicable relationship.

LeHand was born in Potsdam, New York, and was raised in Somerville, Massachusetts. After graduating from high school and secretarial school, she worked in a variety of clerical and secretarial jobs before joining the Democratic National Committee's staff in 1920. There she met Franklin D. Roosevelt, who was then running for vice president. After losing that race, he hired LeHand to help him with his mail. She soon began to undertake other duties and quickly became indispensable, especially after Roosevelt contracted polio in 1921. Serving as a combination secretary-housekeeper-hostess, she accompanied him on his travels as he sought to regain his health, and she actively opposed his return to public life because she feared it would impede his recovery. However, once Roosevelt decided to run for governor of New York in 1928, LeHand supported his career, moving into the governor's mansion and later the White House.

The physical and emotional demands of working around the clock for Roosevelt ultimately undermined LeHand's always fragile health. She suffered two minor breakdowns in the 1920s. In each case, she recovered quickly. However, a severe stroke in 1941 left her an invalid. Although he paid all her medical bills and provided for her in his will, Roosevelt saw LeHand only occasionally after her stroke. When she died of a cerebral embolism in 1944, he did not attend her funeral.

See Also: ROOSEVELT, FRANKLIN D.

BIBLIOGRAPHY

Goodwin, Doris Kearns. *No Ordinary Time: Franklin and Eleanor Roosevelt, The Home Front in World War II.* 1994.

Lash, Joseph P. *Eleanor and Franklin: The Story of Their Relationship, Based on Eleanor Roosevelt's Private Papers.* 1971.

Scharf, Lois. "Marguerite 'Missy' LeHand." In *Franklin D. Roosevelt: His Life and Times, An Encyclopedic View,*

Missy LeHand (center) with Franklin and Eleanor Roosevelt in 1929. FRANKLIN DELANO ROOSEVELT LIBRARY

edited by Otis L. Graham and Meghan Robinson Wander. 1985.

MARY JO BINKER

LEHMAN, HERBERT

Herbert Henry Lehman (March 28,1878–December 5,1963) was a New York businessman who served as governor of New York and United States senator. Lehman was born and grew up in New York City. The son of one of the founders of Lehman Brothers, he worked at the family's investment banking firm and engaged in philanthropy after graduating from Williams College in Williamstown, Massachusetts. A lifelong Democrat and party fundraiser, he was elected as Franklin D. Roosevelt's lieutenant governor in 1928. Four years later he was elected governor of New York, a position he held for ten years.

Under Lehman's leadership, New York state adopted a package of reforms that won recognition as the country's premier "Little New Deal." Some programs, such as public housing, involved state-federal cooperation, but most were exclusively state operations that benefited groups hard hit by the Depression. While some state reforms resembled federal measures, in several cases, notably unemployment insurance and a minimum wage law, New York acted before Washington. In other instances, such as creation of the State Labor Relations Board, New York programs were copied almost verbatim from federal statutes. New York also established a system of price supports for dairy farmers. Other state reforms included restrictions on child labor, as well as state aid, as part of Social Security, for needy people burdened by unemployment, old age, physical disabilities, or fatherless families. Through these programs, New York laid the foundations for a welfare state that became a model for other states.

The Depression provided much of the impetus for New York's reform movement by revealing the impersonal causes of poverty and stimulating a rising demand for government action. Some proposals had been suggested before, but the Depression, which devastated so many people, made the reforms more acceptable. New York proved fertile ground for reform, in part because of its progressive traditions and because it had access to greater taxable wealth than most states. Herbert Lehman also contributed to the success of welfare state reforms, guaranteeing a minimum standard of living to many groups. Despite his wealth, Lehman was genuinely interested in the plight of those in need, seeing "no inconsistency between being a business man and a liberal." Thus, he welcomed the suggestions of social workers and union leaders and in his quiet manner fought doggedly for enabling legislation. On January 6, 1938, the *New York Times* credited the "modest, hard-working and undramatic governor" with guiding passage of "a labor and social program transcending any ever executed in America."

Lehman's reputation as a liberal reformer later helped him win a seat in the U. S. Senate, where he served from 1949 to 1957 and became an outspoken opponent of controversial Republican Senator Joseph R. McCarthy.

See Also: DEMOCRATIC PARTY; ELECTION OF 1928; ELECTION OF 1932.

BIBLIOGRAPHY

Ingalls, Robert P. *Herbert H. Lehman and New York's Little New Deal.* 1975.

Nevins, Allan. *Herbert H. Lehman and His Era.* 1963.

ROBERT P. INGALLS

LEISURE

Americans have always been of two minds about leisure: Too little leisure perhaps makes a dull person, but too much suggests laziness, a lack of purpose. The Depression caused people to question old attitudes about leisure because millions found themselves deprived of work and with time on their hands. Unemployment reached a high of 24.9 percent in 1933; the average workweek simultaneously declined from forty-eight to forty hours. Since women constituted only about one-third of the workforce, more men faced unemployment. Women who worked at home had long since learned to deal with leisure time, but newly unemployed men faced a new challenge. The New Deal attempted to reduce unemployment while at the same time providing outlets for the jobless by creating agencies to address this excess of leisure time. The National Recovery Administration (NRA) instituted employee work codes and fair practices. Despite good intentions, these moves reduced hours at the job, especially overtime. By 1935, two-thirds of NRA-protected employees worked fewer than forty hours a week and thus had increased free time on their hands.

In 1935, the Works Progress Administration (WPA) received the mandate to create meaningful jobs for unemployed citizens. To assist young people, the Roosevelt administration created the National Youth Administration (NYA), which employed thousands of young men and women across the nation. To provide leisure outlets, the government also built parks, playing fields, and recreational areas around the country. Many cities constructed municipal golf courses and softball became popular; late in the decade, five million Americans were playing softball regularly, and almost a quarter of them were women. Millions more attended as fans, and sports equipment manufacturers saw a sales upturn. Swing music, which peaked in popularity during the Depression, encouraged dancing. The jitterbug, along with a host of novelty dances and traditional steps, caused millions to try their skills in the country's many pavilions and dance halls.

Nevertheless, by the early 1930s over a million unemployed people—men and women, young and old—could be found wandering the country. Such roaming hardly qualified as recreational travel, but it resurrected the old frontier custom of moving on in search of something better. At the same time, many other Americans enjoyed jobs and the wherewithal to travel. Tourism prospered, whether by car, bus, train, plane, or luxurious ocean liner—a sharp contrast with the desperation shown by those not so fortunate. Traveling by trailer gained adherents, with thousands of families visiting autocamps and similar sites.

High unemployment and reduced working hours meant that hobbies of every description boomed. Municipalities sponsored hobby clubs, classes, and community garden plots on the theory that regular activities in a structured setting reinforced the work ethic for everyone, even the jobless. Leisure emerged as a form of substitute employment, and newspapers and magazines featured countless how-to columns. Such leisure time activities provided a sense of self-worth to participants, and working at a hobby proved fulfilling. Children who could not afford commercially made toys during the Depression found substitutes. Homemade playthings fashioned from such discarded items as crates, tin cans, old tires, and rope could be one-of-a-kind originals; children passed toy-making ideas on to friends, or found plans and designs in magazines.

Movies also rose in popularity during the Depression, and an average of over seventy-five million Americans, regardless of race or ethnicity, attended the movies every week, often as families. To keep audiences coming during difficult times, theaters cut prices and offered discount passes, premiums, and double features. In addition to movies, a marked rise in sedentary, solitary pastimes occurred. Radio, for example, attracted a growing audience. Approximately six hundred stations broadcast to some twelve million receivers in 1930; by decade's end over eight hundred stations filled the airwaves, and more than fifty-one million sets picked up their signals.

Reading also satisfied leisure needs. Books and magazines of all kinds sold well. By the late 1930s, over 1,200 weekly and some two thousand monthly periodicals vied for the public's attention, jointly circulating 150 million copies, a figure that exceeded the nation's population. In addition, virtually everyone read a daily newspaper, especially the "funnies." With wide distribution and a broad audience, comic strips and comic books constituted a new national literature. In addition, book clubs such as the Literary Guild and the Book-of-the-Month Club flourished. A theme of escapism runs through much of what people read during the Depression, since few wanted reminders of the troubles facing them. Hollywood produced many films based on best sellers, confident that screen images briefly helped audiences escape reality.

Games of every variety thrived. Jigsaw puzzles proved popular, and by 1933 people were buying some ten million a week. The game Pick Up Sticks, introduced in 1936, sold three million sets in less than a year. Board games also saw increased sales; Monopoly, the undisputed champion, made its debut in 1935. Card games, especially contract bridge, likewise rose in popularity; by 1931, over 500,000 individuals had enrolled in bridge lessons at YMCAs, parks, and other locales. Conservative estimates had twenty million people playing the game.

Gambling of various kinds appealed to many. Churches staged bingo in their parish halls, and slot machines, punchboards, and pinball machines gave Americans opportunities to win easy money. A 1939 poll claimed that one-third of the population admitted to occasional gambling.

The value and importance of steady work has long been stressed in American culture. The Great Depression challenged the jobless and the underemployed to deal with the stigma of being out of work, and forced them to learn to manage increased quantities of free time and to find leisure activities that carried meaning, reinforced self-esteem, and distanced them from idleness.

See Also: COMICS; FAMILY AND HOME, IMPACT OF
   THE GREAT DEPRESSION ON; HOLLYWOOD
   AND THE FILM INDUSTRY; LITERATURE;
   MONOPOLY (BOARD GAME); MUSIC; RADIO;
   SPORTS; UNEMPLOYMENT, LEVELS OF.

BIBLIOGRAPHY

Allen, Frederick Lewis. *Since Yesterday: The Nineteen-thirties in America, September 3, 1929–September 3, 1939.* 1940.

Congdon, Don, ed. *The Thirties: A Time to Remember.* 1962.

Gelber, Steven M. "A Job You Can't Lose: Work and Hobbies in the Great Depression." *Journal of Social History* 24 (1991): 741–766.

Kennedy, David M. *Freedom from Fear: The American People in Depression and War, 1929–1945.* 1999.

O'Dell, John. *The Great American Depression Book of Fun.* 1981.

Steiner, Jesse F. *Research Memorandum on Recreation in the Depression.* 1937.

Wecter, Dixon. *The Age of the Great Depression, 1929–1941.* 1948.

Young, William H., with Nancy K. Young. *The 1930s* (American Popular Culture through History). 2002.

WILLIAM H. YOUNG

LEWIS, JOHN L.

John Llewellyn Lewis (February 12, 1880–June 11, 1969), the son of Welsh immigrants, was raised in poverty in the coalfields of Lucas County, Iowa. In the 1890s the family relocated for several years to Des Moines, but upon the family's return to Lucas County, Lewis began work in the mines and in 1901 became secretary of his United Mine Workers (UMW) local. Lewis married the daughter of a local physician, Myrta Bell, and in time the couple raised three children. By 1907 the Lewis family had resettled in the mining town of Panama, Illinois. Three years later Lewis became president of Panama's large Local 1475, which was a springboard for his union career.

Lewis was a stalwart supporter of UMW president John White, who appointed him union statistician in 1917. By the end of that year, White had resigned, and his replacement, Frank Hayes, named Lewis UMW vice president. When Hayes himself resigned in January 1920, Lewis became head of the nation's largest union. Lewis would hold the post of UMW president for the next forty years.

The 1920s and early 1930s were disastrous for the UMW. Facing fierce competition from non-union coalfields, union operators demanded wage reductions. In dealings with operators Lewis pursued a failed policy of "no backward step." Miner militancy could not overcome market forces that generated low wages and unemployment. As membership plummeted, Lewis faced challenges to his leadership. In 1926 the attack came to a head when John Brophy ran against Lewis for the union presidency. Lewis showed no hesitation in centralizing his authority, red baiting his opponents, and stuffing ballot boxes to defeat Brophy.

Although a Republican, Lewis exploited Franklin Roosevelt's 1932 electoral victory. Lewis played a critical role in securing the labor provision of the National Industrial Recovery Act (1933), and he used the law's section 7a to organize miners in the southern coalfields. Throughout the Depression years, Lewis demonstrated skill in bargaining with both employers and the state, and he used the NRA's code hearings to extend membership, reduce regional differentials, and increase wage rates. UMW success under the New Deal fueled Lewis's ambition to expand unionism dramatically in mass-production industries. He urged the craft unionists who dominated the American Federation of Labor (AFL) executive council to abandon their narrow interests and launch vigorous campaigns in automobiles, steel, rubber, electrical appliances, and other industries. When craft unionists refused to sanction the industrial union campaign at the 1935 AFL convention, Lewis foreshadowed the future of American labor by punching the Carpenters' president Bill Hutcheson in the face.

In November 1935 Lewis and others formed the Committee for Industrial Organization (CIO), an industrial union pressure group within the AFL. With Lewis in the limelight, the CIO erected permanent unions in the major mass-production industries and established Labor's Non-Partisan League to re-elect Roosevelt in 1936. In early 1937 Lewis played decisive roles in both the United Automobile Workers' successful sit-down strike against General Motors, and the collective bargaining agreement signed between U.S. Steel and the Steel Workers' Organizing Committee (SWOC). On the heels of these major victories, however, came several setbacks. The spring 1937 "Little

Steel" defeat of SWOC, the 1937 to 1938 recession, and the 1938 AFL decision to expel the CIO killed the aura of invincibility that had surrounded Lewis and the CIO.

After the CIO recast itself as the Congress of Industrial Organizations in 1938, Lewis became increasingly disillusioned with other CIO leaders and with the Roosevelt administration. One week before the November 1940 presidential elections, Lewis urged union members to support the Republican candidate, Wendell Willkie. After Roosevelt's victory, Lewis resigned as CIO president, although he remained a pivotal figure in the labor movement as president of the UMW.

During World War II and the late 1940s Lewis repeatedly used the strike weapon to advance UMW interests. Although he voiced support for labor's "no strike pledge" during the war, he violated that pledge in 1943 with mining strikes that roused the enmity of politicians and led directly to passage of the Smith-Connally Act. In the late 1940s mining strikes were commonplace, sometimes resulting in union advances but at other times yielding stiff fines and threats of state takeover of the mines. In the 1950s Lewis's strategy shifted to one of collaboration with employers, and the earlier patterns of authoritarian rule and corruption became increasingly prominent. When Lewis retired in 1960, the UMW was in decline, reflecting the increasingly poor health of the coal industry and the corruption that had seeped into the administrative apparatus. Lewis died in 1969 in Washington D.C.

See Also: AMERICAN FEDERATION OF LABOR (AFL); COLLECTIVE BARGAINING; CONGRESS OF INDUSTRIAL ORGANIZATIONS (CIO); UNITED MINE WORKERS OF AMERICA (UMWA).

BIBLIOGRAPHY

Alinsky, Saul D. *John L. Lewis: An Unauthorized Biography.* 1949.

Dubofsky, Melvyn, and Warren Van Tine. *John L. Lewis: A Biography.* 1977.

Laslett, John H. M., ed. *The United Mine Workers of America: A Model of Industrial Solidarity?* 1996.

Zieger, Robert H. *John L. Lewis: Labor Leader.* 1988.

CRAIG PHELAN

LINDBERGH, CHARLES

In 1927 Charles Lindbergh (February 4, 1902–August 26,1974) was the first pilot to complete a transatlantic flight. He was born in Detroit to Evangeline and C. A. Lindbergh, a lawyer who served as a U.S. congressman from Minnesota. In his early twenties, Lindbergh briefly studied engineering and learned to fly a plane. In 1923, Lindbergh, along with hundreds of others, bought surplus World War I Curtiss Jenny airplanes from the U.S. Army, which he used to barnstorm and entertain the American public. In 1925, he became the chief pilot for Robertson Aircraft in St. Louis, Missouri, and began to fly the airmail. Two years later, backed by a group of St. Louis businessmen, Lindbergh built a special plane called the Spirit of St. Louis. On May 20, 1927, he flew solo in his new plane from New York to Paris in thirty-three and a half hours.

Four million people welcomed him when he returned to New York, and Lindbergh was an instant hero and attractive celebrity. The media and public focused on his achievement and later his marriage and travels with his copilot wife, Anne Morrow. Lindbergh's flight catapulted America into an aviation frenzy. According to aviation historian Henry Ladd Smith, investors rushed to buy into an industry that was not yet necessary to the public, investing nearly $400 million dollars in 1929 alone. The industry collapsed in the summer of 1929.

In March 1932, Lindbergh's infant son was kidnapped in what became known as the "crime of the century." Two years later, Bruno Richard Hauptmann, a German carpenter, was arrested, tried, and executed for the kidnapping and murder of the baby. Many have questioned the fairness of the trial, arguing that Lindbergh's tremendous popularity may have influenced the outcome.

Lindbergh, a Republican, and President Franklin D. Roosevelt came into public conflict over two issues during the 1930s. In 1934 Lindbergh and Roosevelt disagreed over the "Spoils Conferences," a series of airmail contracts granted to new airline corporations in 1930. Lindbergh, who was employed by one of the airlines, accused Roosevelt of damaging the industry when the president broke the contracts and assigned the Army to fly the mail.

With Lindbergh's support, the Black-McKellar Act returned the airmail to the commercial airlines, a defeat for the President.

Between 1935 and 1939, Lindbergh lived in Europe and visited Germany, publicly meeting with leaders of Germany's Luftwaffe. In 1939, Lindbergh advised the U.S. Army Air Corps to develop high-speed aircraft to deter attacks by other powers. A second conflict with Roosevelt ensued when Lindbergh, a spokesman for the America First Committee, regularly broadcast his isolationist views on the radio. In response to his speeches, the administration questioned Lindbergh's patriotism and intimated that he had a relationship with the Nazi government. In April 1941, Lindbergh resigned from his position as a colonel in the U.S. Air Corps Reserves. That September he accused the British, Jews, and Roosevelt of pushing the country toward war, a move that significantly damaged his image with the American public.

Throughout the Depression Lindbergh was a hero to the American public because of his famous flight and his image as a handsome, intelligent, and resourceful individual. For many, Lindbergh symbolized the possibilities of new technology, ideas about American manhood, and, with his wife and son, modern marriage and family. His isolationist views, while initially shared by many Americans, diminished his popularity. After the Depression, Lindbergh worked with military and commercial aviation interests and engaged in nature conservation efforts until his death in 1974.

See Also: HEROES; ISOLATIONISM.

BIBLIOGRAPHY

Berg, A. Scott. *Lindbergh.* 1998.

Gray, Susan. *Charles Lindbergh and the American Dilemma: The Conflict of Technology and Human Values.* 1988.

Luckett, Perry D. *Charles A. Lindbergh: A Bio-Bibliography.* 1986.

Mosley, Leonard. *Lindbergh: A Biography.* 1976.

Smith, Henry Ladd. *Airways: The History of Commercial Aviation in the United States.* 1942. Reprint, 1965.

LIESL MILLER ORENIC

LITERATURE

Few events have had a more immediate impact on the cultural life of the United States than the Great Depression. When the stock market crashed in October 1929, American literature was in the closing days of a now legendary renaissance, a period in which some of the most significant writers of the twentieth century—T. S. Eliot, F. Scott Fitzgerald, Ernest Hemingway, Langston Hughes, and Robert Frost, to name but a few—first came to prominence. Yet, despite the fact that many of these figures expressed sincere hostility toward the commercial values prevalent in the culture of their day, the writers of the 1920s were deeply dependent on the booming economy of the decade, often for their subject matter as well as for material support. The economic upheaval of the thirties changed that situation fundamentally. Not only did the stagnant economy shake up the publishing industry, leading to important, long-term changes in the literary profession, widespread and persistent suffering forced American writers to question their basic assumptions about the United States and its cultural and political values and brought new ideas and voices to the fore. In the words of the prominent critic Edmund Wilson, "the economic crisis" had been "accompanied by a literary one." As a result, the Great Depression gave rise to a new cohort of important American writers. John Dos Passos, Zora Neale Hurston, William Faulkner, John Steinbeck, Thomas Wolfe, and Richard Wright all did their most important writing in the thirties. Oftentimes their work spoke directly to the social and political conflicts that had been created by the era's economic catastrophe.

LITERATURE AND POLITICS

Perhaps the most evident and controversial feature of Depression-era writing was the self-conscious politicization of literature. For many American writers, as Alfred Kazin explained at the time, the Depression was "an education in shock." Struggling to come to grips with the stagnation and confusion they saw throughout American society, many assumed that capitalism and liberal democracy had not merely suffered setbacks, but had been proven conclusive failures. Many looked to communism or socialism for the promise of a better world, and, hoping to make art more than a diversion or a refuge, many writers sought to make their work a useful tool for improving society. In the words of the radical writer Joseph Freeman, they strove to overcome "the dichotomy between poetry and politics," so that "art and life" might be "fused."

One consequence of that politicization was that throughout the thirties the American literary world was divided by fierce battles between contending factions on the left and by antagonistic theories of literature. At the extreme end of the spectrum stood writers associated with the Communist Party who, advocating a controversial program of "proletarian literature," demanded that art become "a class weapon." Looking to the Soviet Union for the model of a rationally planned society, these writers celebrated the resilience of the working class and extolled the solidarity, enlightenment, and "revolutionary élan" promised by communism. In novels such as Michael Gold's *Jews without Money* and Clara Weatherwax's *Marching! Marching!*, or in plays like Clifford Odets's *Waiting for Lefty*, they described a capitalist world that was exploitative, unjust, and corrupt, and told stories of how their long-suffering protagonists came to see the truth and join the struggle. Their underlying vision was always revolutionary, and their stories typically ended with the promise of cataclysm and violent transformation. "O workers' Revolution," Gold's novel concludes, "You will destroy the East Side when you come, and build there a garden for the human spirit."

Despite the fervor of its proponents, however, the movement for "proletarian" literature never took deep hold in American letters. It was most successful in the field of drama, where the revolutionary demand for immediacy and action revitalized the theater and nurtured such writers as Odets and directors as Harold Clurman, whose influence would be felt long after the 1930s ended. Proletarian poetry, on the other hand, and, in particular, proletarian fiction, where the movement staked its greatest hopes, were far less successful. With the exception of *Jews without Money*, which went

through eleven printings when it was published in 1930, very few proletarian novels found a wide readership, and most lacked the genuine power and eloquence of Gold's often nostalgic account of growing up in the tenements of New York's Lower East Side. The best-selling novels of the thirties—historical romances like Hervey Allen's *Anthony Adverse* and Margaret Mitchell's *Gone with The Wind*—dealt with the Depression in a different way, by allowing readers to escape into another time, where spunky individuals triumphed over great adversity. Proletarian writers, who preferred to stress the significance of class struggle, never reached a popular audience. Nor were they successful with sophisticated readers, who were often offended by the dogmatic simplicity of novels that tended to see workers as inherently good and the bourgeoisie as evil. After 1935, proletarian literature died a quick death, the victim of both Communist Party policy (which, following the directives of the Soviet Comintern, turned away from advocating revolutionary struggle and toward supporting a "Popular Front" of communists, socialists, and liberals against fascism) and the success of Franklin D. Roosevelt's New Deal. Radical writers now spoke not of proletarian, but of "people's literature," and claimed that the central issue of the day was not class struggle, but the contest between fascism and democracy.

Yet, though a small and short-lived phenomenon, the proletarian movement exercised disproportionate influence over the literature of the 1930s because radical writers spoke with energy and conviction when so many of their peers were confused. For many writers, the misery of the Depression made literature seem a useless luxury. Defenders of "proletarian" literature like Gold—who was a harshly polemical critic as well as a novelist—provided an emphatic answer to this anxiety. They repudiated the subtlety and literary sophistication that characterized much of American writing in the 1920s and demanded instead that literature deal "with the real conflicts of men and women." Almost regardless of their political allegiance, American writers tended to share that conviction and to be impressed by the commitment of the era's radicals. Many worried that in the pursuit of technical excellence, American literature had become too preoccupied with aesthetic problems and too narrowly focused on the concerns of a small and highly privileged segment of society. Indeed, shaken by the Depression and increasingly troubled over the course of the decade by the growing threat of fascism in Europe, many writers who had achieved renown during the 1920s adopted left-leaning political views and shifted their work to follow suit. In *Tender is the Night,* for example, F. Scott Fitzgerald continued to write about characters who longed for glamour and wealth, but he now saw their world less as the romantic vision he described in *The Great Gatsby* and more as a crumbling edifice built atop a structure of economic exploitation. Similarly, in his novel about the Spanish Civil War, *For Whom the Bell Tolls,* Ernest Hemingway turned from the individual alienation he had portrayed in such "lost generation" novels as *The Sun Also Rises* and now celebrated his hero's commitment to "absolute brotherhood" in the struggle against fascism. Many of their contemporaries followed a similar path. Even Wallace Stevens, perhaps the most aristocratic and purely aesthetic writer of his generation, declared in 1935 that he hoped his poetry was "heading left."

The proletarian movement also helped inspire a widespread interest in the literature of social protest by writers who were less radical or less doctrinaire than the artists associated with the Communist Party. Among the most impressive literary achievements of the decade, for example, was John Dos Passos's trilogy of novels, *U.S.A.* Dos Passos's massive effort to depict the whole of American civilization was far more complex and politically ambiguous than any example of proletarian literature, but it shared the proletarian writers' sense that American society had been profoundly damaged by capitalism and harshly divided along class lines. "They have the dollars the guns the armed forces the power plants," Dos Passos charged with grim satisfaction, "all right we are two nations." Something similar was true of the most explosive work of the decade, Richard Wright's bestselling novel *Native Son,* which sold 215,000 copies in the first three weeks after it was published and went on to become an extraordinary best seller. Wright's portrait of the simmering Black anger exemplified by his protagonist Bigger Thomas deliberately rejected

Communist Party orthodoxy in favor of Bigger's dreams of "personal" freedom and self-assertion. But Wright's career had been nurtured invaluably by the proletarian movement, and his work reflected genuine sympathy for the Marxian vision of interracial, working-class solidarity. In his most utopian moments, Bigger imagines himself "standing in the midst of a crowd of men, white men and black men and all men" as "the sun's rays melted away the many differences, the colors, the clothes, and drew what was common and good upward toward the sun."

THE PEOPLE, YES

Other prominent writers sought to address "the real conflicts of men and women" in still more direct ways, embracing a documentary realist style of writing that aimed to transmit true reports of Depression conditions. The atmosphere of crisis had created a great demand for reliable information about the suffering and the political attitudes of ordinary Americans, and throughout the decade a new genre of non-fictional literature flourished in which writers sought to answer that need by searching out representatives of the figure Franklin Delano Roosevelt had famously called "the forgotten man." In such works as Sherwood Anderson's *Puzzled America,* Louis Adamic's *My America,* and James Agee and Walker Evans's *Let Us Now Praise Famous Men,* writers traveled the nation's back roads and hinterlands and reported to their readers about the neglected, real people they had found there.

Over the course of the 1930s, the desire to search out, to celebrate, and sometimes to sentimentalize ordinary people became an ever more prevalent feature of American literature. It was encouraged by the Popular Front and, more importantly, by the New Deal, which not only celebrated the common man, but which, through the Federal Writers Project of the Works Progress Administration (WPA), paid writers to chronicle the nation's local cultures and regional differences. But the widespread literary yearning to connect with ordinary people and, as Michael Gold put it, plant "roots in something real," also reflected a more deep-seated reaction to the Depression. Believing that economic collapse had revealed the destructiveness of America's competitive society and the failure—or, still worse, the parasitism—of the nation's elite, many writers looked to plebian Americans for the vitality and good will that seemed otherwise absent from the national culture. Carl Sandburg brought this trend to its apotheosis when he published his much-loved book of poems *The People, Yes* in 1936. Likewise, believing that the Depression had revealed the emptiness and disorganization of urban civilization, many other writers searched for visions of deep-rooted, meaningful ways of life and found them in the nation's folkways and rural communities.

That search was evident in many places during the thirties, as writers eagerly sought out diverse folk cultures across the various regions of the nation. It was apparent, for example, in a new interest in stories by and about ethnic Americans, as such writers as James T. Farrell, Pietro DiDonato, Henry Roth, and William Saroyan chronicled the distinctive cultures of the nation's immigrant communities and their struggles to enter the American mainstream. It was still more evident in the new vogue for Southern literature. In his great novels of the 1930s—*As I Lay Dying, Absalom, Absalom!,* and *Light in August*—William Faulkner created the era's most complex and tragically divided portrait of the South's unique cultural inheritance. But many other writers of the moment offered less ambivalent accounts. Among them was the movement of "Agrarian" writers led by Allan Tate, John Crowe Ransom, and Robert Penn Warren. Echoing the decade's left-wing writers, the Agrarians denounced America's industrial civilization, but against it they advocated a highly conservative vision of an "organic" society that they believed survived in Southern culture. Zora Neale Hurston's fiction focused on the exuberant vitality that Hurston perceived in the region's Black peasantry, but especially in her great novel *Their Eyes Were Watching God,* Hurston also praised the distinctive folkways and communal life that persisted in the rural South. So, too, in varying degrees did a whole crop of new Southern writers, including James Agee, Carson McCullers, Erskine Caldwell, and, not least significantly, Margaret Mitchell.

The celebration of folk culture and of popular resilience took on its most emphatic form, however, in John Steinbeck's hugely successful novel *The Grapes of Wrath,* which is in many ways the most representative of American literary works from the 1930s. Telling the epic tale of the "Okie" migration from the dust bowl of the southwest to southern California, *The Grapes of Wrath* is a protest novel like Dos Passos's *U.S.A.* and Wright's *Native Son.* It indicts the callousness of a social system that rendered millions homeless and that left hungry people to starve while farmers who could not sell their crops were forced to destroy them. And, at its ideological center, in a portrait of a government camp that offers Steinbeck's protagonists a brief respite in their hopeless search for home and work, it provided a defense of the New Deal programs that sought to address the nation's farm crisis. But the true heart of the novel lies in its stirring vision of the goodness and brotherhood among ordinary people struggling to survive. As Steinbeck's Ma Joad says in one of the novel's most celebrated lines, "We're the people—we go on."

A PORTRAIT OF AMERICA

In the long run, the most important achievement of American literature during the Great Depression may have been the way works by Steinbeck and Wright, Faulkner and Hurston, Gold and Dos Passos combined to create what the New Deal administrator Harry Hopkins called, in his praise of the Writers Project, a new "portrait of America." Over the course of the twentieth century, the United States had become an increasingly complex and culturally diverse society. But it was not until the 1930s that American literature began to reflect and, indeed, to glory in that diversity. In fact, one of the most significant literary consequences of the Great Depression was the way the atmosphere of crisis and, more importantly, the federal funding for the arts first provided by the New Deal, brought to prominence many new authors, from previously neglected segments of the population. During the 1930s, those writers contributed to the creation of a new, populist vision of America as, at its best, a multiethnic and fraternal society. But even after the Depression had passed and that populist vision had disappeared along with it, American literature would remain the broad based and diverse field that it had only first become in the thirties.

See Also: ADAMIC, LOUIS; AGEE, JAMES; CALDWELL, ERSKINE; COMMUNIST PARTY; DOS PASSOS, JOHN; EVANS, WALKER; FAULKNER, WILLIAM; *GONE WITH THE WIND*; *GRAPES OF WRATH, THE*; HURSTON, ZORA NEALE; POETRY; POPULAR FRONT; SOCIALIST PARTY; STEINBECK, JOHN.

BIBLIOGRAPHY

Aaron, Daniel. *Writers on the Left: Episodes in American Literary Communism.* 1961.

Bloom, James D. *Left Letters: The Culture Wars of Mike Gold and Joseph Freeman.* 1992.

Denning, Michael. *The Cultural Front: The Laboring of American Culture in the Twentieth Century.* 1996.

Filreis, Alan. *Modernism from Left to Right: Wallace Stevens, the Thirties, and Literary Radicalism.* 1994.

Foley, Barbara. *Radical Representations: Politics and Form in U. S. Proletarian Fiction, 1929–1941.* 1993.

Kazin, Alfred. *On Native Grounds: An Interpretation of Modern American Prose Literature.* 1942.

Klein, Marcus. *Foreigners: The Making of American Literature, 1900–1940.* 1982.

Nelson, Cary. *Repression and Recovery: Modern American Poetry and the Politics of Cultural Memory, 1910–1945.* 1989.

Pells, Richard. *Radical Visions and American Dreams: Culture and Social Thought in the Depression Years.* 1973.

Rideout, Walter B. *The Radical Novel in the United States, 1900–1954: Some Interrelations of Literature and Society.* 1956.

Stott, William. *Documentary Expression and Thirties America.* 1973.

Szalay, Michael. *New Deal Modernism: American Literature and the Invention of the Welfare State.* 2000.

SEAN MCCANN

LITTLE CAESAR

Mervyn LeRoy's 1930 film (released in January 1931) about an aspiring criminal who works his way up through the underworld hierarchy, following an alternate path toward the American dream of success, became the prototype for the gangster film genre that blossomed in the early years of the Great Depression.

There had been several films about urban crime in the silent era, but *Little Caesar*, with the tough-talking, ruthless, self-centered Cesare Enrico Bandello ("Little Caesar"), masterfully portrayed by Edward G. Robinson, set the tone for the genre in the era of sound. The film was such a hit that in 1933 critic Dwight MacDonald called it "the most successful talkie that has been made in this country."

Robinson's Rico, unlike other gangster protagonists, such as those portrayed by James Cagney in *The Public Enemy* (1931) and subsequent films, is unsympathetic. Rico's ruthless self-aggrandizement clearly associated him with the business tycoons of the 1920s, who had just fallen into public disfavor as the Depression was tightening its grip on the nation. Little Caesar's purposes in life are to make money and dominate others—to "be somebody." His selfish, amoral ways parallel those the public was increasingly associating with the business world. At one point in the film, Rico makes this connection explicit by proclaiming, "I ain't doin' too bad in this business, so far." His rapid rise and even more rapid fall parallel the trajectory of business from the late 1920s into the early 1930s.

Rico is a classic tough guy, but with a twist. He is very much concerned with demonstrating masculinity and avoiding anything that might make him seem "soft." "Dancin'. . .ain't my idea of a man's game," Rico says to his friend Joe Massara (Douglas Fairbanks, Jr.). "Ahh, love—soft stuff!" Rico says with disgust. Yet Little Caesar never shows any manly interest in women and there are clear, if subtle, indications that he has a homosexual desire for his friend Joe. Rico's decline begins when he refuses to shoot Joe, and he analyzes his own fall tellingly when he says, "This is what I get for likin' a guy too much."

As the conventions of the time required, *Little Caesar* told its audiences that crime doesn't pay by having Rico killed at the end. Significantly, though, in terms of its message to Depression-era viewers, the biggest criminal of them all, the top business executive, who is referred to simply as the Big Boy, is left untouched.

In a famous closing line, as he dies after taking a hail of police bullets, Little Caesar cries, "Mother

Edward G. Robinson in Mervyn LeRoy's 1931 film Little Caesar. THE KOBAL COLLECTION

of Mercy, is this the end of Rico?" Rico's end marked the beginning for a hugely successful genre that reflected the anti-business and anti-government attitudes of the early 1930s.

See Also: GANGSTER FILMS; GENDER ROLES AND SEXUAL RELATIONS, IMPACT OF THE GREAT DEPRESSION ON; HOLLYWOOD AND THE FILM INDUSTRY; ROBINSON, EDWARD G.; VALUES, EFFECTS OF THE GREAT DEPRESSION ON.

BIBLIOGRAPHY

Bergman, Andrew. *We're in the Money: Depression America and Its Films.* 1971

Mason, Fran. *American Gangster Cinema: From Little Caesar to Pulp Fiction.* 2003.

McElvaine, Robert S. *The Great Depression: America, 1929–1941,* rev. edition. 1993.

Munby, Jonathan. *Public Enemies, Public Heroes: Screening the Gangster from Little Caesar to Touch of Evil.* 1999.

Ruth, David E. *Inventing the Public Enemy: The Gangsters in American Culture, 1918–1934.* 1996.

ROBERT S. MCELVAINE

LITTLE STEEL STRIKE

In the wake of several remarkable labor victories in 1937, unionization of the steel industry seemed to be simply a matter of time. But the determined and ultimately successful resistance of Republic Steel, Youngstown Sheet and Tube, and Inland Steel—collectively known as the Little Steel firms to distinguish them from the giant U.S. Steel—in a devastating standoff sent the burgeoning Committee for Industrial Organization (CIO) into an unanticipated retreat. Coming at this crucial moment, the Little Steel Strike revealed the limitations of organized labor and federal labor policy. Along with the recession of 1937 to 1938, it temporarily halted the growing economic and political power of industrial workers.

The success of the chaotic sit-down strikes in the automobile industry in early 1937 had led U.S. Steel chairman Myron C. Taylor to negotiate with CIO president John L. Lewis an orderly recognition of the Steel Workers' Organizing Committee (SWOC) as its members' sole bargaining agent. The resulting contract, signed on March 2, 1937, led to union recognition at several other companies. Jones & Laughlin, a company known for its aggressive anti-labor practices, capitulated in May after only a two-day strike and a Supreme Court ruling against it, a ruling that also definitively upheld the National Labor Relations Act. Having successfully resisted independent unions in the past, the remaining Little Steel firms, however, refused to be bullied. As SWOC prepared for a strike, Republic and Youngstown Sheet and Tube stockpiled weapons and hired additional guards.

On May 26, 75,000 steelworkers walked out of their plants across the Midwest. Tensions culminated in Chicago, where Republic kept its mill in operation with strikebreakers. At a rally on May 30 police fired into an unarmed crowd of strikers and their sympathizers, killing ten and wounding another thirty, including two women and a child. The Memorial Day Massacre, as it was known, galvanized organized labor. In June SWOC members walked out of Bethlehem Steel's Johnstown, Pennsylvania, plant. Claiming that the Little Steel firms violated the National Labor Relations Act in their refusal to collectively bargain with their workers' representatives, SWOC and CIO leaders sought federal assistance. President Franklin Roosevelt's refusal to intervene beyond appointing a powerless Federal Steel Mediation Board marked a shift away from his tacit support of the CIO, whose participation in Labor's Non-Partisan League had greatly contributed to his re-election.

Efforts by state and local officials to find a compromise also proved fruitless. A national public re-

lations campaign attacked Lewis's vocal presence in the strike as divisive, while back-to-work drives and citizens' committees organized by businessmen slowly swung public opinion in local communities against the strike. Discouraged by the lack of progress and continuing violence (eighteen steelworkers died that summer), strikers returned to work by the end of July. While defeated in the Little Steel Strike, SWOC eventually won its case before the National Labor Relations Board, which granted recognition, back pay, and reinstatement of fired union members. By 1942 further organizing drives secured collective bargaining agreements at all four companies. Still, union leaders had learned that federal protection would not be as vigorous as they previously had expected.

See Also: BLACK METROPOLIS; COLLECTIVE BARGAINING; MEMORIAL DAY MASSACRE; ORGANIZED LABOR; STEEL WORKERS' ORGANIZING COMMITTEE (SWOC).

BIBLIOGRAPHY

Bernstein, Irving. *Turbulent Years: A History of the American Worker, 1933–1941.* 1969.

Clark, Paul; Peter Gottlieb; and Donald Kennedy; eds. *Forging a Union of Steel: Philip Murray, SWOC, and the United Steelworkers.* 1987.

Green, James. "Democracy Comes to 'Little Siberia': Steel Workers Organize in Aliquippa, Pennsylvania, 1933–1937." *Labor's Heritage* 5 (1993): 4–27.

Speer, Michael. "The 'Little Steel' Strike: Conflict for Control." *Ohio History* 178 (1969): 273–287.

Zieger, Robert. *The CIO, 1935–1955.* 1995.

EDUARDO F. CANEDO

LOMAX, ALAN

Alan James Lomax (January 31, 1915–July 19, 2002), folk song collector, folk music scholar, and one of the founders of modern ethnomusicology, was born in Austin, Texas. He received his early background in folk music from his father, John Avery Lomax, with whom he went on collecting expeditions throughout most of the United States in the early 1930s. Much of their work included the re-

Among the many American musicians whom Alan Lomax recorded and photographed was Wilson "Stavin' Chain" Jones, photographed in 1934 in Lafayette, Louisiana. LIBRARY OF CONGRESS, PRINTS & PHOTOGRAPHS DIVISION, LOMAX COLLECTION

cording and publication of cowboy songs from the American West and songs of prisoners and other subcultural groups in the South. They also helped establish the popularity of Huddie Ledbetter ("Leadbelly"), Jelly Roll Morton, and other ethnic American performers.

In the mid- to late 1930s, the elder and younger Lomax served as curator and associate curator, respectively, of the Archive of American Folksong at the Library of Congress, in Washington, D.C. That repository, founded in 1928, had been supported entirely by private contributions and consisted of only a few small collections prior to the arrival of the Lomaxes. Under their direction, it began receiving government endowments and was greatly expanded, in no small measure by the hundreds of recordings that they had made on their collecting

expeditions. Those recordings remain among the most valuable primary sources for the study of American folk music.

Alan Lomax completed college at the University of Texas in 1936, then returned to Washington and the Library of Congress. Beginning in 1939, he hosted "Wellsprings of America" and "Back Where I Come From," both on CBS Radio.

Lomax served in the U.S. Armed Forces in World War II. In 1947, he was appointed director of folk music at Decca Records and continued his folk song collecting. During the 1950s, he helped produce several series of folk song recordings on a number of different labels.

While much of Lomax's most valuable work dates from after the Great Depression, both his interests and his personal views underlying his later efforts were forged during the Depression. Beginning in 1959, he set out to elucidate fully American Southern folk music, especially that of marginalized racial and economic groups. His efforts culminated in the eighty-hour, seven-volume *Southern Heritage Folk Series* that later was re-released as a four-CD set titled *Sounds of the South*.

Lomax also was one of several investigators who revolutionized ethnomusicology during the 1960s by championing the study of folk and non-western music in ways that did not involve comparisons to European and Euro-American art music. His greatest contribution to musical scholarship was the systematic linking of music to its social context. During the 1960s and early 1970s he developed a means of assessment and classification known as cantometrics. The central thesis of that system is that vocal musical performance practices reflect the characteristics of the culture from which they emerged. Lomax died near Tarpon Springs, Florida, on July 19, 2002.

See Also: GUTHRIE, WOODY; MUSIC.

BIBLIOGRAPHY

Lomax, Alan, with John A. Lomax, eds. *American Ballads and Folk Songs*. 1935.

Lomax, Alan, *Cantometrics*. 1976.

Lomax, Alan, and John Avery Lomax, eds. *Cowboy Songs and Other Frontier Ballads*. 1938.

Lomax, Alan. *Folk Style and Culture*. 1968.

Lomax, Alan. *Folk Songs of North America.* 1960.

J. MARSHALL BEVIL

LONDON ECONOMIC CONFERENCE OF 1933

The London Economic Conference of 1933 had its origins in President Herbert Hoover's 1931 call for an international conference to discuss how to raise prices and to reduce tariffs. The internationalists in Hoover's cabinet hoped that once these issues were addressed economic recovery would set in. Interest overseas in the proposal grew in Europe in the summer of 1931 amid speculation that Hoover's administration had finally recognized that reparations and war debts were interconnected. The British government took the lead in securing a final reparations settlement at the Lausanne Conference of July 1932, with the expectation that a settlement on war debts with the United States would soon follow. To bring the Americans on board, the call for an economic conference was enshrined in Article Five of the Lausanne Conference.

Preparations for the meeting began in October 1932. Britain's departure from the gold standard in the summer of 1931 ensured that much of the preparatory discussions for the monetary portion of the agenda focused on the question of how to persuade Britain back onto gold. But the monetary landscape changed significantly after the U.S. dollar left gold in April 1933. As a consequence, European countries still committed to gold found their currencies under renewed pressure and begged Britain and the United States to do something about it.

In May 1933, the United States offered to negotiate a temporary stabilization agreement between the world's leading currencies so that deliberations at the London Conference would not be disrupted by speculation against particular currencies on the world's exchanges. However, France rejected the U.S. offer, demanding instead a permanent stabilization agreement. The issue remained unresolved as representatives from sixty-five different countries, plus assorted international agencies, trooped into London's Geological Museum on June 15, 1933 to begin their deliberations.

Within a matter of days, the world's attention switched from the conference hall to the Bank of England where negotiations for a new temporary stabilization agreement were underway. The bankers thought a deal was within their grasp when Franklin Roosevelt's infamous "bombshell message," made public on July 3, 1933, arrived. In it the president condemned the "old fetishes of so-called international bankers" for the gold standard and underlined his commitment to currency depreciation as a means of invigorating the international economy. The message also demonstrated Roosevelt's growing frustrations with European nationalism. France had persisted with its stubborn advocacy of gold standard orthodoxy, while Britain continued to call for the abolition of war debts. Britain also rejected Secretary of State Cordell Hull's ground-breaking proposal for a Reciprocal Tariff Act Agreement (RTAA) between Britain and the United States based on a flat rate reduction of 10 percent of existing barriers. The RTAA formally became law in 1934, but it took until 1938 for the United States to overcome Britain's political and economic objections to an Anglo-American RTAA. The RTAA became a major plank of U.S. economic foreign policy. By 1945, twenty-nine RTAA treaties had been secured, reducing U.S. tariffs by around 45 percent.

U.S. planning for a new economic order to be established after World War II was shaped by the experience of the London Conference. The U.S. administration was now determined to take the lead and "force" countries to cooperate together for the good of the international economy. In sharp contrast to 1933 it also demonstrated leadership and attempted to break away from the *ad hoc* character of interwar economic cooperation by creating international institutions, such as the International Monetary Fund and the World Bank, to help the world to work together in times of crisis.

See Also: EUROPE, GREAT DEPRESSION IN; GOLD STANDARD; INTERNATIONAL IMPACT OF THE GREAT DEPRESSION; MONETARY POLICY.

BIBLIOGRAPHY

Clavin, Patricia. "The World Economic Conference 1933: The Failure of British Internationalism." *The Journal of European Economic History* 20 (1991): 489–527.

Clavin, Patricia. *The Failure of Economic Diplomacy: Britain, Germany, France and the United States, 1931–36.* 1996.

Simmons, Beth. *Who Adjusts? Domestic Sources of Foreign Economic Policy in the Interwar Years.* 1994.

PATRICIA CLAVIN

LONG, HUEY P.

Huey Pierce Long (The Kingfish; August 30, 1893–September 10, 1935) served as governor and United States senator from Louisiana. Born into a large, contentious, middle-class family in Winnfield, Louisiana, Long became the most famous figure in Louisiana politics. During the era of the Great Depression he energized politics, ingrained corruption in an already corrupt state, and served as a disruptive force in the national Democratic party. Long was planning to challenge President Franklin D. Roosevelt for the presidency when he was assassinated in 1935.

Long gained a rudimentary education at Winnfield high school and in Shreveport schools, relying on his prodigious memory rather than consistent study. Honing his future political skills as a traveling salesman, Long married Rose McConnell, a Shreveport secretary, when he was nineteen years old. The couple had three children: Rose, Palmer, and Russell. Russell Long served a long career in the U. S. Senate, becoming one of the nation's more powerful politicians during the 1960s and 1970s.

Without attending college, Huey Long took courses at the Tulane University Law School for less than a year and was admitted to the bar at twenty-one after passing a special oral examination. Returning to Winnfield, he established a small law practice and won his first political office in 1919, election to the Railroad Commission, which regulated transportation, utilities, and pipelines. Long earned a reputation by championing independent oil companies and attacking the near-monopolistic Standard Oil Company, the state's largest corporation.

GOVERNOR OF LOUISIANA

Long ran for governor in 1923 and finished a close third statewide, but he finished first in the rural sections of the state. In 1928 he ran again and won. At thirty-four, he was the second youngest governor in Louisiana's history. Long owed his political success largely to motivation and drive, a brilliant mind, ruthlessness, unlimited ambition, and after 1928, repression and corruption. The 1928 election was the only relatively fair election the Long machine won.

Louisiana was polarized into rural and urban factions. The rural faction, which was much larger, was fragmented by region, religion, class, and ethnicity, and had never united under a single politician. Long gained support by out-promising his opponents: He vowed to give free schoolbooks to children, build an improved road and bridge system, and furnish cheap natural gas to New Orleans. The other half of his appeal relied on his personal charisma, invective against opponents, and relentless energy.

Long built the most tightly controlled state-level political machine in the United States. He employed nepotism, patronage, vote stealing, repression (once calling out the state guard to cow New Orleans), personal magnetism, kidnappings, and a vast political campaign chest. The Long machine maintained a "deduct" box consisting of compulsory contributions deducted from the salaries of state workers. Long's abuses and powerful enemies, such as Standard Oil, combined to lead to his impeachment by the Louisiana House of Representatives in 1929. The Senate adjourned without voting on the charges after Long produced a round-robin petition signed by more than one third of the senators, who vowed they would not vote to convict regardless of the evidence. Two thirds of the vote was needed to convict.

Long's enemies, and critical historians, have focused largely on his corrupt methods and obsession with power, while his supporters, including some historians, have pointed to his accomplishments. In the context of the Great Depression, the public works he constructed loomed large. Long browbeat the creaky Louisiana legislature into enacting his program, which included new highways and bridges, free textbooks, cheaper gas for New Orleans, a new governor's mansion, a new state capitol, and increased appropriations for Louisiana State University. The governor wanted to finance more public works with a massive bond issue presented at a special legislative session in 1930.

UNITED STATES SENATOR

After the legislature balked, Long decided to run for the office of U. S. senator in the 1930 Democratic primary against the incumbent, James E. Ransdell. Ironically, Long based his campaign for national office on state issues, calling the election a referendum on his state program. Long defeated Ransdell easily, his program passed the legislature, and the opposition surrendered. He was truly Kingfish of Louisiana, a nickname he applied to himself after listening to the popular radio program *Amos 'n' Andy*.

At odds with his lieutenant governor, Long did not take his seat in Washington for nearly two years, ostensibly remaining both governor and senator-elect. Even after taking the oath as U.S. senator in 1932, he continued to control Louisiana through his puppet governor, O. K. Allen.

In his brief national career, Long gained notoriety, but little actual power, by emphasizing a single issue, maldistribution of wealth, which he blamed for the Great Depression. The Louisianan worked for the nomination and election of New York Governor Franklin D. Roosevelt because he believed Roosevelt shared his views on breaking up huge fortunes and wealth sharing. The two soon broke, however, because Roosevelt considered Long dangerous, erratic, and a disloyal Democrat. Long came to detest Roosevelt as an aristocrat whose 1932 promise to dismantle large fortunes had been made in bad faith. More important, Long coveted the presidency, but to become president, he had to challenge Roosevelt, which he planned to do in 1936. Long planned to seek the Democratic Party's nomination, failing which he planned to run as a third party candidate, drawing away enough votes from Roosevelt to elect a conservative Republican. After the Republican wrecked the country as Herbert Hoover had purportedly done, the voters would be ready to elect Huey Long in 1940.

Long used the U.S. Senate as a platform for his promises to share the wealth. He failed to enact a single bill; the most votes any of his bills attracted was twenty in a chamber of ninety-six senators. The Louisianan thrilled the galleries with his attacks on millionaires, but the Democratic leadership disliked him. Roosevelt and Long met only twice, and Long was charmed by the New Yorker, but their relationship foundered on competing ambitions. Each loved power too much to coexist comfortably with the other. Roosevelt began funneling New Deal patronage to Long's political opponents in Louisiana and resumed an investigation into tax evasion by Long and his allies that had been initiated by the Hoover administration.

The Kingfish believed he could obtain power by appealing directly to the people, beyond the reach of Roosevelt and the Democratic party. Long delivered radio speeches, published an autobiography, and forecast the actions of a Long presidency in *My First Days in the White House*. Long's most effective tool in national politics was his Share Our Wealth Society, incorporated in 1934. It was based on a plan to solve the economic problems of the nation by restructuring income and assets from the top down. By confiscating yearly income above $1 million and total assets beyond $5 million, Long would provide every family with a home, an automobile, and a radio worth at least $5,000, an annual income of $2,500, and free college educations. There would also be a veterans' bonus and a war on disease led by the Mayo brothers. No one would pay taxes except millionaires.

All one had to do to join the Share Our Wealth Society was to write to Long. There were no dues, but Huey accepted donations. Members received Long's autobiography, speeches, buttons, and instructions on how to create local affiliates to work for enaction of the plan. Long hired Gerald L. K. Smith, a Shreveport minister and bombastic orator, as his national organizer. The Society gained 200,000 members within a month and by the spring of 1935 boasted seven and a half million members. Long received more mail than all other senators combined, even more than the president. Long hoped that the society would serve as the engine for a potent national vote-gaining machine in 1936, particularly if Long found allies in other dissidents, such as the radio priest Father Charles E. Coughlin and Dr. Francis E. Townsend, an advocate of pensions for the aged.

LONG'S IMPACT

Long never had the opportunity to test his national political prowess. Returning to Louisiana in September 1935 to whip the Louisiana legislature into line, he was shot in the state capital, probably by a lone assassin, a young physician, Carl Austin Weiss. The dynasty Long founded continued on the state level until 1960, when racial issues replaced the bifactionalism of those who supported and opposed Long's program. Long's influence lasted even longer on the local and national levels, where Long remained a magic name to Louisiana voters. Huey's younger brother Earl served three terms as governor.

The Longs remain controversial and aspects of Longism are still debated. Many do not accept the conclusion that Carl Austin Weiss alone assassinated Huey Long. Some claim Long's bodyguards accidentally or deliberately killed the Kingfish, possibly after Weiss punched him. They point out that Weiss did not fit the typical assassin's profile of an alienated loner, but was a happy young man with much to live for. The 1935 state police investigation that blamed Weiss was reopened in 1993, the murder weapon and some accompanying bullets found, and Weiss's body was exhumed and his remains examined for clues to the assassination. State police captain Don Moreau, who headed the new investigation, concluded that his findings did not change the basic conclusions of the earlier investigation. As to motive, Weiss knew that Long was gerrymandering his father-in-law, Judge Benjamin Henry Pavy, a state judge, out of office; moreover, Weiss might have learned that Long had circulated rumors that the Pavy family was part black.

A further issue is Long's place in history. Early biographers tended to be highly critical, comparing the Kingfish to European fascist leaders. In 1969 historian T. Harry Williams won a Pulitzer Prize for his biography of Long, which was based upon prodigious research that included about three hundred interviews. Williams's depiction of Long as an earli-

er version of a 1960s radical gradually lost favor, although it remains influential. Later biographies by Alan Brinkley, William Ivy Hair, and Glen Jeansonne were more critical of Long's abuses of power in the wake of Watergate and the Vietnam War. Jeansonne has observed that Long might have had bipolar disorder, a chronic mental disorder believed to be inherited through the female line. This observation is based on the facts that Huey's brother Earl was diagnosed with the illness and that Long had classic symptoms: insomnia, supercharged energy, mood changes, rapid speech, and a quick wit coupled with impatience. If this is the case, Long's untreated condition explains in part many of his liabilities and assets, including his lack of inhibition, his charisma, his capacity to hate, and his relentless drive. If so, it might lead scholars to be less judgmental of Long and provide insights into his motivations and accomplishments.

See Also: COUGHLIN, CHARLES; SMITH, GERALD L. K.; TOWNSEND PLAN.

BIBLIOGRAPHY

Beals, Carleton. *The Story of Huey P. Long.* 1935.

Brinkley, Alan. *Voices of Protest: Huey Long, Father Coughlin, and the Great Depression.* 1982.

Davis, Forrest. *Huey Long: A Candid Biography.* 1935.

Dethloff, Henry C., ed. *Huey P. Long: Southern Demagogue or American Democrat?* 1967.

Deutsch, Hermann B. *The Huey Long Murder Case.* 1963.

Graham, Hugh Davis, ed. *Great Lives Observed: Huey Long.* 1970.

Hair, William Ivy. *The Kingfish and His Realm: The Life and Times of Huey P. Long.* 1991.

Harris, Thomas O. *The Kingfish: Huey P. Long, Dictator.* 1938.

Jeansonne, Glen, ed. *Huey at 100: Centennial Essays on Huey P. Long.* 1995.

Jeansonne, Glen. *Messiah of Masses: Huey P. Long and the Great Depression.* 1993.

Kane, Harnett T. *Louisiana Hayride: The American Rehearsal for Dictatorship, 1928–1940.* 1941.

Long, Huey P., Papers. Louisiana State University Library, Baton Rouge.

Long, Huey P. Scrapbooks. Louisiana State University Library, Baton Rouge.

Long, Huey P. *Every Man a King.* 1933.

Long, Huey P. *My First Days in the White House.* 1935.

Martin, Thomas P. *Dynasty: The Longs of Louisiana.* 1960.

Opotowsky, Stan. *The Longs of Lousiana.* 1960.

Reed, Ed. *Requiem for a Kingfish.* 1986.

Sindler, Allan P. *Huey Long's Louisiana: State Politics, 1920–1954.* 1956.

Smith, Webster. *The Kingfish: A Biography of Huey P. Long.* 1933.

Williams, T. Harry. T. Harry Williams Papers. Louisiana State University Library, Baton Rouge.

Williams, T. Harry. *Huey Long.* 1969.

Zinman, David H. *The Day Huey Long Was Shot.* 1963.

GLEN JEANSONNE

LOUIS, JOE

Joe Louis (May 13, 1914–April 12, 1981), heavyweight champion and one of the most admired prizefighters in history, was born near Lafayette, Alabama, the seventh of eight children of farmer Munn Barrow and Lillie Barrow. He first took up the sport of boxing as a young teenager in Detroit, Michigan, where his divorced mother had moved with him and his siblings. He fought as an amateur for two years, establishing a reputation as an extraordinarily gifted boxer and powerful puncher.

Louis turned professional in 1934. Under the direction of his trainer and good friend Jack "Chappie" Blackburn and his managers John Roxborough and Julian Black, Louis fought many memorable bouts and suffered only three losses over a career that spanned seventeen years. He captured the world heavyweight championship in 1937 against James Braddock, and defended the title a record twenty-five times. In 1938 Louis knocked out Max Schmeling in the first round, avenging a loss to the German heavyweight just two years earlier. In 1941 Louis recorded a thrilling last-round knockout of Billy Conn and six years later earned a controversial decision over Jersey Joe Walcott. Louis retired as champion in 1949, but monetary burdens eventually forced him to return to the ring, where he lost to new champions Ezzard Charles and Rocky Marciano.

Louis's numerous ring triumphs were of great symbolic importance to the African-American community in particular and American society more generally. Although some African Americans were seemingly troubled by what they viewed as Louis's acquiescence to the white establishment, the large majority of African Americans considered Louis a champion of heroic proportions. In the throes of the Depression, when white citizens were exhibiting racial intolerance and ignoring the needs of the African-American community, Louis became a much-needed example of black achievement and a symbol of possibility. To African Americans caught in the midst of economic crisis, Louis appeared messianic—a great champion who dramatized the black struggle against white aggression and indifference. African Americans gathered at local stores and in neighbor's homes to hear the broadcasts of his fights, vicariously shared in his victories, and honored his ring triumphs with literally hundreds of songs and poems. Richard Wright, Charles Johnson, and other African-American intellectuals wrote of being inspired and filled with hope by Louis's apparent invincibility in the ring. Tellingly, Louis's ring triumphs were often applauded by whites as well. His 1938 victory over Max Schmeling was crucially important to Americans of all races who viewed the German's defeat as a symbolic triumph of American values over Nazi racism and totalitarianism. In large measure, Louis became America's national representative, something no African American, athlete or non-athlete, had ever experienced before. Louis was introduced to American soldiers during World War II as "the first American to K.O. a Nazi."

Unfortunately, like many boxers, Louis's life outside the ring was often filled with disappointment and heartache. Married four times, Louis experienced persistent financial problems as a result of bad investments, poor advice, and lack of marketable skills. At one point, he owed some $1,250,000 in back federal taxes. Once his boxing career was over, Louis attempted to support himself financially and maintain a meaningful existence through a series of jobs and business opportunities. He was for a time a pro wrestler, operated a failed fast-food business, and acted as a front man for boxing promoter James Norris. In 1970, Louis's life seemingly hit rock bottom and he was committed for five months to a psychiatric hospital. He spent

Joe Louis, 1941. CREDIT: LIBRARY OF CONGRESS, PRINTS & PHOTOGRAPHS DIVISION, CARL VAN VECHTEN COLLECTION. PHOTOGRAPH BY CARL VAN VECHTEN. REPRODUCED BY PERMISSION OF THE ESTATE OF CARL VAN VECHTEN

the last few years of his life as an official greeter at Caesar's Palace in Las Vegas.

See Also: AFRICAN AMERICANS, IMPACT OF THE GREAT DEPRESSION ON; LEISURE; OWENS, JESSE; RACE AND ETHNIC RELATIONS; SPORTS.

BIBLIOGRAPHY

Astor, Gerald. *"And a Credit to His Race": The Hard Life and Times of Joseph Louis Barrow, a.k.a. Joe Louis.* 1974.

Bak, Richard. *Joe Louis: The Great Black Hope.* 1996.

Capeci, Jr., Dominic J., and Martha Wilkerson. "Multifarious Hero: Joe Louis, American Society, and Race Relations during World Crisis, 1935–1945." *Journal of Sport History* 10 (1983): 5–25.

Gilmore, Al-Tony. "The Myth, Legend, and Folklore of Joe Louis: The Impression of Sport on Society." *South Atlantic Quarterly* 82 (1983): 256–268.

Mead, Chris. *Champion: Joe Louis, Black Hero in White America.* 1985.

Sammons, Jeffrey T. "Boxing as a Reflection of Society: The Southern Reaction to Joe Louis." *Journal of Popular Culture* 16 (1983): 23–33.

Sammons, Jeffrey T. *Beyond the Ring: The Role of Boxing in American Society.* 1988.

DAVID K. WIGGINS

LUCE, HENRY

Henry Robinson Luce (April 3, 1898–Feb. 28, 1967), editor and publisher, was one of the most innovative figures in American magazine publishing in the twentieth century. As head of Time Incorporated, Luce presided over an empire that included *Time* magazine, *Fortune, Life,* and *Sports Illustrated,* as well as the "March of Time" radio and newsreel programs, book publishing companies, and broadcasting stations.

Born in Tengchow, China, to missionary parents, Luce in later years strongly attacked communism and, in particular, Communist China. After attending boarding school in England and the Hotchkiss School in Connecticut, he graduated from Yale University in 1920 and studied at Oxford University. In 1923 Luce co-founded *Time* as a new kind of weekly newsmagazine with an opinionated style.

In spite of the Depression Luce succeeded at media ventures. He had a sure sense of his audience's interests. Though Luce was surprised by the stock market crash in 1929, he went ahead and launched *Fortune,* an expensive monthly magazine, in February 1930. Aimed at business executives, the magazine succeeded by reporting on American capitalism's surmounting economic woes. Recognizing public interest in broadcasting and film, Luce started a weekly radio show in 1931, followed by a monthly newsreel in 1935. Both were called "The March of Time," and reenacted news events. His greatest achievement was creation of the immensely popular *Life* magazine, begun in 1936, which specialized in photojournalistic essays that appealed to ordinary Americans. Initially a supporter of Franklin D. Roosevelt, Luce disagreed with New Deal ideas on business and became an avid Republican, using his publications to attack Roosevelt's third-term reelection bid in 1940. His second wife, Clare Boothe Luce, a playwright, was a Republican member of Congress from 1943 to 1947. Although well known, Luce himself had little influence on public policies during the Depression.

See Also: COMMUNICATIONS AND THE PRESS.

BIBLIOGRAPHY

Baughman, James L. *Henry R. Luce and the Rise of the American News Media.* 1987.

Herzstein, Robert E. *Henry R. Luce.* 1994.

Swanberg, W. A. *Luce and His Empire.* 1972.

MAURINE H. BEASLEY

LYNCHINGS

Lynching, the practice of illegal killing by a mob of three or more persons motivated by notions of justice, race, or tradition, persisted into the 1930s. The rate of lynching had been declining since the first decade of the twentieth century. However, during the early and mid-Depression years, the practice briefly surged and several well-publicized mob killings occurred outside of the South. The National Association for the Advancement of Colored People (NAACP) continued efforts begun in the 1910s to lobby for a federal anti-lynching bill. Although southern Democrats in the Senate thwarted the passage of anti-lynching legislation, lynching waned in the latter years of the Great Depression due to large-scale trends that discouraged lynching violence.

Thousands of mob killings occurred during the Reconstruction era after the Civil War and again at the end of the nineteenth century. Lynching was concentrated in the South, where white southerners collectively murdered blacks they accused of resisting white supremacy and of interracial criminality. Yet a significant number of lynchings also occurred in the West and Midwest, as whites skeptical of legal process collectively killed whites, Mexicans, Native Americans, Chinese, African-Americans, and Sicilians. After a great frenzy of lynchings in the 1890s, the frequency of mob violence had steadily declined, with a brief exception during the heightened social and racial tensions of the World War I era.

The United States averaged nearly seventeen reported lynchings per year in the mid to late 1920s, but the number of mob killings spiraled to twenty-one in 1930, to twenty-eight in 1933, and then to twenty in 1935, with lesser tallies of mob victims in

Men and women stand silently in front of the Daughters of the American Revolution Memorial Hall in Washington, D.C., in 1934 to protest the failure of the attorney general's national conference on crime to include lynching on its program. BETTMANN/ CORBIS

the years in between. Most of the lynchings in the early 1930s occurred in the South. But highly-publicized lynchings performed by crowds of thousands in Marion, Indiana, in August 1930; in Maryville, Missouri, in January 1931; in Princess Anne, Maryland, in October 1933; and in San Jose, California, in November 1933 raised fears that mob violence was not only growing in frequency but also spreading once again beyond the boundaries of Dixie. However, after 1935, the rate of lynching declined markedly; an average of six persons a year were reported lynched between 1936 and 1940.

The dramatic increase in lynchings in 1933 inspired the NAACP, under the leadership of Walter White, to push anew for Congress to pass anti-lynching legislation. The effort in the mid to late 1930s focused on the Costigan-Wagner and Gavagan anti-lynching bills, which stipulated fines and prison terms for law officers that abetted mobs or

failed to protect prisoners, and fines for counties where lynchings occurred. Anti-lynching bills passed in the House in 1937 and 1940, but were defeated in the Senate by filibuster, or threat of filibuster, by southern Democrats. Some of the failure to enact a federal anti-lynching law was due to the tepid public support offered by President Franklin D. Roosevelt. Although Roosevelt occasionally spoke publicly against lynching and at times voiced support for such legislation behind the scenes, he refused to alienate southern Democrats by officially endorsing these measures. The federal anti-lynching bill was also hindered by the ambivalence of southern white liberals who opposed lynching, such as Dr. Will Alexander and the Commission on Interracial Cooperation, and Jesse Daniel Ames and the Association of Southern Women for the Prevention of Lynching, who feared that a federal approach would alienate white southerners.

The Great Depression initially precipitated social disruption and a heightened ambivalence toward governmental authority that may have contributed to the surge in lynching. Yet long-term trends that discouraged lynching continued and intensified during the era. An emerging mass culture and media integrated the country and sapped the localistic tendencies in which lynching had flourished; lynchings were now immediately publicized throughout the country and could be an embarrassing stain on a state's image. By the end of the decade, lynching went underground, as smaller secretive mobs performed the fewer collective killings that occurred. Moreover, through the New Deal, Americans in the 1930s came to accept a greater role for the federal government, state authority, and law in their lives. Lethal punishment performed by a mob without due process of law came increasingly to be seen as an unbearable anachronism. Finally, the liberal currents of the New Deal contributed to an increasing awareness of how racial injustice, particularly the oppression of African Americans in the South, mocked the ideals of American democracy. Happily, 1935 would be the last year of the twentieth century in which more than ten persons were lynched in the United States.

See Also: AFRICAN AMERICANS, IMPACT OF THE GREAT DEPRESSION ON; ANTI-LYNCHING LEGISLATION; NATIONAL ASSOCIATION FOR THE ADVANCEMENT OF COLORED PEOPLE (NAACP).

BIBLIOGRAPHY

Hall, Jacquelyn Dowd. *Revolt against Chivalry: Jesse Daniel Ames and the Women's Campaign against Lynching,* rev. edition. 1993.

McGovern, James R. *Anatomy of a Lynching: The Killing of Claude Neal.* 1982.

Raper, Arthur. *The Tragedy of Lynching.* 1933.

Zangrando, Robert L. *The NAACP Crusade against Lynching, 1909–1950.* 1980.

MICHAEL J. PFEIFER

MARCANTONIO, VITO

Vito Anthony Marcantonio (December 10, 1902–August 9, 1954) was the most successful U.S. radical politician of the twentieth century. The eldest child of a first-generation immigrant working-class family, Marcantonio was elected to Congress from New York's ethnically Italian and Puerto Rican East Harlem district; he held office longer than any other third party radical, serving seven terms from 1934 to 1950. Colorful and controversial, Marcantonio captured national prominence as a powerful orator and brilliant parliamentarian. Often allied with the U.S. Communist Party, he was an advocate of civil rights, civil liberties, labor unions, and Puerto Rican independence. He supported social security and unemployment legislation, calling for what later was called a *living wage* standard. And he annually introduced anti-lynching and anti-poll tax legislation a decade before it became respectable. Marcantonio also opposed the House Un-American Activities Committee, red baiting, and anti-Semitism, and he fought for the rights of the foreign-born Americans.

Marcantonio was a shrewd tactician in the labyrinth of New York politics, managing the mayoral election in 1933 of Fiorello La Guardia, organizing political coalitions, and ultimately becoming Manhattan's preeminent political power broker as leader of the American Labor Party (ALP). Like his mentor La Guardia, Marcantonio first ran for office in 1934 as a Republican, in opposition to the corrupt Democratic Tammany machine. Marcantonio was defeated for reelection in 1936 in the Roosevelt New Deal landslide (an irony, in that Marcantonio was among the most fervent supporters of New Deal legislation). Out of office and growing more radical, he served two years as president of International Labor Defense, the Communist-aligned civil rights and trade union support organization known for its defense of the eight "Scottsboro Boys." In 1938 he returned to Congress, running as both the Republican and ALP candidate, and he became an enrolled member of the ALP. Although Marcantonio developed a system of service for his impoverished constituents that was nationally acclaimed, his focus remained local. He never abandoned his neighborhood or his friends—even some who were organized crime figures. Marcantonio's career was finally destroyed by the anti-Communism of the Cold War 1950s.

In many ways Marcantonio was an exemplar of the insurgent New Yorker when the city itself was a metaphor for national aspirations. In the post-Depression, postwar years, those visions were lost—transfigured as much by middle-class affluence and suburbanization as by anti-unionism (Marcantonio was one of the House floor managers in the failed fight against the 1947 Taft-Hartley Act) and anti-Communism. Marcantonio continued to plump for political empowerment and equal opportunity. He demanded practical improvements in the quality of life: affordable housing, quality education, health care, and the right to a job. Despite a fervid campaign for the mayoralty of New York in 1949, Marcantonio lost. In 1950 he was defeated for reelection to Congress, but only when Democrats and Republicans united behind another candidate. Out of office, Marcantonio served as defense counsel for leftist union officials, Puerto Rican nationalists, and, most notably, for W. E. B. Du Bois. Planning a comeback, Marcantonio died of a heart attack in 1954 at the age of fifty-one.

See Also: AMERICAN LABOR PARTY; DU BOIS, W. E. B; CIVIL RIGHTS AND CIVIL LIBERTIES; LA GUARDIA, FIORELLO H.

BIBLIOGRAPHY

Marcantonio, Vito. *I Vote My Conscience: Debates, Speeches, and Writings of Vito Marcantonio, 1935–1950,* edited by Annette T. Rubinstein and associates. 1956.

Meyer, Gerald. *Vito Marcantonio: Radical Politician, 1902–1954.* 1989.

Walzer, Kenneth Alan. "The American Labor Party: Third Party Politics in New Deal-Cold War New York, 1936–1954." Ph.D. diss., Harvard University, 1977.

JOHN J. SIMON

MARX BROTHERS

A madcap comedy team, the Marx Brothers—Leo (Chico, 1887–1961); Adolph (Harpo, 1888–1964); Julius Henry (Groucho, 1890–1977); and Herbert (Zeppo, 1901–1979)—began their careers in vaudeville before becoming motion picture stars in the 1930s. Born in New York City, the sons of German-Jewish immigrants, the brothers received a boost in their career from their uncle, Al Shean of the comedy duo "Gallagher and Shean." Billed as "The Four Marx Brothers" they worked in vaudeville until 1925, when they starred in the Broadway production of *The Cocoanuts,* a musical comedy written expressly for them by George S. Kaufman and Irving Berlin. Another Broadway hit followed with *Animal Crackers* in 1928. Though their screwball, improvisational style of comedy had evolved in front of the live audiences of vaudeville and Broadway, the Marx brothers made a successful transition to motion pictures with the release of a film version of *The Cocoanuts* (1929), followed a year later by *Animal Crackers* (1930). Their first two films were shot at Paramount's Long Island studios so that the brothers could continue to work on the New York stage. But for their third film, *Monkey Business* (1931), they relocated to Hollywood, California, where they would spend the rest of their careers.

Throughout the 1930s the Marx Brothers produced a string of successful motion pictures that rank among the most celebrated of Depression-era comedies: *Horse Feathers* (1932), *Duck Soup* (1933), *A Night at the Opera* (1935), *A Day at the Races* (1937), *Room Service* (1938), *At the Circus* (1939), and *Go West* (1940). They also displayed distinct comic personas: Chico was a wisecracking clown with an Italian accent; Groucho, with grease-paint mustache and cigar, often impersonated authority figures, maintaining a constant stream of one-liners and comic asides; Harpo, garbed in fright wig, trench coat, and crushed top hat, renounced speech altogether, preferring a bicycle horn and an absurdist sense of visual humor; Zeppo, the youngest brother, was the good-looking foil and occasional love interest in their films. Chico and Harpo were also accomplished musicians, and each of their films included a scene in which they performed, often to audiences of adoring children. Such moments punctuate the fast-paced verbal and visual humor of their films with intervals of musical and emotional poignancy. But the popularity of the Marx Brothers was based primarily upon the team's ability to lampoon authority figures and skewer the pretensions of the wealthy and powerful.

See Also: HOLLYWOOD AND THE FILM INDUSTRY; HUMOR.

BIBLIOGRAPHY

Louvish, Simon. *Monkey Business: The Lives and Legends of the Marx Brothers.* 1999.

Marx, Groucho. *Groucho and Me.* 1959.

Groucho Marx (standing) with Chico and Harpo (sitting right) in the 1937 film A Day At the Races. Bettmann/CORBIS

Marx, Groucho, and Richard J. Anobile. *The Marx Brothers Scrapbook.* 1973.

Marx, Harpo. *Harpo Speaks!* 1961.

John Parris Springer

MARXISM

The era of the Great Depression saw the rejuvenation of Marxism as a legitimate article of political faith, but also the emergence of Marxist theory as an intellectual and even academic endeavor for the first time. The predictions of Marxism seemed, throughout the decade, to have been legitimated by the severity of economic decline and the scant prospects for capitalist revival, and intellectuals as well as many workers, including pockets of African Americans along with immigrants and the children of immigrants, were drawn toward various parts of the Left. During the early Depression years, movements of unemployed workers and campus antiwar activities were among the most dramatic manifestations, yielding to struggles for industrial unionism. The Socialist and Communist parties held onto only a small fraction of those who moved in and around their extended circles; but they (especially the Communists, from 1935 onward) were able to exert influence far beyond their numbers by providing a framework and talented activists.

An acute section of the generation of intellectuals coming of age during the 1920s and early 1930s plunged into organizing activities on broad fronts, trained themselves or were trained in college classes or leftwing academies, and even studied the Marxist classics while preparing to write films. But creative approaches had only begun in various theoretical areas when the era came crashing to an end. War approached and future repression lay dead ahead.

Ideas about Marxism in the United States before the 1930s had been primitive at best, mainly diluted reiterations of European views since the 1870s. Communist emphasis on theory was negated by the drift toward rigidity and the virtual exclusion of competing views from circulation. The first (non-Yiddish) Marxist journal of note, *The Marxist Quarterly*, quickly dissolved over political differences, and a successor of sorts, *Science and Society*, survived only by adapting to shifting Communist moods.

Yet, on a practical level, assorted adaptations of Marxism rapidly became extraordinarily useful in many ways. The Communist International's shift to the Popular Front in 1935 legitimated positive approaches to American historic themes, and the burst of creativity that spread from radical theater to Works Progress Administration arts programs, modern dance, and even Hollywood inspired thousands of the nation's most energetic young artists and intellectuals. The rash of dramatic strikes in 1934 and the subsequent rise of industrial unionism seemed to lend further credence to the central Marxist notion of working-class self-realization.

These successful uses of Marxist ideas brought a small handful of intellectual classics. W. E. B. Du-Bois's *Black Reconstruction* (1935) stands foremost, but several other works can also be counted as having fairly predicted the trends of Marxist thought to follow, including Sidney Hook's *Towards the Understanding of Karl Marx* (1933), an early exploration of the master's theoretical background; Granville Hicks's *The Great Tradition: An Interpretation of American Literature since the Civil War* (1933); and arguably the first edition of John Howard Lawson's classic *Theory and Technique of Playwriting* (1936). The selected proceedings of the League of American Writers and Congress of American Artists, as well as the pages of better-remembered and less-remembered journals, respectively, the *Partisan Review* and *New Theater*, contain much fascinating and highly creative discussion.

Marxism had not entered the mainstream of intellectual life in the United States as it had in many other societies. But its influences could be surprisingly subtle, as it was in the shrinking but still considerable world of Yiddish culture, or within immigrant working-class groups from Eastern or Southern Europe and from Puerto Rico. Marxism had entered the wide world of arts and criticism, not only at upper levels but most importantly at the levels of popular presentation, theater and film to music (both folk and jazz) and murals. In a society where "politics" remained suspect and popular culture substituted for political discussion, this counted greatly. Marxism deeply influenced many of the Depression era's most important artists and intellectuals, including Dashiell Hammett, Dorothy Parker, Clifford Odets, Woody Guthrie, Aaron Copland, and DuBois. It was, in short, a monumental advance in a short time.

See Also: COMMUNIST PARTY; DU BOIS, W. E. B; LITERATURE; POPULAR FRONT.

BIBLIOGRAPHY

Buhle, Mari Jo; Paul Buhle; and Dan Georgakas. *Encyclopedia of the American Left,* 2nd edition. 1997.

Buhle, Paul. *Marxism in the United States: Remapping the History of the American Left,* rev. edition. 1991.

PAUL BUHLE

MASON, LUCY RANDOLPH

Lucy Randolph Mason (July 26, 1882–May 6, 1959) was a southern reformer and labor rights activist. As general secretary for the National Consumers' League (NCL) from 1932 to 1937, Mason linked the women's reform work of the Progressive years to the broader labor and civil rights activism of the New Deal era. She saw the New Deal as an opportunity to secure protective and minimum wage laws for workers. When the Congress of Industrial Organizations (CIO) launched its drive to organize southern textile workers, Mason became the publicity and public relations representative for the CIO in the South. She belonged to the group of progressive southerners who believed interracial unionism, along with New Deal reforms, could transform the region's politics and race relations.

Born in Alexandria, Virginia, Mason was the daughter of an Episcopal minister and was a descendant of George Mason, author of the Virginia Declaration of Rights, the model for the Bill of Rights. Mason, however, emphasized that she had not been "born with a silver spoon" in her mouth. Her parents instilled in her strong religious convictions and a sense of social responsibility. As a young woman, Mason participated in women's suffrage activities and became interested in improving conditions for workers. Mason served as industrial secretary for the Richmond Young Women's Christian Association (YWCA) from 1914 to 1918, and as general secretary of the Richmond YWCA from 1923 to 1932.

By 1937, Mason desired to leave the NCL and return to the South to work directly with workers and interracial groups. As CIO public relations director, Mason traveled throughout the region, speaking to union members, investigating civil rights violations, and educating local community leaders about the labor movement. Mason also served on the Southern Policy Committee that wrote the *Report on the Economic Conditions in the South,* and she helped to organize the Southern Conference for Human Welfare in 1938.

See Also: CONGRESS OF INDUSTRIAL
    ORGANIZATIONS (CIO); SOUTHERN
    CONFERENCE FOR HUMAN WELFARE (SCHW).

BIBLIOGRAPHY

Mason, Lucy Randolph. *To Win These Rights: A Personal Story of the CIO in the South.* 1952.

Salmond, John. *Miss Lucy of the CIO: The Life and Times of Lucy Randolph Mason, 1882–1959.* 1988.

Storrs, Landon R. Y. *Civilizing Capitalism: The National Consumers' League, Women's Activism, and Labor Standards in the New Deal Era.* 2000.

Sullivan, Patricia A. *Days of Hope: Race and Democracy in the New Deal Era.* 1996.

LARISSA M. SMITH

MAVERICK, MAURY

Fontaine Maury Maverick (October 23, 1895–June 7, 1954) was a U.S. Congressman, mayor of San Antonio, Texas, and a federal bureaucrat during World War II. His last name described his political agenda. Maverick was a liberal Texas Democrat who vociferously advocated civil rights for Mexican Americans and African Americans, defended the rights of blue-collar workers, and argued against the centralization of the economy. His political style was often abrasive, winning him few allies and making it difficult to transform his vision of social justice into legislative reality.

After being admitted to the state bar of Texas, serving with distinction in World War I, and undertaking a business career, Maverick became the tax collector for Bexar County, Texas, winning election to that post in 1929 and 1931. He spent much of the early Depression working for local relief. His efforts included the establishment in 1932 of the Diga Colony, a communally organized relief camp for World War I veterans. The camp was built about five miles from San Antonio on land Maverick leased from Humble Oil Company for one dollar a year. Housing for the residents was constructed from abandoned boxcars. Maverick hoped that the residents would be radicalized by their poverty and would work for long-term systemic reform; he was disgruntled when he discovered that they cared more for food, employment, and shelter. The Diga Colony disbanded in 1933.

In 1934, Maverick was elected to the U.S. House of Representatives, where he became known both as an avid New Dealer and as a leader of insurgent liberals and radicals who found the president's relief agenda too tame. His efforts were largely rhetorical; however, he did force the U.S. Census Bureau to count the Mexican-American population of his district as white, rather than "negro." Furthermore, he was a constant supporter of federal anti-lynching legislation and other civil rights measures. Defeated for reelection in 1938 because he angered conservative power brokers within San Antonio and the state, Maverick returned to San Antonio where he was elected mayor in 1939. Promising expanded public housing and public health programs, Maverick accomplished little because conservatives in the city blocked his efforts. His support for a Communist speaker's right to address a local audience ended his political career as mayor. He was defeated in his reelection bid. Maverick spent the war years working with various federal agencies, including a stint as director of the Smaller War Plants Corporation. He returned to Texas after the war and was a vocal leader of the liberal faction of the state's Democratic Party.

See Also: DEMOCRATIC PARTY; ELECTION OF 1934; LATINO AMERICANS, IMPACT OF THE GREAT DEPRESSION ON.

BIBLIOGRAPHY

Henderson, Richard B. *Maury Maverick: A Political Biography.* 1970.

Maverick, Maury. Papers. Center for American History. University of Texas at Austin.

Maverick, Maury. *A Maverick American.* 1937.

Weiss, Stuart L. "Maury Maverick and the Liberal Bloc." *Journal of American History* 58 (1971): 880–895.

NANCY BECK YOUNG

MCWILLIAMS, CAREY

Carey McWilliams (December 13, 1905–June 27, 1980) was a writer, lawyer, and administrator, and one of the most important leftists in Depression-era California. McWilliams was born in Colorado, but moved to southern California in 1922. Like many other intellectuals, McWilliams became attracted to left-wing ideas during the Great Depression. At the beginning of the 1930s, McWilliams worked as a lawyer at a conservative Los Angeles firm, but he wrote literary criticism in his free time. By the end of the decade, he was a prominent activist, journalist, and government official who was well known for his advocacy of civil liberties, racial equality, and labor unions.

McWilliams's involvement in California's agricultural labor conflicts transformed his life. The organization of farm workers in the state during the 1930s met with resistance so intense that McWil-

liams later dubbed it "farm fascism," referring to the brutal and illegal suppression of a predominantly minority workforce. In the early 1930s, under the auspices of the American Civil Liberties Union, McWilliams performed pro bono legal services for Mexican-American farm workers. In the mid-1930s, he traveled across the state reporting for magazines on the conditions of agricultural labor. In 1939, he published *Factories in the Field,* a best-selling history of farm labor in California. The book received widespread attention as the nation was then becoming attuned to the plight of California's Dust Bowl migrants and it was seen by many as the nonfiction counterpart of John Steinbeck's wildly popular novel, *The Grapes of Wrath,* which was published the same year. Yet, unlike Steinbeck, McWilliams stressed the structural and racial aspects of the exploitation of migrant farm workers.

Though best known for *Factories in the Field,* McWilliams's activities were not limited to his work on agricultural labor. For instance, during the 1930s, he advocated full citizenship rights for Asian immigrants, wrote a pamphlet criticizing anti-Semites in Los Angeles, helped organize the left-wing Western Writers' Congress, and worked with Hollywood's Popular Front liberals to support the antifascist side in the Spanish Civil War. In 1939, California governor Culbert Olsen appointed McWilliams chief of the Division of Immigration and Housing, a post he held until 1943. McWilliams's radicalization during the Great Depression shaped the rest of his long and important career. In the 1940s, he wrote a number of significant works on the issue of race in America, notably *Brothers under the Skin* (1943), and also authored two important histories of California. In 1950, McWilliams left California for New York City, where he served as editor for the liberal weekly *The Nation* from 1955 to 1975.

See Also: LATINO AMERICANS, IMPACT OF THE GREAT DEPRESSION ON; MIGRATORY WORKERS.

BIBLIOGRAPHY

McWillams, Carey. *The Education of Carey McWilliams.* 1979.

McWilliams, Carey. *Fool's Paradise: A Carey McWilliams Reader,* edited by Dean Stewart and Jeannine Gendar. 2001.

Starr, Kevin. "Carey McWilliams's California: The Light and the Dark." In *Reading California: Art, Image, and Identity, 1900–2000,* edited by Stephanie Barron, Sheri Bernstein, and Ilene Susan Fort. 2000.

DANIEL GEARY

MEANS, GARDINER C.

Economist Gardiner Coit Means (June 8, 1896–February 15, 1988) challenged orthodox economic ideas about corporations, prices, and economic planning. Born in Windham, Connecticut, as the son of a Congregational minister, Means entered Harvard University, graduating in absentia in 1918. After joining the army in 1917, Means worked for the Near East Relief helping Armenians in Turkey after the war. In the early 1920s, he founded a blanket making company. In 1924, Means went back to Harvard to study economics formally, earning a master's degree in 1927 and a Ph.D. in 1933.

Means accepted a 1927 invitation from Adolf A. Berle, Jr., at Columbia Law School to assist in researching *The Modern Corporation and Private Property* (1932). They argued that by 1930, two hundred U.S. corporations controlled half of corporate wealth and 43 percent of corporate income. While only two thousand men out of 125 million Americans managed these corporations, real control lay in the hands of several hundred managers. The corporate revolution separated ownership and control. Concentration and control by managers (not stockholders) suggested that competition, individualism, self-regulation, and stockholder control were outmoded.

In the 1933 to 1934 period, while working with the Department of Agriculture and the Consumers' Advisory Board of the National Recovery Administration, Means researched prices to develop his theory of "administered pricing." Two forms of pricing existed. Small businesses and farmers changed prices in response to changing market demand. Concentration in some industries, on the other hand, meant managers set prices based on profit concerns rather than market demand or price competition. Farm prices had declined drastically since 1929, yet many industrial prices had remained stable due to administered pricing. Social responsibility and even market forces had given way to profit maximization.

Between 1934 and 1940, Means worked with the Industrial Committee of the New Deal planning agency (the National Resources Planning Board). Building an economic model based on research on consumer income and industrial structure, Means argued for government industrial policy making. He wanted to adopt multi-industry planning to counterbalance corporate control. After New Deal planners opted for compensatory spending policy, Means went to work for the fiscal division of the Bureau of the Budget in 1940 and 1941.

After 1941, Means engaged in research, writing, and speaking. Between 1943 and 1958, he worked for the Committee for Economic Development, a private sector economic research institution. On February 15, 1988, he died in Vienna, Virginia. Means's work on corporate concentration, separation of ownership and control, administered pricing, and national economic planning represented an alternate path for New Deal economic policy.

See Also: BERLE, ADOLF A., JR.; CONSUMERISM; NEW DEAL.

BIBLIOGRAPHY

Hawley, Ellis W. *The New Deal and the Problem of Monopoly: A Study in Economic Ambivalence.* 1966. Reprint, 1995.

Lee, Frederic S. "A New Dealer in Agriculture: G. C. Means and the Writing of *Industrial Prices.*" *Review of Social Economy* 46 (1988): 180–202.

Lee, Frederic S. "From Multi-Industry Planning to Keynesian Planning: Gardiner Means, the American Keynesians, and National Economic Planning at the National Resources Committee." *Journal of Policy History* 2 (1990): 186–212.

Lee, Frederic S. "Administrative Hypothesis and the Dominance of Neoclassical Price Theory: The Case of the Industrial Prices Dispute." *Research in the History of Economic Thought and Methodology* 17 (1999): 23–42.

Lee, Frederic S., and Warren J. Samuels, eds., with Caroline F. Ware and Steven G. Medema. *The Heterodox Economics of Gardiner Means: A Collection.* 1992.

McCraw, Thomas K. "In Retrospect: Berle and Means." *Reviews in American History* 18 (1990): 578–596.

Andrew Mellon (left) with Ogden Mills outside the United States Capital in Washington, D.C., in 1927. LIBRARY OF CONGRESS, PRINTS & PHOTOGRAPHS DIVISION

Reagan, Patrick D. *Designing a New America: The Origins of New Deal Planning, 1890–1943.* 2000.

Rosenhof, Theodore C. *Economics in the Long Run: New Deal Theorists and Their Legacies, 1933–1993.* 1997.

Samuels, Warren J., and Steven G. Medema. *Gardiner C. Means: Institutionalist and Post-Keynesian.* 1990.

PATRICK D. REAGAN

MELLON, ANDREW

Andrew William Mellon (March 24, 1855–August 26,1937) was a financier, public official, art collector, and philanthropist who was best known as the longest serving secretary of the treasury in U.S. history. Mellon was lauded during much of his tenure as the greatest treasury secretary since Alexander Hamilton.

Born in Pittsburgh, Pennsylvania, one of five surviving sons of Thomas and Sarah Jane Negley Mellon, he attended Western University of Pennsylvania (later the University of Pittsburgh), before joining his father's private banking firm in 1874; he assumed control of T. Mellon and Sons in 1882. Six years later, Mellon became trust executive for the $4 million family fund. The following year, he helped found Union Trust Company and Union Savings Bank of Pittsburgh.

Mellon financed and advised new enterprises in steel, coal, coke, oil, aluminum, and synthetic abrasives. In 1900, he married Nora McMullen of the Guinness Stout family. They had two children—Ailsa born in 1901, and Paul in 1907—before their divorce in 1912. In 1902 T. Mellon and Sons became the Mellon National Bank, which rapidly came to dominate financial institutions in western Pennsylvania; it later merged with Union Trust. As a memorial to their father, Mellon and his brother established the Mellon Institute of Industrial Research in 1913 to foster cooperation between scientific research and industry to create new and improved consumer products; in 1967, the institute merged with the Carnegie Institute of Technology to form Carnegie-Mellon University.

Active in local and regional Republican Party politics, Mellon led local fundraising activities and served as a delegate to the presidential nominating convention in 1920. President Warren G. Harding chose him as secretary of the treasury, a post he retained during the administrations of Calvin Coolidge and Herbert Hoover.

Harding and Coolidge deferred to Mellon on financial policy. Mellon's primary goals, articulated in the "Mellon Plan" presented to the House Committee on Ways and Means in November 1923, called for reduction of the national debt, curtailment of government expenditures, and lowering of taxes. He further explicated his ideas in 1924 in *Taxation: The People's Business.* Mellon believed that reducing taxes on those in the upper income brackets would encourage investment that would lead to increased production and, with it, more jobs and an improved standard of living. The Revenue Acts of

1924, 1926, and 1928 significantly altered the tax structure; they reduced inheritance taxes from 40 to 20 percent, repealed capital stock and gift taxes, reduced income taxes by 25 percent, and dropped the surtax by more than half. The national debt had exceeded $24 billion in 1920; by the end of Mellon's time at the Department of the Treasury, it was down to $16 billion. Government expenditures had been reduced by half. Meanwhile, corporate profits and dividends rose by more than 60 percent between 1921 and 1929.

Consistent with his opposition to what he regarded as government interference in the economy, Mellon favored limitations on antitrust activities and resisted federal involvement in the development of hydroelectric power at Muscle Shoals in Alabama, the problems of particular industries, and the mounting agricultural depression.

Mellon remained aloof from the stock market, both in his personal investments and in policy matters. Since the market was subject to the laws of the state of New York rather than the federal government, Mellon found no need to comment publicly on runaway stock prices. Congressional investigation of questionable banking and investment practices did not begin until 1932, as his time at the Department of the Treasury ended.

With the onset of the Great Depression, President Hoover resisted Mellon's advice to allow wholesale liquidation. Hoping instead to stabilize business, industry, banking, labor, and agriculture, Hoover increasingly relied on Undersecretary Ogden Mills, who was named secretary when Mellon became ambassador to Great Britain in February 1932, a post he held until the change of administrations in 1933. While in London, Mellon proved helpful to American oil interests in the Middle East.

Government investigations of Mellon's finances in the 1930s revealed his enormous wealth, but suits for back taxes uncovered no fraud and a grand jury refused to indict him. A collector of fine art since 1880, Mellon devoted his last years to the creation of the National Gallery of Art. He provided initial funds, was influential in the selection of architect John Russell Pope, supervised of construction of the building on the mall in Washington, D.C., established a foundation to maintain the Gallery, and donated a collection of art valued at more than $35 million. The National Gallery opened in 1941, with Mellon's longtime assistant David Edward Finley as its first director. Mellon's children continued his benefactions to the National Gallery.

See Also: BUSINESSMEN; LAISSEZ-FAIRE; STOCK MARKET CRASH (1929).

BIBLIOGRAPHY

Finley, David Edward. *A Standard of Excellence: Andrew W. Mellon Founds the National Gallery of Art at Washington.* 1973.

Hersh, Burton. *The Mellon Family: A Fortune in History.* 1978.

Koskoff, David E. *The Mellons: The Chronicle of America's Richest Family.* 1978.

Mellon, Andrew W. *Taxation: The People's Business.* 1924.

Mellon, Paul. *Reflections in a Silver Spoon: A Memoir.* 1992.

O'Connor, Harvey. *Mellon's Millions, the Biography of a Fortune: The Life and Times of Andrew W. Mellon.* 1933.

SUSAN ESTABROOK KENNEDY

MEMORIAL DAY MASSACRE

In the midst of the Great Depression many industrial workers clung to their vision of the American dream while continuing their daily struggles for survival. To achieve both goals they turned to strikes, unionization, and labor politics. However, these initiatives provoked violent reactions by some big businessmen and their allies. The Little Steel Strike of 1937, which included the Memorial Day massacre, exemplified this trend.

Although violence characterized many labor struggles during the 1930s, the Memorial Day massacre become a major and enduring symbol, particularly to partisans of the Committee for Industrial Organizations (CIO), of a system that condoned the use of firearms by company guards and police in subduing heroic and peaceful working-class demonstrators. Most workers at Republic Steel's South Chicago mill struck as a protest against their terrible working conditions and the autocratic demeanor of company president Tom Girdler. Girdler not only refused to sign a written contract with the Steelworkers Organizing Committee (SWOC), but he used nonstriking workers to continue production. In addition, company officials and the Chicago police collaborated on a policy to protect the new labor force, to stifle mass picketing, and to defeat the strikers.

Lacking sufficient resources to cope with management's wealth and power, the strikers and SWOC sought external allies. They contacted President Franklin Roosevelt, but he rejected their request for a federal investigation. Chicago mayor Edward Kelly's support of the city's police added to the strikers' woes.

Nevertheless, on Memorial Day over fifteen hundred strikers, family members, and supporters demonstrated for the right of strikers to picket peacefully. Well-armed guards and a large contingent of Chicago police confronted them. Soon a few rock throwers targeted a cluster of police, who responded with tear gas and gunfire. Some marchers evaded the police, but ten demonstrators died and sixty more suffered severe wounds. All the police escaped death and serious injury.

The incident climaxed a series of clashes between workers and the police, and heightened their mutual antagonism. Both parties sought to gain public approval; in this contest, the police had decisive advantages, including the support of Mayor Kelly, the approval of the state's attorney, and the concurrence of the coroner's jury. These sources legitimated the self-image of the police as innocent victims of a violent mob unleashed by the inflammatory rhetoric of communists and other "outside agitators." Newspapers, especially the *Chicago Tribune,* disseminated this official version of the incident, which won widespread acceptance from the mainstream press, the public, and members of Congress.

The strikers and the SWOC gained support from John L. Lewis and other top CIO leaders, from the magazines the *Nation* and the *New Republic,* and from Chicago liberals and progressive clergy. Senator Robert M. La Follette Jr.'s Subcommittee on the Violation of Free Speech and the Rights of Labor, which was investigating the denial of civil liberties to dissidents, provided confirmation of the strikers' criticism. Many committee witnesses, workers, and journalists, rejected the police version of the incident. However, the most dramatic evidence supporting the strikers' perspective was a Paramount newsreel that graphically displayed police violence and showed that many of the dead and wounded had injuries on their backs. Nevertheless, this evidence failed to persuade the public and the majority of politicians because of the late release of the newsreel footage and the continuing adherence of the mainstream press to the official version.

The Memorial Day massacre and its aftermath seriously undermined the South Chicago strike, contributed to strike losses in other venues, and damaged the reputation of the CIO. The massacre joined the Railroad Strike of 1877 and the Haymarket affair of 1886 as prime examples of the pro-business sympathies and propensity for violence of the Chicago police. Finally, the partnership of Lewis and Roosevelt, best exemplified by the 1936 presidential election, began to unravel as Lewis supported the strikers, while Roosevelt condemned both sides. In response, Lewis castigated Roosevelt for his failure to see that the election and the strike were interconnected elements of their mutual fight against "economic royalists," Roosevelt's term for authoritarian and greedy big businessmen.

See Also: COLLECTIVE BARGAINING; LITTLE STEEL STRIKE; SIT-DOWN STRIKES; STEEL WORKERS' ORGANIZING COMMITTEE (SWOC); STRIKES.

BIBLIOGRAPHY

Auerbach, Jerold S. *Labor and Liberty: The La Follette Committee and the New Deal.* 1966.

Cohen, Stephen. "The Little Steel Strike of 1937: A Struggle for Industrial Unionism." Ph.D. diss., The Manchester Metropolitan University, 1999.

Galenson, Walter. *The CIO Challenge to the AFL: A History of the American Labor Movement, 1935–1941.* 1960.

Newell, Barbara Warne. *Chicago and the Labor Movement: Metropolitan Unionism in the 1930's.* 1961.

Sofchalk, Donald G. "The Memorial Day Incident: An Episode in Mass Action." *Labor History* 6 (winter, 1965): 3–43.

IRWIN M. MARCUS

MEN, IMPACT OF THE GREAT DEPRESSION ON

In one of his more memorable lines, Franklin D. Roosevelt spoke in a 1932 campaign radio address of "the forgotten man at the bottom of the economic pyramid." In fact, large numbers of men during the Great Depression had good reason to feel forgotten—or worse.

FORGOTTEN MEN?

The Great Depression had, of course, extremely adverse effects on large fractions of the population of both sexes, but those effects were not entirely alike. The types of employment that had traditionally been classified as "men's work," particularly manufacturing jobs in heavy industry, were hit especially hard by the economic collapse and a resultant sharp drop in demand for most manufactured products. Many of the occupations previously defined as "women's work," on the other hand, such as teaching, clerical work, and domestic service, were not as hard hit. This differential left men facing problems beyond the direct economic ones that their loss of income produced.

It has often been argued that men's roles in society have to be artificially created and so are fragile and in constant danger. "It is impossible to strip [the woman's] life of meaning as completely as the life of a man can be stripped," anthropologist Margaret Mead wrote in 1932. For many men, the Great Depression went a long way toward stripping their lives of meaning. What had traditionally given meaning to men's lives were their roles as providers and protectors. Unemployment—or even the serious threat of soon becoming jobless, a potentiality that could be readily seen all around the men who did manage to hang onto their positions—quickly eroded one of these key components of male self-definition. If a man could not provide, was he really a man?

As John Steinbeck put it in *The Grapes of Wrath* (1939), men are more "breakable" than women. "Women and children knew deep in themselves that no misfortune was too great to bear if their men were whole," Steinbeck wrote. "The women watched the men, watched to see whether the break had come at last."

For many men in the 1930s, the break did come. Men who could not provide for their families during the economic Depression often fell into psychological depression. "Pa and Uncle John standing helplessly gazing at the sick man" at the end of Steinbeck's novel symbolizes the situation in which many men felt the Depression had left them. The women, Steinbeck indicated, could continue to do what they were supposed to do, which the author symbolized by having Rose of Sharon breast-feed an old man. The men, though, felt helpless. "I ain't no good any more," Pa Joad says earlier in the novel. "Funny! Woman takin' over the fambly. Woman sayin' we'll do this here, an' we'll go there. An' I don't even care."

MEN AT HOME AND ON THE ROAD

Filled with self-blame, their sense of being "real men" beaten down, many men spent more time at home, in the sphere that was traditionally the woman's place. Their presence there both increased the chances for friction between spouses and underscored the man's apparent inability to fulfill his expected role. He would not, after all, be hanging around at home during normal working hours if he were doing what a "real man" was expected to do.

"My father he staying home," a twelve-year-old Chicago boy wrote in a 1936 letter to the president and first lady that nicely captures the desperate and unaccustomed position into which many American men fell during the Depression. "All the time he's crying because he can't find work. I told him why are you crying daddy, and daddy said why shouldn't I cry when there is nothing in the house. I feel sorry for him." A man whose son feels sorry for him is not one who is likely to see himself as a "man" in the traditional sense.

Many married men took to the road, initially seeking work, but also escaping from the reminders that home and family constituted of their lack of success in their expected roles. Although most husbands who left home to try to find work presumably did so with the intention of returning, it was not unusual for them to disappear permanently. Desertion by men of their families increased markedly during the 1930s.

During the Depression many fathers became desperate to provide for their children. This young father, a Missouri sharecropper, was evicted from his farm in 1939 after drought caused his crops to fail. LIBRARY OF CONGRESS, PRINTS & PHOTOGRAPHS DIVISION, FSA/OWI COLLECTION

Transient men wait in line for the evening meal at a Dubuque, Iowa, mission in 1940. LIBRARY OF CONGRESS, PRINTS & PHOTOGRAPHS DIVISION, FSA/OWI COLLECTION

For those men who were not yet married, avoiding such responsibilities at a time when they had scant prospects of being able to meet them often seemed to be the most prudent course. And many young women did not seek to marry men who could not fulfill their traditional role. "I don't want to marry. I don't want any children. So they all say. No children. No marriage," writer Meridel LeSueur said of young women in a 1932 article. "The man is helpless now," she wrote. "He cannot provide. If he propagates, he cannot take care of his young."

A WORLD WITH NO PLACE FOR KNIGHTS

Men under such circumstances longed to return to what they believed to be the proper role for their sex. As "forgotten men," they wanted to be remembered—and restored to what they took to be their rightful position. That desire of men during the years of the Depression for a return to "the way things ought to be" in terms of the traditional roles of the sexes can be seen in a wide variety of the decade's popular culture. In the late-1930s Los Angeles depicted in Raymond Chandler's classic detective novel, *The Big Sleep,* Philip Marlowe finds himself in an environment that does not value traditional male virtues. He yearns for a world with a place for knights—a world in which men can play their roles as protectors, a world of damsels in distress, a world in which there are two kinds of women and a man can separate the virgins from the whores. He wants to be able to live up to his ideal-

Many unemployed men found work with the Civilian Conservation Corps. This CCC member planted trees as part of a reforestation project in Montana's Lolo National Forest in 1933. FRANKLIN DELANO ROOSEVELT LIBRARY

ized male role, which he perfectly expresses as: "I work at it, lady. I don't play at it." To his deep dismay, he finds instead that "knights had no meaning in this game. It wasn't a game for knights." The game in which men found themselves by the 1930s was one in which the male-drawn line between virgins and whores had been blurred to the point where the only women in distress seemed to be whores. Chandler does not give us any of the more complex women who fit into neither category: From his binary perspective, if the weak, pure, helpless virgins are gone, all women must be whores. What Chandler wanted was what so many other men in the 1930s wanted: that people would "Remember My Forgotten Man." The song of that title, from the Warner Brothers movie *Gold Diggers of 1933,* well stated the male view of the way things ought to be: "Ever since the world began, a woman's got to have a man."

Men who felt threatened and insecure in their masculinity were prone to lash out, and a common target of their wrath was women. Women, Steinbeck wrote, "knew that a man so hurt and perplexed may turn in anger, even on people he loves." In his 1937 song, "Me and the Devil Blues," Mississippi bluesman Robert Johnson sang, "I'm gonna beat my woman, till I'm satisfied." The long-standing denial of the customary perquisites of manhood that led some African-American males to express such sentiments was spreading to a much larger segment of the male population as unemployment undercut the masculinity of millions of American men. Reflective of this change was the fact that men hitting women became a staple in Depression-era films, especially in the late 1930s. It seems that such vicarious assertions of masculinity struck a chord with men who were feeling insecure because of the Depression's undermining of their positions.

THE NEW DEAL AND THE VISION OF PROPER MASCULINITY

For its part, the New Deal, despite its progressivism in some areas (and notwithstanding the efforts of Eleanor Roosevelt to influence policy in ways that took the varying needs of women more into account), took a very traditional view of the proper roles of men and women. Although there were exceptions, New Deal programs were for the most part designed to provide work and income for men and to restore their position as "breadwinners." New Deal art often depicted such an ideal.

The psychological crisis that men faced during the Great Depression created a pent-up desire for a return to "normal" masculinity. World War II provided an outlet for this desire for a large number of men, but the postwar construction of a hyper-traditional family in which "every woman needs a man" was a significant legacy of the unsettling effects the Great Depression had on men.

See Also: CHANDLER, RAYMOND; FAMILY AND HOME, IMPACT OF THE GREAT DEPRESSION ON; GENDER ROLES AND SEXUAL RELATIONS, IMPACT OF THE GREAT DEPRESSION ON; *GRAPES OF WRATH, THE*; PSYCHOLOGICAL IMPACT OF THE GREAT DEPRESSION; "REMEMBER MY FORGOTTEN MAN"; WOMEN, IMPACT OF THE GREAT DEPRESSION ON.

BIBLIOGRAPHY

Bird, Caroline. *The Invisible Scar.* 1966.

Chandler, Raymond. *The Big Sleep.* 1939.

McElvaine, Robert S. *Down and Out in the Great Depression: Letters from the "Forgotten Man."* 1983.

McElvaine, Robert S. *Eve's Seed: Biology, the Sexes, and the Course of History.* 2001.

Melosh, Barbara. *Engendering Culture: Manhood and Womanhood in New Deal Public Art and Theater.* 1991.

Mettler, Suzanne. *Dividing Citizens: Gender and Federalism in New Deal Public Policy.* 1998.

Steinbeck, John. *The Grapes of Wrath.* 1939.

ROBERT S. MCELVAINE

MENCKEN, H. L.

Henry Louis Mencken (September 12, 1880–January 29, 1956) was a newspaperman, magazine editor, literary critic, political pundit, language scholar, and curmudgeon. He was known as the "Sage of Baltimore," the city where he was born and where he died. Mencken resisted all attempts to lure him away from his native town to more lucrative literary pursuits in New York. He hated New York, loved Baltimore, and wrote of it with affection, nostalgia, and at times brutal honesty. He remains one of the city's most famous authors.

Mencken began his journalistic career in 1899 as a reporter for the Baltimore *Morning Herald*, and when that paper folded in 1906 he joined the Baltimore *Sun*, where he remained for the rest of his life. In 1908 he became book editor of the *Smart Set* magazine, and in 1914 he and his friend and colleague, George Jean Nathan, became its co-editors. They left the magazine in 1924 to found *The American Mercury*, which Mencken continued to edit until 1933.

Mencken's bludgeon-like, hammer-blow style, which he used to attack democracy and the "genteel tradition" in American literature, made him the most famous (and also the most hated) critic of the 1920s. But while engaged in these demolition projects he was also turning out edition after edition of a great scholarly work, *The American Language* (first published in 1919), in which he studied the way that English had developed in the United States.

Mencken's popularity and immense influence came to an end with the Depression for the simple reason that he refused for a long time to admit that anything had happened. When he could no longer ignore the Depression, he claimed that its effects were being greatly exaggerated by the "incompetent unemployed." His fanatical hatred of Franklin

D. Roosevelt made him reject and ridicule all the New Deal programs to restore the economy; he blamed Roosevelt for saddling the country with an impossible load of debt and for dragging it into World War II. But Mencken paid a heavy price for this attitude: By the mid-1930s his lone dissenting voice was largely ignored and forgotten.

Mencken came back in the early 1940s with three delightful volumes of autobiography (the *Days* books) and a new edition and two huge supplements of *The American Language*. These brought him a new, more solid reputation and a wider audience. But the publication of his *Diary* in 1989, with its blatant anti-Semitism, turned him once more, thirty-three years after his death, into a highly controversial figure.

See Also: COMMUNICATIONS AND THE PRESS; LITERATURE.

BIBLIOGRAPHY

Fecher, Charles A. *Mencken: A Study of His Thought.* 1978.

Fitzpatrick, Vincent. *H. L. Mencken.* 1989.

Hobson, Fred. *Mencken: A Life.* 1994.

CHARLES A. FECHER

MEXICO, GREAT DEPRESSION IN

The Great Depression had a profound and long lasting impact on Mexico's economy and society. Proof of this is the drastic redirecting of the Mexican government's economic, labor, and social policies in the 1930s from an essentially passive view of the responsibility of the state in economic matters to a direct commitment to promote growth. Mexican foreign policy also experienced a marked change during this decade. In particular, the nation's relationship to the United States made a 180-degree turn towards friendship, in contrast to the open hostility that prevailed in the 1920s.

The Great Depression in the United States was to the New Deal what *Cardenismo* was to Mexico. The term *Cardenismo* is associated with the period (1934–1940) in which Lázaro Cárdenas (1895–1970) served as president of Mexico. Cárdenas led the na-

tionalization of the foreign owned oil industry in 1938, fomented a radical agrarian reform, encouraged the creation of national industrial unions, and promoted socialist public education. Most of these measures had been fought for during the Mexican Revolution of 1910 to 1920, but they had only been partially and timidly put into practice. In a sense, the impact of the Depression operated as an accelerator of the revolution itself.

From a Latin American perspective, the impact of the Great Depression in Mexico did not reach the dramatic character of Cuba's or Chile's experience. Those countries suffered more because of the extreme dependence of their economies on a single raw material, sugar in Cuba and copper in Chile. For Latin American countries, the "merchandise-lottery" of their typical exports, as the economist Carlos Díaz Alejandro put it, explained a lot about the performance of their economies as a whole. Mexico, like Brazil and Argentina, and to some degree Colombia, Peru, and Costa Rica, implemented programs of import substitute industrialization, processes that accelerated during the isolationist period of World War II and continued well into the 1960s.

In Mexico, the Great Depression had lasting effects in various key areas of the national economy: agriculture (particularly in regions linked to production for export); mining; various branches of manufacturing, especially the textile industry; and the reorganization of labor markets, especially with regard to the dislocation caused by unemployment and waves of migration, both internal and external

ECONOMIC DECLINE

Measuring the Mexican gross national domestic product (GDP) during the 1930s reveals little about the dominant economic situation because a large amount of the economic activity was not officially recorded, as in the case of subsistence agriculture, which did not follow the commercial channels. Nonetheless, the domestic product, as recorded, had negative growth figures between 1928 and 1939: -3.33 percent in 1929, -6.77 percent in 1930, and a surprising -16.22 percent in 1932. In the early 1930s, approximately one-fifth of the domestic product was composed of goods relating to

Mexican President Lázaro Cárdenas (center) meets with oil labor leaders in the Tamaulipas state in 1938. BETTMANN/CORBIS

agricultural or livestock. Mining and petroleum made up nearly 9 percent of the GDP, a proportion that dropped to approximately 7 percent in the latter part of the decade. Meanwhile, manufacturing and the public sector significantly increased their share of the total economic activity, rising from 11 percent to 15 percent and from 5 percent to 7 percent, respectively, of the GDP. This helps explain the emphasis that has been placed on both the process of industrialization brought on by the Depression and the small but significant increase in the state's influence on total economic activity. Yet, how did the Depression spread into the Mexican economy? The eye of the hurricane was located, no doubt, in the external sector.

The volume of Mexico's exports contracted 37 percent between 1929 and 1932. The impact of this contraction was magnified by the deterioration of the *terms of trade* (the relationship of export prices

to import prices) an additional 21 percent, reaching a nearly 50 percent cut in the buying capacity of Mexican exports. Moreover, given the structural dependence of Mexican fiscal policy on export taxes, the decline of the external sector produced tremendous pressure on government income, which fell from 322 million pesos in 1929 to 179 million in 1932, despite every effort made to increase domestic revenues. This impact, however, should not be overemphasized. The army's expenses were still a large part of the government budget: The forced cuts in this sector represented one of the structural outcomes of the Depression. However, the state was not yet able to significantly influence overall mechanisms of economic development.

Agriculture. The majority of agricultural products were affected by the crisis, although those products having principally foreign markets, such as cotton, sisal (a plant grown for fiber), and coffee, were especially affected. As for corn, its production level was essentially tied to domestic factors, the most relevant of which was political instability arising from the uncertainty of land ownership. With several crops the drop in prices would nullify the increase in volume produced; such was the case with sugar, for which the price in 1931 was 42 percent less than it had been on average during the five-year period from 1925 to 1929, with coffee down 12 percent, corn down 23 percent, and wheat down 41 percent. Credit was simply frozen. Although the average bank interest rate was 12 percent, private and non-bank interest rose to more than 60 percent. The typical farmer could not count on any security.

The behavior of export oriented agricultural products was heterogeneous between 1928 and 1939. With such crops as sisal, a combination of long-term factors, including the substitution of synthetic fibers, determined the drop in international demand. On the other hand, cotton, one of the products most seriously affected by the crisis, was able to recover toward the later part of the decade.

Political instability in several agricultural regions was rendered sharper by the Depression and facilitated the implementation of Cárdenas's radical agrarian reform program. Although the precedent for the demand for land had been set during the armed revolution, the political and military defeat of the most important peasant leaders (Emiliano Zapata and Francisco Villa) had introduced an impasse in reform efforts, with the exception of states like Morelos, where the guerrillas never entirely disappeared. During the Great Depression—and this fundamentally in connection with commercial export crops—land lost its previous value, and this facilitated the expropriation projects of *Cardenismo.* It is no coincidence that the geography of the great *Cardenista* nationalization drive toward collective *ejidos* (nationalized land that could only be worked by agricultural families living on the land) corresponded to the commercial agricultural zones—cotton in La Laguna and Valle del Yaqui, Sonora; sisal in the Yucatán Peninsula; sugar in Los Mochis, Sinaloa, and Morelos.

Manufacturing and mining. The crisis was also manifested in the manufacturing sector through a pre-dictable channel: a reduction in domestic demand. At the end of the 1920s, virtually all of the manufactured products in Mexico were being consumed domestically. The impact of manufacturing on exports was practically nil; thus, the fluctuations of international protectionism during the Great Depression had no direct effect on Mexican industry. One of the unique aspects of the crisis in manufacturing was the greater impact suffered by the subsector dedicated to the production of consumer goods compared to the subsector oriented toward the production of intermediary goods, especially cement and steel. These managed to sustain acceptable levels of production based on government support through public works.

The crisis generated a process of classical industrial concentration in several cases, such as tobacco and the brewing industry, already an important branch of Mexican manufacturing. As for its regional impact, the manufacturing sector most affected by the crisis was the cotton textile industry. Textiles was the oldest manufacturing industry in Mexico. Its origins during colonial times in the so-called wool mills or obrajes was in large part in response to the demand for cloth and clothing for the remote mining centers and farms. During the nineteenth century, the struggle between liberals and conservatives over protectionism and free trade exposed the limits of technological development in the textile factories. Always lagging in efficiency compared to industrialized countries, Mexico's textile industry principally served the domestic market. Thus, the textile industry experienced a type of turnaround through a drop in demand for cloth and clothing as a result of a drop in the income of the middle and lower classes. This drop began to cause warehouses to fill up. The decline in employment in this sector was relatively mild—around 15 percent between 1929 and 1932. Cuts were made, especially in the number of hours worked, with the customary forty-eight hour workweek sometimes cut in half. The years that followed were characterized by a combination of defensive solutions, such as the cut in working hours, throughout industry, with the active participation of the workers, usually at the shop floor level.

The pattern—a profound impact from the economic crisis, forced readjustments, and rapid recovery—repeated itself. In general, workers did not wait passively for the recession to end. Instead, Mexico experienced militant resistance to the recession. One important result of the decade's labor struggles was the approval and later implementation of a new Federal Labor Law, proclaimed in 1931, which included the legal right to strike, maximum work hours, and minimum wage limits among its provisions. Granted, these advances were long fought for by workers at the shop floor level, as Jeffrey Bortz has shown, but the catalyst for federal approval was the Great Depression (as it was in many countries around the world).

The railroads. A logical result of the contraction of the export sector—of mining in particular and of the trade of raw materials in general—was the reduction in the volume of freight transported by the railroads. Mineral products represented one-third of the total freight moved by this mode of transportation around 1929 and 1930, when the decline in activity became apparent. The remainder of the freight was divided more or less as follows: 25 to 27 percent was agricultural products, 9 to 10 percent was timber products, 7 percent came from processing industries, and the rest (20 to 23 percent) was inorganic products, such as oil, asphalt, lime, cement, and salt. The 14.3 million tons of freight transported in 1929 were reduced to 9.2 million in 1932; similarly, the figure of 21.1 million passengers transported in 1929 dropped to 15.2 million in 1932, or 28 percent less. The number of passengers per kilometer fell by an estimated 43 percent; train cars were often half empty, and the average income from passenger fares dropped by 20 percent. As one analyst put it, from 1930 to 1932 the administration of the railroads not only dispatched the trains, but it also dispatched thousands of workers. The drop in employment throughout the economy was undoubtedly the most significant negative result, from a social perspective, of the crisis. The difficulties of the labor market were reinforced by the massive repatriation of Mexicans from the United States.

The repatriates. The incoming wave of Mexicans expelled from the United States reached a minimum of 300,000. To put this figure in perspective, it is helpful to consider that Mexico's total population in 1930 was 16,526,000, of which only 5,352,000 were economically active, and of these a mere 692,000 were employed in industry.

There was tremendous insecurity concerning work on the part of Mexican residents in the United States. A conservative estimate places at 28 percent the average number of Mexican residents in the United States who had either resorted to repatriation or had found themselves without work and with few expectations of finding any. Reports from Mexican consulates in the United States become repetitive when evaluating the almost nonexistent job options, repeated city by city, county by county. For example, a special envoy in Phoenix, Arizona, reported that "in not one of the places belonging to this district does there exist even the remotest possibility that Mexicans will find work." In Galveston, Texas, people applying for jobs had to not only vouch for their nationality, but also provide proof of having paid taxes to the Unites States Treasury. The selection criteria for obtaining work put emphasis on the payment of taxes, both income and sales, as well as the location of purchases.

Most Mexican repatriates ended up with their paternal or maternal families, who had to share their scarce resources with their relatives. The majority of the special projects initiated by the Mexican government in agricultural settlements in the country's interior were failures. In addition, the incorporation of the displaced people created intense family tensions between the repatriates and the heads of households who took them in. Whereas the recently arrived family members had aspirations linked to a material culture based on a wage ethic (a car, a radio, clothes), those taking them in had expectations based on working the land. This tension caused many repatriates to decide to repeat the adventure of emigration to the north.

One of the paradoxical aspects of this mass exodus that has received little attention was the repatriates' loss of property in the United States. As job possibilities disappeared, principally in the suburbs of such cities as Los Angeles or San Francisco, the families who undertook the return to Mexico had to abandon land and homes that had been obtained after much effort. Many lost their houses and small properties because they could not make mortgage payments; others were forced to sell their homes and land at extremely low prices. That these purchases had been made in territory that had previously belonged to Mexico strengthened the immigrants' sense of frustration. The repatriation process vividly showed the international impact of the Depression. Nationalistic responses, both popular and elite based, appeared in every country, exacerbating the suffering of the "foreign" poor.

Oil. The oil industry was another important sector of the Mexican economy in which the Great Depression caused a decline. Mexico's oil production, built almost entirely by and for U.S. and British capital, had already gone through one period of spectacular growth and another of sharp decline during its brief existence. The period of its peak performance coincided with the increase in the price of oil from less than $1 per barrel to more than $3 between 1915 and mid-1920. From this point on there began a slow but persistent drop to approximately $1.15 per barrel between 1928 and 1930. Throughout the 1930s the price of oil increased slowly. It did not experience a new boom until the period between 1946 and 1958.

At the beginning of the 1920s, the Mexican oil industry was highly concentrated in the hands of a few multinational firms. The three giants—Huasteca Petroleum Company, the Compañía Mexicana de Petróleo El Aguila (British), and the Penn Mex Fuel Company—represented nearly three-fourths of production in 1918. Of course, the Depression had a major impact on new oil field exploration and the crude oil extraction rate. As a whole, whereas in 1920, the peak of the Mexican oil boom, the industry employed around fifty thousand laborers and other personnel, by 1935 the number had dropped to fifteen thousand. Even in 1938, the year the petroleum industry was expropriated, it had a mere 17,600 workers, 2,800 of whom were temporary.

Nationalization of the oil interests was made possible by such factors as the decline in the value of the fields, the closeness of the *Cardenista* project to the U.S. New Dealers (one of which, Josephus Daniels, was ambassador to Mexico during that time), and the growing fear of war in Europe. In addition, the support of Mexican workers for the mea-

sure was virtually unanimous, and oil became an important engine to internal industrialization.

GOVERNMENT RESPONSE

The severity of the impact of the crisis in numerous sectors of the economy affected the economic policies that the Mexican government implemented. Financial pressures on the budget, in particular, had two long-lasting effects: the postponement of payments to international financial creditors—that is, a moratorium on the public debt service; and the reduction and subsequent reorganization of the state's bureaucratic apparatus. Pressure to create new state-sponsored institutions followed and became the origin, eventually, of several developmental agencies and banks, such as those oriented towards agriculture (Banco de Crédito Ejidal), housing (Banco Nacional Hipotecario), and small enterprises (Nacional Financiera). Public education became a high priority through the Secretaría de Educación Pública, and agrarian reform was pushed forward through irrigation works and new highways.

These policies, which would later be defined as Keynesian, took shape as a pragmatic response to the Depression rather than as a result of some intellectual vision. After two years (1930–1932) of disastrous orthodox fiscal policies, the Ministry of Finance applied new anti-cyclical policies that resembled the orientation of the United States's New Deal. Years later, in lectures prepared for the department of economics at the National University, Mexico's secretary of the treasury from 1935 to 1946, Eduardo Suárez, would severely criticize the previous orthodox policy—the "balanced budget approach." According to that view, money "would have to be kept in refrigerators and isolated from any vibration with the same care given to keeping the platinum and iridium bar in the International Office of Weights and Measures in Paris that serves as the basis of the decimal metric system." Mexico, instead, joined the proactive policies of a group of countries in Latin America and elsewhere that responded to the Depression by increasing the state's intervention in the economy, taking advantage of the social mobilization that was taking place in the countryside and in the cities. However, the peculiarity of the Mexican case was that the import substitutive industrialization was combined with significant social reforms that were pushed forward from below.

See Also: CANADA, GREAT DEPRESSION IN; KEYNESIAN ECONOMICS; LATIN AMERICA, GREAT DEPRESSION IN; LATINO AMERICANS, IMPACT OF THE GREAT DEPRESSION ON.

BIBLIOGRAPHY

Aguila, Marcos T. "The Great Depression and the Origins of Cardenismo in México. The Case of the Mining Sector and Its Workers, 1927–1940." Ph.D. diss., University of Texas, Austin, 1997.

Aguila, Marcos T., and Alberto Enríquez Perea, editors. Perspectivas sobre el Cardenismo: Ensayos sobre economía, trabajo, política y cultura en los años treinta. 1996.

Bortz, Jeffrey. "The Genesis of the Mexican Labor Relations System: Federal Labor Relations Policy and the Textile Industry, 1925–1940." The Americas (July 1995).

Bortz, Jeffrey, "'Without Any More Law Than Their Own Caprice' Cotton Textile Workers and the Challenge to Factory Authority during the Mexican Revolution," International Review of Social History 42, no. 2 (1997): 253-88.

Calderón, Miguel A. El impacto de la Crisis de 1929 en México. 1982.

Cárdenas, Enrique. La industrialización mexicana durante la Gran Depresión Depresión. 1987.

Carr, Barry. "The Mexican Communist Party and Agrarian Mobilization in the Laguna, 1920–1940: A Worker-Peasant Alliance?" Hispanic American Historical Review 67, no. 3 (1987): 371–404.

Carreras de Velasco, M. Los mexicanos que devolvió la crisis, 1929–1932. 1974.

Córdova, Arnaldo. En una época de crisis, 1928–1934: La Clase obrera en la historia de México. 1980.

Díaz Alejandro, Carlos. "Latin America in the 1930's." In Latin America in the 1930's: The Role of the Periphery in World Crisis, edited by Rosemary Thorpe. 1984.

Freeman, Robert S. The United States and Revolutionary Nationalism in Mexico, 1916-1932. 1972.

Haber, Stephen H. Industry and Underdevelopment: The Industrialization of Mexico, 1890–1940. 1989.

Hamilton, Nora. The Limits of State Autonomy: Postrevolutionary Mexico. 1983.

Knight, Alan. US-Mexican Relations, 1910–1940: An Interpretation. 1987.

Knight, Alan. "The Politics of the Expropiation." In The Mexican Petroleum Industry in the Twentieth Century, edited by Jonathan C. Brown and Alan Knight. 1992.

Knight, Alan. "State and Popular Culture in Revolutionary Mexico, 1910–1940." HAHR 74, no. 3: 393–444.

Meyer, Lorenzo. México y los Estados Unidos en el conflicto petrolero (1917–1942). 1972.

Meyer, Lorenzo. Su Majestad británica contra la Revolución Mexicana, 1900–1950: El fin de un imperio informal. 1991.

Schuler, Friedrich E. Mexico between Hitler and Roosevelt: Mexican Foreign Relations in the Age of Lázaro Cárdenas, 1934–1940. 1998.

MARCOS T. AGUILA

MICHEAUX, OSCAR

In a career that began in 1919, Oscar Micheaux (January 2, 1884–March 26, 1951) produced more than forty "race movies"—motion pictures made for African-American audiences—a record unmatched in American cinema history. What little is known of his early life is derived from scattered sources such as family lore, a few elusive public records, and autobiographical themes and sequences in several of his movies, and from seven self-published, often thinly veiled, autobiographical novels. An adherent of Booker T. Washington's ideology of black entrepreneurship and "self-help," Micheaux spent much of his youth homesteading on the Rosebud Indian reservation in South Dakota, doing a stint as a railroad porter on Pullman sleeping cars, and as the author and publisher of his novels. Beginning with his first movie, The Homesteader (1919), he took up themes that Hollywood filmmakers ignored: social dramas rooted in racial issues, tales of black striving and achievement, and plots that sometimes turned on false or mistaken racial identities.

At first the stock market crash of 1929 and the ensuing Depression stifled Micheaux and other makers of race movies. In addition to audiences shrunken by their economic plight and a paucity of sources of capital, the new medium of "talkies" also proved a daunting obstacle, at least until the Harlem theater owner Frank Schiffman backed Micheaux's reentry into production. The Great Depression thereafter reenergized Micheaux's work and sharpened its focus on his familiar themes of black ambition woven into episodes of his own life story. *The Exile* (1931) was typical of his work during this period in that its sources were Micheaux's own autobiographical novel *The Conquest* (1913) and a reworking of his silent film *The Homesteader*. In another instance of his using the Depression as an inspiration for a remake, Micheaux reworked *Birthright* (1924, 1938), a "story of the Negro in the South," that he derived from a novel by the white Pulitzer Prize-winning populist writer T. S. Stribling. As adapted by Micheaux, its story centered on a black Harvard graduate who struggles against Southern racial morés in an attempt to found a school for African-American children.

The Depression touched Micheaux in yet another way. He began to relocate his settings in northern cities, where he created a tension between black plight at the hands of the white South as against the new perils of life in the North, where poverty was accompanied by black crime, violence, and the breakup of the family under the stress of urban life. His heroes were often achievers and go-getters, while the heavies were criminals who preyed upon African Americans, as in *The Girl from Chicago* (1932). Or, as in *Underworld* (1937), the movies were cautionary tales warning of a too hasty rejection of the sturdy values of "the Southland" in favor of the hollow glamour of the urban underworld. Sometimes, a familiar genre such as a backstage romance in which the hero strives to crash Broadway—as in his *Swing* (1938)—also included a subplot that took up some social issue such as, in this instance, the abuse of women by black men idled by slumping urban economies even as their women became breadwinners as domestic servants.

With the onset of World War II and a consequent liberalizing of racial depictions in Hollywood movies, race moviemakers suffered. Micheaux offered his services to the government's propaganda arm, the Office of War Information, pointing out that "we are never shown on the screen in . . . the war effort," but with no recorded response from Washington. Thus Micheaux's work during the Great Depression constituted both a high moment in the history of the race movie as well as its swan song.

See Also: AFRICAN AMERICANS, IMPACT OF THE GREAT DEPRESSION ON.

BIBLIOGRAPHY

Bowser, Pearl; Jane Gaines; and Charles Musser; eds. *Oscar Micheaux and His Circle: African-American Filmmaking and Race Cinema of the Silent Era.* 2001.

Bowser, Pearl, and Louise Spence. *Writing Himself into History: Oscar Micheaux, His Silent Films, and His Audiences.* 2001.

Cripps, Thomas. *Slow Fade to Black: The Negro in American Film, 1900–1942.* 1977.

Gaines, Jane M. *Fire and Desire: Mixed Race Movies in the Silent Era.* 2001.

Green, J. Ronald. *Straight Lick: The Cinema of Oscar Micheaux.* 2000.

VanEpps-Taylor, Betti Carol. *Oscar Micheaux: Dakota Homesteader, Author, Pioneer Film Maker, A Biography.* 1999.

THOMAS CRIPPS

MIDDLETOWN IN TRANSITION

In June 1935 Robert S. Lynd returned to Muncie, Indiana, to conduct a second in-depth sociological study of this "typical" midwestern city. This was to be a sequel to the pioneering work he and his wife, Helen M. Lynd, carried out from 1924 to 1925. Their 1929 report, *Middletown: A Study in Modern American Culture*, had been an unexpected best-seller. Their publisher, Alfred Harcourt, encouraged them to revisit Muncie to document how the city had changed in the intervening decade, particularly from the impact of the Great Depression.

Muncie was a community of approximately fifty thousand people. The overwhelming majority were white Protestants of native stock. The city contained few immigrants or minorities of any kind. In this striking homogeneity, Muncie was hardly a representative American community. It also was more prosperous than most. Though hard hit by the Depression, its main employer manufactured glass jars for home canning—one of the few industries that thrived during hard times.

The original Middletown study involved extensive data gathering. Lacking both time and funding, the second study was less empirical and more dependent on information gained from local "informed sources." Lynd departed after spending only three months in the field. *Middletown in Transition: A Study in Cultural Conflicts* was published in 1937. It was organized around the same six areas as its predecessor: getting a living, making a home, training the young, using leisure time, religious practices, and community activities. One innovation was an analysis of the power exercised by the Ball family (identified in the book only as "the X family"), who directly employed about 10 percent of the town's workers and supported many of its leading institutions.

The Lynds described a community with deep class divisions. The "business class" dominated local affairs. The "working classes" lacked power and seldom openly gave voice to their grievances. Despite economic setbacks, class conflict in Muncie remained beneath the surface. Trends identified in the earlier study continued but had not altered materially. The Lynds concluded that "basically the texture of Middletown's culture has not changed." One must agree with the Italian sociologist, Rita Caccamo, who asked in *Back to Middletown: Three Generations of Sociological Reflections*, "What transition?"

The two Middletown studies are widely cited by sociologists as models for empirical community study. Historians have found a wealth of evidence in their pages for the growing impact of advertising and the spread of the consumer culture. The Lynds' portrait of Middle America in the first half of the twentieth century remains a monumental work of social documentation.

See Also: ADVERTISING IN THE GREAT DEPRESSION; CONSUMERISM; MIDWEST, GREAT DEPRESSION IN THE; SOCIAL SCIENCE.

BIBLIOGRAPHY

Caccamo, Rita. *Back to Middletown: Three Generations of Sociological Reflections.* 2000.

Hoover, Dwight W. *Middletown Revisited.* 1990.

PAUL T. MURRAY

MIDWEST, GREAT DEPRESSION IN THE

In major respects the Great Depression's course and impact in the Midwest (comprising the states of Ohio, Indiana, Illinois, Michigan, Wisconsin, Minnesota, Iowa, Missouri, Kansas, Nebraska, South Dakota, and North Dakota) resembled its course and impact in the United States as a whole. Like other areas, the Midwest suffered from acute and persisting distress, had much difficulty in devising ways to deal with it, and underwent Depression-related reforms that affected its future development. Yet there were also differences. Although some contemporary sociologists considered the region to have more national character traits than any other, it, too, had its peculiarities, evident particularly in its cultural ideals and tensions, its mix of industry and agriculture, its institutional development, and its geographical features. All of these affected both the impact of and responses to the Depression, the result being some significant regional divergences from what was happening elsewhere.

DESCENT AND EARLY RESPONSE, 1929–1932

In the Midwest the Depression arrived more slowly than in America's eastern cities, with conditions during the winter of 1929 to 1930 producing relatively little alarm. By 1931, however, rising unemployment, burgeoning relief needs, and shrinking farm incomes were generating considerable alarm, and by 1932 the region was suffering the severest economic contraction in its history. Unemployment approached 20 percent and in the mining areas and industrial centers was much higher. In Minnesota's iron ranges and Illinois's coal districts unemployment was over 70 percent, and in Chicago, the region's unofficial "capital," it stood at an estimated 40 percent. Midwestern cities had become scenes of suffering and want. And the rural Midwest, already somewhat depressed in 1929, now faced disaster. Farm prices had fallen to all-time lows, and farm income had shrunk by nearly 60 percent, aggravating debt and tax burdens and undermining the vitality of rural service centers.

By 1932, moreover, the inadequacy of existing relief systems was glaringly apparent. The relief ca-

Transient men say prayers before a meal at the Dubuque, Iowa, city mission in 1940. LIBRARY OF CONGRESS, PRINTS & PHOTOGRAPHS DIVISION, FSA/OWI COLLECTION

pacities of private charities, welfare capitalists, and local poor law overseers soon collapsed and could not be revived by the informational and coordinative agencies established at higher levels. Federal support for agricultural marketing associations and emergency stabilization corporations failed to curb rural decline. And numerous cities faced bankruptcy if new sources of funding could not be found. Daily relief allowances shrank to fifteen cents per person in Detroit, Chicago's teachers went unpaid, and in these cities and others shantytowns multiplied while scrounging in garbage cans and city dumps became common. Yet proposals for state and federal aid were still widely viewed as departures from the American way. As of mid-1932 only Illinois and Wisconsin had appropriated state relief

money, and even when federal relief loans became available in late 1932 a number of the region's states were slow to secure them.

As the economy shrank, the region's jobless and dispossessed frequently blamed themselves and retreated into resignation and apathy. Some, however, found scapegoats in the business and political establishments, and smoldering resentment could sometimes burst into violence. Hunger marches and food looting occurred in several cities. Unemployed Councils, under Communist leadership, harassed urban relief authorities, and in early 1932 a march on the Ford Motor plant in Dearborn, Michigan, demanding that it take on more workers, resulted in bloody fighting between marchers and the police. In the hinterland, moreover, particularly the western reaches of the corn belt, some farmers were now ready to challenge established authority. In the "cow war" of 1931, Iowa used martial law to enforce regulations concerning tubercular cattle. And at Des Moines in May 1932, militants formed the Farmers' Holiday Association, a group ready to use violence in support of farm strikes and the halting of foreclosure proceedings.

Depression discontent also threatened the regional political dominance long exercised by the Republican Party. In 1929 the Republicans controlled state government in eleven of the twelve states, all except South Dakota. But in 1930 and 1931 this dominance underwent serious erosion. A resurgent Democratic Party elected governors in Ohio, Nebraska, and Kansas and made substantial gains elsewhere. A Farmer-Labor Party won control in Minnesota, installing Floyd B. Olson as governor there. Progressive Republicans reemerged on top in Wisconsin, where Philip F. La Follette became governor. And the political climate was now such that independents could not only run for high office but also stand a chance of winning. In the Kansas election of 1930, Dr. John R. Brinkley, whose claims for the sexual rejuvenation power of goat glands had cost him his medical license, nearly won the governorship with an independent, anti-establishment campaign that appealed particularly to the state's old populist areas.

In November 1932 the Republican rout seemed virtually complete. A region that had voted overwhelmingly for Herbert Hoover in 1928 now voted solidly against him, and in state contests most remaining Republican governors were ousted. The only winner was Alfred M. Landon of Kansas, in part because of another Brinkley run as an independent. Some special legislative sessions were also meeting now, searching for ways to trim governmental costs, raise new revenue, and provide debt relief. But the more general pattern was to wait and see what might be forthcoming from the change in national administrations. In the winter of 1932 to 1933, unemployment kept mounting, relief funds became still more inadequate, violence flared anew in the corn and dairy lands, and a new wave of bank runs, beginning in Michigan in February 1933, brought "bank holidays" in state after state. Recov-

Many farms in the Midwest, including this one photographed in 1936 near Liberal, Kansas, were rendered uncultivable by drought and soil erosion during the 1930s. LIBRARY OF CONGRESS, PRINTS & PHOTOGRAPHS DIVISION, FSA/OWI COLLECTION

ery seemed farther away than ever and political action more necessary.

REFORM FROM ABOVE AND BELOW, 1933–1940

In the next seven years, political action brought reform and relief but recovery was elusive. Upturns in mid-1933 and on a greater scale in 1935 and 1936 proved short-lived, the result being unemployment rates that never got below 14 percent. In the Midwest, moreover, especially in its western borderlands, the period brought severe drought as well as continued economic depression. The years 1934 and 1936 were the driest that the area had known since such records had been kept, and adding now to its rural misery were seared and withered crops, scorching temperatures, starving livestock, and "black blizzards" that altered the landscape and left dust inches thick on almost everything. By 1940 the Dakotas had lost approximately 150,000 people. Not only farms but towns had been abandoned, and a substantial proportion of those left behind

A Farm Security Administration county supervisor discusses a farm plan with a rehabilitation client in Grant county, Wisconsin, in 1939. LIBRARY OF CONGRESS, PRINTS & PHOTOGRAPHS DIVISION, FSA/OWI COLLECTION

had been reduced to propertylessness, if not abject poverty.

Still, if hard times persisted, Franklin D. Roosevelt's New Deal brought much more federal assistance to the area. Federal money came to the rescue in the form of relief grants, works projects, crop allotment checks, purchasing programs, and special credits for needy farmers, homeowners, and businesses. Market controls came in the guise of industrial codes, agricultural adjustment contracts, fair labor standards, bank deposit guarantees, and more federal regulators. And erected by 1940 was a new if incomplete structure of social insurance, the federal government having now joined with the states to provide employment services, old-age pensions, unemployment compensation, and expanded aid to

handicapped and dependent groups. Midwesterners, like other Americans, had become more dependent on their national government than they or their ancestors had ever been, and the result for many was a mixture of gratitude with concerns about alien influences and the loss of individual freedom, local autonomy, and cultural identity.

Throughout the region, moreover, the coming of federal relief brought significant institutional reform. To meet matching requirements and help administer the programs, the states found new sources of revenue and established a new and more professional array of emergency relief, social welfare, and intrastate regulatory agencies, a number of which became permanent additions to state government. Also serving as administrative partners was a new complex of business and labor associations, farmer committees, and community groups, which significantly affected the area's organizational development. And while these partnerships usually involved and benefited local elites rather than the "grassroots" allegedly being mobilized, there were exceptions. Through its support of industrial unions, rural resettlement, Indian tribal councils, and greater opportunities for women and minority groups, the New Deal helped to advance a kind of democracy often opposed by the area's elites and thus to alter to some degree its power relationships.

Not all reform, however, came from above. Reform coalitions also appeared at lower levels, producing, in some states, "little New Deals" that featured greater tax equity, farm debt moratoria, small business protection, new welfare benefits, and bans on unfair employer practices. Going the farthest in this direction were the governorships of Floyd Olson in Minnesota, Philip La Follette in Wisconsin, and Frank Murphy in Michigan. Regional "wets" also helped to end national prohibition of alcoholic beverages and to shrink drastically the area still subject to state and local "dry" laws. And transforming industrial workplaces and communities was a new labor militancy grounded in the capacity of Depression woes and renewed hope to override long-standing ethnic divisions and produce working-class support for industrial unionism. The region's automobile, rubber, and steel plants became the sites of bitter conflict; its sit-down strikes, at Akron, Ohio, and Flint, Michigan, became milestones in the rise of the new Congress of Industrial Organizations; and in its leading industries and cities organized labor now emerged as a major force.

Labor's rise, moreover, seemed to be turning the Depression-induced political realignment into an enduring one. Democrats continued to win, and in 1936 Roosevelt again carried every state in the region. By this time, however, a vociferous opposition, particularly strong in the region's small cities and small towns, was also denouncing the New Deal as un-American subversion of the nation's traditional liberties and natural recuperative powers. And beginning in 1937, a new economic downturn combined with new labor difficulties, new

fears of dictatorial action, and new concerns about foreign involvement worked to undermine the area's fragile reform coalitions and return Republicans to power. Their older dominance was not completely reestablished, since the movement of blacks and labor into the Democratic Party proved relatively enduring. But by 1940 seven of the twelve states had Republican governors, and in that year seven voted against Roosevelt's reelection.

As the New Deal lost the region's support, the limited achievements of reform, whether from above or below, also became apparent. Conditions had been alleviated and progress made toward creating an organizational order capable of renewed economic growth. But the "industrial democracy" that came to the Midwest's factories operated within and was dependent upon a new bureaucratic framework. Urban political machines drew strength from New Deal programs, most notably in Chicago and Kansas City. The poor law relief system made a comeback as the federal government withdrew from providing relief for unemployables. And much of the discriminatory structure limiting opportunities for women and racial minorities remained in place. Nor did the visions of a restored and vibrant rural civilization, to be achieved through rural resettlement, ever come close to realization. Instead, the bulk of the New Deal programs worked to restart the process of rural depopulation.

CULTURAL CHALLENGE AND COMPROMISE
Long a scene of rural-urban conflict, the Midwest was also experiencing now another kind of cultural dissonance. Its "main streets" had been the strongholds of a culture primarily associated with an older middle class of local businessmen, small-town professionals, and family farmers. There, more so than anywhere else, the ideals of progress through hard work, self-reliance, and community boosterism had held sway. But now these were being undercut, one challenge coming from conditions under which meeting the idealized social responsibilities had become exceedingly difficult, another from what seemed necessary for survival. With rescue had come dependence upon new structures of power, acting through a newer middle class of administrative officials, special agents, and

trained experts with their own notions of what constituted social progress and how to engineer it. Such aid seemed essential, but accepting it seemed to require the abandonment of ideas regarded as fundamental to sensible living.

These perceived threats often underlay the region's notorious critiques of the New Deal. They became standard fare in both a conservative and a neo-populist rhetoric. Yet only a few of the critics were ready to renounce federal support. They looked instead toward compromises that could somehow combine an older independence and traditional ways with new schemes of bureaucratic order and social engineering. And given the vulnerability of the New Deal state to anti-bureaucratic critiques and small-town nostalgia, arrangements were forthcoming to incorporate local initiatives and vetoes and thus to make the new dependence seem less threatening. The elaborate participatory structures created for agricultural adjustment eased concerns about the machinations of distant planners. So did similar structures for undertaking works projects, and in some places, like Fort Wayne, Indiana, for example, pragmatic Republican regimes met New Deal needs while persuading voters that they provided needed curbs on potential tyranny.

Also helping to ease feelings of cultural loss was the emergence of a compensatory art and literature, in which satires of the small town gave way to its celebration and the folkways and traditions of the "heartland" became the true essence of Americanism. One promoter of this was the New Deal state itself, especially through its state guidebooks as produced by the WPA Federal Writers' Project and through the support that other projects gave to fostering a "people's art." But involved as well were local leaders and groups, who found solace in incorporating such art into public monuments, rituals, and commemorations. And facilitating matters was the emergence of an appropriate artistic sensibility, epitomized in what such painters as Grant Wood and Thomas Hart Benton were putting on canvas and in Sherwood Anderson's move from the grim tales of *Winesburg, Ohio* (1919) to being "glad of the life on the farm and in small communities."

For some intellectuals this artistic expression was also part of a larger "revolt of the provinces,"

believed potentially capable both of saving valuable regional ways and creating a national pluralism resistant to mass culture and standardization. In this vision the Midwest and other regions were to restructure resource usage so as to support a revitalization and continuance of traditional ways, with the process to be facilitated by movement educators, artists, and planners. The Depression, it was thought, had created the necessary opening. But action consisted chiefly of academic conferences and treatises, events like the National Folk Festival in Saint Louis, and some effort to guide the federal supports for rural resettlement, river development, and cultural enrichment along this path. Intellectual regionalism in the Midwest stands as an interesting Depression phenomenon, which left behind interesting artistic and intellectual monuments. But its hopes for the region's future were to go unrealized.

The Midwest, then, was not spared the blighted lives, shrunken hopes, and other ravages of the Great Depression. Nor was it spared a degree of Depression-induced social and political transformation. Yet its experience did have regional peculiarities. Its suffering bore the peculiar marks of a pre-existing agricultural depression, a devastating drought, and exceptionally fierce commitments to an outmoded relief system. And its empowerment of new groups left room for a Republican comeback and required a complex accommodation with a sturdy and persisting system of small-town and older-middle-class values. While becoming a different Midwest, it still retained much of its earlier distinctiveness.

See Also: AMERICAN SCENE, THE; CITIES AND SUBURBS; DUST BOWL; FEDERAL WRITERS' PROJECT; LA FOLLETTE, PHILLIP; MINNESOTA FARMER-LABOR PARTY; MURPHY, FRANK; NORTHEAST, GREAT DEPRESSION IN THE; RURAL LIFE; SIT-DOWN STRIKE; SOUTH, GREAT DEPRESSION IN THE; WEST, GREAT DEPRESSION IN THE AMERICAN.

BIBLIOGRAPHY

Bauman, John F., and Thomas H. Coode. *In the Eye of the Great Depression: New Deal Reporters and the Agony of the American People.* 1988.

Biles, Roger. *Big City Boss in Depression and War: Mayor Edward J. Kelly of Chicago.* 1984.

Brock, William R. *Welfare, Democracy, and the New Deal.* 1988.

Cohen, Lizabeth. *Making a New Deal: Industrial Workers in Chicago, 1919–1939.* 1990.

DiLeva, Frank D. "Frantic Farmers Fight Law." *Annals of Iowa* 32 (October 1953): 81–109.

Dorman, Robert L. *Revolt of the Provinces: The Regionalist Movement in America, 1920–1945.* 1993.

Glad, Paul W. *The History of Wisconsin,* Vol. 5: *War, a New Era, and Depression, 1914–1940.* 1990.

Glick, Frank Z. *The Illinois Emergency Relief Commission: A Study of Administrative and Financial Aspects of Emergency Relief.* 1940.

Jones, Alan. "The New Deal Comes to Iowa." In *The New Deal: Viewed from Fifty Years,* edited by Lawrence E. Gelfand and Robert J. Neymeyer. 1983.

Koch, Raymond L. "Politics and Relief in Minneapolis during the 1930s." *Minnesota History* 41 (winter 1968): 153–170.

Lynd, Robert S., and Helen Merrell Lynd. *Middletown in Transition: A Study in Cultural Conflicts.* 1937.

Maurer, David J. "Relief Problems and Politics in Ohio." In *The New Deal: The State and Local Levels,* edited by John Braeman, Robert H. Bremner, and David Brody. 1975.

Mitchell, Franklin D. *Embattled Democracy: Missouri Democratic Politics, 1919–1932.* 1968.

Morgan, Iwan. "Fort Wayne and the Great Depression." *Indiana Magazine of History* 80 (1984): 122–145, 348–378.

Nash, Gerald D. *The Great Depression and World War II: Organizing America, 1933–1945.* 1979.

Odum, Howard W., and Harry Estill Moore. *American Regionalism: A Cultural-Historical Approach to National Integration.* 1938.

Ortquist, Richard T. *Depression Politics in Michigan, 1929–1933.* 1982.

Patterson, James T. *The New Deal and the States: Federalism in Transition.* 1969.

Schruben, Francis W. *Kansas in Turmoil, 1930–1936.* 1969.

Simmons, Jerold. "Dawson County Responds to the New Deal, 1933–1940." *Nebraska History* 62 (spring 1981): 47–72.

Stock, Catherine McNicol. *Main Street in Crisis: The Great Depression and the Old Middle Class on the Northern Plains.* 1992.

Tweton, D. Jerome. *The New Deal at the Grass Roots: Programs for the People in Otter Tail County, Minnesota.* 1988.

ELLIS W. HAWLEY

MIGRATION

During the Great Depression more than two and one-half million Americans, many of them poverty-stricken, took to the road. They moved from country to city and sometimes from the city back to the country, from the South to the North and from the North and South to the West, within states and from state to state, leaving one region for another, in pursuit of elusive opportunities elsewhere. Families as well as single individuals set forth with what little they had, stealing rides in boxcars, bartering their few remaining possessions to obtain gasoline for decrepit jalopies, hitchhiking down dusty highways. In general, they left areas affected by declining manufacturing output, adverse weather conditions, soil erosion, farm foreclosures, boll weevil ravages, mechanization forcing laborers off the land, and stifling racial segregation.

The trend toward interregional migration began before the Depression. Migration rates were considerably higher in the United States from 1920 to 1930 than from 1930 to 1940. In the 1920s the population of the Northeast and North Central states grew, in part because of an influx of immigrants from abroad. During the same period native-born migrants headed to the North and West, fleeing drought and other agricultural devastation in the middle and southern portions of the nation. African Americans left the South in response to both adverse changes in farming and legalized discrimination.

Manufacturing cutbacks of the 1930s brought net declines in population to the Northeast and North Central regions as closed factory doors prompted migration from industrialized states. At the same time migrants continued to head out of the South and the parched Dust Bowl of the Southwest where howling winds scooped up dry topsoil. With its promise of orange groves and fertile fields, California beckoned as a particularly attractive destination for some 400,000 migrants called *Okies*. These were farmers, blown off their land in Oklahoma and parts of Missouri, Kansas, Colorado, and Texas, who headed west on Route 66 in old automobiles.

During the Great Depression, thousands of African Americans left the South in response to both adverse changes in farming and legalized discrimination. These migrants from Florida were photographed in 1940 in South Carolina on their way to New Jersey.
FRANKLIN DELANO ROOSEVELT LIBRARY

In a 1944 report, the federal Social Security Board estimated population shifts in the United States due to migration totaled more than 5,800,000 from 1920 to 1930. This figure was cut nearly in half during the Depression, with the comparable estimate given as 2,576,000. Nevertheless, the fact that migration remained significant from 1930 to 1940 showed that thousands of Americans saw no way to improve their plight except to move.

Different and confusing names characterized those who crossed state lines looking for work from 1930 to 1940. Initially, interstate migrants were somewhat differentiated from seasonal migrant laborers who traditionally had moved from place to place to harvest crops. In the early days of the De-

pression, those on the road commonly were called *transients*. They also were referred to by such terms as nonresident indigents or the unattached. Sometimes they were lumped together with hobos and tramps, social outcasts who were long-term wanderers.

When the New Deal pushed through its Federal Emergency Relief Act in May 1933, it contained provision for a Federal Transient Program to help those who had left their homes. The program lasted for two years, functioned in forty-four states, and, at its height, offered assistance to more than 300,000 persons. It ended when the Roosevelt administration changed its approach to relief from direct aid to work-oriented projects centered in local communities. This left the floating population without legal rights to benefits, although the Resettlement Administration (which became part of the Farm Security Administration in 1937) provided some camps for migrants.

As the 1930s unfolded, the term *migrant* was used increasingly in place of the word *transient*. In 1940 the U.S. House of Representatives looked into the problems facing migrants. Its Select Committee to Investigate the Interstate Migration of Destitute Citizens held hearings from New York to California. Its five hundred witnesses dealt with deplorable conditions faced by transients, some of whom had become migratory agricultural workers. The hearings had little impact on legislation because the advent of World War II ended mass unemployment, but the committee's work made it plain that migration was changing the face of the United States.

DEMOGRAPHIC PATTERNS

The 1944 Social Security Board report provided a statistical picture of migration within the United States for the two decades prior to World War II. It pointed out that twenty-one states and the District of Columbia gained population from 1930 to 1940, acquiring a total of 2,567,000 new residents due to migration. At the same time the majority of states, twenty-seven, lost population as residents left to seek improved circumstances. In the early years of the Depression, migration in the Northeast took place from large cities and industrial areas, where workers had lost their jobs, to selected agricultural areas where migrants hoped to be self-sufficient. This trend shifted back somewhat toward the end of the decade with improvements in business and industrial conditions.

During the 1930s the industrialized Northeast and the North Central states lost population, as did most of the South with the exception of Florida. Virginia and Maryland grew in population, benefiting from the expansion of government employment in the neighboring District of Columbia. But it was the West, including both the mountain and Pacific states, that scored the biggest increase, adding a total of 1,322,000 residents. California alone gained l,052,000 residents during the 1930s. Figures in-

cluded both foreign-born and native persons, although immigration into the United States and emigration from it offset each other from 1930 to 1940. This contrasted with the previous decade when immigrants from abroad played a pronounced role in population growth. Clearly, during the Depression, when birth rates were particularly low, states that gained population did so due to interregional migration.

From 1930 to 1940 relatively modest migration increased the population of New Hampshire, Connecticut, Indiana, Minnesota, Delaware, Virginia, Tennessee, Louisiana, Texas, Idaho, Wyoming, Colorado, New Mexico, Arizona, and Nevada. Many of these states served as magnets for the unemployed from industrial areas. Only a few states added more than 100,000 individuals. These included Maryland, Oregon, and Washington, along with the District of Columbia. Florida attracted 334,960 new residents by the end of the decade.

With some exceptions these migratory trends represented a continuation of patterns already in place. The nine states that had the largest gains in population from 1930 to 1940— California, Oregon, Washington, Nevada, Arizona, Indiana, Connecticut, Maryland, and Florida—also had the largest increases in the preceding decade (from 1920 to 1930). While the annual rate of migration to these states declined during the Depression, it picked up again during World War II. From 1920 through 1940 a total of twenty states had continuous losses in population—Maine, Vermont, Pennsylvania, North Carolina, South Carolina, Georgia, Alabama, Mississippi, Arkansas, Kentucky, West Virginia, Iowa, Missouri, North Dakota, South Dakota, Nebraska, Kansas, Oklahoma, Wisconsin, and Montana; this trend also continued into World War II.

AFRICAN-AMERICAN MOVEMENT

The Depression slowed, but did not stem, the general movement of African Americans from the South to the North and from rural to more urban areas within Southern states. Journalist Lorena Hickok, an undercover investigator of Depression conditions for the Roosevelt administration, noted the latter phenomena. She reported that white Southerners claimed that New Deal relief programs drew low-paid agricultural workers, many of them African Americans, out of the cotton fields and into nearby cities where they found little employment. More to the point, many white planters pocketed money paid to them by Roosevelt's Agricultural Adjustment Administration for taking land out of production. By refusing to share payments with their tenants and sharecroppers, as they were supposed to do, planters forced them off the land. In some cases they replaced laborers with machinery. Thus, the New Deal unwittingly contributed to displacements that encouraged migration already underway.

Nearly 500,000 African Americans fled the South from 1910 to 1920 when jobs opened to them in northern industry. The following decade an additional 750,000 exited to escape harsh economic and social conditions. During the 1930s the South lost about 350,000 African Americans, less than half the previous decade's total. The mass exodus of African Americans from the South did not come until the 1940s and 1950s when about three million people moved North and West, initially drawn by work in World War II defense plants. Nevertheless, the Depression did not halt redistribution of the African-American population outside the South, a movement that led to sweeping political changes and the end of segregation.

MIGRATION SYMBOLISM

No group of migrants captured the feel of the Depression in the popular imagination to as great an extent as the *Okies*. The documentary photographer Dorothea Lange took a widely reproduced picture of a toil-worn Okie mother and her hungry children. Titled "Migrant Mother," it appeared in *An American Exodus: A Record of Human Erosion* (1939), a book written by Lange and her husband, economist Paul Taylor. Lange's photograph still is used to symbolize the destitution faced by millions during the 1930s.

John Steinbeck's best-selling novel *The Grapes of Wrath* (1939), subsequently made into a popular movie, familiarized the nation with the tribulations of the penniless Joad family as they strove to find a new life in California. The Joad family's fictional travails represented those of thousands of uprooted individuals who tried to better themselves by moving. Although many eventually established themselves in their new surroundings, the chronicles of downtrodden migrants in the 1930s remain a heart-wrenching part of American history.

See Also: DUST BOWL; *GRAPES OF WRATH, THE;* MIGRATORY WORKERS; OKIES; TRANSIENTS.

BIBLIOGRAPHY

Asch, Nathan. "Cross-Country Bus." *New Republic* 87 (April 25, 1934): 301–304.

Committee on Care of Transient and Homeless. Records of the National Urban League. Part I. Series 4, Box 3, Manuscript Division, Library of Congress, Washington, D.C.

Conrad, David E. *The Forgotten Farmers: The Story of Sharecroppers in the New Deal.* 1965.

Kennedy, David M. *Freedom from Fear: The American People in Depression and War, 1929–1945.* 1999.

Lange, Dorothea. "The Making of a Documentary Photographer." Oral history interview with Suzanne Riess. University of California Regional Oral History Office, Berkeley, 1968.

Lisca, Peter. *John Steinbeck: Nature and Myth.* 1978.

Lowitt, Richard, and Maurine Beasley, eds. *One Third of a Nation: Lorena Hickok Reports the Great Depression.* 1981.

Olson, James S., ed. *Historical Dictionary of the New Deal: From Inauguration to Preparation for War.* 1985.

Peeler, David P. *Hope among Us Yet: Social Criticism and Social Solace in Depression America.* 1987.

Shindo, Charles J. *Dust Bowl Migrants in the American Imagination.* 1997.

Schomburg Center for Research in Black Culture. *The New York Public Library African America Desk Reference.* 1999.

Smith, Jessie Carney, and Carrell Peterson Horton, eds. *Historical Statistics of Black America.* 1995.

Stott, William. *Documentary Expression and Thirties America.* 1973.

Woytinsky, W. S. "Internal Migration during the War." Report prepared for the Bureau of Employment Security, Social Security Board. Records of the National Urban League, Part I. Series 3, Box 18, Manuscript Division, Library of Congress, Washington, D.C.

MAURINE H. BEASLEY

MIGRATORY WORKERS

The images of the Dust Bowl migrants, made famous in John Steinbeck's best selling novel *The Grapes of Wrath* (1939), tend to dominate the historical memory of migrant workers during the Great Depression era. However, while thousands of Okies and Arkies did take to the road in search of survival, they joined migrant workers who had traveled the nation in search of work long before the Depression and who would continue to do so for decades thereafter. These migrants, many of them racial and ethnic minorities, had always worked for low wages and lived in horrible conditions. The Great Depression merely exacerbated their harsh circumstances.

Assessing the absolute number of migrant workers during any decade is difficult. In 1937, sociologist Paul S. Taylor tentatively estimated that there were between 200,000 and 350,000 migrant workers traveling yearly throughout the United States. Although many migrants worked in California, where some would be displaced by incoming Dust Bowl migrants, migrant labor was not just a West Coast phenomenon. For example, thousands of Mexican and Mexican-American migrant workers toiled throughout the nation—from the cotton fields of Texas to the sugar beet fields of Colorado, Michigan, and Ohio. Thousands of southern African Americans and whites (mostly displaced sharecroppers from Georgia and Alabama) regularly worked along the Atlantic Coast, toiling in the winter months in Florida's Everglades and in the northern states during the summer. And finally, thousands of other migrant workers traveled less clear paths throughout dozens of states in search of work.

The Great Depression, which had begun in the 1920s for many of the nation's agricultural regions, worsened the difficulties migrant workers faced. While the numbers of workers in search of work rose during the Depression, the amount of land in production decreased. Moreover, farmers who also faced economic difficulties—falling prices for their crops, higher taxes, and increased debt—looked for places to cut costs, and reducing workers' wages was often the only option they had. The surplus labor (in 1933 in California there were roughly 2.36 workers for each available job) made it extremely difficult for workers to get paid for the full value of their labor. As a result, wages throughout the nation fell during the Depression. Migrant workers in California who had been making 35 cents per hour in 1928 made only 14 cents per hour in 1933. Sugar beet workers in Colorado saw their wages decrease from $27 an acre in 1930 to $12.37 an acre three years later. In Texas, migrant families during the Depression could expect yearly earnings of between $278 and $500, hundreds of dollars below what experts at the time estimated it would cost a family of four merely to survive.

In addition to earning low wages—the lowest of any workers in the country—migrant workers also tended to live in horrible conditions. It was not uncommon for farmers to house migrant workers in shanties, shacks, chicken coops, barns, portable wagons, and even open fields. Those who found shelter inside small cabins or abandoned farm houses often had to contend with broken windows, torn screens, missing doors, and leaky roofs. Most migrants, whether living by themselves in the fields or in specially designated migrant camps, remained isolated from the surrounding communities. Often viewed as racial and class outcasts, migrant workers were shunned by the local communities.

While the nation's industrial workers could look to the New Deal to address some of their problems, migrant workers found themselves largely outside of the scope of most of the programs and legislation. When discussing the status of migrant workers in the United States, historian Cindy Hahamovitch argued that they were, in fact, "stateless." Unlike industrial workers who gained the right to organize unions and bargain collectively, migrant workers were left outside of the bounds of the most important New Deal legislation. Neither section 7a of the 1933 National Industrial Recovery Act nor the 1935 National Labor Relations Act included migrant agricultural workers. When Congress passed the Fair Labor Standards Act instituting minimum wage provisions in 1938, agricultural workers were once again exempted from the federal protections afforded other kinds of workers. Certainly the political clout of agricultural interests

A family of migrant agricultural workers boards a freight car near Roseville, California, in 1940 on their way to Utah where they hope to find work in the sugar beet fields. NATIONAL ARCHIVES AND RECORDS ADMINISTRATION

A migrant agricultural worker carries a basket of peas to the weigh station in a field near Calipatria, California, in 1939. LIBRARY OF CONGRESS, PRINTS & PHOTOGRAPHS DIVISION, FSA/OWI COLLECTION

helped to keep agricultural workers outside of the New Deal protections. Idealistic notions about agricultural labor and rural America may have also made it difficult to pass legislation to protect or empower migrant workers. Even legislation passed explicitly to address the problems plaguing rural America—the Agricultural Adjustment Act—did little to help migrant workers. In fact, the Agricultural Adjustment Administration (AAA) probably worsened the conditions for many migrant workers who saw their jobs disappear along with the crop reductions required by the AAA. In addition, the jobs of many agricultural workers were eliminated when farmers used their government stipends to

buy new machinery. The only New Deal agency that attempted to address the needs of migrant workers was the Resettlement Administration, which was replaced by the Farm Security Administration (FSA). By 1942, the FSA had built ninety-five camps, which could house approximately 75,000 workers. Many of these camps provided housing, health services, schools, laundry facilities, and adult-education programs.

With the exception of the FSA camps, when migrant workers looked to the state for relief, they faced an uphill battle. Racist private and public relief agencies throughout the nation, but especially in the South and West, often denied migrant work-

This newly constructed Farm Security Administration camp for seasonal workers, photographed in 1940 near Yuba City, California, boasted steel shelters, rather than the tents found in many older camps. The camp also included a clinic. NATIONAL ARCHIVES AND RECORDS ADMINISTRATION

ers benefits or granted them benefits much lower than those awarded to other workers. Even the federal relief agencies, including the Works Progress Administration and the Federal Emergency Relief Administration, worked in conjunction with local officials to schedule relief benefits according to the growing seasons. Migrant workers often found their meager benefits cut at the same time that their labor would be needed in the fields. In this way, the federal government helped to maintain a vulnerable, low-income workforce.

Mexican and Mexican-American migrant workers felt the full force of state power during the

Great Depression. As non-citizens, many Mexicans were banned from public works projects available to other destitute workers. Moreover, communities looking for a scapegoat to explain the Depression often blamed Mexicans. Working together, private relief charities, municipal governments, and Mexican consuls helped to repatriate thousands of Mexicans and even Mexican Americans back to Mexico. Many of these men, women, and children had been migrant workers.

Even though migrant workers were excluded from the National Labor Relations Act, thousands joined unions and engaged in strikes to garner better wages and living conditions. In fact, in the early years of the Depression, the number of agricultural unions increased, as did the number of strikes. In his exhaustively researched study on unions in agriculture, Stuart Jamieson recounted ten strikes involving 3,200 workers in 1932. The following year, 1933, over 56,800 workers in seventeen different states took part in at least sixty-one strikes. By 1935 nearly one hundred agricultural unions represented thousands of workers. Although California remained the bastion of labor organizing among agricultural workers, states in the Midwest and East, including Michigan and New Jersey, also witnessed unions and strikes. This militancy is essential for understanding the experiences of migrant workers during the Great Depression. Even though they were often viewed as the bottom rung of society, traveling from place to place and doing jobs others would not do, and even though they were excluded from the benefits awarded other workers, migrant workers nonetheless tried to make a New Deal of their own.

See Also: MIGRATION; OKIES; TRANSIENTS.

BIBLIOGRAPHY

Deutsch, Sarah. *No Separate Refuge: Culture, Class, and Gender on an Anglo-Hispanic Frontier in the American Southwest, 1880–1940.* 1987.

Foley, Neil. *The White Scourge: Mexicans, Blacks, and Poor Whites in Texas Cotton Culture.* 1997.

Guerin-Gonzales, Camille. *Mexican Workers and American Dreams: Immigration, Repatriation, and California Farm Labor, 1900–1939.* 1994.

Hahamovitch, Cindy. *The Fruits of Their Labor: Atlantic Coast Farmworkers and the Making of Migrant Poverty, 1870–1945.* 1997.

Jamieson, Stuart Marshall. *Labor Unionism in American Agriculture.* 1945.

Jones, Jacqueline. *The Dispossessed: America's Underclasses from the Civil War to the Present.* 1992.

McWilliams, Carey. *Ill Fares the Land: Migrants and Migratory Labor in the United States.* 1942.

Reisler, Mark. *By the Sweat of Their Brow: Mexican Immigrant Labor in the United States, 1900–1940.* 1976.

Surfin, Sidney C. "Labor Organization in American Agriculture, 1930–1935." *American Journal of Sociology* 43 (1938): 544–549.

Taylor, Paul S. "Migratory Farm Labor in the United States." *Monthly Labor Review* 44 (1937): 537–549.

Weber, Devra. *Dark Sweat, White Gold: California Farm Workers, Cotton, and the New Deal.* 1994.

KATHY MAPES

MILITARY: UNITED STATES ARMY

In 1929, the U. S. armed services received more funding than the armed services of any other nation, despite the absence of a discernible enemy. The 1920 National Defense Act, which was the nation's first true military policy, had authorized the War Department to recruit 280,000 enlisted personnel and 17,043 officers. Shrinking appropriations during the 1920s lowered the totals in 1930 to 136,216 enlisted and 12,000 officers. In 1935 the enlisted figure had shrunk by executive action to 118,750. The 1920 Act also federalized the 135,000-man National Guard, and by 1933 there was a National Guard Bureau within the War Department. Douglas MacArthur, who became chief of staff of the Army in 1930, could also expect, in an emergency, the activation of 101,000 organized reservists, 127,000 reserve officers, and 28,000 members of the Citizens Military Training camps. In addition, existing war plans included a civilian draft and mandated an initial 4.5 million-man Army with 225,000 officers. Such a force would require one year to assemble, and even longer to reach full production of supplies and weaponry.

Army budgets increased during Herbert Hoover's first two years as president. In 1930, a congressionally-mandated War Policies Commission, the most thorough peacetime war planning inquiry to that date, reviewed mobilization plans and procurement policies. Administered by the assistant secretary of war, prototype legislative drafts defined war rationing, a draft, and government control of the economy. In 1933, MacArthur published a new field manual that established four regular field armies, built upon the nine corps areas. He centralized authority under the chief of staff, inserted Army command over assembling divisions, and provided steps for a partial mobilization, if necessary.

As the Depression deepened, Hoover exercised executive authority to decrease expenditures, but concern over domestic strife and Hoover's long-held theory that public works would speed economic recovery led him to treat the Army in kinder fiscal fashion than other federal agencies. During the Hoover administration, new construction from work relief funds began replacing decaying World War I facilities. The Depression also increased the purchasing power of the dollar and so augmented military funding. Only Hoover's dictated furloughs and later wage cuts for federal agencies gave the Army reason to suffer and protest. By 1935, however, wages were restored. Between 1932 and 1935, maintenance budgets protected the core of the War Department.

The military establishment struggled to absorb new technologies generated by World War I, but MacArthur's commitment to infantry in this environment of curtailed personnel and materiel led to a subordination of armor, chemicals, light weapons, and airplanes. Rather than maintain a separate tank corps, MacArthur integrated mechanized armor into the infantry and bypassed more effective models. The 1926 Air Corps Act had established a five-year plan to secure 1,800 planes. Congress approved the purchase of hundreds more of the fragile machines, but, given their quickly obsolescent designs and high number of crashes, the mandated goal was not realized until 1937. In the same year, Congress increased the number to 2,300. Furthermore, the Air Corps's growing personnel requirements continued to conflict with the General Board's infantry preference. As with the tanks, the planes were scattered among field troops. In 1935 the General Headquarters Air Force, designed as a strategic support for land forces, concentrated the Air Corps command, with a plan for dispersal at the outbreak of a war. That same year Congress passed the National Frontier Defense Act, which authorized the construction of ten huge regional air-dromes to strengthen security, especially in the West Coast. Work relief projects throughout the decade greatly enhanced Army air fields and land support structures.

Other events, such as the 1932 Bonus March and the use of regular and guard troops to quell strikes, soured civilian attitudes and harmed the Army's public image. In 1933, the Army vehement-ly opposed the use of its facilities and personnel by the Civilian Conservation Corps. By 1935, however, Army leaders had discovered that the CCC was a useful source for funds to replace old expended materiel. In addition, officers such as George C. Marshall gained experience in mass mobilization as tens of thousands of CCC recruits were processed. The CCC also contributed to an improved quality of Army inductees during the Depression years.

Difficulties with procurement contracts caused the removal in 1936 of Air Corps chief Benjamin Foulois. In addition, with the exception of the B-17, the aviation industry failed to provide world-class pursuit planes and bombers, and corporate delays hampered delivery of contracted models. After severe congressional pressure, the Army moved to completely motorize the infantry and adopted a semiautomatic rifle (the M-1) in 1935. That same year, Congress authorized an increase of the Army to 165,000 enlisted men, while maintaining 11,500 officers on active duty. The Army could now fully man four divisions, each with 11,500 soldiers. Other divisions remained only partially manned until required by a war to expand. The War Department also used personnel for support bureaus, the Air Corps, and regiments to garrison the country's island possessions and the Panama Canal Zone. Recruit overcrowding and Roosevelt's fiscal fears prolonged full realization of Congress's plan for three years.

Malin Craig, who became chief of staff in September 1935, emphasized a forward vision and a greater realization of the time required for war preparation; he also argued that the shape of national defense was determined by staff decisions and congressional actions made years earlier. As the naval arms limitation treaties faded in 1936 and the Axis Powers emerged, the Army benefited from a general rearming that was led by Congress. From fiscal year 1934 onward, total annual military and naval expenditures averaged over a billion dollars. Although the War Department still estimated a year or more would be required to reach full production in the event of war, by 1939 the United States possessed a well-trained Army and increasingly modern military facilities. Infantry tactics and pilot training had advanced, although defense command remained divided as Army and Navy feuding continued. Contemplating a two-front war, one in the Pacific and another in the Atlantic, at the end of the 1930s the U.S. military profited from excellent noncommissioned officers and a strong cadre of younger officers. The depressed job markets had encouraged the enrollment of both.

See Also: BONUS ARMY/BONUS MARCH; ISOLATIONISM; MILITARY: UNITED STATES NAVY; WORLD WAR II AND THE ENDING OF THE DEPRESSION.

BIBLIOGRAPHY

Brown, Jerold E. *Where Eagles Land: Planning and Development of U.S. Army Airfields, 1910–1941.* 1990.

Griffith, Robert K., Jr. *Men Wanted for the U.S. Army: America's Experience with an All Volunteer Army between the World Wars.* 1982.

Killegrew, John W. *The Impact of the Great Depression on the Army.* 1979.

Kreidberg, Marvin A., and Henry G. Merton. *History of Military Mobilization in the United States Army, 1775–1945.* 1955.

Shiner, John F. *Foulois and the U. S. Army Air Corps, 1931–1935.* 1983.

Vander Meulen, Jacob A. *The Politics of Aircraft: Building an American Military Industry.* 1991.

Wilson, John R. M. *Herbert Hoover and the Armed Forces: A Study of Presidential Attitudes and Policy.* 1993.

HENRY C. FERRELL, JR.

MILITARY: UNITED STATES NAVY

In 1929, as its first line of defense, the United States owned the world's most balanced navy, equally developed in all its elements. The U.S. Navy possessed the most modern battleship fleet, although it was limited in tonnage by the Five-Power Naval Limitation Treaty, adopted by Great Britain, France, Italy, Japan, and the United States after the 1922 Washington Conference. The U.S. Navy continued perfecting new technical applications in communications and engine designs, and under the direction of William Moffett, the Navy's Bureau of Aeronautics also cultivated the first carrier force. Develop-

ment of the fast carriers, with speeds beyond thirty knots, would doom the reconditioned but slow battleships to secondary status. Yet, both elements struggled for appropriations and personnel assignments. Congressional calls for a unified air force caused additional career anxieties among Navy professionals. Aside from these internal bureaucratic tiffs, the Department of the Navy continued its competition with the Army, and both services squabbled over whose planes would defend the coasts.

William Veazie Pratt, chief of naval operations from 1930 to 1933, promoted a plan for systematic new construction to replace the common practice of irregular and spontaneous building, and he called for the improvement of cruisers and the construction of oceangoing submarines. Pratt's endorsement of the 1930 London Naval Treaty with France, Great Britain, Italy, and Japan to limit naval armaments recognized the political reality of Herbert Hoover's intention to reduce both armaments and federal expenditures. Those who supported a larger navy attacked the president and raised questions as to the Navy's size and effectiveness. But the Navy proved more popular than the Army with the public, and Hollywood romanticized the service in a series of movies.

When Franklin Roosevelt became president in 1933, Carl Vinson, chair of the House Committee on Naval Affairs, led Congress and the Navy to initiate a massive ship replacement program. An even larger building effort followed the Japanese withdrawal in 1936 from the naval treaties. The Vinson Trammell Act of 1934 and the Supplemental Navy Bill of 1938 were benchmarks, but other authorizations, some financed by relief funds, contributed as well. Between 1933 and 1940 Congress appropriated $4.2 billion for the construction of 238 combatant ships and forty-five auxiliaries. Personnel increases occurred regularly after 1936, and by 1939 dozens of air fields were constructed and 4,500 planes had been authorized. In addition, the Marine Corps, which averaged seventeen thousand enlisted men and one thousand officers, was intent upon developing amphibious landing techniques.

By December 1939, the Navy could call upon fifteen battleships, six carriers, eighteen heavy cruisers, nineteen light cruisers, 185 destroyers, and sixty-four submarines. Other ships were authorized and built, but the department decided during the 1937 to 1939 period to construct six battleships at the expense of more carriers. Still, the USS York-town, commissioned in 1938, became a prototype for dozens of carriers in the next decade.

Working with Congress, William Leahy proved more effective as chief of naval operations than his predecessor, William Harrison Standley. In 1938, Leahy warned the congressional appropriations and Navy service committees of the double dangers growing in the Atlantic and Pacific, as evidenced by Japan's aggression in Asia and the sinking of the American ship Panay on the Yangtze in 1937. In response, the Navy developed a series of defensive schemes directed at possible opponents. The plan to deal with Japan was called Plan Orange, and it anticipated a Japanese surprise offensive that might include an attack on Pearl Harbor. According to the plan, the United States could withstand the loss of the Philippines and Guam, and would rally by moving across the Pacific, seizing Japanese bases and confronting its battle fleet and air force. In line with these projections, ship designs, especially for new cruisers, accentuated range and durability. These defensive plans served as training paradigms throughout the Depression era. In the late 1930s, the Orange Plan evolved into a series of so-called Rainbow Plans, which involved attacks by several nations, defense of the Western Hemisphere, and possible abandonment of U. S. possessions in the far Pacific. On October 14, 1939, Roosevelt agreed to this amended strategy, which moved the Navy from a defensive to an offensive stance.

See Also: ISOLATIONISM; MILITARY: UNITED STATES ARMY; WORLD WAR II AND THE ENDING OF THE DEPRESSION.

BIBLIOGRAPHY

Baer, George W. One Hundred Years of Sea Power: The U.S. Navy, 1890–1990. 1994.

Dove, Robert W., Jr., ed. The Chiefs of Naval Operations. 1980.

Gardiner, Robert, and Roger Chesneau, eds. Conway's All the World's Fighting Ships, 1922–1946. 1980.

Kaufman, Robert Gordon. Arms Control during the Pre-Nuclear Era: The United States and Naval Limitations between the Two World Wars. 1990.

Levine, Robert H. The Politics of American Naval Rearmament, 1930–1938. 1988.

Major, John. "The Navy Plans for War." In In Peace and War: Interpretations of American Naval History, 1775–1984, 2nd edition, edited by Kenneth J. Hagan. 1984.

Miller, Edward. War Plan Orange. 1991.

Rosen, Philip T. "The Treaty Navy, 1919–1937." In In Peace and War: Interpretations of American Naval History, 1775–1984, 2nd edition, edited by Kenneth J. Hagan. 1984.

Trimble, William F. Admiral William A. Moffett: Architect of Naval Aviation. 1994.

Wilson, John R. M. Herbert Hoover and the Armed Forces: A Study of Presidential Attitudes and Policy. 1993.

HENRY C. FERRELL, JR.

MILLS, OGDEN

Ogden L. Mills (August 23, 1884–October 11, 1937) lawyer, politician, and United States Treasury official, was born in Newport, Rhode Island. After completing an undergraduate degree (1905) and a law degree (1907) at Harvard, he entered law practice in New York City. He became active in Republican politics and won a seat in the New York state Senate in 1914. After war service in the U. S. Army, he was elected in 1920 to represent the 17th District of New York in the U.S. House of Representatives, a position he held until 1927 when he became under-secretary of the Treasury in the Coolidge administration.

President Herbert Hoover, who took office in March 1929, retained his predecessor's Treasury team with Mills as under-secretary and Andrew W. Mellon as secretary. (Mills was to succeed Mellon in the secretaryship in 1932.) Mellon was uncompromising in his opposition to unconventional interventions to stimulate a depressed economy. By contrast, Mills approached economic policy-making with much greater intellectual flexibility. He was a party to Hoover's decision in mid-1931 to declare a moratorium on debt repayments to the

United States by World War I allies if these governments temporarily waived their claims to reparations from Germany. Mills contributed to the architecture of the Reconstruction Finance Corporation, (RFC), an institution created in 1931 to lend to banks (and other financial institutions) and to railroads, which was a pioneering exercise in off-budget financing. In mid-1932, Mills was the point man in a failed effort to persuade Congress to authorize RFC to function as an investment banker by lending to private businesses to fund capital formation. He was also involved in shaping legislation allowing the Federal Reserve to use government securities, rather than gold, as backing for its currency issues.

Perhaps Mills's most significant contribution to Depression-fighting occurred after he had technically left high office. In the interregnum between President Franklin D. Roosevelt's election in November 1932 and his inauguration in March 1933, an epidemic of bank failures swept over the country. The near paralysis of the financial system threatened the nation's ability to maintain gold convertibility of the dollar, a commitment that Hoover regarded as sacrosanct. Mills anticipated that this position was likely to become untenable and prepared contingency plans for executive orders to suspend gold payments and to close commercial banks until public confidence had been restored. The Bank "Holiday" declared by the Roosevelt administration in March 1933 drew heavily on the script that Mills had written.

See Also: BANKING PANICS (1930–1933); GOLD STANDARD; MELLON, ANDREW.

BIBLIOGRAPHY

Barber, William J. *From New Era to New Deal: Herbert Hoover, the Economists, and American Economic Policy, 1921–1933.* 1985.

Fausold, Martin L. *The Presidency of Herbert C. Hoover.* 1985.

Kennedy, Susan. *The Banking Crisis of 1933.* 1973.

WILLIAM J. BARBER

MINNESOTA FARMER-LABOR PARTY

The Minnesota Farmer-Labor Party still ranks as America's most successful state level third party. It began in 1919 as something of an organizational conglomerate, functioning as the electoral wing of the national Nonpartisan League (a farm protest movement that originated in North Dakota), the locally strong Minneapolis Socialist Party, and the Minnesota state Federation of Labor. As those organizations disappeared or weakened, the Farmer-Labor Party took on a life of its own as party leaders created a permanent organization known as the Farmer-Labor Association to plan the party's direction. Until the mid-1920s the Farmer-Labor Party was the Republican Party's rival for control of state's congressional delegation. In 1924 the Farmer-Labor Party also supported the independent presidential campaign of Robert La Follette.

During the second half of "Prosperity Decade," membership in the Farmer-Labor Association dropped, the state Federation of Labor withdrew its formal affiliation, and the party's newspaper was sold off. Attractive candidates stopped calling attention to their affiliation with the party. Then, in 1930, the party's 1924 gubernatorial candidate, Floyd B. Olson, ran again. Olson had served for many years as attorney for Hennepin County, a jurisdiction that includes Minneapolis. As an adolescent working as a harvest hand in North Dakota, Olson had joined the Industrial Workers of the World (IWW). He also enjoyed good relations with the tightly knit Jewish community of Minneapolis. Later, Olson was an early leader in the American Civil Liberties Union, whose founders sought to protect the right of free political speech for left-wing radicals in the Nonpartisan League, the Socialist Party, and the Communist Party, and to protect the civil liberties of labor organizers and labor strikers. Photographs and films from the era show a ruddy, strapping, and evidently gregarious man. Olson had a commanding radio voice, but he was just as good in a convention hall or on the stump. He was elected governor in 1930.

Olson's political heyday ran from 1931 to August 1936, during which time he rose to national prominence. He died in office, however, from stomach cancer. During this period the Farmer-Labor Party gained control of the state's congressional delegation, and by 1936 the party had elected, for the first time, two full-term senators. The party also made rapid progress in mobilizing voters to support candidates for all state-wide executive offices, including treasurer, secretary of state, attorney general, and lieutenant governor.

The Farmer-Labor Party permanently changed the political economy of Minnesota. The party established collective bargaining in the state and protected farmers before passage of the 1933 federal Agricultural Adjustment Act. Two other constituencies of the Farmer-Labor Party that had joined its coalition in the late 1920s and early 1930s were small business owners facing competition from chain stores, and rural bankers facing the prospect of sale of their establishments to larger banks in better condition. For them, the Farmer-Laborites backed anti-chain store legislation and discouraged the acquisition of independent banks by large Twin Cities or out-of-state banks.

In the areas of industrial relations and agricultural income security, the Farmer-Labor Party engaged in close collaboration with dynamic social movements pushing for bold new policies. They did not achieve their goals in the end, but with help from the Farmer-Labor Party, public policy moved far in the direction preferred by the leaders of these movements.

As governor, Floyd Olson used a key executive resource—command of the state National Guard—to recast industrial relations in the Twin Cities and elsewhere in the state, particularly in Duluth, on the Iron Range, and in the meat-packing and processing centers in southeastern Minnesota. American governors had historically used this authority to break strikes by enforcing anti-picketing injunctions issued by the courts, thus helping employers withhold recognition of a strike leadership's authority. In several cases, governors had used state military force to assault strike picketers directly. Olson, however, used the Minnesota National Guard during the 1934 truckers' strike in Minneapolis to unravel an "open-shop" anti-union system that had thrived in the Twin Cities for two decades.

Olson did the same in 1935, as did the two succeeding Farmer-Labor governors: Hjalmar Petersen, the lieutenant governor who assumed the governorship after Olson's death in 1936 and held office until January 1937, and former banking commissioner and U.S. Senator Elmer Benson, who held the governorship from 1937 to 1939. Minnesota's three Farmer-Labor governors established a labor record that is rare, if not unique, in the history of American gubernatorial politics. Because they transformed the state National Guard into a neutral instrument for preserving public order in a context of increased labor militancy, they essentially distanced the police power of the state government from its traditional pro-employer role. This change facilitated the rapid increase in trade union strength and the development of modern collective bargaining in Minnesota.

A similar pattern of collaboration between the party and various movements occurred in agriculture in 1932 and 1933 when many commercial farmers in Iowa, the Dakotas, Minnesota, and elsewhere in the north central states and the Plains faced mortgage foreclosure. Prices for corn, milk, and other commodities rapidly sank in the general deflation. In Iowa and Minnesota, protests emerged, partly through the Farmers Holiday Association. This association was an offshoot of the Farmers Union and had been set up to shield the union from legal liability for actions that its members might take in connection with the protest movement. The new organization named itself after the presidential moratorium on bank transactions, euphemistically called the "bank holiday." If bankers could take a holiday from their jobs in order to gain economic relief, impoverished farmers reasoned that they could do the same.

Farmers blocked roads, hoping to dramatize their plight and cause food shortages at regional farm markets. They also mobbed public foreclosure sales of farms, and would either prevent completion of sale or force sale at a ridiculously low price that the original farmer could easily afford. In addition, they organized protest marches on state capitols to bring their cause to the attention of governors and legislators.

One important response, taken by both the Republican and Farmer-Labor parties, was tax relief through homestead exemption legislation, which provided a standard property tax exemption. In February 1933, after several months of issuing sometimes fiery statements of sympathy for the farmers' plight, Olson proclaimed a one-year moratorium on foreclosure sales in Minnesota, acting on the basis of the state's police power. Olson's actions placed considerable pressure on the state legislature; the Farmer-Labor Party controlled only one house, the House of Representatives. Nonetheless, on April 18, 1933, Olson was able to sign the Minnesota Mortgage Moratorium Act.

Harry Peterson, the Minnesota attorney general, who was elected as a Farmer-Laborite, defended the Minnesota Mortgage Moratorium Act when the U.S. Supreme Court accepted an appeal brought from the Supreme Court of Minnesota, which had upheld the statute. In describing the scope and depth of economic distress in Minnesota, the resulting distortion of mortgage contracts undertaken in different times, and the public interest in restoring order and confidence in property rights, the Minnesota attorney general played a key role in the case's presentation. The U.S. Supreme Court was persuaded to break from a tradition of strict construction of the Constitution's contract clause. In an opinion written by the chief justice, the Court affirmed the judgment of the Minnesota Supreme Court. The U.S. Supreme Court's decision, *Home Building and Loan Association v. Blaisdell* (1934), gave support to the large number of moratoria enacted throughout the country. It is today a basic undergirding of government regulation.

In contrast to this legal contribution to national policy, the Farmer-Labor Party had little effect on congressional politics, despite its control of the Minnesota delegation in both the House and the Senate. The one exception is its role in the Depression-era debate over unemployment insurance, in which a Farmer-Labor congressman, Ernest Lundeen, defined the radical end of the policy debate. Lundeen used his assignment to the subcommittee on unemployment insurance of the House Committee on Labor to publicize his plan for government and employers to replace all wages lost to unemployment, with the administration of insurance funds to occur through local workers' and farmers'

councils. Thousands of American Federation of Labor locals expressed support for the Lundeen bill. It applied to all workers and farmers "without discrimination because of age, sex, race, color, religious or political opinion or affiliation," and it covered workers who became unemployed due to maternity, sickness, accident, or old age. Remarkably, the House Committee on Labor reported the bill favorably after holding hearings on it in 1934 and 1935. However, the bill never received a rule for floor consideration after the Roosevelt administration denounced it, and the bill died when it was defeated as a proposed amendment to the Social Security Act.

The Farmer-Labor Party was a vital organization that left a deep imprint on Minnesota politics and on national regulatory doctrine. Today its vision of social security still inspires scholarly comment and research. The history of the Farmer-Labor Party shows the extent to which some Americans were willing to break from two-party traditions and allegiances if a well-organized, viable, and resilient alternative was available. That alternative ended when the party's leaders merged their organization with the Democratic Party in 1944, creating today's Minnesota Democratic Farmer-Labor Party.

See Also: ELECTION OF 1934; LA FOLLETTE, ROBERT
    M., JR.; FARMERS' HOLIDAY ASSOCIATION
    (FHA); OLSON, FLOYD B; UNEMPLOYMENT
    INSURANCE.

BIBLIOGRAPHY

Dobbs, Farrell. *Teamster Rebellion*. 1972.

Faue, Elizabeth. *Community of Suffering and Struggle: Women, Men, and the Labor Movement in Minneapolis, 1915–1945*. 1991.

Gieske, Millard L. *Minnesota Farmer-Laborism: The Third-Party Alternative*. 1979.

Haynes, John Earl. *Dubious Alliance: The Making of Minnesota's DFL Party*. 1984.

Mayer, George H. *The Political Career of Floyd B. Olson*. 1951.

Morlan, Robert L. *Political Prairie Fire: The Nonpartisan League, 1915–1922*. 1955. Reprint, 1985.

Tweton, D. Jerome, *The New Deal at the Grass Roots: Programs for the People in Otter Tail County, Minnesota*. 1988.

Valelly, Richard M. *Radicalism in the States: The Minnesota Farmer-Labor Party and the American Political Economy.* 1989.

RICHARD M. VALELLY

MISSOURI EX REL. GAINES V. CANADA

On January 4, 1936, the National Association for the Advancement of Colored People (NAACP) launched its sustained challenge against state-imposed school segregation by filing a petition for a writ of mandamus for Lloyd L. Gaines against the University of Missouri to gain admission for him to its law school. The university had refused to admit Gaines the previous September because of his race. Missouri had no law school for African Americans, who were barred from all graduate and professional schools in the state. So Gaines's attorneys, Sidney R. Redmond, Henry D. Espy, and Charles Hamilton Houston, on March 27 filed a new suit, *Missouri ex rel. Gaines v. Canada,* to force the university to admit him.

This struggle was spurred by the NAACP's unprecedented victory in 1935 in the case of Donald Gaines Murray, a Baltimore resident, who had been denied admission to the University of Maryland Law School because he was black. Representing Murray, Charles Houston, the NAACP's special counsel, and Thurgood Marshall, a young attorney with the Baltimore NAACP branch, won a writ of mandamus from the Baltimore City Court ordering the university to admit Murray at once. The attorneys sued within the "separate but equal" concept that the U.S. Supreme Court established in the *Plessy v. Ferguson* case in 1896. The university had offered to pay for Murray's education at an institution outside Maryland, but he rejected the offer. Upholding the Baltimore City Court's order, the Maryland Court of Appeals ruled that duly qualified African Americans "must at present" be admitted to the one school provided for the study of law—the law school of the University of Maryland." The university had contended that the law school was not a governmental agency and that provisions for

racial segregation in education automatically excluded African Americans. But Maryland's high court held that "there is no escape from the conclusion that the school is now a branch or agency of the state government." The university did not appeal the ruling to the U.S. Supreme Court, and Murray was admitted without further incident.

The *Gaines* case, however, did reach the U.S. Supreme Court. Gaines was a citizen of Missouri and had graduated from Missouri's Lincoln University, a Jim Crow school. Reaffirming the lower court's denial of his application, the Missouri Supreme Court explained that under state law, Lincoln University could "open any necessary school or department" its curators deemed advisable. Where no alternative had been provided, the state was required to pay the African-American resident's tuition "at any university of any adjacent state." Kansas, Illinois, Iowa, and Nebraska, it noted, all had law schools that admitted blacks. Gaines was therefore accorded equal protection of law. Thus the Supreme Court of Missouri denied him relief.

The U.S. Supreme Court, however, reversed the state court's decision. Writing for the six to two majority in what *The Crisis* considered "the most significant victory for Negro rights in the highest court of the land in the past decade," (January 1939) Chief Justice Charles Evans Hughes concluded, "The admissibility of laws separating the races in the enjoyment of privileges afforded by the State rests wholly upon the equality of the privileges which the laws give to the separated groups within the State. The question here is not of a duty of the State to supply legal training, or of the quality of the training which it does supply, but of its duty when it provides such training to furnish it to the residents of the State upon the basis of an equality of right." Consequently, Gaines "was entitled to be admitted to the law school of the State University in the absence of other and proper provision for his legal training within the State." Unlike Murray in Maryland, Gaines did not enter the law school. He disappeared and was not seen again.

The precedent established the test for all educational facilities in the country and applied to the nineteen states and the District of Columbia that maintained separate schools for the races in the section of the country where almost 80 percent of African Americans lived. The *Gaines* decision was a major step on the road to the 1954 decision in *Brown v. Board of Education of Topeka.* The opinions in the series of cases from *Gaines* to *Brown* defined the constitutional rights of African Americans as citizens. They furthermore broadened the interpretation of constitutional rights for all citizens under the Fourteenth Amendment in ways that eventually also extended civil liberties to whites, women, the elderly, gays, and the disabled.

See Also: HOUSTON, CHARLES; NATIONAL ASSOCIATION FOR THE ADVANCEMENT OF COLORED PEOPLE (NAACP); SUPREME COURT.

BIBLIOGRAPHY

"Gaines Case Won." *The Crisis* (January 1939): 10.

"The Inevitable Mr. Gaines." *The Crisis* (February 1939): 51.

Kluger, Richard. *Simple Justice: The History of* Brown v. Board of Education, *the Epochal Supreme Court Decision that Outlawed Segregation, and of Black America's Century-long Struggle for Equality under Law.* 1976.

Marshall, Thurgood. "Equal Justice Under Law." *The Crisis* (July 1939): 199–201.

Miller, Loren. *The Petitioner: The Story of the Supreme Court of the United States and the Negro.* 1966.

Missouri ex rel. Gaines v. Canada et al., 305 U.S. 337.

NAACP Annual Report, 1935.

New York Times, 13 December 1938, sec. I, p. 24.

New York Times, 18 December 1938, sec. IV, p. 10.

"Press Comment on the Gaines Case." *The Crisis* (February 1939): 52–53, 61.

"University of Missouri Case Won." *The Crisis* (January 1939): 10–12, 18.

DENTON L. WATSON

MITCHELL, ARTHUR W.

As the first black American to serve in Congress as a Democrat, Arthur Wergs Mitchell (December 22, 1883–May 9, 1968) pioneered black Americans' transition from the Republican to the Democratic Party.

Born in Roanoke, Alabama, Mitchell possessed great intelligence and ruthless ambition. He attended Tuskegee Institute for two years and received his teaching certificate from Alabama's Snow Hill Institute in 1903. Later that year, Mitchell founded the West Alabama Normal and Industrial Institute in Panola County. The school suffered from financial mismanagement and poor relations with the local black community. When a fire destroyed the school's main building in 1915, Mitchell fled with the insurance money and headed to the Armstrong Agricultural Institute in Choctaw County. At Armstrong, Mitchell's haughty behavior alienated poor blacks and whites alike, resulting in his leaving for Washington, D.C., in 1919 with $10,000 from the school's reserves.

After a successful real estate career in Washington, Mitchell moved to Chicago in 1928 to become active in local Republican politics. Chicago Republicans, however, possessed too many established black politicians for Mitchell to move up as quickly as he desired, so Mitchell switched to the Democratic Party. Mitchell's arrival coincided with a push by local Democrats to convert Chicago blacks to the Democratic cause. Consequently, Mitchell moved up the ranks quickly, becoming in 1934 the first black Democrat to be elected to Congress.

From the start, Mitchell suffered from poor relations with his black constituents at home and across the country. Aside from his ardent support for the New Deal, Mitchell did little to address the economic deprivations blacks faced during the Depression. The black press frequently criticized Mitchell for his "lack of aggressiveness" on civil rights. He feuded with the National Association for the Advancement of Colored People, which he labeled a "vicious" organization. Finally, Mitchell's anti-labor sentiments led Associated Negro Press reporter George F. McCray to characterize Mitchell's labor policy as "reckless, and unenlightened."

Mitchell shifted towards a moderate civil rights stance later in his career, becoming a vocal critic of the poll tax and lynching. In 1937, after being forced to ride in a segregated railroad car in Arkansas, Mitchell defied his political bosses in Chicago by launching a personal damage suit against three Chicago-based railroad companies that observed Jim Crow seating arrangements in the South. The Supreme Court decided in Mitchell's favor in 1941, but Mitchell's unwillingness to drop the case cost him the support of Chicago's Democratic leadership. Knowing he could not win reelection without party support, Mitchell announced his retirement and moved to his country estate in Petersburg, Virginia, in 1942.

See Also: AFRICAN AMERICANS, IMPACT OF THE GREAT DEPRESSION ON; CIVIL RIGHTS AND CIVIL LIBERTIES; DEMOCRATIC PARTY; DE PRIEST, OSCAR; FAUSET, CRYSTAL BIRD.

BIBLIOGRAPHY

Barnett, Claude. Papers. Chicago Historical Society, Chicago, Illinois.

Drake, St. Clair, and Horace R. Cayton. *Black Metropolis: A Study of Negro Life in a Northern City,* rev. edition. 1993.

Grimshaw, William J. *Bitter Fruit: Black Politics and the Chicago Political Machine, 1931–1991.* 1992.

Nordin, Dennis S. *The New Deal's Black Congressman: A Life of Arthur Wergs Mitchell.* 1997.

CHRISTOPHER E. MANNING

MOLEY, RAYMOND

Raymond Charles Moley (September 27, 1886–February 18, 1975) was a scholar, a New Deal public servant, a journalist, and an author. Born in Berea, Ohio, Moley grew up in Olmsted Falls. In 1906, he graduated with a bachelor's degree from Baldwin-Wallace College in Cleveland. For a short time thereafter, Moley served as superintendent of schools in his hometown. In 1909, he became ill with tuberculosis and moved to New Mexico and Colorado for health reasons. By 1912 he was cured and decided to pursue his education again, first getting his master's degree in political science at Oberlin College in Ohio, and later his Ph.D. at Columbia University in New York. He taught for a short time at Western Reserve University in Cleveland, then returned to Columbia in the 1920s.

In 1919, Moley became director of the Cleveland Foundation, where he studied and wrote on the court system and the criminal justice system. He eventually became a member of the New York State Crime Commission, where he participated in the Seabury investigation into corruption in the New York City government. While in New York, Moley met Louis Howe, who introduced him to Franklin D. Roosevelt, then governor of New York. Moley and Roosevelt came to know each other better, and Moley offered to help Roosevelt in his 1932 presidential campaign. At the instigation of Samuel Rosenman, Moley put together Roosevelt's famous Brains Trust. Consisting of Moley, Rexford Tugwell, and Adolf Berle, the Brains Trust was designed to help educate Roosevelt for the 1932 campaign and to keep him informed on the most current solutions being offered to resolve the Great Depression. The three men also served as speech-writers for Roosevelt, and it was Moley who actually coined the term *New Deal.* Moley was particularly helpful in drafting Roosevelt's "Concert of Interests" speech in 1932. During the campaign, Moley emphasized the need for business and government to cooperate in overcoming the economic crisis. After the election, Moley continued calling for such cooperation, while working closely with Roosevelt in both domestic and foreign policy matters. Officially, Moley became assistant secretary of state to Cordell Hull, with whom he disagreed on numerous policy matters.

Moley's star began to fall rapidly during 1933 London Economic Conference. Disagreeing with the president on monetary and world issues, Moley was undermined by Roosevelt's famous "bombshell" message to the Conference announcing that the United States would pursue a domestic program to solve the Depression. Angered and hurt, Moley returned home and gradually began to move out of the Roosevelt inner circle. By 1936, Moley had turned towards Herbert Hoover and the Republican Party. In 1939, he published his memoirs, *After Seven Years,* criticizing Roosevelt, and in 1940 he openly supported Republican candidate Wendell Wilkie for the presidency. Thereafter, Moley, working as an editor at *Today* and an associate editor at *Newsweek,* continued to support Republican candidates and often attacked Roosevelt and the Democratic Party. He died in 1975.

See Also: BRAIN(S) TRUST; LONDON ECONOMIC CONFERENCE OF 1933; NEW DEAL.

BIBLIOGRAPHY

Moley, Raymond. *After Seven Years.* 1939.

Moley, Raymond. *The First New Deal.* 1966.

Moley, Raymond. *Realities and Illusions, 1886–1931: The Autobiography of Raymond Moley,* edited by Frank Freidel. 1980.

Rosen, Elliot A. *Hoover, Roosevelt, and the Brains Trust: From Depression to New Deal.* 1977.

MICHAEL V. NAMORATO

MONETARY POLICY

In the United States, heterodox proposals for monetary manipulation tend to flourish in times of economic crisis. The farm lobbies, in particular, have been disposed to back such measures when seeking relief from agricultural distress. They had done so in the 1870s when supporting the Greenback movement to expand the currency issue. They did so again in the 1890s when rallying behind the Populists and then William Jennings Bryan's campaigns for "free silver."

In 1932, this tradition took on a renewed vitality. The argument for inflationary policies to pump up farm prices was now articulated in more sophisticated form. Through the research of Cornell University agricultural economist George F. Warren and his collaborator, F. A. Pearson, doctrines that could formerly be dismissed as the work of "cranks" and "amateurs" were given at least a pseudoscientific veneer. From their base at the state of New York's land grant college, Warren and Pearson enjoyed proximity and visibility to the state's political establishment. And they had won converts to their views among some who would later occupy high positions in President Franklin D. Roosevelt's administrations—most notably, Henry Morgenthau, Jr., a future secretary of the treasury.

Warren and Pearson rested their arguments on elaborate statistical investigations of the behavior of commodity prices, on the one hand, and the price of gold, on the other. Their findings suggested that there was a high positive correlation between the two. It thus seemed to follow that the answer to depressed farm prices could be found in raising the price of gold. This approach to policy, however, would be incompatible with a U. S. commitment to gold convertibility of the dollar at a fixed parity.

Another version of this line of argument was supplied by Yale University's Irving Fisher, an economist recognized for his analytic ingenuity, though one who was also regarded as a bit suspect for his eccentricities (such as his ardent advocacy of prohibition and the eugenics movement) and for his unfortunate pronouncement in September 1929 that the stock market had reached a permanently high plateau. Fisher's empirical studies in the mid-1920s had indicated that the general price level—with a lag of seven months or so—led changes in the volume of aggregate economic activity. More specifically, a rising price level stimulated the volume of trade, and a declining price level depressed it. Since 1930, the American economy had experienced severe deflation: It was thus not surprising that the Depression had deepened. By 1932, Fisher was convinced that the remedy for this condition was to be found in "reflating" the general price level back to its pre-Depression elevation. When the targeted price level had been reached, the price level should be stabilized and the economy would thereafter enjoy stability. He insisted that monetary expansion—when no longer constrained by the gold standard—could produce the needed reflation. Raising the price of gold should be one of the measures deployed for this purpose.

The state of the American financial system when Roosevelt was inaugurated in March 1933 provided a moment of opportunity when suspension of the dollar's gold convertibility was both necessary and acceptable. Between his election in November 1932 and his assumption of the presidency, the nation had experienced unprecedented runs on banks and drains on the country's gold reserves serious enough to threaten their exhaustion. In the face of this crisis, Roosevelt was obliged to declare a "bank holiday" and to suspend gold convertibility, which he did by executive order as his first substantive official act. Measures taken in the months immediately thereafter effectively nationalized the monetary gold stock by outlawing private holdings.

Rupturing the tie to gold meant that economic policymakers had a much freer hand to experiment.

Congress further widened the president's range of options with the passage of an amendment to the Agricultural Adjustment Act of 1933 (known as the Thomas Amendment, in recognition of the Oklahoma senator who sponsored it). This legislation conveyed discretionary power to the president to: (1) issue up to $3 billion in greenbacks (a currency without metallic backing); (2) establish the gold content of the dollar with the restriction that it could not be reduced by more than 50 percent; and (3) fix the value of silver and provide for its unlimited coinage and establish bimetallism. It was not clear, however, which of these powers (if any) would be exercised.

GOLD AND SILVER PURCHASE PROGRAMS

On October 22, 1933, Roosevelt announced that he had ordered a government agency to buy gold "at prices determined from time to time," that "this was a policy and not an expedient," and that this action was "not to be used merely to offset a temporary fall in prices." (The presence of Warren and of James Harvey Rogers—a Yale economist who shared Fisher's views—when this initiative was launched indicated that reflation of the price level was the objective of the exercise.) On each business day in the ensuing weeks, Roosevelt met with Morgenthau to fix the day's buying price. When price-elevating bidding was terminated in January 1934, the price of gold had reached $35 per ounce, at which point it was pegged. Before the country left the gold standard, its official price had been $20.67. Despite this activity, the general price level had not risen as the advocates of the gold purchase program had predicted.

In early 1934, the Roosevelt administration was confronted with mounting political pressures—particularly from senators representing silver-mining constituencies—to do something to raise the price of silver. There was a fundamental difference between the gold purchase program mounted in the autumn of 1933 and the silver purchase program that was later adopted. The former was an instance of a deliberate policy of preference that allegedly had some analytic mooring. The latter was undertaken reluctantly in response to congressional pressures that were difficult to contain. Administra-

tion officials counted it as a success that they had at least managed to forestall enactment of legislation that would mandate purchase of prescribed quantities of silver. The agreement struck with Congress in May 1934 instead set out a general goal: Treasury purchases should aim at an accumulation in which silver amounted to one-third of the value of the gold stock. However, no timetable for this outcome was specified. Though the Department of the Treasury was slow to implement this policy, it managed to spend $1.6 billion on silver acquisitions between 1934 and 1941.

Between them, gold and silver acquisitions substantially augmented the nation's monetary base and made major contributions to the swelling of excess reserves in commercial banks. By contrast, the Federal Reserve's contribution to monetary ease in 1933 and 1934 was slight. The Federal Reserve—without enthusiasm—did acquire a modest quantity of government securities between May and November 1933 and then suspended open market operations until 1937. The 1933 purchases appear to have been motivated by the Board's fear that, in the absence of some activity on its part, the administration might be provoked to issue greenbacks. The discount rate, which stood at 3.5 percent in March 1933, was reduced by seven of the twelve District Banks and, in New York, it fell to 2 percent.

RESHAPING THE FEDERAL RESERVE SYSTEM

The Federal Reserve's role began to change in 1935 with passage of a Banking Act that reorganized its structure. This legislation was largely the handiwork of Marriner Eccles, a Utah banker whose views on depression-fighting called for enlarged government spending financed through deficits, who had been recruited to Washington to serve as its chairman. The Banking Act of 1935 was designed to serve three purposes: (1) to change the composition of the governing body by displacing two *ex officio* members—the secretary of the treasury and the comptroller of the currency—and by restyling the Federal Reserve Board as the Board of Governors of the Federal Reserve System; (2) to restructure the Open Market Committee by placing its decisive weight with the Board of Governors in Washington by reducing the voting strength of the

Federal Reserve District Banks; and (3) to increase the power of the central Board over the determination of discount rates and to widen its discretionary latitude over required reserve ratios.

Eccles did not delay long in using his new authority over required reserve ratios. It was then believed that the Board's capacity to restrain lending by commercial banks would be compromised when they held abnormally large sums in excess reserves, as appeared to be the case in 1936 and early 1937. Accordingly, the Board of Governors acted to increase its leverage by exercising its newly-conveyed power to double required reserve ratios. Board action was taken in two steps: (1) required reserve ratios were raised half the distance toward the legal maximum in August 1936; and (2) increases to the full limit allowed by law were ordered in the spring of 1937. All of this was seen as precautionary and not as a retreat from monetary ease. After all, the discount rate in New York in September 1937 was 1 percent and it was set at 1.5 percent by the other District Banks. Eccles insisted that the "supply of money to finance increased production [was] ample."

THE RECESSION OF 1937 AND 1938

The Board's decisions on this matter have been faulted on grounds that they provoked the recession of 1937 and 1938, which set in when the economy was operating well below its full employment capacity. Two latter-day commentators, Milton Friedman and Anna Jacobson Schwartz, have assigned major responsibility for this sharp downturn to the Federal Reserve's actions in doubling required reserve ratios. Their argument rests on the view that excess reserves, which the Board held to be needlessly excessive, were, in fact, desired as liquidity cushions in circumstances of depression. Hence, the Board's intervention in shrinking them led banks to constrain lending activities. A different interpretation—favored by New Deal contemporaries—held that the recession had been triggered by a turnaround in government's fiscal impact on the economy: that is, from being expansionary in 1936 to contractionary in 1937.

The administration's policy response to the recession—when announced in April 1938—emphasized fiscal stimulants in a "spend-lend program." Then, for the first time, Roosevelt embraced deficit financing as a positive good, rather than an unavoidable evil. The Federal Reserve participated by lowering required reserve ratios by one-third. Subsequently the volume of excess reserves again grew. It was not until November 1941, however, that the Board once more set required reserve ratios at the maximum level allowed by law.

See Also: BANK PANICS (1930–1933); ECCLES, MARRINER; ECONOMY, AMERICAN; FEDERAL RESERVE SYSTEM; GOLD STANDARD; MORGENTHAU, HENRY T., JR.; RECESSION OF 1937.

BIBLIOGRAPHY

Barber, William J. *Designs within Disorder: Franklin D. Roosevelt, the Economists, and the Shaping of American Economic Policy, 1933–1945.* 1996.

Blum, John Morton. *From the Morgenthau Diaries,* Vol. 1: *Years of Crisis, 1928–1938*; Vol. 2: *Years of Urgency, 1938-1941*; Vol. 3: *Years of War, 1941–1945.* 1959–1967.

Chandler, Lester V. *America's Greatest Depression, 1929–1941.* 1970.

Eccles, Marriner S. *Beckoning Frontiers: Public and Personal Recollections.* 1951.

Friedman, Milton, and Anna Jacobson Schwartz. *A Monetary History of the United States, 1867–1960.* 1963.

Johnson, G. Griffith. *The Treasury and Monetary Policy, 1932–1938.* 1939.

Roose, Kenneth D. *The Economics of Recession and Revival: An Interpretation of 1937–38.* 1954.

WILLIAM J. BARBER

MONOPOLY (BOARD GAME)

The Monopoly game was first published by Parker Brothers in 1935 and quickly became the nation's most popular board game. Its success was actually enhanced by the Great Depression: Millions of people from Maine to California found its vicarious promise of wealth to be irresistible, in stark contrast to the grim economic realities of their daily lives. Few realized that its board spaces were named after

A MONOPOLY® board from 1935, the year Parker Brothers first published the game.

counterparts in one specific community (Atlantic City, New Jersey), and fewer still knew that the game's predecessor dated back to the turn of the century.

Parker Brothers acquired the game from an un-employed steam-heating repairman, Charles Dar-row of Mount Airey (Philadelphia), Pennsylvania. Darrow was the first to publish Monopoly, which evolved from Elizabeth Magie-Phillips's Landlord Game. Her 1903 game espoused Henry George's single tax theory (that only real estate should be taxed). Monopoly became a fixture at certain east-ern colleges, and homemade copies, which usually featured street names from the maker's hometown, found their way eventually to Atlantic City, New Jersey. Darrow played this early version with his friends, then began to make and sell copies, which preserved the street names from Atlantic City, to

others. Realizing the potential to provide income for his family, Darrow invested in five hundred printed copies and sold them through a few stores, most notably FAO Schwarz toy stores and the John Wanamaker department store in Philadelphia. Word of the game's success reached Parker Broth-ers. The firm acquired Darrow's version and its sub-sequent patent. It also acquired Mrs. Phillips's pa-tent on the Landlord Game and the rights for a few other similar games. By 1936, Parker Brothers owned a monopoly on Monopoly.

Parker Brothers, the nation's best-known game company, had been founded by sixteen-year-old George Parker in 1883, but it was on the verge of bankruptcy when Monopoly arrived in 1935. Locat-ed in the Boston suburb made famous by the witch trials of the 1600s (Salem, Massachusetts), the firm went from begging for printing business in Boston to running its presses around the clock, seven days a week, to keep up with demand for this one game. (It requested and obtained the approval of the Catholic Church in Salem to employ its workers on Sundays.) Within eighteen months, more than two million copies had been sold. Standard editions sold for $2.50 and deluxe editions went for as much as $25.00.

The game published in 1935 is remarkably similar to the standard edition published today. Its object is to bankrupt all of the opposing players. Its game board features a continuous track of forty spaces, twenty-eight of which are properties represented by title deeds. Players buy these spaces and attempt to collect complete color groups in order to charge ever-higher rents by building houses and hotels on them. (Players are obligated to pay rent when landing on an opponent's properties.) Trading of properties is encouraged. Many believe that Monopoly owes its enduring appeal to what happens off of the game board—the social interaction amongst its players. Nearly two hundred million copies of Monopoly had been sold worldwide by the year 2000.

See Also: FAMILY AND HOME, IMPACT OF THE GREAT DEPRESSION ON; LEISURE.

BIBLIOGRAPHY

Orbanes, Philip, *The Monopoly Companion,* 2nd edition. 1999.

PHILIP E. ORBANES

MORGAN, J. P., JR.

John Pierpont Morgan, Jr. (September 7, 1867–March 13, 1943) was a prominent American banker and financier who served as head of the Morgan investment banking house for thirty years. John Pierpont Morgan, Jr., or "Jack," was the eldest son of John Pierpont Morgan, the most powerful American banker and financier of the late nineteenth and early twentieth century. The most important American financier of his day, Jack was the target of both politicians' barbs and an assassin's bullets during his career.

After graduating from Harvard University in 1889, Jack joined his father's firm in 1892 and worked in the firm's London branch for eight years. When his father died in 1913, Jack took over the firm. Morgan secured billions in loans during and after World War I for Britain and France. Unabashedly pro-British in his public sentiments, in July 1915 Morgan was the target of a mentally deranged German sympathizer who shot and wounded him. In 1929, Morgan served on the Committee of Experts to advise the Reparation Commission about Germany's war reparations.

At the onset of the Depression, Morgan's firm helped prevent retail banks from closing their doors and tried to save several companies from failing. Nonetheless, Morgan was frequently the subject of suspicion and conspiratorial rumors and he became a leading target of politicians who sought scapegoats for the nation's economic woes. Even Nazi anti-American propaganda accused Morgan of contributing to Germany's problems. Morgan's public statements supporting laissez-faire business views did little to help his image or that of the banking industry. From 1933 to 1941, congressional committees conducted a series of investigations into Morgan-managed foreign loans. The Senate Banking and Currency Committee, which retained Ferdinand Pecora as special counsel in 1933, launched an investigation into the activities of the securities business and the stock market. The Pecora Committee was dismissed by some as political theater, but not before Pecora tried to discredit Morgan by publicly examining his business affairs in an attempt to find wrongdoing. Pecora's efforts failed to turn up anything illegal, but he did succeed in tarnishing the reputation of both Morgan and his company. The committee's finding that the twenty Morgan partners had paid nothing in federal income tax for the previous two years (all perfectly legal but seen as somehow dishonest and immoral) contributed to the passage of the Glass-Steagall banking bill, which separated investment from commercial (deposit) banking. The Morgan firm elected to become a private commercial bank.

In 1934 allegations surfaced that the financial community had been instrumental in maneuvering the United States into World War I on the side of the Allies. Some argued that American bankers did this in order to protect the huge loans they floated to the Allies. Senator Gerald P. Nye, chair of the Munitions Committee, spent a month closely questioning Morgan and two of his associates over their role as "merchants of death." The Nye Committee finally decided that there was no evidence of wrongdoing. The stress of the hearings may have directly contributed to the heart attack Morgan suffered four months later. In all, Morgan and his firm faced at least four congressional investigations.

By the time of the Nye Committee, Morgan was semi-retired from the day-to-day operations of his company. As war approached, he scaled back his holdings as he watched his fortune continue to shrink. In 1940, he turned J.P. Morgan & Co., a private banking firm, into J.P. Morgan & Co., Inc., a publicly traded corporation, to help protect its assets. The change also lightened his workload considerably. He spent his remaining years traveling and working.

See Also: BANKING PANICS (1930–1933); BUSINESSMEN; GLASS-STEAGALL ACT OF 1933.

BIBLIOGRAPHY

Burk, Kathleen. "The House of Morgan in Financial Diplomacy: 1920–1930." In *Anglo-American Relations in the 1920s: The Struggle for Supremacy,* edited by B. J. C. McKercher. 1987.

Chernow, Ron. *The House of Morgan: An American Banking Dynasty and the Rise of Modern Finance.* 1990.

Forbes, John Douglas. *J. P. Morgan, Jr., 1867–1943.* 1981.

Leuchtenburg, William E. *Franklin D. Roosevelt and the New Deal, 1932–1940.* 1963.

Morgan, J. P., Jr. Personal Papers. Morgan Library, New York, NY.

Strouse, Jean. *Morgan: American Financier.* 1999.

JAMES G. LEWIS

MORGENTHAU, HENRY T., JR.

Henry T. Morgenthau, Jr., (May 11, 1891–February 6, 1967) was secretary of the treasury from 1934 to 1945 under presidents Franklin D. Roosevelt and (briefly) Harry S. Truman. Morgenthau's father was from a German-Jewish family that immigrated to the United States in 1865. Henry Morgenthau, Sr., amassed a considerable fortune through investment in real-estate properties in the New York City boroughs of the Bronx and Harlem. He and his wife, Josephine Sykes, were activists in the Democratic Party and in social welfare causes, including the Henry Street settlement, the Bronx House, and fire safety conditions in New York City. Henry Morgenthau, Sr., also served as head of finance for the Democratic National Committee in 1912 and again in 1916, and as ambassador to Turkey during World War I

Henry Morgenthau, Jr. was born in New York City, the third and only son of four children. He entered Phillips Exeter Academy in New Hampshire in 1904 but did not do well, completing his college preparation at the Sachs Collegiate Institute in New York City. In 1909 he enrolled at Cornell University to study architecture, but completed only two years. His father then found him work at various jobs, including volunteer service with Lillian D. Wald at the Henry Street Settlement.

In 1911 Morgenthau contracted typhoid fever and went to Texas to recuperate. Life in rural Texas convinced him that he wanted to build a career as a gentleman farmer, even if that meant defying his father's wish that he take up the family businesses. After another brief stint at Cornell, and a tour of farming districts throughout the United States, he returned to New York, where he acquired some 1,700 acres in Dutchess County, New York. There, at age twenty-two, he began a career in agriculture, working hard to make his largely depleted lands along the Hudson River productive and profitable. During World War I he accepted a largely honorary commission as a naval lieutenant, and after the war helped Herbert Hoover's U.S. Food Administration provide tractors to French farmers.

By 1915 Morgenthau had met a neighbor, Franklin Roosevelt, who unsuccessfully urged him to get involved in politics. Their common Democratic Party and humanitarian interests nonetheless helped in forging a close relationship, the younger Morgenthau becoming intensely loyal and devoted to Roosevelt and eager to promote his friend's political career. In 1916 Morgenthau married a childhood friend, Elinor Fatman, a highly able and accomplished graduate of nearby Vassar College. Elinor Morgenthau and Eleanor Roosevelt also formed a close friendship, working together in various welfare and educational activities.

In 1922 Morgenthau purchased a failing journal, the *American Agriculturalist.* Through the journal he became known as a leading advocate of progressive scientific farming. It thus was almost predictable that when Roosevelt was elected governor of New York in 1928 he named Morgenthau chairman of the Agricultural Advisory Committee, asking him in addition to work at strengthening the Democratic Party in the economically depressed rural areas of the state. In 1930 Roosevelt moved Morgenthau to the post of conservation commissioner for the state. There Morgenthau worked closely with Harry L. Hopkins, helping to establish a state reforestation project that created employment for thousands of men and served as a model for the popular New Deal Civilian Conservation Corps.

Morgenthau was deeply disappointed in 1933 when the newly-elected President Roosevelt did not appoint him secretary of agriculture. He nonetheless accepted a post as head of the Federal Farm Board. In November the illness of William Woodin led Roosevelt to appoint Morgenthau acting secretary of the treasury. Within a few months it was clear that Woodin could not return and Morgenthau became secretary. He continued as secretary of the treasury for the next eleven years, longer than any of his predecessors except Andrew Mellon.

Morgenthau led the Department of the Treasury through perhaps the most turbulent era since the Civil War, that of the Great Depression and World War II. He had unparalleled access to the president, the two taking lunch together each Monday. His was a major voice in encouraging the president to devalue the dollar in late 1933 and early 1934, a policy recommended by the inflationist monetary theories of Cornell agricultural economists George F. Warren and Frank A. Pearson.

Well-schooled in progressivism, the secretary of the treasury was devoted to efficiency and economy in government. He saw a balanced federal budget as the best indicator of success in both and

Henry Morgenthau, Jr., with Franklin D. Roosevelt in Ithaca, New York, in August 1931. FRANKLIN DELANO ROOSEVELT LIBRARY

took upon himself the task of accomplishing it. Early in 1937 the economic indices were suggesting that the recovery was solid, and Morgenthau began plans for balancing the budget. That fall, however, the economy took a serious plunge. Morgenthau responded by insisting even more strongly that the budget be balanced, now not as a happy consequence of, but as an instrument of, recovery. When Roosevelt ignored him and took the advice of Harry Hopkins and Federal Reserve Chairman Marriner S. Eccles to renew spending in April 1938, Morgenthau threatened to resign.

World War II involved the Department of the Treasury continuously in key issues. Morgenthau opposed the relocation of West Coast Japanese Americans in 1941. He was an early advocate of American aid to the allies, and helped to establish the War Refugee Board to assist Jews and other refugees from Europe. Most controversial, however, was his Morgenthau Plan for dealing with postwar

Germany. The secretary proposed the complete demilitarization of Germany, the dismantling of its industries, and its division into two agricultural states. The plan was opposed by President Truman and others, whose argument that a strong postwar Germany was needed for stability in Europe carried the day. Morgenthau was a key participant in the Bretton Woods Conference of July 1944, which led to the establishment of the International Monetary Fund and the World Bank.

Finding that Truman opposed the Morgenthau Plan, and resentful that the president did not invite him to attend the Potsdam Conference, Morgenthau resigned in July 1945, returning to his farm in Dutchess County. After his wife Elinor died in 1949, he married Margaret Puthon Hirsch. In retirement he devoted much of his time to philanthropies, directing the United Jewish Appeal between 1947 and 1950, and chairing the board of governors of the American Financial and Development Corporation for Israel from 1951 to 1954. He died in Poughkeepsie, New York, in 1967.

See Also: DEFICIT SPENDING; MONETARY POLICY; ROOSEVELT, FRANKLIN D.

BIBLIOGRAPHY

Blum, John Morton. *From the Morgenthau Diaries,* 3 vols. 1959–1967.

Blum, John Morton. *Roosevelt and Morgenthau.* 1970.

Everest, Allan Seymour. *Morgenthau, the New Deal and Silver: A Story of Pressure Politics.* 1950.

May, Dean L. *From New Deal to New Economics: The American Liberal Response to the Recession of 1937.* 1981.

Sowden, J. K. *The German Question, 1945–1973: Continuity in Change.* 1975.

DEAN L. MAY

MOSES, ROBERT

During the 1930s, Robert Moses (December 18, 1888–July 29, 1981), acting under the title commissioner of parks, not only dotted New York City with hundreds of new parks, playgrounds, and swimming pools, but also permeated much of New York state with his vision of public recreational facilities linked by parkways, causeways, and bridges. From 1933 to 1939, Moses probably exercised control over a greater amount of public funds than any unelected official ever had. And the elected officials he "served" were glad to let him do it.

Moses's strong-minded and independent mother, Isabella, gave him his most salient personality traits. He was an extraordinarily industrious student at Yale from 1905 to 1909, despite the fact that being Jewish left him at the edges of Yale society. After Yale he went to Oxford, where he decided to focus on public administration and made himself an expert on the British colonial system, which he saw as a model of efficient government.

Though he was a lifelong Republican, Moses rose to power under Democratic administrations in New York, particularly those of Al Smith and Franklin D. Roosevelt. Having grown up during the height of the Progressive era, Moses was always to remain an idealist. Thus, he was able to maintain his early value as a public official through his judicious and successful sponsorship of reform measures, particularly in the area of banking in the first years of the Depression. It also did not hurt that the studious Moses knew more about the issues at hand than anybody else did. When federal money poured into New York City in the mid-1930s under the auspices of the Public Works Administration, Moses was given almost total freedom to build his most ambitious projects to date. These included the building of the Triborough Bridge, an expansion of the subway system, the construction of the city's first public housing project, and an extensive renovation of the city's parks.

Moses's reclamation of part of Long Island as a 118-mile-long public playground in the late 1920s set the model and tone for how he would work during the 1930s and after. First, he would think big, fitting every detail of his plan into his macrocosmic vision. Second, he would see potential in tracts of land that others had dismissed as unworthy of development. His Jones Beach project was exemplary in this regard. Third, he would overcome all opposition to his plans, even though this opposition often came in the form of powerful estate owners and politicians. Lastly, he would consolidate the authority for all of these public works under himself. This led to greater efficiency in administration, but left him open to charges of autocracy. The primary example in this regard is the Triborough Bridge Authority, over which he took complete charge when he was appointed city parks commissioner by Mayor Fiorello La Guardia in 1934.

Critics of Moses have pointed out that his parks, roads, and public facilities have subsequently led to unexpected blights upon the landscape, and to greater congestion in places where he had hoped to create a free flow of movement. However, these problems might have been caused by factors of urban (and suburban) expansion that were beyond even "The Commissioner's" extensive control. Robert Moses finally left state government in 1968 when Nelson Rockefeller shuffled the cards of the New York bureaucracy and forced him out. However, by then Moses had left his indelible stamp upon the city and state, and had become the most influential environmental planner of the twentieth century.

See Also: CITIES AND SUBURBS; HOUSING; PUBLIC WORKS ADMINISTRATION (PWA); TRANSPORTATION.

BIBLIOGRAPHY

Caro, Robert A. *The Power Broker: Robert Moses and the Fall of New York.* 1974.

Krieg, Joann P., ed. *Robert Moses: Single-Minded Genius.* 1989.

Ladner, Joyce A. *The New Urban Leaders.* 2001.

Rodgers, Cleveland. *Robert Moses: Builder for Democracy.* 1952.

Schwartz, Joel. *The New York Approach: Robert Moses, Urban Liberals, and Redevelopment of the Inner City.* 1993.

MICHAEL T. VAN DYKE

MOSKOWITZ, BELLE

Belle Lindner Israels Moskowitz (October 5, 1877–January 2, 1933) was a social and industrial reformer and a political strategist. As New York Governor Alfred E. Smith's strategist during the 1920s, Belle Moskowitz helped develop Smith's legislative and administrative policies. These policies later influenced the state's early responses to the Great Depression under Smith's successors, Franklin D. Roosevelt and Herbert H. Lehman. Moskowitz also ran Smith's reelection and 1928 presidential campaigns, working through a post she created in 1924—publicity director of the New York State Democratic Committee. In the process she trained Democratic Party women, including Eleanor Roosevelt and Mary (Molly) Dewson, in campaign techniques they later used to win support for the New Deal.

Belle Lindner was born in Harlem and educated at city schools, at the Horace Mann High School for Girls, and for a year at the Teachers' College of Columbia University. She worked in a social settlement on Manhattan's Lower East Side before marrying Charles Israels, an architect, in 1903. While raising her children she pursued social reforms, primarily through the Council of Jewish Women. In 1912, she joined the Progressive Party and served as a ward captain. From 1913 to 1916, she worked as a grievance arbitrator in the dress and waist trade.

In 1914, three years after her first husband died, she married Henry Moskowitz, a former settlement worker and industrial pacifist. In 1918, because of Smith's strong pro-labor record, the couple decided to support him for governor. Belle Moskowitz organized the women's vote for Smith and after his victory she proposed a reconstruction commission to plan the state's peacetime economy. Smith accepted Moskowitz's idea and appointed her the commission's executive secretary. Its reports formed the core of Smith's legislative program.

After Smith's defeat in 1928, Moskowitz tried to help him retain party leadership. She produced the publicity for the Empire State Building, a symbol of hope in the growing Depression. She also organized Smith's attempt to win the nomination in 1932. Franklin D. Roosevelt's capture of the nomination, and Smith's increasing bitterness over his political failures, were deeply disappointing to her. Her health declined, and while recovering from a fall she suffered an embolism and died. In 1936 Henry Moskowitz publicly announced that he could no longer support his old friend Al Smith, who by then was vigorously opposing the New Deal.

See Also: DEMOCRATIC PARTY; ELECTION OF 1928; SMITH, ALFRED E.

BIBLIOGRAPHY

Perry, Elisabeth Israels. *Belle Moskowitz: Feminine Politics and the Exercise of Power in the Age of Alfred E. Smith.* 1987.

Slayton, Robert A. *Empire Statesman: The Rise and Redemption of Al Smith.* 2001.

ELISABETH ISRAELS PERRY

MR. SMITH GOES TO WASHINGTON

Released by Columbia Pictures Corp. in late 1939, this 126-minute film (screenplay by Sidney Buchman) was directed by Frank Capra, then at the height of his renown. Leading players were James Stewart as the eponymous hero, and Jean Arthur, Claude Rains, and Edward Arnold. The film is a classic example of "Capra corn"—the director's populist paen to an America in which "the little people" triumph.

Stewart portrays Jefferson Smith, a naïve but dedicated young man who heads the Boy Rangers in his state and is appointed to the unexpired term of a deceased U.S. senator. In Washington he is assigned a savvy, cynical secretary (well-played by Arthur), who initially mocks Smith's enthusiastic idealism but is won over. Smith's naïveté results in a cynical press corps drubbing him cruelly. His idol, the state's senior senator (Rains), worked with Smith's murdered father for many a worthy but lost cause, now is secretly in cahoots with the state's corrupt boss (Arnold).

Attempting to escape the "honorary stooge" label pinned on him by the press corps, Smith introduces a bill that would create a national Boys Ranger camp, at a site that would interfere with the boss's pocket-lining real estate deal. Smith rebuffs attempts to have the camp placed elsewhere. The senior senator is part of the boss's maneuver to frame Smith and get him expelled from the Senate. Smith undertakes a filibuster in hopes of arousing public opinion in his state, but the boss manages to keep the truth about his graft from the state's citizens. After twenty-four hours of his one-man filibuster, Smith collapses on the Senate floor. His former idol's conscience having been revived by the filibuster, the senior senator attempts suicide, confessing that everything Smith had said about corruption and graft in the state is true. It is a victory for Smith and what he stands for.

The film garnered very positive reviews, winning eleven Oscar nominations, and has since been judged "among the foremost 'message' films of 1930s Hollywood." But there was a darker side to its contemporary reception. The American media praised the film, but the Washington press corps took umbrage at how it was presented, and various senators attacked the film, among them Alben Barkley (D-KY), who called its portrayal of the Senate "silly and stupid," and James Byrnes (D-SC), who labeled it "outrageous."

See Also: CAPRA, FRANK; HOLLYWOOD AND THE FILM INDUSTRY.

BIBLIOGRAPHY

Capra, Frank. *The Name above the Title.* 1980.

Carney, Raymond. *American Vision: The Films of Frank Capra.* 1986.

McBride, Joseph. *Frank Capra: The Catastrophe of Success.* 1992.

DANIEL J. LEAB

MUMFORD, LEWIS

Lewis Mumford (October 19, 1895–January 26, 1990) was a New York humanist, intellectual, architectural critic, journalist, and the author of numerous critically acclaimed works on architecture and the history of urban culture. In 1923 Mumford cofounded the Regional Planning Association of America (RPAA), and for much of the twentieth

James Stewart (right) as an idealistic young senator in Frank Capra's 1939 film Mr. Smith Goes to Washington. THE KOBAL COLLECTION/COLUMBIA

century he provoked America to think creatively and comprehensively about the social and physical form of the modern urban community and about building a more humane urban and regional civilization.

Mumford was born in New York City, the illegitimate son of a Jewish businessman. Raised in semi-poverty by his mother, Elvina, the daughter of German immigrants, Mumford attended but never graduated from the City College of New York. He believed that his main education came from long solitary walks through the city, during which he carefully observed and studied urban life and architecture. At City College Mumford encountered the works of the Scottish biologist and urban theorist Patrick Geddes and he became a close disciple of

Geddes and his comprehensive, biological view of the city and its region as a living organism.

After World War I Mumford married Sophie Wittenberg (his lifelong companion), moved to Greenwich Village, and worked as a book reviewer for *Dial* magazine. During the 1920s Mumford established himself as one of America's leading intellectuals and social commentators through his books *The Story of Utopias* (1922), *Sticks and Stones* (1924), and *The Golden Day* (1926), and his architectural criticism in the *New Republic*. His communitarianism, a byproduct of his apostleship of Geddes and his conviction that architecture must serve social ends, led him to Charles Whitaker, Clarence Stein, Henry Wright, and Benton MacKaye, with whom he founded the RPAA, an informal body of social planners influenced by the ideas of Ebeneezer Howard, Raymond Unwin, Barry Parker, and the British Garden City Movement. The RPAA sponsored several garden communities including Sunnyside, New York, where Mumford and Sophie lived from 1925 to 1936.

When the Great Depression struck America in the 1930s, Mumford, like many progressive, left-of-center intellectuals, hoped that the crisis of capitalism might shift the nation from a privatistic economy toward a more cooperative one modeled somewhat on the new regionalism espoused by the RPAA. In Mumford's brilliant Depression-era writings *The Brown Decades* (1931), *Technics and Civilization* (1934), and *The Culture of Cities* (1938), he explored the role of the machine (technology) in shaping modern urban civilization. These works revealed Mumford's essential optimism that humankind was capable of shaping truly humane, equitable, and socially efficient living environments that Mumford labeled the new "biotechnic" order. For evidence of this progress he pointed to Europe, in particular Letchworth and Welwyn in England and Romerstadt in Germany, the modern, low-density cooperative housing communities he had visited in 1930 and 1932 when he toured Europe with his then paramour, the houser Catherine Bauer.

This was the "new world" Mumford hoped President Franklin D. Roosevelt and his New Deal would bring to America during the 1930s. When Roosevelt's New Deal housing programs failed to realize this dream, Mumford lashed out at the New Deal in his column in the *New Republic*. He also assailed the rise of fascism in Europe. Mumford branded Adolf Hitler and Benito Mussolini as "barbarians," and he became a strident voice in favor of American military intervention. After the war Mumford continued his prodigious literary output that included his opus *The City in History* (1961) and numerous books of social and architectural criticism aimed particularly at American housing, highway, and urban renewal policy.

See Also: BAUER, CATHERINE; HOUSING; PLANNING; REGIONAL PLANNING ASSOCIATION OF AMERICA (RPAA).

BIBLIOGRAPHY

Miller, Donald L. *Lewis Mumford: A Life.* 1989.

Mumford, Lewis. *Sketches from Life: The Autobiography of Lewis Mumford.* 1982.

Spann, Edward K. *Designing Modern America: The Regional Planning Association of American and Its Members.* 1996.

Thomas, John L. "Lewis Mumford, Benton MacKaye, and the Regional Vision." In *The American Planner: Biographies and Recollections,* 2nd edition, edited by Donald A. Krueckeberg. 1994.

JOHN F. BAUMAN

MURPHY, FRANK

Frank Murphy (April 13, 1890–July 19, 1949) held more high public offices than almost any other resident of Michigan in the entire history of the state. He served successively as first assistant U. S. attorney for the Eastern District of Michigan (1919-1922), judge of the Detroit Recorder's Court (1924-1930), mayor of Detroit (1930-1933), last governor-general of the Philippines and first United States high commissioner to the Philippines (1933-1936), governor of Michigan (1937-1938), attorney-general of the United States (1939-1940), and justice of the U. S. Supreme Court (1940-1949).

The dominating event of Murphy's Detroit mayoralty was the Great Depression. No mayor in the nation did more to deal with the Depression than Murphy did. Detroit was one of the few cities in the nation at the time that provided public relief, and Murphy extended city aid to the needy to the extent that funds permitted, the Welfare Department at one point assisting 229,000 persons. The department's efforts were supplemented by the Murphy-created Mayor's Unemployment Committee, which registered the unemployed, maintained a free employment bureau, distributed clothing and emergency relief to those in need, maintained emergency lodges for homeless men, initiated a school lunch program for indigent children, provided legal aid for the poor, and sponsored a successful thrift garden program. As Detroit neared bankruptcy—the city defaulted on its bonds in 1933—Murphy convened a conference of U.S. mayors in an effort to secure federal aid. This action led to the establishment of the U.S. Conference of Mayors, with Murphy as its first president.

Murphy helped to restore faith in Detroit's government at a time when civic morale was at a low ebb. He provided Detroit with honest, economical, and efficient government; made excellent appointments that accorded recognition to the city's blacks, Jews, and white ethnic minorities; extended the city's merit pay system; improved the city's police force; ousted the last remaining competitor of the city-owned transportation system; initiated a process leading to lower utility rates; and protected the rights of free speech and freedom of assembly in a time of trouble.

When Murphy became Michigan's governor in January 1937, the critical General Motors sit-down strike was already underway, and Murphy played the crucial mediatory role in bringing the strike to an end on February 11 on terms that amounted to a victory for the United Automobile Workers. As governor, Murphy sought to bring the New Deal to Michigan. Long a proponent of social security, he provided the impetus for the enactment by a lame-duck legislature in December 1936 of a liberal state unemployment compensation system, and the next year the legislature liberalized the state's old-age assistance law. The massive impact on Michigan of the recession of 1937 and 1938 led Murphy to call for increased aid from the Works Progress Administration, and the federal government responded to his importunities. Murphy's Michigan New Deal also included a substantial hospital building program, the expansion of public health services, an occupational disease law, rural electrification, liberalized housing legislation, the establishment of a Consumers Bureau, and a consumer-minded Public Utilities Commission.

Murphy raised the tone of state government while he was governor. He was responsible for the enactment and effective implementation of a model state civil service system, the most significant structural reform of his governorship. His administration also provided the state with its first effective budget system, an efficient and nonpolitical purchasing system, an excellent corrections system, an efficiently operated Liquor Control Commission, and a well-managed Corporation and Securities Commission.

Despite his achievements as governor, Murphy, a Democrat, was defeated for reelection in Republican Michigan in 1938. The next year, Roosevelt appointed Murphy to be the nation's attorney general, and he served a notable year in that capacity. He created what became the Civil Rights Division of the Department of Justice, and he successfully crusaded against crime and corruption, prosecuting such notable figures as Kansas City's Democratic boss Tom Pendergast and newspaper publisher Moses Annenberg.

When Supreme Court Justice Pierce Butler died in 1939, Roosevelt appointed Murphy to replace Butler. The appointment, to be sure, perfectly fit the prescription for a successor to Butler, a Catholic from the Midwest, just as it met Roosevelt's general criteria for selecting Supreme Court justices: loyalty to the New Deal, "a libertarian and egalitarian philosophy of government under law," and, with war looming, support for the president's "war aims." It may be, however, that Roosevelt wished to rid himself of an attorney general whose successful prosecution of city bosses and threatened prosecution of others posed a threat to the president's third-term ambitions. Murphy was unanimously confirmed by the Senate on January 16, 1940, and took his judicial oath on February 5. Murphy remained on the Court until his death in 1949.

See Also: CITIES AND SUBURBS; SIT-DOWN STRIKES; SUPREME COURT; UNEMPLOYMENT INSURANCE.

BIBLIOGRAPHY

Fine, Sidney. *Frank Murphy,* Vol. 1: *The Detroit Years;* Vol. 2: *The New Deal Years;* Vol. 3: *The Washington Years.* 1975–1984.

Howard, J. Woodford. *Mr. Justice Murphy: A Political Biography.* 1968.

Lunt, Richard D. *The High Ministry of Government: The Political Career of Frank Murphy.* 1965.

SIDNEY FINE

MURRAY, PHILIP

Philip Murray (May 25, 1886–November 9, 1952) was the founding president of the United Steelworkers of America (USA) and president of the Congress of Industrial Organizations (CIO) from 1940 to 1952.

Murray was born in Scotland, where he began mining coal at age ten. In 1902, he immigrated with his family to western Pennsylvania, where he followed in his father's footsteps to become a union activist. Murray was elected president of a United Mine Workers (UMW) local in 1904 and began a quick rise through the ranks to a district presidency in 1916, and to the vice presidency in 1920.

Over the ensuing two decades Murray worked closely with UMW president John L. Lewis. He became an effective adjunct to Lewis's flamboyant leadership by mastering the technical details of the coal industry, union organization, and government policy. Although a staunch fighter for union members' interests, as a devout Catholic, Murray rejected radical solutions to industrial conflict for the papal vision of cooperation between labor and management. His belief in the sanctity of contracts and his abilities as a conciliator earned the respect of employers while his honesty and tough negotiation skills secured his popularity among union members.

Murray believed that a strong union and government intervention in the coal market would be mutually beneficial to workers and mine owners. When the Great Depression hit he became an early advocate of national legislation to regulate the industry. His efforts bore fruit with the early New Deal when the UMW used section 7a of the National Industrial Recovery Act to regain its membership and Murray took a leading role in writing the coal code under the National Recovery Administration.

Murray was a key player in the creation and success of the CIO. His experience and close relationship with Lewis placed him at the head of the Steel Workers' Organizing Committee (SWOC), one of the CIO's major initiatives. By early 1937 the SWOC negotiated an agreement with industry giant U. S. Steel, but failed to do so in the rest of the industry. Murray's skilled leadership of SWOC and ability to work with the government finally organized these "little steel" companies in 1941. The next year he founded the USA with himself as president. Unlike many other CIO unions that were born of rank-and-file action, the USA was a more hierarchical and bureaucratic entity from the start. To a great degree this suited Murray's vision for a labor movement that had to survive in conflict with similarly organized large corporations.

Murray took the reigns of the CIO in 1940, after Lewis followed through on a promise to resign the CIO presidency if Franklin Roosevelt won a third term. In this position he maintained his ties to the administration and succeeded in stabilizing the organization and seeing to its growth during the war years and successful institutionalization thereafter. Worried that early Cold War-era attacks on the CIO's left-led unions would compromise the organization, Murray expelled eleven tainted organizations in 1949. He remained in charge of the CIO until his death in 1952.

See Also: COLLECTIVE BARGAINING; CONGRESS OF INDUSTRIAL ORGANIZATIONS (CIO); NATIONAL INDUSTRIAL RECOVERY ACT (NIRA); NATIONAL RECOVERY ADMINISTRATION (NRA); STEEL WORKERS' ORGANIZING COMMITTEE (SWOC); UNITED MINE WORKERS OF AMERICA (UMWA).

BIBLIOGRAPHY

Bernstein, Irving. *The Lean Years: A History of the American Worker, 1920–1933.* 1960.

Bernstein, Irving. *Turbulent Years: History of the American Worker, 1933–1941.* 1970.

Zieger, Robert H. *The CIO, 1935–1955.* 1995.

ANDREW A. WORKMAN

MUSEUMS, ART

Daniel Catton Rich, director of the Art Institute of Chicago, declared at the 1955 American Federation of Arts convention that American art museums were in an "age of innocence" until after 1925. Rich was referring to the lack of professionalism and concrete philosophies in the country's art museums, which had tended simply to follow European models. The American Federation of Arts, founded in 1909 by Elihu Root, had dedicated itself to developing American art, but the European nature of American art collections was reinforced when tariff laws eliminated duties on art entering the country, thus stimulating the growth of public and private collections that contributed to museum collections. During this time, American art museums purchased most of their acquisitions using tax deductible donations.

In 1920, the United States had only a few art museums that were comparable to Europe's best. The directors were generally retired artists, professors, or museum corporate officers who operated on the basis of personal dynamism or the whims of benefactors, and applied little scholarship to their work. At the time, the American arts establishment of dealers, collectors, and museums considered impressionist artists skeptically, post-impressionists out of the question, and American works second-rate. Old concepts of the fine arts and the "casual age" of museum keeping began to end when Paul J. Sachs of Harvard's Fogg Museum developed a course in museum management that he taught from 1916 to 1955, thereby creating professional museology and a new generation of strong American directors and curators intent on renovating art institutions and collections.

The photographer Alfred Stieglitz helped gain acceptance for modern art and photography through his New York galleries from 1908 to 1946. The famous 1913 Armory Show in New York, Boston, and Chicago, recognized over three hundred artists, most of them American and many whom the art establishment had rejected. About this time, the Art Institute of Chicago began to expand its holdings with works by European modernists and previously neglected American artists. A. E. "Chick" Austin curated the first group show of surrealist art in the United States at the Wadsworth Atheneum in Hartford, Connecticut, in 1932.

Sachs worked with Abby Aldrich Rockefeller, Lizzie P. Bliss, and Mrs. Cornelius J. Sullivan to charter the Museum of Modern Art (MoMA) in New York in 1929. MoMA's President A. Conger Goodyear and Director Alfred H. Barr recruited members from other cities to foster interest in contemporary visual and industrial arts with traveling exhibitions beginning in 1932. Other independent arts organizations evolved, including the Boston Museum of Modern Art (now called the Institute of Contemporary Art) in 1936, the Museum of Modern Art Gallery of Washington in 1937, and the Modern Art Society in Cincinnati (later called the Contemporary Art Center) in 1939. At first, most of these were modeled on the Kunsthalle, mounting temporary exhibitions, rather than building permanent collections.

New York City's Whitney Museum of American Art opened in 1930 with Juliana Force as director of Gertrude Vanderbilt Whitney's collection of approximately six hundred works. The Whitney Museum's mission was "gaining for the art of this country the prestige which heretofore the public has devoted too exclusively to the art of foreign countries and of the past." The Whitney began an annual show of contemporary art in 1932. The Solomon R. Guggenheim Foundation Museum of Non-Objective Painting opened in New York in 1939, followed in 1942 by Peggy Guggenheim's Art of This Century Gallery, which featured modern art rescued from Europe on the eve of World War II.

Roosevelt created the Public Works of Art Project in 1933 to pay weekly wages to more than four thousand artists, who produced some fifteen thousand works that same year. The Treasury Department's Section of Painting and Sculpture, established in 1934, took over public projects; it was renamed the Section of Fine Arts in 1938 and the Public Buildings Administration in 1939. Harry Hopkins's Works Progress Administration (WPA) organized the Federal Art Project, headed by Holger Cahill, which commissioned artists to bring art out of the museum by creating murals, reliefs, and other works in railway terminals, airports, post offices, and schools. The Federal Art Project's goals included educating art students, expanding programs beyond cities, and researching America's cultural heritage. The WPA also helped expand and maintain museums around the country.

During the 1930s, efforts in the development of art museums were led by philanthropists, professional museologists, and the federal government; these projects paralleled the preservation of old historic houses and public places for living history museums. Americans discovered and learned to value their country's culture and history as never before during the Depression.

See Also: ART; FEDERAL ART PROJECT (FAP); HISTORY, INTERPRETATION, AND MEMORY OF THE GREAT DEPRESSION; MUSEUMS AND MONUMENTS, HISTORIC; PHOTOGRAPHY; POST OFFICE MURALS.

BIBLIOGRAPHY

Lynes, Russell. *Good Old Modern: An Intimate Portrait of the Museum of Modern Art.* 1973.

O'Conner, Francis V. *Federal Art Patronage, 1933–1943.* 1966.

Pach, Walter. *The Art Museum in America.* 1948.

BLANCHE M. G. LINDEN

MUSEUMS AND MONUMENTS, HISTORIC

Preservation of historic sites with a patriotic focus was in its infancy in the 1920s, although many states had historic house museums run by antiquarians. Preservation efforts reached a fever pitch during the years of the Great Depression, however. The Society for the Preservation of New England Antiquities (SPNEA), founded in 1910 and headed by William Sumner Appleton, was devoted to preserving the region's architectural heritage. Although many projects were stalled during the early years of the Depression, Appleton's work served as a catalyst for other such efforts around the country. SPNEA's *Old-Time New England,* the nation's first preservation magazine, also appeared in 1910 and was highly influential. Largely financed by philanthropists, preservation efforts aimed to create "a usable past" in an era of rampant change as old buildings fell into decay or were threatened with demolition.

Henry Ford sponsored a number of major restoration projects, beginning with Sudbury's Wayside Inn in Massachusetts in the early 1920s, his Michigan boyhood home in 1923, and the Botsford Tavern near Detroit in 1924. Ford also designed the Greenfield Village and Museum in Dearborn, Michigan, which opened in 1933 as a work in progress. By the time he died in 1947, Ford had invested millions in moving historic buildings and duplicating others. Ford aimed to create an "animated textbook," where actors or "interpreters" playing "living history" roles would inspire America's young people.

Similar outdoor museums followed, with or without site-specific buildings. Sewing machine magnate Stephen C. Clark determined to make Cooperstown, New York, a cultural "shrine," and persuaded the State Historical Association to move there in 1938. Clark also supported the National Baseball Hall of Fame and the Cooperstown Farmer's Museum, which showcased early nineteenth-century rural life.

The founding of *Antiques* magazine in 1922 and the opening of the American decorative arts wing at New York's Metropolitan Museum of Art in 1924 signaled a growing interest in the country's historic material culture. Henry Francis du Pont pledged his fortune in 1928 to construct the Winterthur Museum on his Delaware country estate, which opened in 1951 as a nonprofit educational institution.

William A. R. Goodwin introduced John D. Rockefeller, Jr., to Virginia's old capital of Williamsburg in 1926 and persuaded him to underwrite a restoration project run by professionals using state-of-the-art preservation methods. Colonial revival architects collaborated with museologists, archaeologists, and historians, who aimed for authenticity in restoring Williamsburg's governor's palace, capitol, and houses and gardens to reflect "the spirit of the past." Williamsburg became a laboratory in restoration techniques and the research of colonial life, although some details of the site were later proved to be historically inaccurate.

Albert Wells of Southbridge, Massachusetts, an avid collector of historic machinery and other "old and odd things" made his home the Wells Historical Museum in 1935. In 1938 Wells incorporated Old Sturbridge Village to celebrate the "arts and industry of early rural New England." Advised by

Goodwin and Kenneth Chorley, he hired Perry, Shaw, & Hepburn as well as Arthur Shurcliff to create a historical village from the early 1800s by moving vernacular buildings from neighboring states and constructing others copied from regional models. The village opened in 1946, complete with craftspeople and actors in an educational outdoor museum.

The restoration staff of Colonial Williamsburg consulted around the country on the restoration of old taverns, mills, and plantations, including a more accurate restoration of George Washington's home for the Mount Vernon Ladies' Association from 1931 to 1938 after Hoover signed a bill making it a national monument in 1930. Kenneth Chorley, who served as president of Colonial Williamsburg from 1935 through the 1940s, became adviser and mentor for similar restoration projects around the country, including Deerfield, Massachusetts, where piecemeal restoration work began in 1930, and Saint Augustine, Florida. Fiske Kimball, director of the Pennsylvania Museum of Art, became a pioneering professional by first restoring old Philadelphia houses and then advising the Thomas Jefferson Memorial Foundation, which bought Monticello in 1923.

Kimball helped the National Society of the Colonial Dames of America refurnish Dumbarton Oaks, their Washington, D.C., headquarters in 1928. The Dames and the Daughters of the American Revolution supported state and local preservation efforts, as did some state federation of women's clubs. The United Daughters of the Confederacy formed the Robert E. Lee Memorial Foundation in 1929 with private donations and funds from Virginia and Tennessee for the restoration of the general's birthplace, Stratford Hall on the Potomac.

Laurence Vail Coleman of the American Association of Museums traveled widely, studying and encouraging the establishment of historic house museums, despite difficulties raising money to buy, restore, and maintain endangered properties. In 1934, the Old Fort Niagara Association in Youngstown, New York, renovated a colonial fort on Lake Ontario. A coalition of SPNEA, the Trustees of Public Reservations, Colonial Dames, and the Mas-

sachusetts Society of Architects mustered funds in 1935 to create the Gore Place Society, saving a great Federal estate near Boston from developers. Trustees of Public Reservations' Laurence B. Fletcher saved the Old Manse in Concord, Massachusetts, appealing to school children to fund purchase in 1939. Horace M. Albright became director of the National Park Service (NPS) in 1929 and widened its focus to include historic sites and buildings. The NPS hired Verne E. Chatelain in 1931 as the first historian in its Education and Research Branch, which later included archaeologists, architects, and landscape architects. In 1930, Herbert Hoover authorized the establishment and restoration of the Colonial National Monument, which includes Jamestown, Williamsburg, and Yorktown.

After Roosevelt's 1933 inauguration, NPS director Arno B. Cammerer received expanded authority over national military parks, battlefields, and cemeteries, sites that had previously been administered by the War and Agriculture departments. The first new military park was the Morristown National Historical Park in New Jersey, where Washington's Continental Army wintered in 1779. The NPS hired more historians, used Civilian Works Administration funds to start the Historic American Buildings Survey under Thomas C. Vint, and put eight hundred Civilian Conservation Corps (CCC) laborers to work on historic sites. The Historic Sites, Buildings, and Antiquities Act of 1935 extended NPS authority over far-flung projects, including aid to the city of Charleston, South Carolina, which had passed a landmark historic district zoning ordinance in 1931. The NPS also designated the Salem, Massachusetts, waterfront as the first National Historic Site in 1937.

Urged on by Secretary of the Interior Harold L. Ickes, acquisitions of historic sites were funded through both private donations and congressional appropriations. NPS staff helped state efforts as CCC units began working in more and more national and state parks. The WPA began an Illinois Museum Extension Project to reconstruct the Cahokia Courthouse with help from the state architect's office. In addition, Ickes created the Appomattox Court House National Historic Monument in 1940, but the war halted its restoration for a time.

State and local efforts also gained momentum. In 1929 Illinois bought one of Abraham Lincoln's log cabins, restoring it to its 1840s appearance. The state also began reconstructing New Salem village, where Lincoln lived in the 1830s. Pennsylvania acquired Pennsbury Manor, the forty-acre home of William Penn, its first governor, and colonial revival architect Brognard Okie restored it. In 1931, Tombstone, Arizona, began raising funds to recreate the history of the Old West. The San Antonio Conservation Society used municipal funds to open the Spanish Governor's Palace in 1929 and worked on the San Jose Mission from 1933 to 1935 under the Public Works Administration. A 1933 county public works project in Syracuse rebuilt the Jesuit mission to the Iroquois, Sainte Marie de Gannentaha's fort and crafts shops. The Museum of the City of New York, which was established in 1923, helped charter the Historic Landmark Society in 1935, opening the Old Merchant's House museum in 1936. Louisiana amended its constitution in 1936 to permit the Vieux Carré Commission to preserve New Orleans's French Quarter. The state of California purchased the Monterey Custom House in 1937 as part of a master plan for historic preservation.

With 1928 congressional legislation, the nation's capital underwent renovations under the Commission of Fine Arts. Plans for a Thomas Jefferson Memorial gained momentum after the 1926 centennial of Jefferson's death; the National Capital Park and Planning Commission chose a Tidal Basin site in 1935, and John Russell Pope's design, inspired by the Pantheon in Rome, was selected for the monument. Although criticized as "empty classicism," Pope's design won congressional approval in 1938. Dedication of a sarcophagus at Arlington National Cemetery's Tomb of the Unknown Soldier took place in 1931. The War Department transferred Bedloe's Island, the site of the Statue of Liberty, to the NPS in 1937.

Renovation of historic houses and preservation of historic sites, as well as the construction of living history museums, created jobs during the Depression, and such efforts had wide popular appeal. The American Guide series, a state-by-state series of guidebooks prepared by the WPA's Federal Writers' Project, published its first volume in 1937. The series cultivated popular interest in historic places. Americans auto-toured in search of nature and nostalgia, antidotes for the problems of the present.

See Also: AMERICAN GUIDE SERIES; LEISURE.

BIBLIOGRAPHY

Barrington, Lewis. *Historic Restorations of the Daughters of the American Revolution.* 1941.

Becker, Carl. *Every Man His Own Historian.* 1935.

Coleman, Laurence Vail. *Historic House Museums.* 1933.

Crowther, Samuel. "Henry Ford's Village of Yesterday." *Ladies' Home Journal* 45 (September 1928).

Fitzpatrick, John C., ed. *Some Historic Houses.* 1939.

Hosmer, Charles B., Jr. *Presence of the Past: A History of the Preservation Movement in the United States before Williamsburg.* 1965.

Hosmer, Charles B., Jr., *Preservation Comes of Age: From Williamsburg to the National Trust, 1926–1949.* 1981.

BLANCHE M. G. LINDEN

MUSIC

The year 1929 began with a sense of optimism that was reflected in the popular song "Happy Days Are Here Again" by Milton Ager and Jack Yellen. Soon, however, other songs reflected a grim reality. In 1931 Jay Gorney and E. Y. "Yip" Harburg wrote a song called "Brother, Can You Spare a Dime?," which came to symbolize the hopelessness and indignity many Americans felt in the face of unemployment and severe economic hardship. After President Franklin Roosevelt's morale boosting pronouncement, "The only thing we have to fear is fear itself," the song "Who's Afraid of the Big Bad Wolf?" became popular. This was ironic inasmuch as the song was from the cartoon *The Three Little Pigs* (1933), produced by the arch conservative Walt Disney. Not long thereafter, prohibition was repealed, giving rise to a culture of bars and cocktail lounges, which was reflected in such songs as "Soft Lights and Sweet Music," "Night and Day," and "Deep Purple."

Ultimately, the Depression proved to be an era rich in musical composition, innovation, and vari-

Popular Depression-era film and stage composer Richard Rodgers (seated at piano) with lyricist Lorenz Hart in 1936. LIBRARY OF
CONGRESS, PRINTS & PHOTOGRAPHS DIVISION, NEW YORK WORLD-TELEGRAM AND THE SUN NEWSPAPER PHOTOGRAPH COLLECTION

ety. In particular, numerous music publishers who were clustered in New York City's Tin Pan Alley were dependent on the sale of sheet music, since recordings were rare. In order to produce a hit song, a composer had to write a good song, sell it to a popular singer, and hope for financial success. Successful Depression-era Tin Pan Alley songs included George Gershwin's "I Got Rhythm" (1930) and "Embraceable You" (1930); Jerome Kern's "All the Things You Are" (1939), "Smoke Gets in Your Eyes" (1933), and "I Won't Dance" (1934); Irving Berlin's "God Bless America" (1938); and Richard Rodgers's "Falling in Love with Love" (1938) and "This Can't Be Love" (1938).

During the same years, many of these composers also wrote Broadway musicals that featured songs of lasting popularity. These include Jerome Kern's *Roberta* (1933, "Smoke Gets in Your Eyes"), George Gershwin's *Porgy and Bess* (1935, "Summertime"), Richard Rodgers and Lorenz Hart's *Babes in Arms* (1937, "My Funny Valentine"), and Cole Porter's *Red, Hot and Blue!* (1936, "It's De-Lovely"). Another composer of note, Kurt Weill, a refugee from Adolf Hitler's Germany, composed *Knickerbocker Holiday* with Maxwell Anderson and gave the world the memorable "September Song" in 1938.

Many singers became successful radio performers during the Depression years, introducing popu-

A jazz orchestra performs at the Savoy Ballroom in Chicago in 1941. LIBRARY OF CONGRESS, PRINTS & PHOTOGRAPHS DIVISION, FSA/

OWI COLLECTION

lar songs that became identified with them. Kate Smith, for example, was associated with the songs "When the Moon Comes over the Mountain" and "God Bless America." Bing Crosby became linked with "When the Blue of the Night Meets the Gold of the Day." Other popular Depression-era singers include Rudy Vallee, Vaughan McRae, and Frank Sinatra. Sinatra was the first singer to use a microphone to startling advantage; earlier singers tended to belt out songs in the style of Al Jolson, but the microphone made subtlety possible, and Sinatra began a new trend in vocal style. Sinatra and other singers generally got their start by singing with big bands, including those led by Harry James, Tommy Dorsey, Guy Lombardo, and Paul Whiteman.

BLUES AND JAZZ

Blues music arose from people who had known hard times, exploitation, and violence long before the Depression. Blues songs were considered crude by many listeners in the first part of the twentieth century when they were first heard in such cities as New Orleans, Saint Louis, and Mobile, Alabama. But many Depression-era listeners responded to blues music because it was about life and release from troubles. The rhythms are danceable, requiring only a guitar and some type of percussion. Among the most important blues musicians in terms of his legacy for later American music, including rock and roll, was legendary Mississippian Robert Johnson. Such Johnson songs as "Me and

A homesteader teaches a Work Projects Administration music class to local children in Pie Town, New Mexico, in 1940. LIBRARY OF CONGRESS, PRINTS & PHOTOGRAPHS DIVISION, FSA/OWI COLLECTION

the Devil Blues" (1937) inspired countless later musicians.

Both ragtime, a rhythmic piano-based music, and jazz, a multi-faceted musical form, derived from blues, and both exhibit the energy and rhythm of African music—handclapping, dancing, singing, and improvisation. Jazz surpassed blues in popularity during the 1930s, and many jazz musicians became well known and greatly in demand. In 1915, jazz was generally considered a form of folk music played primarily in the Deep South. Before long, however, such early jazz musicians as Jelly Roll Morton, Sidney Bechet, and King Oliver became national stars. They could play, and they could im-

provise; improvisation is the very heart of jazz, making it spontaneous and dramatic.

Louis Armstrong mastered the improvisatory style on trumpet, sang as well as he played, and is credited with inventing scat singing. Armstrong came to prominence in the 1920s and 1930s, and he remained creative and popular until his death in 1971. One of Armstrong's contemporaries, Edward Kennedy "Duke" Ellington, became an established entertainer, composer, and band leader by 1930. Gathering the best musicians he could find, Ellington led a band for fifty years and paid its members well so that he could hear his compositions as soon as he wrote them. Many of Ellington's compositions have become standards, including "Mood Indigo," "Satin Doll," "Black and Tan Fantasy," and "Sophisticated Lady."

Jazz bands evolved into big bands during the swing era, which began in the 1920s and lasted until after World War II. Popular big bands included Red Nichols and his Five Pennies, the Wolverines, and the Chicago Rhythm Kings. Swing music, which combined basic New Orleans jazz with the smoother Chicago style, employed a fast tempo, making the music appealing to dancers. Important swing bands included those led by Tommy and Jimmy Dorsey, Duke Ellington, Artie Shaw, Glenn Miller, and Benny Goodman, who became known as the King of Swing.

Boogie-woogie, a fast-paced blues-influenced piano style with a steady, driving left-hand rhythm, was introduced in the mid-1930s. Originating in Chicago and Kansas City, boogie-woogie is a style for both listening and for frenzied dancing.

FOLK MUSIC AND THE WPA

During the 1930s, the Federal Music Project of the Works Progress Administration (WPA) kept musicians employed by paying them to give concerts and music lessons, to compose original works, and to talk to the public about music. The Federal Music Project collaborated with the WPA Federal Writers' Project to collect, catalogue, and research the nation's folk materials. As part of these efforts, the WPA authorized its employees to collect American folk songs, both old songs and new ones arising from the trying experiences of the 1930s. This project, particularly the contributions of Alan Lomax, resulted in a wealth of folk songs, many of which are available in state archives and the Library of Congress. The most comprehensive of these compilations of Depression-era songs is *Hard Hitting Songs for Hard-Hit People*, compiled by Lomax and edited by Pete Seeger, with commentary by Woody Guthrie. Folksongs are often born of hardship and poverty, and the songs in this collection are no exception. Most of them have a strong blues component, as indicated by many of the titles, including "I Aint Got No Home in This World Anymore," "Depression Blues," "Hard Times in the Mill," and "Wanderin'."

Folksinger and songwriter Woody Guthrie traveled around the United States during the De-

pression, forming his musical ideas in hobo camps, where he listened to drifters and the dispossessed, learning songs passed down through many generations and giving a voice to the downtrodden, the poverty-stricken, and the hopeless. He wrote and sang about what he saw and experienced, with many songs expressing social commentary and love for America, including the familiar "God Blessed America," commonly known as "This Land Is Your Land."

Another major influence in folk music during the Depression years was Huddie Ledbetter, better known as Leadbelly. Leadbelly was discovered by folklorists John and Alan Lomax while he was serving a prison sentence in the Louisiana State Penitentiary in 1933. The Lomaxes recorded hundreds of his songs, which eventually would include "Where Did You Sleep Last Night" and "Goodnight Irene," and brought him and his music to the attention of a worldwide audience by the second half of the 1930s.

COUNTRY MUSIC

Singing comes easily to country people—songs that tell stories, songs that have been handed down through oral tradition, songs that break the monotony of farm life. Country music developed in the rural South and in America's isolated mountain regions, often remaining unchanged for generations, until improved methods of communication were introduced. The term *hillbilly music* became popular in the early 1900s and referred to a type of music that was sincere, if raw, and that spoke of God, home, unrequited love, and real life occurrences.

Jimmie Rodgers is known as the Father of Country Music. A country boy from Mississippi, his entire life was disjointed, unsettled, and frequently sad. However, he combined all these experiences with humor, a simple and straightforward singing style, and his own signature "blue yodel," a cross between a Swiss Alpine yodel and a blues moan. Rodgers's songs were a mixture of random tunes, blues, and jazz, a legacy of inimitable modern country music. Even though poverty was rampant in the South, it is said that during the Depression the standard order in general stores was "a sack of flour, a slab of bacon, and the latest Jimmie Rodgers record."

CLASSICAL MUSIC

By 1929, composers in the United States were seeking to produce original American music that reflected American culture and did not simply imitate European styles. Some composers looked for inspiration in Anglo-American folk music; others looked to African-American spirituals, blues, and jazz, all of which were now well established in American culture.

Aaron Copland set about to develop a musical style with a distinctly American sound. In the 1920s, his compositions incorporated influences from jazz and blues. During the Depression years, Copland adopted a leftist, populist outlook that was evident in such works as the ballet *Billy the Kid* (1938). His best-known composition, *Appalachian Spring* (1943–1944), continued in the same folk-inspired tradition.

William Grant Still studied composition at Oberlin College in Ohio and in New York with Edgard Varese. William Still played in theater and nightclub orchestras, an experience he combined with his formal training in composition to produce his symphonic works, which included *Africa* (1930), *Afro-American Symphony* (1931), the opera *Blue Steel* (1933), and *Lenox Avenue* (1937). All these works reflected Still's African-American culture and traditions.

Other important composers of the period include Howard Hanson, longtime director of the Eastman School of Music in Rochester, New York, who composed several symphonies, two of which premiered in the 1930s, forming milestones for the post-Romantic movement. Randall Thompson is recognized for choral and symphonic works. He composed his *Second Symphony* in 1931 and the *Peaceable Kingdom,* an a cappella piece for mixed voices, in 1936. In 1940 Thompson composed *Alleluia,* a choral number that became well established in the repertoire of American choirs. Roy Harris, who was classically trained in harmony and orchestration, heard his *First Symphony* performed in Boston in 1934 under the baton of Serge Koussevitsky. His *Second Symphony* was performed in 1936, and his *Third Symphony* in 1939. Harris wrote the overture "When Johnny Comes Marching Home" in 1934 to "express . . . emotions particularly American and in an American manner."

Virgil Thomson studied music at Harvard University and composition with Nadia Boulanger in Paris. Thomson later formed a friendship with the author Gertrude Stein in Paris, and the two collaborated in writing the opera *Four Saints in Three Acts,* which made Thomson famous. This opera premiered in Hartford, Connecticut, in 1934, and transferred to Broadway twelve days later, where it was an immediate success. Thomson's other compositions include music for theater, film, and ballet, as well as religious choral music.

See Also: ANDERSON, MARIAN; ARMSTRONG, LOUIS; BIG BAND MUSIC; "BROTHER CAN YOU SPARE A DIME?"; ELLINGTON, DUKE; FEDERAL MUSIC PROJECT (FMP); GERSHWIN, GEORGE AND IRA; GOODMAN, BENNY; GUTHRIE, WOODY; HOLIDAY, BILLIE; JAZZ; LOMAX, ALAN; RADIO.

BIBLIOGRAPHY

Conte, Bob. *Portrait of American Music: Great Twentieth-Century Musicians.* 1989.

Cowell, Sidney Robertson, compiler. *California Gold: Northern California Folk Music from the Thirties.* American Folklife Center, Library of Congress. Available at: www.memory.loc.gov/ammem/afccchtml/cowhome.html

Green, Stanley. "The Thirties." In *Songs of the 30's: Piano, Vocal, Guitar.* 1989.

Lloyd, Norman. *The Golden Encyclopedia of Music.* 1968.

Lomax, Alan, compiler, and Pete Seeger, ed. *Hard Hitting Songs for Hard-Hit People.* 1967.

Reid, William, Jr. *Popular Music in American History.* 1981.

NATOMA N. NOBLE

MUSSOLINI, BENITO

Benito Mussolini (July 29, 1883–April 28, 1945) was founder and leader of the *Facsci di Combattimento,* the Italian fascist movement. A successful journalist and former socialist, he became Italian prime minister on October 29, 1922. He remained in power

Benito Mussolini (left) with Adolf Hitler in Munich, Germany, in 1940. NATIONAL ARCHIVES AND RECORDS ADMINISTRATION

until July 24, 1943. Although the Nazis attempted to rescue him, Mussolini was executed by Italian partisans on April 28, 1945.

MUSSOLINI'S RISE TO POWER

The impact of World War II accelerated the decomposition of liberal, middle-class politics in Italy. The country was suffering as early as 1917 when it was gripped by widespread industrial strikes over rising prices and food shortages, fear of a communist revolution thanks to events in Russia, and a crushing military defeat for the Italian forces at Caporetto in October. Victory in World War I also left most Italians bitter because the Allies subsequently refused to grant Italy territories promised to it to bring the nation into the war. After 1918 the country was overwhelmed by a host of social and economic problems: urban unemployment, high rents for tenant farmers in the north, land-hunger among peasant farmers in the south, spiraling inflation, and increased violence. Neither Italy's established liberal parties nor the structure of constitution could cope with the crisis. Mussolini successfully exploited the sharp divisions that emerged, presenting his party as a force for peace by breaking strikes and "disciplining" labor, and himself as a new kind of strong and efficient national leader. (His claim to act as a peacemaker was disingenuous given the role played by his armed gangs in the rising tide of violence.) Although Mussolini came to power more than ten years before Hitler, their rise shared common features: an ability to exploit deep-seated political divisions, economic upheaval, and the acquiescence, if not support, of powerful elite groups, such as industrialists, who feared communism and were desperate to escape the prolonged crisis.

ITALY'S RESPONSE TO THE GREAT DEPRESSION

Despite his grand claims to a revolutionary vision that had, in Mussolini's words, "the sanctity of heroism" at its heart, Italian fascism was largely tied to the existing capitalist economic and social order. While Mussolini clamped down hard on his left-wing opponents, his fascist economics offered little that was new. The regime did institute a new set of institutional arrangements intended to integrate capital and labor in hierarchical units, called "corporatism," linked to the Ministry of Corporations, but the system only enhanced the power of big business. Mussolini's rhetoric proclaiming innovation proved hollow, too, when Italy joined the gold standard in 1927, a step which prompted greater fascist intervention in the economy as the regime acted to push down food prices and force workers to accept wage cuts of up to 20 percent.

Nor was Mussolini able to shelter Italy from the effects of the collapse in world trade and pressures that mounted on the gold standard after 1929. By the summer of 1931 Italy had experienced a serious crisis in its commercial banking sector, although, in sharp contrast to events in central Europe, Mussolini was able to conceal the development from the Italian people. The state loaned the banks one million lira and established an Instituto Mobilare Italiano to support the banks and an Instituto per la Riconstruzione Industriale to strengthen the ties between government and industry.

But the Depression continued to bite. By 1934 more than 15 percent of Italian workers found themselves out of work, with unemployment rising to almost 18 percent in the northeast and central regions of the country. The regime's efforts to help Italian farmers also failed. Mussolini's regime resorted to a system of exchange controls, quotas, and clearing agreements that took on a renewed importance once Italy invaded Abyssinia in 1935 and intervened in the Spanish Civil War in 1936. This ambitious foreign policy soaked up surplus Italian labor and gave the economy an important boost, but at a price. Italy was forced officially to abandon the gold standard in October 1936 (a painful blow to Mussolini's ego), and by 1937 inflation was dramatically on the rise.

Intervention in the Spanish Civil War brought Mussolini closer to Hitler. The struggle in Spain emphasized the ideological common ground between the two leaders, notably their deeply felt hostility towards communism. A highly choreographed visit to Berlin in September 1937 further impressed Mussolini to the ambition and the military power underpinning the German regime, and the two countries signed a military alliance, the Pact of Steel, in May 1939. Despite the fact that the Pact committed Italy to come to the immediate support of its ally "with all its military forces on land, sea and in the air," Mussolini always claimed he had agreed to the alliance only on the understanding that there would be no major war until 1942. Italy's foreign adventures in the 1930s had sapped its strength and remained neutral in World War II until June 1940 when, after the fall of France, a German victory appeared assured. Italy's subsequent intervention in the war in Greece and in North Africa proved disastrous—Hitler had to send German troops to prevent an Italian collapse—and on July 25, 1943, after a string of military defeats, Mussolini was dismissed as Italy's leader by King Victor Emmanuelle.

See Also: DICTATORSHIP; EUROPE, GREAT DEPRESSION IN; FASCISM; SPANISH CIVIL WAR; WORLD WAR II AND THE ENDING OF THE GREAT DEPRESSION.

BIBLIOGRAPHY

Cohen, Jon, and Federico, Giovanni. *The Growth of the Italian Economy, 1820–1960.* 2001.

De Grand, Alexander. *Fascist Italy and Nazi Germany: The "Fascist" Style of Rule.* 1995.

Forstyth, Douglas. *The Crisis of Liberal Italy: Monetary and Financial Policy, 1914–1922.* 1993.

Gregor, A. James. *Young Mussolini and the Intellectual Origins of Fascism.* 1979.

Mack-Smith, Denis. *Mussolini.* 1980.

Morgan, Philip. "The Party Is Everywhere: The Fascist Party in Economic Life, 1926–40." *English Historical Review* 114 (1999): 85–111.

Zamagni, Vera. *The Economic History of Italy.* 1993.

PATRICIA CLAVIN

MUSTE, A. J.

Labor and peace activist Abraham Johannes Muste (January 8, 1885–February 11, 1967) was born in the Netherlands. His father, a coachman, moved the family to the Dutch community at Grand Rapids, Michigan, in 1891. The boy trained to be a Dutch Reformed minister and was ordained in 1909. The rest of his life was the story of a steady movement leftward, in both theology and politics. By the time of World War I, Muste had become a Quaker and an unyielding pacifist.

During the next twenty years, Muste devoted himself principally to the American labor movement. Starting as an observer of the Lawrence textile strike (1919), he became the leader of the Brookwood Labor College of Katonah, New York (1921), and, now a full-fledged Trotskyite, a thorn in the side of the much more conservative American Federation of Labor. Muste left Brookwood in 1933 for two other radical organizations that he had helped found: the Conference for Progressive Labor Action (established in 1929), whose members became known as "Musteites," and the American Workers Party (founded in 1933), which merged with the Trotskyites, who then ousted Muste from leadership.

While traveling in Europe in 1936 Muste experienced a kind of religious revelation that directed him away from Marxist class conflict and labor agi-tation and back to nonviolent, Christian pacifism. He worked with the Fellowship of Reconciliation, opposed World War II, and urged draft resistance. After the war he increased, rather than reduced his activism. He opposed Senator Joseph McCarthy's investigations into Communist influence in the United States, organized for the civil rights movement, and was the titular and symbolic father of the effort to limit nuclear weapons and end nuclear testing. Not surprisingly, he was one of the first opponents of the United States's war in Vietnam.

Lean, energetic, and deadly serious, Muste, "the American Gandhi," won the respect and admiration of thousands of devoted followers. Even those who detested his work acknowledged the purity of his motives and the tirelessness of his efforts. He died in New York City while trying to organize a massive demonstration against the Vietnam war.

See Also: PEACE MOVEMENT.

BIBLIOGRAPHY

Muste, A. J. *The Essays of A. J. Muste,* edited by Nat Hentoff. 1967.

Robinson, Jo Ann. *Abraham Went Out: A Biography of A. J. Muste.* 1981.

Rosenzweig, Roy. "Radicals and the Jobless: The Musteites and the Unemployed Leagues, 1932–1936." *Labor History* (winter 1975): 52–77.

DAVID W. LEVY

NAM. *See* NATIONAL ASSOCIATION OF
MANUFACTURERS.

NATIONAL ASSOCIATION FOR THE ADVANCEMENT OF COLORED PEOPLE (NAACP)

The National Association for the Advancement of
Colored People (NAACP) was founded on February 12, 1909, on the fringes of the progressive
movement at Charity Organization Hall in New
York City. The organization evolved with the
changing social milieu as it struggled to implement
its egalitarian philosophy with programs designed
to obtain basic citizenship rights for African Americans. The programs developed along two distinct
paths: (1) agitation and education, which would become the organization's well-defined political
course, and (2) legal, which would define its constitutional foundation. As the NAACP stated in its
tenth annual report, its goal was "to reach the conscience of America" in seeking racial equality. Until
June 26, 1934, when he resigned from the organization, W. E. B. Du Bois led the NAACP in developing
its agitation and education program. Du Bois accomplished his mission through the organization's
official magazine, *The Crisis*, which he edited;

through his prolific writings and speeches; and
through his founding of Pan Africanism.

By 1930, despite the financial ravages of the
Great Depression, the NAACP was a major force in
the burgeoning liberal phalanx that included the
expanding organized Congress-labor movement
and the socialist forces that would create the New
Deal. Walter Francis White, who succeeded James
Weldon Johnson that year as executive secretary,
demonstrated the NAACP's growing political
strength by launching the struggle that defeated
President Herbert Hoover's nomination of Judge
John J. Parker of North Carolina to the U.S. Supreme Court by a thirty-nine to forty-one vote in
the Senate. Challenging Hoover's "lily-white policies" and his indifference to the black electorate,
the NAACP opposed the nomination because of a
speech Parker had given ten years earlier endorsing
black disenfranchisement.

The Parker fight marked the coming to political
maturity of African Americans who previously were
ignored. *The Washington Post* published a lengthy
feature on May 18, 1930, noting the development.
The Crisis targeted several senators who had supported Parker's nomination and were running for
reelection in 1930, 1932, and 1934. Eleven were defeated, but as *The Crisis* noted in its December 1934
issue, three "escaped" by winning reelection. White
observed in his 1948 autobiography, *A Man Called*

White, "Out of these effective hard-hitting and uncompromising campaigns two changed political attitudes came." White politicians "were forced to recognize that the Negro voter no longer was gullible, purchasable, or complacent as before and would have to be recognized as an increasingly potent force in the American political scene." Furthermore, African Americans "found new hope and dignity" when "hitherto their efforts had been crowned at best with purely 'moral' victories." In "the Parker fight victory had been achieved and a philosophy and aura of success had replaced the purely protest values of preceding battles." Editorials in the black press confirmed the transformation. William Hastie, a member of the NAACP national board, concluded that victory strengthened the NAACP's belief that the ballot was "the most important phase of the Negro's effort to improve his status in America."

Economic inequality, though, remained a burning issue. Franklin D. Roosevelt's presidential victory in 1932 further confirmed that concern; it also marked the beginning of the seismic shift of African Americans away from the Republican to the Democratic Party, a shift that became dramatic in Roosevelt's 1936 reelection. The Great Depression and the New Deal confirmed the maturity of the NAACP as a civil rights organization, a national bureaucratic machine with branches in every state. The deterioration of the economic position of African Americans, however, forced the NAACP to begin reexamining its strategy and emphasizing the economic needs of the masses. "We are becoming concerned," an NAACP statement declared, "that we are able to accomplish so little. . . .We are going to continue to agitate. . . .But we believe what the Negro needs primarily is a definite economic program."

The endemic discrimination of the New Deal's alphabet soup of programs opened the NAACP to intense criticisms from young radical black intellectuals, including John P. Davis, head of the Joint Committee on National Recovery, who pushed the association to further shift its focus to economic issues. The most prominent of these radicals, who were centered at Howard University in Washington, D.C., were economist Abraham L. Harris, soci-

ologist E. Franklin Frazier, and political scientist Ralph J. Bunche. As Bunche noted, "the New Deal for the first time gave broad recognition to the existence of the African American as a national problem and undertook to give special consideration to this fact in many ways, though the basic evils remained untouched." Another prominent critic was Charles Hamilton Houston, associate dean of Howard University Law School, who also pressed the NAACP to shift its focus from anti-lynching to economic issues.

In 1933, the NAACP held a second Amenia Conference at the Troutbeck estate of Joel E. Spingarn, its president, in upstate New York, to develop a broader civil rights program and strategy. Unlike the first Amenia Conference held in 1916, which was integrated, the second was all-black. The conference concluded that a union of black and white workers was needed in the labor movement to direct America's economic and political life. The following year, the NAACP began implementing this program by appointing a Committee on Future Plan and Program of the NAACP, headed by Harris. The organization's economic program included the launching in 1936 of a sustained legal battle in Baltimore, Maryland, against unequal salaries for African-American teachers.

At the same time, under Houston's direction, the NAACP launched its legal campaign against educational inequalities. In 1935, Houston and his protégé Thurgood Marshall (later to become the first black justice on the U.S. Supreme Court) won in the Baltimore City Court the NAACP's trailblazing legal challenge to segregation at the University of Maryland Law School. Their success helped set the stage for subsequent NAACP's court challenges that led to the landmark victory in 1954 in *Brown v. Board of Education of Topeka,* in which the U.S. Supreme Court ruled that the "separate but equal" doctrine, established in the 1896 *Plessy v. Ferguson* case, was unconstitutional. To accomplish that goal, Houston recommended to the NAACP that it attack the unequal funding of schools in the South in order to make maintaining segregation within the context of "separate but equal" so expensive that the region would be forced to abandon its Jim Crow education system. His recommendation, more limited and direct, varied from that of Nathan Margold of Harvard University, a white expert in constitutional law, who had earlier urged the NAACP to abandon its case-by-case attack on discrimination by directly challenging the constitutional validity of the "separate but equal" doctrine.

Part of the reason the NAACP reacted slowly during the Depression to increasing demands from blacks for assistance was that its leaders feared infiltration by Communists, and the NAACP was anxious to avoid fly-by-night projects. White, furthermore, had strong reservations about embracing a more "mass-oriented" program. Nevertheless, the NAACP could not disregard the obvious inequalities in the implementation of New Deal programs, including wage differentials sanctioned by the National Recovery Administration; the exclusion of black sharecroppers from the benefits of the Agricultural Adjustment Act; and the exclusion of black-dominated occupations, such as agricultural and domestic work, from Social Security coverage. The programs of other New Deal agencies, such as the Works Progress Administration, the National Youth Administration, and the United States Housing Authority, helped attract blacks to the Democratic Party, but the party itself, especially its southern wing, remained discriminatory. Most of the NAACP's effort to end discrimination in New Deal agencies was waged through the Joint Committee on National Recovery, which was composed of twenty-two national racial and interracial organizations.

White, furthermore, established a solid and warm working alliance with First Lady Eleanor Roosevelt, enabling the NAACP to garner added respect and ready access to the White House. This access was essential because, as White explained, "the President was frankly unwilling to challenge the Southern leaders of his party."

As a member of the NAACP national board of directors, Eleanor Roosevelt remained fully attuned to the thinking of blacks with the help of her friend, Mary McLeod Bethune, spiritual leader of the New Deal's Black Cabinet. Mrs. Roosevelt worked tirelessly to influence the course of government for the benefit of the NAACP and African Americans. A noteworthy challenge for her was the refusal in 1939 by the Daughters of the American Revolution (DAR) to permit the African-American contralto Marian Anderson to sing in Constitution Hall. Roosevelt protested the decision by resigning from the DAR. With the president's blessing (and at Eleanor's nudging), the Department of the Interior approved the use of the Lincoln Memorial for the concert, which was held under the auspices of the NAACP. Characteristically, White relished another victory over bigotry. Nothing made him happier, however, than Anderson's exquisitely beautiful performance, which brought tears of joy streaming down the face of one young girl who said, "If Marian Anderson could do it . . . then I can, too."

The NAACP's activities during the Great Depression considerably strengthened its political and legal programs, enabling it in the 1940s to become an early leader in the modern civil rights movement. Its Depression-era programs contributed to the reaffirmation by the federal courts of the principle of equality under the Fourteenth Amendment, and to the subsequent adoption by the federal government of civil rights policies, and the enactment of a comprehensive package of new laws to protect those rights.

See Also: AFRICAN AMERICANS, IMPACT OF THE GREAT DEPRESSION ON; BETHUNE, MARY MCLEOD; DEMOCRATIC PARTY; ELECTION OF 1936; *MISSOURI EX REL. GAINES V. CANADA*; ROOSEVELT, ELEANOR; WHITE, WALTER.

BIBLIOGRAPHY

Bunche, Ralph J. "The Negro in the Political Life of the United States." *The Journal of Negro Education* 10 (1941): 580.

Du Bois, W. E. B. "The Immediate Problem of the American Negro." *The Crisis* (April 1915): 310–312.

Hastie, William H. "A Look at the NAACP." *The Crisis* (September 1939): 263–264.

Kellogg, Charles Flint. *NAACP: A History of the National Association for the Advancement of Colored People*, Vol. 1: *1909–1920*. 1967.

Lawrence, Charles Radford. "Negro Organizations in Crisis: The Depression, New Deal, World War II." Ph.D. diss., Columbia University, 1952.

McNeil, Genna Rae. *Groundwork: Charles Hamilton Houston and the Struggle for Civil Rights*. 1983.

Meier, August, and John H. Bracey, Jr. *The Journal of Southern History* 59, no. 1 (1993): 3–30.

"Negro Editors on Communism." *The Crisis* (April 1932): 117–119.

Watson, Denton L. *Highlights of NAACP History: 1909–1979.* 1979.

Watson, Denton L. *Lion in the Lobby: Clarence Mitchell, Jr.'s Struggle for the Passage of Civil Rights Laws.* 1990.

White, Walter. "The Negro and the Communists." *Harper's Magazine* (December 1931); NAACP Reprint 10.

White, Walter. *A Man Called White.* 1948.

Wolters, Raymond. *Negroes and the Great Depression: The Problem of Economic Recovery.* 1970.

DENTON L. WATSON

NATIONAL ASSOCIATION OF MANUFACTURERS (NAM)

The National Association of Manufacturers (NAM) was founded in 1895 as a collection of small- and medium-sized firms with common interests in two areas of public policy: achieving protectionist trade measures and strengthening the power of management vis-à-vis organized labor. After World War I and during the 1920s, the NAM conducted a high-profile campaign in favor of the open shop, striking back at organized labor's efforts to increase union membership. Hit hard by the Great Depression, member firms resigned from the NAM at a high rate; by 1933 membership had declined to fewer than 1,500 firms, down from five thousand in 1920.

During the Great Depression, the NAM was led by Robert Lund, president of Lambert Pharmaceutical. Due to the decline in its traditional membership base of smaller firms in textiles, shipbuilding, and the metal trades, the NAM increasingly fell under the influence of larger firms from the tobacco, automobile, steel, chemical, and food processing industries. By 1936, these latter firms provided about 40 percent of the NAM's annual revenues, which grew by 1937 to $1.5 million a year, up from $250,000 in 1933. Lund, who assumed leadership of the NAM in 1931, mobilized it against the New Deal. The NAM opposed Franklin D. Roosevelt every time he ran for president, and objected to aspects of major New Deal policies, including the National Industrial Recovery Act (1933), National Labor Relations Act (1935), and the Fair Labor Standards Act (1938). By 1937, 55 percent of the NAM's budget went to spending on public relations, carrying the NAM's vision of business-government relations to the broader public. The NAM also focused its energies on lobbying the government, attempting to directly influence events on Capitol Hill. Unlike such business figures as Edward Filene and Gerard Swope, the NAM entertained little sympathy for the rights of organized labor. The NAM portrayed government as parasitic and organized labor as proponents of social agitation and disorder, contrasting them with an image of business leaders as paragons of expertise, social harmony, and reasoned decision making. Although the NAM made little headway against the New Deal, its organizing efforts, publicity campaigns, and improved financial health placed it in a position to advance its goals during and after World War II.

See Also: BUSINESSMEN; ORGANIZED LABOR.

BIBLIOGRAPHY

Fones-Wolf, Elizabeth. *Selling Free Enterprise: The Business Assault on Labor and Liberalism, 1945–1960.* 1994.

Gordon, Colin. *New Deals: Business, Labor, and Politics in America, 1920–1935.* 1994.

Tedlow, Richard S. "The National Association of Manufacturers and Public Relations during the New Deal." *Business History Review* 50 (1976): 25–45.

JASON SCOTT SMITH

NATIONAL COMMITTEE TO ABOLISH THE POLL TAX

Founded in 1941, the National Committee to Abolish the Poll Tax was a coalition of labor, liberal, and civil rights organizations dedicated to expanding federal protection of voting rights in the South. The poll tax was one of a variety of methods adopted by southern states at the turn of the century to restrict voter participation. The cost of the poll tax varied from state to state, and became increasingly restrictive during the Depression. Since there were other

A Depression-era billboard in Dubuque, Iowa, promotes the National Association of Manufacturers. LIBRARY OF CONGRESS, PRINTS & PHOTOGRAPHS DIVISION, FSA/OWI COLLECTION

laws and customs specifically designed to bar blacks from voting, such as the white primary, the poll tax was especially effective in disfranchising poor and working-class whites. In 1939, the *Louisville Courier Journal* estimated that as many as 64 percent of the white adult voters had been disfranchised in poll tax states.

When it was founded in 1938, the Southern Conference for Human Welfare made abolition of the poll tax its top priority. The Conference established a Committee on Civil Rights, headed by Joseph Gelders and Virginia Durr, to oversee this effort. Gelders and Durr, both natives of Alabama, concentrated their efforts on getting a bill introduced in Congress that would ban the poll tax in federal elections. With the support of California Congressman Lee Geyers, Durr and Gelders built a broad base of support among major labor, liberal, and civil rights organizations for anti-poll tax legislation.

In 1941, Durr and Gelders incorporated their coalition into the National Committee to Abolish the Poll Tax. Gelders soon enlisted in the army. As vice chairman of the National Committee to Abolish the Poll Tax, Durr led in orchestrating a major lobbying and educational effort. The Committee's supporting organizations included the National Association for the Advancement of Colored People, the National Negro Congress, the American Federation of Labor, and the League of Women Voters. Eleanor Roosevelt was among the prominent figures who lent her active support to the effort. The National Committee to Abolish the Poll Tax published a newsletter, *The Poll Tax Repealer,* and recruited a staff of volunteers, including a number of college students.

The struggle around the poll tax reflected the divide between the New Deal coalition within the Democratic Party and conservative southern Democrats. From 1941 to 1948, the Committee succeeded in getting three major bills introduced in Congress. The first bill, sponsored by Lee Geyers and Senator Claude Pepper of Florida, initiated the first full-scale congressional debate on federal protection of voting rights since the defeat of the Lodge election bill in 1890. Southern conservatives mounted a vigorous opposition, arguing that the bill was unconstitutional, and warning that any federal tampering with voting restrictions would ultimately compromise the South's ability to restrict black voter participation. Anti-poll tax legislation passed the House by increasingly wide margins, only to be tabled in the Senate by southern-led filibusters.

By the time it disbanded in 1948, the National Committee to Abolish the Poll Tax had succeeded in forging a broad liberal-labor coalition that would play an increasingly important role in securing national support for the federal protection of civil rights and voting rights in the South.

See Also: CONSERVATIVE COALITION; CIVIL RIGHTS AND CIVIL LIBERTIES; SOUTHERN CONFERENCE FOR HUMAN WELFARE (SCHW).

BIBLIOGRAPHY
Lawson, Steven F. *Black Ballots: Voting Rights in the South, 1944–1969.* 1976.

PATRICIA SULLIVAN

NATIONAL FARMERS UNION (NFU)

The National Farmers Union (NFU), founded in Texas in 1902, was one of the three most important farmers' organizations in the United States during the 1930s. The NFU's base of support could be found among various small producers, including small family farmers, tenant farmers, and sharecroppers, as well as undercapitalized wheat growers in the Midwest. In 1930, John Simpson of Oklahoma was voted in as president of the NFU. In this position, he worked hard to convince Washington to provide credit relief to farmers and to stop the farm foreclosures that were forcing small producers

off the land. Simpson also insisted that the long-term problems of farmers could only be solved with legislation that would directly raise farm prices. To that end, he proposed that Congress pass a cost-of-production plan to provide minimum prices for farmers. According to this plan, each farmer would be allocated a certain production quota, with surpluses sold overseas in the open market.

Simpson's cost-of–production plan placed him at odds with other factions within the NFU, most importantly those who advocated the strengthening of large marketing cooperatives and those who were hostile to state intervention. Simpson was also at odds with the Roosevelt administration. Simpson's premature death in 1934 catapulted E. H. Everson of South Dakota to the presidency of the NFU. Everson mostly continued Simpson's anti-New Deal policies by supporting William Lemke for president in 1936. (Lemke was running as the official candidate of the Union Party, created by Father Charles E. Coughlin.) Everson's own tenure in office proved short, and he was succeeded by John Vesecky of Kansas in 1937. Vesecky's rise to power marked a turning point for the NFU and its relationship to Roosevelt and organized labor. Beginning in 1937, the NFU abandoned its calls for currency inflation and cost-of-production measures, and the union began to support Roosevelt's agricultural policies. This allowed the NFU to forge a closer relationship with the Roosevelt administration and marked a transition in NFU ideology from one of agricultural fundamentalism (the idea that production and farmers formed the base of society) to one of agricultural liberalism (the idea that consumption, full employment, and state-directed fiscal policies determined the well-being of society).

See Also: AGRICULTURE; FARM POLICY; UNION PARTY.

BIBLIOGRAPHY
Crampton, John A. *The National Farmers Union: Ideology of a Pressure Group.* 1965.

Flamm, Michael W. "The National Farmers Union and the Evolution of Agrarian Liberalism, 1937–1946." *Agricultural History* 68 (1994): 54–81.

Mast, Charles Anthony. "Farm Factionalism over Federal Agricultural Policy: The National Farmers Union,

1926–1937." M.A. thesis, University of Maryland. 1967.

Saloutos, Theodore, and John D. Hicks. *Agricultural Discontent in the Middle West, 1900–1939.* 1951.

KATHY MAPES

NATIONAL HOUSING ACT OF 1934

The enactment of the National Housing Act on June 27, 1934, began the modern involvement of the federal government in the American housing market. It represented the early New Deal's most important attempt at short-term pump priming of the economy, but it also had long-term significance as a shaping influence on the development of urban America.

The main rationale for the legislation was to revive the ailing construction industry, which accounted for about a third of the total unemployed, and whose recovery would have important consequences for supply industries like wood, cement, and electrical appliances. New housing starts, which averaged 900,000 a year in the 1920s, had plummeted as a result of the Great Depression to 90,000 in 1933. Testifying in support of the legislation before the House Banking and Currency Committee, Federal Emergency Relief administrator Harry Hopkins confirmed that "a fundamental purpose of this bill is an effort to get people back to work."

The legislation was devised by a task force headed by Utah banker Marriner Eccles, a special assistant to Secretary of the Treasury Henry Morgenthau on credit and monetary matters. From the framers' perspective, the best way to revive construction was not through a mass program of public housing but through the use of federal insurance programs to encourage private ventures. This was also the solution preferred by President Franklin D. Roosevelt. The National Housing Act created two important federal housing agencies. The Federal Savings and Loan Insurance Corporation spent $275 million to insure the mortgages that federally chartered savings and loan associations made. Under the law's provisions these associations were mandated to institute an important reform of housing finance by inaugurating the long-term amortized loan, which eliminated the daunting balloon payment that was hitherto due at the end of the loan period. The other agency created by the legislation, the Federal Housing Administration (FHA), was the New Deal's most direct intervention in the housing market. It aimed to encourage mortgage lending by banks and other bodies through extending low-premium federal insurance against default by borrowers.

The steady growth of annual housing starts to 800,000 by 1940 indicated that the National Housing Act had helped substantially in reviving the construction industry. Nevertheless, the problematic consequences of its long-term effects were also becoming evident by then. While never intended as a social reform to improve the quality of low-income inner-city housing, the legislation arguably made things worse for slum dwellers by hastening suburban development and white flight from the cities. Under conservative leadership drawn from the business and banking industries, the FHA discriminated against inner-city districts, especially those settled by African Americans, through the institution of a red-lining regime that prohibited insurance on housing in neighborhoods that lacked social and economic stability. It was the white suburbs that benefited primarily from the $119 billion in mortgage insurance that the FHA issued in the first four decades of its existence. The consequences of the New Deal's neglect of the inner cities would become evident in the 1960s.

See Also: CITIES AND SUBURBS; ECCLES, MARRINER; FEDERAL HOUSING ADMINISTRATION (FHA); HOUSING.

BIBLIOGRAPHY

Eccles, Marriner S. *Beckoning Frontiers: Public and Personal Recollections.* 1951.

Gelfand, Mark I. *A Nation of Cities: The Federal Government and Urban America, 1933–1965.* 1975.

Jackson, Kenneth T. *Crabgrass Frontier: The Suburbanization of the United States.* 1985.

IWAN MORGAN

NATIONAL INDUSTRIAL RECOVERY ACT (NIRA)

In early 1933 the United States was mired in the Depression. One-fourth of the nation's workers were unemployed, and industry was operating at only a fraction of its capacity. Yet during the month following his inauguration on March 4, 1933, President Franklin D. Roosevelt gave little attention to a program for industry in his efforts to stimulate recovery. His advisors had yet to coalesce around one or even two plans that would enable him to choose a course of action, and Roosevelt hoped the banking, relief, agricultural, and monetary policies he was developing might be sufficient to get the economy back on track. To his thinking, an industrial policy, while desirable, was not necessary to spur general recovery, and he did not want to be rushed into a program in the face of the often conflicting ideas for industrial recovery that were being presented.

Trust-busting progressives, such as Professor Felix Frankfurter of the Harvard Law School, believed that monopolistic rigidity in the economy had brought on the Depression through excessive profits, over saving, and reduced consumer spending. In their view an emphasis upon the restoration of competition with vigorous enforcement of the antitrust laws, limits on the size of businesses, progressive taxation, and controls over financial and business practices would achieve recovery by unleashing free markets. Senators Robert Wagner of New York and Robert LaFollette Jr. of Wisconsin and Secretary of Labor Frances Perkins favored large-scale public works spending to pump purchasing power into the economy and put men back to work. Spokesmen for organized labor called for legislation limiting working hours and prescribing minimum wages in the belief it would spread jobs, stabilize labor standards, and give workers more money to spend. Others advocated plans to "restart industry," either by means of government loans to businesses for reemployment purposes or government guarantees against losses for firms increasing their work forces. Still others, most notably Assistant Secretary of Agriculture Rexford Tugwell, had talked about industrial planning by which a national industrial council made up of government officials or organized non-business groups would exhort business to more responsible behavior. Finally, business elements proposed industrial self-government based on trade association control of markets. Persuaded that overproduction and destructive competition had brought on the Depression, they argued that businessmen, coordinated and assisted by the federal government, could stabilize the price system and spur recovery through agreements limiting competition and raising labor standards.

Industrial self-government had first been utilized on a large scale during World War I by the War Industries Board (WIB) to mobilize industry for war. In the 1920s businessmen had used voluntary agreements, or codes, of fair practices in an attempt to minimize cutthroat competition in some industries. But in the absence of any legal sanctions these agreements often collapsed. With the Depression, businessmen from the cotton textile, petroleum, and other industries that faced chaotic conditions from excessive production called for the suspension of the antitrust laws to permit trade associations to draft effective agreements on production, pricing, and marketing. They were supported by labor leaders in "sick" industries, such as bituminous coal and the needle trades, who believed that if operators could fix minimum prices and set production quotas they could afford to pay higher wages.

Roosevelt was finally stirred to action on industrial recovery in April 1933. Economic indices were slipping, and Congress was ready to move on industrial recovery despite the lack of a presidential initiative. In the Congress, debate focused on a bill introduced by Senator Hugo Black of Alabama that would mandate a maximum thirty-hour-work week. Based on the notion that available work should be shared and that a shorter workweek would create a labor shortage and push up wages, the Black bill had strong support among the Democratic Party majorities in both houses of Congress. It was approved by the Senate on March 30 and seemed likely to be approved by the House of Representatives. However, Roosevelt was skeptical about the Black bill. In his view, it was probably unconstitutional and overly rigid and would not necessarily lead to wage increases. But he was reluctant to embarrass his Democratic supporters in the Congress by opposing it. As a result, he used his political clout to tie up the bill in the House, where it eventually died, and he instructed Assistant Secretary of State Raymond Moley, a principal advisor, to analyze the various proposals for industrial recovery and come up with an alternative to the Black measure.

Moley ultimately concentrated on two plans. One, put together by a group led by Wagner and Assistant Secretary of Commerce John Dickinson and drawing upon ideas from an assortment of business, labor, and government figures, centered on public works spending, government loans to industry, and industrial self-government. It also guaranteed labor's right to collective bargaining. The other plan was largely crafted by Hugh Johnson, a businessman who had represented the army on the WIB, and Donald Richberg, a Chicago lawyer with close ties to the railroad brotherhoods. It likewise called for public works spending and industrial self-government. But in contrast to the Wagner-Dickinson plan, which saw industrial self-government as a partnership between government and business, with business as the senior partner, the Johnson-Richberg plan envisioned a stronger role for government, including presidential authority to license businesses.

At a meeting on May 10, Roosevelt listened to arguments for the two plans from the major drafters and then ordered Johnson, Richberg, Dickinson, Wagner, Perkins, Tugwell, and Budget Director Lewis Douglas "to shut themselves up in a room" and not come out until they had settled on a common plan for industrial recovery. The conferees completed their work on the plan on May 14. The provision for government loans to industry was dropped. Otherwise, it was an amalgamation of the two proposals, with provisions for public works, industrial self-government, and government sanction of unions.

Roosevelt endorsed the plan on May 15 and sent a bill to implement it to Congress on May 17. Strongly supported by business and labor groups, the bill was approved by the House on May 26 by a vote of 325 to 76. In the Senate rural progressives

and antitrusters led by Senator William E. Borah of Idaho mounted a fierce attack against the bill, arguing it would create a giant system of cartels that would stifle any competition and ignore the interests of labor and consumers. Roosevelt, however, had enough votes in the Senate to approve the bill, and on June 13 the Senate passed the measure by a vote of 46 to 37. Three days later Roosevelt signed it into law.

Officially known as the National Industrial Recovery Act (NIRA), the law contained three titles. Title II authorized a $3.3 billion public works program, and Title III provided for a new system of capital stock and excess profits taxes to finance it. Title I, the most publicized feature of NIRA, implemented the program of industrial self-government. Limited to two years, it permitted industries to draft agreements, or codes, governing business and labor practices that were exempt from the antitrust laws and had the force of law once they received the president's signature. Although not stated explicitly, trade associations were anticipated to have the major role in drafting and administering the codes. Little was said about the specific provisions in codes except for Section 7, which stated that codes were to include provisions for maximum hours, minimum wages, and the right of workers to organize and bargain collectively. Section 4 gave the president the power to license industries for a period of one year, and Section 9 gave him the power to remake any code when he thought it was necessary or to impose one on an industry.

In signing NIRA, Roosevelt pronounced it the "most important and far-reaching legislation ever enacted by the American Congress." Brought about by the blight of the Depression, it marked a major step away from the competition of free enterprise capitalism and offered a vision of economic cooperation and social harmony. Business looked forward to the use of price and production controls to restore profits, and workers saw the prospect of higher wages, shorter workdays, full employment, and the growth of unions. Though it was promising, NIRA failed to meet the hopes of its supporters. The public works program, implemented by the Public Works Administration, was run by Administrator Harold Ickes in a tight-fisted fashion that dribbled money into the economy and did not significantly jump start reemployment. Title I, little more than an enabling measure, was too vague to be a coherent guide to meet the disparate goals of business, labor, and consumers. As implemented by the National Recovery Administration under the leadership of Hugh Johnson, industrial self-government was generally dominated by larger firms, which put in place practices that often hindered recovery and thwarted the aspirations of labor. By the fall of 1933 industrial self-government was enmeshed in controversy that did not end until May 1935 when the U.S. Supreme Court, in the case of *Schechter Poultry Corporation v. United States*, declared Title I unconstitutional on the grounds that it was an invalid delegation of legislative power to the president and exceeded the authority of the federal government to regulate intrastate commerce.

See Also: COLLECTIVE BARGAINING; ECONOMY, AMERICAN; INDUSTRY, EFFECTS ON THE GREAT DEPRESSION ON; JOHNSON, HUGH; MOLEY, RAYMOND.

BIBLIOGRAPHY

Bellush, Bernard. *The Failure of the NRA.* 1975.

Brand, Donald R. *Corporatism and the Rule of Law: A Study of the National Recovery Administration.* 1988.

Freidel, Frank. *Franklin D. Roosevelt, Vol. 4: Launching the New Deal.* 1973.

Hawley, Ellis W. *The New Deal and the Problem of Monopoly: A Study in Economic Ambivalence.* 1966.

Himmelberg, Robert F. *The Origins of the National Recovery Administration: Business, Government, and the Trade Association Issue, 1921–1933.* 1976.

Huthmacher, J. Joseph. *Senator Robert F. Wagner and the Rise of Urban Liberalism.* 1968.

Johnson, Hugh S. *The Blue Eagle from Egg to Earth.* 1935.

Moley, Raymond. *The First New Deal.* 1966.

Ohl, John Kennedy. *Hugh S. Johnson and the New Deal.* 1985.

Schlesinger, Arthur M., Jr. *The Age of Roosevelt, Vol. 2: The Coming of the New Deal.* 1958.

Vadney, Thomas E. *The Wayward Liberal: A Political Biography of Donald Richberg.* 1970.

JOHN KENNEDY OHL

NATIONAL LABOR RELATIONS ACT OF 1935 (WAGNER ACT)

Franklin Roosevelt signed the National Labor Relations Act (NLRA) into law on July 5, 1935. Also known as the Wagner Act after its chief sponsor, Senator Robert F. Wagner, a New York Democrat, the law marked a major milestone in the history of the American trade union movement. The NLRA went beyond earlier legislative declarations in the Railway Labor and Norris-LaGuardia acts to demonstrate that U.S. public policy favored workers joining unions and engaging in collective bargaining by providing government protection of the right to organize. Although many historians credit the NLRA with contributing significantly to the quadrupling in union membership that occurred in the twenty years following the law's adoption, some critics see the labor law regime established by the NLRA as ultimately constricting the development of the labor movement and creating the context for the steady decline of trade unions that occurred after the mid-1950s.

Wagner first introduced a Labor Disputes bill in the Senate in March 1934. His proposal was in reaction to the labor turmoil that had followed in the wake of the adoption of section 7(a) of the National Industrial Recovery Act. Section 7(a) asserted the right of employees "to organize and bargain collectively through representatives of their own choosing." The precise meaning of that right, however, soon became a matter of controversy and led to President Roosevelt's appointment of a National Labor Board, headed by Wagner, to interpret the law and mediate disputes. The National Labor Board's lack of clear authority and frequent disagreements with the leadership of the National Recovery Administration led Wagner to propose a separate bill to establish a more effective labor board and to clarify the protections to be provided to workers attempting to organize. Rather than supporting Wagner's proposed legislation, Roosevelt in 1934 favored the adoption of a stopgap measure, Public Resolution No. 44, that allowed him to create a revamped labor tribunal, the National Labor Relations Board (NLRB), but which continued to lack effective enforcement powers.

Continuing frustration with the implementation of section 7(a) led Wagner to introduce a revised version of his Labor Disputes bill in the Senate in February 1935. Wagner drafted the new NLRA with the assistance of his legislative aide, Leon Keyserling, American Federation of Labor counsel Charlton Ogburn, and NLRB lawyers Calvert Magruder, Philip Levy, and P.G. Phillips. Representative William P. Connery, Jr., sponsored the bill in the House. In spite of strong support for the bill in both houses of Congress and from the leadership of organized labor, Roosevelt remained unenthusiastic about the legislation until the Supreme Court ruled the entire National Industrial Recovery Act unconstitutional in May 1935, thus creating a void in New Deal labor policy.

The NLRA as finally passed established an independent three-person National Labor Relations Board that, in contrast to its predecessors, could go directly to the courts to enforce its orders. The law banned certain specified "unfair labor practices" by employers that might interfere with or obstruct employees' "right to self-organization." Such unfair practices included employer-dominated or financed company unions. The NLRB was given authority to determine the appropriate bargaining unit and to conduct secret ballot elections to determine who, if anyone, the majority of workers in the unit wanted as exclusive bargaining agents. The specific language relating to the determination of bargaining units made possible the growth of industrial unions, but ruled out the development of industry-wide collective bargaining.

Most employers strongly opposed the NLRA and then actively resisted the law through legal suits challenging the law's constitutionality. The law thus did not become fully effective until the Supreme Court in 1937 upheld its constitutionality in *National Labor Relations Board* v. *Jones & Laughlin Steel Corp.*

Some critics of the NLRA see the law as part of a corporate liberal strategy to defuse the radical potential of what had become a militant labor movement by channeling that movement into a narrowly constricted form of collective bargaining. Although organized labor strongly supported passage of the NLRA, several labor leaders in 1935 expressed concern about the long-term consequences of relying on the state to define and protect labor's rights. The passage in 1947 of the Taft-Hartley amendments to the NLRA demonstrated the dangers of making unions subject to government regulation. Wagner, however, saw the law not as a means of controlling labor, but rather as a matter of justice, and he supported it because he believed strong unions would boost wages and thereby contribute to the growth of purchasing power needed for a healthy economy. Without the NLRA, it is hard to imagine either unions or workers making the gains they did after the law's passage.

See Also: COLLECTIVE BARGAINING; FAIR LABOR STANDARDS ACT; NATIONAL INDUSTRIAL RECOVERY ACT (NIRA); NATIONAL LABOR RELATIONS BOARD (NLRB); NORRIS-LA GUARDIA ACT; WAGNER, ROBERT F.

BIBLIOGRAPHY

Bernstein, Irving. *New Deal Collective Bargaining Policy.* 1950.

Gordon, Colin. *New Deals: Business, Labor, and Politics in America, 1920–1935.* 1994.

Gross, James A. *The Making of the National Labor Relations Board,* Vol. 1: *A Study in Economics, Politics, and the Law.* 1974.

Keyserling, Leon H. "The Wagner Act: Its Origin and Current Significance." *George Washington Law Review* 29 (1960): 199–233.

Klare, Karl. "Judicial Deradicalization of the Wagner Act and the Origins of Modern Legal Consciousness, 1937–1941." *Minnesota Law Review* 62 (1978): 265–339.

National Labor Relations Board. *Legislative History of the National Labor Relations Act, 1935.* 1949.

Tomlins, Christopher L. *The State and the Unions: Labor Relations, Law, and the Organized Labor Movement in America, 1880–1960.* 1985.

Vittoz, Stanley. *New Deal Labor Policy and the American Industrial Economy.* 1987.

LARRY G. GERBER

NATIONAL LABOR RELATIONS BOARD (NLRB)

The National Labor Relations Board (NLRB) is a governmental agency that was founded in July 1935

Government and labor officials oversee the NLRB election for union representation at the River Rouge Ford plant in Dearborn, Michigan, in 1941. LIBRARY OF CONGRESS, PRINTS & PHOTOGRAPHS DIVISION, FSA/OWI COLLECTION

for the purpose of enforcing the National Labor Relations Act, also called the Wagner Act after its main architect, Senator Robert F. Wagner, a progressive Democratic from President Franklin Delano Roosevelt's home state of New York. The National Labor Relations Act was supposed to give teeth to workers' collective bargaining rights, and during the "Second" New Deal the NLRB was successful in safeguarding workers' rights to select their bargaining representatives and in ensuring the compliance of management with the law. The NLRB also facilitated the formation of the Congress of Industrial Organizations (CIO), which could compete with the American Federation of Labor (AFL) for the votes of minorities, many of whom had been used by management in mass production

industries—such as steel, automobiles, mining, and rubber—as strikebreakers.

The economic hardship and suffering that characterized the Great Depression had impelled workers during the "First" New Deal to unionize and to oppose the labor practices that management had utilized for decades—practices that included court injunctions, "yellow dog" contracts, blacklists, strikebreakers, company unions, and other coercive measures to limit the bargaining effectiveness of unions. Thus, the Roosevelt administration adopted pro-union policies through one of its key agencies, the National Recovery Administration (NRA). During the NRA's two years of existence, it engendered the unionization of labor, and numerous, sometimes violent, strikes took place in the country from

1933 to 1935 as a consequence. In response, Roosevelt created the National Labor Board, headed by Senator Wagner. Although the Board enjoyed some initial success, it eventually collapsed because of the stubborn resistance of business leaders to independent unions.

Although business was able to receive insulation from antitrust laws, section 7(a) of the 1933 National Industrial Recovery Act, which had created the NRA, affirmed the right of unions to "organize and bargain collectively through representatives of their own choosing." The NRA's minimum wages and maximum hours codes, however, were jettisoned by the Supreme Court in the 1935 *Schechter* case, which found the National Industrial Recovery Act unconstitutional, primarily because it attempted to regulate interstate commerce and because of its broad delegation of legislative power. In 1937 a divided Supreme Court, in a broad interpretation of interstate commerce, upheld the constitutionality of the National Labor Relations Act by a five to four margin in *NLRB v. Jones and Laughlin Steel.*

Despite the NLRB's successful role in promulgating pro-union policies during the late 1930s, its policies created a conservative backlash against labor after 1945. Following a major victory in 1946, Republicans passed the Taft-Hartley Act over President Harry Truman's veto. The Taft-Hartley Act effectively compromised the union movement. Furthermore, by 1986 the NLRB was dominated by President Ronald Reagan's pro-management appointees, with the net effect of eviscerating federal support for the collective bargaining power of unions.

See Also: COLLECTIVE BARGAINING; FAIR LABOR STANDARDS ACT; NATIONAL LABOR RELATIONS ACT OF 1935 (WAGNER ACT); NEW DEAL, SECOND.

BIBLIOGRAPHY

Bernstein, Irving. *New Deal Collective Bargaining Policy.* 1950.

Bernstein, Irving. *Turbulent Years: A History of the American Worker, 1933–1941.* 1969.

Fraser, Steve, and Gary Gerstle. *The Rise and Fall of the New Deal Order, 1930–1980.* 1989.

Leuchtenberg, William E. *Franklin D. Roosevelt and the New Deal, 1932–1940.* 1963.

VERNON J. WILLIAMS, JR.

NATIONAL LAWYERS GUILD

During the Depression years there were approximately 140,000 lawyers in the United States, almost half of whom had incomes below the poverty line. Four out of five were not members of the American Bar Association, the national conservative association that at the time admitted few women and no African Americans.

In 1936 about 1,200 lawyers met in New York City in support of President Franklin D. Roosevelt's "court-packing plan," which aimed to add new members to the Supreme Court who would no longer rule that New Deal legislation was unconstitutional. The group that met in New York included unemployed lawyers in the Lawyers Security League, which was pressing for Works Progress Administration positions and unemployment compensation; lawyers representing new labor unions affiliated with the CIO; law professors who taught and advocated legal realism; various New Deal lawyers and elected officials; members of the Communist Party Lawyers Club, who were committed to Marxism and to developing new tactics to win difficult political cases; African-American members of the National Bar Association and the National Association for the Advancement of Colored People who were excluded from renting downtown office space in some cities and from using libraries in the South; many Jewish members of the International Juridical Association, which included women; and some Socialist lawyers.

This meeting led to founding the National Lawyers Guild in Washington, D.C., in 1937. The Guild's goals included "to aid in making the United States and state constitutions . . . the law," and all government and judicial agencies "responsive to the will of the American people." The Guild also hoped "to protect and foster our democratic institutions and civil rights and liberties of all the people; to aid in the establishment of governmental . . .

agencies to supply adequate legal service to all . . . ; to advance the economic well-being of the members of the legal profession, and to improve the relations between the legal profession and the community at large; to encourage, in the study of the law, a consideration of the social and economic aspects of the law; [and] to improve the ethical standards which must guide the lawyer." Finally, the National Lawyers Guild was formed to promote the ideal that "human rights shall be more sacred than property rights." The organization elected Wisconsin Governor Philip F. La Follette and Washington Senator Homer T. Bone to its temporary executive committee. It then elected Minnesota Supreme Court justice John P. Devaney as its first president.

Guild members in private practice fought political deportations and anti-strike injunctions (risking disbarment in Ohio), while government lawyers in the National Labor Relations Board faced open defiance in the South. A few Guild members also fought in the Abraham Lincoln Brigade during the Spanish Civil War. In 1939 Morris Ernst, a leader of the America Civil Liberties Union (and a friend of FBI director J. Edgar Hoover), demanded a resolution from the Guild expressing opposition to "Communism, Fascism, and Nazism," a proposal that the executive board rejected unanimously as divisive. Amid innumerable subpoenas to appear before the new Dies Un-American Activities Committee in the U.S. Congress and similar state committees, most government lawyers resigned from the Guild. Robert Kenny, who later became California attorney general, then became Guild president.

During World War II, Guild members worked for the War Labor Board, joined the military services and demanded an end to racial segregation, represented unions struggling against race and sex discrimination, and called for an excess profits tax on war industries. The Guild strongly supported Roosevelt's "four freedoms" and worked for a full employment law, Social Security coverage for lawyers and other self-employed workers, a fair employment practices commission, anti-lynching legislation, a constitutional amendment to outlaw southern poll taxes, a public defender system for indigent criminal defendants, and low-cost neighborhood law offices. The Guild strongly supported Roosevelt's proposal, with Winston Churchill and Joseph Stalin, for a United Nations organization to work against all future wars.

Immediately after World War II, Attorney General Herbert Brownell sought to put the National Lawyers Guild on a list of "subversive" organizations. The Guild defeated this effort, but by 1956 had declined to only about five hundred members nationally. The National Lawyers Guild is one of the very few New Deal-era organizations that survived into the twenty-first century. In 2003, the Guild had some seven thousand members and chapters in every state. Among its members were lawyers, law professors, law students and legal workers.

See Also: LEGAL PROFESSION; SUPREME COURT "PACKING" CONTROVERSY.

BIBLIOGRAPHY

Emerson, Thomas I. *Young Lawyer for the New Deal: An Insider's Memoir of the Roosevelt Years.* 1991.

Ginger, Ann Fagan. *Carol Weiss King: Human Rights Lawyer 1895–1952.* 1993.

Ginger, Ann Fagan, and Eugene M. Tobin, eds. *The National Lawyers Guild: From Roosevelt through Reagan.* 1988.

Lazarus, Isidore. "The Economic Crisis in the Legal Profession." *National Lawyers Guild Quarterly* 1, no. 1 (December 1937).

National Lawyers Guild v. Attorney General Brownell, 215 F. 2d 485 (CA DC 1954); 225 F. 2d 552 (CA DC 1955), cert. den. 351 U.S. 927 (1956).

ANN FAGAN GINGER

NATIONAL NEGRO CONGRESS

The idea of a representative assembly for all of black America began with John P. Davis, a militant civil rights activist of the 1920s and 1930s. At a Howard University conference in Washington, D.C., in 1935, Davis, Ralph Bunche, and other prominent African Americans decided to push ahead. A year later the first National Negro Congress met in Chicago and included some 817 delegates representing 585 religious, labor, civic, and fraternal groups.

They intended to pursue racial justice at home and abroad by securing "the right of the Negro people to be free from Jim Crowism. . .and mob violence" and otherwise promoting "the spirit of unity and cooperation between Negro and white people." Prominent members included not only Bunche and Davis, who served as executive secretary, but A. Philip Randolph of the Brotherhood of Sleeping Car Porters. Randolph was elected president.

If this ambitious coalition held great promise given the particular problems black Americans faced during the Great Depression years, its scope also made it vulnerable to factionalism. Predictably, the nation's most prominent civil rights group, the National Association for the Advancement of Colored People (NAACP), saw the National Negro Congress as a rival and kept its distance. Roy Wilkins, nonetheless, attended the Chicago convention as an observer and several local NAACP activists were more directly involved. Davis had more success courting the National Urban League and the Congress of Industrial Organizations (CIO), focusing on a working-class constituency that the NAACP largely ignored even during the Depression's depths. That focus, however, led to an increasing Communist Party presence.

The National Negro Congress's accomplishments were substantial given the constraints of the times. On the grassroots level, the Congress helped organize boycotts, rent strikes, and other direct-action protests against racial discrimination. Meanwhile, Davis convinced the CIO to recruit black members and the WPA Federal Writers Project to guarantee positions for black writers. Whether organizing voting drives in New York or condemning imperialism in Africa and fascism in Germany, the National Negro Congress was very active through the late 1930s, emerging as a force that could not be ignored. With President Franklin D. Roosevelt sending greetings to its annual meetings, even the NAACP's Walter White felt compelled to participate.

Yet, the National Negro Congress fell apart as quickly as it had come together. The Nazi-Soviet Pact of 1939 led to a raucous debate culminating in Randolph's decision to leave the organization and begin work on an all-black March on Washington movement. When other prominent members left and general membership plummeted, what was left of the National Negro Congress remained largely in Communist hands. In 1946, the Congress joined two other organizations, the International Labor Defense and the National Federation for Constitutional Liberties, to form the Civil Rights Congress. Under pressure from the Federal Bureau of Investigation, the House Committee on Un-American Activities, the Subversive Activities Control Board, and the Internal Revenue Service, the Civil Rights Congress closed its doors for good in 1956, citing declining membership and the legal costs of defending itself against the Cold War's investigatory apparatus.

See Also: AFRICAN AMERICANS, IMPACT OF THE GREAT DEPRESSION ON; BUNCHE, RALPH; RANDOLPH, A. PHILIP.

BIBLIOGRAPHY

Jensen, Hilmar L. "The Rise of an African American Left: John P. Davis and the National Negro Congress." Ph.D. diss., Cornell University, 1997.

FBI File on the National Negro Congress. Microfilm ed. Wilmington, Del.: Scholarly Resources, Inc.

National Negro Congress Papers. Schomburg Center for Research in Black Culture. New York Public Library.

KENNETH O'REILLY

NATIONAL RECOVERY ADMINISTRATION (NRA)

On June 16, 1933, President Franklin D. Roosevelt signed the National Industrial Recovery Act (NIRA), an ambitious effort to hasten recovery from the Depression and cure economic ills through public works spending and industrial self-government. The program for industrial self-government, which harked back to World War I when business and government had cooperated through the War Industries Board to mobilize American industry for war, was based on the assumption that businessmen, coordinated and assisted by the federal government, could bring about

A restaurant worker posts an NRA blue eagle sign in a window in 1934 to show the establishment's support for the government program. FRANKLIN DELANO ROOSEVELT LIBRARY

industrial recovery and social progress. Under industrial self-government, representatives of business, labor, and government would draft agreements, or codes, of "fair" business and labor practices for each of the nation's major industries. Among other things, the codes could include provisions for controls on prices, production, and marketing and were required to include provisions for minimum wages, maximum hours, and the right of workers to organize and bargain collectively. Through the codes, it was hoped, cutthroat competition, overproduction, labor conflict, and deflationary prices would be checked, leading the nation into a new era of prosperity and industrial harmony.

Roosevelt entrusted responsibility for implementing industrial self-government to the newly formed National Recovery Administration (NRA). Headed by Hugh S. Johnson, a former army officer and businessman, it had to chart a path through a bewildering maze of conflicting business and labor pressures. Less prosperous industries, such as cotton textiles and petroleum, generally favored codification in the hope that it would restore profitability. More prosperous industries, for example steel and automobiles, were less interested in codification than in putting brakes on it to forestall unwanted government interference. There were inter-industry conflicts between new and declining industries and intra-industry conflicts between large and small firms, regions or sections, and manufacturers and distributors. Moreover, labor expected to benefit greatly from the NIRA, while many businessmen were determined to minimize the influence of unions.

Johnson was in a difficult position for dealing with the conflicting pressures. The NIRA included coercive measures such as federal licensing and presidential authority to impose or modify codes to keep business, which under the ideology of industrial self-government would have the dominant voice, from turning code making into an orgy of profit taking at the expense of workers and consumers. But concerned about the constitutionality of NRA, Johnson was reluctant to use the coercive features out of fear they could lead the U.S. Supreme Court to rule against the NRA. In addition, he believed businessmen had to have the prospect of reasonable profits if they were to afford the higher labor costs inherent in NRA. Thus Johnson decided to depend upon the voluntary cooperation of business in codification and hope it would not lose sight of the public interest in its desire to restore profitability.

The NRA initially concentrated on those industries that were either strong supporters of industrial self-government or sufficiently organized through trade associations to permit speedy codification. The code for the cotton textile industry was the first to be completed. Approved by Roosevelt in July 1933, it provided for collective bargaining, reduced working days, and minimum wages. It also abolished child labor, achieving something that neither law nor constitutional amendment had been able to do in forty years. Despite these gains for labor, the Cotton Textile Institute, the industry trade association, dominated the drafting process and fashioned a code to its liking with the strong backing of Johnson, who wanted to get the industry codified quickly and use this bell-weather industry to let business know it had nothing to fear from the NRA. As a result, the industry got nearly everything it wanted, including strong production controls and industry dominance of the code enforcement agency.

During the summer and fall of 1933 codes for the nation's other largest industries as well as hundreds of smaller industries were drafted. With some exceptions, they followed the general pattern of the cotton textile code. Businessmen possessed a monopoly of information about their own industries, and when combined with "a lack of state capacity" and the weakness of labor, they held sway in the code-making process. Labor received some benefits in the form of maximum hours, minimum wages, and the right to have unions, although in many cases the wages were at very low levels, and unions were circumscribed by crippling qualifications or the steadfast determination of business to resist unionization on anything but its own terms. In return for these small concessions to workers, business got all manner of price, production, and marketing restrictions and was largely invested with the enforcement of the codes. The code for the burlesque industry even went so far as to restrict the number of times a stripper could remove her clothes each day. For the most part, representatives of organized labor and spokesmen for consumers were largely ignored in the drafting process and had little standing with the code authorities, the bodies that were charged with enforcement of the codes and were dominated by trade association members. In effect, when the nation was mired in the Depression and in need of immediate expansion of production, jobs, and income, the NRA permitted business to put in place restrictive policies that would actually hinder recovery.

As industries were drafting specific codes, they were asked by the NRA to adhere to a voluntary blanket code (the President's Reemployment Agreement) that Johnson introduced for all industries in July 1933. Providing for minimum wages and maximum hours, it was designed to speed codification, which was lagging in many industries, and inject some badly needed confidence into the economy. The code was to be in effect from August 1 to December 31, 1933, or until the employer's specific industry was codified. Businessmen who agreed to abide by the blanket code were to display the symbol of the NRA, a Blue Eagle accompanied by the words "We Do Our Part," on a placard in their window or on their products. Consumers were to give their business only to those firms that adhered to the code.

Johnson mobilized the nation behind the Blue Eagle with a war mobilization psychology reminiscent of the liberty bond drives of 1917 and 1918. The NRA orchestrated a great outpouring of ballyhoo and patriotic appeal replete with radio speakers, motorcades, torchlight processions, mass rallies, parades, and a nationwide speaking tour by Johnson. Businessmen and the public quickly enlisted in the NRA's army of Depression fighters. The Blue Eagle appeared on posters, billboards, flags, movie screens, magazines, newspapers, and numerous products. Beauty contestants had the Blue Eagle stamped on their thighs, and in Philadelphia fans cheered a new professional football team dubbed the Eagles after the NRA's icon. The Blue Eagle campaign was a success. The national surge around it helped quicken the pace of code drafting, and, according to NRA data, payrolls grew. The boomlet, however, did not last. Neither government nor private spending injected enough purchasing power into the economy to sustain it, and before long many of those who had been recently hired were again unemployed.

By the fall of 1933, the NRA was mired in controversy. Johnson, a highly emotional individual and prone to erratic behavior, drank too much, appeared to have an improper relationship with his secretary, and feuded with other government officials, businessmen such as Henry Ford who refused to cooperate with the NRA, and members of the press. Economists and consumer representatives claimed that businessmen were raising prices faster than wages. Labor leaders charged that businessmen were perverting workers' right to form unions by herding them into company unions. Problems with code compliance were widespread, and when the NRA did respond it seemed to crack down on the "little guy" and permit larger firms to violate the codes at will. In the cotton textile industry, for example, mill owners fired employees and rehired them as "apprentices," who could be paid less than the minimum wage. Former President Herbert Hoover and Senator Huey P. Long of Louisiana compared the NRA to fascism, an absurd charge but one many took seriously. Even many of the business supporters of industrial self-government began to lose confidence in the NRA as the agency's labor and consumer advisory boards started to raise disturbing questions about code provisions and call for greater participation by labor and con-

sumer groups in the code authorities. If business could not run industrial self-government as it saw fit, many businessmen preferred to see the NRA scrapped. Reflecting the growing disenchantment with the NRA, many said the initials NRA had come to mean "No Recovery Allowed"; to others, they stood for "National Run Around."

The controversy engulfing NRA came to center on the price problem and labor policy. The NRA offered business the prospect of higher profits through price increases, and Johnson believed price increases were necessary if business was to afford the higher wages workers had been promised. Consequently, he consented to numerous price protection provisions in codes, including price controls through prohibition of sales below costs and, in a few industries, direct price-fixing. Taking advantage of these provisions, business began to raise prices substantially.

Opposition to the price-control measures developed quickly. Within the NRA the Consumers' Advisory Board and the Research and Planning Division criticized the price concessions made to business and called for Johnson to protect the interests of consumers. On Capitol Hill, Senators William Borah of Idaho and Gerald Nye of North Dakota charged that NRA's price policies were undercutting small businesses by eliminating the lower prices they often used to compete with larger firms. The National Industrial Recovery Board, a special board set up in early 1934 to look into the price issue, also lashed out at the NRA for hurting small businesses. Unable to quiet the growing clamor over prices, Johnson issued Office Memorandum 228 on June 7, 1934. It prohibited price-fixing arrangements in future codes, but because more than 90 percent of NRA-subject industries had already been codified, the memorandum had little practical effect. Nevertheless, it indicated that future NRA price policy would no longer be directed at large-scale price regulation.

In the matter of labor policy, the NRA followed a pro-management approach. Labor read Section 7a of the NIRA, which gave workers the right to have unions led by representatives of their own choosing, to mean workers could form their own independent unions and that if a union successfully organized a majority of workers in a company it could speak for all the workers. Johnson, meanwhile, said that workers were free to have a union, whether it be an independent or a company union, or not have a union, that employers were not under any obligation to reach an agreement with a union, and that individuals or minorities were free to do their own bargaining and make agreements separate from the union. Encouraged by Johnson's interpretation of Section 7a, business used company unions, multiple representation (more than one union representing workers in a company), the open or nonunion shop, and intimidation of workers to resist the organizing drives of those favoring independent unions. Except for limited gains in the coal, automobile, and steel industries, most organizing drives were unsuccessful.

To adjudicate disputes arising out of Section 7a, Roosevelt in August 1933 established the National Labor Board (NLB). Before long, however, Johnson and the NLB were at odds, for the NLB refused to support his position on multiple representation and was less tolerant of company unions. Frustrated by the intransigence of business and the failure to gain the full support of NRA, labor increasingly looked to strikes rather than the NRA to advance its interests. As strikes spread, Johnson rushed into disputes in the automobile, coal, textile, and steel industries, helping to arrange settlements that generally left labor disappointed and convinced that the NRA was a tool of management. In response to labor's criticism of NRA's policies, Roosevelt in June 1934 replaced the NLB with the National Labor Relations Board. Separate from NRA, it was to investigate and mediate labor disputes and hold elections for workers to decide what representation they desired, relegating the NRA to a secondary position in labor policy.

By the summer of 1934 it was obvious that Johnson, now on the verge of physical and mental collapse, had outlasted his usefulness. Officials inside and outside of the NRA said they could no longer work with Johnson, and heeding their warnings that he was dragging down NRA, Roosevelt removed him from the NRA in September. Johnson's removal eliminated a major sore spot for the NRA, but the more fundamental problems regarding policy remained.

Some believed the program of industrial self-government was so bankrupt it should be allowed to expire in June 1935 when the NRA's two-year charter was scheduled for renewal. Others concluded that Roosevelt should let the NRA die and preserve its best features through separate enactments. Roosevelt decided in February 1935 to ask Congress to renew the NRA on a more progressive basis than the original version, with specific requests for retaining Section 7a, restriction of price and production controls, and the application of the antitrust laws against monopolies. By this time Congress was cooling toward the NRA. Six weeks of hearings in the spring of 1935 by the Senate Finance Committee, which was stacked with opponents of the agency, provided critics with a field day to attack NRA. The hearings were accompanied by the release of a damaging report from the Brookings Institution. While granting that the NRA might have instilled some optimism into the economy in the summer of 1933, it castigated the program for retarding recovery, hurting wage earners, and reducing the volume of production. The combination of the Finance Committee's hearings and the Brookings report shattered what was left of the NRA's support on Capitol Hill.

Before Congress could act on Roosevelt's request, the Supreme Court brought an abrupt end to the NRA. Johnson had avoided testing the constitutionality of the NRA out of fear the court would rule against the agency. Roosevelt, however, believed the NRA's constitutionality must be confirmed if the codes were to be enforced. He choose a case involving the Schechter brothers of Brooklyn, New York, who had violated the live poultry code by ignoring wage and hour regulations, filing false sales and price reports, and selling diseased chickens. For the latter reason it came to be known as the "sick chicken" case. Johnson's original concern proved correct. On May 27, 1935, in a nine to nothing decision, the justices found that Title I of NIRA, the enabling measure for NRA, was an invalid delegation of legislative power to the president and an unconstitutional regulation of intrastate commerce. The ideal of industrial self-government did not die completely with the NRA, though. During the next two years Congress passed legislation continuing NRA-type price-and-production controls for the coal, petroleum, and retail trades industries. But beyond these industries, there was little support for industrial self-government as a means for overall economic recovery or social progress.

In its early months the NRA helped check the deflationary spiral and provided a temporary psychological boost to the economy and the nation's spirit. It also consolidated social innovations like the abolition of child labor, the right of workers to have unions, and the elimination of unfair trade practices. But ultimately the NRA failed. Its failure can be explained in part by Johnson's leadership. In the final analysis, however, the NRA failed because of its underlying premise. Industrial self-government was grounded in the belief that the various segments of the economy could look beyond their own interests and work together for the national welfare. This belief was naïve in the case of organized business. Starved for profits and often unwilling to accept labor as even a junior partner, it pursued its own interests and used the NRA to restrict production, raise prices, and thwart labor's aspirations. If the NRA had endured, the likely result, in the words of Ellis Hawley, "would have been economic stagnation, permanent unemployment, and the perpetuation of a depression standard of living, at least for the majority of the people."

See Also: BUSINESSMEN; COLLECTIVE BARGAINING; CONSUMERISM; JOHNSON, HUGH; NATIONAL INDUSTRIAL RECOVERY ACT (NIRA); NATIONAL LABOR RELATIONS BOARD (NLRB); SUPREME COURT.

BIBLIOGRAPHY

Bellush, Bernard. *The Failure of the NRA.* 1975.

Bernstein, Irving. *The Turbulent Years: A History of the American Worker, 1933–1941.* 1970.

Blanchard. Margaret A. "Freedom of the Press and the Newspaper Code: June 1933-February 1934." *Journalism Quarterly* 54 (1977): 40–49.

Brand, Donald R. *Corporatism and the Rule of Law: A Study of the National Recovery Administration.* 1988.

Fine, Sidney. *The Automobile under the Blue Eagle: Labor, Management and the Automobile Manufacturing Code.* 1963.

Galambos, Louis. *Competition and Cooperation: The Emergence of a National Trade Association.* 1966.

Hawley, Ellis W. *The New Deal and the Problem of Monopoly: A Study in Economic Ambivalence.* 1966.

Johnson, Hugh S. *The Blue Eagle from Egg to Earth.* 1935.

Johnson, James P. *The Politics of Soft Coal: The Bituminous Coal Industry from World War I through the New Deal.* 1979.

Lyon, Leverett S., et al. *The National Recovery Administration: An Analysis and Appraisal.* 1935.

Martin, George. *Madam Secretary: Frances Perkins.* 1976.

Moody, Jesse Carroll, Jr. "The Steel Industry and the National Recovery Administration: An Experiment in Industrial Self-Government." Ph.D. diss., University of Oklahoma. 1965.

Ohl, John Kennedy. *Hugh S. Johnson and the New Deal.* 1985.

Richberg, Donald R. *My Hero: The Indiscreet Memoirs of an Eventful but Unheroic Life.* 1954.

Robbins, William G. "The Great Experiment in Industrial Self-Government: The Lumber Industry and the National Recovery Administration." *Journal of Forest History* 25 (1981): 128–143.

Roos, Charles Frederick. *NRA Economic Planning.* 1937.

Schlesinger, Arthur M., Jr. *The Age of Roosevelt,* Vol. 2: *The Coming of the New Deal.* 1958.

Skocpol, Theda, and Finegold, Kenneth. "State Capacity and Economic Intervention in the Early New Deal." *Political Science Quarterly* 97 (1982): 255–278.

Vadney, Thomas E. *The Wayward Liberal: A Political Biography of Donald Richberg.* 1970.

Wolvin, Andrew Davis. "The 1933 Blue Eagle Campaign: A Study in Persuasion and Coercion." Ph.D. diss., Purdue University. 1968.

JOHN KENNEDY OHL

NATIONAL RESOURCES PLANNING BOARD (NRPB)

Between 1933 and 1943, the National Resources Planning Board (NRPB) served as the only national planning agency in U.S. history. Created in July 1933, the NRPB had consistent leadership from planner Frederic A. Delano, political scientist Charles E. Merriam, and economist Wesley Clair Mitchell. In 1936, business leaders Henry S. Dennison and Beardsley Ruml replaced Mitchell. The board evolved from public works planning to broader social and economic planning.

NRPB advisory national planning became a policy process bringing together social scientists, executive and legislative branches, and private and public institutions. A small staff of experts, temporary consultants, and field branches conducted studies of land use, multi-use water planning, natural resources, population, industrial structure, transportation, science, and technology that provided the first national inventories of significant American resources. Regional planning groups were created in New England and the Pacific Northwest. Most states established planning agencies, while planning boards emerged in many cities.

The NRPB responded to key national needs: new policy in reaction to the recession of 1937 to 1938, reorganization of the executive branch (the Reorganization Act of 1939), industrial site location studies in wartime, and postwar planning. Funded with emergency monies until 1939, the NRPB worked under the direction of President Franklin D. Roosevelt. Rising tensions between Congress and the president led to controversy over wartime and postwar planning that culminated in a 1943 abolition of the board.

Drawing on a social science research network built in the 1900 to 1933 period, the NRPB's planning vision reflected the evolution of a new political economy centered on interest-group competition, cooperation, and conflict. NRPB legacies included compensatory spending policy, executive reorganization, wartime and postwar planning, an early version of the G.I. Bill of Rights, the Second (Economic) Bill of Rights (a manifesto for postwar liberalism), and an institutionalized policy planning process via the Council of Economic Advisers and the annual federal budget process established by the Employment Act of 1946.

See Also: PLANNING; RECESSION OF 1937; REORGANIZATION ACT OF 1939.

BIBLIOGRAPHY

Clawson, Marion. *New Deal Planning: The National Resources Planning Board.* 1981.

Lepawsky, Albert. "Style and Substance in Contemporary Planning: The American New Deal's National Resources Planning Board as a Model." *Plan Canada* 18 (September/December 1978): 153–187.

Reagan, Patrick D. *Designing a New America: The Origins of New Deal Planning, 1890–1943.* 2000.

Warken, Philip W. *A History of the National Resources Planning Board, 1933–1943.* 1979.

PATRICK D. REAGAN

NATIONAL URBAN LEAGUE

The National Urban League was established in 1911 through the merger of three related organizations: the Committee on Urban Conditions among Negroes in New York, the National League for the Protection of Colored Women, and the Committee for Improving Industrial Conditions among Negroes. Between the time of its founding and the Great Depression, the National Urban League focused on a range of goals, which included: changing the interracial status quo by encouraging whites "to work with African Americans for their mutual advantage and advancement," establishing a social work program at Fisk University to train African-American social workers, securing financial support for local Urban League branches from local community chests such as the United Way, and the establishment of *Opportunity* magazine in 1925 as a publicity vehicle for presenting "factual data on African-American life to businessmen, government officials, labor leaders, and organized and unorganized white workers."

The Depression and the New Deal had an enormous impact on the National Urban League's activities, policies, and programs. By the time of the stock market crash of 1929, close to 300,000 black industrial workers were unemployed. Less than a third of these would find work through employment offices. The majority of the jobs that the National Urban League was able to secure were for African-American women in domestic work. The Depression years pushed the League to the brink of bankruptcy. That it survived was due in large part to the heroic efforts of its executive board and a few staunch contributors. The crisis prevented the National Urban League from cutting back on activities so the staff had to return a portion of their salaries. With so many white people out of work, employers could hardly be expected to listen to appeals from the Urban League. The League was forced to change its strategy from industrial relations to protecting African-American jobs from the invasion of white workers.

African Americans benefited from the New Deal, but not without a struggle in which the Urban League played a major role by assuring that African Americans received equal treatment for programs responsible for economic relief. From the beginning, the National Urban League criticized New Deal programs for neglecting to curtail widespread discrimination against African Americans.

The Depression and New Deal legislation, along with the groundswell of African-American frustration, forced the National Urban League to break with its tradition of polite interpersonal diplomacy in the worlds of business and labor. It shifted to protest and embraced the strategy and tactics of mass letter-writing campaigns, petitions, and the lobbying of members of Congress for the benefit of African Americans. As a result, the Urban League was able to maintain influence among African Americans suffering from the effects of the Depression and the racial exclusion of New Deal programs.

Part of the Urban League's new strategy was the establishment of emergency advisory councils and workers councils in key urban centers throughout the country and the building of alliances between African Americans and organized labor. In 1933 the League joined other interracial and African-American organizations to form the Joint Committee on National Recovery. Limited by lack of funds and staff, the Committee nonetheless managed to lobby in Washington, D.C., on behalf of African Americans and expose the public to the failure of New Deal programs to address the needs of African Americans.

The National Urban League contributed its share to the recovery efforts by providing crucial studies and African-American specialists to advise the Roosevelt administration. The organization believed that New Dealers needed accurate information about racial problems before they could provide solutions. This data was also used by the Urban League to buttress its case for administrative and legislative reforms.

Throughout most of the Depression the Rockefeller, Carnegie, and the Friedsam foundations funded more that half of the National Urban League's annual budget. African-American organizations did their share as well, on both local and national levels. The Delta Sigma Theta sorority worked with and financially supported the League. Robert S. Abbott, editor of the *Chicago Defender*, and A. Phillip Randolph, head of the Brotherhood of Sleeping Car Porters, worked with the National Urban League to protect the rights of black workers in New Deal programs. Locally, the Michigan People's Finance Corporation in Detroit provided the Detroit Urban League with free rent throughout the Depression.

See Also: AFRICAN AMERICANS, IMPACT OF THE GREAT DEPRESSION ON; RACE AND ETHNIC RELATIONS.

BIBLIOGRAPHY

Giddings, Paula. *In Search of Sisterhood: Delta Sigma Theta and the Challenge of the Black Sorority Movement.* 1988.

Strickland, Arvarh E. *History of the Chicago Urban League.* 1974.

Thomas, Richard W. *Life for Us Is What We Make It: Building the Black Community in Detroit, 1915–1945.* 1992.

Trotter, Joe William, Jr. "From A Raw Deal to a New Deal, 1929–1945." In *To Make Our World Anew: A History of African Americans,* edited by Robin D. G. Kelly and Earl Lewis. 2000.

Weiss, Nancy J. *The National Urban League: 1910–1940.* 1974.

RICHARD W. THOMAS

NATIONAL WOMEN'S PARTY

After the Nineteenth Amendment provided for woman's suffrage in 1920, most activists reorganized as the League of Women Voters. A few militant activists, however, wanted more for women than suffrage, and they pursued that goal through the National Women's Party, which was formed in 1916 by Alice Stokes Paul and others. Although membership never topped fifty thousand, the National Women's Party was active and vocal, promising to support female political candidates but never putting up its own.

In 1921, the National Women's Party declared its primary objective to be the passage of a national equal rights amendment (ERA) to the U.S. Constitution. Paul drafted an amendment in 1923 to eliminate gender discrimination in federal, state, and local laws: "Men and women shall have equal rights throughout the United States and every place subject to its jurisdiction." Although a few congressmen sponsored the bill, by 1938 it had only been reported to the House Judiciary Committee three times.

During the 1920s, the National Women's Party tried to enlist the League of Women Voters and other women's groups to lobby through the Women's Joint Congressional Committee for the passage of the ERA and other legislation of interest to women, including child labor laws, nondiscriminatory civil service classifications, the formation of a federal bureau of education, and the establishment of uniform marriage and divorce laws. Members of the Women's Joint Congressional Committee, however, adamantly opposed the ERA. Many women's groups, including the League of Women Voters, the National Women's Trade Union League, the National Federation of Business and Professional Women's Clubs, the American Association of University Women, the General Federation of Women's Clubs, and the National Council of Jewish Women opposed the ERA on the basis that it would be detrimental to existing legislation that protected women. The National Women's Party, on the other hand, considered such protective laws, such as those limiting women's working hours, as discriminatory and advocated "not removal of protection, but removal of the sex basis in protective laws." Opponents to the ERA also claimed the amendment would allow women to be drafted into the army, would endanger child custody, and would force women to pay alimony.

The National Women's Party lost ground during the Depression as many businesses ruled against the employment of married women, who were accused of taking jobs from men, the "bread-winners." The 1932 Economy Act, which allowed the firing of married women whose husbands were employed by the government, was not repealed until 1937. In addition, half of the states prohibited married women from working and three-fourths of states banned married women from being hired as teachers. National Women's Party member Alma Lutz charged that the enemies of married women workers were not men but single women "obsessed with the idea that their salvation depends upon barring married women from paid labor."

The National Women's Party also tried to fight discrimination against women in New Deal programs. The National Recovery Administration's (NRA) Labor Advisory Board codes, for example, allowed lower wages for women doing the same work as men, while section 213 of the National Industrial Recovery Act forced two-thirds of women civil service workers to resign. The Civilian Conservation Corps was open only to men, and did not hire any of America's four million unemployed women. Secretary of Labor Frances Perkins and Eleanor Roosevelt's network of women also held firm against the National Women's Party and its goals. Only the National Federation of Business and Professional Women's Clubs broke ranks, finding that protective laws hindered business and professional women as the 1938 Fair Labor Standards Act gave minimum wage and maximum hours protection to both sexes.

Frustrated with the party's lack of success in the United States, Paul expanded activism internationally as chair of the Nationality Committee of the Inter-American Commission on Women, on the executive committee of Equal Rights International in Geneva, and on the Committee on Nationality of the League of Nations. Perkins, however, squelched National Women's Party efforts to put the ERA before the 1936 Buenos Aires Inter-American Peace Conference. There were steps forward, however, when the Democratic Party endorsed the ERA in 1944, and Eleanor Roosevelt withdrew her opposition to the amendment. Although the 1945 United Nations Charter had an equal rights for women resolution, the ERA was not approved by the U.S. Congress until 1972. Thereafter, the amendment was sent to the states for ratification, but was not approved.

See Also: GENDER ROLES AND SEXUAL RELATIONS, IMPACT OF THE GREAT DEPRESSION ON; WOMEN, IMPACT OF THE GREAT DEPRESSION ON.

BIBLIOGRAPHY

Chambers, Clarke A. "The Campaign for Women's Rights in the 1920s." In *Our American Sisters: Women in American Life and Thought,* 3rd edition, edited by Jean E. Friedman and William G. Shade. 1982.

Perkins, Frances. "So Women in Industry Need Special Protection? Yes." *Survey* 55, no. 10 (1926): 529–531.

Sicherman, Barbara, and Carol Hurd Green, eds. *Notable American Women: The Modern Period.* 1980.

Sochen, June. *Movers and Shakers: American Women Thinkers and Activists, 1900–1970.* 1973.

Ware, Susan. *Beyond Suffrage: Women in the New Deal.* 1981.

Woloch, Nancy. *Women and the American Experience.* 1984.

BLANCHE M. G. LINDEN

NATIONAL YOUTH ADMINISTRATION (NYA)

When in May 1934 Eleanor Roosevelt admitted her fear that the United States was in danger of losing a whole generation of young people, there was good reason for her anxiety. Available statistics indicated that as many as 50 percent of Americans between sixteen and twenty-four years old who were in the labor market were unemployed. Unskilled and untrained, they were seemingly incapable of becoming productive adults. Though the Franklin D. Roosevelt administration had moved swiftly to deal with the worst aspects of the problem, most notably with the creation in 1933 of the Civilian Conservation Corps (CCC), these first measures were little more than stopgaps, catering to the most desperate cases only. The National Youth Administration (NYA) was the New Deal's attempt to combat the problem of youth unemployment on a more long-term basis.

Created by executive order on June 26, 1935, as part of the new Works Progress Administration (WPA), the NYA had twin functions from the start.

One goal was to help needy young people stay in school or in college, enabling them both to develop their skills and talents and to keep out of the hopelessly swollen labor market. The second, more difficult function was to provide assistance to young people no longer in school, but out of work. Such youths needed both immediate relief and job training that would be useful once recovery came. To head the new agency, Roosevelt selected the outspoken Southern liberal Aubrey Willis Williams. Already the WPA's deputy-director, Williams remained the NYA's head throughout its existence. Clearly identified with the New Deal's left wing, Williams was determined to use the new agency to help black youths and white youths equally. Symbolic of this commitment was the early appointment of the distinguished black educator Mary McLeod Bethune to an important position in the agency's administrative structure.

The student work program was relatively easy to organize. It was largely run by the schools and colleges themselves, and by early 1937 more than 400,000 young people were receiving regular stipends in return for performing useful tasks on their various campuses. In all, more than two million young people completed their education while receiving NYA assistance. The program for out-of-school youth was more difficult to manage. The first work projects were often high-labor low-capital-outlay affairs like cleaning up public buildings or developing local parks. Such projects were useful to the communities involved, but failed to impart practical job skills. As soon as possible, therefore, Williams redirected the NYA's emphasis into the acquirement of permanent skills, and, after 1939, even more specifically into training youth for defense industry work. As such, the NYA introduced its enrollees to machines, gave them basic shop training, and then poured them into the nation's rapidly reviving industrial plants. By 1942 the NYA had become a crucial adjunct to the war effort, something thousands of employers all over the country enthusiastically attested to.

Congress abolished the NYA in 1943 over the president's strenuous objections. The program was a victim of the drive to prune federal expenditures to the bone, but its cancellation was also an expres-

Young women take typing lessons sponsored by the National Youth Administration in Illinois in 1937. FRANKLIN DELANO ROOSEVELT LIBRARY

sion of distaste for Williams as a symbol of extreme New Dealism. The accomplishments of the NYA had been numerous, however, and it remains one of the best examples of what enlightened, committed people can achieve when they have the public behind them, if only for a short time.

See Also: BETHUNE, MARY MCLEOD; CHILDREN AND ADOLESCENTS, IMPACT OF THE GREAT DEPRESSION ON; WILLIAMS, AUBREY.

BIBLIOGRAPHY

Jacobson, Paul B. "Youth at Work." *Bulletin of the National Association of Secondary School Principals* 25, no. 99 (1941): 114–119.

Lindley, Ernest K., and Betty Lindley. *A New Deal for Youth: The Story of the National Youth Administration.* 1938. Reprint, 1972.

Reiman, Richard A. *The New Deal and American Youth: Ideas and Ideals in a Depression Decade.* 1992.

Salmond, John A. *A Southern Rebel: The Life and Times of Aubrey Willis Williams, 1890–1965.* 1983.

JOHN A. SALMOND

NATIVE AMERICANS, IMPACT OF THE GREAT DEPRESSION ON

Before the Great Depression and the Indian New Deal, ethnocidal policies devastated Native-American individuals and nations. Between 1887 and 1933, over half of the tribal land base was lost to land thieves, tax sales, and governmental sales of "surplus lands." These policies launched a cycle of poverty that continues at the beginning of the twenty-first century. Thus, lack of education and ill health became hallmarks of tribal societies in the United States. But these racist missionary and civilizing policies did not bring the benefits of American civilization to Native-American people. Instead, many native peoples strengthened their resolve to nurture and cleave to their old traditional ways.

This period of ethnocide or "forced assimilation" was the worst period of Native-American civil rights. In spite of constitutional affirmations, Native-American property rights, free speech, and free exercise of religion were denied. On a more fundamental level, the right of Native-American tribes to continue their distinct tribal status was violated systematically. To this day, the damage to native individuals and communities and the economic rights of Native Americans has not been mended.

INDIAN CITIZENSHIP ACT

After World War I, some enlightened Native Americans and white individuals decided to reform these oppressive "assimilation" policies with new legislation. Although many Native Americans had become U. S. citizens through "competency commissions" and treaties, Congress unilaterally granted citizenship to all Native Americans in 1924. However, many natives were wary of being declared citizens through "competency" since it often meant that their federal land allotments and treaty rights were no longer protected and thus subject to

confiscation or sale. A significant amount of the tribal estate was taken from Native Americans through fraud and state tax sales. In fact, thousands of newly created Native-American citizens saw their lands removed from federal protection and sold out from under them during the 1920 and 1930s.

Many Native-American leaders asserted that the American Indian Citizenship Act of 1924 was a mischief-maker in Native-American policy. They did not like the way it was imposed without consultation and consent from native communities. The Tuscarora chief, Clinton Rickard, summarized the views of many Native Americans by stating:

> The Citizenship Act did pass in 1924 despite our strong opposition. By its provisions all Indians were automatically made United States citizens whether they wanted to do so or not. This was a violation of our sovereignty. Our citizenship was in our own nations. We had a great attachment to our style of government. We wished to remain treaty Indians and reserve our ancient rights. There was no great rush among my people to go out and vote in the white man's elections. Anyone who did so was denied the privilege of becoming a chief or clan mother in our nations.

Although the 1924 American Indian Citizenship Act granted citizenship unilaterally, it did not end federal protection of native lands and governmental entities. Hence, Native Americans acquired a new status as American citizens while maintaining their privileges and rights as members of distinct Native-American political units. However, native policymakers in 1924 assumed that tribal governments would wither away when Native Americans became U. S. citizens. But most tribal governments did not disappear as anticipated and native peoples continue to enjoy a special dual citizenship.

Poverty, poor education, and ill health characterized the existence of most Native Americans in the 1920s. When native lands were allotted, the federal government assured communities that they would be supported during the transition from communal ways to the individualistic mores of Euro-American society. But government promises were not kept, and many Native Americans contin-

A Native-American mother and child stand next to their home in 1936 on the Mescalero reservation in New Mexico. LIBRARY OF CONGRESS, PRINTS & PHOTOGRAPHS DIVISION, FSA/OWI COLLECTION

ued to reject American individualism and cling to traditional group-oriented values. In some cases, native communities were devoured by their more greedy and competitive white neighbors. By the end of the 1920s, many reformers and Native-American leaders understood that instilling private property through allotment and Christianity

through missionization had wreaked havoc in Native-American country.

THE MERIAM REPORT

In 1928, the federal government commissioned a study of Native-American policy. The resulting Meriam Report catalogued the woeful conditions of

This Native-American family of migrant farm laborers worked in the blueberry fields near Little Fork, Minnesota, in 1937. LIBRARY OF CONGRESS, PRINTS & PHOTOGRAPHS DIVISION, FSA/OWI COLLECTION

native peoples. In health care, Native Americans were found to be without even rudimentary services. Infant mortality rates were twice the national average. Native Americans were also seven times more likely than the general population to die of tuberculosis. Sanitary conditions were bad, and many native peoples were disease-ridden. The Meriam report also criticized Native-American boarding schools as "grossly inadequate." From 1800 to 1926, the Bureau of Indian Affairs separated Native-American children from their parents in a cruel attempt to Christianize and civilize them. The Meriam Report pointed out the harsh discipline heaped on Indian children. Basically, the boarding schools forbade Native-American children to speak their own languages, practice their religions, or wear traditional clothes. Violators of these rules were subject to physical abuse. Male American-Indian survivors of this period, such as Rupert

Costo (Cahuilla), joked that upon arriving at boarding schools a missionary teacher would point to a picture of Jesus Christ with long flowing hair and state that they were to become like this man and then order that the boys' long hair be cut. In addition, most Christian boarding schools ruthlessly exploited Native-American child labor throughout much of the first half of the twentieth century. The Meriam Report characterized boarding schools as overcrowded and staffed with unqualified personnel who provided poor medical care, an unhealthy diet, and substandard education. Under these harsh conditions, Native-American literacy rates remained low. Boarding schools were also a direct attack on native families since they separated Native-American youths as early as the age of five from their families and often forbade children from even visiting their reservations and families during the summer.

A Native-American tenant farm family, photographed in 1939 at their farmhouse in McIntosh county, Oklahoma. LIBRARY OF CONGRESS, PRINTS & PHOTOGRAPHS DIVISION, FSA/OWI COLLECTION

Furthermore, no economic or legal structure appeared to be in place to protect the rights of Native Americans. The Meriam Report found that only 2 percent of all Native Americans earned in excess of $500 per year and that 96 percent of all Native Americans made less that $200 per year. Almost half of all Native Americans had lost their land to unscrupulous people who were manipulating the law to take advantage of allotted Native American lands. Legal authorities were unsure where cases involving natives and non-natives as defendants and plaintiffs should be heard—on reservations or off reservations. Often, when such cases were adjudicated, justice was not the result.

Having diagnosed this staggering array of problems, the Meriam Report recommended an infusion of funds to correct the ills of the system. It called for a new office in the Bureau of Indian Affairs to institute new programs and monitor existing ones. The report also stated that the government and especially the Bureau of Indian Affairs had exhibited an extremely hostile attitude towards native families and native culture. The allotment system, a cornerstone of Native-American policy since 1887, was found to be the major cause of chronic Native-American poverty.

THE INDIAN NEW DEAL

The Meriam Report documented a national scandal, showing that the deplorable conditions on reservations were a byproduct of governmental policies and neglect. Thus, the Meriam Report became a major blueprint for the Indian New Deal. In the 1930s, Native-American policy was taken out of the hands of missionaries and transferred to white social scientists. Most Native-American leaders of the time pointed out that Native-American affairs were still not in the hands of native peoples. Native leaders also knew that the persistence of Native-American ways depended on maintaining the land base and traditional tribal identity, and they looked to the Bill of Rights for the legal machinery to facilitate this survival process. The white religious reform community was largely responsible for these excesses since they had backed the discredited allotment policies and the Indian Citizenship Act.

The reforms that emerged in the 1930s were built on the idea that native culture and nations had a place in twentieth-century America. President Franklin D. Roosevelt's new commissioner of Indian affairs, John Collier, instituted a policy to restore the vitality of Native-American governments through the Indian Reorganization Act (IRA) of 1934. The IRA renounced the old allotment policies and encouraged tribes to promulgate their own constitutions. In addition, Native-American governments were recognized as the basic way to foster federal Native-American policies. New Deal reforms also sought to create nondenominational day schools on reservations, rather than continue to fund religious boarding schools that destroyed Native-American traditional family values. In these ways, the right of Native Americans to maintain distinct tribal communities was sustained. The idea that tribes and tribal values would eventually disappear was no longer the underlying assumption behind United States Native-American policy during the 1930s.

Paradoxically, federal officials during the 1930s often pursued goals of Native-American autonomy with an enthusiasm that limited the Native Americans' right of choice. In his zeal for social change, Collier pushed for the adoption of Native-American constitutions that reflected bureaucratic opinions as to how older tribal structures could be converted into contemporary constitutional structures. As a result, IRA constitutions were forced upon many tribes that clearly opposed such measures. During the 1930s, most Native Americans continued to be suspicious of governmental programs to aid them. Many large tribes, such as the Navajos, rejected the Indian New Deal because it did not address the very real economic and resource management issues on large reservations. Unemployment on most Native-American reservations continued to be well over 50 percent throughout the 1930s.

Despite these concerns, the reforms of the 1930s continued. Tribal governments were revitalized and their political authority over reservation life was reinvigorated. Gradually, native peoples started to recover from the devastations of the allotment policy, and health and education programs improved. But these reforms were short-lived.

As the Great Depression ended and World War II began, the United States turned away from

Native-American issues. The budget for the Bureau of Indians Affairs was cut, and conservative politicians attacked Collier's policies of empowering Native-American societies. Racism played an important role in this backlash, as did non-native businessmen who had lost their ability to plunder Native-American resources and lands during the 1930s. The cost of reforming the administration of Indian affairs was also a source of friction. An ideological attack against Native Americans emerged out of the anticommunist hysteria of the day. The attack painted Native-American ways as un-American and communistic. These ideological critiques aided another attack on native societies in the late 1940s and early 1950s, reversing many of the gains secured during the Indian New Deal. These conservative political attacks on native peoples would pave the way for radical civil rights and self-determination movements like the American Indian Movement in the 1960s.

See Also: COLLIER, JOHN; INDIAN NEW DEAL; INDIAN REORGANIZATION ACT OF 1934; RACE AND ETHNIC RELATIONS.

BIBLIOGRAPHY

Barsh, Russel Lawrence, and James Youngblood Henderson. *The Road: Indian Tribes and Political Liberty.* 1980.

Canby, William C. *American Indian Law in a Nutshell,* 3rd edition. 1998.

Cohen, Felix S. *Felix S. Cohen's Handbook of Federal Indian Law.* 1982.

Cornell, Stephen. *The Return of the Native: American Indian Political Resurgence.* 1988.

Getches, David H.; Charles F. Wilkinson; and Robert A. Williams, Jr. *Cases and Materials on Federal Indian Law,* 4th edition. 1998.

Jaimes, M. Annette. *The State of Native America: Genocide, Colonization, and Resistance.* 1992.

Lyons, Oren, et al. *Exiled in the Land of the Free: Democracy, Indian Nations, and the U. S. Constitution.* 1992.

Pevar, Stephen L. *The Rights of Indians and Tribes: The Basic ACLU Guide to Indian and Tribal Rights,* 2nd edition. 1992.

Price, Monroe E., and Robert N. Clinton. *Law and the American Indian: Readings, Notes, and Cases,* 2nd edition. 1983.

Shattuck, Petra T., and Jill Norgren. *Partial Justice: Federal Indian Law in a Liberal Constitutional System.* 1991.

United States Commission on Civil Rights. *American Indian Civil Rights Handbook,* 2nd edition. 1980.

West, W. Richard, Jr., and Kevin Gover. "The Struggle for Indian Civil Rights." In *Indians in American History: An Introduction,* edited by Frederick E. Hoxie. 1988.

Wunder, John R. *"Retained by the People": A History of American Indians and the Bill of Rights.* 1994.

Ziontz, Alvin J. "After Martinez: Indian Civil Rights Under Tribal Government." *U. C. Davis Law Review* 12, no. 1 (1979).

DONALD A. GRINDE, JR.

NAZI-SOVIET PACT

The Nazi-Soviet Pact, signed during early morning hours on August 24, 1939, formed the historical gateway between the Great Depression and World War II. Ostensibly a mere nonaggression treaty between Germany and the USSR, the agreement contained an unpublished protocol that gave independent Poland a death sentence by carving up Eastern Europe. In the United States, the entente placed a permanent cloud over the Communist Party's leadership of the anticapitalist left.

The Pact had roots in appeasement of Nazi Führer Adolf Hitler by European democracies. Germany's annexation of Austria in 1938 went uncontested. Later that year, Great Britain and France ignored Soviet Foreign Commissar Maxim Litvinov's call for collective action to protect Czechoslovakia's Sudetenland, a border region with a sizable German-speaking minority. On September 30, in a conference at Munich, Germany, the two Western powers surrendered the region to Hitler in exchange for a promise to maintain peace. From that point on, he sought to seize Poland, certain that Britain and France would not fight a major war to defend that nation. The Munich Pact caused Soviet Communist Party General Secretary Joseph Stalin to consider a treaty with Germany. For the next year, the British and French made no serious effort toward any accord with Moscow to contain the Nazis, causing Stalin to suspect they wanted Hitler to attack the USSR. Germany's need for raw materials, plus Stalin's anger at the democracies, led to a Russo-German trade agreement in August 1939. At that point, Soviet Prime Minister Vyacheslav Molotov proposed a nonaggression pact.

The concord was written by four persons: Hitler in Berlin, and his Foreign Minister Joachim von Ribbentrop, Stalin, and Molotov in Moscow. They drafted the document in haste. Germany was planning an early invasion of Poland, and Stalin gleefully exploited Hitler's impatience to exact territorial concessions. The text, therefore, contained unusually straightforward language. A preamble cited a 1926 neutrality agreement between Germany and the Soviet Union as historical precedent. Seven articles followed. The first article abjured aggression, each nation upon the other, whether severally or jointly with other powers. The second clause provided that if an outsider attacked either, the signatories would not lend support. This gave Hitler carte blanche to address "provocations" by Germany's eastern neighbor. The third section promised an open channel of communication between Russia and the Reich. The fourth provided that neither would join any grouping of powers aimed directly or indirectly at the other—blatantly ignoring Germany's Anti-Comintern Pact with Italy and Japan against the USSR. Article five affirmed that disputes would be settled by arbitration commissions. A sixth gave the agreement a ten-year life, with an automatic five-year extension, if neither side objected. The final clause put the Nazi-Soviet Pact in force immediately upon signature by Ribbentrop, Molotov, and Stalin, thereby hastening the attack on Poland.

The secret protocol partitioned Poland, also handing the USSR Belorussian and Ukrainian lands lost in her 1920 war with the Poles. In addition, the unpublished portion ceded to Stalin the Romanian province of Bessarabia, as well as Latvia, Estonia, and Finland. Subsequent negotiations brought Lithuania under Russian rule as well.

One can scarcely overstate the Nazi-Soviet Pact's historical significance. World War II erupted just days after its signing, when Germany invaded Poland and Britain and France declared war on Germany. The conflict killed eighty million people. It destroyed fascist governments in Italy, Germany, and far-off Japan. It left the European continent in rubble, and fatally undermined European colonialism everywhere. The ultimate victory by the Soviet Union, which was foolishly attacked by Germany—her 669-day ally—on June 22, 1941, marked the rise of a new Russian empire that lasted until 1989.

In the United States, the Nazi-Soviet Pact, and blind support of it by the American Communist Party (CPUSA), ended the Popular Front against fascism. For nearly six years, leftists of various stripes had put aside differences to resist the spread of Hitlerism. The CPUSA had become the largest anticapitalist party, with influence ranging far beyond a membership that never surpassed 100,000. The Pact belied the CPUSA's claim to leadership of democratic, progressive forces. Support for the USSR's treaty with Nazi Germany raised the question of where the party's primary loyalty lay. It put Communists under the same type of expanded federal surveillance that domestic fascist groups faced. It also prompted a miniature red scare and cemented ideological foundations that Senator Joseph McCarthy and other political opportunists built upon a decade later. Paradoxically, the war that devastated so much of the world ended America's Great Depression and brought unprecedented prosperity thereafter.

See Also: COMMUNIST PARTY; HITLER, ADOLF; POPULAR FRONT; STALIN, JOSEPH; WORLD WAR II AND THE ENDING OF THE DEPRESSION; EUROPE, GREAT DEPRESSION IN.

BIBLIOGRAPHY

Gorodetsky, Gabriel. *The Grand Delusion: Stalin and the German Invasion of Russia.* 1999.

Ierace, Francis A. *America and the Nazi-Soviet Pact.* 1978.

Kolasky, John. *Partners in Tyranny.* 1990.

Read, Anthony, and David Fisher. *The Deadly Embrace: Hitler, Stalin, and the Nazi-Soviet Pact, 1939–1941.* 1988.

Roberts, Geoffrey. *The Unholy Alliance: Stalin's Pact with Hitler.* 1989.

Suziedelis, Saulius, ed. *History and Commemoration in the Baltic: The Nazi-Soviet Pact, 1939–1989.* 1989.

JAMES G. RYAN

The National Youth Administration, an important New Deal agency, was established in 1935 to provide vocational training and employment for young men and women. These men attended an NYA mechanics class in Phoenix, Arizona, in 1936. FRANKLIN DELANO ROOSEVELT LIBRARY

NEW DEAL

The United States in the 1920s, argued William E. Leuchtenburg, "had almost no institutional structure to which Europeans would accord the term 'the State.'" As one journalist had observed, "nobody would have thought of calling the sleepy inconsequential Southern town that Washington was in Calvin Coolidge's day the center of anything very important." An economist noted that "The only business a citizen had with the government was through the Post Office. No doubt he saw a soldier

or a sailor now and then, but the government had nothing to do with the general public."

THE TRANSFORMATION OF THE FEDERAL GOVERNMENT

Franklin D. Roosevelt confronted the worst economic depression in American history with this feeble state apparatus. A generation before, Grover Cleveland had responded to a similar crisis. As in 1933, the president had been faced in 1893 with armies of the unemployed, desperate farmers, and frightened financiers. Cleveland had resolutely

The Civilian Conservation Corps, one of the earliest New Deal programs, was established in 1933 to provide jobs in conservation projects for young men around the country. These CCC members were photographed at California's Rock Creek Camp in June 1933. FRANKLIN DELANO ROOSEVELT LIBRARY

maintained a policy of sound money and strict economy, and he steadfastly resisted demands for government assistance. His courage won Cleveland the praise of conservatives everywhere, but it split his Democratic Party, brought it electoral disaster, and condemned the Democrats to national minority status until the 1930s.

Roosevelt ignored this model. Instead, he drew on the Progressive traditions of the need for government to confront the problems of modern industrial society and to protect the disadvantaged—what Daniel Rodgers has called a "new social poli-

tics." Roosevelt also drew on the model of what the federal government had done during World War I when it mobilized men and resources to fight a European war. Herbert Hoover had drawn on many of the same traditions and had mobilized government agencies to check the deflationary spiral after 1929, just as he had as secretary of commerce in 1921 to combat recession. But Hoover's activism was to promote voluntary cooperation. Roosevelt's was not so constrained: He cheerfully, albeit unsystematically, sought federal government remedies and, if necessary, federal government coercion to tackle the Depression.

As a result, American citizens who had had so little experience with the federal government now saw it deeply interwoven in their daily lives. Between 1933 and 1938 the New Deal that Roosevelt had promised the American people when he accepted the Democratic nomination in 1932 profoundly altered the relationship between individuals and their government and shaped the political economy of the United States for the next fifty years.

American farmers were told what they could and could not plant by federal officials. They received checks for not planting crops, or even for destroying what they had already planted. Many had access to electricity for the first time. Farm owners, like homeowners across the nation, renegotiated their mortgages with federal agencies. Tenants could borrow to buy their own farms. Millions of workers were employed by the government on public works and work relief projects. They voted in federal elections for union representation. Their minimum wage was determined by the government. They were eligible for unemployment compensation and received old-age pensions. Most Americans paid income taxes to the federal government for the first time in the 1930s and 1940s. Businessmen could no longer fight unions with every weapon at their disposal and could no longer simply ignore them. They were told what they had to pay their workers, and, for a short time, how much they could produce. Their banking and securities operations were strictly monitored. At the same time, they had unprecedented access to cheap credit from the Reconstruction Finance Corporation (RFC) and had their bank deposits underwritten. Virtually every community in the United States bore the physical imprint of the New Deal: a public housing project, a new high school stadium, a new airport, a new road, a new dam.

This transformation of the role of the federal government and the notions of the legitimate function of government was eventually accepted by the federal courts. The exact timing of the "Constitutional Revolution" of the 1930s, and the motivation of the judges who appeared to switch sides, remains open to dispute, but the constitutional consequences were clear. The restrictions on what the

federal government could regulate under the commerce clause were largely removed. In 1942 the U.S. Supreme Court ruled that an Ohio chicken farmer growing twenty-three acres of wheat, all of which would be fed to his chickens and consumed in his backyard, so affected interstate commerce that the secretary of agriculture could impose marketing penalties on him. Before 1937 the Court had savaged economic and social legislation, notably the great industrial and farm recovery acts of 1933. Since 1937 it has never overturned legislation involving economic regulation and between 1937 and 1946 it reversed thirty-two of its earlier decisions in the economic and social arena.

The American people made the same decision as the judges. The majority of Americans welcomed this assumption of active responsibility by the federal government for the welfare of ordinary Americans and responded by electing Roosevelt as president four times. American voters made the Democratic Party the national majority party for a generation and supported presidents—Harry Truman, John F. Kennedy, and Lyndon Johnson—who campaigned in the shadow of Roosevelt and sought to complete the unfinished business of the New Deal. Until the 1960s most Americans believed that the federal government could be relied on to do the right thing.

HISTORIANS

The first generation of New Deal historians (Tugwell, Freidel, Burns, Schlesinger, Leuchtenburg) largely shared this perspective. They were mainly liberal activists for whom the Depression and World War II were their formative political experiences. Because of Roosevelt's sense of history and the creation of the presidential library in Hyde Park, New York, historians could accomplish archive-based work on the Roosevelt presidency far more quickly than on any previous president. By 1950, 85 percent of Roosevelt's papers had been cleared and could be studied—some five years before the Library of Congress was able to release some of its Lincoln papers and seventeen years before serious archival assessments of the Hoover presidency started. It was inevitable that these historians should put Roosevelt at center stage: The need to establish a coherent narrative of the vast array of legislation and the agencies that proliferated dictated their emphasis on the president and the dynamics of policy formulation. Their tone was largely celebratory. "Something magical," recalled one historian, happened in the 1930s when the federal government came to the rescue of ordinary Americans. They were not uncritical: They regretted the lack of greater planning and coherence in the New Deal, felt that Roosevelt was sometimes too clever by half and sacrificed long-term strategic goals for short-term political gains, and noted that many who needed help most were excluded from the benefits of the New Deal. Nevertheless the overall portrait of Roosevelt and the New Deal was heroic. At a time of unprecedented prosperity after 1945, the New Deal legacy of economic management through fiscal activism seemed successful. At a time when ideology and mass movements—fascism, communism, McCarthyism—seemed so dangerous, these historians could see great value in the apparently pragmatic, non-ideological New Deal that "brokered" the demands of the competing interests groups who mediated between the government and the people.

Radical historians (Zinn, Bernstein, Conkin, Kolko) of the 1960s lamented what the liberals had celebrated. The one-third of a nation that Roosevelt had identified in 1937 as ill-housed, ill-clothed, and ill-fed remained poor. Neither racism nor the power of capitalism had been checked. To these historians the New Deal, like other reform movements in twentieth century, had merely served to sustain the hegemony of corporate capitalism. To the radical historians of the 1960s, the New Deal failure was particularly tragic because, echoing the radicals of the 1930s, they believed that there had never been a better time for a radical overhaul of the American economic and political system. Capitalism had collapsed. American workers and farmers were more disillusioned than ever before or since with traditional business leadership. For once corporate leaders could not solve their problems through overseas economic expansion, since foreign markets had collapsed. They feared that the alternative domestic remedies for depression in a mature economy, therefore, would involve the radical redistribution of wealth and power if America's persistent overproduction were to be solved. To forestall that radical change, New Left historians argued, corporate leaders were not the targets of New Deal reform; rather they were the driving force behind the New Deal. These corporate leaders sought to patch up, not tear down, the old economic system to ensure that power remained largely in traditional hands. Shrewd business leaders supported industrial stabilization, labor legislation, and social security legislation because they could afford increased labor costs that would drive under their smaller competitors. To defuse the angry discontent of workers, farmers, and the poor, they supported the most minimal welfare measures possible. Limited concessions would avert the threat of disorder and undercut the appeal of radicals. This interpretation continued to resonate in graduate schools in the United States, even though it did not yield a major overview of the New Deal. In the 1990s historians of American business like Colin Gordon resurrected a more sophisticated version of the analysis.

If New Left historians lamented the limited nature of New Deal change and viewed it as a decisive "missed opportunity" for radical change, critics on the right lamented that the New Deal had initiated entirely too much change and that the 1930s had marked the "Big Bang" of the federal government. Critics from Herbert Hoover to economic historians such as Robert Higgs in the 1980s and 1990s argued that Roosevelt artificially created a crisis in 1933, then used the analogy of wartime powers and foisted economic regimentation and government control on the American people. The New Deal was a decisive wrong turn in American history that set the nation firmly on the road to collectivism and the creation of a Leviathan—the modern, insatiable, bureaucratic state. As a result, conservative critics and historians argued, the commitment of both ordinary Americans and their leaders to individualism, free markets, and limited government suffered a blow from which the nation has never recovered.

In fact, few New Deal programs were implemented by an army of federal officials faithfully carrying out orders from Washington. Programs were often administered by state administrators, by local officials more sensitive to local mores than to

Washington diktat, or by people, such as farmers and businessmen themselves, whom the programs were intended to regulate. State and local case studies of the New Deal and particular agencies have shown that change that looked impressive in Washington did not necessarily have the same impact at the local level. Studies that focus on social groups rather than on their leaders and politicians, "the inarticulate many" rather than "the articulate few," show grassroots radicalism and the agency of ordinary Americans, but they also show the persistence of conservative traditions of deference and individualism amid extraordinary economic distress. Studies that focus on policymaking rarely show the enlightened capitalists as the driving force behind New Deal reforms. Historians who have attempted overviews that take advantage of these studies (McElvaine, Badger, Biles) have tended to emphasize the limitations of the changes wrought by the New Deal. In that sense they resemble the New Left historians. But, unlike those historians, they tend to stress not the conservative intent of policymakers or the malign influence of corporate capitalists, but the external constraints imposed by the political and economic environment: the lack of a sufficient state apparatus, the strong forces of localism, the great difficulty of policymaking in an economic emergency, and entrenched conservative leadership in Congress.

THE EFFORTS AT RECOVERY

What judgments on the New Deal can be made against this background? The overriding imperative in 1933 was to produce economic recovery quickly—to reopen the banks and to check the downward deflationary spiral of wages and prices. The microeconomic intervention in agriculture and industry aimed to restore purchasing power to farmers by controlling production under the Agricultural Adjustment Administration (AAA) and to eliminate destructive competition in industry by setting a floor under wages and prices through National Recovery Administration (NRA) codes. Various schemes of "quick fixes" by currency manipulation, to which Roosevelt was always attracted, had little effect. The NRA codes may have checked the deflationary spiral, but they did not generate additional purchasing power that would create extra jobs.

Public works spending by the slow moving Public Works Administration (PWA) did not compensate. Microeconomic policies were largely abandoned after the end of the NRA in 1935. Unemployment figures never fell below 10 percent until well into 1941. It would take the demands of preparedness and the defense industries during the war to generate the purchasing power to create new jobs and full employment.

In agriculture, the mix of credit, production control programs, parity payments, and price support loans under the 1933 and 1938 Farm Acts rescued rural America. Federal assistance enabled farm owners to stay on the land in the 1930s when there were no alternative economic prospects off the land. But those on the land who were always poor—tenants and sharecroppers in the South, migratory farm workers in Florida and California, small farmers in the Appalachians—did not receive proportionate assistance from the AAA or the cash-strapped Resettlement Administration (RA) and its successor, the Farm Security Administration (FSA). Farm programs, which were largely to remain in place for the next fifty years, eliminated much of the risk of unpredictable weather and markets for American farmers but they did not in themselves bring prosperity. It was World War II that solved the farm problem: It produced the urban demand that absorbed surplus farm production and the non-farm jobs that absorbed the surplus rural population.

Nevertheless, there were important New Deal economic legacies. The reforms in banking and securities eliminated most of the excesses that had produced financial instability in the 1920s. The stabilization of the financial system lasted until deregulation in the 1980s. The New Deal was also a "laboratory of economic learning." Roosevelt did not allow unbalanced budgets before 1937 as a conscious economic policy: They were emergency measures and he hoped to balance the budget in fiscal 1937. The defense buildup and the need to escape the 1937 to 1938 recession once more made deficit spending an imperative. By now a version of Keynesian economics had influential backers in the administration. Previously they had believed that the mature American economy did not have the capacity to expand dramatically: Unemployment would always be with them. Now they believed that the necessary injection of purchasing power through government spending could create the demand to put all Americans back to work. The war showed that government spending could indeed create full employment. The New Deal left a legacy of macroeconomic tools that would produce nearly full employment until the late 1960s.

THE WELFARE STATE

The mixed record on the economy was not what brought the New Deal overwhelming electoral endorsement. What more than anything bound lower-income voters to the Democratic Party, including for the first time African-American voters in the northern cities, were the welfare programs of the New Deal. Before 1933 the United States was a welfare "outlier" in the Western industrial world: Private charity and county poor-law provision all too often constituted the sum total of assistance to the unemployed. There was no social insurance—no unemployment compensation in operation at the state or federal level, no old-age insurance, no health insurance. Under the Federal Emergency Relief Administration (FERA) the federal government made grants, not loans, to the states for relief. The Civil Works Administration (CWA) in 1933 and 1934 and the Works Progress Administration (WPA) after 1935 provided jobs for as many as four million of the unemployed. The Social Security Act of 1935 provided unemployment compensation, old-age insurance, and matching funds for categorical assistance to the needy aged, the blind, and dependent children. The New Deal, as James Patterson concluded, "responded with a level of public aid scarcely imaginable in 1929."

The welfare state the New Deal launched was, however, in many ways a ramshackle affair. New Dealers disliked welfare and wanted to replace the dole with jobs and social insurance. But work relief programs never provided jobs for more than 40 percent of the unemployed and welfare did not wither away: Indeed, aid to dependent children would in time be unrecognizable as a program that was aimed at the children of worthy widows. Relief programs, whether under federal direction from 1933

to 1935 or under state control thereafter, were always handicapped by occasionally incompetent, sometimes corrupt, often niggardly state and county administrators. Social insurance was funded by the contributions of the workers themselves and not by general tax revenues. The immediate impact of payroll taxes was deflationary and regressive. There were wide variations in state generosity and eligibility requirements, and Social Security failed to cover many of the most needy in the United States—agricultural laborers and domestic servants, who were disproportionately African American. The emerging welfare state offered nothing for health care and very little for low-income housing—staples of the welfare state in western European countries.

WORKERS

The New Deal may not have achieved a dramatic redistribution of wealth, but there was a radical edge and a class base to politics in the 1930s. American workers flocked to unions in the 1930s: Union membership tripled. Even more important, the great majority of unskilled and semiskilled, often immigrant, workers in the mass production, basic manufacturing industries were organized. Before 1933 organized labor had been hemmed into sick industries and into craft unions of skilled workers. By 1940 the great primary industries of autos, steel, rubber, and electrical goods, which were dominated by hostile open shop national corporations, had been organized in industrial unions under the Congress of Industrial Organizations (CIO). These new unions were overtly and aggressively political in contrast to the traditional nonpartisan stance of the American Federation of Labor (AFL). By 1940 labor funds made the largest contribution to the Democratic Party's campaign chest, union members were a crucial element of a class-based New Deal electoral coalition, and in many northern cities union organizing drives and Democratic election campaigns were virtually interchangeable. Labor leaders could demand representation at the highest levels of government policymaking.

These labor gains owed much to a newfound militancy on the part of American workers, a militancy that was developed and channeled by union organizers, many of whom were Communists and Socialists. Before 1933 vulnerable immigrant workers, no matter how much they resented their job insecurity or the arbitrary power of foremen on the shop floor, had been no match for the unfettered power of employers determined to smash unions. But the Depression solidified class solidarity and subordinated ethnic divisions. Any loyalty to employers from the benefits of welfare capitalism disappeared when those benefits were eliminated as employers cut costs. Explosions of militancy in 1933 and 1934 were in part stimulated by the rising expectations encouraged by the NRA. But rank-and-file militancy was not enough to secure long-term organization. What workers needed was the protection afforded by the Wagner Act of 1935, which outlawed many of the traditional anti-union practices of the employers, and by the political power exercised by labor within the Democratic Party, which meant sympathetic federal, state, and local governments. Governors and sheriffs no longer inevitably protected strikebreakers or used troops or the courts to defeat labor. The sit-down strikes were allowed to succeed. Even defeats during the 1937 to 1938 recession did not mean the complete destruction of unions, as in the past. Employers bitterly resisted and seldom realistically bargained, even after union recognition. But faced with the determined stance of government and the need to maintain production and profits during the war, they did come to terms with unions. They continued to seek to protect managerial prerogatives after the war, but also came to see benefits in stable and predictable industrial relations with "responsible" unions.

INFRASTRUCTURE

The New Deal also made important investments in the nation's infrastructure. Public works projects built the roads, government buildings, and airports that revenue-starved localities could not. Long before federal aid to education, New Deal programs built school and university facilities, paid teachers' salaries and, through the National Youth Administration (NYA), put thousands through school. The New Deal may not have built many units of public housing, but its credit to homeown-

ers not only saved homes for owners who would otherwise have lost them but paved the way for long-term mortgages that revived the private construction industry in the late 1930s and, in due course, gave the United States the highest percentage of home ownership in the world. Multipurpose dams like those in the Tennessee Valley brought water resource development and cheap power that not only transformed agriculture in the West and the South but also stimulated industrialization. The Reconstruction Finance Corporation made credit available to regional entrepreneurs in the Sunbelt who would spearhead economic development in the late 1930s and 1940s.

ACHIEVEMENTS AND LIMITATIONS

The New Deal had major achievements: immediate relief for the unemployed, a welfare state, long-term safeguards for commercial farmers, financial stability, the macroeconomic tools for long-term growth, the creation of a countervailing power to business in the form of organized labor, and investment in the infrastructure. But these achievements have to be set against confusions in policy, the restoration of the power of big business in World War II, the failure to tackle rural poverty with as much vigor as farm recovery, the failure to challenge segregation and disfranchisement of African Americans in the South, and the inadequacies of the welfare revolution.

The limitations of the New Deal were perfectly clear to younger New Dealers. Roosevelt inspired a remarkably talented and largely incorruptible cohort of young academics, economists, lawyers, and social workers into government service, including the first generation of influential women at the federal government level. They were self-critical and willing to learn. It was their own investigations that first uncovered the extent of rural relief needs. Critics of the impact of New Deal policy on southern tenancy were brought into the government. Advocates of social security were conscious of taking first steps: They would extend coverage and bring in health insurance later. Rural planners intended to tackle the problem of urban under-consumption and to shift farmers out of high-cost production. Advocates of the Tennessee Valley Authority (TVA)

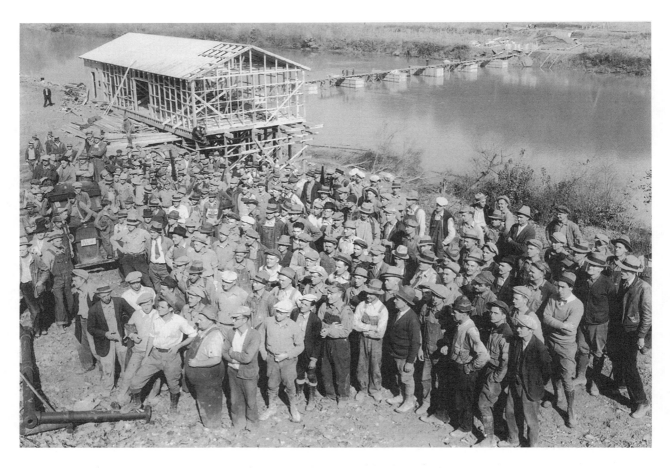

The Tennessee Valley Authority, a major New Deal agency, was established in 1933 to build dams, provide electricity, and develop the resources of the Tennessee Valley region. Large numbers of unemployed laborers were hired to work on TVA projects, including these men who showed up for work at the Norris Dam site in November 1933. NATIONAL ARCHIVES AND RECORDS ADMINISTRATION

wanted to see it replicated in all the major river valleys of the country. Radical southerners saw that prosperity in the South needed political and economic democracy in the region, which meant, at the least, the end of black disfranchisement. Their faith in federal solutions made sense, given the narrow-minded, venal, and amateurish politics of so many state governments. But a remarkably lean federal bureaucracy and a recurrent faith in participatory democracy in the form of, for example, farmer committees, crop control elections, National Labor Relations Board elections, and Native-American self-government accompanied their faith in federal solutions.

That the New Dealers failed to overcome the limitations they themselves identified was sometimes the result of missed opportunities, of excessive deference to southern congressional leaders, of a lack of interest in domestic politics during World War II, of too great a willingness to compromise, and of a lack of valor against vested interests like the American Medical Association or white southerners. But the limitations were also the result of the economic emergency of 1933 and the lack of preexisting "state capacity." The need to act quickly meant working with, not against, bankers, businessmen, and farm leaders; it meant cultivating and strengthening southern conservative leaders. The lack of central government expertise and resources precluded top-down central planning or purely federal solutions.

The political realignment that the New Deal created was inevitably a partial realignment. The Democratic Party might be a class-based party of lower-income voters linked with middle-class consumers behind policies that accepted the necessity of increasing mass purchasing power. But the power of southern county-seat elites and their control of congressional leaders were still intact. Some scholars now argue that a Third New Deal from 1937 onwards attempted to achieve the full-scale political realignment, the strengthening of state capacity and executive power, and the policy prescriptions that would have enabled the New Deal reform aspirations to be more completely met through executive reorganization, the court-packing plan of 1937, and the attempt to purge the Democratic Party of conservatives in the primaries of 1938. The president would have had more control over the executive through the budget bureau, a planning board, and control of the regulatory agencies. A reformed Supreme Court would have ensured that rulemaking authority could be delegated to this new streamlined executive. The purge attempted to nationalize party politics and overcome localism and inertia. In the North, issue-oriented politics espoused by young New Dealers had replaced the patronage-oriented politics of the older generation of Democrats. Roosevelt hoped to facilitate the same change in the politics of the South. The policy complement to this administrative thrust was the National Resource Planning Board's report of 1943, *Security, Work, and Relief*, which called for guaranteed minimums for all American citizens, health care, and low-cost housing. Full employment, the elimination of the weaknesses of Social Security, and a structural assault on rural and urban poverty would ensure that the first steps of the New Deal were not last steps.

THE ANTI-STATIST COALITION

But a full-scale political realignment, the creation of a liberal nation-wide Democratic Party, and the triumph of a social democratic agenda was ultimately checked by a powerful anti-statist coali-tion that had developed right from the start of the New Deal. Conservative businessmen had backed the Association Against the Prohibition Amendment (AAPA) because of prohibition's unacceptable degree of federal control and interference in individual rights. A billion-dollar industry had been destroyed and assets confiscated without compensation. AAPA Democrats, such as John Raskob and Jouett Shouse, supported Al Smith in his attempt to block Roosevelt's nomination in 1932. They hoped to link up with southern states-rights advocates of rigid governmental economy, such as Harry Byrd of Virginia. They viewed the New Deal's exercise of power in the same light as prohibition—a massive infringement of property rights and freedom of contract. They soon sought like-minded businessmen to join them in the Liberty League in outright rejection of the New Deal.

But, on the whole, businessmen were on the defensive in the 1930s: Those who worked with the New Deal largely did so to try and restrain New Deal reforms. They regrouped in the late 1930s to redress the political balance that had produced the Wagner Act of 1935. They tapped into long-term middle-class hostility to strikes and trade unions and managed to drive a wedge between working-class and middle-class Americans. In the 1930s working-class and middle-class Americans were seen as united consumers and producers, protecting their incomes against privileged corporations. In the 1940s businessmen mounted a carefully orchestrated campaign to link inflation to union demands and the labor/middle-class coalition was never restored, except for a brief period in the mid-1960s.

Republicans could capitalize on these developments. The logic of their defeat in 1932 and 1936 should have been to moderate their conservatism, to move the party to the center to compete with the Democrats. But hard-line conservatives dominated the party machinery and the New Deal's constitutional changes, especially court reform, reawakened old guard Republican concerns in defense of the Constitution and the courts. Rural and small-town conservatives continued to dominate Republican representation in Congress, especially in the House. Western progressive Republicans, who had deserted Hoover in 1932 and rejoiced in Roosevelt's bold leadership in 1933, were nevertheless opposed to the direction of the non-emergency New Deal. Powerful anti-statist sentiments shaped their hostility to the expansion of federal power in the late 1930s.

Just as businessmen whose financial institutions had been rescued by the government disliked state intervention, so American farmers were capable of significant dissonance between their dependence on government support and their distaste for statism. For example, in the Dakotas not a single person survived the droughts of the 1930s without the government's intervention, and the federal government spent more money per capita there than in all but six other states. But sociologists noted that few Dakotans were prepared to admit that they had received government assistance. This rural celebration of self-help was as powerful in the West as it was among conservative elites in the South. Just as a wedge was driven between workers and middle-class consumers, so a wedge was driven between farmers and labor. The hostility of farmers to statism led them to be a prominent part of the anti-New Deal, anti-labor coalition.

The power of that anti-statist coalition was cemented by the presence of the southern Democrats. Some, notably Harry Byrd, Carter Glass, and Josiah Bailey had opposed the New Deal as unconstitutional from the start of the first "Hundred Days" of the Roosevelt administration. Most southern congressmen, especially committee chairmen, had welcomed New Deal measures in the economic emergency. But they cooled over the non-emergency direction of the New Deal that seemed to benefit northern cities and labor at their expense, and to threaten traditional patterns of dependency and control in the South. But the original conservatives, Glass and Bailey, saw an even greater danger of federal intrusion in Roosevelt's plans to reform the Supreme Court. They predicted that not merely would newly appointed judges expand the federal power to intervene in interstate commerce but that they would also interfere in the South's traditional pattern of race relations. This fear seemed far-fetched in 1937, given the New Deal's caution on racial issues, yet Roosevelt's appointees on the Court proved those fears prescient in the long run

This anti-statist coalition represented in Congress by Republicans and southern Democrats would for a quarter of a century check any significant expansion of the New Deal. It ensured that New Deal first steps would generally be last steps. But it also shaped the liberal legacy of the New Deal. Faced with these challenges and the success of government policy in creating seventeen million new jobs in World War II, New Dealers increasingly came to champion "commercial" rather than "social" Keynesianism. They felt that they had the fiscal tools to create continued economic growth which in itself would solve many of the social, including racial, ills of America. There was no need in this formulation of Keynesianism to redistribute income or reshape capitalist institutions. Unlike ambitious New Deal goals of planning encapsulated in the National Resource Planning Board's 1943 report, liberal post-1945 policy did not require constant involvement in the affairs of public institutions or the drastic expansion of federal regulations. They acquiesced in a limited statist vision.

The New Deal was a dramatic response to economic crisis, the most dramatic democratic response in the industrialized world in the 1930s. Its recovery and relief programs may have been flawed, but they enabled millions of Americans to survive the Depression. The response of Franklin Roosevelt and his government and the radical, participatory nature of politics in the 1930s checked temporarily what was the steady erosion of popular participation and faith in politics throughout the twentieth century. The New Deal revolutionized the agenda of American politics. There were permanent new roles for the federal government. Social Security through contributory taxes by the workers themselves would prove impossible, just as Roosevelt intended, for future congresses to cut. Farm programs would prove almost as difficult to dislodge, given the strategic position in both the legislature and the executive that organized farmers occupied. Members of the U.S. House of Representatives, up for reelection every two years, soon learned that the provision of government services and infrastructure projects to their constituents would bring even more political rewards for incumbents than the patronage politics of the pre-New Deal period, which involved the appointment of postmasters and the delivery of civil war pensions. But a powerful anti-statist coalition checked the more systematic and social democratic expansion of the New Deal envisaged by reformers between 1937 and 1945.

See Also: CAUSES OF THE GREAT DEPRESSION; CONSERVATIVE COALITION; HOUSING; HUNDRED DAYS; NEW DEAL, SECOND; NEW DEAL, THIRD; ORGANIZED LABOR; ROOSEVELT, FRANKLIN D.; TRANSPORTATION.

BIBLIOGRAPHY

Badger, Anthony J. *The New Deal: The Depression Years, 1933–40.* 1990.

Bernstein, Barton J. "The New Deal: The Conservative Achievements of Liberal Reform." In *Towards a New Past: Dissenting Essays in American History.* 1967.

Biles, Roger. *A New Deal for the American People.* 1991.

Brinkley, Alan. *The End of Reform: New Deal Liberalism in Recession and War.* 1995.

Burns, James McGregor. *Roosevelt: The Lion and the Fox.* 1956.

Conkin, Paul K. *The New Deal.* 1968.

Freidel, Frank. *Franklin D Roosevelt*, Vol. 1: *The Apprenticeship*; Vol. 2: *The Ordeal*; Vol. 3: *The Triumph*; Vol. 4: *Launching the New Deal.* 1952–1973.

Gordon, Colin. *New Deals: Business, Labor, and Politics in America, 1920–1935.* 1994.

Higgs, Robert. *Crisis and Leviathan: Critical Episodes in the Growth of American Government.* 1987.

Kolko, Gabriel. *Main Currents in Modern American History.* 1976.

Leuchtenburg, William E. *Franklin D Roosevelt and the New Deal, 1932–1940.* 1963.

Schlesinger, Arthur M., Jr. *The Age of Roosevelt*, Vol. 1: *The Crisis of the Old Order, 1919–1933*; Vol. 2: *The Coming of the New Deal*; Vol. 3: *The Politics of Upheaval.* 1956–1960.

Schwarz, Jordan. *The New Dealer: Power Politics in the Age of Roosevelt.* 1993.

Tugwell, Rexford G. *The Democratic Roosevelt: A Biography of Franklin D. Roosevelt.* 1957.

Zinn, Howard, ed. *New Deal Thought.* 1966.

TONY BADGER

NEW DEAL, SECOND

In analyzing the New Deal and its development, historians have often distinguished between a "First New Deal" of 1933 and a "Second New Deal" of 1935. (Subsequently scholars also identified a "Third New Deal" that began in 1937.) In the First and Second New Deal model, the First New Deal, enacted during the first "Hundred Days" of the administration of President Franklin D. Roosevelt in the spring of 1933, especially involved efforts to achieve economic recovery by means of national planning and controls and to provide "relief" assistance to the unemployed and impoverished. The key programs of the First New Deal were the National Recovery Administration (NRA) and the Agricultural Adjustment Administration (AAA), designed to bring balanced recovery in the industrial and agricultural sectors, and the Federal Emergency Relief Administration (FERA), to provide assistance to the needy. Other important First New Deal programs were the Tennessee Valley Authority (TVA), the Civilian Conservation Corps (CCC), the Glass-Steagall Banking Act of 1933, and the Securities Act of 1933.

A second major burst of New Deal legislation, concerned especially with social reform, came in 1935. The defining programs of this Second New Deal began with the Emergency Relief Appropriation Act of April 1935, which produced the Works Progress Administration (WPA), followed in the spring and summer by a number of programs enacted in the "Second Hundred Days." These included the Social Security Act, the National Labor Relations Act (or Wagner Act), the Revenue Act (or "Wealth Tax") of 1935, the Banking Act of 1935, and the Public Utilities Holding Company Act.

But while scholars have generally agreed that the two major periods of New Deal reform came in 1933 and 1935, they have disagreed about other aspects of the First and Second New Deals. One view maintains that the New Deal moved in a more radical policy direction in 1935, with its emphasis on social-democratic programs to provide economic security, to support organized labor, and to implement more progressive taxation. Another version holds that while the New Deal became politically more radical in 1935, with anti-business rhetoric and appeals to the working class, it actually became more conservative ideologically and programmatically by moving away from federal planning and controls and towards regulatory efforts to ensure a more competitive market economy.

The disagreement about just what the First New Deal and the Second New Deal entailed helps explain why New Deal scholars have typically concluded that matters were more complicated than a simple First and Second New Deal dichotomy would suggest. Neither the 1933 nor the 1935 legislation was so coherent as the model suggests, and important continuities can be found between the two periods. Though a few New Dealers had envisioned thoroughgoing federal economic planning and controls, most had not, and the NRA and AAA in practice had cooperated with big business and farmers and often acted upon their preferences. Significant elements of the First New Deal (relief, agricultural policy, some planning, regulation of banking and securities, for example) continued into the Second, while much of the Second New Deal (including work relief, social security, progressive taxation) had been in the planning stages almost from the beginning. Moreover, Roosevelt had been an advocate of public utilities regulation since he was governor of New York, and New York Senator Robert F. Wagner had provided powerful impetus for more far-reaching New Deal labor policy beginning in 1933.

The First and Second New Deal framework thus seems to oversimplify and therefore to distort the nature and development of the New Deal. Policymaking was more complicated and had more continuity than the model suggests, and changing circumstances rather than ideological change largely accounted for the differences between the First and the Second New Deals. Yet the framework nonetheless remains a useful one that identifies the two principal, and different, periods of New Deal policymaking. The Second New Deal had a greater social-democratic character, with programs that aimed especially at economic security and at the working classes. In addition to the Wagner Act that enabled the growth in size and power of organized labor, the Social Security Act, with its old-age in-surance, unemployment compensation, and public assistance provisions, constituted a major change laying essential foundations of the modern regulatory-welfare state.

To be sure, the programs of the Second New Deal did not do all that many claimed that they did or desired that they do. The Social Security Act, for example, did not cover large groups of people, agricultural and domestic workers most importantly. Surviving spouses initially had no benefits, and African Americans often held jobs not covered by the act. Benefits were relatively small, and the old-age and unemployment insurance were financed largely by regressive payroll taxes. The act did not include health insurance. In the reworking of social reform policy in 1935, "unemployables" (including such groups as children, the elderly, and the blind) fell to state responsibility, though the Social Security Act provided for matching grants for such categories of the needy. Other Second New Deal programs also had important limits. The "Wealth Tax" turned out to be something of a misnomer, for after Congress revised it, the legislation had little redistributionist character and did little to reduce concentrations of corporate wealth and power. The Public Utilities Holding Company Act also underwent significant revision, though ultimately it did help to decentralize the utilities industry and end some of the worst monopolistic practices.

But the programs of the Second New Deal nonetheless had a profound impact. The work relief programs of the WPA gave work and income to millions of people—not only in the varied construction programs of the WPA, but also in its programs for writers, theater workers, musicians, and artists. The WPA also implemented the National Youth Administration, which helped young people gain education and skills, and the Rural Electrification Administration, which ultimately helped to transform the American countryside. The Social Security Act provided the beginnings of an old-age insurance program that, starting with 1939 amendments, would expand in various ways over subsequent decades, and its other provisions had large future implications as well. The Wagner Act, and the National Labor Relations Board it created, played an instrumental role in the growing size and power of organized labor—both the American Federation of Labor (AFL) and the new Congress of Industrial Organizations (CIO). The Banking Act of 1935 substantially increased the power of the Federal Reserve Board over the banking system and thus enhanced its ability to support the economy. The 1935 legislation also contributed to Roosevelt's landslide reelection victory in the election of 1936.

The idea of a Second New Deal thus usefully focuses on the important legislation of 1935 and helps to illuminate what was different and important about it. But the First and Second New Deal concept has another advantage: it provides a chronological framework that enables understanding of the dynamics of New Deal policymaking and the development of the New Deal.

To a significant extent, the programs of the Second New Deal came as a result of policy planning underway for some time. That was certainly the case with the Social Security Act, recommended by the Committee on Economic Security formed in 1934 but with roots going back well before that. In the case of the WPA, the New Deal had begun work-relief programs in 1933, and Roosevelt and Relief Administrator Harry Hopkins preferred work relief over direct relief as a way to safeguard self-respect and build the national infrastructure. Roosevelt had been concerned about progressive taxation and utilities regulation long before 1935, and for some time Senator Robert Wagner had advocated stronger labor policy and a National Labor Relations Board with real authority and power. The Supreme Court's invalidation of the NRA in 1935 (and with it Section 7(a) of the National Industrial Recovery Act that had provided some protection for organized labor) required policy adjustments and paved the way for the passage of the Wagner Act.

But the Second New Deal was a product of politics as well as of policy planning and adjustment. By 1935 the efforts at national unity of the early New Deal had dissipated. Much of business had soured not only on the NRA but also on Roosevelt and the New Deal, and for his part, Roosevelt was no longer inclined to propitiate business. As anti-New Deal rhetoric escalated among businessmen, so did anti-business rhetoric increase among New Dealers.

While business, the wealthy, and conservatives increasingly criticized Roosevelt and the New Deal for doing too much, leaders on the left, often reflecting discontent among the poor, the working class, and the lower middle-class criticized the New Deal for doing too little. Especially prominent were Louisiana Senator Huey P. Long with his redistributionist "Share Our Wealth" program, California physician Francis Townsend and his plan for generous federal old age pensions, and the Michigan "Radio Priest" Father Charles Coughlin and his populist attacks on the New Deal and calls for monetary reform. These men attracted millions of followers and reflected widespread sentiment that the New Deal should do more to help struggling Americans. Despite economic improvement since 1933, unemployment had only fallen from 25 percent to 20 percent by 1935, and New Deal programs had only begun to provide assistance to the impoverished and unemployed.

To some degree, the Social Security Act, the "Wealth Tax," and other Second New Deal programs can be understood as responses to the criticisms and proposals of Long, Townsend, and Coughlin and as efforts to undercut their apparently growing political appeal. But while Long and the others did help focus attention on such measures and help build momentum for them, planning for Social Security, progressive taxation, and other 1935 legislation did not arise from their agitation. Moreover, policymaking in 1935 was also strongly affected by the outcome of the 1934 elections. Typically parties winning the presidency had lost significant strength in the subsequent off-year congressional elections; in earlier twentieth-century off-year elections, the president's party had lost an average of some three dozen seats in the House and three or four in the Senate. In 1934, however, Democrats gained an additional nine Congressmen and nine Senators (on top of the great increases in 1930 and especially 1932). Those results reflected both a vote of confidence in FDR and a desire for more reform—and produced a Congress that was more Democratic and more liberal than the Congress elected in 1932—and a Congress in which urban liberals in particular had significantly more power. Led by Senator Wagner, urban liberals provided both leadership and support for the programs of the Second New Deal.

The Second New Deal was thus a product of many forces—longstanding policy planning, the continued ravages of the Great Depression, the inadequacies or termination of some First New Deal programs, growing tension between the Roosevelt administration and business, pressure from such leaders as Long, Townsend, and Coughlin, and the election of 1934. Reflecting such factors, the legislation and programs of 1935 had a different character than those of 1933 and great importance for politics and government thereafter. Whatever its flaws, the First and Second New Deal framework thus does provide a way to understand the nature and importance of the 1935 legislation and the policy and political dynamics that shaped it.

See Also: NEW DEAL; NEW DEAL, THIRD; PUBLIC UTILITIES HOLDING COMPANY ACT; SOCIAL SECURITY ACT; TAXATION; WORKS PROGRESS ADMINISTRATION (WPA).

BIBLIOGRAPHY

Badger, Anthony J. *The New Deal: The Depression Years, 1933–1940.* 1989.

Graham, Otis. L., Jr. "Historians and the New Deals," *Social Studies* 54 (1963): 133–40.

Kennedy, David M. *Freedom from Fear: The American People in Depression and War, 1929–1945.* 1999.

Leuchtenburg, William E. *Franklin D. Roosevelt and the New Deal, 1932–1940.* 1963.

Schlesinger, Arthur M., Jr. *The Coming of the New Deal.* 1959.

Schlesinger, Arthur M., Jr. *The Politics of Upheaval.* 1960.

Wilson, William H. "The Two New Deals: A Valid Concept?" *The Historian* 28 (1966): 268–88.

JOHN W. JEFFRIES

NEW DEAL, THIRD

Historians have long distinguished between the "First New Deal" of 1933 and the "Second New Deal" of 1935 in tracing the development of the New Deal programs of President Franklin D. Roosevelt. A number of New Deal scholars later identified a "Third New Deal" that began in 1937. As with the First and Second New Deal typology, the idea of a Third New Deal has involved different interpretations and can suggest too great a discontinuity in priorities and programs from previous New Deal policy. But also as with the First and Second New Deal framework, understanding the notion of a Third New Deal helps to understand the dynamics of New Deal policymaking and the nature and legacy of the New Deal. While the First and Second New Deals laid the foundations for the modern regulatory-welfare state, the Third New Deal entailed both a new liberal agenda based on Keynesian fiscal policy and a more conservative political context that would be central to wartime and early postwar American politics.

Historians have identified at least two versions of an "intended" Third New Deal that did not materialize. One involved efforts to enlarge the policy planning and coordinating capacity of the executive branch and thus to implement a more powerful administrative state. Early in 1937, FDR sent Congress two measures towards that end: the Executive Reorganization Bill and the Judiciary Reorganization (or "Court-Packing") Bill. The Court-Packing Bill created a furor, and ultimately Roosevelt got only a shadow of what he had requested (though the bill may have contributed to creation of a more liberal Court in the next few years). In the context of the Court fight and of an emerging conservative coalition in Congress wary about expanding federal and presidential power, the Executive Reorganization Bill also stood little chance. A substantially watered down, though still significant, Executive Reorganization Act was passed in 1939. Some New Dealers also wanted to enhance the anti-monopoly power of the federal government, but little came of the Temporary National Economic Committee established in 1938 and of other anti-trust efforts.

Another version of an intended but essentially unsuccessful expansion of the New Deal, consistent with Roosevelt's second inaugural address in 1937 in which he talked about "one-third of a nation ill-housed, ill-clad, ill-nourished," was to enlarge the welfare state. The sharp and shocking recession of

1937 and 1938 reinforced the priority that social reformers gave to expanding social welfare and public assistance programs. But those efforts encountered effective opposition in the late 1930s, and then wartime prosperity seemed to make them unnecessary.

The more powerful administrative state and an expanded social welfare state failed to win approval largely because of the unexpected strength of conservatism in Washington and the nation after the overwhelming landslide victory of Roosevelt and the Democrats in 1936. In Congress, a conservative coalition of Republicans and conservative Democrats, enhanced by GOP gains in the election of 1938, stymied efforts to expand the New Deal. Among the forces creating this increased conservative opposition to liberal reform were the court-packing controversy and the recession of 1937 and 1938, though other events (for example, the sit-down strikes of the Congress of Industrial Organizations and Roosevelt's effort to "purge" conservative Democrats in the 1938 elections) played a role, too.

The recession of 1937 and 1938 was an especially important event in shaping the Third New Deal, for besides strengthening conservatives it also helped change the liberal agenda. Influenced by the British economist John Maynard Keynes, a number of influential New Deal policymakers became persuaded that the recession had occurred because Roosevelt had cut back on spending programs that had unbalanced the budget and contributed to the economic expansion (though far short of full recovery) between 1933 and 1936. In the spring of 1938, they persuaded FDR to return to a spending program, especially to provide relief assistance to the poor and jobless, and the deficits helped to reverse the recession. This sequence of events strengthened the belief that fiscal policy was vital to the performance of the economy. It also convinced many policymakers that compensatory fiscal policy could produce both reform and recovery—that deficit spending on desired social programs might also provide the economic stimulus for economic growth. During World War II, the massive deficits to finance mobilization (which dwarfed the relatively small and mostly unintended deficits of the 1930s) at last ended the Depression, restored prosperity, and created a full-production, full-employment economy. Keynesian fiscal policy thus became central to the liberal agenda of the Third New Deal of the late 1930s and beyond.

See Also: CONSERVATIVE COALITION; KEYNESIAN ECONOMICS; NEW DEAL; NEW DEAL, SECOND; RECESSION OF 1937.

BIBLIOGRAPHY

Brinkley, Alan. *The End of Reform: New Deal Liberalism in Recession and War.* 1995.

Jeffries, John W. "A 'Third New Deal'? Liberal Policy and the American State, 1937–1945." *Journal of Policy History* 8(4) (1996): 387–409.

Graham, Otis. L., Jr. "Franklin D. Roosevelt and the Intended New Deal." In *Essays in Honor of James MacGregor Burns,* edited by Michael R. Beschloss and Thomas E. Cronin. 1989.

Karl, Barry D. "Constitution and Central Planning: The Third New Deal Revisited." In *The Supreme Court Review, 1988,* edited by Philip B. Kurland, Gerhard Casper, and Dennis J. Hutchinson. 1989.

Milkis, Sidney M. *The President and the Parties: The Transformation of the American Party System since the New Deal.* 1993.

JOHN W. JEFFRIES

NEW MASSES

New Masses was the predominant intellectual journal of the Left from the mid-1920s to the mid-1940s. *New Masses* played a catalytic role in allowing a range of voices little heard in American "high" culture except in parody into the center of that culture. While this may seem unremarkable today, it was revolutionary then.

New Masses first appeared in late 1926 as a monthly cultural magazine that also featured considerable reportage. As the name suggests, its founders saw it as revival of the radical Greenwich Village bohemia embodied in the journals *The Masses* and *The Liberator*. Like *The Liberator* before it, *New Masses* viewed the Communist Party of the United States of America (CPUSA) as the leading vehicle of social change—a connection that would become increasingly close.

New Masses soon moved toward a more proletarian and less regionally parochial stance, particularly with the ascension of Mike Gold to the position of editor-in-chief in 1928. The most notable aspect of Gold's editorship over the next few years was his invitation to working-class writers (and would-be writers) across the country to tell their stories in their own voices. With the onset of the Great Depression in 1929, *New Masses* powerfully recorded the economic, social, and political crisis in a wide range of American accents.

In 1932, faced with a financial crisis, *New Masses* was transformed into a weekly political journal with a strong cultural interest modeled after *The New Republic.* It was increasingly aimed at white-collar workers. Nonetheless, the editors of *New Masses* retained a considerable attachment to the notion of promoting a working-class literature.

These alterations in format and intended audience lent themselves well to the Popular Front era that emerged in the mid-1930s. The magazine was closely aligned with both the antifascist struggle epitomized by the Republican cause in the Spanish Civil War and the organization of workers in the new industrial labor unions of the Committee for Industrial Organization (later the Congress of Industrial Organizations, or CIO). *New Masses* was able to reach a large segment of the liberal non-Communist intelligentsia not only because of a general antifascist zeitgeist, but also because the period saw the first successful large-scale attempts to organize white-collar workers into such left-influenced unions as the Screenwriters Guild, the Newspaper Guild, the Teachers Union, and the Office and Professional Employees Union.

This Hitler-Stalin pact in 1939 marked the end of the Popular Front era at the magazine in some respects. *New Masses* still strove to reach non-Communist activists in the arts, the labor movement, and the civil rights movement—and to build support for the Soviet Union. However, negative reaction to the pact provided a major boost to an anti-Stalinist Left critique of the CPUSA and *New Masses* within intellectual and artistic circles.

This anti-Stalinism, most prominently displayed in the pages of *The Partisan Review*, painted *New Masses* as a middlebrow tool of Soviet foreign policy. *New Masses* was able to deflect some of this criticism once the Soviet Union and the United States became allied against the Nazis. However, the journal's core constituency was weakened and increasingly isolated, a weakness that became apparent once World War II ended and the Cold War began in earnest. *New Masses* retrenched to a weekly cultural journal and then merged in 1947 with the leftist cultural journal *Mainstream* to form *Masses and Mainstream.*

See Also: COMMUNIST PARTY; POPULAR FRONT.

BIBLIOGRAPHY

Aaron, Daniel. *Writers on the Left: Episodes in American Literary Communism.* 1961.

Denning, Michael. *The Cultural Front: The Laboring of American Culture in the Twentieth Century.* 1996.

Foley, Barbara. *Radical Representations: Politics and Form in U.S. Proletarian Fiction, 1929–1941.* 1993.

North, Joseph, ed. *New Masses: An Anthology of the Rebel Thirties.* 1969.

Pells, Richard H. *Radical Visions and American Dreams: Culture and Social Thought in the Depression Years.* 1974.

Wixson, Douglas. *Worker-Writer in America: Jack Conroy and the Tradition of Midwestern Literary Radicalism, 1898–1990.* 1994.

JAMES SMETHURST

NEW YORK WORLD'S FAIR (1939–1940)

The New York World's Fair of 1939 to 1940 in Flushing Meadow, Queens, celebrated a utopian vision of the "World of Tomorrow" that touted American machine-age industrial prowess. Organized by New York's business elite beginning in 1935, the fair was originally conceived as a celebration of the 150th anniversary of George Washington's inauguration in New York City. The organizers hoped that the fair would boost the local economy and alleviate Depression-era anxieties about the role of industry in American society. The emulation of an idealized past typical of other international expositions gave way, however, to an optimistic vision of the future in which the availability of machine-made consumer goods created conditions for widespread prosperity and democracy. The only remnant of the original theme was a monumental statue of George Washington, depicted as if gazing into the future, that provided a link between 150 years of democratic traditions and modern American prosperity. Overall, the fair's modernist utopian vision predominated, symbolized by the Trylon and Perisphere that became the icons of the exposition.

Fair planners aimed to structure visitors' experience to reinforce the ideology of a machine-age consumer prosperity. Situated at the heart of a series of color-coded zones, the Perisphere housed the exposition's theme center. Here, visitors encountered the "Democracity," a vision of the planned communities of the future in which an efficient highway system linked a commercial urban core to suburbs designed for the modern living of the "average" American family. Industry pavilions underscored the significance of new technologies such as television and FM radio in creating consumer goods that would facilitate a distinctly American "way of life."

The World of Tomorrow was presented as a product of an industry-government coalition. One of the most popular exhibitions was the Futurama at the General Motors pavilion. Created by industrial designer Norman Bel Geddes, Futurama seated visitors in plush armchairs and conveyed them past a 36,000 square foot model of the American landscape as it would look in 1960. The efficient system of highways showed viewers the possibilities that could be realized by the automobile if government funding would create the infrastructure.

The fair touted federal and state accomplishments in its government zone amidst international exhibitions from more than sixty countries. Here, the backdrop of the war in Europe disrupted the fair's vision of a prosperous and peaceful future. Germany was notably absent from the lineup of European exhibitors, and the pavilions of Poland and Czechoslovakia remained open despite the Nazi takeover of those countries.

The streamlined modernism that characterized the fair's architecture and consumer goods was complemented by art of all styles throughout the fair grounds. Drawing on Works Progress Administration arts projects that stressed the integration of art and everyday life, fair planners made sculpture integral to the design of the fair; murals by Fernand Leger, Willem de Kooning, Stuart Davis, and others decorated the pavilions. With additional exhibitions of contemporary American and old master paintings, the fair became an art event that linked cultural achievement and American industrial innovation.

The amusement zone was a prime attraction and planners stretched unsuccessfully to connect its spectacles to the fair's utopian theme. Billy Rose's Aquacade, for example, was pure spectacle—an aquatic variety show with elaborate synchronized swimming held in a ten-thousand-seat amphitheater. Other displays attracted viewers with risqué offerings, such as Norman Bel Geddes's Crystal Lassies, a modern peep show enhanced by an elaborate system of mirrors, and Salvador Dali's Dream of Venus, a nonsensical surrealist "fun house" that featured semi-nude figures.

The World of Tomorrow was a financial disaster. Attendance fell short of expectations and organizers had lost millions of dollars by the time the fair closed on October 27, 1940. Many people, it seemed, found the admission price too high. Those who did come further disappointed organizers by seeking their own experience of the exposition rather than conforming to the planned vision. Nevertheless, the fair's legacy included new technologies and consumer goods that transformed daily life, and widespread acceptance of modernism in the areas of art, architecture and industrial design. The World of Tomorrow also popularized the idea of the "average" American, affecting corporate marketing strategies and Americans' own understanding of themselves.

See Also: SCIENCE AND TECHNOLOGY.

BIBLIOGRAPHY

Gelernter, David H. *1939: The Lost World of the Fair.* 1995.

Harrison, Helen A., ed. *Dawn of a New Day: The New York World's Fair, 1939/40.* 1980.

Rosenblum, Robert; Rosemarie Haag Bletter; et. al *Remembering the Future: The New York World's Fair from 1939 to 1964.* 1989

Rydell, Robert W. *World of Fairs: The Century-of-Progress Expositions.* 1993.

Wurts, Richard, et al., photographers, and Stanley Applebaum, ed. *The New York World's Fair, 1939/1940 in 155 Photographs.* 1977.

ISADORA ANDERSON HELFGOTT

NFU. *See* NATIONAL FARMERS UNION.

NIEBUHR, REINHOLD

Karl Paul Reinhold Niebuhr (June 21, 1892–June 1, 1971) was the most significant American-born Protestant theologian of the twentieth century, and during the Depression an important political activist, thinker, and writer. Son of an immigrant minister of the German Evangelical Synod of North America, Niebuhr grew up in Missouri and Illinois and attended the Synod's Eden Seminary (Bachelor of Divinity, 1913) and Yale Divinity School (B.D. 1914, M.A. 1915). His studies confirmed him as a liberal and a modernist in theology—both anti-Calvinist and anti-supernaturalist. During World War I he was an ardent supporter of Woodrow Wilson's liberal internationalism and a militant Americanizer within the German-American community. In the 1920s, while serving as pastor of the middle-class Bethel Evangelical Church in Detroit, he became a leading voice of liberal Protestantism. A determined foe of Henry Ford's labor policies, he preached social justice and racial tolerance from pulpits around the country and in the pages of the national weekly magazine *The Christian Century.*

Even before leaving Detroit in 1928 for a professorship in Christian ethics at Union Theological Seminary in New York, Niebuhr had embraced a gradualist socialism. Once in New York he became a main contributor to the socialist weekly *The World Tomorrow.* In 1930 he ran for the state Senate on the Socialist Party ticket, and in 1932 he was a Socialist candidate for Congress (both were "educational" campaigns that garnered few votes). But with the rise of fascism Niebuhr moved toward the New Deal coalition, voting for Roosevelt reluctantly in 1936, and enthusiastically thereafter. During the Depression he wrote his most influential books, while also laboring tirelessly as a political organizer and journalist. *Moral Man and Immoral Society* (1932), *Beyond Tragedy* (1937), and *The Nature and Destiny of Man* (1941) were pivotal works in the rethinking of American reform politics in relation to Protestant theology. He blended the liberal hope for expanded justice and equality with "the tragic sense of life," a sensibility usually associated with conservatism. Niebuhr effected the same ideological merger in founding the Fellowship of Socialist Christians (1931), the Union for Democratic Action (1941), and *Radical Religion* (1935) and *Christianity and Crisis* (1941) magazines. By the time he appeared on the cover of *Time*'s twenty-fifth anniversary issue in 1948, the word *Niebuhrian* had come to mean a persistent commitment to social responsibility in a world of chastened expectations.

See Also: CIVIL RIGHTS AND CIVIL LIBERTIES; RELIGION; SOCIALIST PARTY.

BIBLIOGRAPHY
Beckley, Harlan. *Passion for Justice: Retrieving the Legacies of Walter Rauschenbusch, John A. Ryan, and Reinhold Niebuhr.* 1992.

Fox, Richard Wightman. *Reinhold Niebuhr: A Biography.* 1997.

Lovin, Robin. *Reinhold Niebuhr and Christian Realism.* 1995.

Meyer, Donald B. *The Protestant Search for Political Realism, 1919–1941,* 2nd edition. 1988

RICHARD WIGHTMAN FOX

NIRA. *See* NATIONAL INDUSTRIAL RECOVERY ACT.

NLRB. *See* NATIONAL LABOR RELATIONS BOARD.

NORRIS, GEORGE

The Depression years witnessed the fulfillment of the public career of George William Norris (July 11,

1861–September 2, 1944). Already in his seventies, he played a major role in the enactment of many of his legislative aspirations both in Washington and in Lincoln, Nebraska.

Elected to the House of Representatives in 1902 and to the Senate in 1912, Norris first came to public attention as a member in opposition; he opposed the power of the speaker of the house in 1910 and the nation's entrance into World War I, as well as the peace treaty that followed the war. During the 1920s Norris continued as an opposition leader, fighting against the disposal of government properties, including a dam under construction during World War I at Muscle Shoals, a series of swift rapids in the Tennessee River in northern Alabama. The dam was unfinished when the war ended. Norris also opposed individuals and groups interested in the private development of the dam's hydroelectric potential and what he considered flawed efforts to provide assistance to distressed rural America. However, by the last years of the Hoover administration, as the Great Depression unfolded with progressive Republicans holding the balance of power in the Senate, the Norris-La Guardia Anti-Injunction Act (1932) became law, and a measure championed by Norris for over a decade calling for an amendment abolishing the "lame duck" sessions of Congress was approved and then ratified in 1933 as the twentieth amendment to the U.S. Constitution.

With the election of Franklin Delano Roosevelt, Norris saw more of his dreams coming true. Most important was the creation of the Tennessee Valley Authority (TVA), which called for multipurpose development of the Tennessee River Valley. In Nebraska, Norris championed the Tri-County Project and other public power projects, creating in effect a miniature TVA that helped make Nebraska, like Tennessee, an all-public-power state. In 1934, Norris stumped the state calling for the creation of a unicameral legislature and was on hand for the convening of its first session in 1936.

An ardent supporter of the New Deal, Norris cosponsored measures calling for the permanent establishment of the Rural Electrification Administration. He also supported a farm forestry law, and endorsed funding for agencies and projects providing assistance to rural America. Norris supported measures to regulate corporations and to guarantee labor's right to organize, and he also supported the establishment of a system of social security, as well as appropriations providing work for the unemployed. Reluctantly, because he believed that "only God can change the Supreme Court," Norris voted for the president's court-packing scheme to secure justices more sympathetic to the New Deal. In 1936, seeking a fifth term, Norris abandoned his Republican Party affiliation and ran as an independent, becoming the first senator to be elected as an independent. President Roosevelt, campaigning in Omaha, endorsed Norris over his own party's candidate.

Defeated for reelection in 1942, Norris returned to his hometown, McCook, where he prepared his autobiography and maintained until his death an active interest in public affairs and the concerns of rural America.

See Also: NORRIS-LA GUARDIA ACT; TENNESSEE VALLEY AUTHORITY (TVA).

BIBLIOGRAPHY

Lowitt, Richard. *George W. Norris.* Vol. 1: *The Making of a Progressive, 1861–1912.* 1963. Vol. 2: *The Persistence of a Progressive: 1913–1933,* 1971. Vol. 3: *The Triumph of a Progressive: 1933–1934,* 1978.

Norris, George W. *Fighting Liberal: The Autobiography of George W. Norris.* 1945.

RICHARD LOWITT

NORRIS-LA GUARDIA ACT

Signed into law by President Herbert Hoover on March 23, 1932, the Norris-La Guardia Act culminated a decades-long struggle by the American labor movement to restrict the use of anti-union injunctions in labor disputes. First introduced in the Senate by George W. Norris in 1928 and later sponsored in the House of Representatives by Fiorello La Guardia, the act presaged the National Labor Relations Act by proclaiming as the public policy of the United States support for the efforts of workers to form their own unions and engage in collective bargaining. The law severely limited the power of federal judges to issue injunctions in labor disputes and also rendered so-called yellow dog contracts, which made employment contingent upon an employee agreeing not to join a union, unenforceable in the federal courts.

The issuance of injunctions against sympathy strikes, boycotts, and other tactics used by organized labor had become increasingly common after 1880. Over four thousand such injunctions were issued between 1880 and 1930. The elimination of labor injunctions had thus become a top priority for the American Federation of Labor (AFL) after its founding in the 1880s. Leaders of the AFL believed they had accomplished this objective with the 1914 Clayton Act amendments to the Sherman antitrust law. However, subsequent judicial interpretation negated the effectiveness of the Clayton Act, so that almost as many injunctions were issued in the 1920s alone as in the previous four decades combined. Although Norris supported the AFL's basic objectives, he rejected a specific AFL proposal to make unions and labor disputes virtually immune from any form of judicial intervention. Instead, he relied on labor lawyer Donald Richberg, economist Edwin Witte, and law professors Felix Frankfurter, Herman Oliphant, and Francis Sayre to draft a more narrowly framed law that was consistent with the approach to labor law reform soon to be adopted by the New Deal.

In response to the tremendous increase in the use of labor injunctions during the 1920s and the change in political climate resulting from the impact of the Great Depression, both the House and Senate approved the Norris La Guardia Act by overwhelming margins in 1932. Although Hoover had previously opposed the bill, he grudgingly signed it, stating at the time that the courts would ultimately determine the act's constitutionality. The Supreme Court later upheld the law in *Lauf v. E.G. Shiner & Co.* (1938).

See Also: AMERICAN FEDERATION OF LABOR (AFL); COLLECTIVE BARGAINING; ORGANIZED LABOR.

BIBLIOGRAPHY

Bernstein, Irving. *The Lean Years: A History of the American Worker, 1920–1933.* 1960.

Ernst, Daniel. "The Yellow-Dog Contract and Liberal Reform, 1917–1932." *Labor History* 30 (1989): 251–274.

Forbath, William E. *Law and the Shaping of the American Labor Movement.* 1991.

Frankfurter, Felix, and Nathan Greene. *The Labor Injunction.* 1930.

O'Brien, Ruth. *Workers' Paradox: The Republican Origins of New Deal Labor Policy, 1886–1935.* 1998.

LARRY G. GERBER

NORTHEAST, GREAT DEPRESSION IN THE

Given its place at the heart of the American economic system, the Northeast (comprising the states of Connecticut, Rhode Island, Massachusetts, Maine, New Hampshire, Vermont, New York, Pennsylvania, and New Jersey) suffered mightily during the Great Depression. An argument could be made that as a region the Northeast bore the brunt of the economic crisis, particularly because New York City reigned as the capital of global finance. Not only did the American people look to the financiers on Wall Street to bail them out of the crisis, but the entire world hoped that a economic recovery would begin in New York City.

The Great Depression also had a psychological impact on the United States, and news of the economic chaos was spread through newspapers and radio. Since the nation's media spotlight emanated from and shined brightly on New York City, the city's newspapers covered the Great Depression from front row seats that intensified the glare. A reporter for one of New York City's many daily newspapers did not have to travel far to see or feel the devastation—thousands of citizens formed breadlines on a daily basis.

Up and down the Northeast, from the important port cities of Boston and Philadelphia to the financial capital of New York City, the region symbolized the massive human suffering endured during the era. Prior to the stock market crash, the *New York Times* and the *Wall Street Journal* had trumpeted the success of the market and kept tabs

Unemployment in the major cities of the Northeast forced many people to seek charitable help during the Depression. These men lined up for free food at a New York City mission in 1932. FRANKLIN DELANO ROOSEVELT LIBRARY

on the stock market's movers and shakers. Despite the widespread panic gripping the nation after the collapse, newspapers across the region were filled with reassuring stories about the long-term viability of the market system.

Psychologically, money was at the center of American culture in the 1920s. Brokers and investment bankers were society's new heroes—the kinds of people flocking to the financial centers in the Northeast, particularly New York City, Boston, and Philadelphia. Markets fluctuations, hot stocks, and trading exploits became juicy gossip items in

the era. The growing consumer culture required money. The impulse to live it up necessitated an ever-growing cash flow. Thus, many relied on stocks and a line of credit to finance their new lifestyles. The banking industry, centered in New York City, gained a tremendous amount of power in determining the economic fortunes of the nation. The "get rich quick" mentality lured people into the market. They hoped for the big score that would take them away from everyday toil.

The bond drives that took place during World War I opened the public's eyes to the power of investment. The large commercial banks were more than willing to facilitate these trades. Win or lose, the big banks and brokerages would receive their cut. In addition, the expanding opportunities to acquire goods on credit familiarized average citizens with the concept of buying stocks on margin.

STOCK MARKET COLLAPSE

Wall Street represented a new religion in the United States. Its priests were the men who ran Wall Street's successful brokerages and investment banks. They formed a sort of exclusive gentleman's club, each belonging to the same clubs, vacationing together, and mainly living on the Upper East Side of Manhattan. The ultimate club was the New York Stock Exchange, with a mere 1,100 seats. The only way in was to purchase an existing seat from one of the members or investment banks that owned the seat. The men who controlled Wall Street had deep ties to the Northeast. Most had attended the private schools and elite colleges dotting the region.

While Wall Street's leaders breezed through an insulated world high above the trading floor, an entirely different kind of trader fueled the stock overspeculation that would lead to the crash. Many traders only cared about stock fluctuation, borrowing enough money to buy and sell, then quickly moving the stock to make money on the difference. Timing, not knowledge, mattered most. By the summer of 1929, stock market value hit $67 billion, up from $27 billion two years earlier.

The economic freefall that took place in and after October 1929 decimated the American economy. Within three years, 75 percent of the value of all securities—a whopping $90 billion—disappeared. The year after the crash, more than twenty-six thousand businesses went bankrupt, surpassed in 1931 by more than twenty-eight thousand failures. In December 1930, the Bank of the United States went bankrupt, wiping out approximately 400,000 depositors.

Early relief efforts advocated by the administration of Herbert Hoover were a mix of public and private cooperation. In November 1930, Philadelphia's most influential citizens formed a committee under the leadership of Horatio Gates Lloyd, a partner in the city's branch of the J. P. Morgan con-

glomerate. The group raised an initial $4 million, which it doled out to various charitable organizations. Lloyd also participated in a city effort to raise money for the needy. To the dismay of the Hoover administration and the private organizers, such programs did little to stem the disaster. Although the Lloyd committee raised an additional $7 million to fight Philadelphia's economic woes, the money ran out in a little over a year. And even though it raised another $10 million and received $2.5 million more from the state, the committee had disbanded by June 1932. Philadelphia's relief efforts failed, as did the efforts of similar charitable organizations across the region, and with them went the hopes of the Hoover administration for a public-private partnership to end the crisis.

AWASH IN FEAR

As debilitating as the stock market crash was to the nation's economy, the crushing blow came from the way it demoralized the American people. The collapse shocked everyone and shook people's faith in the national economic system. Businessmen and corporations, many headquartered in New York, reacted by making drastic cuts, while anxious consumers virtually stopped spending on anything beyond bare necessities. Millions of workers lost their jobs as businesses desperately cut their operations to the bare essentials. Construction in New York City, for example, came to a near halt as 64 percent of construction workers were laid off soon after the stock market collapsed. Unemployment in 1929 was slightly over 3 percent, but by 1932 the figure had reached 24 percent. Millions more were involuntarily working in part-time positions.

In 1931, nearly 200,000 New Yorkers were evicted from their apartments for failure to pay rent. Many who were not evicted sold off their valuables so they could pay their rent, or they moved from apartment to apartment. If their furniture had been purchased on credit, owners left it behind when they could no longer make payments. Philadelphians experienced 1,300 evictions per month during the year following the crash.

The psychological toll unemployment took on the American people caused high levels of stress and anxiety. While some took to the streets to sell

Unemployed steel workers and their families (photographed in 1938 in Midland, Pennsylvania) were forced to live in tarpaper shacks because of a housing shortage. LIBRARY OF CONGRESS, PRINTS & PHOTOGRAPHS DIVISION, FSA/OWI COLLECTION

whatever they could gather, others turned to crime in an effort to find food. In Pittsburgh, a man stole a loaf of bread to feed his children, and then later hanged himself in shame. In New York City, hundreds of thousands of unemployed or underemployed workers turned to soup kitchens. By October 1933, New York City counted 1.25 million people on relief. Even more telling is that another one million were eligible for relief, but did not accept it. Six thousand New Yorkers tried to make money selling apples on the streets. But by the end of 1931, most street vendors were gone. Grocery store sales dropped by 50 percent during the Depression. Many urban dwellers scoured garbage cans and dumps looking for food. Studies estimated that 65 percent of the African-American children in Harlem were plagued by malnutrition during the era.

Tens of thousands of people in New York City were forced to live on the streets or in shantytowns located along the banks of the East River and the Hudson River. These clusters of makeshift abodes were dubbed *Hoovervilles*—a backhanded tribute to the president. The city's largest camp was in Central Park. Ironically, the Central Park shantytown became a tourist attraction and featured daily performances by an unemployed tightrope walker and other out-of-work artists.

Even the rich were not immune to the harsh realities of the Great Depression. From his Manhattan palace, steel king Charles M. Schwab openly admitted his fear. By the early 1930s, the situation was so glum that it became fashionable among the wealthy to brag about how much they had lost in the crash. Even professions one would think were insulated from economic hardship were affected during the Depression. In Brooklyn, one-third of all doctors were forced out of business.

When people learned of the role business leaders had played in the stock market crash, they quickly changed their formerly favorable opinions to outright scorn. The Wall Street collapse proved that these exalted financial leaders did not know what they were talking about in the years leading up to that fateful October as they continually hyped the market. Remarkably, in the days immediately after the collapse, the nation's business leaders (from Sears, AT&T, and General Motors, among others) issued cheery reports about swelling sales and stability in an attempt to bolster public confidence.

The Depression in the Northeast was not confined to the region's urban centers. Farming—still accounting for one-fourth of the U.S. population—had been depressed for nearly a decade. Farmers suffered as exports, crop prices, and land values all dropped. The Great Depression hit farmers and rural areas in the Midwest and West much harder than the Northeast because those areas depended much more on farming as part of the regional economy. In addition, many of the farmers who left their land during the crisis headed west to find a better life in California's agricultural regions and urban centers.

The bleak economic conditions in the Northeast led to direct confrontation between those who were suffering and various authorities. The Communist and Socialist parties, for instance, agitated unemployed workers to rise up against those controlling the economy. While party bosses, like the Communist leader William Z. Foster, dreamed of the end of the capitalist system, hungry and fearful workers demanded food, jobs, and some form of meaningful relief. In early 1930, Communist activists staged rallies against unemployment that drew protestors in New York, Washington, D.C., Boston, and many other cities. At some sites, demonstrators fought with police, who used force against the agi-

tators, including tear gas in the nation's capital. New York police used nightsticks to break up a crowd of thirty-five thousand who had turned out in Union Square to hear Foster speak.

The administration of Franklin D. Roosevelt was not immune to agitation, even though it fought to alleviate the problems plaguing the economy. In 1933 and 1934, unions organized around the country to fight for better wages, working conditions, and hours. On Labor Day in 1934, more than 300,000 textile workers from New England to the southern states staged a strike that became the most violent strike in American history. In Fall River, Massachusetts, approximately ten thousand protestors surrounded a mill, trapping the strikebreakers inside. Riots broke out across New England, and at many sites corporate guards, special deputies, and the police fought with strikers and their supporters. As the violence increased, the National Guard was mobilized in every New England state except New Hampshire and Vermont. President Roosevelt had to personally intervene to end the confrontation between owners and workers.

THE NEW DEAL

Given the state's place at the heart of the financial and psychological turmoil of the Great Depression, it is ironic that a New Yorker, then Governor Roosevelt, rose to challenge incumbent Herbert Hoover in the 1932 presidential election. The public perception that Hoover did not fully grasp the enormity of the economic crisis led to a landslide victory for Roosevelt, who came from a long line of New York aristocrats.

Roosevelt took office in the midst of a banking crisis, but with a deft touch and a supportive Congress, he got the Emergency Banking Act passed, which allayed depositors' fears and gave banks a shot of confidence. Next, Roosevelt used a series of fireside chats to calm the nation, and he created programs that put people back to work and gave them hope for the future.

The Roosevelt administration heard the pleas of those who wanted to work, but could not find jobs. Roosevelt championed the Civil Works Administration and within two weeks 800,000 people were put to work. Several months later, more than

This federal housing project, photographed in 1942, was built during the Depression for low-income families in New Bedford, Massachusetts. LIBRARY OF CONGRESS, PRINTS & PHOTOGRAPHS DIVISION, FSA/OWI COLLECTION

four million were working in the program, which focused on construction of roads, bridges, schools, playgrounds, and hospitals. Roosevelt and his aides realized that hunger was not negotiable and putting people to work would relieve some of the doldrums the nation confronted.

In early 1933, the Civilian Conservation Corps (CCC) began operations with an initial enrollment of 250,000 at a cost of $500 million. The next summer, Roosevelt enlarged the group to 350,000, then to half a million in 1935. CCC "soil soldiers" built roads, installed telephone lines, planted trees, and worked for several federal agencies. In New York and Vermont, they supported the Army Corps of Engineers in building much needed flood control projects. Although the CCC was a nationwide effort, it helped ease the plight of northeastern urban centers by relocating young unemployed men out of the cities.

The federal government also supported public works efforts by doling out money from the Public Works Administration (PWA), established in 1933. New York City received more PWA money than any other municipality because of Mayor Fiorello La Guardia's close relationship with President Roosevelt. In all, the city was given $116 million in grants and another $136 million in loans. The improvement projects ranged from new playgrounds and housing complexes to the $42 million Triborough Bridge, linking Queens, Manhattan, and the Bronx.

Later, Roosevelt pushed through the Emergency Relief Appropriation of 1935, which enabled him to create the Works Progress Administration (WPA). Although the WPA cost more than making direct payments to the poor, the program helped lift people's spirits, in the Northeast and elsewhere, making them feel worthy of having a job.

See Also: BUSINESSMEN; CITIES AND SUBURBS; COMMUNICATION AND THE PRESS; HOMELESSNESS; HOUSING; MIDWEST, GREAT DEPRESSION IN THE; PSYCHOLOGICAL IMPACT OF THE GREAT DEPRESSION; SOUTH, GREAT DEPRESSION IN THE; STOCK MARKET CRASH (1929); STRIKES; WEST, GREAT DEPRESSION IN THE AMERICAN.

BIBLIOGRAPHY

Bernstein, Michael A. *The Great Depression: Delayed Recovery and Economic Change in America, 1929–1939.* 1987.

Bird, Caroline. *The Invisible Scar.* 1966.

Ellis, Edward Robb. *A Nation in Torment: The Great American Depression, 1929–1939.* 1970.

Green, Harvey. *The Uncertainty of Everyday Life, 1915–1945.* 1992.

Klein, Maury. *Rainbow's End: The Crash of 1929.* 2001.

Klingaman, William K. *1929: The Year of the Great Crash.* 1989.

McElvaine, Robert S. *The Great Depression: America, 1929–1941,* rev. edition. 1993.

Watkins, T. H. *The Great Depression: America in the 1930s.* 1993.

Watkins, T. H. *The Hungry Years: A Narrative History of the Great Depression in America.* 1999.

BOB BATCHELOR

NRA. *See* NATIONAL RECOVERY ADMINISTRATION.

NRPB. *See* NATIONAL RESOURCES PLANNING BOARD.

NYA. *See* NATIONAL YOUTH ADMINISTRATION.

ODUM, HOWARD

Howard Washington Odum (May 24, 1884–November 8, 1954) was an educator, sociologist, and research director, and the first individual to undertake an organized, social scientific research program of the American South. Born near Mount Pleasant, Georgia, to a family of small fundamentalist farmers, Odum imbibed southern patriotism from his grandfathers, both Civil War veterans. An opportune family move allowed him to attend Emory College, where he received a bachelor's degree in classics. Odum earned a master of arts degree at the University of Mississippi, where a psychologist mentor directed him first to G. Stanley Hall at Clark University and then to Franklin Giddings at Columbia University. Odum's Clark dissertation in psychology in 1909 and his sociology dissertation from Columbia in 1910 were both based on African-American folktales. These writings reflected Odum's interest in African Americans, but he assumed their natural inferiority. Until near the end of his life, Odum, despite his membership in the Commission for Interracial Cooperation, was unable to transcend his prejudices, although he came to view black inferiority as a function of environment rather than genetics.

After short stays at several academic institutions, Odum went in 1920 to the University of North Carolina at Chapel Hill, where he would remain for the rest of his life. Within his first five years at Chapel Hill, Odum founded the department of sociology, the school of public welfare, the *Journal of Social Forces,* and the Institute for Research in the Social Sciences. He excelled at raising money, receiving $1.25 million from Rockefeller foundations alone.

Odum was popular with foundations because he focused completely on specific social problems. He emphasized "objective measurement," and when he served as an assistant director for the 1929 President's Research Committee on Social Trends, he demanded totally factual contributions in line with Herbert Hoover's demands. Ironically, "impressionistic" analysis was central to Odum's own work.

By the 1930s Odum identified *sectionalism,* a self-enforced isolation that inculcated prejudice and caused people to reject outside help, as the South's greatest problem. He accused the Southern Agrarians of championing exactly such a view, and advocated the concept of regionalism, or the breaking up of the nation's complexity into smaller, cooperating regions. Using research teams to collect data in 648 categories, Odum wrote the influential *Southern Regions* (1936) and *American Regionalism* (1938). Despite Odum's extensive research and problem-solving orientation, he lacked a willingness to take into account political and economic power.

By the 1940s, Odum had returned to work on his initial subject of folkways, and he added the concept of *technicways* to reflect technological society and its culture, which he despised. Odum continued to write until the time of his death.

See Also: EDUCATION; SOUTH, GREAT DEPRESSION IN THE.

BIBLIOGRAPHY

Challen, Paul. *A Sociological Analysis of Southern Regionalism: The Contributions of Howard W. Odum.* 1993.

O'Brien, Michael. *The Idea of the American South, 1920–1941.* 1979.

Singal, Daniel J. *The War Within: From Victorian to Modernist Thought in the South 1915–1945.* 1982.

Tullos, Allen. "Politics of Regional Development." In *Lewis Mumford: Public Intellectual,* edited by Thomas P. Hughes and Agatha C. Hughes. 1990.

MARK C. SMITH

OKIES

Okies is a term applied generally to people from the American Southwest who migrated to the Pacific Coast, particularly to California, during the Great Depression. This pattern became associated with Oklahoma because that state provided a plurality of migrants from 1935 to 1940, the peak of the phenomenon. Texas, Arkansas, Missouri, Kansas, Nebraska, Colorado, and the Dakotas all contributed heavily to the numbers trekking west, not only to California, but also to Arizona, Washington, Oregon, and Idaho. Though this migration was commonly associated with the Dust Bowl (vividly portrayed in Pare Lorentz's 1936 documentary *The Plow that Broke the Plains*), the impelling forces were complex. Drought conditions on the Plains, starting in the early 1930s and intensifying in mid-decade, were surely a cause for leaving. But a larger number of Oklahoma migrants, for example, came from the more humid, though drought-stricken, southeastern part of the state than from the Dust Bowl region of the northwest and panhandle. Many of the migrants from the Plains and Southwest farmed marginal land. In drought conditions the topsoil blew away and the land became even less likely to support crops. A large number of these farmers were tenants—60 percent of Oklahoma farmers rented their farms—and consequently were less rooted. Mechanization of farming, especially the introduction of tractors, pushed people off the land. Moreover, when the Agricultural Adjustment Administration paid farmers not to grow crops, it was often the tenants who would be left landless. Finally, at least in southeastern Oklahoma, farmers possessed a migratory habit of mind and simply continued their pattern of moving west.

The Okies were drawn to California by a vision of the West as a land of greater opportunity, especially the chance to own a small plot of fertile soil. But there were more substantive draws. Both jobs and relief seemed to be paying more in California, and the migrants' friends and relatives who had moved to the Golden State in large numbers in the 1920s invited them to enjoy a better life.

The migration started in earnest in 1935, peaking in 1937 and 1938. The essential optimism of the people, always hoping for better weather and a better crop next year, probably kept them from moving earlier. But as the weather got worse and their personal economic situations became desperate, the Okies took action. They packed up what belongings they could get into the family truck or car and began the three-day (or more) trip to California along Route 66.

Not all of the migrants were farmers (a Farm Security Administration [FSA] survey indicated that unemployment more than drought caused the migrants to relocate), and a substantial number of the Okies made their way to the cities. Almost 100,000 of the 252,000 migrants to California followed Highway 66 to its western terminus in Los Angeles where they largely blended in and quickly lost any identity as Okies. Angelinos noticed their arrival. In 1936 the Los Angeles Police established a Bum Blockade at all the major entrances to the state. Short-lived and embarrassing to Los Angeles, it nonetheless hinted at the harsher reception for those better-remembered migrants who settled in the San Joaquin Valley.

This Oklahoma family found work in the pea fields near Nipomo, California, in the spring of 1937. LIBRARY OF CONGRESS, PRINTS & PHOTOGRAPHS DIVISION, FSA/OWI COLLECTION

Though some ended up in oil and others in construction, most of the migrants to this fertile central California valley became farm laborers, replacing Mexican and Filipino workers in the orchards and cotton fields. The Okies were welcomed as cheap labor, but despised as residents. The worst off lived along the banks of irrigation ditches in abject squalor. A few found lodging in the sixteen permanent and nine mobile FSA government camps. As time went on the migrants themselves were able to construct modest homes for themselves in Okievilles.

The Okies were segregated by class and stereotyped as rigidly as any disdained racial or ethnic group. The California Citizens Association, orga-

nized to stem the influx of migrants, succeeded in upping the relief requirement from one year's residence to three. The Associated Farmers battled against the possibility that the migrants might be organized into a meaningful force by the United Cannery, Agricultural, Packing, and Allied Workers of America, a Congress of Industrial Organizations union. They criticized (accurately) FSA camps as organizing grounds and fought the several strikes that broke out in the late 1930s. Okies, however, were not much interested in unionization. Though often demoralized, they were still independent enough to reject the blandishments of organizers.

The Okies probably fared best in the area of culture. Novelist John Steinbeck brought the plight of the migrants with full force to the American public in 1939 with the novel *The Grapes of Wrath*, which described the journey of the Joad family from Oklahoma to California, where they were met with disdain and hostility, except in a government camp. Dramatic photographs of Okies by the FSA's Dorothea Lange and the widely heard folk songs of Oklahoma native Woody Guthrie reinforced Steinbeck's pleas on behalf of the migrants. Director John Ford reworked *The Grapes of Wrath* into a more optimistic and populist presentation in his 1940 film.

As World War II loomed, the Okies began substantially to assimilate. Many entered defense industries in the larger metropolitan areas, but many remained in the San Joaquin Valley scoring some cultural victories. A streak of common-man political conservatism, the emergence and popularization of country music, and the burgeoning of conservative Protestant religious groups mark the impact of the migrants on the society that had despised them.

See Also: DUST BOWL; MIGRATION; WEST, GREAT DEPRESSION IN THE AMERICAN.

BIBLIOGRAPHY

Gregory, James N. *American Exodus: The Dust Bowl Migration and Okie Culture in California.* 1989.

Hurt, Douglas R. *The Dust Bowl: An Agricultural and Social History.* 1981.

Manes, Sheila G. "Pioneers and Survivors: Oklahoma's Landless Farmers." In *Oklahoma: New Views of the Forty-sixth State,* eds. Anne Hodges Morgan and H. Wayne Morgan. 1982.

Shindo, Charles J. *Dust Bowl Migrants in the American Imagination.* 1997.

Stein, Walter J. *California and the Dust Bowl Migration.* 1973.

Weisiger, Marsha L. *Land of Plenty: Oklahomans in the Cotton Fields of Arizona, 1933–1942.* 1995.

Worster, Donald. *Dust Bowl: The Southern Plains in the 1930s.* 1979.

WILLIAM H. MULLINS

OLD-AGE INSURANCE

On August 14, 1935, Franklin D. Roosevelt signed into law the Social Security Act, creating the first federal old-age insurance system in the United States. The Federal Old-Age Benefits program was one of seven new federal entitlement programs created by the Social Security Act, to be administered by a newly created Social Security Board. The old-age benefits were funded initially by a payroll tax of 1 percent levied on both employees and employers, with the first revenues collected in 1937 and the first benefits paid in 1940.

Interest in old-age insurance as a means to alleviate old-age poverty grew in the early twentieth century in response to the increasing number of individuals living into old age and the diminished employment opportunities for older workers. The numbers of Americans over the age of sixty-five increased dramatically, from 1.1 million people in 1870 (3 percent of the population) to 6.7 million (5.4 percent) in 1930. Improvements in public health and medicine increased life spans, but individuals often found it difficult to maintain themselves financially in old age. By law and custom, families became the chief form of assistance to needy older relatives. For those without kin able to support them, the dreaded county poor house remained the means of last resort.

During the Progressive era, Americans looked to the examples of Germany and England, where old-age insurance programs had been established in 1889 and 1908 respectively. Advocates of social insurance argued that certain hazards of life, such as old age, were social problems best addressed by using actuarial principles to distribute the risk and financial burden across society. Early advocates, such Columbia University professor Henry Rogers Seager, author of *Social Insurance: A Program of Social Reform* (1910), and social theorist Isaac Rubinow, author of *Social Insurance* (1913), educated a generation of economists, politicians, academics, and social reformers on the benefits of social insurance as a rational approach to addressing social ills. In the 1920s, the American Association for Labor Legislation, which included such prominent labor economists as John R. Commons, John B. Andrews, and Richard T. Ely, continued to support the concept of old-age insurance, though it focused its efforts on winning the passage of state old-age pension laws funded by general revenues on a pay-as-you-go basis. Old-age insurance advocates found a cool reception among politicians in the 1920s, but Rubinow and Abraham Epstein, former research director of the Pennsylvania Old Age Commission and executive secretary of the American Association for Old Age Insurance (founded in 1927), continued as outspoken and persistent advocates for an American system of old-age insurance.

By 1930, only 33.1 percent of men and 8.1 percent of women over sixty-five participated in the labor force while the majority of old people relied on savings, investment income, or relatives to support them. However, the failure of financial institutions, the bankruptcy of corporate pension plans, and the crash of the stock and real estate markets eliminated the savings and income of many old people, increasing the financial burden placed on family, friends, and public relief. Individual families, poor relief, and private charity strained to aid the swelling ranks of the impoverished aged. Popular organizations, such as the Townsend clubs, led by Dr. Francis E. Townsend, mobilized millions of old people in support of proposals for immediate, generous payments by the federal government to the nation's older citizens.

The federal government responded to the crisis of old-age poverty as part of a broader economic security program. On June 29, 1934, Roosevelt signed Executive Order 6757 creating the Committee on Economic Security to prepare comprehensive legislation addressing the major causes of economic insecurity. To the New Dealers designing the Economic Security Act, social insurance would be the key component of the administration's bill. Assistant Secretary of Labor Arthur Altmeyer and Dr. Edwin Witte, executive director of the Committee on Economic Security, both of whom oversaw the day-to-day development of the Act, were long-time social insurance advocates who had studied under John R. Commons at the University of Wisconsin. Franklin Roosevelt himself spent part of the spring of 1934 reading Rubinow's *Quest for Security* (1934), a work that convinced him of the value of social insurance. The president instructed Witte, Altmeyer, and Secretary of Labor Frances Perkins that the long-term program to assist senior citizens must be financed through contributions rather than general revenues to enhance its financial stability and ensure its political future by making its benefits appear to be an earned right. After months of research and several attempts to craft a workable bill, the Committee on Economic Security delivered its final report and the text of the Economic Security Act to the president on January 15, 1935. The final version of the bill, modified by both the House and Senate and renamed the Social Security Act, emerged from the House on August 8 and the Senate on August 9, and was signed into law five days later.

The Social Security Act created a dual system of immediate and long-term programs to provide old-age security. The old-age assistance program (Title I) allocated $49,750,000 in matching grants to states to pay benefits immediately to needy old people. The Old Age Benefits program (Title II) created a contributory old-age insurance system designed to provide payments to current workers when they reached old age. The program was to be entirely self-supporting with payroll taxes that would gradually rise to handle the growing elderly population. Initially, the program provided assistance primarily to white, male industrial employees. By excluding certain occupations from coverage, especially farmer laborers and domestic workers, the old-age insurance program initially excluded 60 percent of all African-American workers and 80 percent of all African-American women workers from coverage. Women, though only 30 percent of the workforce, accounted for 60 percent of those excluded from coverage.

Though initially limited in scope, the Social Security Act marked the culmination of a three-decade long campaign for social insurance in the United States. Building on the 1935 provisions, Congress would amend the old-age insurance program numerous times, gradually liberalizing benefits and broadening coverage to more workers and their dependents. The old-age insurance provisions of the Social Security Act continue to be an effective program for reducing the insecurity and poverty of old age in America.

See Also: ELDERLY, IMPACT OF THE GREAT DEPRESSION ON THE; ORGANIZED LABOR; SOCIAL SECURITY ACT; TOWNSEND PLAN.

BIBLIOGRAPHY

Achenbaum, Andrew W. *Old Age in the New Land: The American Experience since 1790.* 1978.

Altmeyer, Arthur J. *The Formative Years of Social Security.* 1966.

Berkowitz, Edward D. *Creating the Welfare State: The Political Economy of Twentieth Century Reform.* 1980.

Burg, Steven B. *The Gray Crusade: The Townsend Movement, Old Age Politics, and the Development of Social Security,* Ph.D. diss., University of Wisconsin, Madison. 1999.

Chambers, Clarke. *Seedtime of Reform: American Social Service and Social Action, 1918–1933.* 1963.

Haber, Carole, and Brian Gratton. *Old Age and the Search for Security: An American Social History.* 1994.

Gordon, Linda. *Pitied but Not Entitled: Single Mothers and the History of Welfare, 1890–1935.* 1994.

Katz, Michael B. *In the Shadow of the Poorhouse: A Social History of Welfare in America.* 1986.

Orloff, Ann Shola. *The Politics of Pensions: A Comparative Analysis of Britain, Canada, and the United States, 1880–1940.* 1993.

Quadagno, Jill. *The Transformation of Old Age Security: Class and Politics in the American Welfare State.* 1988.

Social Security Online. *The History of Social Security.* Available from http://www.ssa.gov/history

Witte, Edwin. *The Development of the Social Security Act: A Memorandum on the History of the Committee on Economic Security and Drafting and Legislative History of the Social Security Act.* 1963.

STEVEN B. BURG

OLSON, FLOYD B.

Floyd Bjornstjerne Olson (November 13, 1891– August 22, 1936), governor of Minnesota, was born in Minneapolis, Minnesota, the only child of Paul Olson, a railroad worker, and Ida Marie Nelson. He grew up in a poor area of North Minneapolis, an experience that influenced his later career in politics. After completing high school in Minneapolis, Olson attended the University of Minnesota for one year in 1910, but left for financial reasons and worked at a series of jobs in Alaska, the Canadian Northwest, and in Seattle. He returned to Minneapolis in 1913 and resumed his legal studies at night at Northwestern Law College. He graduated at the head of his class in 1915 and joined the law firm of Frank Larrabee and Otto Davies. In 1917 he married Ada Krejci, with whom he had one daughter, Patricia.

In May 1919, at the age of twenty-eight, Olson was appointed assistant county attorney for Hennepin County. In 1920 he succeeded William Nash as county attorney, easily winning reelection in 1922 and 1926. As the leading prosecuting attorney for the state's most populous county throughout the 1920s, Olson enjoyed high visibility and steadily increasing stature as an honest, hardworking public official who was not afraid to tackle challenging cases. He led an investigation into the activities of the Ku Klux Klan in 1923 and obtained several indictments against local Klan leaders.

Olson's interest in the welfare of the common person led him to join the fledgling Minnesota Farmer-Labor Association, which gained strength in the years immediately following World War I. Olson's impressive speaking abilities and his hard-earned reputation as someone who would represent common people made him highly attractive to the Farmer-Laborites. In the 1924 gubernatorial election, Olson lost by 40,000 votes to the Republican candidate, Theodore Christianson. Olson remained affiliated with the Farmer-Labor Association, but declined to run in the 1928 election.

With the onset of the Depression in 1929 Olson believed the Farmer-Laborites could win in the 1930 election in Minnesota. He ran a conservative campaign, emphasizing his interest in appointing people to office who would be nonpartisan and committed to the welfare of all Minnesotans. Although he won handily in 1930—and would be reelected twice more—Olson's party never controlled the Minnesota legislature. Indeed, throughout his three terms as governor, Olson constantly fought the more conservative elements in the Minnesota legislature. In spite of this, he signed a number of bills relating to expanding public works, regulating securities, encouraging cooperative enterprises, and conserving natural resources.

Olson greatly admired the new president, Franklin D. Roosevelt, and during his last two terms as governor he sought to have his state's program mirror that of the New Deal. Toward this end he gained passage of a mortgage moratorium, a state income tax, allocation of fifteen million dollars in direct relief to the destitute, and congressional re-apportionment. As his legislative agenda progressed, Olson became more enthusiastic about reform to the point that he declared himself a "radical" in a speech to the 1934 Farmer-Labor state convention. He soon realized that his rhetoric of radical reform was discomforting to many voters, and he abruptly toned down his speeches and advocated a more moderate approach for reform during his last years in office.

Although often mentioned as a possible third-party nominee for the 1936 presidential election, Olson had no desire to oppose Roosevelt, and instead began his campaign for the 1936 Senate contest. Late in 1935, however, he was diagnosed with pancreatic cancer, and in August 1936 he died at the Mayo Clinic in Rochester, Minnesota.

Standing six-feet-two-inches tall, handsome and blue-eyed with impressive speaking skills, Floyd Olson was a pragmatic politician whose words were often more radical than his deeds. Popular with voters throughout his political career, his reputation for personal generosity and honesty enabled him to work effectively with an often hostile legislature in passing numerous laws that expanded the role of state government in the lives of Minnesotans.

See Also: MINNESOTA FARMER-LABOR PARTY.

BIBLIOGRAPHY

Jansen, Steven Donald. "Floyd Olson: The Years Prior to His Governorship, 1891–1930." Ph.D. diss., University of Kansas, 1985.

Mayer, George H. *The Political Career of Floyd B. Olson.* 1951. Reprint edition, 1987.

McGrath, John S., and James J. Delmont. *Floyd Bjornsterne Olson: Minnesota's Greatest Liberal Governor, A Memorial Volume.* 1937.

EDWARD A. GOEDEKEN

OLYMPICS, BERLIN (1936)

Shortly after Adolf Hitler took power in Germany in 1933, many Americans questioned the propriety of supporting the Nazi-hosted Olympic Games scheduled for Berlin in 1936. In response to reports of Jewish persecution, the American Jewish Congress, the Jewish Labor Committee, and the non-sectarian Anti-Nazi League held protest rallies that called for an Olympic boycott. By 1934, support for a boycott had spread abroad. It was supported by many newspapers, including *The New York Times,* anti-Nazi groups, and such Catholic lay leaders as Al Smith of New York and Governor James Curley of Massachusetts. The African-American press opposed a boycott, pointing to the hypocrisy of not first addressing discrimination at home. African-American journalists further argued that black athletic success at the Olympics would undermine Nazi racial views and foster a new sense of black pride at home.

Avery Brundage, president of the American Olympic Committee, opposed a boycott, arguing that politics had no place in sports. He blamed the proposed boycott on a Jewish-Communist conspiracy. In 1934 Brundage investigated the German sports program, and after a series of closely controlled interviews, he reported that Jewish athletes were treated fairly and that the games should go on. Judge Jeremiah Mahoney, president of the Amateur Athletic Union (AAU), argued that Germany had broken Olympic rules forbidding discrimination, and he opposed participation as an endorsement of Nazism. The boycott issue came to a head on December 8, 1935, when the AAU voted by a slim margin to not boycott the Olympics. The following summer, Ernest Lee Jahncke, an American member of the International Olympic Committee (IOC) who had come out strongly against the Berlin games, became the only person ever expelled from the IOC. He was replaced by Brundage.

The winter games were held in February at Garmisch-Partenkirchen in the Bavarian Alps. The United States faired poorly, winning only one gold medal in two-man bobsledding, and bronze medals in two-man bobsledding, the 500-meter skating race, and hockey.

German spectators salute Adolf Hitler at the opening ceremonies of the Berlin Olympics in August 1936. NATIONAL ARCHIVES AND RECORDS ADMINISTRATION, COURTESY OF UNITED STATES HOLOCAUST MEMORIAL MUSEUM PHOTO ARCHIVES

The summer team's voyage to Germany started off badly when Brundage dismissed Eleanor Holm Jarrett from the team for drinking. She was a 1932 Olympic swimming champion, a world record holder, a married woman, and a movie starlet.

There were nearly five thousand athletes from forty-nine countries at the Berlin Games. The 383-member American team was strong in track and field and basketball, but weak in other areas, including boxing, a traditional American strength. Jesse Owens, the star of the games, captured four gold medals. Owens won the 100-meter dash in 10.3 seconds (wind aided), the 200-meter dash in 20.7 seconds, and the broad jump with a jump of 26 feet 5 5/16 inches; Owens also ran on the 4x100-meter relay team. All but the 100-meter dash were world records. The first black champion of the

games was high jumper Cornelius Johnson, who leaped 6 feet 8 inches. Johnson was later snubbed by Hitler, who had previously congratulated every winner. Thereafter Hitler was advised by IOC president Count Baillet-Latour not to recognize any champion. The eighteen African-American athletes in track and field, demeaned by the German press as America's "Black Auxiliary," won thirteen medals. The women's track squad was led by sprinter Helen Stephens, who set a world record in the 100-meter dash and anchored the victorious 400-meter relay. The United States won a total of twenty-four gold, twenty silver, and twelve bronze medals for 124 points, a distant second to Germany's thirty gold medals and 181 points.

The main controversy involving the United States team was the benching of Jewish sprinters

A pedestrian in New York City in November 1935 reads a sign urging Americans to boycott the 1936 Berlin Olympics in protest of Nazi persecution of German Jews. The sign announced a meeting to discuss the issue at New York's Mecca Temple. NATIONAL ARCHIVES AND RECORDS ADMINISTRATION, COURTESY OF UNITED STATES HOLOCAUST MEMORIAL MUSEUM PHOTO ARCHIVES

Marty Glickman and Sam Stoller from the 4x100-meter relay the day before the event. They were replaced by Owens and Ralph Metcalfe, the team's two fastest men. Coach Dean Cromwell of the University of Southern California claimed that the Germans were hiding a team of superstars, so the United States needed to use their top men. Glickman, however, believed anti-Semitism was the motivation; he maintained that the coaches wanted to avoid embarrassing Germany by dropping the only Jewish-American track competitors. The other two runners, Frank Wykoff and Foy Draper, were from the University of Southern California, as was Cromwell, so favoritism may have played a factor in Cromwell's choice to keep them in the race. The team easily won the relay in a world record 39.8 seconds.

The Olympics provided a perfect arena for Nazi propaganda. The Games went off flawlessly, full of lavish pageantry and rituals, punctuated with great athletic achievements. German director Leni Riefenstahl's monumental film *Olympia* has preserved the pomp, circumstance, and athleticism of the Berlin Games. The spectacle gave the Nazis, as well as fascist Italy, Hungary, and Japan, a field on which to demonstrate the alleged superiority of their social, economic, and political systems. The Berlin Olympics also made a hero out of Jesse Owens, who defeated the racist Nazis on their home field, and encouraged Americans to respect the accomplishments of African Americans.

See Also: ANTI-SEMITISM; HITLER, ADOLF; LEISURE; OWENS, JESSE; SPORTS.

BIBLIOGRAPHY

Baker, William J. *Jesse Owens: An American Life.* 1986.

Guttmann, Allen. *The Olympics: A History of the Modern Games.* 1992.

Mandell, Richard. *The Nazi Olympics.* 1971.

The Nazi Olympics, Berlin 1936. An online exhibit sponsored by United States Holocaust Memorial Museum, Washington, D.C. Available at: http// www.ushmm.org/olympics/

STEVEN A. RIESS

ORGANIZED LABOR

The ranks of organized labor expanded enormously over the course of the Great Depression. The number of employees represented by unions grew from 3.6 million to 10.5 million between 1930 and 1941. As a percentage of the non-agricultural labor force, union membership rose from 11.6 percent in 1930 to 27.9 percent in 1941. The labor movement's progress, however, was hardly steady or inexorable. Throughout the 1930s workers alternately encountered success and failure, employer resistance and cooperation, ineffective and responsive labor leadership, and a protective but ultimately constrained federal government.

After a steep decline in the early 1920s, unions had begun to recover by the end of the decade. The American Federation of Labor (AFL), the umbrella association of craft unions that represented the vast majority of organized workers, had worked successfully to develop amicable relations with employers. This was a practical strategy when the economy was healthy but it left the AFL completely unprepared for the economic crisis that accompanied the stock market crash of 1929. Rather than proposing aggressive strategies for tackling unemployment and employers' wage cuts at the onset of the Depression, AFL president William Green pleaded for labor-management cooperation, a thirty-hour workweek, and a public works program; he was late in supporting unemployment insurance and refused to endorse a candidate in the 1932 presidential election. As jobs became scarce and labor leadership failed to respond effectively, union membership steadily dropped to 3.2 million in 1932, its lowest level in over fourteen years. Workers appeared demoralized and withdrawn, displaying none of the radicalism that had characterized their response to the earlier depressions of the 1870s and 1890s. Whereas prior depressions featured prominent national strike waves, fewer than 200,000 workers, a new low, took part in work stoppages in 1930.

Federal legislation and the efforts of a rising cadre of industrial unionists breathed new life into the labor movement. In 1932 Congress passed the Norris-LaGuardia Act, which gave employees the

Police battle with striking teamsters in June 1934 in Minneapolis. NATIONAL ARCHIVES AND RECORDS ADMINISTRATION

right of association, outlawed "yellow-dog" contracts that stipulated that workers could not join unions, and restricted the use of federal injunctions to stifle pickets or boycotts. Although its effects arguably were less profound, the National Industrial Recovery Act of 1933 provoked a far greater reaction from unions. Its famed section 7(a) required that the industrial codes drawn up under the law grant employees the right to bargain collectively with employers without coercion or discrimination. Unions felt that the federal government, at last, had become a tool rather than weapon to be used against them. Organizers from the United Mine Workers (UMW), distorted the law's meaning but demonstrated its rallying potential in recruitment

signs that announced "The President wants you to join a union."

Well before many codes were drawn up, workers began returning to the labor movement. There were more work stoppages in 1933 than the previous two years combined. By 1934 violent strikes demanding union recognition had broken out in the steel, automobile, textile, lumber, and shipping industries. San Francisco faced a city-wide general strike in which longshoremen, led by Harry Bridges, broke from the AFL, set up the independent International Longshoremen and Warehousemen's Union, and won a favorable settlement. Rank-and-file unionists (i.e., those who were not leaders or officers) and their insurgent leaders threatened not

These Tennessee Valley Authority employees, photographed in 1942, were members of the Electrical Workers Union in Sheffield, Alabama. LIBRARY OF CONGRESS, PRINTS & PHOTOGRAPHS DIVISION, FSA/OWI COLLECTION

only employers, who resisted forcefully, but the AFL's authority within the labor movement.

Unable to harness the anger and excitement of ordinary workers, the AFL also suffered from its own tactical errors. The national textile strike of 1934 (the largest in American history at that date) was prematurely called off, sacrificing critical momentum, when President Franklin Roosevelt promised an investigation into working conditions. The AFL's rigid attachment to craft unionism, in which an industry's employees were split off into separate unions on the basis of occupation, cost it the loyalty of workers who had organized and formed relationships across job categories and did not care about the national unions' jurisdictional boundaries. As a result, thousands of workers who had taken part in strikes gradually dropped out of the unions after the immediate conflict was resolved.

John L. Lewis, president of the UMW, argued that the AFL's single-minded focus on craft workers came at the expense of the unskilled and semiskilled operatives prevalent in the mass-production industries. A more promising approach lay with industrial unionism, which held that a single union should encompass all workers in a given industry. Most importantly, Lewis decried the AFL's disinclination to mount aggressive organizing campaigns until jurisdictional issues were resolved. When the leadership of the AFL irreconcilably fragmented, Lewis and his associates announced on November 9, 1935, the formation of the Committee for Industrial Organization (CIO), an alliance of some of the AFL's most militant unions, and vigorously began recruiting industrial workers. The split was later completed when the CIO permanently became the Congress of Industrial Organizations.

The CIO's efforts were greatly assisted when Congress passed the National Labor Relations Act of 1935, also known as the Wagner Act. The Act reaffirmed the protections of labor that had been implemented in the National Industrial Recovery Act (which the Supreme Court declared unconstitutional that same year), granting labor the right to organize and bargain collectively with employers, but it also extended those protections by creating the National Labor Relations Board (NLRB) to investigate complaints of unfair labor practices, enforce the right to form unions, and oversee the election of representatives by employees. Unlike earlier pro-labor legislation that merely removed constraints to labor organization, the National Labor Relations Act committed the federal government to supporting union activity within established limits.

There is considerable debate about the contribution of the National Labor Relations Act to the subsequent escalation of industrial unrest. Some historians believe that the law and the hearings of the La Follette Civil Liberties Committee, which were chaired by Senator Robert M. La Follette, Jr., of Wisconsin in order to support the National Labor Relations Act by compiling evidence of employer violence and industrial espionage, encouraged ordinary workers to defend their interests. Once the law was upheld on April 27, 1937, by the Supreme Court in *NLRB v. Jones and Laughlin Steel Company*, the NLRB energetically began to enforce the law that employers previously had disobeyed openly. Between 1935 and 1945, the board handled 36,000 cases of unfair labor practices and held 24,000 elections, 83.9 percent of which resulted in the certification of unions.

Others historians attribute the success and abrupt rise of rank-and-file militancy to the CIO's organizing campaigns and the competition for members that finally mobilized the AFL. Certainly, Lewis's efforts in forming Labor's Non-Partisan League in 1936 helped politicize workers and contributed to Roosevelt's landslide re-election. More decisively, the CIO's on-the-ground organizing led to the resurgence of the labor movement. Its innovative approach included promoting interracial solidarity, appealing to ethnic workers by expanding the concept of Americanism, utilizing the radio to spread its message, and cooperating with Communist and Socialist activists who proved to be some of its most effective organizers.

The first test of the nascent alliance came in late 1936 when militant autoworkers at a General Motors plant in Flint, Michigan, staged a nonviolent sit-down strike. Recognizing its broader implications in one of the nation's vital non-unionized industries, Lewis quickly championed the strike, which spread throughout the company. When bloodshed seemed imminent, Lewis interceded, secured the support of Roosevelt and Governor Frank Murphy, and on February 11, 1937, won an agreement whereby for the first time General Motors recognized the United Automobile Workers (UAW) as the bargaining agent for its members. Worried about similar disruptions, U.S. Steel, the target of the CIO's most aggressive organizing campaign, settled an equally historic agreement on March 2, 1937, that recognized a CIO union (one that would become the United Steelworkers of America), raised wages by 10 percent, and introduced a forty-hour workweek. These two victories galvanized workers throughout the country, who struck for union recognition, as well as better wages and improved conditions. Even the AFL got busy organizing mass-production industries, responding to the demands of its own energized membership and the success of the CIO. By the end of 1937, the CIO claimed 3.7 million members and the AFL another 3.4 million, together more than doubling the union membership of 1932.

The momentum of 1936 and 1937 proved difficult to sustain. Although cumulative union membership continued to grow through the end of the Depression, several high-profile organizing failures and the economic downturn of late 1937 and 1938 hurt the labor movement. Collective bargaining reached its limit when employers refused to negotiate with labor representatives in good faith. Layoffs shrank the membership of some industrial unions and forced others to accept wage concessions; the AFL, meanwhile, withstood the recession with fewer setbacks. Roosevelt's waning interest in broad social and economic reform also took a toll. By the late 1930s, Roosevelt shifted his attention to diplomacy, which widened the growing split between the pacifist CIO and the interventionist administration. Tensions mounted until Lewis, who once had been a vocal supporter of the president, declared his endorsement of Republican Wendell Willkie in the 1940 election.

The rank and file took its own path in the election. Working-class voters, even those in Lewis's own UMW, overwhelmingly cast their ballots in support of Roosevelt. Indeed, throughout the decade ordinary workers took matters into their own hands, often without consulting or despite the con-

trary wishes of union leaders. Early in the Depression the paralysis of AFL leadership sometimes was broken by spontaneous strikes touched off by local incidents and popular radicalism. Many of the alliances that workers formed at the local level were improvisational and unconventional. For instance, in 1934 strikers in Toledo, Ohio, secured the support of A. J. Muste's Unemployed League to win union recognition. Later efforts by the CIO proved so successful in part because they merged the resources of national unions with sensitivity to local community autonomy. The CIO not only generated but identified and supported rank-and-file militancy.

While workers displayed more enthusiasm than union officials for direct action, they often were motivated by less radical social values. Whereas union leaders, particularly those in the CIO, sometimes supported a wide range of reforms and political philosophies, workers themselves often cared only about their specific demands. Their activism, therefore, arose out of a defense of the implicit prerogatives they had established with employers in prior decades. Social transformations also indirectly increased participation in union activity. Ethnic divisions that inhibited unionization earlier in the century fell away after immigration was severely curtailed in the early 1920s. The arrival of mass consumption allowed workers to develop a separate working-class culture with ties beyond their neighborhoods.

All workers did not share equally in the advances made by organized labor. Workers in the South and West remained much less organized than those in the Northeast and Midwest. Union organizers targeted several industries, such as textiles and garments, that employed women in great numbers and others, such as automobile, rubber, and metalworking, that employed few, but increasing numbers of, women. Nevertheless, unions remained led by men and oriented toward the interests of male workers. For instance, many unions embraced discriminatory employment policies in which women were laid off first under the assumption that men provided their household's primary income. Long ignored or discriminated against by AFL unions, African Americans and Mexican

Americans were slow in joining the labor movement. The CIO made great efforts to attract them, however, partly because it understood that by using African-American strikebreakers employers had fostered racism to divide workers. The CIO's concern for unskilled and semi-skilled industrial workers also led to its particular interest in African Americans and Mexican Americans, who disproportionately filled those positions. Still, racism was not absent altogether from even the CIO unions. Moreover, the single major union dominated and led by African Americans was part of the AFL. In line with the AFL's craft constituency, A. Philip Randolph's Brotherhood of Sleeping Car Porters represented relatively prosperous railway workers, though it also would become an institutional channel for the integration of the AFL Executive Committee and was a forerunner of civil rights activism.

Few could have predicted in the early 1930s that by the decade's end more than a quarter of the workforce would be unionized and that collective bargaining would be protected by the federal government. Nevertheless, the Depression years also amply illustrated the limitations of American unions and anticipated future troubles. But before confronting these enduring difficulties the labor movement would enjoy yet another prolonged resurgence during World War II.

See Also: AMERICAN FEDERATION OF LABOR (AFL); BROTHERHOOD OF SLEEPING CAR PORTERS (BSCP); COLLECTIVE BARGAINING; CONGRESS OF INDUSTRIAL ORGANIZATIONS (CIO); LABOR'S NON-PARTISAN LEAGUE; NATIONAL LABOR RELATIONS ACT OF 1935 (WAGNER ACT); STRIKES.

BIBLIOGRAPHY

Bates, Beth Tompkins. *Pullman Porters and the Rise of Protest Politics in Black America, 1925–1945.* 2001.

Bernstein, Irving. *The Lean Years: A History of the American Worker, 1920–1933.* 1960.

Bernstein, Irving. *Turbulent Years: A History of the American Worker, 1933–1941.* 1969.

Brody, David. *Workers in Industrial America: Essays on the Twentieth Century Struggle,* 2nd edition. 1993.

Cohen, Lizabeth. *Making a New Deal: Industrial Workers in Chicago, 1919–1939.* 1990.

Dubofsky, Melvyn, and Foster Rhea Dulles. *Labor in America: A History,* 6th edition. 1999.

Faue, Elizabeth. *Community of Suffering and Struggle: Women, Men, and the Labor Movement in Minneapolis, 1915–1945.* 1991.

Fine, Sidney. *Sit-Down: The General Motors Strike of 1936–1937.* 1969.

Fraser, Steve. *Labor Will Rule: Sidney Hillman and the Rise of American Labor.* 1991.

Gerstle, Gary. *Working-Class Americanism: The Politics of Labor in a Textile City, 1914–1960.* 1989.

Kessler-Harris, Alice. *Out to Work: A History of Wage-Earning Women in the United States.* 1982.

Lichtenstein, Nelson. *The Most Dangerous Man in Detroit: Walter Reuther and the Fate of American Labor.* 1995.

Lynd, Alice, and Staughton Lynd, eds. *Rank and File: Personal Histories by Working-Class Organizers.* 1973.

Nelson, Bruce. *Workers on the Waterfront: Seamen, Longshoremen, and Unionism in the 1930s.* 1988.

Pope, Liston. *Millhands and Preachers: A Study of Gastonia.* 1942.

Ruiz, Vicki L. *Cannery Women, Cannery Lives: Mexican Women, Unionization, and the California Food Processing Industry, 1930–1950.* 1987.

Tomlins, Christopher L. *The State and the Unions: Labor Relations, Law, and the Organized Labor Movement in America, 1880–1960.* 1985.

Zieger, Robert H. *The CIO, 1935–1955.* 1995.

EDUARDO F. CANEDO

OUR DAILY BREAD

Our Daily Bread, released in late 1934 through United Artists, was an eighty-minute film produced and directed by the respected 40-year-old King Vidor. His then wife Elizabeth Hill is credited with the screenplay. The film's leading players were Karen Morley, Tom Keene, and Barbara Pepper. Vidor had struggled unsuccessfully to find an interested studio and finally financed production himself. Vidor, determined to make a film that would depict "the struggles of a typical young American couple in this most difficult period," believed that people working together could beat the hard times, and the film is, among other things, a plea for cooperatives. The film was well received critically, won a League of Nations prize, was shown to President Franklin D. Roosevelt at the White House, and turned a small profit.

The storyline is simple and, according to *Variety*, concurred with "the views of various public persons." City dwellers John and Mary, victims of the hard times, accept an offer from her uncle to farm some undeveloped land he owns. John and Mary struggle to make a go of it. John, realizing how ill-equipped they are for farming, offers a transient dispossessed farmer a place to live and a share of the crop in exchange for his expertise. Soon there are dozens of families on the farm working together, living in hand-built shacks. Sally, a slatternly attractive blonde, turns up in a rainstorm searching for her boyfriend. A compassionate Mary takes her in.

The people on the farm overcome various crises, but despair sets in because an unrelenting drought threatens to annihilate the crop. John falls into self-doubt, is seduced by Sally, and with her leaves the farm. En route together he discovers a stream some miles away and, returning to the farm, convinces the people that working together they can divert the stream, irrigate the land, and save the crop. In an exciting and superbly directed and edited ten-minute sequence, representing some days of around-the-clock effort, water is brought to the parched crop. The depiction of this massive effort draws heavily on contemporary Soviet film technique and the ideology underlying it. The farm is saved. So too is the marriage of John and Mary, but it faces a more rosy future than the cooperative which, like American society at the time, still has many problems to overcome.

See Also: HOLLYWOOD AND THE FILM INDUSTRY.

BIBLIOGRAPHY

Dowd, Nancy, and David Shepard. *King Vidor (A Directors Guild of America Oral History).* 1988.

Vidor, King. *A Tree Is a Tree.* 1953.

DANIEL J. LEAB

OWENS, JESSE

In an era of rigid racial segregation of all the major team sports in the United States, track star and Olympic champion James Cleveland "Jesse" Owens (September 12, 1913–March 31, 1980), along with heavyweight boxing champion Joe Louis, was the most prominent African-American athlete of the 1930s. Owens, the youngest of ten children born to Henry and Emma Owens in Oakville, Alabama, moved with the family in the early 1920s to Cleveland, Ohio, where he received the nickname of "Jesse" from an elementary school teacher who misunderstood his drawled pronunciation of J. C. In junior high school an energetic physical education teacher, Charles Riley, taught Owens the mechanics of athleticism, as well as proper manners and good citizenship.

A spectacular high school career in track propelled Owens to Ohio State University, where he enrolled in 1933 on a work-study arrangement. As a sophomore (his first year of varsity eligibility), he broke three world records and tied another in the Big Ten finals at Ann Arbor, Michigan. Just over a year later, Owens dominated the Berlin Olympics, winning four gold medals with new world records in the 100-meter and 200-meter dashes, the broad jump, and the 400-meter relay.

These successes were all the sweeter because they occurred under the nose of Nazi leader Adolf Hitler. Owens disproved Hitler's theory of Aryan supremacy, and Hitler was reported to have snubbed Owens by refusing to shake his hand. In truth, American sportswriters concocted the snub story for patriotic readers, thus creating one of the most enduring of all American legends. While hotels refused admission to Jesse Owens's parents who had come to New York City to welcome their son home from Berlin, the Hitler snub story allowed racist Americans to focus on bigotry abroad.

After rousing receptions in New York City, Columbus, and Cleveland, the youthful Owens faced the ominous task of finding a job. By now his amateur athletic career was officially finished because the Amateur Athletic Union banned him for refusing to participate in a post-Olympics fund-raising tour of European cities. Instead, Owens rushed home to capitalize on various stage and screen offers. All those proposals turned out to be insubstantial, but Republican presidential candidate Alf Landon paid Owens handsomely to rally black voters in the election of 1936.

That failed effort appropriately represented Owens's unsatisfactory experience from 1937 to the outbreak of World War II. He barnstormed with several athletic and musical groups, supervised a public recreational program in Cleveland, and ran exhibition races at professional baseball games. Often his athletic efforts were clownishly framed on the order of an infamous race against a horse in Havana, Cuba, on the day after Christmas in 1936, and two years later a farcical loss to Joe Louis in a sprint in Chicago between games of a Negro League doubleheader. Owens established a dry-cleaning business in Cleveland, but saw it go bankrupt in 1939; he re-enrolled at Ohio State, but within a week of the Japanese attack on Pearl Harbor in December 1941, Owens gave up his dream of earning a baccalaureate degree.

Had the Cold War and the civil rights movement not cast Owens's Depression-era feats in a new light, he might well have been forgotten. As American-Soviet rivalries turned the Olympic Games into a symbolic war, Owens became a premier showpiece of American success. His modest, conservative style made him an effective antidote to radical blacks, especially after the black-power salutes of two American sprinters at the Mexico City Olympics of 1968. Owens's mature years saw him comfortably active as a public speaker and as a spokesperson for a dozen or so major corporations.

See Also: AFRICAN AMERICANS, IMPACT OF THE GREAT DEPRESSION ON; LOUIS, JOE; OLYMPICS, BERLIN (1936); SPORTS.

BIBLIOGRAPHY

Baker, William J. *Jesse Owens: An American Life.* 1986.

McRae, Donald. *In Black and White: The Untold Story of Joe Louis and Jesse Owens.* 2002.

WILLIAM J. BAKER

PATMAN, WRIGHT

John William Wright Patman (1893–1976) served in Congress for forty-seven years from 1929 until 1976, advocating on behalf of small business owners on the economic periphery. In the 1920s he served briefly in the Texas legislature and as a district attorney. After his 1928 election to Congress, Patman refused to work with the seniority system, and instead he carved out a leadership position for himself. Patman's career was shaped by the Depression-era economics of scarcity. His legislative agenda included immediate payment of the World War I soldiers' bonus, the impeachment of Treasury Secretary Andrew Mellon, the elimination of chain stores, and government ownership of the Federal Reserve System. Permeating each of these concerns was a commitment to the Democratic Party and liberal economic populism.

Patman believed that World War I veterans had not received just compensation. He argued that immediate payment of the soldiers' bonus, passed in 1924 as an insurance policy due in 1945, could also be used to expand the currency, thus remedying the nation's economic woes. Patman was tenacious in his advocacy and came into conflict with Mellon, who attacked the measure as financially unsound. Patman therefore pushed unsuccessfully for Mellon's impeachment, but created enough of a con-

troversy to cause Mellon to resign from his appointment as ambassador to Great Britain. Patman's bonus advocacy generated other political problems: He encouraged the June 1932 Bonus March to Washington, D.C. that resulted in a military attack on the World War I veterans and proved to be a fiasco for Hoover's 1932 re-election bid. After Franklin D. Roosevelt's election, Patman continued to push for the measure despite presidential opposition. In 1936, Congress enacted the bonus, without the inflationary provisions, over Roosevelt's veto.

During the 1930s Patman turned his attention to the problems of economic concentration within the private and public sectors. He become a leader in the antimonopoly movement, and conducted three legislative campaigns—one successful and two not: the first to amend the Clayton Antitrust Act of 1914; the second to implement a progressive tax on the earnings of chain stores; and the third to require government ownership of the Federal Reserve. The Robinson-Patman Act, passed in 1936, sought to eliminate discriminatory wholesale pricing whereby large retailers received discounts unavailable to smaller merchants. The measures dealing with chain stores and the Federal Reserve failed. Patman fought for reform of the Federal Reserve System, though, until his death, fearing that private bankers exerted too much influence over the nation's monetary supply.

See Also: BONUS ARMY/BONUS MARCH; FEDERAL RESERVE SYSTEM.

BIBLIOGRAPHY

Patman, Wright. *Bankerteering, Bonuseering, Melloneering.* 1934.

Schwarz, Jordan A. *The New Dealers: Power Politics in the Age of Roosevelt.* 1993.

Wright Patman Papers. Lyndon Baines Johnson Presidential Library, Austin, Texas.

Young, Nancy Beck. *Wright Patman: Populism, Liberalism, and the American Dream.* 2000.

NANCY BECK YOUNG

PEACE MOVEMENT

Because the Treaty of Versailles fell short of the Wilsonian liberal internationalist vision, Americans were receptive to proposals to avoid future wars. In the 1920s, the organized peace movement campaigned for a reduction in military appropriations, for disarmament, and for outlawing war. Peace activists supported the signing of the Kellogg-Briand Pact in 1928, under which the United States, France, and eventually more than sixty other countries committed to seeking peaceful solutions to international differences. Women's peace groups conducted large-scale petition campaigns for disarmament in 1931 and 1932. Aggressive acts by Japan, Italy, and Germany in the 1930s, however, led to fears that the United States would be drawn into war, but also concern that the world was becoming more unjust, unstable, and dangerous.

Dorothy Detzer, the executive secretary of the Women's International League for Peace and Freedom, persuaded Senator Gerald Nye to launch his influential 1934 investigation focusing on the role of the munitions industry in the United States' entry into World War I. In April 1935, fifty thousand veterans marched in Washington for peace and 175,000 students conducted a student strike for peace. Students also campaigned against military training and took the Oxford Oath to refuse to support any war the government might conduct. The Communist-initiated American League against War and Fascism organized a peace demonstration in August 1935 that brought together fifty thousand activists from labor, women's, and religious groups. Students strikes grew even larger in the next three years and involved a majority of college students. Pacifists and liberal internationalists joined in the Emergency Peace Campaign in 1937 and allied with isolationist members of Congress in an unsuccessful effort to get the Ludlow Amendment reported out of the House of Representatives. Defeated by the narrow margin of 209 to 188 in the House, the amendment would have required a national referendum prior to war except when the United States was attacked. In 1938 Socialists joined with isolationists in a campaign to "Keep America Out of War" but found their effort eclipsed by the conservative isolationist America First Committee.

Other groups campaigning for peace included religious-based pacifist groups, such as the Fellowship of Reconciliation, and secular pacifist groups, such as the Women's Peace Union and the War Resisters League. Moderate, nonpacifist peace groups included the League of Nations Association and the Carnegie Endowment for Peace. The National Council for the Prevention of War, led by pacifist Frederick Libby, had numerous affiliated organizations and a significant Washington presence. Carrie Chapman Catt initiated the National Committee on the Cause and Cure of War, which included women's organizations with a total of five million members.

Peace groups divided over the issues of strict versus flexible neutrality, whether to embrace collective security against fascist aggression, particularly in the case of Spain, and how to respond to Nazi anti-Semitism and events such as the Nazi-Soviet Pact and the fall of France. As the United States moved toward war, the broad peace coalitions disintegrated and membership in all but the absolute pacifist peace groups declined significantly. The latter groups played important roles in assisting conscientious objectors during the war, while other peace groups increased their activity only after the war.

See Also: MUSTE, A. J.

BIBLIOGRAPHY

Alonso, Harriet Hyman. *Peace as a Women's Issue: A History of the U.S. Movement for World Peace and Women's Rights.* 1993.

Chatfield, Charles. *For Peace and Justice: Pacifism in America, 1914–1941.* 1971.

Cohen, Robert. *When the Old Left Was Young: Student Radicals and America's First Mass Student Movement, 1929–1941.* 1993.

Eagan, Eileen. *Class, Culture, and the Classrooom: The Student Peace Movement of the 1930s.* 1981.

Wittner, Lawrence S. *Rebels against War: The American Peace Movement, 1933–1983.*1984.

MARTIN HALPERN

PECE. See PRESIDENT'S EMERGENCY COMMITTEE FOR EMPLOYMENT.

PECORA, FERDINAND

From 1932 to 1934, Ferdinand Pecora (January 6, 1882–December 7, 1971) led an exhaustive investigation that exposed corrupt practices in U.S. financial services, garnered national press coverage, and contributed significantly to New Deal legislation that regulated and reformed the banks and stock exchanges.

A Sicilian immigrant, Pecora grew up in New York City, where he studied to become an Episcopalian priest before turning to the law. Active in Theodore Roosevelt's Progressive Party in 1912, he later joined the Democrats and served as an assistant district attorney for New York County.

Following the stock market crash of 1929, President Herbert Hoover urged congressional Republicans to investigate rumors that Democratic "bear raiders" had profited by driving down the markets. The Senate Banking Committee launched an investigation, but it quickly foundered, unable to substantiate the charges. After dismal performances by its first two counsels, the committee hired Pecora in January 1933 to prepare a final report. Convinced that much more remained to be investigated, Pecora won a brief extension. He assembled several tal-ented lawyers and dispatched them to the National City Bank in New York, where they combed through the bank's records before Pecora called its president, Charles Mitchell, to testify in Washington. Under tough questioning, Mitchell admitted that the bank's security house had unloaded poor stocks onto unsuspecting investors, conceded his own income tax evasion, and resigned as bank president.

Headlines from the Mitchell hearings convinced the incoming Democratic majority on the Banking Committee to let Pecora continue the investigation. The counsel called a long list of prominent financiers to inquire into their questionable banking and brokerage practices. When a circus promoter slipped a midget into the lap of banker J. P. Morgan, Jr., during a brief recess of the committee, widely printed news photographs symbolized the congressional humbling of the mightiest bankers. Pecora's probe put human faces on the economic catastrophe of the Depression and spurred public demands for reform. The hearings' well-documented findings had a direct impact on passage of the Glass-Steagall Banking Act (1933), the Securities Act (1933), the Securities and Exchange Act (1934), and the Public Utilities Holding Company Act (1935).

President Franklin D. Roosevelt appointed Pecora to the Securities and Exchange Commission (SEC) in 1934, but the former investigator was dismayed when a notorious stock trader, Joseph P. Kennedy, became its chairman. Voting mostly in the minority on the SEC, Pecora resigned after six months to accept a seat on the New York Supreme Court. In 1950 he ran unsuccessfully as the Democratic candidate for mayor of New York.

See Also: GLASS-STEAGALL ACT OF 1933; PUBLIC UTILITIES HOLDING COMPANY ACT; SECURITIES REGULATION.

BIBLIOGRAPHY

Pecora, Ferdinand. *Wall Street under Oath.* 1939.

Ritchie, Donald A. "The Pecora Wall Street Exposé." In *Congress Investigates: A Documented History,* edited by Arthur M. Schlesinger, Jr., and Roger Bruns. 1975.

DONALD A. RITCHIE

PENDERGAST, TOM

Thomas Joseph Pendergast (1872–1945) was the powerful and notorious political boss of Kansas City, Missouri, which, with a population of 400,000, was the largest city in the United States west of the Mississippi River during the Depression. "Tom's Town," as the media dubbed Kansas City, was wide-open and utterly corrupt: In 1939, FBI director J. Edgar Hoover called the situation in Kansas City more dangerous to American institutions than world communism.

In 1911, after a long apprenticeship, Pendergast assumed control of a local political faction, the Goat Democrats, which had been started in the 1880s by his brother, James Pendergast. By 1926, he had combined several Democratic factions in Kansas City into the all-powerful Pendergast machine. (To be on the safe side, he also held sway over the small local Republican Party.) The Pendergast machine had block captains—political workers who handled relations between neighborhood residents and city hall—on every block in Kansas City. Under its rule, there were no free elections in Kansas City. As many as 60,000 illegal ghost voters helped keep the invisible machine in control. Enforcers stifled dissent—during the 1934 city election they killed four people at the polls.

Pendergast, a short and brutish former saloon bouncer, lived lavishly in a large mansion with his wife and three children and ran Kansas City as if it were his own personal business. He dominated the construction and wholesale liquor businesses and had a forced presence on the boards of numerous corporations. The local underworld, which had considerable influence in the police department, was allied with Pendergast's machine, and Pendergast claimed to have 20,000 informants. He required all legal and illegal businesses in Kansas City to pay a percentage of their annual gross to machine collectors; he received over $30 million a year in tainted money from gambling, prostitution, and narcotics. Pendergast never held public office after leaving the city council in 1915, but he was a major force in the Missouri and national Democratic Party and started Harry S. Truman, a member of his machine, on the road to the presidency. Inside Missouri, he had so much power at the state level that he controlled almost all the New Deal relief jobs in the state.

Pendergast experienced serious health problems in 1936, from which he never entirely recovered. In 1937 and 1938, the federal government moved against the Pendergast machine, convicting 259 campaign aides of voter fraud. Pendergast, addicted to gambling and purportedly the biggest better on racehorses in the country, became reckless in his need for ready cash. In 1939, he pled guilty to income tax evasion and served a year in the federal penal system. His machine collapsed at the municipal level and he died in disgrace of heart trouble on February 25, 1945.

See Also: DEMOCRATIC PARTY.

BIBLIOGRAPHY

Dorsett, Lyle W. *The Pendergast Machine.* 1968.

Larsen, Lawrence H., and Nancy J. Hulston. *Pendergast!* 1997.

Milligan, Maurice M. *Missouri Waltz: The Inside Story of the Pendergast Machine by the Man Who Smashed It.* 1948.

Reddig, William M. *Tom's Town: Kansas City and the Pendergast Legend.* 1986.

LAWRENCE H. LARSEN

PEPPER, CLAUDE

Claude Denson Pepper (September 8, 1900–May 30, 1989) was a loyal and outspoken supporter of President Franklin D. Roosevelt's Depression-era program of reform and relief. Raised in rural Alabama in near poverty, Pepper matured in a legacy of populism that became for him a lifetime political commitment to that strain of liberalism that was the underpinning of New Deal political philosophy.

After graduating from the University of Alabama, Pepper went to Harvard Law School with the help of government aid he was awarded as a result of an army training accident. Following a short period teaching law, Pepper entered law practice in rural north Florida and was elected to the state legislature in 1928. Defeated after one term, he nevertheless established himself as a Democratic Party stalwart. He moved to Tallahassee, Florida, and developed a statewide network of professional and political relationships. In 1934 he ran for the U.S. Senate, losing an exceptionally close race. In the process, he established himself as a rising star in the state's Democratic Party structure. Two years later, both of Florida's U.S. senators died within a month of each other, and Pepper was nominated without opposition in the Democratic primary for one of the vacated seats, a feat tantamount to election in the South's one-party system of the period.

The new Florida senator was quickly confronted with Roosevelt's "court packing" plan to enlarge the Supreme Court in order to obtain favorable judicial review of New Deal legislation. After some hesitation over the radical proposal, Pepper strongly supported the plan. This gained presidential favor and established him as a New Dealer. Thereafter, he never wavered in his support of administration measures. In the face of widespread southern opposition in 1938, Pepper made his support of the Fair Labor Standards Act, a controversial New Deal labor proposal, a principal issue in his reelection campaign. His overwhelming primary victory re-ignited congressional support for the nearly lost measure, further strengthening his position as an administration insider.

In the face of rising isolationism in 1939, Pepper advocated intervention in the early stages of World War II on the side of Britain and France against Germany, a politically courageous course of action that aided Roosevelt's efforts to prepare the nation for war. In 1950, at the height of the Cold War, Pepper was defeated for reelection largely because of his earlier conciliatory posture toward the Soviet Union. In 1963, he was elected from a Miami district to the U.S. House of Representatives and served continuously until his death in 1989. Pepper rose to be chairman of the House Select Committee on Aging, and was later chairman of the powerful House Rules Committee. As a self-styled "last of the New Dealers," he made himself the political guardian of the nation's social security program, which is today the principal legacy of the New Deal.

See Also: DEMOCRATIC PARTY; ELECTION OF 1938.

Frances Perkins (right) in New York City in 1931 with Eleanor Roosevelt and Mrs. Percy Pennypacker. FRANKLIN DELANO ROOSEVELT LIBRARY

BIBLIOGRAPHY

Danese, Tracy E. *Claude Pepper and Ed Ball: Politics, Purpose, and Power.* 2000.

Kabat, Ric A. "From New Deal to Red Scare: The Political Odyssey of Senator Claude D. Pepper." Ph.D. diss., Florida State University, 1995.

Kennedy, David. M. *Freedom from Fear: The American People in Depression and War.* 1999.

Pepper, Claude Denson. *Pepper: Eyewitness to a Century.* 1987.

TRACY E. DANESE

PERKINS, FRANCES

Frances Perkins (April 10, 1880–May 14, 1965), Franklin D. Roosevelt's secretary of labor from 1933 to 1945 and the country's first female cabinet member, molded New Deal welfare and labor legislation. Daughter of Susan Bean and Fredrick W. Perkins, a businessman, Fannie Perkins (she later changed her name to Frances) was born in Boston, raised in Worcester, and attended Mount Holyoke College in Massachusetts from 1898 to 1902. In 1910, Perkins received a master's degree in economics and sociology from Columbia University in New York, and became executive secretary of the New York City Consumers League, where she lobbied for maximum work hours, workplace safety, and other labor laws. Outraged by the 1911 Triangle Shirtwaist factory fire, Perkins and others demanded that the state legislature act, leading to creation of the Factory Investigation Commission, cochaired by state senator Robert F. Wagner and assembly leader Alfred E. Smith. Perkins testified before the commission as an expert witness, became its chief investigator, and arranged surprise factory visits for lawmakers. Based on the commission's findings, New York enacted more than thirty laws protecting industrial workers.

When Smith became governor of New York in 1919, he appointed Perkins to the state Industrial Commission and heeded her advice on labor and welfare policies. In 1929, Governor Franklin D. Roosevelt elevated Perkins to the post of industrial commissioner of New York. Once the Depression hit, Commissioner Perkins became a leading advocate for unemployment insurance and direct federal aid to the jobless.

As President Roosevelt's secretary of labor, Perkins helped establish the Civilian Conservation Corps, the Public Works Administration, and the Federal Emergency Relief Administration. She insisted that the National Recovery Administration (NRA) codes include wage and hour standards and that they prohibit child labor. After the Supreme Court declared the NRA unconstitutional, Perkins backed the Wagner Act, guaranteeing labor's right to collective bargaining. She also had Labor Department lawyers draft a minimum wage, maximum hour, child labor-banning bill. A modified and weakened version of the bill passed Congress in 1938 as the Fair Labor Standards Act.

In June 1934, President Roosevelt created the Committee on Economic Security, with Perkins as its chairperson, to formulate a social security program. Working with scores of experts and state and federal officials, often with conflicting views and interests, Perkins delivered to the President recommendations that became the basis for the 1935 Social Security Act. Disappointed by the law's exclusion of farm, domestic, and some other workers, she fought for the rest of her life to extend social security to everyone.

Rising labor militancy and the split between the American Federation of Labor and the Congress of Industrial Organizations complicated Perkins's job. Though she was neutral and urged reconciliation between the AFL and CIO, each accused her of favoring the other. On her advice, Roosevelt refused to use force in the 1934 San Francisco Longshoremen's and general strike and in the wave of sitdown strikes. This angered management and conservatives, as did Perkins's refusal summarily to deport Harry Bridges, the radical leader of the San Francisco strike. In 1938, the House Committee on Un-American Activities demanded her impeachment, but dropped the matter after a few hearings.

Perkins's and the Labor Department's role diminished during World War II as Roosevelt created independent wartime agencies to mobilize industry and labor and to curtail strikes. President Harry S. Truman accepted Perkins's resignation as secretary of labor in July 1945, subsequently appointing her to the Civil Service Commission, where she stayed until 1953. Perkins remained active, writing, lecturing, and teaching at Cornell University, until two weeks before her death. In 1965, Secretary of Labor Willard Wirtz summarized her importance: "Every man and woman in America who works at a living wage, under safe conditions, for reasonable hours, or who is protected by unemployment insurance or social security, is her debtor."

See Also: ORGANIZED LABOR; WOMEN, IMPACT OF THE GREAT DEPRESSION ON.

BIBLIOGRAPHY

Altmeyer, Arthur. *Reminiscences of Arthur Altmeyer.* Oral History Collection, Columbia University, New York.

Lubin, Isador. *Reminiscences of Isador Lubin.* Oral History Collection, Columbia University, New York.

Martin, George. *Madam Secretary: Frances Perkins.* 1976.

Perkins, Frances. *The Roosevelt I Knew.* 1946.

Perkins, Frances. *Reminiscences of Frances Perkins.* Oral History Collection, Columbia University, New York.

Severn, Bill. *Frances Perkins: A Member of the Cabinet.* 1976.

BARBARA BLUMBERG

PHILANTHROPY

In 1934, millions of ordinary Americans gathered eagerly around a radio set to listen to Louisiana politician Huey Long rail against the rich. The idea that the wealth of families like the Rockefellers only had to be shared to end the Depression was economic nonsense, but it was highly appealing. Most people would have been enormously surprised had they known the truth: In 1929, the net worth of John D. Rockefeller, Jr., principal heir to the Standard Oil fortune, was almost $1 billion. By 1934, that figure had been cut in half.

Bankruptcy never loomed as a possibility for the Rockefellers, nor for most of the country's richest families. However, many wealthy Americans sought to economize in the wake of their declining net worth. The most important characteristic of philanthropy during the 1930s was its relative diminution. Nonetheless, while the Depression overwhelmed many charitable ventures, New Deal tax policy spurred the creation of new nonprofit foundations. And during years when other institutions were starved for cash, a few philanthropies promoted agendas with important consequences for generations to come.

Throughout American history, only a minority of those with money gave any substantial amount of it away. Nonetheless, wealthy American families such as the Rockefellers, Dukes, Milbanks, Carnegies, Sages, Harknesses, and Kelloggs had been far more generous with their assets before 1929 than had most of their contemporaries, and they continued to give, sometimes at reduced rates, as the nation's surplus wealth shrank. However, the network of private charitable organizations that they and thousands of other donors supported reeled under the combination of increased need and de-

clining contributions. Orphanages, for instance, historically had helped significant numbers of poor families cope with a crisis by keeping young children for a limited period of time, usually less than six months. "Orphans" rarely lacked living parents. After 1932, however, once a child gained a much sought-after place in an orphanage, he or she remained, on average, seven years. The harried superintendent of one of the few private orphanages left open in Kentucky during the 1930s reported that lucky children slept two to a bed, and the rest in his hugely overcrowded institution slept on the floor. During the Depression, pleas for clothing, food, or emergency housing deluged hundreds of municipally based charity organizations, which, like orphanages, did not have sufficient resources to meet need. To complicate matters, corporate "welfare work" collapsed. During the early twentieth century, progressive businesses had pioneered systems of fringe benefits for employees, including free health care, profit-sharing, or educational scholarships for workers' children. Few businesses were able to maintain such benefits after 1931.

Private philanthropy's inability alone to respond to the crisis spurred an accelerated development of an American "welfare" state, which, in turn, reshaped philanthropic giving during the Depression. In 1929 only about 250 philanthropic foundations existed in the country. A decade later, another three hundred had been added. Before the stock market crash, tax advantage had not been a powerful inducement to charity in the United States; by 1935, it was. Significant increases in taxes began during the Herbert Hoover administration, with the Revenue Act of 1932. Prior to that year the maximum rate the richest Americans paid on annual income was 20 percent. The 1932 bill raised the rate to 55 percent and made stock that was distributed as a dividend subject to income tax. The Revenue Act of 1934, which took effect in January 1935, raised the maximum tax rate on incomes of more than $1 million to 63 percent and imposed a hefty estate tax as well. For the first time in American history, tax avoidance through charitable deductions was a significant incentive to philanthropy. Spurred by the need to reduce taxable income, several foundations that would remain among the country's largest and most influential philanthropies for the rest of the twentieth century received charters in the mid-1930s, notably the Alfred P. Sloan Foundation in 1934, the Ford Foundation in 1936, and the Lilly Endowment in 1937.

Most charitable giving in the United States had limited goals: a scholarship pledge to a patron's favorite college or a check to build a wing on the local hospital, for example. That was true in the 1930s as well, but, prompted by the mixed motives of self-interest and civic obligation, a small number of national foundations developed much larger agendas, with long-term repercussions. Most importantly, a few foundations began to champion such causes as improvement of race relations, a greater international role for the United States, and the development of research hospitals.

During a decade when Jim Crow segregation retained its firm grip, the Chicago-based Rosenwald Fund continued its aggressive program of building Rosenwald Schools. By 1939, almost 750,000 black children were studying in more than 5,300 clean, brightly-lit schoolhouses scattered throughout fourteen southern states. The Rosenwald Fund, along with the Rockefeller-supported General Education Board, also provided grants to sustain black colleges. During a decade when many American hospitals refused admittance to minority patients, the Rosenwald Fund built several regional health centers throughout the South to serve blacks.

In 1937, the Carnegie Corporation commissioned Swedish economist Gunnar Myrdal to begin a major examination of the problem of race in America. Myrdal's lengthy two-volume study, finally published in 1944, argued that Americans had to resolve their central "dilemma" by making their intellectual endorsement of equality a social reality for the country's African Americans.

If Depression-era philanthropy help to sow the seeds of a later civil rights crusade, it also nourished internationalism during an era that shunned formal external alliances. The Rockefeller and Kellogg foundations, two of the country's largest philanthropic organizations, funded projects throughout Asia and Latin America to promote improved public health. The Guggenheim Foundation expanded a fellowship program formerly restricted to Ameri-

can citizens so that South Americans could study in the United States. The Rockefeller Institute mounted a major worldwide campaign against yellow fever, and foundation-supported scientists created the first vaccine against the disease in 1937.

Philanthropy not only battled yellow fever and other insect-borne scourges, it helped to reshape healthcare during the 1930s. Prior to the early twentieth century, physicians visited most sick Americans in their own homes. Hospitals were considered charity institutions for the poor. Only in the 1920s did the middle class begin to trickle into hospitals, led by women wanting to use the "Twilight Sleep" process to give birth painlessly. Philanthropy accelerated that trend during the 1930s by supporting the idea that hospitals should not only treat paying patients but should be centers for advanced medical research and teaching as well.

One of the most popular songs of the Great Depression asked, "Brother can you spare a dime?" Philanthropy's "dime" was not sufficient to solve the era's complex problems. It was, however, a significant player in the decade's events.

See Also: CHARITY; EDUCATION.

BIBLIOGRAPHY

Beito, David. *From Mutual Aid to the Welfare State: Fraternal Societies and Social Services, 1890–1967.* 2000.

Clotfelter, Charles, and Thomas Erlich. *Philanthropy and the Nonprofit Sector in a Changing America.* 1999.

Fosdick, Raymond. *The Story of the Rockefeller Foundation.* 1952.

Harr, John Ensor, and Peter Johnson. *The Rockefeller Century.* 1988.

Kiger, Joseph. *Philanthropic Foundations in the Twentieth Century.* 2000.

Lagemann, Ellen Condliffe, ed. *Philanthropic Foundations: New Scholarship, New Possibilities.* 1999.

Macdonald, Dwight. *The Ford Foundation: The Men and the Millions.* 1956.

JUDITH SEALANDER

PHOTOGRAPHY

The technologies of photography changed immensely in the first four decades of the twentieth

Gordon Park's memorable portrait of a government-employed cleaning woman, photographed in Washington, D.C., in 1942.

LIBRARY OF CONGRESS, PRINTS & PHOTOGRAPHS DIVISION, FSA/OWI COLLECTION

This famous image, shot by Arthur Rothstein in 1936, shows a farmer and his sons on their Oklahoma farm during the Dust Bowl. FRANKLIN DELANO ROOSEVELT LIBRARY

century, increasing the sorts of pictures that could be taken and printed for mass distribution. Among the innovations was the portable 35-millimeter Leica, introduced in the 1920s, which permitted rapid, unobtrusive, spontaneous use. In addition, photoelectric exposure meters, which came on the market in the early 1930s and soon became standard equipment, allowed photographers to measure luminance and determine proper lens aperture (called f-stop) calibration. The annual *U.S. Camera* charted the modernization in photography beginning in 1935 with the best new photographic work chosen by juries chaired by photographer Edward Steichen. During the 1930s, the annual included works by Arnold Genthe, M. F. Agha, Paul Outer-

bridge, Charles Sheeler, and Edward Weston. It remains the comprehensive, primary-source overview of the era's developments.

The "big picture" magazine was a further innovation that helped broaden the profession of the news photographer, photojournalist, and commercial photographer beyond the fashion and celebrity photographs by Steichen and Baron A. De Meyer that appeared in *Vogue, Vanity Fair,* and similar magazines, or Nickolas Muray's work for *Harper's Bazaar* and *McCall's.* Photography in advertising was in its infancy in the 1920s. J. Stirling Getchell worked for the J. Walter Thompson agency until he opened his own from in 1932. *Advertising and Selling* credited him in 1934 with a revolutionary use of

Lewis Hine's well-known photograph of a homeless man sleeping on a dock in New York City in 1935. FRANKLIN DELANO ROOSEVELT LIBRARY

photography and inventing tabloid layouts with work by Steichen, Anton Bruehl, and Margaret Bourke-White. Berenice Abbott, Charles Sheeler, and others contributed to a "futuristic" style of dramatized, cubistic, or manipulated image. Commercial photography became a recognized profession by 1938. Henry Luce, publisher of *Time,* launched *Fortune* in 1929 and hired the German photographer Erich Salomon, a pioneering Leica user, as staff photographer. Bourke-White rose to fame with her Leica work for *Fortune,* which included innovative journalistic realism and aerial photography.

When Luce began publishing the weekly *Life* in 1936 he developed the *picture essay,* a collaboration of editors, photographers, and writers who worked according to a shooting script. Luce described *Life*'s mission as, "to see the world; to eyewitness great events; to watch the faces of the poor and the gestures of the proud; to see strange things . . . to see man's work." Bourke-White produced the photographs for *Life*'s first cover story, which described the lives of the workers constructing Montana's Fort Peck Dam. Bourke-White also served as associate editor, believing in Luce's theory of the "mind-guided camera." Other staff photographers at *Life* included Alfred Eisenstaedt, Thomas D. McAvoy, and Peter Stackpole. The magazine became so popular that Luce had to print over a million copies of each issue to meet demand.

One of the most celebrated Depression-era images is this portrait of a migrant mother, photographed by Dorothea Lange in Nipomo, California, in 1936. LIBRARY OF CONGRESS, PRINTS & PHOTOGRAPHS DIVISION, FSA/OWI COLLECTION

In 1937 Gardner "Mike" Cowles, Jr., and his brother John began publishing the monthly *Look*, which became *Life's* most successful competitor. Immediately popular, *Look* went biweekly as circulation soared to two million by 1938. By 1939, however, *Look's* fortunes had plunged, with circulation cut in half as more than a dozen new picture magazines appeared on newsstands. *Look* also lost readers because of its failure to use quality paper and printing and its poor layout design. By 1940, however, *Look* had gained new professional staff members and a new editor, Dan Mich, and the magazine prospered during the war years.

In addition to these commercial photographic ventures, several New Deal agencies promoted photography during the Depression. The Federal Art Project of the Works Progress Administration, for example, hired New York photographer Bere-

nice Abbott to prepare a portrait of the metropolis, which was published as *Changing New York* in 1939. Abbott used as large a view camera as possible to capture the city's minute details.

In 1935, Rexford Tugwell, head of the Resettlement Administration (RA), formed a historical section within the RA to produce a "pictorial documentation of our rural areas and rural problems." Tugwell was especially interested in recording the consequences of the Dust Bowl. He appointed Roy Emerson Stryker to head what became the Farm Security Administration's (FSA) documentary photography unit. Stryker began the project with the photographers Arthur Rothstein, Carl Mydans, and Walker Evans. Dorothea Lange, who had documented the plight of migrant workers for the state of California, joined the FSA team, along with Paul Carter, Theodor Jung, Russell Lee, Ben Shahn, Arthur Siegel, John Vachon, and Marion Post Wolcott, and later Jack Delano, John Collier, Gordon Parks, and others. Stryker assigned projects but left the choice of equipment, technique, and style to the photographers, who were directed "to speak as eloquently as possible of the thing to be said in the language of pictures." The FSA distributed the pictures free to newspapers and magazines to win support for New Deal programs and aid for the rural poor. FSA photographers amassed thousands of images, which are now held by the Library of Congress.

Steichen observed in 1938 that the FSA photography unit produced "a series of the most remarkable human documents ever rendered in pictures." These photographs "told stories and told them with [such] simple and blunt directness that they made many a citizen wince"; they conveyed "a feeling of a living experience you won't forget." In 1940, documentary filmmaker Pare Lorentz described the FSA photographs as showing "group after group of wretched human beings, starkly asking for so little and wondering what they will get." Some critics, however, labeled them "subversive." Was it art, they asked, or rather sociology, journalism, history, education, or propaganda?

In many cases, writers teamed with photographers to add depth to the documentation. John Steinbeck's 1938 pamphlet about California migrant workers was illustrated with Lange's photographs, and Horace Bristol took a series of photos while traveling with Steinbeck on a research trip for *The Grapes of Wrath*. The writer Erskine Caldwell teamed up with Bourke-White for a book on Deep South poverty called *You Have Seen Their Faces* (1937). Archibald MacLeish provided a poem to accompany FSA photos in *Land of the Free* (1938). Lange collaborated with Paul Taylor on *An American Exodus: A Record of Human Erosion* (1939), in which some photographs were set alongside the subject's own words. James Agee and Evans investigated the lives of southern tenant farmers in *Let Us Now Praise Famous Men* (1941).

Depression-era photographers also won acclaim as artists. From 1929 till his death in 1946, Alfred Stieglitz, the guru of American photography, presided over a gallery called An American Place in New York. Stieglitz encouraged Ansel Adams's career with a one-man show in 1936, a year after Adams's book on technique, *Making a Photograph*, appeared. Adams, Imogen Cunningham, John Paul Edwards, Willard Van Dyke, and Weston founded Group f.64 (f.64 is a lens aperture setting that produces great detail) in California in 1932; the group was dedicated to "pure" or "straight" photography using view cameras with super-speed panchromatic film, and close control over the printing process. Lange, William Simpson, and Stackpole later joined Group f.64. Weston won the first Guggenheim Fellowship for photography in 1937; Evans received a Guggenheim in 1940; Lange, in 1941.

During the 1930s, art museums began to value photography and started adding prints to their collections. The Museum of Modern Art in New York organized an exhibit of Evans's photographs of vernacular and Victorian architecture in 1934, and gave his work another show in 1938. The Baltimore Museum of Art mounted an exhibit of Steichen's work in 1938. Adams curated the Pageant of Photography exhibition at San Francisco's 1939 Golden Gate Exposition. In 1940, Adams helped Beaumont Newhall create the Museum of Modern Art's Photography Department.

As World War II erupted, photographers mustered. Lange documented the internment of Japanese-Americans on the West Coast. The U.S. Navy commissioned Steichen to organize photography of the war at sea. New picture magazines covered it all.

See Also: EVANS, WALKER; FARM SECURITY ADMINISTRATION (FSA); LANGE, DOROTHEA; HINE, LEWIS; ROTHSTEIN, ARTHUR.

BIBLIOGRAPHY

American Memory: America from the Great Depression to World War II, Black-and-White Photographs from the FSA-OWI, 1935–1945. Prints and Photographs Division, Library of Congress. Available at http://memory.loc.gov/ammem/fsahtml/fahome.html

Anderson, James C., ed. *Roy Stryker: The Humane Propagandist.* 1977.

Baldwin, Sidney. *Poverty and Politics: The Rise and Decline of the Farm Security Administration.* 1968.

Curtis, James. *Mind's Eye, Mind's Truth: FSA Photography Reconsidered.* 1989.

Edey, Maitland. *Great Photographic Essays from LIFE.* 1978.

Evans, Walker, et al. *The Years of Bitterness and Pride: Farm Security Administration, FSA Photographs, 1935–1943.* 1975.

Fleischhauer, Carl, and Beverly W. Brannan, eds. *Documenting America, 1935–1943.* 1988.

Hurley, F. Jack. *Portrait of a Decade: Roy Stryker and the Development of Documentary Photography in the Thirties.* 1973.

O'Neal, Hank. *A Vision Shared: A Classic Portrait of America and its People, 1935–1943.* 1976.

Rothstein, Arthur; Roy Emerson Stryker; and John Vachon. *Just before the War: Urban America from 1935 to 1941 as Seen by Photographers of the Farm Security Administration.* 1968.

Steichen, Edward, ed. *The Bitter Years, 1935–1941: Rural America as Seen by the Photographers of the Farm Security Administration.* 1962.

Stott, William. *Documentary Expression and Thirties America.* 1973.

Stryker, Roy Emerson, and Nancy Wood. *In This Proud Land: America 1935–1943, as Seen in the FSA Photographs.* 1973.

BLANCHE M. G. LINDEN

PLANNING

In the twentieth century, planning entered the mainstream of American life in the wake of industrialization, urbanization, and modernization. Many planners started in the city planning movement of the Progressive era. During the wartime mobilization of 1917 and 1918, American planners became aware of the limits of a federalist system built on the bedrock of anti-statist values. Government committees sponsored by Herbert Hoover explored the potential of planning throughout the 1920s, and landmark social science studies at the end of the decade led to the creation of the first national planning agency in U.S. history. Between 1933 and 1943, national planners participated in the New Deal response to the crises of the Great Depression and World War II.

THE NEW DEAL AND PLANNING

Between 1929 and 1941, the American economy suffered dramatic declines in investment, production, employment, income, and consumption. Unwilling to entrust the future to Republican Herbert Hoover, millions of Americans voted for Democrats in the congressional elections of 1930 and 1932, and Democrat Franklin D. Roosevelt won the presidential election of 1932 after promising a "new deal" for the American people. In this changed economic and political climate, the possibilities for planning seemed promising. Historian Charles A. Beard, business leaders Gerard Swope and Owen Young, and activist Rexford Tugwell sparked a national debate over planning.

In July 1933, Roosevelt appointed the National Planning Board under Title II of the National Industrial Recovery Act. The name, structure, and funding of the planning agency changed over time from the National Planning Board (1933–1934) to the National Resources Board (1934–1935) to the National Resources Committee (1935–1939) to the National Resources Planning Board (1939–1943). Roosevelt and Secretary of the Interior Harold L. Ickes sought people with professional expertise to serve on the board, and New Deal planning maintained continuity of leadership and vision from exceptional people with backgrounds in significant areas of American life. Frederic A. Delano, Roosevelt's uncle, had worked in railroad management, city planning in Chicago, and regional planning in New York and Washington, D.C. Political scientist

Charles E. Merriam built a social science network at the University of Chicago and founded the Social Science Research Council in 1923. Economist Wesley Clair Mitchell conducted business cycle research, founded the National Bureau of Economic Research in 1920, and led the President's Research Committee on Social Trends from 1929 to 1933. Boston manufacturer Henry S. Dennison experimented with firm-specific planning, helped professionalize business management by founding the American Management Association, and participated in a range of advisory roles. Philanthropic manager Beardsley Ruml used his leadership of the Laura Spelman Rockefeller Memorial during the 1920s to create and fund a national social science network in collaboration with Merriam. Between 1921 and 1933, all five men worked on Hooverian projects that led to their appointment to Roosevelt's National Planning Board. New Deal planning represented more than a short-term response to the Depression—it emerged from a complicated institutional network of private and public groups built since 1900.

THE NEW DEAL PLANNERS

During the nineteenth century, most Americans assumed that laissez-faire economic distinctions between private and public sector activity lay at the core of institutional life. New Deal planners came to see that modernization of the nation's economy, society, and culture called for new kinds of cross-sectoral institutions that would allow cooperation and coordination between business, government, social scientists, and public policy actors using private funds to shape public policy. Delano, Merriam, Mitchell, Dennison, and Ruml represented a new generation of policy actors.

Delano had moved up the managerial ranks of the Chicago, Burlington, and Quincy Railroad to join the social elite of turn-of-the-century Chicago. Active in Daniel Burnham's famous Chicago Plan, by the end of the 1920s Delano helped lead the National Capital Park and Planning Commission in Washington, D.C., and the Regional Plan of New York and its Environs.

Merriam, the first political scientist hired by the new University of Chicago, established his reputation through a series of research projects, often using Chicago as his social science laboratory. Although his political career as alderman and mayoral candidate proved short-lived, Merriam moved into advisory work during and after World War I. In the 1920s, Merriam, Ruml, Mitchell, and other social scientists made the University of Chicago one of the premiere research institutions in the world when they established the new Social Science Research Council.

Mitchell, an institutional economist trained at the University of Chicago, began his professional career at the University of California at Berkeley, studying fluctuations in the business cycle. Shortly after moving to Columbia University in New York, Mitchell published his seminal work, *Business Cycles* (1913). In the 1917 to 1918 period, Mitchell worked with Dennison and economic historian Edwin F. Gay in the Price Section of the War Industries Board. Frustration with the inadequacies of federal statistical analysis led Mitchell and Gay to co-found the National Bureau of Economic Research in 1920. In 1927, Mitchell succeeded Merriam as head of the Social Science Research Council.

Dennison co-founded the Twentieth Century Fund (1920), experimented with countercyclical business planning, and worked with a variety of private and public groups that brought him in touch with other Hooverian planners.

After finishing a doctorate in psychology at the University of Chicago, Ruml moved into applied psychology at the Carnegie Institute of Technology and the Committee for the Classification of Personnel in the Army, where he designed tests to place draftees in military occupation slots. After he was noticed by Raymond B. Fosdick, adviser to John D. Rockefeller, Jr., Ruml was hired as director of the Laura Spelman Rockefeller Memorial. Between 1921 and 1933, Ruml brought together social scientists (Social Science Research Council), business firms (the Dennison Manufacturing Company), philanthropies (Laura Spelman Rockefeller Memorial, Rockefeller Foundation, the Carnegie Corporation, and the Russell Sage Foundation), and research institutes (the National Bureau of Economic Research and the Brookings Institution) in a national social science network.

These five planners came together under the leadership and vision of Herbert Hoover in the 1920s during Hoover's tenure as secretary of commerce. Hooverian committees conducted studies of the business cycle, unemployment relief, and countercyclical public works planning in reaction to the short recession of 1920 to 1921. These planning institutions, funded with private philanthropic monies, brought together social scientists, new cross-sectoral institutions, representatives of the business community, and the public. These efforts culminated in two landmark social science studies, the first national inventories of their kind—*Recent Economic Changes* (1927–1929) and *Recent Social Trends* (1929–1933). Hoover's voluntarist, ad hoc planning during the 1920s laid the foundation for a shift toward a more statist national planning in the 1930s.

THE ACHIEVEMENTS OF NATIONAL PLANNING

The Depression served as a catalyst that made possible the transition from New Era to New Deal planning. Between 1929 and 1933, economic, social, and political conditions changed dramatically. Under Roosevelt, the Democratic Party and New Deal reformers brought planning to the federal government. Using pre-1933 experiences in social science research, personal and professional contacts, and institutional networks in business, the social sciences, and philanthropy as their base, Roosevelt's planners came together in 1933 as an advisory planning body.

Between 1933 and 1939, New Deal planners engaged in a flurry of activity, taking inventory of natural, technological, and economic resources; expanding physical planning to broader social and economic planning; establishing regional planning bodies in New England and the Pacific Northwest; and creating planning agencies in most of the states. Rather than developing rigid blueprints for the future, they saw planning as a national policy process that would create cooperation among interest groups, coordinate policy recommendations by experts, and buttress democracy through leadership by the president and Congress. Delano, Dennison, and Ruml led efforts to formulate the new policy of compensatory spending in response to the recession of 1937, while Merriam led the fight for executive branch reorganization. During mobilization for World War II, the National Resources Planning Board conducted defense production planning, industrial site location studies, and established a national roster of scientific experts. Postwar planning reports recommended broadening social security coverage, compensatory spending to launch the consumer society, and benefits for military and home front veterans.

Perhaps the most lasting and significant of the planners' efforts came in the form of a second "Economic Bill of Rights" that not only served as the cornerstone of Roosevelt's 1944 campaign but also as the agenda for postwar liberalism. The New Deal planners argued that postwar Americans should have the right to work, food, clothing, shelter, medical care, and security; freedom from "irresponsible private power, arbitrary public authority, and unregulated monopolies"; freedom of speech and association; equality before the law; and opportunities for education and recreation. As practical legacies, the planners left the country with public works planning, compensatory spending policy, executive reorganization, the federal income withholding tax, the G.I. Bill of Rights, and the Employment Act of 1946. However, the New Deal planners overlooked rising tensions between the executive and legislative branches, the bureaucratic turf wars within and between federal agencies, the country's historic anti-statist fear of centralized power, and the complexities of the modern American political economy.

Congress abolished the New Deal planning board in 1943. Once presidential support and monies faltered, the planners fell victim to resurgent congressional conservatism. Conservatives in Congress used rhetorical ploys of red baiting, indirect attacks on Roosevelt, and accusations of waste, duplication of effort, and creeping socialism to bury the agency by sending its records to the dustbins of the National Archives.

Delano and Merriam had both come to national planning in part through city and regional planning. Since 1900, planners had created a range of organizations, including the American Planning and Civic Association (1904), the National Confer-

ence on City Planning (1909), the American City Planning Institute (1917), the American Institute of Planning (1934), and the American Society of Planning Officials (1935). City planning in Chicago and Washington, D.C., and regional planning in New York centered on housing, roads, and economic infrastructure. Professional architects, landscape architects, engineers, and city planners brought economy, efficiency, rationality, and industrialism to their work. But not all planners assumed these same values. Members of the Regional Planning Association of America (1923–1933) hoped to bring greenbelt cities to Depression-era America. Disillusioned by the technocratic nature of modern life, these planners sought to combine community, cooperation, and decentralization in human-scale cities called "new towns."

THE REGIONAL PLANNING ASSOCIATION AND GREENBELT TOWNS

Inspiration for the Regional Planning Association of America (RPAA) came from Charles Whitaker, editor of the *Journal of the American Institute of Architects,* and Clarence Stein, a skilled organizer. Whitaker, head of the New York City planning committee, brought together a small group of visionaries that included Robert Kohn, director of housing production for the Emergency Fleet Corporation of the U.S. Shipping Board during World War I. Conservationist Benton MacKaye, educated in forestry at Harvard, provided a broad naturalist perspective seen in his 1921 proposal for an Appalachian hiking trail. Through the Appalachian Trail Conference in 1925, MacKaye helped found hundreds of Mountain Clubs that built most of the Appalachian Trail by the mid-1930s. New York City developer Alexander Bing founded the City Housing Corporation to build RPAA-inspired new towns in Sunnyside, Queens, New York (1924), and Radburn, New Jersey (1927). Bing's financial skills complemented the writing of Lewis Mumford, who served as the public voice of the RPAA. Henry Wright used his experience as landscape architect and subdivision designer in Saint Louis, Missouri, to analyze and evaluate RPAA plans. These people worked to create an alternate vision of city and regional planning that was showcased in a special May 1925 issue of *Survey Graphic* and in work on

Governor Al Smith's 1926 New York State Commission on Housing and Regional Planning.

Lewis Mumford became the most influential RPAA member as he wrote about the possibilities of the modern city. Growing up in the laboratory of New York City, Mumford was strongly influenced by the work of Scottish biologist and urbanist Patrick Geddes and by Ebenezer Howard's Garden City movement. From his base in Sunnyside (1925–1936) and later the small town of Leedsville in upstate New York, Mumford drew on the RPAA's twice-weekly meetings to mold his urban vision. Although the RPAA held high hopes for early New Deal projects, most members quickly became disenchanted with the administration's limited program for new towns and the narrowness of the regional planning of the Tennessee Valley Authority. Through his influential "The Skyline" column in *The New Yorker* magazine (1931–1963), Mumford critiqued mainstream city and regional planning. He initially hoped to use modern technology—electricity, the automobile, and roads—as a complement to small communities that were enveloped by a natural belt of greenery, where residents could walk, garden, and engage in recreation.

Under Rexford Tugwell, the Resettlement Administration built three experimental towns to provide models for the future: Greenbelt, Maryland, near Washington, D.C.; Greenhills, Ohio, near Cincinnati; and Greendale, Wisconsin, near Milwaukee. Drawing on the British Garden City ideal and the model of the RPAA's Radburn, New Jersey, these towns demonstrated how to bring together the best features of urban and rural living in a new kind of suburban life that mixed cars and people, housing and walkways, roads and trees, planners and citizens, private builders and government officials. Yet even these few projects proved highly controversial. Critics derided the Greenbelt towns as too expensive, too much like socialism, and too thoroughly New Deal inspired. All three towns were sold to private developers in the early 1950s, yet they remain highly regarded communities to home buyers and models for urban planners.

THE LEGACY OF PLANNING

Members of the RPAA presented an alternate vision of decentralized community building best seen in Mumford's commentaries. Planning in the 1930s brought together a diverse set of people, ideas, institutions, and projects. National planning directed by experts in city and regional planning, social science, organized philanthropy, and business management engaged in advisory planning through cross-sectoral institutions to promote natural resources planning, a range of national inventories, compensatory spending policy, executive reorganization, wartime use of expertise, and planning for postwar consumer culture. Yet planning remained highly controversial in a society and culture that historically feared centralized, public power. Romanticizing the voluntarist vision of an older agricultural republic, many Americans remained wary of statist planning. During a decade wracked by the destructive actions of Communists and fascists, conservatives in Congress used this fear of collectivism to attack planners, the New Deal planning agency, and the RPAA planning vision. In 1943, Congress abolished the only national planning agency in U.S. history. By the early 1950s, the greenbelt towns, now owned by private developers, expanded the crabgrass frontier of suburban America. After World War II, planning continued through private and cross-sectoral institutions that scholars have only begun to study.

See Also: GREENBELT TOWNS; MUMFORD, LEWIS; NATIONAL RESOURCES PLANNING BOARD (NRPB); REGIONAL PLANNING ASSOCIATION OF AMERICA (RPAA).

BIBLIOGRAPHY

Alchon, Guy. *The Invisible Hand of Planning: Capitalism, Social Science, and the State in the 1920s.* 1985.

Arnold, Joseph L. *The New Deal in the Suburbs: A History of the Greenbelt Towns Program, 1935–1954.* 1971.

Birch, Eugenie Ladner. "Advancing the Art and Science of Planning: Planners and Their Organizations, 1909–1980." *Journal of the American Planning Association* 46 (1980): 22–49.

Brinkley, Alan. *The End of Reform: New Deal Liberalism in Recession and War.* 1995.

Clawson, Marion. *New Deal Planning: The National Resources Planning Board.* 1981.

Conkin, Paul K. *Tomorrow a New World: The New Deal Community Program.* 1959.

Eden, Joseph A., and Arnold R. Alanen. "Looking Backward at a New Deal Town: Greendale, Wisconsin,

1933-1980." *Journal of the American Planning Association* 49 (1983): 40–58.

Fairbanks, Robert B. "Cincinnati and Greenhills: The Response to a Federal Community, 1935-1939." *Cincinnati Historical Society Quarterly* 36 (1978): 223–242.

Graham, Otis L., Jr. *Toward a Planned Society: From Roosevelt to Nixon.* 1976.

Hawley, Ellis W. *The New Deal and the Problem of Monopoly: A Study in Economic Ambivalence.* 1966.

Hawley, Ellis W. *The Great War and the Search for a Modern Order: A History of the American People and Their Institutions, 1917–1933,* 2nd edition. 1992.

Hughes, Thomas P., and Agatha C. Hughes, eds. *Lewis Mumford: Public Intellectual.* 1990.

Knepper, Cathy D. *Greenbelt, Maryland: A Living Legacy of the New Deal.* 2001.

Krueckeberg, Donald A., ed. *The American Planner: Biographies and Recollections,* 2nd edition. 1994.

Lubove, Roy. *Community Planning in the 1920's: The Contribution of the Regional Planning Association of America.* 1963.

Miller, Donald L., ed. *The Lewis Mumford Reader.* 1986.

Miller, Donald L. *Lewis Mumford: A Life.* 1989.

Myhra, David. "Rexford Guy Tugwell: Initiator of America's Greenbelt New Towns, 1935 to 1936." *Journal of the American Institute of Planners* 40 (1974): 176–188.

Parsons, Kermit C. "Collaborative Genius: The Regional Planning Association of America." *Journal of the American Planning Association* 60 (1994): 462–482.

Platt, Harold L. "World War I and the Birth of American Regionalism." *Journal of Policy History* 5 (1993): 128–152.

Reagan, Patrick D. "The Withholding Tax, Beardsley Ruml, and Modern American Public Policy." *Prologue* 24 (Spring 1992): 18–31.

Reagan, Patrick D. *Designing a New America: The Origins of New Deal Planning, 1890-1943.* 2000.

Schaeffer, Daniel, ed. *Two Centuries of American Planning.* 1988.

Spann, Edward K. *Designing Modern America: The Regional Planning Association of America and Its Members.* 1996.

Sussman, Carl, ed. *Planning the Fourth Migration: The Neglected Vision of the Regional Planning Association of America.* 1976.

Warken, Philip W. *A History of the National Resources Planning Board, 1933–1943.* 1979.

PATRICK D. REAGAN

POETRY

Poetry published in the United States during the 1930s was, as in any other era, extremely varied aesthetically and ideologically. However, in general it was marked by social engagement and a concern for history, ethnicity, race, and region. It was also a period in which writing associated with the organized Left, particularly the Communist Party, in no small part set the poetic agenda.

The economic crisis of the Great Depression and the various political crises that the financial collapse engendered brought politics and ideology into the foreground of much 1930s poetry. This was not only true of the work of such left-wing poets as Muriel Rukeyser, Joy Davidman, Edwin Rolfe, Langston Hughes, Sterling A. Brown, and Horace Gregory, but also that of writers with announced right-wing, sometimes even fascist, sympathies, such as Ezra Pound and Wallace Stevens. Also, left-wing institutions that supported the work of radical poets, such as the journal *New Masses,* gained an increased prominence. At the same time, "mainstream" institutions became more open to the Left and poetry of social engagement generally. For example, a number of radical poets, including Rukeyser, Davidman, and Margaret Walker, won the prestigious Yale Younger Poets award during this period. The leading poetry magazine, *Poetry,* featured "social realist" issues edited by prominent leftist poets.

The political engagement of many poets, both left and right, had a tremendous impact on the form of poetry in the 1930s. An overriding concern for poets of the era was the relationship between high literary culture and the new popular culture industries that came of age by the end of the 1920s (e.g., sound film, pulp fiction, radio, comic books, advertising, phonograph recordings). Some poets, generally the more politically conservative ones, such as Wallace Stevens, T. S. Eliot, Ezra Pound, Alan Tate, and John Crowe Ransom, maintained a "high modern" antagonism to popular culture and often looked back to an idealized vision of an earlier historical moment, whether the Holy Roman Empire or the pre-Civil War South, for a model of organic society.

The more Left-influenced poets, including some of the older modernist generation (e.g., William Carlos Williams, Archibald MacLeish, and Langston Hughes), as well as the younger radicals, often, though not universally, engaged popular culture in a more positive fashion. These writers considered how to address the working class, "the people," or some other oppressed group (e.g., African Americans), whether in modernist or traditional high literary forms, in adaptations of folk culture or popular commercial culture, or some amalgamation of the above. The manner in which various poets answered the question of how one might speak by, for, of, and to the people had tremendous implications for poetic diction, rhythm, rhyme, received forms (whether the sonnet or the blues), theme, intertextual relationships, voice, the arrangement on the page—and in fact what constitutes poetry. Of course, such poets as Carl Sandburg and Vachel Lindsay (and Walt Whitman for that matter) had considered these issues decades earlier, but the question of audience, form, and cultural work took on a new intensity in atmosphere of the Great Depression.

Leftist influence during this era can be roughly divided into two periods. The first, from about 1928 to 1935, was dominated by the notion of an oppositional culture that was rooted in a workers' or folk tradition that allegedly existed outside of commercial culture. Left-influenced artists who subscribed to this approach tended to look for or imagine "folk" cultures or a "worker" culture that lay outside of mass consumer culture—though they were often also influenced by the formal artistic radicalism of the early twentieth-century modernists (who, as mentioned earlier, often looked back to an idealized pre-capitalist community). They were not only interested in folklore and documentary, but in recreating a distinctive working-class or folk voice in a manner that was paradoxically engaged and objective. For example, the African-American poet Sterling A. Brown in the title poem of his 1932 volume *Southern Road* combines the form and subjectivity of the blues and the collectivity of the chain gang call-and-response song.

The second period was the Popular Front era of the later half of the 1930s. A notable aspect of Pop-

ular Front aesthetics was a cultural mixing of the "high" and the "low," of the "popular" and the "literary," of Walt Whitman and the early T. S. Eliot, of folk culture and mass culture, of literary and non-literary documents, of different genres and different media. This mixing of high and low frequently functioned satirically, as seen, for example, in the work of Kenneth Fearing, Frank Marshall Davis, and Langston Hughes, which often made use of a pastiche of the diction and rhetorical styles of hard-boiled fiction, advertising, journalism, newsreels, political speechmaking, and radio drama. Although the relation of these artists to mass culture was less adversarial than that of their high modernist predecessors, a critique of mass culture that highlighted some awareness of the costs of using the resources of mass culture was an important part of even those artists who seemed most sanguine about the possibilities of such a usage.

Another important feature of much Popular Front art is an interest in race and ethnicity and the relation of racial identity and ethnic identity to American identity. This aspect of the Popular Front has often been misunderstood in that Popular Front constructs of "the people" have been set in opposition to particularized ethnic or racial identity. However, when one considers the poetry of Sterling A. Brown, Don West, Aaron Kramer, Frank Marshall Davis, Langston Hughes, Waring Cuney, and Margaret Walker, to name but a few of many examples, it is clear that race and ethnicity remain overriding concerns during the Popular Front, albeit concerns that are as much about transformation of identity as they are tradition.

Finally, many of the artistic, literary, or quasi-literary works of the Popular Front era are marked by concerns with place and history in American identity, an interest that is often closely connected to the above mentioned concern with race and ethnicity. While the place represented, recreated, and dissected is most commonly a specific city or urban neighborhood, such representations are frequently rural, as seen in Don West's poems of the southern mountains. These concerns mark not only the work of poets commonly associated with the Left of the 1930s, but also the work of older writers, including Ezra Pound, William Carlos Williams, and, more obliquely, Wallace Stevens, as well as that of the conservative poets, including Alan Tate and Robert Penn Warren, who were associated with the Agrarian literary circle of Vanderbilt University in Nashville. Interestingly, Tate, Warren, Cleanth Brooks, and others associated with the Agrarians published some of the seminal works of the New Criticism during this period, particularly Warren's and Brooks's 1938 *Understanding Poetry,* which enshrined a formalist modernism detached from author and social engagement as the dominant model for literary evaluation.

As noted above, there were considerable aesthetic and ideological differences among poets during the 1930s. Even among writers who could be considered leftist, or among those who could be seen as conservative, there were different emphases in aesthetics and political concerns. However, poets of the era generally examined the generic limits of poetry, often with questions concerning who poetry is written for and what poetry can do in the mind. Certainly these questions had been asked and answered before the 1930s, particularly in the modernist era preceding the 1930s. What is unusual about these poets, and the radical poets, critics, and journals of the 1930s generally, is that they placed these questions in the foreground.

See Also: FOLKLORISTS; LITERATURE; POPULAR FRONT.

BIBLIOGRAPHY

Filreis, Alan. *Modernism from Right to Left: Wallace Stevens, the Thirties, and Literary Radicalism.* 1994.

Nelson, Cary. *Revolutionary Memory: Recovering the Poetry of the American Left.* 2001

Nelson, Cary. *Repression and Recovery: Modern American Poetry and the Politics of Cultural Memory, 1910–1945.* 1989.

Nelson, Cary, ed. Modern American Poetry homepage: an online journal and multimedia companion to the *Anthology of Modern American Poetry,* Oxford University Press, 2000. Department of English, University of Illinois, Champaign-Urbana. Available at: www.english.uiuc.edu/maps/

Perkins, David. *A History of Modern Poetry: Modernism and After.* 1987.

Smethurst, James. *The New Red Negro: The Literary Left and African-American Poetry, 1930–1946.* 1999.

Thurston, Michael. *Making Something Happen: American Political Poetry between the Wars.* 2001.

JAMES SMETHURST

POLITICAL REALIGNMENT

American political scientists have often analyzed the two major U.S. parties according to three internal dimensions: the party as an organization, the party in government, and the party in the electorate. The study of political realignments, or realigning elections, is concerned with a rare, significant, long-term change in the voting behavior and party identification of the electorate. Such a change also affects the party as an organization (e.g., the chairmanship, activities, finances, and apparatus of the Democratic National Committee [DNC] or Republican National Committee [RNC]) and the party in government (e.g., partisan control of the presidency and Congress and the policy agenda identified with a party through its national platforms and legislative behavior).

In a 1955 journal article on critical elections and a 1959 article on secular realignment, political scientist V. O. Key, Jr., defined a critical election as "a type of election in which there occurs a sharp and durable electoral realignment between parties" (Key 1955, p. 3). In adopting the term "secular realignment" in his 1959 article, Key characterized a critical or realigning election as a "secular shift in party attachment," that is, "a movement of the members of a population category from party to party that extends over several presidential elections and appears to be independent of the peculiar factors influencing the vote at individual elections" (Key 1959, p. 199).

Since Key's articles were published, political scientists and historians have disagreed about several aspects of realignment, but there is scholarly consensus that enduring changes occurred in U.S. voting behavior and party identification from 1928 to 1936 that benefited the Democratic Party and made it the majority party until the 1968 presidential election.

According to some scholars, the presidential election of 1928 foreshadowed the New Deal realignment that was eventually confirmed by the 1936 presidential and congressional elections. Al Smith, the Democratic presidential nominee of 1928, was a Catholic, antiprohibition governor of New York who lost decisively to Herbert Hoover. Not only did Smith fail to carry his home state in the electoral college, but he also lost several normally Democratic border and southern states to Hoover. Smith, however, did carry the two most Catholic states, Massachusetts and Rhode Island, and proved to be more attractive to non-Irish Catholics, African Americans, Jews, immigrant women, and industrial workers than previous Democratic presidential nominees. In short, according to this interpretation, the urban, northern, multiethnic base of Smith's popular vote in 1928 served as as the demographic foundation for the later, New Deal realignment of the Democratic Party.

The widespread, severe economic suffering caused by the Great Depression contributed to the Democrats winning control of the U.S. House of Representatives in 1930 and both houses of Congress and the presidency in 1932. The Democrats also gained congressional seats in 1934, a rare accomplishment for the president's party in a midterm election. Until the results of 1936 presidential and congressional elections were analyzed, however, it was not certain during Roosevelt's first term if a long-term realignment of voting blocs establishing the Democratic Party as the new majority party had been effected. For example, African Americans, who were suffering economically more than whites, voted about 65 percent Republican for president in 1932. Leaders of political movements of economic protest criticized Roosevelt, the New Deal, and the Democratic Party for being too cautious, moderate, and ineffective in combating the Great Depression, and they threatened his re-election.

But Roosevelt was re-elected with more than 60 percent of the popular vote and carried 46 of the 48 states in the electoral college. While maintaining the pre-New Deal Democratic loyalty of southern whites and Irish Catholics, Roosevelt received overwhelming majorities from African Americans, Jews, non-Irish Catholics, urban residents in general, and labor union members. The New Deal's social welfare programs, public works projects, and labor reforms, especially the Wagner Act of 1935, were instrumental in developing organized labor as a major source of votes, campaign finance and services, and interest group strength for the Democratic Party during and long after the New Deal realignment.

As a consequence of the 1936 election results, the Democratic Party became the nation's majority in voter registration for the first time since 1856. Many rural, non-southern white Protestants who had voted Democratic from 1932 to 1936 began to return to the Republican Party in 1938, and there was a steady decline in the national Democratic Party's electoral appeal to southern whites after World War II and, to a lesser extent, to Catholics by the late 1960s. Nonetheless, the political realignment of voting blocs, party identification, and electoral behavior stemming from the Great Depression, the New Deal, and Franklin D. Roosevelt enabled the Democratic Party to dominate the presidency, Congress, and policymaking, and even to influence the internal politics of the Republican Party long after the Great Depression.

See Also: DEMOCRATIC PARTY; REPUBLICAN PARTY.

BIBLIOGRAPHY

Key, V. O., Jr. "A Theory of Critical Elections." *Journal of Politics* 17 (1955): 3–18.

Key, V. O., Jr. "Secular Realignment and the Party System." *Journal of Politics* 21 (1959): 198–210.

Savage, Sean J. *Roosevelt: The Party Leader, 1932–1945.* 1991.

SEAN J. SAVAGE

POPULAR FRONT

In 1935 the Seventh World Congress of the Communist International (Comintern) announced the opening of the "Popular Front." The campaign called for an international alliance against fascism and shifted Communist emphasis away from building proletarian revolution. In the United States, the Communist Party responded by reducing opposition to the New Deal, re-concentrating efforts in the mainstream of the trade union movement, and building alliances against fascism in Germany, Japan, Italy, and Spain. Internationally, the Popular Front took multiple forms. In Spain, the Popular Front organized to defeat fascist forces under Francisco Franco. In Chile, the Popular Front political party organized workers against old ruling parties and won the 1938 presidential election. In China, Soviet influence persuaded Chinese Communists to compromise with the Nationalist Party to defeat Japanese imperialism. In August 1939, the Comintern retracted its popular front campaign after Stalin and Hitler signed a nonaggression pact. In 1941, Germany attacked Russia, and a "democratic" antifascist emphasis returned to international communism's line.

Its populist undertones and democratic rhetoric made the Popular Front the high point of Communist influence in U.S. history. Earl Browder, general secretary of the Communist Party of the United States (CPUSA), famously declared during the Popular Front that "Communism is Twentieth-Century Americanism." Browder's 1938 book *The People's Front* invoked mainstream liberal American appeals: support for Roosevelt and trade unions, freedom of the press, democracy and the constitution. Abraham Lincoln was embraced as an American freedom fighter during the Popular Front, and American leftists, including the poet Langston Hughes, volunteered to fight in the Abraham Lincoln Brigade in Spain. Black Americans also responded to the Popular Front's appeal for interracial solidarity against fascism. In 1936 the Communist Party helped to organize the National Negro Congress in Chicago and opened its "Negro People's Front," a companion movement to the larger Popular Front. James Ford, the black vice-presidential candidate for the CPUSA in 1932 and 1936, published *The Negro and the Democratic National Front* in 1938, praising Communist efforts in the Congress of Industrial Organizations (CIO), the Southern Negro Youth Movement, and the defense of Ethiopia against Italy.

The Popular Front also promoted "people's culture." The American Writers' Congress was created by the CPUSA in 1935 to replace its John Reed clubs. Shortly thereafter the Popular Front League of American Writers was formed. League work was carried on by a broad range of American writers: Nelson Algren, Kenneth Rexroth, Meridel Le Sueur, Franklin Folsom, among others. African-American writers were among the league's most enthusiastic supporters: Richard Wright, Langston Hughes, Gwendolyn Brooks, Margaret Walker, Arna Bontemps, and Frank Marshall Davis were members. In the visual arts, the Mexican Popular Front artists Diego Rivera, Jose Orozco, and David Siqueiros and the American populist Thomas Hart Benton impressed folk materials and a progressive representational style on American painting. Swing, jazz, and folk music, particularly the ballads of Paul Robeson, were enlisted against fascism, if not for communism, during the Popular Front.

The Popular Front remains the most vexing period in U.S. Communist history: Detractors perceive its ideological compromises as fatal to international proletarianism, while admirers value its capacity for progressive political and cultural alliances.

See Also: COMMUNIST PARTY; FASCISM.

BIBLIOGRAPHY

Browder, Earl. *The People's Front.* 1938.

Denning, Michael. *The Cultural Front: The Laboring of American Culture in the Twentieth-Century.* 1996.

Drake, Paul W. *Socialism and Populism in Chile, 1932–52.* 1978.

Ford, James W. *The Negro and the Democratic Front.* 1938.

Kelley, Robin D. G. *Hammer and Hoe: Alabama Communists during the Great Depression.* 1990.

Mullen, Bill V. *Popular Fronts: Chicago and African-American Cultural Politics, 1935–46.* 1999.

Naison, Mark. *Communists in Harlem During the Great Depression.* 1983.

BILL V. MULLEN

POST OFFICE MURALS

In October 1934 the Section of Painting and Sculpture was established within the U.S. Department of

A mural by Ann Hunt Spencer adorns a post office in 1942 in Southington, Connecticut. LIBRARY OF CONGRESS, PRINTS & PHOTOGRAPHS DIVISION, FSA/OWI COLLECTION

the Treasury. From 1938 until its closure in 1943 it was referred to as the Section of Fine Arts. The Section was assigned one percent of construction funds to decorate new federal buildings, many of which were post offices. Although involved in prestigious projects decorating government buildings in Washington, D.C., the Section of Fine Arts is best known for the post office art that it commissioned. In total, the Section decorated buildings in more than one thousand American cities and towns.

Edward Bruce was the director of the Section of Fine Arts. A businessman, artist, and ardent New Dealer, Bruce had been director of the Public Works of Art Project that was attached to the Civil Works Administration during 1933 and 1934. Bruce's strong convictions about government funding of

the arts influenced the Section's work. He believed that federal sponsorship needed to be justified through work of high quality, and although the Section of Fine Arts aided many artists, in contrast to the Federal Art Project of the Works Progress Administration, it did not prioritize the provision of relief. Commissions were awarded through competitions of invited artists, a practice that was intended to favor established artists. Of the 850 artists employed by the Section of Fine Arts, only one-sixth were women and only three were African Americans. Bruce was also prescriptive about the style of art that would decorate the post offices. An enthusiast for realism and the American Scene, he approved only one abstract mural—by Lloyd R. Ney in New London, Ohio.

The aim of the post office murals was to make "art a part of daily life." This was achieved at the outset through the artists working in public spaces, interacting with the community, and demystifying the creative process. Generally, the muralists worked either with oil and canvas that was glued to the wall, in *buon fresco* that involved painting directly on wet plaster, or in *fresco secco* in which paint was applied to a dry wall. In addition, some murals were relief sculptures, using wood, plaster, or stone.

The post office was a major focus of American communities and an obvious link between the people and the federal government. However, the Section of Fine Arts did not proclaim federal authority through triumphal symbolism or, normally, through explicit references to the New Deal and its programs. Rather, the murals reflected local community characteristics, registered their histories, and celebrated their citizens. The murals contained powerful mythic images of the United States as expressed in representations of the family, pioneers, farmers, and workers, and they embedded such values as liberty, democracy, individualism, and opportunity. Although the artists of many post office murals were inspired by the Mexican revolutionary muralists—Diego Rivera, David Alfaro Siqueiros, and Jose Clemente Orozco—their work tended to lack similar critical perspectives. Rarely did the murals engage with the impact of the Depression, and they tended to omit representations of conflict based on race, class, and gender. As such, they not only confirmed the strong bonds between localities and the state, they also proclaimed the vitality and strength of national values and institutions, offering hope for the future beyond the economic crisis.

See Also: AMERICAN SCENE, THE; ART; FEDERAL ART PROJECT (FAP); RIVERA, DIEGO.

BIBLIOGRAPHY

Beckham, Sue Bridwell. *Depression Post Office Murals and Southern Culture: A Gentle Reconstruction.* 1989.

Contreras, Belisario R. *Tradition and Innovation in New Deal Art.* 1983.

Marling, Karal Ann. *Wall-to-Wall America: A Cultural History of Post-Office Murals in the Great Depression.* 1982.

Marling, Karal Ann. "A Note on New Deal Iconography: Futurology and the Historical Myth." In *Prospects* 4 (1979): 421–440.

McKinzie, Richard D. *The New Deal for Artists.* 1973.

Park, Marlene, and Gerald E. Markowitz. *Democratic Vistas: Post Offices and Public Art in the New Deal.* 1984.

STUART KIDD

POUR. *See* PRESIDENT'S ORGANIZATION FOR UNEMPLOYMENT RELIEF.

PRESIDENT'S COMMITTEE ON SOCIAL TRENDS

Established in 1929 by the newly inaugurated Herbert Hoover, the President's Committee on Social Trends was a group of leading social scientists and foundation officials whose task was to collect data on leading social institutions and behavior. Hoover had utilized this survey approach since his days as food administrator during World War I, and he had made it a keystone of his work as secretary of commerce. Hoover's view of social science perceived the collection and description of facts as leading automatically to obvious conclusions. On several occasions he noted his intentions of basing his social policies upon the data of the social trends study.

The chairman of the committee was Columbia University economist and director of the National Bureau for Economic Research Wesley Mitchell. Mitchell and Hoover had known each other since their government service in World War I. Like Hoover, Mitchell believed in the slow accumulation of statistical facts that could eventually lead to social improvement. The committee's vice-chairman was Charles Merriam, founder of the Social Science Research Council (SSRC) and long-time collaborator with Mitchell on social science committees. Almost all of the contributors had a close relationship with the SSRC.

More significant for the actual writing of the report were the director and assistant directors of research, William Ogburn and Howard Odum, both possessors of doctorates in sociology from Columbia. Ogburn, in particular, insisted upon absolute objectivity and absence of opinions. His favorite chapters included little beyond statistics. Fearing that some chapters would include recommendations, Ogburn sent out a memorandum promising to prevent acceptance of any chapter with conclusions or recommendations. While the more politically astute Mitchell and Merriam blocked his veto in several cases, almost all of the chapters bore Ogburn's imprint.

The Committee's final product, *Recent Social Trends*, finished in early 1932, was thirty chapters and over 1,500 pages. The subjects ranged from agricultural and forest lands to taxation and public finance. While most reviews were complimentary, others noted its limitations. Adolf Berle, soon to become a member of Franklin D. Roosevelt "brains trust," stated that the work needed a "master" to interpret the data and develop specific policies. The historian Charles Beard saw *Recent Social Trends* as a crisis in the empirical method. Berle and Beard's predictions were borne out. The book did not provide a basis for social reform or legislation, even in the Great Depression, but it does serve as a splendid overview of American society at the beginning of the 1930s.

See Also: SOCIAL SCIENCE.

BIBLIOGRAPHY

Bannister, Robert C. *Sociology and Scientism: The American Quest for Objectivity, 1880–1940.* 1987.

Karl, Barry D. "Presidential Planning and Social Research: Mr. Hoover's Experts," in *Perspectives in American History* 3 (1969): 347–409.

Karl, Barry D. *Charles E. Merriam and the Study of Politics.* 1974.

MARK C. SMITH

PRESIDENT'S EMERGENCY COMMITTEE FOR EMPLOYMENT (PECE)

The President's Emergency Committee for Employment (PECE) was President Herbert Hoover's first organizational response to the economic crisis that became the "Great Depression." In October of 1930, Hoover appointed Colonel Arthur Woods to head PECE, a federal "employment committee," modeled on a similar federal organization established during the recession of 1921 and 1922 (also created by then Secretary of Commerce Hoover and chaired by Woods).

PECE's stated goal was "job-creation." This aim was to be accomplished by expanding federal employment, encouraging the expansion of locally financed public construction, and stimulating private sector job-creation schemes. The committee's literature urged Americans to "give a job" and "spread the work." Local governments were called upon to initiate construction projects already planned, and PECE officials advocated a large increase in federal public works spending. The committee also encouraged local private relief efforts and served as a clearinghouse for information on relief. However, the PECE did not raise relief funds directly nor did it attempt to encourage needed public appropriations for direct aid to the unemployed.

In hindsight, the PECE has been viewed as an ineffectual response to the emerging Depression, an example of Herbert Hoover's outdated "voluntarism" (reliance on private initiatives) and his resistance to a more aggressive federal policy. But in the fall of 1930, the Depression was not yet "great," and the PECE's re-employment proposals seemed to most Americans to be adequate, even innovative, experiments.

By the spring of 1931, however, the administration's anti-Depression policies were in disarray. Unemployment had reached unprecedented levels; private industry was laying off workers rather than creating jobs; and financially strapped local governments were reducing public employment. There was growing sentiment in the social work community and in Congress that a federal relief appropriation might soon be necessary. In April, PECE chairman Arthur Woods, disillusioned by the administration's refusal to fund a more generous federal public employment program, resigned. In August 1931 the PECE was reorganized and renamed the President's Organization for Unemployment Relief (POUR).

See Also: HOOVER, HERBERT; UNEMPLOYMENT, LEVELS OF.

BIBLIOGRAPHY

Bremer, William W. *Depression Winters: Social Workers and the New Deal.* 1984.

Brown, Josephine C. *Public Relief, 1929–1939.* 1939.

Burner, David. *Herbert Hoover: A Public Life.* 1984.

Grim, Carolyn. "The Unemployment Conference of 1921: An Experiment in National Cooperative Planning." *Mid-America* 55 (1973): 83–107.

Hayes, E. P. *Activities of the President's Emergency Committee for Employment, 1930–1931.* 1936.

Mullins, William H. *The Depression and the Urban West Coast, 1929–1933.* 1991.

JEFF SINGLETON

PRESIDENT'S ORGANIZATION FOR UNEMPLOYMENT RELIEF (POUR)

The President's Organization for Unemployment Relief (POUR), created in August of 1931, was the Hoover administration's second federal committee to promote voluntarist solutions to the unemployment crisis. Although the POUR resembled its predecessor, the President's Emergency Committee on Employment (PECE), there were important differences between the two committees. The PECE, created in October 1930, had played a minimal role in national relief policy, focusing instead on encouraging local public employment and private sector job creation. The POUR's mandate, by contrast, was to organize a national fundraising campaign to finance local relief for the unemployed.

The POUR fund drive was, in large measure, a response to the growing demand for a federal relief appropriation. The issue had been raised in late 1930 during a congressional debate over drought relief to farmers and by the fall of 1931 support in Congress for a more active federal role in the unemployment emergency was growing.

The administration's response to these pressures was a national fund drive modeled on the Liberty Loan campaigns of World War I and the Community Chest drives of the 1920s. During the fall of 1931, advertising agencies prepared full-page ads that the POUR distributed to newspapers and magazines. Press services and newspapers donated space for publicity. Thousands of billboards throughout the country carried POUR's slogan, "Of Course We Can Do It." Over one hundred colleges organized benefit football games and air shows were staged throughout the country to raise funds for the unemployed.

The POUR raised significant sums, as private spending for relief nearly doubled during the winter of 1931 and 1932. But the national private relief drive was not only inadequate to meet the needs of the mass of unemployed, it was counterproductive. By portraying the unemployed as needy and advertising the existence of large relief funds, the POUR drive encouraged mass applications for aid. The large urban relief organizations established in November and December of 1931 with POUR funds were on the verge of collapse by the following spring, generating a relief crisis that required federal intervention.

See Also: HOOVER, HERBERT; PRESIDENT'S EMERGENCY COMMITTEE FOR EMPLOYMENT (PECE); UNEMPLOYMENT, LEVELS OF.

BIBLIOGRAPHY

Brown, Josephine. *Public Relief, 1929–1939.* 1940.

Burner, David. *Herbert Hoover: A Public Life.* 1984.

Hamilton, David E. "Herbert Hoover and the Great Drought of 1930." *Journal of American History* 68 (1982): 850–875.

Hawley, Ellis. "Neo-Institutional History and the Understanding of Herbert Hoover. " In *Understanding Herbert Hoover: Ten Perspectives,* ed. Lee Nash. 1987.

Schwartz, Bonnie Fox. "Unemployment Relief in Philadelphia, 1930–1932: A Study of the Depression's Impact on Voluntarism." In *Hitting Home: The Great Depression in Town and Country,* ed. Bernard Sternsher. 1970.

Singleton, Jeff. *The American Dole: Unemployment Relief and the Welfare State in the Great Depression.* 2000.

JEFF SINGLETON

PRODUCTION CODE ADMINISTRATION (HAYS OFFICE)

In the early 1920s notorious sex scandals, as well as racy movie content and advertising, raised strong cries for state and federal regulation of the movies. To forestall official intervention, the motion picture industry committed to self-regulation under a so-called czar: Will Hays, an influential Republican politician and prominent Presbyterian elder, headed a new trade organization, the Motion Picture Producers and Distributors Association (MPPDA), soon known as the Hays Office.

Self-regulation failed to mute critics, however, who found the continuing preoccupation with sex and crime in the movies a baleful influence on American culture and society, and especially on the nation's youth. Hays periodically found it necessary to reinforce the industry's moral façade. In 1924 he announced a "formula" to ensure that only material of "the right type" would be filmed. In 1927 the Hays Office issued a set of "don'ts" and "be carefuls" to govern filmmaking. In 1930 a production code was promulgated—primarily the work of Jesuit priest Daniel Lord and influential Catholic trade publisher Martin Quigley—that stressed "no picture will be produced which will lower . . . moral standards."

None of these documents functioned adequately, as industry critics recognized, and by 1933 some forty religious, civic, and educational organizations were calling for government regulation of the movie industry. In late 1933 American Catholic bishops, concerned about the moral values depicted in motion pictures, organized the Legion of Decency (joined in its goals by many non-Catholic groups), which undertook to boycott films violating the production code's strictures. This decency campaign, accepted by Hays in preference to government intervention, benefited from the Church's hierarchical structure, as well as the industry's economic slump resulting from the Great Depression, and it quickly put teeth into the code, which could no longer be disregarded.

After mid-1934 all films exhibited in the industry's theatre chains—the vast majority of U.S. motion picture venues—needed Production Code Administration (PCA) approval. By the end of the decade, Hays estimated that 98 percent of films distributed in the United States carried the PCA "seal of approval." Code implementation began with script vetting and continued through production. Code-approved movies respected religion, law enforcement, and the family; avoided miscegenation, nudity, and profanity; and presented "correct standards of life." The co-existence of moral didacticism with box-office necessity meant that "wrong" could be shown provided that before a film's conclusion there were "compensating moral values," such as regeneration, suffering, punishment, or "a lesson learned."

In June 1934 Joseph Breen, a devout 43-year-old Catholic, former Philadelphia newspaperman, and one-time U.S. counselor official, whose church ties had brought him to Hollywood and the MPPDA, became director of the PCA, which after Hays's 1945 retirement became known as the Breen Office. Shrewd and hardworking, Breen remained its head until 1953, except for a 1941 to 1942 industry stint. Throughout his tenure the conservative Breen was concerned with both moral values and political content, a censorship that kept most films bland and noncontroversial. The PCA and the Legion of Decency lost their clout in the early 1950s as a result of economic changes in the industry, shifts in public taste, and anticensorship court rulings.

See Also: HOLLYWOOD AND THE FILM INDUSTRY.

BIBLIOGRAPHY

Bernstein, Matthew, ed. *Controlling Hollywood: Censorship and Regulation in the Studio Era.* 1999.

Black, Gregory D. *Hollywood Censored: Morality Codes, Catholics, and the Movies.* 1994.

Leff, Leonard J., and Jerold L. Simmons. *Dame in the Kimono: Hollywood, Censorship, and the Production Code from the 1920s to the 1960s,* 2nd edition. 2001.

Martin, Olga J. *Hollywood's Movie Commandments: A Handbook for Motion Picture Writers and Reviewers.* 1937.

Schumach, Murray. *The Face on the Cutting Room Floor: The Story of Movie and Television Censorship.* 1964.

Vizzard, Jack. *See No Evil: Life Inside a Hollywood Censor.*
1970.

DANIEL J. LEAB

PROHIBITION

By the onset of the Great Depression, national prohibition was beginning to stagger. The ban on alcoholic beverages was ignored by a sizeable minority
of Americans and disliked by many more. Nevertheless, both politicians and the general public assumed the dry law to be permanently embedded in
United States public policy because of its status as
a constitutional requirement. Not the least of the
unexpected consequences of the Depression was
the creation of circumstances in which national
prohibition was overturned.

THE EIGHTEENTH AMENDMENT AND THE
VOLSTEAD ACT

Advocates of temperance concluded during
a century-long crusade that the only workable
solution to the problem of alcohol abuse was
government-enforced elimination of beverage alcohol. The movement to prohibit drinking attracted
a broad base of support from women, churches,
employers, urban social and political reformers, and
rural nativists. Eager to avoid the backsliding that
had followed earlier local and state liquor bans,
members of the temperance movement began in
1913 to seek a constitutional amendment on the assumption that, once approved by the necessary
two-thirds of Congress and three-fourths of the
states, it could never be repealed. Prohibitionists
benefited from the wartime atmosphere of 1917
and 1918 and achieved ratification in January 1919
of the Eighteenth Amendment to the Constitution,
which banned the manufacture, transportation,
sale, import, and export of intoxicating beverages.
The widespread support for the liquor ban was reflected in its approval by more than two-thirds of
each house of Congress and then by forty-five state
legislatures. Before prohibition took effect one year
later, Congress adopted the Volstead enforcement
act, which defined as intoxicating any beverage

containing more than 0.5 percent alcohol (thus including beer and wine as well as distilled spirits).
Alcohol prohibition appeared to be both absolute
and unshakeable.

PROHIBITION IN PRACTICE

During the 1920s most Americans observed
prohibition most of the time. Alcohol consumption
dropped by nearly two-thirds, according to the best
estimates. Resistance was concentrated in ethnic
communities where recent immigrants saw no
harm in drinking, and among the urban upper
classes who were able to afford the high price of
bootleg liquor and inclined to regard it as culturally
sophisticated to ignore the dry law. Other citizens,
both urban and rural, took advantage of Volstead
Act loopholes allowing the personal use of wine
fermented from natural fruit juices and the prescribing of spirits for medicinal use. Despite the less
than complete observance of the dry law, not to
mention a wave of films and novels depicting
drinking as widespread and fashionable, its constitutional status kept prohibition firmly in place. Its
advocates frequently gave prohibition credit for the
unprecedented prosperity of the 1920s. In the 1928
presidential campaign Democratic candidate Alfred
E. Smith talked of ending prohibition while Republican Herbert Hoover defended it as "a great social
and economic experiment, noble in motive and far-
reaching in purpose" (New York Times, February
24, 1928, p. 1) Hoover's landslide victory was taken
as evidence of continuing support for the liquor
ban.

PROHIBITION CRITICS

Arguments against prohibition predated the
autumn 1929 economic collapse. Opposition to the
dry law came most prominently from the Association Against the Prohibition Amendment (AAPA)
and the Women's Organization for National Prohibition Reform (WONPR). The AAPA complained
that giving federal and state authorities the power
to control an individual's choice of drink was putting too much power into the government's hands.
Furthermore, the liquor ban was producing alarm-
ing enforcement practices, including warrantless
searches of automobiles, wiretapping of telephones, and gun battles between prohibition

agents and bootleggers in which innocents had been killed. The WONPR, worried that prohibition was causing a breakdown of respect for law and the Constitution, echoed these concerns.

THE PRICE OF PROHIBITION

Economic hard times focused attention on the costs of alcohol prohibition, which the AAPA claimed had totaled more than $300 million in enforcement expenses and $11 billion in lost tax revenues by 1931. Enforcing the law increased police costs, jammed federal and state courts, and dramatically expanded the prison population. During the 1920s federal criminal cases more than quadrupled, to more than 85,000 per year; most involved Volstead Act violations. By 1930 two-thirds of those found guilty received only fines, but still federal prisons bulged with twice the number of inmates for which they were designed, and an overflow resided in state and local jails. Not only did taxpayers bear prohibition's considerable direct costs, the AAPA complained, but the outlawing of the liquor trade, once the nation's seventh-largest industry, also eliminated many legitimate jobs and did away with liquor taxes, an important source of government revenue. Ending prohibition, antiprohibitionists argued, could eradicate the federal budget deficit, create employment, and ease the Depression. Temperance advocates responded that the AAPA consisted of wealthy businessmen simply trying to reduce their income taxes. The economic cost of prohibition was unintentionally underscored in 1931 by the successful federal prosecution of the nation's most notorious bootlegger, 32-year-old Alphonse Capone of Chicago. Like many other ambitious young immigrants who found few opportunities open to them in legitimate business or even organized crime (gambling, prostitution, loansharking), Al Capone turned to bootlegging. He prospered in a business that, as he pointed out, satisfied a public demand, and targeted (albeit violently) only rival bootleggers, not paying customers. Despite a great deal of effort, federal prohibition agents were unsuccessful in thwarting him until they apprehended him not for Volstead Act violations, but for income tax evasion. Capone's conviction served as a reminder that bootleggers were not paying taxes on income from an illegal trade, while the government was spending a great deal to enforce prohibition.

INVESTIGATING PROHIBITION

Upon taking office in 1929, President Herbert Hoover appointed a presidential commission to study prohibition and the general problem of crime. By the time the National Commission on Law Observance and Enforcement released its report in January 1931, the U.S. economy was in shambles. Commission chairman George Wickersham and his ten colleagues called for continuation of the liquor ban, but their individual statements revealed skepticism as to whether the law was enforceable, at least at an acceptable cost. Seven of the commissioners indicated that they actually favored immediate or eventual adoption of the Swedish system of licensing responsible drinkers to purchase controlled amounts of alcohol from state dispensaries.

PARTISANSHIP ON PROHIBITION

Despite the Wickersham Commission report, Hoover continued to defend prohibition. The 1932 Republican Party platform pledged continued enforcement of the law, but it also gave tepid support to a qualified proposal for a constitutional amendment that would allow states to exempt themselves from national prohibition. Hoover was widely perceived as the candidate of an alcoholic as well as economic status quo. The Democratic Party struck a different pose. Alfred E. Smith and his supporters, including Democratic National Chairman John J. Raskob, a leader of the AAPA, demanded that the party platform endorse repeal of the Eighteenth Amendment. Franklin D. Roosevelt, who had avoided the issue throughout his career, grudgingly agreed. The party convention embraced a platform plank calling for immediate and unqualified repeal more enthusiastically than it supported Roosevelt's nomination. When Democrats swept to a landslide victory in November 1932, the party position on repeal, one of its clearest contrasts with the Republicans, was given partial credit.

REPEALING PROHIBITION

Congress acted on a prohibition repeal amendment even before Roosevelt took office. The

Seventy-second Congress, meeting in a lame-duck session from December 1932 until March 1933, was unable to agree on measures to deal with a collapsing economy, but it did adopt by more than a two-thirds margin in each house a constitutional amendment overturning the Eighteenth. Congress heeded AAPA and WONPR demands that the proposed amendment not be sent for ratification to state legislatures, where dry sentiment was thought to be still strong; instead, ratification was entrusted to specially elected state conventions. When he took office on March 4, Roosevelt quickly called the Seventy-third Congress into session. One of his first proposals for improving the economy and public spirits involved revising the Volstead Act to allow the manufacture, sale, and taxation of beer with 3.2 percent alcohol content. Promptly adopted, the Beer Bill made weak beer legal beginning April 7, 1933. To many Americans, the worst of prohibition was over. With breweries immediately hiring twenty thousand workers and the federal government receiving $4 million in tax revenue during the first week of sale, the return of beer was hailed as a step toward economic recovery.

Despite the unprecedented requirement of state ratifying conventions, the repeal amendment moved forward rapidly. Most state legislatures quickly agreed to offer voters one slate of convention delegates pledged to support the new amendment and another committed to retaining the Eighteenth. The electorate left no doubt as to its preference. Between April and November thirty-seven states held delegate elections, and nationwide 73 percent of voters expressed a preference for prohibition repeal. Only South Carolina, by a 52 percent margin, favored retaining the alcohol ban. When the final state conventions were held in Pennsylvania, Ohio, and Utah on December 5, 1933, ratification of the Twenty-first Amendment was completed.

Repeal increased legal employment and largely wiped out the illicit liquor trade. During the 1930s alcohol consumption remained well below pre-prohibition levels—some Americans had learned to do without liquor during prohibition, and others found it difficult to afford in the depressed economy. But the end of prohibition was one of the events of 1933 that reduced social discontent and raised spirits.

See Also: ASSOCIATION AGAINST THE PROHIBITION AMENDMENT (AAPA); CAPONE, AL; LAW ENFORCEMENT.

BIBLIOGRAPHY

Blocker, Jack S., Jr. *American Temperance Movements: Cycles of Reform.* 1989.

Burnham, John C. *Bad Habits: Drinking, Smoking, Taking Drugs, Gambling, Sexual Misbehavior, and Swearing in American History.* 1993.

Guthrie, John J., Jr. *Keepers of the Spirits: The Judicial Response to Prohibition Enforcement in Florida, 1885–1935.* 1998.

Haller, Mark H. "Bootleggers and Businessmen: From City Slums to City Builders," in *Law, Alcohol, and Order: Perspectives on National Prohibition,* edited by David E. Kyvig. 1985.

Hallwas, John E. *The Bootlegger: A Story of Small-Town America.* 1998.

Hamm, Richard, "Short Euphorias Followed by Long Hangovers: Unintended Consequences of the Eighteenth and Twenty-first Amendments," in *Unintended Consequences of Constitutional Amendment,* edited by David E. Kyvig. 2000.

Kyvig, David E. *Explicit and Authentic Acts: Amending the U.S. Constitution, 1776–1995.* 1996.

Kyvig, David E. *Repealing National Prohibition.* 2nd ed. 2000.

Martin, James Kirby, and Mark E. Lender. *Drinking in America: A History.* 1982.

Murchison, Kenneth M. *Federal Criminal Law Doctrines: The Forgotten Influence of National Prohibition.* 1994.

Murdock, Catherine. *Domesticating Drink: Women, Men, and Alcohol in America, 1870–1940.* 1998.

New York Times, February 24, 1928, 1.

Pegram, Thomas R. *Battling Demon Rum: The Struggle for a Dry America, 1800–1933.* 1998.

Rose, Kenneth D. *American Women and the Repeal of National Prohibition.* 1996.

Spinelli, Lawrence. *Dry Diplomacy: The United States, Great Britain, and Prohibition.* 1989.

Vose, Clement E. "Repeal as a Political Achievement," in *Law, Alcohol, and Order: Perspectives on National Prohibition,* edited by David E. Kyvig. 1985.

DAVID E. KYVIG

This women in Peoria, Illinois, was photographed by Arthur Rothstein in 1938 as she signaled to a man in the street that she was engaged in prostitution. LIBRARY OF CONGRESS, PRINTS & PHOTOGRAPHS DIVISION, FSA/OWI COLLECTION

PROSTITUTION

During the Progressive era, prostitution came to symbolize broader anxieties having to do with urbanization, mass consumption, and class and gender roles. Although Americans' preoccupation with prostitution diminished after World War I, it resurfaced in the early years of the Great Depression. Increasing concerns about prostitution reflected a broader climate of gender anxiety. Particularly in the early 1930s before the advent of the New Deal, many Americans believed that the economic crisis might lead to social and sexual chaos. Unable to comprehend the vastness of the nation's economic troubles, they often translated them into problems of gender instead. Thus, images of fallen women populate the Depression-era cultural landscape.

Such images directly influenced state policy and action, shaping employment and welfare options not only for prostitutes but for a much broader group of women.

Particularly in the 1930 to 1933 period, prostitution was a topic of widespread comment and concern. Critics drew a direct connection between increasing unemployment and rising rates of vice and crime. A committee of prominent New Yorkers, known as the Seabury Committee, found in 1931 that prostitution was on the increase in their city. They claimed that women were becoming prostitutes because more legitimate jobs were unavailable. A sociologist at Brooklyn College noted that African-American women were at greater risk than white women for becoming prostitutes. Not only were African-American women more financially vulnerable, but urban vice tended to be concentrated in black residential areas like Harlem. Focusing on Chicago, sociologist Walter Reckless noted a similar rise in white and black prostitution. Like the Seabury Committee, he attributed the increase to women's unemployment, but also to the breakdown of traditional family constraints and the allure of urban leisure activities. Reckless downplayed women's financial motives for becoming prostitutes, arguing instead that sexual commerce afforded prostitutes excitement, glamour, and independence, thus appealing to their selfish, modern sensibilities.

For some commentators, even more distressing than the fact of prostitution was the perverse gender arrangements it supported. The Seabury Report on vice in New York expressed concern that pimps and nightclub proprietors relied on prostitutes for their livelihoods. Citing conventional wisdom about the prostitute's relation to male dependents, another writer noted that prostitutes typically supported male pimps, as well as corrupt police and city officials. As such observations suggest, prostitution signified both Depression-induced social instability and the potential reversal of male and female economic roles.

Concerns about the prostitute's usurpation of male economic authority are also evident in fallen woman films, such as *Susan Lenox, Her Fall and Rise* (1931), *Blonde Venus* (1932), and *Baby Face* (1933). In such films, prostitutes obtain wealth and power by sexually emasculating their male associates. The heroines of such films embody negative traits, such as selfishness, moral weakness, and duplicity. By using their sexual wiles for material gain, they wreak havoc on their male counterparts' lives, much as the Depression devastated the lives of much of the male moviegoing public. Narrative closure occurs in these films when masculine authority is restored and the prostitute-heroine is punished for her transgressions.

Concerns about rising rates of prostitution also infused the early Depression discourse on transiency. Many commentators alleged that women's participation in the "transient horde" was on the rise, and that most female transients engaged in prostitution. Thomas Minehan fed such fears with his 1934 volume, *Boy and Girl Tramps of America*. According to Minehan, prostitution was normalized within the transient community, and prostitutes were often young girls who traded sex for food and protection. In another sensational account, female transients prostituted themselves with as many as twenty men at a time, thus making up for the lack of women within the transient community.

Sensationalized accounts of prostitution and female transiency directly influenced early Depression welfare policy. Prior to the New Deal, prostitution was a major focus of municipal relief. Some jobless women objected to the implication embedded in municipal relief policy that they were at risk for becoming prostitutes. Instead of focusing on their supposed sexual exploits, such women suggested, journalists and others might do well to consider women's real relief needs. In a 1931 letter to *The New Republic,* one woman wrote, "The need is for agencies to which women of pride and independence—not potential prostitutes—can turn, and in which they will receive aid uninjurious to their self-respect."

Such women had to wait some time before their pleas for dignified relief were met. Reflecting the broader climate of concern about prostitution, initial New Deal relief policy focused disproportionately on the plight of the sexually vulnerable "woman alone." The needs of single, needy women were a major focus of the White House Conference on the Emergency Needs of Women, convened in November 1933. Rose Schneiderman, president of the Women's Trade Union League, set an urgent tone for the conference when she observed that countless young women lacked not only jobs but shelter, and that many had little recourse but to sell their bodies. First Lady Eleanor Roosevelt reiterated Schneiderman's concern, and following the conference, the newly formed Women's Division of the Federal Emergency Relief Administration prioritized the needs of single, needy women. Only gradually, as the social and sexual panic of the early Depression years subsided, did federal relief administrators redirect their attention to the needs of jobless women who were not at risk for becoming prostitutes, but whose primary concern was supporting their children and other family dependents.

In the early Depression years, the widespread preoccupation with prostitution obscured women's real relief needs and disadvantaged them relative to men. At a time when male citizenship ideals were under stress, figures like the prostitute, the girl tramp, and the fallen woman heroine signified the potential disruptiveness of women in public. Much as the fallen woman film celebrated the restoration of masculine authority while blaming the prostitute-heroine for social chaos, New Deal social policies promoted masculine providership while reinforcing women's subordinate domestic roles. By the late 1930s, Americans no longer believed that the economic crisis would result in widespread social or sexual chaos. Complacency led to diminished visibility for the prostitute, if not to equitable and dignified work and welfare options for a majority of American women.

See Also: FAMILY AND HOME, IMPACT OF THE GREAT DEPRESSION ON; GENDER ROLES AND SEXUAL RELATIONS, IMPACT OF THE GREAT DEPRESSION ON; WOMEN, IMPACT OF THE GREAT DEPRESSION ON.

BIBLIOGRAPHY

"Comments on Prostitution." *New Republic* (December 30, 1931).

Connelly, Mark Thomas. *The Response to Prostitution in the Progressive Era.* 1980.

Federal Emergency Relief Administration. Proceedings of the Conference on the Emergency Needs of Women, November 20, 1933. WPA Women's Division Files (R.G. 69, P.C. 37, entry 8, box 83), National Archives.

Golden, Stephanie. *The Women Outside: Meanings and Myths of Homelessness.* 1992.

Gordon, Linda. *Pitied but Not Entitled: Single Mothers and the History of Welfare, 1890–1935.* 1994.

Green, Alfred E., director. *Baby Face.* 1933.

Hobson, Barbara Meil. *Uneasy Virtue: The Politics of Prostitution and the American Reform Tradition.* 1987.

Jacobs, Lea. *The Wages of Sin: Censorship and the Fallen Woman Film, 1928–1942.* 1991.

Leonard, Robert Z., director. *Susan Lenox: Her Fall and Rise.* 1931.

Minehan, Thomas. *Boy and Girl Tramps of America.* 1934.

Sternberg, Joseph von, director. *Blonde Venus.* 1932.

Ware, Susan. *Holding Their Own: American Women in the 1930s.* 1982.

HOLLY ALLEN

PSYCHOLOGICAL IMPACT OF THE GREAT DEPRESSION

In March 1930 a bone-chilling wind assaulted two thousand men standing outside an Episcopal church on Twenty-ninth Street in Manhattan. The long line twisted its way up Fifth Avenue, filled with people who had heard that the church was dispensing food to the poor. A quarter of them were turned away when the rations ran out. The sight of the long line of needy New Yorkers unnerved the city's residents because many of those waiting for food were clearly in anguish over accepting charity to survive. Many people carried a great psychological burden during the Depression because they had become unwilling participants in the economic breakdown. Americans wanted to work and had believed they would be rewarded for their hard work; most who received welfare aid, from clothing to food and medical supplies, did so reluctantly.

Some critics claimed that people on welfare were freeloaders, but these criticisms did not take into account the shame felt by most able-bodied citizens forced out of work and only able to survive through government welfare programs and private charity. Regardless of class status, many families tried to hide their problems, acting as if they were doing well so those around them would be fooled.

Family life had been changing dramatically during the twentieth century and the transformation continued during the Depression. Family roles were muddled when the traditional male role of breadwinner became unavailable for many men. Merely keeping families together during economic duress became difficult as people lost their homes and livelihood. Some couples delayed weddings due to the uncertainty, while others put off divorce because they could not afford to separate. For many children, the Depression altered their role in maintaining family order. Children had to grow up faster during the crisis; many were forced to forgo formal schooling and get a job at an early age, while also often taking on parental roles to provide solace to those within their own families.

Historian Harvey Green argues that domestic violence and child abuse increased during the Depression. Family disputes over finances, food, and other basic necessities caused tensions to increase. Men and boys often simply fled the home out of embarrassment, frustration, or the inability to cope with the new economic reality. Thousands of people, young and old, became traveling hobos, riding the rails in search of work or some form of relief.

Men's self-image, which had been strengthened by the nation's victory in World War I and the subsequent prosperity of the 1920s, took a beating during the Great Depression. In many cases, men arrived at work to find the doors locked, with little or no explanation. Some families were able to make ends meet by having the wife and children work, a situation that could be humiliating for the husband and father. Studies, such those undertaken by sociologist Mirra Komarovsky for her book *The Unemployed Man and His Family* (1940), revealed that many unemployed or underemployed men suffered from impotence. Both historian T. H. Watkins and writer Edward Robb Ellis also state that the birthrate slipped as unemployment grew.

During the 1920s, many Americans had begun to equate self-worth with material possessions. Therefore, when times turned bad, people felt worthless. The nation's traditional optimistic outlook was replaced by the reality of economic chaos and confusion. Even among those fortunate or wealthy enough to avoid economic disruption, the Great Depression took a psychological toll. According to Green, psychiatrist's offices were packed in the early 1930s with those from the upper classes attempting to cope with the economic mayhem. The confidence of the average American fell to a general malaise and inertia as unemployment grew and the Depression set in. People waited for something to happen, spinning in circles as they fought to survive.

Suicide became a part of everyday conversation, particularly as the stories of bankrupt Wall Street traders jumping from tall office buildings entered the public mindset. Urban legend regarding mass suicides during the Great Depression far outstripped reality. However, the national suicide rate did increase in late 1929 and continued to increase until 1933—from 13.9 per 100,000 to an all-time high of 17.4 per 100,000. In one widely publicized example, James J. Riordan, president of the New

York County Trust Company, killed himself in November 1929 because of the deep shame he felt over losing other people's money, as well as his own loss of funds. Fearing that news of his suicide would cause a run on the bank's deposits, the board of directors did not release a public statement until after the bank closed on Saturday afternoon.

Franklin D. Roosevelt's New Deal began to reverse some of the psychological damage inflicted by the Great Depression. The New Deal relief programs helped people to realize that the collapse was societal, and not the result of individual failure. The New Deal enabled many Americans to deflect some of the guilt they felt for their personal economic failure.

The entertainment industry helped divert people's attention during the Great Depression. Hollywood actually entered a boom period, with about eighty million people going to the movies each week. Popular radio entertainers, including Bing Crosby, George Burns, and Gracie Allen, also helped distract Americans from their difficulties.

The Depression left deep emotional scars on the American psyche. The stock market crash destroyed the nation's feeling of invincibility and left its people anxious and guilt-ridden. For a decade, the Depression defined life in the United States, leaving an imprint on the nation that remains apparent at the beginning of the twenty-first century. Whenever the economy sputters, as with the late 1990s dot-com fallout and subsequent recession, many people are gripped by fears of another Great Depression.

See Also: FAMILY AND HOME, IMPACT OF THE GREAT DEPRESSION ON; GENDER ROLES AND SEXUAL RELATIONS, IMPACT OF THE GREAT DEPRESSION ON; MEN, IMPACT OF THE GREAT DEPRESSION ON; WOMEN, IMPACT OF THE GREAT DEPRESSION ON.

BIBLIOGRAPHY

Bernstein, Michael A. *The Great Depression: Delayed Recovery and Economic Change in America, 1929–1939.* 1987.

Bird, Caroline. *The Invisible Scar.* 1966.

Ellis, Edward Robb. *A Nation in Torment: The Great American Depression, 1929–1939.* 1970.

Green, Harvey. *The Uncertainty of Everyday Life, 1915–1945.* 1992.

Klein, Maury. *Rainbow's End: The Crash of 1929.* 2001.

Klingaman, William K. *1929: The Year of the Great Crash.* 1989.

McElvaine, Robert S. *The Great Depression: America, 1929–1941,* rev. edition. 1993.

Watkins, T. H. *The Hungry Years: A Narrative History of the Great Depression in America.*1999.

BOB BATCHELOR

PUBLIC POWER

Seeking to combat the ravages of the Depression by stimulating employment on the one hand, and by furthering the acceptance of public ownership and regulation of electric utilities on the other, the federal government after 1932 developed huge power projects in widely separated regions of the United States. Using Public Works Administration grants and loans, as well as Works Progress Administration labor and funds, the federal government helped districts and communities around the country either acquire privately-owned power properties or construct public electric facilities to compete with private companies. By the spring of 1939 more than a billion and a quarter dollars in public funds were distributed to more than 1,450 separate projects that established or improved public power facilities. Through Rural Electrification Administration loans, chiefly to farmers' cooperatives, the federal government brought electricity to 462,817 consumers in rural areas by 1940. With the completion of all these projects by 1940, close to nine million kilowatts of new electric generating capacity were added to the nation's generating capacity—approximately a 25 percent increase.

U.S. territory east of the northern Great Plains and above the border states, a region that contained more than half of the nation's electric generating capacity, as well as numerous consumers of electricity, was relatively lacking in major governmental endeavors in electric service. Attempts to develop the Passamaquoddy project in Maine, to produce power and improve navigation along portions of the Saint Lawrence River, to use the New York State Power Authority to harness the Niagara River, and to include power generation as a component of flood control activities in New England were never realized during the Great Depression.

During his 1932 campaign for the presidency, Franklin D. Roosevelt called for public power in a speech in Portland, Oregon: "When a community, a city, a county, or a district is not satisfied with the service rendered or the rates charged by the private utility, it has the undeniable right as one of the functions of government . . . to set up . . . its own governmentally owned and operated service." He further stated that "state owned or federal owned power sites can and should be developed by government itself." With this encouragement, many areas with high rates of electric consumption soon found themselves within transmission range of one or more public power projects. By the 1940s both Tennessee and Nebraska were considered all public-power states. Many of these projects competed with privately-owned electric utilities and provided a "yardstick" to measure rates. In some cases, privately-owned utilities entered into sales agreements that affected all or parts of their facilities.

Three major public power developments were fully launched during the Depression years: the Tennessee Valley Authority (TVA) in the southeastern United States, the Boulder Canyon Project in the southwest, and the Columbia Basin Project in the northwest. To further widespread public acceptance of such projects, the Roosevelt administration undertook the development of a National Power Policy to make electricity "more broadly available at cheaper rates to industry, to domestic, and to agricultural consumers." In furthering this goal the Army Corps of Engineers, the Bureau of Reclamation, and the TVA constructed projects for the public generation and transmission of electricity, and the federal government created agencies to assist states and their political subdivisions in financing acquisitions of existing private facilities, or in constructing duplicate facilities to compete with them.

By 1940 there were twenty-six public power projects sponsored by the federal government, 477 sponsored by the Public Works Administration, 362 by the Works Progress Administration, and 392 by the Rural Electrification Administration. Many of these projects aroused strong opposition from utility companies, southern congressmen devoted to states' rights, and many well-to-do citizens and other Americans fearful of what they called "creeping Socialism." Opponents to the development of public power facilities found an effective voice in the Liberty League, a conservative organization that opposed the New Deal. Much of the opposition focused on the fight of George W. Norris to further public development of the hydroelectric potential at Muscle Shoals in Alabama, which became the locus of the Tennessee Valley Authority with the advent of the New Deal. In addition, the Public Utilities Holding Company Act of 1935, which declared that pyramided holding companies beyond the second level were illegal, caused consternation for many private power companies.

See Also: RURAL ELECTRIFICATION
ADMINISTRATION; TENNESSEE VALLEY
AUTHORITY (TVA).

BIBLIOGRAPHY

Brown, D. Clayton. *Electricity for Rural America: The Fight for REA.* 1980.

Childs, Marquis. *The Farmer Takes a Hand: The Electric Power Revolution in Rural America.* 1952.

Clapp, Gordon R. *The TVA: An Approach to the Development of a Region.* 1955.

Ellis, Clyde T. *A Giant Step.* 1966.

Firth, Robert. *Public Power in Nebraska: A Report on State Ownership.* 1962.

Funigiello, Philip J. *Toward a National Power Policy: The New Deal and the Electric Utility Industry, 1933–1941.* 1973.

Howard, Donald S. *The WPA and Federal Relief Policy.* 1943.

Ickes, Harold L. *Back to Work: The Story of PWA.* 1935.

Lilienthal, David E. *TVA: Democracy on the March.* 1944.

Lilienthal, David E. *The Journals of David E. Lilienthal,* Vol. 1: *The TVA Years, 1939–1945.* 1964.

Lowitt, Richard. "The TVA 1933–1945." In *TVA: Fifty Years of Grassroots Bureaucracy,* edited by Erwin Hargrove and Paul Conkin. 1983.

McGraw, Thomas K. *TVA and the Power Fight, 1935–1939.* 1971.

McKinley, Charles. *Uncle Sam in the Pacific Northwest: Federal Management of Natural Resources in the Columbia River Valley.* 1952.

Neuberger, Richard L. *Our Promised Land.* 1938.

Owen, Marguerite. *The Tennessee Valley Authority.* 1971.

Pitzer, Paul C. *Grand Coulee: Harnessing a Dream.* 1994.

Public Works Administration Division of Information. *America Builds: The Record of PWA.* 1939.

Searle, Charles F. *Minister of Relief: Henry Hopkins and the Depression.* 1963.

Stevens, Joseph R. *Hoover Dam: An American Adventure.* 1988.

Wolf, Donald E. *Big Dams and Other Dreams: The Six Companies Story.* 1996.

RICHARD LOWITT

PUBLIC UTILITIES HOLDING COMPANY ACT

The Public Utilities Holding Company Act of 1935 (PUHCA) was New Deal legislation that broke the grip that a few holding companies had exerted over the nation's natural gas electric power production. The law aimed to simplify the utilities' corporate structure, eliminate absentee management, protect consumer interests, and foster an orderly and efficient national utility system through state and federal regulation. It required any company that generated or sold electricity or gas in interstate commerce to register with the Securities and Exchange Commission (SEC) and to publicly disclose information relating to its finances, operations, and management structure. Purely intrastate utilities were exempt from federal regulation.

The number of private electric companies in the United States more than doubled between 1900 and 1920, reaching 6,500. That trend reversed sharply during the 1920s as holding companies consolidated local electric and gas companies into vast utility empires. Holding companies obtained controlling interest in local power-producing companies and could themselves be owned by other holding companies, creating a pyramid structure in which the top companies could be several layers removed from the actual utility operations. By 1930, a handful of holding-company groups commanded most of the energy generated and sold within the country. Most conspicuously, Samuel Insull chaired multiple boards of directors that controlled utilities in thirty-two states, combinations that made state regulation ineffective. These utility empires freely employed their concentrations of wealth to exert influence over state and local governments and newspapers in order to shape public opinion and policy.

Monopoly status in their localities made gas and electric utilities seem safe investments. They grew even more profitable in the 1920s as technological advancements increased production while the economic boom increased demand for electricity. Despite reductions in the cost of production, however, utility rates rose as holding companies charged their subsidiaries excessively high fees, drained the more profitable utilities to finance their acquisition of additional subsidiaries, and ran up dangerously high debts. The economic downturn following the 1929 stock market crash caused many holding company pyramids to collapse when they could not meet their debts, and their bankruptcies cost investors hundreds of millions of dollars. When Samuel Insull's house of cards collapsed in 1932, he fled the country to avoid arrest.

As early as 1928 the Federal Trade Commission had declared the holding company structure unsound and dangerous for both investors and consumers, but not until the New Deal did the federal government move to regulate utilities. Franklin Roosevelt supported such public power programs as the Tennessee Valley Authority, where government-run operations could serve as "national yardsticks" to measure private power rates. But the Roosevelt administration chose federal regulation instead of nationalization of private power production. Rather than concentrate power in federal hands, the federal government adopted an approach that resembled the antitrust and "antibigness" philosophy of Supreme Court Justice Louis Brandeis. Federal regulation would simplify the utilities' structure and decentralize their management to facilitate state regulation.

Neither the Securities Act of 1933 nor the Securities Exchange Act of 1934 specifically addressed the regulation of public utilities. In 1934, Roosevelt appointed a National Power Policy Committee, chaired by Secretary of the Interior Harold Ickes,

with Benjamin Cohen as its chief counsel. Cohen and Thomas G. Corcoran, who had drafted the earlier securities act, were assigned to draft a public utilities bill. Sponsored by Senator Burton K. Wheeler (Democrat-Montana) and Representative Sam Rayburn (Democrat-Texas), the Cohen-Corcoran draft authorized the Federal Power Commission and the Securities and Exchange Commission to regulate power companies to make them geographically and economically integrated. Since President Roosevelt favored abolishing the holding companies, Cohen and Corcoran added a provision by which the SEC could force holding companies to divest themselves of utilities subsidiaries within five years. This "death sentence" provision triggered intense opposition. On June 11, 1935, the Senate narrowly passed the administration's bill, but twice, on July 2 and August 1, the House defeated the "death sentence" by wide margins. In place of the geographically contiguous utility operations envisioned by the Senate bill, the House substituted a broader concept of "integrated public-utility systems" that might operate over broader regions.

Congress was deluged with so many thousands of telegrams protesting the "death sentence" that supporters of the bill suspected an organized lobbying campaign rather than a grass-roots movement. Alabama Senator Hugo Black chaired a special investigating committee that subpoenaed the records of the telegraph office and proved that the more than 14,000 telegrams had come from only eleven locations. Lobbyists for the utility companies had paid for practically all of them, randomly signing citizens' names without their knowledge. Black's investigation led to the first law requiring lobbyists to register their expenses and objectives publicly, and also contributed to passage of a compromise version of the holding company act.

Harvard law professor Felix Frankfurter and Senator Alben Barkley (Democrat-Kentucky) provided the compromise that allowed holding companies to control two geographically-related systems unless the SEC found them contrary to efficient operations. This shifted the burden of the proof from the companies to the regulatory commission. Both houses accepted the compromise on August 24, and on August 26 President Roosevelt signed the bill into law. PUHCA required all holding companies to register with the SEC and gave the regulatory commission power to force divestiture of any operating subsidiary more than twice removed from a holding company, unless those operations could be demonstrated to serve the public interest. Utilities continued to operate as local monopolies so long as they provided their customers with reliable service at regulated rates. The SEC had the power to regulate any proposed utility merger or holding company effort to purchase utilities' securities or property from another company. The law further prohibited utilities from lending money to their parent holding company.

Even before the SEC could draft regulations, its chairman, James M. Landis, urged utility holding companies to begin voluntarily divesting themselves of their "non-integrated" affiliates. But the companies planned to challenge the new law in the courts, and few holding companies bothered to register with the SEC or comply with its call for self-regulation. As a test case, the bankrupt American Public Service Company petitioned the federal court in Baltimore to review the entire act's constitutionality. One bondholder entered the case to protect his holdings and secured the prestigious Wall Street lawyer John W. Davis as his counsel. Another creditor entered the case in favor of the act's constitutionality and employed a utility company lawyer well known for his opposition to the act. The SEC could enter the case only as a "friend of the court" rather than a participant. In November 1935 a federal judge in Baltimore found the PUHCA "unconstitutional and invalid in its entirety." The SEC responded by selecting the world's largest utility holding company, the Electric Bond & Share Company, as a test of the act's least controversial provisions. After Electric Bond failed to register voluntarily, the SEC filed suit in a more sympathetic court in New York. In January 1937 Judge Julian Mack ruled that holding companies must register with the SEC. The Supreme Court, in *Electric Bond & Share v. SEC* (1938) unanimously upheld the constitutionality of the act.

Assured of sweeping powers, the SEC redesigned the nation's utility systems by ordering divestitures and by splitting electricity and gas operations. PUHCA functioned without major alteration for a half century, but increasingly came under fire from free-market critics who charged that its provisions discouraged competition. Supporters insisted that PUHCA had maintained the public interest by protecting consumers. Congress resisted outright repeal, but the Public Utility Regulatory Policies Act of 1992 significantly loosened federal regulation by exempting wholesale power production and allowing utilities to operate wholesale plants out of their service territories.

See Also: NEW DEAL, SECOND; PUBLIC POWER.

BIBLIOGRAPHY

Funigiello, Philip J. *Toward a National Power Policy: The New Deal and the Electric Utility Industry, 1933–1941.* 1973.

Hawley, Ellis W. *The New Deal and the Problem of Monopoly: A Study in Economic Ambivalence.* 1966.

Lash, Joseph P. *The Dealers and the Dream: A New Look at the New Deal.* 1988.

Seligman, Joel. *The Transformation of Wall Street: A History of the Securities and Exchange Commission and Modern Corporate Finance.* 1982.

DONALD A. RITCHIE

PUBLIC WORKS ADMINISTRATION (PWA)

The Public Works Administration, popularly known as the PWA, was an organizational cornerstone of President Franklin D. Roosevelt's New Deal. During its six years in existence, from June 1933 until 1939, public works projects of all shapes, purposes, and sizes were undertaken in virtually every part of the United States and its territories. From the construction of gigantic dams on the Columbia River in the Pacific Northwest to the construction of post offices and school buildings in small southern towns, PWA administrators worked at pumping federal dollars, and hope, into the nation's economy. It is not an exaggeration to claim that the PWA, along with the other "alphabet soup" recovery agencies, such as the WPA, the TVA, and the CCC, built most of the nation's infra-

This PWA housing project, photographed in 1938 in Omaha, Nebraska, included a playground for children. LIBRARY OF CONGRESS, PRINTS & PHOTOGRAPHS DIVISION, FSA/OWI COLLECTION

structure during the decade of the 1930s. Seventy years later, many of these public works projects continue to function in much the same manner as they did when they were built.

The PWA originated in one of the most important statutes ever passed by Congress, the National Industrial Recovery Act (NIRA) of June 16, 1933. Title I of the Act created a National Recovery Administration (NRA), often referred to as the Blue Eagle Program; Title II authorized the president to expend $3.3 billion on a nationwide program of public works. President Roosevelt appointed General Hugh S. Johnson to administer Title I, and he selected his secretary of the interior, Harold L. Ickes, for the daunting task of putting together a new Public Works Administration. Because Ickes

was interior secretary, the PWA functioned for six years out of offices in the Department of the Interior. Initially, personnel in the Department of the Interior were utilized to implement the emergency legislation.

In addition to the two organizations that President Roosevelt created to implement the NIRA, other emergency statutes passed during the First Hundred Days of the new administration produced still other agencies. Combating the Great Depression required a multifaceted approach on the part of government, so the president selected Harry Hopkins, an aide from his years as governor of New York, to administer the Federal Emergency Relief Act (FERA), which Congress passed in May 1933. Robert Fechner was appointed director of the new

Construction in 1936 on the Bonneville Dam, a major PWA project, on the Columbia River in Oregon and Washington. FRANKLIN DELANO ROOSEVELT LIBRARY

Civilian Conservation Corps (CCC). Thus, from the very beginning of the New Deal there existed considerable overlapping and duplication of functions and responsibilities. Not only were members of the public often confused by the numerous New Deal agencies with similar-sounding titles, so were the administrators. Conflicts over who was doing what, and how appropriations were divided, became a routine and sometimes humorous feature of the New Deal. The competition between FERA administrator Harry Hopkins and PWA administrator Harold Ickes was the most acute, especially after 1935 when Hopkins became head of a newly created program that replaced the FERA, the Works Progress Administration (WPA), thereby creating

more confusion between Ickes's PWA and Hopkins's WPA. In his memoirs, Ickes claimed that the choice of the similar name was intentional on Hopkins's part.

ORGANIZATION AND STAFFING OF THE PWA

The purpose of the PWA was to spend an initial $3.3 billion appropriation not only with dispatch, but on necessary—that is, socially useful—public works projects. This required a staff with expertise in a number of fields, including accounting, engineering, urban planning, and the law. During the summer of 1933, Ickes, along with his deputy administrator, Colonel Henry M. Waite, concentrated on hiring staff at the same time that they began searching for projects on which to expend PWA funds. As the New Dealers often noted, it was a most unusual situation they found themselves in: They had to create organizations that were fully functioning practically overnight. In the space of just two years, from 1933 to 1935, the PWA went from being nonexistent to employing over 3,700 people. PWA offices were set up in all forty-eight states, and in ten regional offices created for the express purpose of reviewing projects on a regional basis. The project review process normally went through state, regional, and national level reviews. Much of the work of the PWA was decentralized, but Administrator Ickes insisted on centralizing most of the legal work involved in the PWA effort. His explanation in *The Secret Diary of Harold L. Ickes* (1953–1954) underscores his unrelenting effort at keeping graft and corruption to a minimum within the organization:

> I decided that instead of selecting lawyers in the states, we would select lawyers for our staff here and let all the legal work come here. . . . There are always a lot incompetent or crooked lawyers with strong political backing, and we can handle that situation better by building up our staff here than by finding a lawyer in each state.

This was not so much the case with engineers and accountants, he noted.

Although Ickes claimed it was purely happenstance, a decision made at the outset turned out to be a key organizational characteristic of the PWA. That was to divide projects into two types: federal and nonfederal. Because of the urgency of getting money pumped into the economy, administrators recognized that working through existing federal agencies would accomplish that objective much more quickly than working through state and local governments. Thus, many of the initial projects funded through the PWA were ongoing federal projects, such as the construction of Hoover (Boulder) Dam on the Colorado River. The Bureau of Reclamation finished this mammoth project ahead of schedule, in 1934, thanks to generous funding through the PWA.

Indeed, the primary beneficiaries of PWA funds throughout the 1930s were the federal government's two principal water resources agencies, the Army Corps of Engineers and the Bureau of Reclamation. In his book *Cadillac Desert: The American West and Its Disappearing Water* (1986), Marc Reisner called the 1930s "The Go-Go Years" of big dam construction. Federal engineers located sites on virtually every major river in the United States, and they proceeded to build dams in record time. Considered by most people at the time to be in the best interests of resource conservation, monumental structures such as the Grand Coulee Dam, the Bonneville Dam, and the Tennessee Valley Authority's several dams became the most visible, and permanent, features of the economic recovery program of the 1930s.

The nonfederal component of the PWA took somewhat longer to organize, yet it too was functioning within months after Congress passed the NIRA. Proposals for needed public works projects from state and local governments arrived in Washington, D.C., where they went through an elaborate screening process. Projects were reviewed by three functional offices: an engineering, a financial, and a legal division. After passing through those reviews, projects were reviewed by a Public Works Board, chaired by Ickes, and finally by President Roosevelt. In his memoirs Ickes noted how impressed he was by the president's careful review of the proposed projects and of his knowledge about them. At least initially, until he had confidence in the new agency and its staff, Roosevelt spent considerable time making sure that public works projects conformed to high standards of the national interest.

REDEFINING FEDERALISM

What was being undertaken by the PWA and other emergency relief agencies during the 1930s was nothing less than a redefinition of federal-state relations. The expenditure of what were at the time huge sums of money not only on federal projects but on public works proposed by state governments, municipalities, other public authorities, and even some private corporations, such as the railroads, was unprecedented in America's history. It amounted to a redefinition of federalism. Although the administrators themselves may not always have appreciated how groundbreaking their work was, others did. The governor of Massachusetts, Joseph Ely, for example, called attention to this fact in communications with the PWA staff as early as August of 1933. As he wrote in a letter to Ickes:

> It has been a very laborious undertaking for Massachusetts to rehabilitate the credit of our municipalities. . . . If you are interested at all in the fundamental theory upon which the federal government was created, and by which the municipalities are created, . . . it would be plain that direct contact between the federal government and the municipalities is an affront to the sovereignty of this Commonwealth.

Governor Ely, who interestingly was a Democrat, had insisted for some time that local projects in Massachusetts be screened by the appropriate state authorities, but to no avail. Both Ickes and the president decided that any number of public and private authorities, including local governments, were eligible for PWA funds.

Of course, a more serious constitutional challenge to the recovery program arose with the U.S. Supreme Court's 1935 invalidation of sections of the National Industrial Recovery Act. A number of emergency programs had to be reformulated after this controversial decision, but the PWA survived the Court's careful scrutiny. A new definition of federalism, often referred to by political scientists and historians as *cooperative federalism,* became firmly established in the nation's political history. Since the New Deal, federal appropriations, in the form of low interest loans or direct grants, have gone to all manner of private entities and public institutions operating at all levels of government.

BUILDERS TO RIVAL CHEOPS

James MacGregor Burns, a Roosevelt biographer, described the president as a "creative thinker in a 'gadget' sense." The president was idealistic yet pragmatic; the projects he cared most about were those that improved the lives of Americans in observable, day-to-day ways: better housing and schools, improved roads and public transit, airports for the new mode of transportation, more parks and forests for recreation, rural electrification, and sanitation systems for the nation's cities. It was a public philosophy shared by most of those who worked in

the Public Works Administration, including Harold Ickes. He too loved building things of permanence that would benefit the greatest number of people in the long run, a quintessentially utilitarian philosophy. While others in Roosevelt's administration concentrated on combating the Great Depression in the most immediate ways—Harry Hopkins, for instance, whose famous statement, "People don't eat in the long run," summed up his role in the New Deal—the PWA functioned with both the short- and the long-term in mind.

The PWA's dual objectives resulted in considerable criticism in the press for the relative slowness with which it operated. An editorial in a 1933 issue of *Business Week,* for example, complained that "Mr. Ickes is running a fire department on the principles of a good, sound bond house." Although such criticism smarted, and Administrator Ickes was not shy about firing back, it was a trade-off he was willing to make. But in addition to insisting that public works projects be of high quality and designed to last, Ickes insisted on keeping corruption out of his organization. This objective, too, resulted in a certain amount of delay in the project review process, but it also produced a federal agency that was remarkably free of corruption. As Roosevelt told his cabinet in December 1934,

> When Harold took hold of public works, he had to start cold. He had no program and he had no organization. It was necessary to develop both. A lot of people thought that all he would have to do would be to shovel money out of the window. There have been a good many complaints about the slowness of the works program and Harold's caution. There hasn't been even a minor scandal in public works and that is some record.

In 1935 Ickes published a book titled *Back to Work: The Story of PWA.* Its purpose was to tell the American public what the agency had accomplished in its first two years in operation. (It also may have been written in anticipation of the 1936 presidential election.) More than 19,000 projects were either completed or underway, he wrote. They were located in all forty-eight states and spread across 3,040 of the nation's 3,073 counties. The U.S. territories, including Alaska, Hawaii, the Virgin Islands, and the Panama Canal Zone all had ongoing projects. A fundamental goal of the PWA was to distribute projects among the states and territories as equitably as possible, so a formula based on the state's population and its percentage of unemployed served as the primary method of determining how many projects each state would be granted per year. Despite these efforts at achieving fairness, critics often complained about inequities in where PWA money was going. One of the agency's most vociferous critics was the publisher and editor of Ickes' hometown newspaper, *The Chicago Tribune*; Colonel Robert McCormick's charges of favoritism produced a long-running and very public row between himself and Administrator Ickes, an individual who never avoided a good political fight.

In addition to the construction of dams previously mentioned, the first 19,000 PWA-funded projects included 522 public schools, 87 hospitals, nearly 600 municipal water systems, 433 sewer lines and sewage disposal plants, and 360 street and highway improvements. But it was in the area of public housing that the agency broke completely new ground: For the first time in America's history, the federal government embarked upon a policy of providing decent, affordable housing for all of its citizens, regardless of race. Ickes was especially enthusiastic about this aspect of his agency, for he had a life-long commitment to racial equality. In the slum clearance and public housing component of the PWA, Ickes, and indeed the president and First Lady Eleanor Roosevelt, found a means to improve dramatically the lives of the nation's most desperately poor. These Americans, as often as not, were minorities.

History was made in October 1934, when the PWA embarked on its first slum clearance project. The sites chosen were in Atlanta, Georgia, and Administrator Ickes was present for the historic occasion. In his *Secret Diary* he described how a small entourage of politicians and administrators proceeded to the two sites scheduled for demolition: One near Atlanta University, a "black college," and the other adjacent to a "white college," Georgia Tech. "There I made another extemporaneous speech from a temporary platform," Ickes recalled, "spoke for a couple of minutes before the newsreel machine, and then blew up another house."

It was an impressive beginning for a program that would continue for four more years. The emergency relief program proved to be so popular with the public, and so needed, that Congress appropriated nearly $5 billion for its continuance in 1935. The bulk of that money went to the new WPA, but PWA also received increased funding. More money was appropriated in 1936, a presidential election year. Roosevelt's landslide victory in the November election was due in no small part to the activities of the PWA and the other emergency relief programs. The 1936 election, often referred to as a realigning election, marked the appearance of a new political coalition in American politics. Due to the administration's efforts at including minorities in all phases of the New Deal recovery programs, support for Roosevelt and the Democratic Party in the 1936 election by minority groups that traditionally voted Republican (if they voted at all) was unprecedented.

THE "ROOSEVELT RECESSION" OF 1937 TO 1938 AND A 1939 REORGANIZATION

Just as the Roosevelt administration contemplated phasing out many of the emergency recovery programs, a severe economic downturn beginning in the fall of 1937 put that idea on hold. The press dubbed it the "Roosevelt Recession," with social conditions approaching those of 1933. In his 1963 book *Franklin D. Roosevelt and the New Deal, 1932–1940*, historian William Leuchtenburg described how 1938 began: "Many Americans once more neared starvation. In Chicago, children salvaged food from garbage cans; in Cleveland, families scrambled for spoiled produce dumped in the streets when the markets closed." Unemployment reached nearly 11 percent, and serious labor unrest appeared in many parts of the country. After months of debating whether to ask Congress for an emergency appropriation, President Roosevelt decided he had no choice but to go ahead once more with "pump-priming."

On June 21, 1938, Congress passed the PWA Extension Act, allotting some $1.5 billion to be spent on public works projects. But the statute also contained stringent deadlines: Applications for projects had to be in Washington by September 30; construction had to commence by January 1, 1939; and all PWA projects were to be completed by July

1, 1940. Legislators thus recognized the necessity of responding to the dire economic conditions of 1938 with additional federal spending, but they also insisted upon a definite conclusion to the program. It was a view shared by Roosevelt, who never considered that the emergency relief effort would become a permanent feature of the federal government. Contrary to popular belief, Roosevelt abhorred deficit spending and resorted to it only because circumstances demanded it.

The PWA met the deadlines imposed by Congress. All totaled, the agency processed some 7,853 projects under the 1938 Extension Act, with the full economic effects felt in 1939 and 1940. With this accomplished, in 1939 Congress passed an important piece of legislation giving the president authority to reorganize the executive branch. Roosevelt had repeatedly asked legislators for such authority, and finally they gave him the opportunity to effect a wide-ranging administrative reorganization. Acting with dispatch, the president merged the PWA and the WPA into a single entity and renamed it the Federal Works Agency (FWA). A new administrator, John Carmody, was appointed to head the agency. In no way reflecting upon his high opinion of Ickes's talents as an administrator, the president chose someone else to run the FWA in order to relieve the 65-year-old Ickes of having to be in charge of both the Department of the Interior and the public works program. Moreover, it was becoming increasingly clear that war was about to erupt in Europe, and this would mean an entirely changed agenda in Washington. The president had other jobs in mind for his secretary of the interior.

With the 1939 reorganization the PWA formally ceased to exist. Its legacy, however, is that of a model government agency, one that not only operated efficiently and effectively, but virtually free of corruption. Two thorough congressional investigations uncovered only one minor case of fraud, for which Administrator Ickes took full responsibility. As President Roosevelt himself said, "That is some record." Seventy years later, it remains "some record" of what government can accomplish for the public good.

See Also: ICKES, HAROLD; NATIONAL INDUSTRIAL RECOVERY ACT (NIRA).

BIBLIOGRAPHY

Clarke, Jeanne Nienaber. *Roosevelt's Warrior: Harold L. Ickes and the New Deal.* 1996.

Freidel, Frank. *Franklin D. Roosevelt: Launching the New Deal.* 1973.

Ickes, Harold L. *The Secret Diary of Harold L. Ickes,* 3 vols. 1953–1954.

Lear, Linda J. "Boulder Dam: A Crossroads in Natural Resource Policy." *Journal of the West* (October 1985): 82–94.

Leuchtenburg, William. *Franklin D. Roosevelt and the New Deal, 1932–1940.* 1963.

Lowitt, Richard. *The New Deal and the West.* 1984.

Patterson, James T. "The New Deal in the West." *Pacific Historical Review* 38 (1969): 317–327.

Perkins, Frances. *The Roosevelt I Knew.* 1946.

Public Building: Architecture under the P.W.A., 1933–39. Washington, D.C.: GPO, 1939.

Reisner, Marc. *Cadillac Desert: The American West and Its Disappearing Water.* 1986. Rev. edition, 1993.

Sitkoff, Harvard. *A New Deal for Blacks: The Emergence of Civil Rights as a National Issue,* Vol 1: *The Depression Decade.* 1978.

Warne, William E. *The Bureau of Reclamation.* 1973. Reprint, 1985.

JEANNE NIENABER CLARKE

PWA. *See* PUBLIC WORKS ADMINISTRATION.

RACE AND ETHNIC RELATIONS

Unemployment more than tripled between 1930 and the beginning of President Franklin Delano Roosevelt's first term in March 1933. Employers slashed hourly wages by more than half, and opportunities for employment were severely limited. Most native-born white Americans suffered greatly during the Great Depression, but many of America's most visible racial and ethnic minorities had a particularly hard lot. African Americans, Native Americans, and Latino Americans not only experienced malnutrition and hunger that resulted in disease and despair, but even the most able-bodied among them were competing for far fewer jobs. Their employment and health problems were compounded when both racism and nativism reared their ugly heads. The lynching of African Americans in the South increased dramatically during the Great Depression, rising more than threefold between 1932 and 1933. Although blacks were systematically discriminated against in the South in the first New Deal relief programs, the second New Deal legislation—especially the Wagner Act of 1935, which facilitated the entry of blacks into the Congress of Industrial Organizations (CIO)—assuaged racial tensions between black workers and white workers and promoted worker solidarity.

The plight of Native Americans, which had been aggravated by the division of their land into small plots as a result of the Dawes Severalty Act of 1887, was exacerbated by an inefficient and corrupt Bureau of Indian Affairs (BIA). In 1933, President Roosevelt appointed John Collier to head the BIA. Collier, who had prior experience in urban reform during the Progressive era, immediately moved to upgrade the BIA and to prevent whites from obtaining Indian land. He secured gainful employment for thousands of Indians with the Civilian Conservation Corps, and used monies from the Public Works Administration to pay for schools. Nevertheless, many tribes, especially the Navajos, protested against the Collier engineered Indian Relief Act because it proposed to force the tribe to help prevent soil erosion by reducing its herds of sheep. Still, the Indian Relief Act permitted Indian tribes once again to gain the status of semi-sovereign nations.

THE PLIGHT OF ETHNIC MINORITIES

In 1930, as the economic catastrophe of the Great Depression became apparent, President Herbert Hoover attempted to halt the rise of unemployment in the United States. Siding with those who advocated immigration restrictions, the president ordered that prospective immigrants who could potentially become public charges be denied visas, a policy that was on the books for the entirety of the Depression. Even under President Roosevelt, Jewish and other refugees from war-torn Europe, including thousands of children, were denied entrance into the United States.

Most Latino Americans—especially Mexicans—had been encouraged to migrate and had formed an integral part of the labor force not only on farms in the southwestern United States, but also in factories in the Midwest and East. During the Depression, many Mexicans left urban areas of the Southwest and attempted to acquire work in small towns and on farms. That action brought them into conflict with native-born white Americans with whom they were competing for scarce employment.

Perhaps the most sophisticated response by a racial minority to the Depression was cultivated by Japanese Americans. Within their niche, they created an infrastructure in which their economy was self-contained and independent of the crisis that beset the larger economy. As a consequence, many Japanese Americans had to accept public assistance during the Great Depression. Nevertheless, after 1931 their presence in California increased the enmity of native-born whites. This resentment culminated in the internment of Japanese Americans in 1942 in the midst of wartime hysteria.

The Great Depression and the New Deal constituted, at best, a mixed picture for Jewish Americans. On the one hand, the 1930s were marked by blatant discrimination against Jews who sought employment in colleges and universities, especially private institutions of higher learning. Nonetheless, many young Jewish Americans were able to obtain employment that was based on competitive merit examinations, and many were hired in Washington, D.C., as public assistants and legal personnel. The resultant cry of "Jew Deal" by other ethnics, as well as Anglo-Saxon Protestants, however, punctured whatever sense of achievement the Jewish men and women might have felt.

Unlike many Jews, most Italians were employed in working-class occupations during the Great Depression and New Deal. Hence, their economic mobility was slower than that of most Jews. The economic position of Italian Americans deteriorated during the Depression, largely due to the huge decline in the construction industry.

RACIAL MINORITIES CONFRONTED BY DISCRIMINATION

The relations between African Americans, Mexican Americans, and Anglo-Americans in relief programs and labor unions were exceedingly complex. Although relief programs, such as those of the Tennessee Valley Authority (TVA), promised to follow a policy of equality of opportunity, they maintained pay differentials, racial employment quota systems, and other forms of blatant discrimination. TVA policies, in short, conformed to the mores of the southern towns in which their white and black workforce was located. Indeed, historian Nancy L. Grant has argued that TVA administrators, by bungling their goals of easing, and thereby transforming, white-black relations in the valley, in reality reinforced older patterns of racial proscription and, as a result, exacerbated tensions not only between members of their racially segmented workforce but also between their workers and the predominantly white communities in which many of them resided.

In Chicago, Milwaukee, Cleveland, and Pittsburgh, and other urban-industrial areas of the Northeast and Midwest, relief work in New Deal agencies, such as the Federal Emergency Relief Administration (FERA), Works Progress Administration (WPA), and the Civil Works Administration (CWA), provided much-needed relief, but also increased conflict between unemployed whites and blacks. Furthermore, after the mid 1930s, when the WPA suffered cuts in its appropriations, the competition between the unemployed of both races became more intense. In 1935, the Harlem Riot in New York City underscored these increasing tensions in race relations.

For many Mexican Americans in the Southwest the New Deal federal relief and work agencies reduced ethnic and racial conflict and ameliorated their economic condition. In New Mexico, for example, the Interdepartmental Rio Grande Board opened up available range land for subsistence farmers. The WPA provided jobs for skilled as well as unskilled workers and stimulated an interest among white Americans in Mexican arts and crafts. Nevertheless, overburdened relief programs resulting from low tax revenues and rising costs increased tensions between Anglo-Americans and Mexicans. Anglo-Americans purveyed the stereotype that most Mexicans were lazy and on the dole. Furthermore, Anglo-American administrators in local governments believed that Mexicans were a temporary source of foreign laborers who were not entitled to relief. As a result, white administrators attempted, with some success, to engender Mexican repatriation. More than 500,000 Mexicans left the United States during the Depression.

Relations between blacks and other minorities and whites in labor unions were also variegated. Although predominantly white craft unions discriminated against blacks, and the New Deal still remained the almost exclusive domain of whites, the industry-wide policies of the CIO and the activities of the Communist Party somewhat reduced racial tensions and hostilities. Interracial unions, which undermined companies' use of nonunion blacks as "scabs," brought minority and white workers together under the banner of similarly vested interests and solidarity.

THE SOCIAL SCIENTIFIC ANALYSIS

In the midst of catastrophic economic disaster, American social scientists attempted to examine, analyze, and find solutions that would help remedy the socioeconomic problems of the country's major ethnic and racial minorities. The Chicago School of Sociologists—led by two of Robert E. Park's students, E. Franklin Frazier and Charles S. Johnson—was the most prominent group of scholars that took on the task of publicizing the plight of African Americans. Franz Boas and his students of anthropology at Columbia University in New York City performed a similar task for the Native Americans of the West.

Although another of Park's students, Emory Bogardus, an expert in race relations and professor of sociology at the University of Southern California, studied Mexican Americans, the most significant contemporary sociological works centered on

African Americans and were penned by E. Franklin Frazier—especially *The Negro Family in Chicago* (1932) and his classic statement, *The Negro Family in the United States* (1939). These two books were intended to demonstrate Frazier's revulsion against older writings that argued that black family patterns were a result of racial or cultural traits that had been acquired in Africa. For Frazier, any explanation of the family behavior of blacks in the United States during the 1930s was a direct product of slavery, emancipation, and urbanization. On the basis of statistical data obtained from the census, social service agencies, the police, the courts, and case histories from social workers, Frazier argued that most black families that were held together solely by the ties of sympathy and habit between mother and child, and those families in which the father's interest was based only upon affectional ties, became disorganized in the urban environment. Furthermore, children from these families often became delinquents, and illegitimacy, which had been a "harmless affair" in rural areas, became a serious economic and social problem in the city. Frazier thought that the patterns of behavior molded by rural folk culture were not adequate to sustain blacks when they moved to severely competitive urban areas. On the other hand, the small group of blacks whose family patterns approximated those of the white middle class generally succeeded in resisting the destructive forces of urban life. Their families tended to remain stable, and some of their children entered the middle class. In light of these findings, Frazier was committed to the argument that middle-class culture was a more valuable resource than rural folk culture for African Americans living in urban environments during times of economic plight.

Charles S. Johnson's *Shadow of the Plantation* (1934), which was a product of his study of hundreds of African-American families in Macon County, Alabama, demonstrated that the sharecropper's life in the 1930s was similar to that of the servile labor force during slavery: African-American farmers, saddled by debt, could not terminate the inexorable movement towards decline. Nevertheless, Johnson argued that there were signs of significant change as some young people migrated to the North; as some who gained education in Tuskegee and Montgomery returned to Macon County; as many young people became literate; and as certain programs of welfare were introduced into the area. By documenting African Americans' assessments of the harsh and often brutal conditions under which they lived, Johnson, like Frazier, in essence discredited the pervasive myth among white Americans of African-American primitivism and replaced it with a sociological analysis that stressed the oppressiveness of the cotton cultivation system.

For both Frazier and Johnson, however, race relations were dynamic: The traditional southern social order was changing—perhaps even breaking up—and the North, where many African Americans had migrated during the 1920s and during the Great Depression years, had an incipient race problem. In 1941, for example, W. Lloyd Warner, a social anthropologist at the University of Chicago, Walter A. Adams, and Buford H. Junker argued that the low social status that characterized the position of African Americans in the South was paralleled in some northern cities, such as Chicago. They noted that African Americans were subordinated in those urban areas as well. The rigid segregation of African Americans and European Americans in residences, playgrounds, schools, and available occupations, as well as the primary and secondary prejudicial beliefs of European Americans towards African Americans, compelled the authors to argue that the system of race relations in Chicago bore a marked resemblance to race relations in the Deep South.

Warner and his associates were correct in pointing to the structural impediments that hampered the socioeconomic mobility of African Americans in both the North and South. Nevertheless, African-American sociologists such as Johnson and Frazier sincerely felt that dynamic forces were altering traditional patterns of race relations—primarily because they could not concede that African Americans, with whose aspirations they were in touch, accepted traditional race relations as part of a natural order. Furthermore, writing at a time when it was apparent that the United States was likely to enter World War II, both black and white liberal and radical sociologists were certain that the status of racial and ethnic minorities would be elevated in the near future. As the United States prepared to confront the Axis Powers, these social scientists knew that discrimination against ethnic and racial minorities in the political and economic spheres was a dangerous liability. In short, they thought—and were correct—that World War II would precipitate fundamental changes in American society in terms of the status of racial and ethnic minorities. African-American participation in the conflict and the desire of the United States government to cleanse its international image would legitimize greater demands for full inclusion in the American mainstream.

See Also: AFRICAN AMERICANS, IMPACT OF THE GREAT DEPRESSION ON; ASIAN AMERICANS, IMPACT OF THE GREAT DEPRESSION ON; LATINO AMERICANS, IMPACT OF THE GREAT DEPRESSION ON; NATIVE AMERICANS, IMPACT OF THE GREAT DEPRESSION ON.

BIBLIOGRAPHY

Acuña, Rodolfo. *Occupied America: A History of Chicanos,* 4th edition. 2000.

Dinnerstein, Leonard, and David M. Reimers. *Ethnic Americans: A History of Immigration,* 4th edition. 1999.

Dinnerstein, Leonard; Roger L. Nichols; and David M. Reimers. *Natives and Strangers: Ethnic Groups and the Building of America.* 1979.

Frazier, E. Franklin. *The Negro Family in Chicago.* 1932.

Frazier, E. Franklin. *The Negro Family in the United States.* 1939.

Higham, John. *Send These to Me: Immigrants in Urban America,* rev. edition. 1984.

Johnson, Charles S. *Shadow of the Plantation.* 1934.

Katz, Michael B., ed. *The "Underclass Debate": Views from History.* 1993.

Meier, Matt S., and Feliciano Rivera. *The Chicanos: A History of Mexican Americans.* 1972.

Olson, James S. *The Ethnic Dimension in American History,* 2nd edition. 1994.

Sitkoff, Harvard. *A New Deal for Blacks: The Emergence of Civil Rights as a National Issue.* 1978.

Warner, W. Lloyd; Buford H. Junker; and Walter A. Adams. *Color and Human Nature: Negro Personality Development in a Northern City.* 1941.

Williams, Vernon J., Jr. *From a Caste to a Minority: Changing Attitudes of American Sociologists Toward Afro-Americans, 1896–1945.* 1989.

VERNON J. WILLIAMS, JR.

RADIO

The most important new mass medium of the Depression era had evolved dramatically in earlier decades. The development of telegraphy in the nineteenth century, along with investigations into electromagnetism, gave rise in the late 1800s to the genesis of wireless communications. At the turn of the century Guglielmo Marconi invented the first devices that transmitted bits of Morse Code via electromagnetic waves, using an oscillating electrical circuit. Wireless telegraphy soon bridged the Atlantic and announced Robert E. Peary's arrival at the North Pole, and it would dominate the wireless scene into the 1910s. Meanwhile, though, American scientists led by Lee De Forest developed vacuum tubes that could receive and reproduce the human voice and other transmitted sound. The Radio Corporation of America (RCA) was formed in 1919, after the military ceased its wartime control of wireless communications. RCA and other companies produced the first crystal radio kits, receivers for individual listeners that required the use of earphones.

The first radio station had been established in San Jose, California, in 1909, but modern radio broadcasting began with the formation in 1920 of KDKA in Pittsburgh. Victrola records were played into a "wireless telephone" or pick-up microphone and *broadcast* (a term invented at KDKA) over a three-state area; a music store soon allowed unlimited playing of its disks in return for on-air promotions. On election night 1920, amplified kits were arrayed in movie houses and other halls where Pittsburghers received returns. By 1922 local stations across the United States were broadcasting concerts, sermons, and political speeches. Vaudeville and musical performers, such as Ed Wynn and Paul Whiteman, soon appeared regularly on radio, and such broadcasters as Milton Cross, Walter Damrosch, and "Major" Edward Bowes also were heard. All remained popular through the Depression era. Bandleaders placed "wires" or radio transmitters into ballrooms and transmitted their music beyond the immediate dance floor. By 1928 shortwave transatlantic broadcasts were possible. Labor unions, political parties, and municipalities began their own stations in this early era of democratic experimentation.

Overlapping frequencies and distorted signals increased the demand for regulation or standardization in radio. While Britain's government nationalized the airwaves in 1922, creating the British Broadcasting Company (BBC), David Sarnoff of RCA and others in the United States pushed for a commercially-sponsored system of radio networks that would dominate programming and the widest-band (AM, or "amplitude modulation") signals. In 1926 RCA's National Broadcasting Company (NBC) became the first radio network. The next year NBC transmitted the Rose Bowl game coast-to-coast. That same year the Radio Act became law, protecting the interests of networks and relegating nonaffiliated local stations to narrower, less-powerful frequencies. NBC actually ran two networks, the Blue and the Red, derived from existing station alliances; these were joined in 1929 by the Columbia Broadcasting System (CBS), founded by William Paley, and in 1934 by the Mutual Broadcasting System. All of them featured predominantly musical programs, often sponsored and funded by a commercial advertiser. Product advertising thus took a quantum leap forward with the arrival of radio's electronic mass-marketing. On the eve of the Depression radio receivers were attached to loudspeakers that allowed families and other groups to listen together, and the problems of airwave static and tinny-sounding pickup microphones were increasingly overcome by technological improvements. Just as Wall Street crashed, radio was becoming a major communications phenomenon.

By the end of the 1920s domestic and small-town melodramas (the first "soap operas," presented by Palmolive and other sponsors), sermons, band and symphony broadcasts, primitive infomercials featuring "blindfold tests," quiz shows, speeches by presidents and other notables, and children's series derived from comic strips were everyday fare for millions. Educators and others condemned the lowbrow content of radio series—"This child of mine is moronic," Lee De Forest lamented—and new legislation sought to regulate the content of children's programming. By the fall

A Tehama county, California, farmer and his daughter (photographed in 1940) listen to their radio, a popular pastime during the Depression years. LIBRARY OF CONGRESS, PRINTS & PHOTOGRAPHS DIVISION, FSA/OWI COLLECTION

of 1929, though, the antics of Amos 'n' Andy, two shiftless and comical Negro caricatures portrayed by the white actors Charles Correll and Freeman Gosden, had conquered the national audience. *Amos 'n' Andy* appeared for a quarter hour at 7:00 P.M. every Monday through Saturday and created an unprecedented following, even among millions of African-American listeners. Supporting characters, such as the Kingfish and Senator Claghorn, helped construct a comical vision of American race relations that reinforced the passivity of most Americans regarding such issues as civil rights and lynching. Vaudeville-style ethnic programming such as *The Rise of the Goldbergs* soon followed, and a culture of celebrity grew up around such crooning variety-show hosts as Rudy Vallée and Bing Crosby. Vallée is credited with popularizing the variety show format, which became standard. Vaudeville comics such as Jack Benny, George Burns and Gracie Allen, Fred Allen, and Bob Hope also became radio stars, and like Vallée and Crosby they also crossed over into successful motion picture careers.

Journalism was a decidedly minor aspect of the networks' programming, despite the efforts of pioneering commentators such as H. V. Kaltenborn and reporters such as Edward R. Murrow and Robert Trout, and it was often obscured by the trivial but wildly popular "reporting" of gossip-dispensers such as Walter Winchell and Louella Parsons. Into the early 1930s, in short, network radio solidified its presence as mass entertainment in a box, bringing ephemeral diversions and capitalism's thirty-second fables into almost every living room and eatery.

Radio nevertheless still showed some diversity. The Depression made it far more difficult for grass-roots local stations to survive, but some were able to continue to offer alternatives to the networks' mass-oriented fare. Union dues and listeners' subscriptions kept dozens of low-wattage stations on the air. In New York City, the Socialist Party's WEVD (named after the party's founder, Eugene V. Debs) dispensed news, discussions, and jazz by both black and white musicians. Regional arrangements targeted subgroups of the national audience as well, such as the syndicated networks that broadcast WMC-Nashville's *Grand Ole Opry* across

the South and WLS-Chicago's *Barn Dance* in the Midwest. Even these regional trends, though, increasingly made radio a homogeneous, standardized corporate product that, like movies, had the effect of "massifying" American culture to an unprecedented degree.

With the deepening of the Great Depression, radio brought basic political discourse into almost every home for the first time. In 1921, as secretary of commerce, Herbert Hoover had been the first American public official to give a radio address. A decade later, now a beleaguered president, Hoover was a regular but notably ineffective presence on the airwaves. He fell prey to the criticisms of such network commentators as Father Charles E. Coughlin of Royal Oak, Michigan, whose NBC-broadcast Sunday sermons became increasingly political and polemical in nature. (High listener ratings—first tabulated in the early 1930s—ensured that Coughlin kept his radio platform for a long time.) In 1932, broadcast political conventions and campaign oratory helped to ensure Hoover's defeat and a landslide victory for Franklin D. Roosevelt.

Roosevelt pioneered the intimate presidential radio address, intended solely for the mass audience in their homes. His first "fireside chat" took place just days after he took office, and he made three more such broadcasts in 1933. In the first two years of his term he spoke on national radio forty times, in public and in "fireside" settings, and his audiences were almost always large. This trend continued into his second term; a fireside chat in March 1937 was heard by a third of the entire radio audience. The intense ideological struggles between Roosevelt's New Dealers and opponents on the political right (such as Hoover and Alfred E. Smith) and on the left (such as Norman Thomas, Huey Long, and Father Coughlin) were serialized in an extended debate over the radio waves, democratizing the great political discourse of the day to an unprecedented degree. However, radio's journalistic coverage of actual grassroots suffering during the Depression was minimal. Meanwhile, radio became increasingly regulated during the New Deal. In 1934 the new Federal Communications Commission (FCC) began more intense scrutiny of the operations of networks and small stations.

Network radio's artistic standards improved markedly in the late 1930s. Executives partially took the critics' scorn to heart and sought out more substantial talent, especially in the field of writing. In 1936 CBS's *Columbia Workshop* began presenting experimental original work by Irwin Shaw, Archibald MacLeish, James Thurber, Steven Vincent Benét, and others, as well as Aldous Huxley narrating an adaptation of his novel *Brave New World.* Bernard Herrmann's musical scores enhanced the program's quality as well. Similar programs such as *The Theater Guild on the Air* (for which Arthur Miller wrote) signaled the increased translation of good drama from stage to sound studio, while the *Lux Radio Theater* adapted high-quality motion pictures to radio, featuring the original screen stars. Norman Corwin began a distinguished career as a creator of thoughtful dramatic programs, while Arch Oboler churned out hundreds of expertly-crafted mysteries, adventure stories, and kitchen-table dramas.

The most notable risk was taken in 1937 by CBS, when Orson Welles, the 22-year-old sensation of the avant-garde theater (and already a veteran radio performer), was given the *Mercury Theater on the Air.* Welles's versions of classic and popular literature caused little controversy until his October 30, 1938, broadcast of H. G. Wells's *War of the Worlds.* By then, Americans had grown familiar with broadcasts of the tirades of Adolf Hitler and Benito Mussolini, and network news departments had intensified their coverage of such world issues as Europe's move toward war. Welles's pseudo-journalistic approach to the martian invasion, featuring a simulated news broadcast that evoked the memorable coverage of the 1937 explosion of the dirigible *Hindenburg* (which, like the "invasion," took place in New Jersey), fooled and terrified thousands of listeners, who were convinced that the war of the worlds had actually begun. The FCC warned the networks not to allow such provocative and clever deceptions in the future. The specter of censorship had also been raised in 1937, when Mae West performed a risqué comedy sketch by Arch Oboler, *The Garden of Eden,* and the FCC received hundreds of complaints. The Welles controversy showed, above all, that radio could be a powerful expression and reflection of a troubled nation's mood.

By the late 1930s radio's prominence as a social force was being acknowledged by cultural commentators and scholars. Princeton University began an Office of Radio Research to explore the content of radio programming and its impact on the attitudes and lives of listeners. Exiled Central European scholars such as Paul Lazarsfeld and Theodor Adorno provided intellectual ballast to Princeton's investigations. Adorno in particular published studies that revealed, through his Marxist critical perspective, patterns of manipulation and degradation in the consciousness of the mass of American listeners. Such perspectives were hotly debated, but they also indicated the growth of a body of critical analysis in mass communications that increasingly shaped the response of educated Americans to radio and other electronic media. It was one more indication of the wide and diverse impact of radio on American culture during the 1930s.

As the 1930s closed, radio continued to evolve. FCC pressure on the networks to surrender their monopolies increased; antitrust legislation would eventually be brought against NBC and force it to divest its Blue network. Despite the dangers of monopolization, however, unaffiliated local radio stations grew in number. Increasingly they pioneered the use of disk jockeys, listener research, and package deals with record companies, while some of them also became guardians of regional and special musical styles, such as country-western and big-band jazz. African-American musicians faced much discrimination in radio, but their invisibility in that medium allowed more bands and soloists to appear than in films or on vaudeville touring circuits. Also before 1940, FM (frequency modulation) radio was introduced, promising more true-to-life transmissions in the near future. Television's stalled development before 1940 also ensured the primacy of radio in America's living rooms. In short, despite the difficulties caused by the Depression and the dominance of the networks—and sometimes because of it—radio made stunning advances and caused decisive transformations in American communications and culture.

See Also: AMOS 'N' ANDY; COMMUNICATIONS ACT OF 1934; COMMUNICATIONS AND THE PRESS; COUGHLIN, CHARLES; FEDERAL

COMMUNICATIONS COMMISSION (FCC); FIRESIDE CHATS; WELLES, ORSON.

BIBLIOGRAPHY

Barnouw, Eric. *A Tower in Babel: A History of Broadcasting in the United States to 1933.* 1966.

Barnouw, Eric. *The Golden Web: A History of Broadcasting in the United States, 1933–1953.* 1968.

Douglas, Susan J. *Inventing American Broadcasting, 1899–1922.* 1987.

Hilliard, Robert L., and Michael C. Keith. *The Broadcast Century: A Biography of American Broadcasting,* 3rd edition. 2001.

MacDonald, J. Fred. *Don't Touch That Dial! Radio Programming in American Life, 1920 to 1960.* 1979.

Smulyan, Susan. *Selling Radio: The Commercialization of American Broadcasting, 1920–1934.* 1994.

Sterling, Christopher H., and John Michael Kittros. *Stay Tuned: A History of American Broadcasting,* 3rd edition. 2001.

Summers, Harrison B., ed. *A Thirty-Year History of Programs Carried on National Radio Networks in the United States, 1926–1956.* 1971.

BURTON W. PERETTI

A. Philip Randolph, 1942. LIBRARY OF CONGRESS, PRINTS & PHOTOGRAPHS DIVISION, FSA/OWI COLLECTION

RANDOLPH, A. PHILIP

Asa Philip Randolph (April 15, 1889–May 16, 1979) was a civil rights leader and the founder of the Brotherhood of Sleeping Car Porters. The younger of two sons, Randolph was born in Crescent City, Florida, to Elizabeth Robinson and James William Randolph, an itinerant African Methodist Episcopal preacher. Randolph graduated from Cookman Institute (later Bethune-Cookman College) in Jacksonville in 1909. Unable to find any but manual labor jobs in the South, Randolph left for New York in 1911. There he came under the influence of Socialists and the International Workers of the World. He took speech lessons, which accounted for his Oxford English speaking style and soon became a soapbox orator, propagandizing on behalf of black unionism and Socialism, beliefs to which he adhered for the rest of his life. In 1913 he married Lucille Campbell Green, whose beauty shop earnings supported his subsequent undertakings.

Randolph opposed the entry of the United States into World War I, and in 1917 he began publishing the *Messenger,* in which he argued that since 99 percent of African Americans were workers their logical affiliation should be with the Socialist Party. Following the 1917 Bolshevik Revolution in Russia, government repression decimated the *Messenger* radical group and left Randolph a confirmed anti-Communist. With declining Socialist support for the *Messenger,* Randolph became more conservative.

In 1925 Randolph was invited to organize the Pullman Company railroad porters, the one occupation in which African Americans held a near monopoly. It was only after the Great Depression brought Franklin Roosevelt and the New Deal to power that Randolph succeeded in gaining recognition for the Brotherhood of Sleeping Car Porters (BSCP) from the American Federation of Labor (AFL) in 1935 and the Pullman Company in 1937. The National Industrial Recovery Act (1933) and National Labor Relations Act (1935), which guaranteed labor the right to organize and select its own bargaining agent without interference from the employer, enabled Randolph to achieve legitimacy for the union. Even before formal recognition of the BSCP by the AFL, Randolph used AFL conventions to denounce racism in the labor movement.

In the depths of the Depression the agreement between Pullman and the porters' union brought some $2 million in income to the porters and their families and prominence for Randolph in both the black and white communities. In 1935 Randolph became president of the National Negro Congress (NNC), an umbrella organization established to help African Americans cope with the economic distress of the Depression. Randolph resigned in 1940, charging that the NNC was Communist-dominated.

By then defense preparations were pulling the country out of the Depression. Blacks, however, denied the opportunity to apply for defense jobs because of racial discrimination, remained disproportionately unemployed. When the Roosevelt administration proved impervious to their entreaties, Randolph conceived the idea of a mass march of African Americans on Washington to demand defense jobs and training. Realizing that the administration could not persuade Randolph to call off the march, scheduled for July 1, 1941, without some tangible gain, Roosevelt issued an executive order that created a temporary wartime Fair Employment Practices Committee, in exchange for which Randolph agreed to cancel the march. Uncertain how many African Americans would actually participate, Randolph was elated at the success of his strategy, and decided to keep his organization, the March on Washington Movement, intact to promote nonviolent civil disobedience in the fight for civil rights.

During the Cold War, Randolph counseled young black men to refuse to register or be drafted into a segregated military establishment. President Harry Truman capitulated, integrating the armed services in 1948. Next, in an effort to speed implementation of the Supreme Court school desegregation decision of 1954, Randolph mounted a prayer pilgrimage in 1957 and two youth marches for integrated schools in the nation's capital in 1958 and 1959. Becoming one of the AFL's two black vice presidents when the federation merged with the Congress of Industrial Organizations (AFL-CIO) in 1955, Randolph launched an all-black labor group, the Negro American Labor Council in 1959 to fight racism within the labor movement. In 1963 Randolph proposed a march on Washington for jobs and freedom to be led by a coalition of civil rights organizations, major religious denominations, and the United Auto Workers. Although it marked the high point of the civil rights movement, the integrated march was somewhat marred for Randolph by his wife's death three months earlier. Afterwards the civil rights coalition dissolved into wrangling over prestige, financial contributions, and Black Power separatism. Randolph retired in 1968, after founding the A. Philip Randolph Institute in 1964 to carry on his ideas and methods.

Taking advantage of the opportunities presented by the Great Depression to form the nation's first black union, Randolph's unique contribution was promotion of nonviolent civil disobedience and a symbiotic relationship between the American labor movement and the cause of racial justice.

See Also: AFRICAN AMERICANS, IMPACT OF THE GREAT DEPRESSION ON; BROTHERHOOD OF SLEEPING CAR PORTERS (BSCP); NATIONAL NEGRO CONGRESS.

BIBLIOGRAPHY

Anderson, Jervis. *A. Philip Randolph: A Biographical Portrait.* 1986.

Bates, Beth Tompkins. *Pullman Porters and the Rise of Protest Politics in Black America, 1925–1945.* 2001.

Harris, William H. *Keeping the Faith: A. Philip Randolph, Milton P. Webster, and the Brotherhood of Sleeping Car Porters, 1925–37.* 1991.

Pfeffer, Paula F. *A. Philip Randolph: Pioneer of the Civil Rights Movement.* 1990.

Randolph, A. Philip. *The Papers of A. Philip Randolph,* edited by John H. Bracey, Jr., and August Meier. 1990.

Randolph, A. Philip. Reminiscences. Columbia Oral History Research Office. Columbia University, New York.

PAULA F. PFEFFER

RAPER, ARTHUR

Arthur Franklin Raper (November 8, 1899–August 10, 1979) was a rural sociologist and reformer whose work mirrored the problems and promise of the American South. Born in Davidson County, North Carolina, Raper attended the University of North Carolina at Chapel Hill, where he studied with sociologist Howard Odum. In 1926, Raper went to work for the Commission on Interracial Cooperation in Atlanta. As research secretary for the commission, Raper monitored race relations throughout the South, described the impact of the agricultural depression of the 1920s and 1930s, and cooperated with various New Deal agencies. From 1932 to 1939, he also taught part-time at Agnes Scott College in Decatur, Georgia.

Raper endeavored to reach a broad audience, making numerous speeches across the South and publishing in both scholarly and popular outlets. Perhaps his most influential work was *The Tragedy of Lynching,* published in 1933. A study of every community where a lynching had occurred during 1930, *The Tragedy of Lynching* was widely reviewed and contributed to the anti-lynching campaign. In addition, Raper wrote three significant books on the rural South: *Preface to Peasantry* (1936), an attack on the plantation system in Georgia's Greene and Macon counties; *Sharecroppers All* (1941), coauthored with African-American sociologist Ira Reid, which portrayed the culture of dependency throughout the region; and *Tenants of the Almighty* (1943), describing Greene County's Unified Farm Program.

Raper's research was intertwined with his activism. He worked closely with the Farm Security Administration and other New Deal agencies that sought to provide relief for farmers and lift them out of tenancy. Raper also regularly challenged prevailing racial mores in his publications and actions. His transgressions of regional racial codes often drew criticism, as in 1935 when he took Agnes Scott students to historically black Tuskegee Institute in Alabama, and in 1941 when he was brought before a Greene County grand jury for using polite titles when addressing African Americans. Raper was an original member of the Southern Conference for Human Welfare.

In 1939, Raper went to work for the Carnegie-Myrdal study on race in America, which led to the publication of *An American Dilemma: The Negro Problem and Modern Democracy* (1944). Raper's report was considered by project director Gunnar Myrdal to be one of the most valuable in the study. In 1940, Raper began a two-year stint as a participant-observer of Greene County's Unified Farm Program, before moving to Washington to work for the U.S. Department of Agriculture's Bureau of Agricultural Economics. After World War II, Raper turned to international rural development, explicitly linking his efforts in land reform and community development to his earlier work in the South.

See Also: AFRICAN AMERICANS, IMPACT OF THE GREAT DEPRESSION; RACE AND ETHNIC RELATIONS.

BIBLIOGRAPHY

Egerton, John. *Speak Now against the Day: The Generation before the Civil Rights Movement in the South.* 1994.

Raper, Arthur F. Papers. Southern Historical Collection, University of North Carolina, Chapel Hill.

Singal, Daniel J. *The War Within: From Victorian to Modernist Thought in the South, 1919–1945.* 1982.

Sosna, Morton. *In Search of the Silent South: Southern Liberals and the Race Issue.* 1977.

CLIFFORD M. KUHN

RASKOB, JOHN J.

John Jakob Raskob (March 19, 1879–October 15, 1950) was an industrialist, financier, chairman of the Democratic National Committee from 1928 to 1932, and cofounder of the American Liberty League. Born in Lockport, New York, Raskob rose from poverty to extraordinary wealth through a combination of ambition, financial acumen, and good luck. Educated at parochial schools and then the Bryant and Stratton Business School, Raskob struggled to support his mother and siblings after his father's death in 1897. In 1900 he became secretary to Pierre S. du Pont, and after 1902 the two men reorganized the financial structures of the family gunpowder company. As treasurer after 1914 Raskob oversaw the investment of some of the DuPont Company's enormous wartime profits into the General Motors Corporation (GMC), and he and Pierre du Pont reorganized the struggling carmaker's operations.

During the 1920s Raskob combined business vision with increasing political activism. His greatest achievement at GMC was the creation in 1919 of the General Motors Acceptance Corporation (GMAC), which lent customers money to buy GMC cars. The first of its kind, GMAC financed two-thirds of all GMC car sales by 1927. Raskob also championed employee stock bonuses and investment plans, and by 1929 he was worth more than $100 million. Politically Raskob contributed heavily to the Association Against the Prohibition Amendment after 1925 and to the political campaigns of Alfred E. Smith, a fellow Catholic, self-made man, and anti-prohibitionist. Prohibition struck Raskob as a dangerous expansion of federal regulatory power and as an infringement of personal liberty. In 1928 Smith, who was the Democratic presidential nominee, appointed Raskob chairman of the Democratic National Committee (DNC). Raskob transformed the DNC into a permanent organization and used his influence to advocate more business-friendly policies within the party.

The Great Depression significantly reduced Raskob's personal fortune and convinced him that the federal government should retrench its expenditures and allow business to recover without government interference. Consequently he gave strong support to conservative Democrats in their fight against Franklin Roosevelt's presidential nomination in 1932. Raskob then became a prominent critic of the New Deal. In 1934 Raskob, du Pont, Smith, and other business leaders founded the American Liberty League to warn Americans of the dangers of federal centralism and government activism. Raskob withdrew from political life after Roosevelt's landslide victory in 1936, and he eased out of his business commitments during the later 1930s. Raskob then devoted himself to his charitable foundations, and died on his country estate in Maryland in 1950. His wife, Helena, and twelve children survived him.

See Also: AMERICAN LIBERTY LEAGUE; CONSERVATIVE COALITION; DEMOCRATIC PARTY; ELECTION OF 1928; ELECTION OF 1930; ELECTION OF 1932.

BIBLIOGRAPHY

Craig, Douglas B. *After Wilson: The Struggle for the Democratic Party, 1920–1934.* 1992.

Dale, Ernest. *The Great Organizers.* 1960.

DOUGLAS CRAIG

REA. *See* RURAL ELECTRIFICATION ADMINISTRATION.

RECESSION OF 1937

In the six months between August 1937 and January 1938 the U.S. economy dropped as sharply as it had during the thirteen months following the stock market crash of 1929. From the peak in March 1937 to the trough in April 1938, stock prices fell 58 percent, employment 28 percent, and payrolls and industrial production 43 percent.

The recession came in the middle of Franklin D. Roosevelt's second term, after an extended period of slow but evident recovery. The president and his advisors understood clearly that the recession's implications for domestic politics and international ideological struggles were potentially of enormous consequence. The New Dealers had carefully constructed their public image as happy days depression busters and pointedly contrasted that with their image of Hoover and the Republicans as the party of gloom and depression. Now it appeared that the Roosevelt administration had its own depression.

Moreover, the apparent economic vitality of the new totalitarian regimes of both the left and right in Europe and Asia cast the recession as a threat not only to New Deal political survival, but to the survival in the world of liberalism itself. It became vital for the United States to demonstrate that liberal capitalism could achieve economic recovery, not only for the economic well-being of its own citizens, but to counter the threats of fascism and communism around the world, a struggle that was highlighted at the time by the civil war in Spain. Faced with the gravest crisis of his administration thus far, Roosevelt seemed immobilized as policy advisors bickered over possible ways to reverse the downturn.

Economic conditions early in 1937 had brought Marriner S. Eccles, chairman of the Federal Reserve Board, and Henry Morgenthau, Jr., the secretary of the treasury, into momentary agreement on federal fiscal and monetary policy. The inflow of newly-instituted Social Security taxes, together with the ending of veterans' bonus payments, had given the appearance of a sharply improved budgetary situation, occasioning a fear of inflationary pressures. The Federal Reserve Board responded by raising reserve requirements and supporting the Department of the Treasury's advocacy of a cutback in federal expenditures to help achieve a balanced budget for 1938.

These policies choked the frail recovery and by August the economy was showing signs of recession. At that point the policy recommendations of Eccles and Morgenthau began to diverge sharply. Since coming to Washington in 1934, Eccles had advocated federal expenditures as the most effective means of stimulating the economy during depression. When the 1937 downturn began, he backed quickly away from the monetary and fiscal constraint he had advocated earlier in the year, and he urged the president to resume spending. Morgenthau had long seen himself as the conscience of his friend and mentor Roosevelt, particularly in matters of fiscal integrity. Morgenthau had advocated balancing the budget early in 1937 as a counter to inflation and a happy consequence of recovery, but, unlike Eccles, his policy recommendations did not change when the economy began to falter. Indeed, they became even more rigid.

Morgenthau's contacts in the financial world had persuaded him that New Deal policies had been discouraging investment and inhibiting full recovery. He believed investors had lost confidence

in the administration because year after year Roosevelt had failed to deliver the balanced budget he had promised since his first campaign for the presidency in 1932. The best thing the president could do to counter the recession, Morgenthau believed, would be to boost business confidence by making a firm commitment to a balanced budget.

These opposing perspectives defined the struggle that continued through the winter of 1937 to 1938. Morgenthau had ready access to the president through their regular Monday luncheons. Early in the recession Roosevelt seemed to be leaning toward Morgenthau's point of view. Eccles, head of an independent regulatory commission, was not part of the White House inner circle, and he made his argument for increased spending through associates with better access to the president, including especially Harry L. Hopkins, a close friend of the president and head of the Federal Emergency Relief Administration since 1933 and the Works Progress Administration since 1935. Eccles corresponded with Hopkins during the latter's surgery and convalescence at the Mayo Clinic that winter. Eccles also maintained regular contact with Hopkins's assistants, Aubrey Williams and Leon Henderson, and with Beardsley Ruml, a former Macy's executive whom Eccles had appointed director of the New York Federal Reserve Bank.

As the depression deepened, the President was shaken by the German takeover of Austria on March 12, 1938, an event, ominous in itself, that precipitated another slide in stock prices. On March 22, Roosevelt left Washington for his traditional retreat at Warm Springs, Georgia. Morgenthau took a vacation to Sea Island, Georgia, at the same time. Hopkins, now recuperated, arranged meetings with the president at Warm Springs, where, armed with memos from Aubrey Williams, Leon Henderson, and Beardsley Ruml, he urged Roosevelt to endorse renewed spending. Hopkins did so not as an expedient response to the recession, but because he saw renewed spending as the foundation for a new direction in government policy where "national intervention to stimulate consumption" would provide purchasing power, making it possible for not just the privileged few but for the "whole culture" to express itself "through actions of individual consumers." Such a policy, Hopkins and others argued, would lead to an increase in public purchasing power, a demand for consumer products, the opening and expansion of production and distribution facilities to meet that demand, jobs to staff those revived industries, and eventually "the abolition of poverty in America."

The argument, well designed to appeal to Roosevelt, was effective. Despite Morgenthau's threats to resign, the president on April 14 announced to Congress and that evening to the public (in his first fireside chat since the previous October) a major new spending program and a request that the Federal Reserve Board reduce reserve requirements. Roosevelt's announcement, which relied heavily on the memos Hopkins and his aides had presented to him at Warm Springs, assured Americans that "dictatorships do not grow out of strong and successful governments, but out of weak and helpless ones." He pointed out that federal expenditures "acted as a trigger to set off private activity." The cost of the new spending program would be minimal, he argued, compared to the enormous loss in national income caused by the recession.

By mid-summer 1938 the economic decline had been halted and recovery was back on track. Although the causes of the "Roosevelt recession" and the subsequent recovery are still debated among economists, there can be no doubt that the recession crisis marked a major turning point in New Deal ideology. The rise of dictatorships in Europe and Asia made adherence to American liberal values a necessary concomitant of a recovery program. A compensatory monetary and fiscal policy fit the bill perfectly, avoiding direct intervention in economic decision-making at the grassroots level and employing only long-accepted macroeconomic instruments of fiscal and economic policy. Though the level of public investment needed to bring about full recovery was well beyond what Roosevelt and his advisors imagined, and would not be implemented until the war, a new credo for American liberalism had been formulated.

See Also: FEDERAL RESERVE SYSTEM; MORGENTHAU, HENRY T., JR.

BIBLIOGRAPHY

Blum, John Morton. *From the Morgenthau Diaries*, 3 vols. 1959–1967.

May, Dean L. *From New Deal to New Economics: The American Liberal Response to the Recession of 1937.* 1981.

Roose, Kenneth D. *The Economics of Recession and Revival: An Interpretation of 1937–38.* 1954.

Stein, Herbert. *The Fiscal Revolution in America.* 1969.

DEAN L. MAY

RECIPROCAL TRADE AGREEMENTS

Spurred by the wave of isolationism and protectionism that swept America in the aftermath of World War I, the United States initiated a series of tariffs in the 1920s that by the end of the decade had brought U.S. import duties to their highest point in American history. The great symbol of this movement towards ever increasing protectionism was the Hawley-Smoot tariff, which was passed in 1930 over the objections of many economists who argued at the time that higher U.S. tariffs would do nothing to alleviate the crisis of the Great Depression, but would in fact impede progress toward a general economic recovery. One individual who spoke out vociferously against high tariff policies was Cordell Hull, who both as a congressman and a senator had consistently opposed the high tariff rates imposed by the Republican congresses during these years.

Given this record, it would come as no surprise that one of Hull's highest priorities after his appointment as U.S. secretary of state in 1933 was to embark upon a program of trade liberalization. In principle, Roosevelt shared Hull's belief in internationalism, and almost immediately after assuming office, Hull instructed his advisors to draw up legislation aimed at granting the president the authority to negotiate trade agreements. It was Hull's hope that this legislation would be passed in time for him to use it as a bargaining chip at the 1933 London Economic Conference, where he intended to negotiate a multilateral reduction in tariff rates. But there were others within the Roosevelt administration who rejected Hull's ideas, including such influential New Dealers as Raymond Moley and George Peek, both of whom argued strongly in favor of protectionism and the need to raise domestic price levels prior to the initiation of any effort to lower trade barriers. Much to Hull's disappointment, Roosevelt came down on the side of the protectionists in the early months of the New Deal and refused to allow Hull to submit his legislation to Congress. This in turn negated any possibility that the secretary would be able to negotiate multilateral tariff reductions at the London Conference, and Hull returned from England in the summer of 1933 a deeply frustrated man.

Convinced by his bitter experience in London that a multilateral approach to freer trade was no longer feasible, Hull now sought legislation that would establish a system of bilateral agreements through which the United States would seek reciprocal reductions in the duties imposed on specific commodities with other interested governments. These reductions would then be generalized by the application of the most-favored-nation principle, with the result that the reduction accorded to a commodity from one country would then be accorded to the same commodity when imported from other countries.

Hull called his new legislation the Reciprocal Trade Agreements Act. Well aware of the lingering resistance to tariff reduction that remained in Congress, Hull insisted that the power to make these agreements must rest with the president alone, without the necessity of submitting them to the Senate for approval. The amount of reduction authorized was based on the 1930 Hawley-Smoot tariff. Under the act, the president would be granted the power to decrease or increase existing rates by as much as 50 percent in return for reciprocal trade concessions granted by the other country.

By the spring of 1934, Roosevelt was more inclined to look with favor on trade liberalization and on March 2 the president announced his support for Hull's legislation. In urging its passage Roosevelt stressed that the powers it granted the executive were necessary because other countries (most notably Great Britain) were using reciprocal agree-

ments to expand their trade at the expense of the United States. To back up his claim, Roosevelt cited the tremendous drop in U.S. exports, which in 1932 alone had fallen to a mere 52 percent of the 1929 volume. Roosevelt also indicated that he regarded the legislation as part of his emergency economic program particularly because a "full and permanent domestic recovery" would not be possible without the revival of international trade.

After the addition of two amendments, the first of which called for hearings of interested parties before a trade agreement could be negotiated, and a second that limited the term of the legislation to three years, the Reciprocal Trade Agreements Act was signed into law on June 12, 1934. Following the passage of the act (and a brief bureaucratic struggle in which George Peek lost out to Hull over who would take the lead on trade policy within the administration), Roosevelt and Hull established the needed governmental apparatus to run the program, including the Committee for Reciprocity Information, which would hear the public representations required by the Senate amendment, and the Committee on Trade Agreements, which was formed to administer the act. Representatives from the departments of State, Commerce, and Agriculture, as well as representatives from the National Recovery Administration, the Tariff Commission, and the newly created Office of the Special Advisor on Foreign Trade, were included on both these committees. Assistant Secretary of State Francis Sayre became head of the Committee on Trade Agreements, while at Hull's urging, Roosevelt appointed Henry Grady as the secretary's special advisor on trade. Following the establishment of the machinery to run the program, the Committee on Trade Agreements soon began to survey the foreign trade field to determine which countries offered the best prospects for negotiations. Under its aegis, a number of country subcommittees were formed to study the trade patterns with a specific nation to ascertain which exports or imports might receive lower duties and the effects that such reductions might have in the domestic market.

Under Hull's guidance, the United States managed to negotiate twenty-two reciprocal trade agreements by the end of 1940. Included in these were agreements with Cuba, Brazil, Belgium, Sweden, Columbia, Canada, the Netherlands, France, Costa Rica, and the United Kingdom. Of these, the two most consequential were the agreements with Canada, signed in 1936, and the United Kingdom, signed in 1938. The latter two were important not only because of the significant volume of trade involved, but also because they were regarded as indicative of growing solidarity among the Atlantic powers in the troubled years leading up to World War II. Hull, like many of his contemporaries, regarded economic nationalism as one of the root causes of war and remained convinced that one way to reduce the likelihood of conflict was to reduce trade barriers. Unfortunately, Hull's efforts at liberalizing world trade had little impact on the dictators, but his belief in the necessity for freer trade gained credence during the war with the result that the United States emerged from the conflict firmly committed to an internationalist foreign economic policy.

See Also: HAWLEY-SMOOT TARIFF; HULL, CORDELL.

BIBLIOGRAPHY

Dallek, Robert. *Franklin D. Roosevelt and American Foreign Policy: 1943–1945.* 1979.

Drummond, Ian M., and Norman Hillmer. *Negotiating Freer Trade: The United Kingdom, the United States, Canada, and the Trade Agreements of 1938.* 1989.

Gellman, Irwin F. *Secret Affairs: Franklin Roosevelt, Cordell Hull, and Sumner Welles.* 1995.

Harrison, Richard. "Testing the Water: A Secret Probe towards Anglo-American Military Co-operation in 1936." *International History Review* 7, no. 2 (1985): 214–234.

Hull, Cordell. *The Memoirs of Cordell Hull.* 1948.

Langer, William L., and S. Everett Gleason. *The Challenge to Isolation: 1937–1940.* 1952.

Pratt, Julius W. *The American Secretaries of State and Their Diplomacy: Cordell Hull, 1933–1944,* 2 vols. 1964.

Schatz, Arthur W. "The Anglo-American Trade Agreement and Cordell Hull's Search for Peace, 1936–1938." *The Journal of American History* 57, no. 1 (1970): 85–103.

DAVID B. WOOLNER

RECONSTRUCTION FINANCE CORPORATION (RFC)

In searching for the causes of the Great Depression, historians regularly cite protective tariffs and their impact on foreign trade, gross agricultural overproduction, speculative mania on Wall Street, and inequitable distributions of national income, but the most significant factor may well have been the instability in the money markets during the 1920s. Intense competition, inadequate capital reserves, real-estate speculation, and inadequately secured loans (especially to farmers) eroded bank assets and brought about the failure of more than five thousand banks between 1920 and 1930. In addition, banks and insurance companies had long invested in railroad bonds, but early in the 1930s, many railroads began defaulting on interest payments. Deeply in debt, burdened by heavy fixed costs, and suffering declines in freight revenues because of competition from long-haul trucks, dozens of major railroads faced bankruptcy. Their plight pulled thousands of banks toward the same fate. Another 1,357 American banks went belly up in 1930. International problems then finished the job. In May 1931 Austria's largest bank declared bankruptcy, and four months later the Bank of England abandoned the gold standard, sending American money markets into a state of panic.

To prevent a complete financial meltdown on Wall Street—and Main Street—that would doom his reelection chances, President Herbert Hoover acted, turning first to the private sector. Working with a number of prominent bankers, he established the National Credit Corporation (NCC), hoping to accumulate up to $500 million for loans to troubled banks. In October and November 1931, however, the NCC loaned out a paltry $10 million, hardly enough to rescue the banking system. Reluctantly, Hoover turned to the federal government. Modeling his plan on the War Finance Corporation of World War I, in January 1931 Hoover proposed and Congress established the Reconstruction Finance Corporation (RFC), endowing it with an initial capital of $500 million and the ability to borrow another $1.5 billion to make loans to banks, mutual savings banks, insurance companies, credit unions, railroads, and savings, building, and loan associations. Determined to avoid political controversy, Hoover gave the RFC a bipartisan board that included Charles G. Dawes, a prominent Chicago banker and former Republican vice president of the United States, and Jesse Jones, a wealthy Houston banker and a power broker in the Texas Democratic Party.

The RFC went to work immediately, but it soon generated bitter political controversy. When the Central Republic Bank of Chicago (of which Charles Dawes had only recently been president) hurtled toward bankruptcy in the spring of 1932, the RFC sprang for a loan of $90 million. The money staved off bankruptcy and prevented a regional financial crisis, but it smacked of corruption, and Democratic politicians pounced on it. The fact that the Hoover administration was so stingy in providing work relief for the unemployed only exacerbated the controversy. While poor people in Chicago starved, so the critique went, Charles Dawes and his minions filled their pockets with federal money. A $19 million loan to the Missouri Pacific railroad precipitated almost as much controversy. Long known for its dishonesty and financial slights-of-hand, the Missouri Pacific enjoyed a particularly stained financial reputation, but the Hoover administration insisted that had the Missouri Pacific defaulted, hundreds of banks and insurance companies would have been drawn into its whirlpool of bankruptcy.

To blunt the controversy, Hoover joined hands with Republican moderates and Democratic liberals in Congress to expand RFC authority. In July 1932, the Emergency Relief and Construction Act authorized the RFC to make up to $300 million in loans to state and local governments to assist them in providing relief to the unemployed, and $1.5 billion in loans to state and local governments to put people to work building such self-liquidating public works as toll roads, bridges, and sewage and water systems. The act also gave the RFC power to extend loans to financial institutions to assist farmers in storing and marketing agricultural goods. But the effort proved to be too little, too late. The $300 million in relief was only the proverbial drop in the bucket compared to total need, and the public

works construction projects took too long to get underway. President Hoover's political fortunes continued to sink.

Although the RFC made nearly $2 billion in bank loans in 1932, instability continued to plague the money markets, with hundreds of banks failing every month, more and more railroads going into default, and commercial loans drying up. In the winter of 1932 to 1933, the RFC's shortcomings came into bold relief. The governors of Idaho, Nevada, Iowa, Louisiana, and Oregon all had to declare statewide banking holidays to stop panic-stricken depositors from making runs on banks, and in March 1933 newly-inaugurated President Franklin D. Roosevelt declared a nationwide bank holiday. The nation's financial system had collapsed, even with $2 billion in RFC loans.

Despite its shortcomings, the RFC was about to undergo a geometric expansion in its power and scope. During the famous First Hundred Days of the Roosevelt administration, the RFC became the heart and soul of the New Deal. Congress established the Federal Emergency Relief Administration to take over and expand the RFC's program of relief loans to state and local governments. The new Public Works Administration assumed responsibility for the RFC public works construction program. The Commodity Credit Corporation took over the RFC loan program to assist farmers in storing and marketing crops. The Emergency Banking Act of 1933, which Congress passed at the outset of the nationwide bank holiday, authorized the RFC to make direct loans to private businesses and to purchase preferred stock in private banks. Within a few years, the RFC owned $1.3 billion in stock and exercised voting rights in 6,200 private commercial banks. Because the money came in the form of investment capital, not loans that had to be repaid in six months, the RFC stock purchases proved to be a godsend. With the RFC, the Banking Act of 1933, and establishment of the Federal Deposit Insurance Corporation, the money markets began to settle down. Bank failures plummeted, and commercial loans, the life blood of an economy, slowly began to increase.

Finally, because the RFC enjoyed a constant flow of capital through loan repayments, it became a source of money almost external to Congress, which President Roosevelt and other New Dealers frequently exploited. By 1937, Jesse Jones headed an RFC empire that included direct control or profound financial influence over the Federal Emergency Relief Administration, the Public Works Administration, the Works Progress Administration, the Commodity Credit Corporation, the RFC Mortgage Company, the Rural Electrification Administration, the Federal Security Administration, the Federal Housing Administration, the Home Owners' Loan Corporation, the Resettlement Administration, the Federal Farm Mortgage Association, the Farm Credit Administration, the Tennessee Valley Authority, the Electric Farm and Home Authority, the Disaster Loan Agency, the Export-Import Bank, and the Federal National Mortgage Association. In 1939, Congress established the Federal Loan Agency to supervise the federal government's vast financial establishment, and President Roosevelt named Jesse Jones to head the new agency. By that time, the RFC and its subsidiaries had made loans in excess of $8 billion, prompting some journalists to refer to the agency as the "Fourth Branch of Government."

Two years later the entrance of the United States into World War II brought extraordinary new powers to the RFC. The economy needed to make, as soon as possible, the transition from Depression to wartime production, and Jesse Jones and the RFC assumed a central role in that effort. A host of new government corporations—all included under the financial umbrella of the RFC—mushroomed to transform the economy; they included the Defense Plant Corporation, the Defense Supplies Corporation, the Metals Reserve Company, the Defense Homes Corporation, the Petroleum Reserves Corporation, the Rubber Reserve Company, the United States Commercial Company, the War Assets Corporation, and the Smaller War Plants Corporation. By the end of World War II, the RFC's total loan volume, to fight the war and the Depression, exceeded $50 billion, making it by far the largest and most powerful federal agency in American history. After the war, however, during the reconversion effort, the RFC lost political traction. In 1953, Congress passed the RFC Liquidation Act, transferring the RFC's loan-making power to the new Small

Business Administration. Four years later, in 1957, Congress dissolved the RFC.

Because of the New Deal's profound impact on American public policy, historians and politicians have spent seventy years debating its meaning and its merits, arguing about whether it was essentially liberal or conservative or radical. But it seems clear that the RFC—by far the most influential of New Deal agencies—was an institution designed to save capitalism from the ravages of the Great Depression. Through the RFC, Roosevelt and the New Deal handed over $10 billion to tens of thousands of private businesses, keeping them afloat when they would otherwise have gone under and deadening the voices of those who saw in socialism a solution to the country's economic mess.

See Also: BANKING PANICS (1930–1933); JONES, JESSE.

BIBLIOGRAPHY

Burns, Helen M. *The American Banking Community and New Deal Banking Reforms: 1933–1935.* 1974.

Jones, Jesse H. *Fifty Billion Dollars: My Thirteen Years with the RFC, 1932–1945.* 1951.

Kennedy, Susan Estabrook. *The Banking Crisis of 1933.* 1973.

Olson, James S. *Herbert Hoover and the Reconstruction Finance Corporation, 1931–1933.* 1977.

Olson, James S. *Saving Capitalism: The Reconstruction Finance Corporation and the New Deal, 1933–1940.* 1988.

JAMES S. OLSON

REGIONAL PLANNING ASSOCIATION OF AMERICA (RPAA)

A loose circle of friends, mainly from the New York City area, and never more that twenty-five members, the Regional Planning Association of America (RPAA) shared a commitment to regionalism—the need to balance the healthy and indigenous cultural values of the hinterland with those of the metropolis, to substitute socialized for speculative land values, and to decentralize congested urban populations into architecturally planned cooperative communities similar to those built during World War I by the United States Housing Corporation and the Emergency Fleet Corporation.

The RPAA was founded in 1923 when, at the urging of the American Institute of Architecture *Journal* editor Charles H. Whitaker, Lewis Mumford had architect Clarence Stein convene at his Dakota apartment in Manhattan a small group of architects, foresters, and economists—many of them alumni of the war housing experiment—to discuss the waste of haphazard urban growth and the prospects for a new regional basis for civilization. By 1925 this mildly socialistic assemblage met variously at Whitaker's Twelve Opossum farm in New Jersey, Stein's Dakota apartment, or the Hudson Guild Farm in Netcong, New Jersey. The group consisted not only of Whitaker, Stein, and Mumford, but also of forester Benton MacKaye, economist Stuart Chase, architects Henry Wright, Russell Van Nest Black, Fred Ackerman, Robert D. Kohn, and Fred Bigger, social scientist Robert Bruere, and housers Edith Elmer Wood and Catherine Bauer.

RPAA members were deeply influenced by the ideas of not only Patrick Geddes, Thorstein Veblen, and Henry George, but also Ebenezer Howard, Raymond Unwin, Barry Parker, and the British Garden City Movement. The greenbelted British garden cities of Letchworth and Welwyn Town, a train ride from London, inspired Wright's and Stein's garden communities in Sunnyside, New York, and Radburn, New Jersey. These communities featured superblock design, interior courts, schools, playgrounds, and other communal facilities.

Although neither Sunnyside nor Radburn achieved working-class affordability, the Great Depression and the New Deal convinced RPAA members that federal intervention would realize a true regional solution to the conundrum of affordable housing. Franklin D. Roosevelt had endorsed regionalism in his speeches, and by 1933 RPAA members Kohn, Ackerman, Stein, and MacKaye all served on New Deal agencies philosophically harmonious with association ideals. These agencies included the Tennessee Valley Authority, the Resettlement Administration, the National Resources Planning Board, and the Public Works Administra-

tion's Housing Division (headed by Kohn). Architecturally, much of the public housing built by the Housing Division met RPAA standards; however, the housing built under the 1937 United States Housing Act fell somewhat short of the mark. In 1935 both Stein and Fred Bigger worked on the design and construction of Greenbelt, Maryland, one of the new towns built by Rexford Tugwell's Suburban Division of the Resettlement Administration. Greenbelt largely recapitulated the agenda of the RPAA. However, by 1933 the RPAA had all but vanished. Stein and Mumford parted disagreeably, Whitaker fell ill, and Bauer shifted to housing activism. However, the association's legacy was indisputable.

See Also: BAUER, CATHERINE; MUMFORD, LEWIS; PLANNING.

BIBLIOGRAPHY

Arnold, Joseph. *The New Deal in the Suburbs: A History of the Greenbelt Town Program, 1935–1954.* 1971.

Conkin, Paul. *Tomorrow a New World: The New Deal Community Program.* 1959.

Lubove, Roy. *Community Planning in the 1920s: The Contribution of the Regional Planning Association of America.* 1963.

Schaffer, Daniel. *Garden Cities for America: The Radburn Experience.* 1982.

Spann, Edward K. *Designing Modern America: The Regional Planning Association of American and Its Members.* 1996.

JOHN F. BAUMAN

RELIGION

POLITICS AND PLURALISM

The period between the stock market crash of 1929 and the beginning of World War II was an important time for the development of a religiously pluralistic United States. The nomination of Al Smith as the Democratic Party candidate in 1928 drew attention to the fact that Catholics living in East Coast cities now held considerable political power and that rural Protestants no longer automatically de-

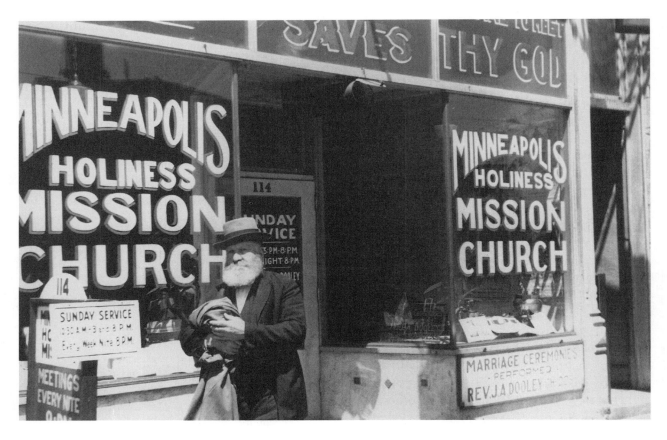

During the Depression, urban mission churches, such as this one photographed in Minneapolis, Minnesota, in 1937, offered spiritual relief, as well as food and temporary shelter, to the needy. LIBRARY OF CONGRESS, PRINTS & PHOTOGRAPHS DIVISION, FSA/OWI COLLECTION

termined presidential candidates. During the 1930s Catholics made up two-thirds of the union membership, and in 1932 Father James Cox led what was then the largest protest march on Washington in American history to draw attention to the needs of suffering workers. Catholic votes would be critical in solidifying Democratic political power, so Catholics gained a presence in Franklin D. Roosevelt's new administration. Of the 196 federal judges that the president appointed, fifty-one were Catholic. During the preceding three administrations only eight Catholics had been appointed to the 214 judicial openings. The president appointed Catholics James A. Farley as postmaster general and Thomas J. Walsh as attorney general. Roosevelt's social initiatives resonated with the pro-labor papal encyclicals of *Rerum Novarum* (1891) and *Quadragesimo Anno* (1931). Two priests committed to Catholic vi-

sions of economic justice, John A. Ryan and Francis J. Haas, sat on New Deal committees. In 1931 Dorothy Day and Peter Maurin founded the *Catholic Worker* newspaper, and by 1942 thirty-two Houses of Hospitality attended to the nation's impoverished.

Spurred on by the economic crisis, Roosevelt looked beyond the Protestant elite to establish an alternative to Herbert Hoover's conservatism. While governor of New York, Roosevelt had been impressed by the reform orientation of many progressive Jews, and he invited some of them to Washington; Louis Brandeis, Felix Frankfurter, Bernard Baruch, Henry Morgenthau, Jr., Samuel Rosenman, Alexander Sachs, J. David Stern, Nathan Straus, and Benjamin Cohen became the president's friends and advisors. Between four and five thousand young Jews who were recently trained in

This Pentecostal church in Olivehurst, California (photographed in 1940 by Dorothea Lange), served migrant agricultural workers, who brought their religious institutions with them from the Midwest and the South. The preacher was an Arkansas native. NATIONAL ARCHIVES AND RECORDS ADMINISTRATION

law, economics, and social work, and who were experiencing difficulty finding employment in the anti-Semitic environment of the period, found welcoming positions in the government.

In contrast to Catholics and Jews, mainline Protestant clergy showed little support for Roosevelt. By 1936 when a *Literary Digest* poll asked "Do you NOW approve the acts and policies of the Roosevelt New Deal to date?" over 70 percent responded "no." Liberal and moderate Protestants—Congregationalists, Methodists, Presbyterians, Lutherans, and Episcopalians—supported any candidate who ran against Roosevelt. Seventy-

eight percent of all Congregationalists, for example, voted for Alfred M. Landon, the Republican candidate for president, in 1936. On the other hand, Baptists and smaller fundamentalist, holiness, and Pentecostal groups consistently voted for Roosevelt. The numbers of these conservative Protestants were rapidly growing throughout the country. Between 1926 and 1940 Southern Baptists grew by 1.5 million, membership in the Assemblies of God increased four fold, and the Church of the Nazarene grew from 63,558 congregants to 165,532. Conservative Protestants voted with the majority of Americans, supporting the president even though he oversaw the dismantling of prohibition in 1933. While Protestant clergy attacked the New Deal for either being too socialist or not socialist enough, the working class and the poor directly benefited from Roosevelt's programs.

GROWTH OF CONSERVATIVE PROTESTANTISM

During the Depression, the number of conservative Protestants increased as a result of their vigorous evangelization efforts and the growth of their educational and parachurch organizations. By 1930 there were approximately fifty nondenominational Bible schools in major cities that not only trained lay workers, Sunday school leaders, and foreign missionaries, but also supplied pastors and printed materials. Evangelicals increasingly sent their children to their own institutions of higher education; the enrollment in seventy of these colleges doubled between 1929 and 1940. A network of Bible conferences offered a mix of piety and recreation during the summer months. Foreign missionary activity was also critical to the evangelical worldview. The *Sunday School Times* listed forty-nine mission agencies in 1931; the number had increased to seventy-six by 1941. When displaced farmers from Oklahoma, Arkansas, and Missouri settled in southern California and Arizona and parts of Washington and Oregon, they brought their evangelical commitments with them. The religious landscape of the nation became permanently altered when southern Protestantism moved into the West because of the Dust Bowl.

A few conservative Protestants preached extremist visions of political and economic systems. Gerald B. Winrod founded the Defenders of the Christian Faith, and in 1938 entered the Republican primary for the United States Senate seat from Kansas. His anti-Jewish, anti-Catholic, and anti-black vitriol combined premillennial fundamentalism with political populism. Gerald L. K. Smith was a Disciples of Christ minister who joined with the governor of Louisiana, Huey Long, to promote his "Share-Our-Wealth" program. William D. Pelley, the son of a Methodist preacher, hoped to establish a Christian (evangelical Protestant) state where Jews would be disfranchised and confined to the equivalent of an American ghetto. Unlike Winrod

and Smith, who stayed close to their fundamentalist roots, Pelley's message also included theosophy, astrology, and spiritualism.

DIVERSIFICATION AND MAINSTREAM DECLINE

African Americans who moved from the South during the Depression also brought their Christian commitments to urban centers. Olivet Baptist church in Chicago was America's largest Protestant congregation. Another Chicago church, Pilgrim Baptist, was one of the nation's ten largest churches by 1930 and managed to liquidate its $150,000 debt during the Depression. New religions emerged in the cities alongside the traditional black denominations. In New York, Father Divine held massive communion feasts and taught his followers the principles of positive thinking. Some African Americans chose to join communities that linked themselves to Islam, but congregational rivalries caused disunity and fragmentation among black Muslims. Others developed communities that used Hebrew scriptures and Jewish rituals. Migration out of the South brought African Americans in contact with Catholics and their parochial school system. In the segregated diocese of Chicago, all black parish schools flourished and contributed to the growing number of African-American converts. White priests at Corpus Christi Church baptized twenty-one adult African Americans in 1920, 131 in 1935, and 322 in 1938. During the Depression, African Americans diversified their religion rather than escaping from it.

While some religious groups flourished during the Depression, liberal and moderate Protestants noted a decline in the critical elements of their religious culture. Between 1916 and 1926 congregations had expanded their physical plants, broadened their services, and increased their staffs. As a result, they experienced a sharp rise in operational costs and debt. With the onset of the Depression, church members withdrew much of their financial support, leaving ministers unable to meet expenses. Funding for foreign and domestic missionary programs also dropped, and it was difficult to find volunteers to venture overseas. Theological disputes drew some congregants into more conservative denominations. Other men and women found that their humanistic impulses could be satisfied outside of the church in the growing fields of social work, education, and government service. From the perspective of ministers and theologians, many of those who remained within their denominations were at best disillusioned and at worst mired in a form of sanctified commercialism.

A similar pattern occurred in American Judaism. In the 1920s and 1930s the Jewish population in the United States grew by 40 percent and the number of synagogues increased from 1,910 in 1917 to 3,748 in 1937. Congregations in areas with large Jewish populations, such as New York City, expanded, but financial support dropped when the crash hit. In order to survive, synagogues raised their membership fees, which caused more Jews to break away from communal worship. Rabbis complained of the spiritual lethargy and intermarriages of their people. On the other hand, "mushroom synagogues" arose in New York City to cater to unaffiliated Jews. Jews in smaller communities had an easier time weathering economic decline because they could more efficiently adapt to the changing economic climate. Zionist organizations increased their membership. While anti-Semitism made Jews feel more sharply that they were outsiders, the reforming spirit of the New Deal brought socialist and labor union Jews closer to the political mainstream.

Native Americans found it easier to participate in their rituals after John Collier was made Commissioner of Indian Affairs in 1933. His "Indian New Deal" included directives that insisted there be no interference with Native American religious life or ceremonial expression. Collier restricted religious instructions—typically conducted by Christian missionaries—in the newly established Indian day schools. He ended compulsory Christian services and supported voluntary instruction in native religions. During his administration, the Native American Church, along with its peyote rituals, was approved to function on the reservations. Although Collier and the Indian New Deal were controversial, there is no question that they helped shift the power on the reservation away from Christian groups and toward traditional ceremonial expression.

MEDIA AND DEVOTIONAL PIETY

The variety of faith communities in the United States and the diversity within those groups made for a complicated religious environment. However, decisions made by the broadcasting industry with the support of older Protestant denominations sought to present America as having only three religious faiths, which were all orderly and controllable. By 1925 there were at least sixty-three church-owned radio broadcasting stations across the country. Economic problems, however, forced many of them to sell. Rather than eliminate religion from the airwaves, the major commercial broadcasting networks NBC and ABC decided to provide free time to representatives of Protestant, Catholic, and Jewish communities. In consultation with liberal Protestants, the networks agreed that religious broadcasting should be nondenominational, should avoid controversial or doctrinal matters, and should stress ecumenical ideals.

In 1934 the Federal Council of Churches assumed the responsibility for network Protestant broadcasting. The *National Radio Pulpit* on NBC presented sermons given by Harry Emerson Fosdick, Ralph Sockman, and David H. C. Read. NBC also broadcast the *Message of Israel* and the *Catholic Hour*. Bishop Fulton J. Sheen began his media career on the *Catholic Hour*, attracting a listening audience of seven million and receiving six thousand letters per day.

Groups whose religious messages did not conform to the network's standards could purchase airtime or struggle to maintain their own broadcasts. In 1926 fundamentalist Bob Shuler installed a radio station in the tower of his church and sent his message out across Los Angeles. His sensationalist exposés of political corruption provoked the Federal Radio Commission to terminate his right to broadcast in 1931. Father Charles E. Coughlin, with the approval of his local bishop, also bought radio time to promote his notions of Catholic piety and economic reform. Less controversial was the preaching of Walter A. Maier during the *Lutheran Hour*. Belonging to the conservative Missouri Synod, Maier preached in English rather than German, and in 1938 listeners sent over 125,000 letters responding to his programming. Other ministers presented music, healing, and testimonials on the radio. Elder Lucy Smith, the founder of the All Nations Pentecostal Church and an important African-American healer in Chicago, broadcast her interracial healing services throughout the 1930s. Many tuned in merely to hear her gospel choir sing. Aimee Semple McPherson continued to have a radio presence during the 1930s and broke with the sermon model of preaching by designing dramatic reenactments of biblical and moral tales. She encouraged her listeners to kneel next to their radios to pray with her and to place their hands on the receiver in order to heal their bodies and souls.

Protestants and Catholics looked to the miraculous to heal themselves and their families during the difficult times. Pentecostal women sent letters to religious magazines where they testified to both their suffering and God's goodness. Others laid the devotional magazines themselves on the afflicted parts of their bodies. Both black and white Pentecostals used handkerchiefs anointed with oil to achieve healing. Catholics flocked to novenas to the saints and the Virgin Mother. In 1938, 70,000 people attended a series of communal prayers offered to Our Lady of Sorrows in Chicago, and devotion to Saint Jude, the patron saint of desperate causes, spread throughout the country. Religious orders of priests and nuns offered to enroll people in devotional societies for their donations, sending the members medals and holy cards. Even Father Coughlin offered masses to be said for those who joined his Radio League of the Little Flower. Replicas of the apparition of the Virgin Mary at Lourdes were built next to churches so that Catholics could imaginatively connect with the healing power of the shrine. The Vatican had encouraged lay piety since the nineteenth century, and during the 1930s increased fervor enabled many churches to not only survive but to make their Catholic world in public space. While people have always used religion to transform suffering into sacrifice and thus give meaning to their lives, during the Depression this need was intensified.

See Also: CHARITY; FATHER DIVINE.

BIBLIOGRAPHY

Burkett, Randall K. "The Baptist Church in Years of Crisis: J. C. Austin and Pilgrim Baptist Church, 1912–1950." In *African-American Religion in the Twentieth Century: Varieties of Protest and Accommodation*, edited by Hans A. Baer and Merrill Singer. 1992.

Feingold, Henry L. *A Time for Searching: Entering the Mainstream, 1920–1945.* 1992.

Flynn, George Q. *American Catholics and the Roosevelt Presidency, 1932–1936.* 1968.

Griffith, R. Marie. "Female Suffering and Religious Devotion in American Pentecostalism." In *Women and Twentieth-Century Protestantism*, edited by Margaret Lamberts Bendroth and Virginia Lieson Brereton. 2002.

Handy, Robert T. "The American Religious Depression, 1925–1935." *Church History* 24 (1960): 13.

Hangen, Tona J. *Redeeming the Dial: Radio, Religion and Popular Culture in America.* 2002.

Heineman, Kenneth J. *A Catholic New Deal: Religion and Reform in Depression Pittsburgh.* 1999.

Joselit, Jenna Weissman. *The Wonders of America: Reinventing Jewish Culture, 1880–1950.* 1994.

Lynd, Robert S., and Helen Merrell Lund. *Middletown in Transition: A Study in Cultural Conflicts.* 1937.

Marty, Martin E. *Modern American Religion*, Vol. 2: *The Noise of Conflict, 1919–1941.* 1991.

Miller, Robert Moats. *American Protestantism and Social Issues, 1919–1939.* 1958.

Orsi, Robert A. *Thank You, St. Jude: Women's Devotion to the Patron Saint of Hopeless Causes.* 1996.

Watts, Jill. *God, Harlem U.S.A.: The Father Divine Story.* 1992.

Wenger, Beth S. *New York Jews and the Great Depression: Uncertain Promise.* 1996.

COLLEEN McDANNELL

"REMEMBER MY FORGOTTEN MAN"

The film *Gold Diggers of 1933,* directed by Mervyn LeRoy and choreographed by Busby Berkeley, was a hugely successful and accordingly oft-imitated pioneer in the genre of musicals. Its generally upbeat story caught the mood of returning hope and "the only thing we have to fear is fear itself" positive thinking that accompanied Franklin Roosevelt's assumption of the presidency and launching of the New Deal the year the film was made. But its long and memorable closing number, "Remember My Forgotten Man," did something highly unusual for a Hollywood musical of the thirties: It addressed the Depression directly.

Berkeley's number reminds viewers of the sacrifices that veterans made for the nation in World War I and suggests that they have been forgotten now, as they suffer the harsh realities of the Depression. Marching soldiers from the Great War morph into hungry men plodding along on a breadline as Joan Blondell sings: "Remember my forgotten man/You put a rifle in his hand/. . ./But look at him today."

Such an attempt at social commentary in a Hollywood backstage musical would be noteworthy in itself, but the real significance of the song is what it says about gender relations and the longings of men during the Depression. Al Dublin's lyrics (the music was composed by Harry Warren) have a woman recalling that she "was happy then," when her man was employed and "the sweat fell from his brow." The reason for her happiness? "He used to take care of me." Such male care of and provision for "their women," Dublin's lyrics affirm, is the natural state of affairs: "Cause ever since the world began/A woman's got to have a man."

The Great Depression had overturned "normalcy" not only by denying men jobs, this song asserted, but by denying them their proper role of providing for and ruling over women. "Won't you bring him back again?" Blondell plaintively sang of the sort of man who was said to have taken care of women before the Depression.

See Also: BERKELEY, BUSBY; GENDER ROLES AND SEXUAL RELATIONS, IMPACT OF THE GREAT DEPRESSION ON; GOLD DIGGERS OF 1933; HOLLYWOOD AND THE FILM INDUSTRY; MUSIC; VALUES, EFFECTS OF THE GREAT DEPRESSION ON.

BIBLIOGRAPHY

Bergman, Andrew. We're in the Money: Depression America and Its Films. 1971.

Cohan, Steven, ed. The Hollywood Musicals: The Film Reader. 2002.

ROBERT S. MCELVAINE

REORGANIZATION ACT OF 1939

The Reorganization Act of 1939 restructured the executive branch in the wake of the New Deal. From March 1936, Louis Brownlow, director of the Public Administration Clearing House (PACH) at the University of Chicago and head of the Public Administration Committee of the Social Science Research Council (SSRC) led the President's Committee on Administrative Management, known as the Brownlow Committee. Political scientist Charles E. Merriam and public administration expert Luther Gulick assisted Brownlow in recommending ways to streamline federal agencies. They used policy ideas developed by the Brookings Institution, the PACH, the SSRC, and the New Deal planning agency (the National Resources Planning Board) to model public institutions along the lines of private firms. In January 1937 they sent recommendations to President Franklin D. Roosevelt.

When Roosevelt introduced reorganization bills in Congress, he met a storm of opposition. Conservative Republicans and southern Democrats let liberal Democrats lead the fight to amend the reorganization bills. The Reorganization Act of 1939 included a series of compromises that watered down the original bills. Even so, the act encompassed the most far-reaching changes in the executive branch to that point in U.S. history. The president could hire six assistants, propose reorganization plans subject to congressional veto, and make economy in government a priority. On April 25, 1939, President Roosevelt submitted Reorganization Plan No. 1, which moved the Bureau of the Budget and the National Resources Planning Board into a newly created Executive Office of the President. Reorganization Plan No. 2, introduced on May 9, 1939, transferred other agencies within existing departments to allay fears of radical restructuring.

The Reorganization Act of 1939 remade the executive branch by making government operations more efficient in terms of structure, process, and cost. Investigations under presidents Harry Truman, Richard Nixon, and Bill Clinton would continue the ongoing attempt to streamline executive branch organization.

See Also: NATIONAL RESOURCES PLANNING
BOARD (NRPB); NEW DEAL, THIRD.

BIBLIOGRAPHY

Arnold, Peri E. *Making the Managerial Presidency: Comprehensive Reorganization Planning, 1905–1996,* 2nd edition. 1998.

Berman, Larry. *The Office of Management and Budget and the Presidency, 1921–1969.* 1979.

Karl, Barry Dean. *Executive Reorganization and Reform in the New Deal: The Genesis of Administrative Management, 1900–1939.* 1963.

Polenberg, Richard. *Reorganizing Roosevelt's Government: The Controversy over Executive Reorganization, 1936–1939.* 1966.

Reagan, Patrick D. *Designing a New America: The Origins of New Deal Planning, 1890–1943.* 2000.

PATRICK D. REAGAN

REPORT ON THE ECONOMIC CONDITIONS OF THE SOUTH

In the spring of 1938, Franklin D. Roosevelt commissioned a report on the economic conditions of the South as part of his effort to defeat leading southern opponents of his reform agenda. A small group of southern policymakers who worked for the Roosevelt administration, most notably Clark Foreman, Clifford J. Durr, and Arthur Goldschmidt, compiled the report. They drew on the work of the region's leading social scientists and prepared the final report in consultation with an advisory commission of prominent southern educators, businessmen, and elected officials. The report, which covered fifteen topics, contrasted the rich natural resources of the South with its chronic underdevelopment and poverty. Citing the report, Roosevelt declared that the South was "the nation's number one economic problem," and he underscored the critical importance of federal aid to advancing economic development in the South and the economic recovery of the nation.

While Roosevelt's efforts to "purge" southern conservatives failed, the report, along with the president's aggressive participation in the 1938 primary elections in the South, succeeded in focusing national attention on the economic and political significance of the region. The report was widely noted and excerpted in the nation's major newspapers, and was reprinted in full in the *New York Times.* Most importantly, the report helped to mobilize southern supporters of the New Deal at a time when conservative southerners were emerging as its most vocal opponents in Congress. In response to the report, white and black southerners representing a broad cross section of southern life met in Birmingham, Alabama, in November 1938 to voice their support for the Roosevelt administration, and to establish the Southern Conference for Human Welfare.

See Also: SOUTH, GREAT DEPRESSION IN THE;
SOUTHERN CONFERENCE FOR HUMAN
WELFARE (SCHW).

BIBLIOGRAPHY

Carlton, David L., and Peter A. Coclanis, eds. *Confronting Southern Poverty in the Great Depression: The Report on Economic Conditions of the South with Related Documents.* 1996

Sullivan, Patricia. *Days of Hope: Race and Democracy in the New Deal Era.* 1996.

PATRICIA SULLIVAN

REPUBLICAN PARTY

The Republican Party entered the 1930s as the heir to a vitalist reform tradition that underscored its historic role as the modernizing "national party." By 1940 this role was in complete eclipse and the party could no longer lay claim to the mantle of "the party of ideas" and the political embodiment of the national destiny. Nevertheless its role in the Great Depression was far more important than once recognized. It was apparent by 1938 that center-right congressional coalitions had a renewed vitality that lent force to a New Deal opposition that had begun to surface in 1935.

The party's assumption of the minority role in American politics had no parallel in its history.

There had been no Democratic landslide under normal conditions since the election of 1852, prior to the formation of the Republican Party. The election of Warren Harding to the presidency in 1920 had brought about a decisive restoration of Republican dominance. Simultaneously, the conservative old guard of the Republican Party, after almost a decade of diminished influence, reassumed its role as the dominant faction in Republican councils. By 1920, adverse reaction to American participation in the League of Nations had drawn most insurgent western Republicans back into the party's fold, finally providing an opportunity to heal the split between conservative eastern Republicans and the western members of the party. Still, as the Depression dawned, the core of Republican old guard strength and control of the party's decision-making apparatus remained in the eastern United States, while the party's western members continued to articulate the discontent of a region visited by chronic agricultural depression. The western insurgents were too few to effectively challenge the conservative national leadership on most issues while the Republicans were the dominant national party during the 1920s. By the 1930s, however, they would take on new importance as the Roosevelt administration attempted to court them in the early days of the New Deal.

THE REPUBLICAN PARTY AND THE ASSOCIATIONAL STATE, 1920–1932

The division between old guard eastern conservatives and the party's western progressives was the party's most visible problem but perhaps not its most important. Throughout the 1920s tension remained in Republican ranks over basic issues of political economy and business-government relations. Some of the party's industrial base was more in sympathy with efforts at business-government "coordination" than the party's executive or congressional leadership. The industrial mobilization policies of the World War I had proven remarkably palatable to major American corporations. While the period occasioned the final abandonment of laissez-faire precepts and formally raised the federal government to the role of director of war-related industry, the very diversity and specialized expertise central to the operation of modern industrial processes gave industrial leaders a systematic advantage in dealing with often hastily constructed government agencies. The successful prosecution of the war effort left an indelible imprint on the minds of industrial managers. The war experience seemed to indicate what could be achieved through industrial self-government when the national economy was largely freed from the restraint of antitrust prosecution and directed toward mutually agreeable ends by the coordinating efforts of a benign government.

It is hardly surprising, then, that the wartime program of industrial self-government would evolve into the "associational" activities of the 1920s. Associationalism involved the deliberate cultivation and encouragement of voluntary institutions—particularly trade associations, professional groups, company unions, and farm cooperatives—to encourage cooperation within particular trades or industries. Throughout the 1920s, Republican leaders strove to implement their vision of an associative state. Indeed, the period after 1925 saw the rapid emergence of powerful trade organizations in a wide variety of basic industries, such as rubber, steel, and mining.

The onset of the Depression, however, would demonstrate the clear limits of voluntary associationalism during a period of privation and scarcity. As industrial profits declined, the Republican precedent of encouraging effective coordination among industrial groupings through governmental sponsorship would enable such interests to formulate demands for forms of governmental assistance that most elements of the Republican Party had never envisioned. Unwittingly, Republican associationalism had introduced business groupings to a form of cooperative planning that, under the impact of economic crisis, would carry many of them away from the GOP as the political realignment of the 1930s began.

THE REPUBLICAN ELECTORAL COALITION AND THE GREAT DEPRESSION

The American economy suffered its most severe and enduring contraction during the period that began in October 1929. By 1931 it was apparent that voluntary efforts to maintain wage, employment, and price levels had been unsuccessful and that the Depression could no longer be viewed as normal in either duration or effect. Rising evidence of market failure and the continued existence of anti-statist impulses were reflected in a series of calls for planned production under the auspices of trade associations, which would be granted immunity from antitrust laws. This would permit industry's use of production quotas, pricing agreements, and entry controls, along with the legalization of formulas for the establishment of "reasonable prices" by corporate groupings. As these business groupings began to urge that they be given new power to plan and rationalize their own operations with government assistance, President Herbert Hoover continued to champion his lifelong belief in voluntary arrangements and refused to endorse the proposals for cartelization now suggested by both the Chamber of Commerce and the National Association of Manufacturers.

These divergent attitudes reflected a widening schism within conservative groupings that would hinder the Republican Party's desperate campaign efforts in the 1932 and its later attempts to oppose the recovery proposals of the early New Deal. Arrayed against the tradition of classical economics and the enduring pull of partisan loyalty was the notion of a cooperative effort to manage economic affairs in a fashion that recalled the unity of the wartime experience. The very lack of precision surrounding such notions of planning allowed interest groups that were traditionally hostile to government direction to view such efforts as little more than an exercise in self-direction. While Hoover would continue to command an absolute majority of support within the business community, in part due to his support of the protective tariff, the ever-growing clamor for positive intervention in economic affairs threatened permanent disruption of the Republican electoral coalition as the 1932 campaign approached. Paradoxically, Hoover's efforts to stimulate industrial cooperation through the development of trade associations in the 1920s had now placed him in the position of opposing the policy recommendations of many of the very groups he had helped foster.

THE REPUBLICAN ELECTORAL DISASTER OF 1932 AND ITS AFTERMATH

On November 8, 1932, Roosevelt carried forty-two states with 472 electoral votes, while Hoover carried six states with fifty-nine electoral votes. The only states outside New England that Hoover carried were Pennsylvania and Delaware. While the western United States clearly did not determine the electoral outcome, the capture of all of its electoral votes by Roosevelt broke down the northeastern-western alliance that had enabled Republicans to dominate presidential elections since 1896. Moreover, the turnover in Congress was considerably more dramatic and conclusive than had been predicted only days before. The Republicans lost 103 House seats, where the balance now stood at 313 Democrats to 117 Republicans. Most of these seats were lost in the Midwestern region of the country. In the Senate, Republican control was decisively repudiated, as the party lost twelve seats, ten in the midwestern and western states. Even amidst severe economic depression, the electoral results were shocking to individual Republicans grown accustomed to persistent electoral success.

By 1934, the pattern of early New Deal legislation was becoming more clearly discernable. One distinguishing feature was its effort to induce economic recovery through the use of the largest existing institutional structures capable of having an immediate effect. The early New Deal coalition sought the inclusion of all groups and classes, while attempting to effect a kind of political truce that recalled the unity and cohesion of wartime planning efforts. The crisis politics of the administration also sought the abatement of partisan political conflict in the name of a broader national unity.

By early 1934, the administration's recovery policies had substantially strengthened the cooperative farm bureaus and industrial trade associations conceived in the 1920s. These traditionally Republican constituencies had been quick to seize the opportunities provided by the pragmatic recovery approach of the early New Deal. During the first six months of the National Recovery Administration (NRA), for example, American industry developed codes of fair competition that covered the vast percentage of American industry and trade. While the creation of the NRA had reflected a variety of reform impulses, organized business was in the best position to seize the initiative in the code-drafting process.

The practical effect of the administration's incorporation of potential political opposition was felt throughout the Republican electoral coalition as 1934 dawned. Widespread approval by farmers of governmental limitations on agricultural production and the substantial business support accorded to the NRA code-drafting process further constricted the Republican Party's base of popular political support.

THE 1934 CONGRESSIONAL ELECTIONS

During early 1934 it was clear that the national committee's conservative leadership desired a congressional campaign that focused on the alleged excesses of the New Deal. This reflected the old guard view that much support of the New Deal was predicated on the "emergency" conditions that had existed during the 1933 to 1934 period. By this analysis, the general success of conservative appeals to the electorate remained self-evident despite the party's recent reversals, and efforts to "stagger to the left" could only result in the abrogation of both political principle and success at the polling booths. Even a partial restoration of prosperity and business confidence would diminish support for the Roosevelt administration; accordingly, substantial modification of electoral appeals was both unnecessary and unwise. The adoption of a policy of "holding fast" in the face of insurgence had been successful as recently as the election of 1920, and the old guard felt that such tactics would ultimately foster similar results. While entertaining no hope of "rolling back" the entire New Deal following the 1934 congressional elections, the old guard felt that the abatement of emergency conditions would result in Republican congressional gains. To the Republican's dismay, the Democrats, in defiance of both off-year tradition and contemporary expectations, again gained seats in Congress. The GOP's already diminished senatorial contingent fell from thirty-five to twenty-five.

There seemed to be few, if any, positive portents for the Republican Party as 1935 dawned. The all-class coalition of the early New Deal had inaugurated political movement that had been almost entirely away from the Republican electoral coalition. By the middle of that year, however, it was apparent that the administration's effort to maintain an all-class coalition of interests was beginning to break down. Despite the initial success of American industry in structuring the NRA to further trade association objectives, its fragile unity had broken down by early 1935. Once the sense of panic characteristic of 1932 and 1933 passed, it gradually became clearer to American industry that the price exacted for exemption from the antitrust laws was higher than had been anticipated. The administration's sympathy toward efforts to raise wage rates and encourage industrial unionism, as well as its ability to license business through the NRA code-making process, limited the previous prerogatives of industrial managers. It was becoming apparent to business leaders that the administration of the NRA apparatus involved input from groups, such as organized labor, that stressed political agendas beyond trade association control. Ultimately, individual business enterprise had submitted only to a process that it felt it could control; when the rise of other political forces made this difficult, enthusiasm rapidly waned. Thus, the pattern of government support so eagerly courted by industrial leaders after 1930 was being abruptly reconsidered as the NRA experience unfolded.

THE REPUBLICAN PRESIDENTIAL CAMPAIGN OF 1936

Throughout 1935, Republican strategists were preoccupied with efforts to regain the western states that had deserted the party's presidential candidate in 1932. It was felt that such efforts required the selection of a presidential candidate from a western state who would also be acceptable to the party's eastern wing. Republican preconvention maneuvering was shaped by the rapprochement that had been achieved between eastern conservatives and the representatives of the Republican governor of Kansas, Alfred Landon.

It rapidly became apparent that Landon was the only available candidate who was acceptable to eastern conservatives and who also offered the prospect of regaining the party's lost western base.

A former Bull Mooser who had since maintained a record of party regularity, Landon could not be immediately identified as a candidate from either the conservative or progressive wing of the party. From its inception, the Landon movement progressed with the benign tolerance of eastern party leaders and scored an easy first ballot victory at the Republican convention of 1936. Thus, while the original Landon effort has been correctly identified as reflecting the influence of younger, more liberal elements within the party, its easy march to the nomination had been the result of deliberate abstention on the part of the party's eastern conservative leaders. As the Landon forces attempted to lay the basis for an effective nationwide campaign, however, it would become apparent that the remarkable first ballot victory and the acceptance of a platform with a liberal tinge had only masked the fundamental division over political strategy.

Roosevelt's overwhelming victory in 1936 is an excellent example of historical event that, by upstaging the uncertainties that preceded it, appears after the fact to have been inevitable. Little seemed inevitable in mid-1936, however. Despite the removal of the threat posed by a possible Huey Long candidacy, political conditions continued to be subject to a wide variety of interpretations. Nor was the situation at all clarified by the public opinion polls then in operation. In July 1936 the Gallup poll accorded President Roosevelt the support of only 51.8 percent of the electorate. This represented a drop of four points since Gallup's June poll. When electoral sentiment was analyzed by the Gallup organization on a state-by-state basis, thirteen states, with a total of ninety-nine electoral votes, were said to be "safely Republican." Even more significant was the fact that the Gallup organization credited Landon with leads in eleven additional states, representing a total of 173 electoral votes. If these analyses of "trends" were accurate, the Republicans would amass 272 electoral votes and win the election. The now renowned 1936 *Literary Digest* poll, whose 1932 counterpart had come within a percentage point of forecasting the actual popular vote that year, continued throughout the campaign to predict a massive Landon victory. Confusion over the direction of political trends was also frequently reflected in much serious journalistic commentary.

Although the *New York Times* announced editorial support for Roosevelt, its electoral analysis continued to forecast a close, hard-fought election. Massive Republican congressional gains were predicted in the *New York Times* throughout the year.

THE 1936 ELECTION RESULTS

Republican leaders, who had anticipated at least the restoration of the party as a competitive force, were suddenly instead faced with a devastating electoral repudiation. The Landon-Knox ticket had succeeded in carrying only the states of Maine and Vermont and had garnered over 45 percent of the vote in only four states. Overall, the Republican presidential ticket had won but 36.5 percent of the popular vote. The election results were also devastating to the party's already drastically reduced congressional contingent. Republicans found their numbers in the House reduced from 104 to eighty-nine and in the Senate from twenty-five to sixteen.

In one day, patterns of electoral analysis that had guided Republican political strategists since the election of 1896 had been abruptly overturned. The Democratic electoral coalition had been decisively established as the majority party within the electorate. Subsequently, Republicans would continue to travel a road of reevaluation and reassessment, while awaiting a turn of political fortune that might enable the party to bid for majority status.

The Republican Party's efforts at electoral adjustment were aided by an intellectual transformation occurring within the business community. By 1935 much of American heavy industry had experienced a strong negative reaction to the increased role of government in macroeconomic management. This had dramatically affected the ability of the Republican Party to alter electoral appeals. But with the introduction after 1936 of Keynesian principles of economic management, important segments of the business community came to gradually support an activist fiscal and monetary policy. The gradual adoption of these attitudes by a number of business elites presaged a substantial modification of the polarized political debates over political economy characteristic of the early 1930s and the 1936 election.

After 1936, then, new efforts to reestablish a government-business alliance were undertaken.

These patterns of positive response again suggest the impact of attitudinal changes by political elites on the formulation of mass political appeals. In 1939, *Fortune's* "Round Table" surveys of executive opinion found that stagnation and chronic unemployment were now regarded as the greatest dangers facing the economy.

THE 1938 ELECTIONS

For the first time since 1928 the Republican Party gained seats in the congressional elections of 1938. The party, apparently moribund in 1937, scored remarkable gains throughout the nation the following year. In senatorial races the GOP won eleven of twenty-seven contests for a net gain of eight seats. The minority contingent in the Senate increased from fifteen to twenty-three, and six of the eight new Republican senators displaced reliable liberal supporters of the administration. The Republicans also registered substantial gains in the House of Representatives, where they almost doubled their strength, increasing their numbers from 89 to 169. Many of the defeated Democrats had come from the industrial sections of the East and Midwest, and many were recently elected congressmen who had been swept into office by the 1932, 1934, and 1936 Democratic landslides. The Republican restoration greatly enhanced the prospects for cooperation with conservative Democrats, thus establishing a pattern of political deadlock that would subsequently become the norm in American political life.

Despite its decent to minority status after 1932, the Republican Party had retained its historical connection to political power while invoking symbolic identification with national values and belief systems that were meaningful to millions of voters. The abrupt succession of Republican electoral defeats had concealed the extent to which the party still reflected general attitudes of a somewhat wider nature. While the fear evoked by economic crisis had produced a call for government assistance, even from conservative groups, the abatement of this sense of emergency by 1937 demonstrated the persistence of previous ideological patterns. Even the disastrous dislocation of the 1930s did not dispel decades of support for the idea of limited government activity. The notions of individualism, self-help, and the general legitimacy of entrepreneurial activity remained important components of the American belief system.

Given the persistence of these belief patterns, any voter reaction against the administration after 1936 had the potential of resulting in GOP electoral gains. The rise of a candidly urban liberalism after 1936 had finally enabled Republicans to minimize their own internal divisions and to develop cohesive party responses to efforts to expand the New Deal. Simultaneously, a downward trend in the business cycle, increased divisiveness within the enlarged Democratic Party, and a general unease with the continued exercise of larger-than-life efforts by Roosevelt presented the Republicans with opportunities not of their own making. Thus, the events of 1937 to 1938 had done more than reawaken submerged feelings of congressional independence; they had given renewed intensity to expressions of partisanship on the part of the minority party. After the success achieved in the 1938 elections, the Republican congressional delegation remained cohesive, providing some three-quarters of the anti-administration votes on most major controversial measures by 1939. Revived Republican partisanship thus became the indispensable component of the modern conservative congressional coalition. The party's return to competitive status also suggested clear limitations to the reform impulse that flourished in the Congress and the nation from 1932 through 1937.

By the election of 1940 an important transformation of the ideological wings of the Republican Party was underway. Essentially the GOP had to come to terms with the new centers of urban power established by the New Deal. As a result, the urbanized northeastern wing of the party would come to be represented by a Dewey-Rockefeller liberal wing that stood in contrast to the old guard representation of the 1930 period. Changes in the western Republican contingent came to be symbolized by the rise of Robert Taft, who stood in vivid contrast to the Republican insurgents of the pre–New Deal period. Thus, the modern postwar Republican Party can be said to be a result of the New Deal's electoral success.

See Also: ELECTION OF 1928; ELECTION OF 1930; ELECTION OF 1932; ELECTION OF 1934; ELECTION OF 1936; ELECTION OF 1938; ELECTION OF 1940; POLITICAL REALIGNMENT.

BIBLIOGRAPHY

Berkowitz, Edward, and Kim McQuaid. *Creating the Welfare State: The Political Economy of Twentieth-Century Reform.* 1992.

Graham, Otis L. *Toward a Planned Society: From Roosevelt to Nixon.* 1976

Hawley, Ellis. *The New Deal and the Problem of Monopoly: A Study in Economic Ambivalence.* 1966.

Hawley, Ellis. "Herbert Hoover, the Commerce Secretariat and the Vision of an 'Associative State.'" *Journal of American History* 61 (1974): 116–40.

Hawley, Ellis. "The New Deal and Business." In *The New Deal: The National Level,* edited by John Braeman, Robert H. Bremner, and David Brody. 1975.

Himmelberg, Robert R. *The Origins of the National Recovery Administration: Business, Government, and the Trade Association Issue, 1921–1933.* 1976.

Keller, Morton. *In Defense of Yesterday: James Beck and the Politics of Conservatism.* 1958.

Kennedy, David. *Over Here: The First World War and American Society.* 1980.

Leuchtenburg, William E. *Franklin D. Roosevelt and the New Deal 1932–1940.*1963.

Leuchtenburg, William E. "The New Deal and the Analogue of War" In *Change and Continuity in Twentieth-Century America,* edited by John Braeman, Robert Bremner, and Everett Walters. 1966.

Literary Digest 18 (January 1936): 10–11.

Overacker, Louise. "Campaign Funds in a Depression Year." In *American Political Science Reviewer* 27 (1933): 772.

The Regulation of Businessmen: Social Conditions of Government Economic Control, edited by Robert Lane. 1954.

Romasco, Albert U. *The Politics of Recovery: Roosevelt's New Deal.* 1983.

Wolfskill, George. *The Revolt of the Conservatives: A History of the American Liberty League, 1934–1941.* 1962.

CLYDE P. WEED

RESETTLEMENT ADMINISTRATION (RA)

President Franklin D. Roosevelt established the Resettlement Administration (RA) by executive order on May 1, 1935. The new organization consolidated programs relating to land use planning and rural relief from several federal departments. To head the RA the president appointed brains truster and undersecretary of agriculture Rexford G. Tugwell, who recruited Will W. Alexander of the Commission on Interracial Cooperation as assistant administrator. The way the RA was assembled, its mix of activities, and the objectives of its leaders would make it the New Deal's comprehensive rural anti-poverty program.

The RA was formed as the New Deal was reordering several agricultural and relief programs. After the firing of liberal lawyers from the Agricultural Adjustment Administration (AAA) in February 1935, Tugwell was ready to leave the Department of Agriculture (USDA). Heading the RA, he could oversee an independent agency with jurisdiction over his chief interest, land classification and planning. Accordingly, all such functions of the USDA, AAA, and the National Resources Planning Board were assigned to the RA, which was charged with retiring sub-marginal lands from agriculture and resettling farmers from those lands. Meanwhile, as the Federal Emergency Relief Administration (FERA) was being discontinued in favor of the new Works Progress Administration, its rural rehabilitation division was attached to the RA. Since 1934 that program had aided chronically impoverished farmers, tenants, and laborers, and by the spring of 1935 it had about 210,000 clients, mostly in the South. This assignment of rehabilitation, largely determined by Alexander's agreement to take charge of it, expanded the RA and set its course as an anti-poverty agency. The RA also received miscellaneous programs, including subsistence homesteads from the Department of the Interior, suburban "greenbelts" around four cities, and cooperative farm communities started by the FERA.

The centerpiece of the RA's anti-poverty work was its standard rehabilitation loan. Estimates of borrowers served by the mid-1940s range from 695,000 to 825,000. The loans, usually a few hundred dollars per year, underwrote farm operations, while additional credit might assist home improvements or the purchase of tools or livestock. To safeguard loans, credit was conditioned on supervision;

A tenant farmer in Plaquemines Parish, Louisiana, in 1935 shows off the mule he obtained with help from the Resettlement Administration. LIBRARY OF CONGRESS, PRINTS & PHOTOGRAPHS DIVISION, FSA/OWI COLLECTION

the RA's field staff advised clients on farming methods and annual budgets, and required them to plant gardens and preserve their produce. Clients' progress was measured by increased family income and net worth, and improved farming ability.

Much smaller than rehabilitation lending was the RA's resettlement program, comprising about 150 projects by 1937. Some of the most prominent of these were in the lower Mississippi Valley, including eight plantation projects leasing government-owned land to resettled farmers under varying plans of cooperation. As Donald Holley has shown, RA projects rarely deviated from a pattern of individually operated acreages, had difficulty establishing a cooperative outlook among participants, and often experienced large cost overruns. They also drew heavy fire from congressional conservatives who condemned them as socialistic. In its 1944 appropriations Congress ordered all reset-

tlement work disbanded, along with fifty-two client associations for leasing privately held land.

From its beginning the RA had sought authority to help tenants buy farms. Even before joining the RA, Alexander had helped develop the Bankhead bill of 1935, an ambitious plan for government acquisition of land for resale to supervised tenants. Although the bill failed in Congress, RA leaders hoped to revive and implement it. But the Bankhead-Jones Act that was passed in July 1937 was a severely limited measure that ultimately provided only 44,300 loans in eight years. Nevertheless, the lending program was assigned to the RA, which was renamed the Farm Security Administration (FSA).

Administered by Alexander from 1936 to 1940 and Calvin B. Baldwin from 1940 to 1943, the RA-FSA expanded its array of anti-poverty programs. It promoted improved land tenure for tenants and

This housing project under construction in Greenhills, Ohio, in 1937 was one of numerous Resettlement Administration initiatives.

LIBRARY OF CONGRESS, PRINTS & PHOTOGRAPHS DIVISION, FSA/OWI COLLECTION

encouraged clients to form cooperatives for purchasing supplies, machinery, or breeding stock. It organized innovative small group medical plans covering almost 110,000 families by 1942. But the agency's wide-ranging programs were not sufficient to reach all poor farmers. Indeed, despite repeated efforts to assist the most impoverished, the FSA moved increasingly toward selecting better credit risks as new borrowers.

The RA-FSA was never popular with congressional conservatives and they attacked it repeatedly. As Sidney Baldwin has pointed out, the agency never had an adequate statutory foundation. The Bankhead-Jones Act authorized only farm purchase lending, land retirement work, and rehabilitation loans using diverted relief money; otherwise FSA programs depended on the continued willingness of Congress to fund them. That willingness declined markedly as the New Deal waned and war priorities took precedence. After inflicting devastating budget cuts in 1943, Congress ended the FSA in 1946, continuing some farm purchase lending under a new Farmers Home Administration.

See Also: BANKHEAD-JONES FARM TENANT ACT OF 1937; FARM SECURITY ADMINISTRATION (FSA).

BIBLIOGRAPHY

Baldwin, Sidney. *Poverty and Politics: The Rise and Decline of the Farm Security Administration.* 1968.

Banfield, Edward C. "Ten Years of the Farm Tenant Purchase Program." *Journal of Farm Economics* 31 (1949): 469–86.

Dykeman, Wilma, and James Stokely. *Seeds of Southern Change: The Life of Will Alexander.* 1962.

Gray, L. C.; John D. Black; E. G. Nourse; et al. (U.S. National Resources Committee). *Farm Tenancy: Report of the President's Committee.* 1937.

Holley, Donald. *Uncle Sam's Farmers: The New Deal Communities in the Lower Mississippi Valley.* 1975.

Larson, Olaf F., and the U.S. Bureau of Agricultural Economics. *Ten Years of Rural Rehabilitation in the United States.* 1947.

Maddox, James G. "The Farm Security Administration." Ph.D. diss., Harvard University. 1950.

Mertz, Paul E. *New Deal Policy and Southern Rural Poverty.* 1978.

PAUL E. MERTZ

REUTHER, WALTER

Best known as president of the United Auto Workers (UAW) union from 1946 until his death in a plane crash in 1970, Walter Philip Reuther (September 1, 1907–May 9, 1970) struggled during the Great Depression to find a focus for his considerable skill and energy before eventually immersing himself in the cause of organizing Detroit automobile workers. Born in Wheeling, West Virginia, Reuther left a tool and die apprenticeship in his hometown at age nineteen to seek work in Detroit. Despite his age, Reuther was highly skilled and gained a position of responsibility at Ford's Highland Park Plant. Reuther attended high school after work, and, with his younger brother Victor, took classes at Detroit City College (which became Wayne State University). Displaying his activist inclination and the influence of his Socialist father, Reuther fought to defend free speech rights at the college, opposed segregation at a pool near campus, and campaigned for supported Socialist Norman Thomas in the 1932 presidential campaign.

The Great Depression made employment insecure even for skilled workers like Reuther. With an uncertain future in Detroit, and lured by the prospect of a viable workers' state in the Soviet Union, Walter and Victor left Detroit in January 1933 for what would become an amazing journey of over two and a half years through Europe and Asia. The Reuthers arrived in Germany during the Nazi takeover, then bicycled around Europe for nine months waiting for their visas to enter the Soviet Union. Observing the rise of fascism only strengthened Walter Reuther's tendency to see the best in the alternative Soviet model. In the Soviet Union, the Reuthers worked on a massive industrialization project in Gorky and were moved by the cooperation they observed between management, union leaders, and the state, as well as by the spirit of Soviet workers. The Reuthers did not observe the most brutal aspects of Soviet industrialization—although they eventually saw enough to cause concern—and Walter's praise for the Soviet system provided fodder for both American opponents of unionization and, in the 1930s, conservative union rivals. Reuther's relationship with Communists and communism remains a topic of historical debate. Communists were vitally important to the rise of industrial unionism, primarily as organizers, and many UAW Communists had been close to Reuther. But Reuther's outspoken opposition to Communists in the UAW in the early Cold War era, whether principled or opportunistic, undoubtedly helped him become president of the union.

Upon returning to Detroit in 1935, Reuther joined a UAW local—without actually working in a plant—and was elected to the UAW executive board. In early 1936, Reuther married May Wolf, who was equally dedicated to organizing autoworkers. Later that year, Reuther helped organize a sit-down strike at Kelsey-Hayes Wheel Company. The strike resulted in few tangible gains, but much favorable publicity, especially after the more successful sit-down strike at General Motors (GM) in Flint, Michigan, which began shortly after the settlement at Kelsey-Hayes. Reuther received national attention in May 1937 when he and three other UAW officials were savagely beaten by Ford security personnel in the famous "Battle of the Overpass." Photographers documented the attack, but it nevertheless took four more years for Reuther and the UAW to overcome Ford's resistance to unionization.

After supporting Norman Thomas for president in 1936, but seeing merit in Franklin Roosevelt's pro-worker rhetoric, Reuther ran unsuccessfully for the Detroit city council in 1937. None of the four labor candidates was elected, and Reuther finished third among them. Even in the late 1930s, Reuther was but one of many labor notables in Detroit, and he might today remain a somewhat obscure figure if not for his high-profile postwar career.

From 1937 to 1939, Reuther contended with the UAW's factional infighting and the severe recession that almost eliminated both automobile production and the union. Only 6 percent of the UAW's GM employees paid union dues in 1939. In May 1939 Reuther, as the new director of the UAW's GM department, helped the union regain strength by organizing a strike of skilled tradesmen, without whose labor the company could not produce any cars for the 1940 model year. GM was forced, once again, to recognize the UAW, just in time for the production boom that accompanied World War II. Reuther's fame grew proportionately throughout the next thirty years.

See Also: AMERICAN FEDERATION OF LABOR (AFL); CONGRESS OF INDUSTRIAL ORGANIZATIONS (CIO); LABOR'S NON-PARTISAN LEAGUE; ORGANIZED LABOR; UNITED AUTOMOBILE WORKERS (UAW).

BIBLIOGRAPHY

Barnard, John. *Walter Reuther and the Rise of the Auto Workers.* 1983.

Barnard, John. "Rebirth of the United Automobile Workers: The General Motors Tool and Diemakers' Strike of 1939." *Labor History* 27 (1986): 165–187.

Boyle, Kevin. "Building the Vanguard: Walter Reuther and Radical Politics in 1936." *Labor History* 30 (1989): 433–48.

Boyle, Kevin. *The UAW and the Heyday of American Liberalism: 1945–1968.* 1995.

Lichtenstein, Nelson. *The Most Dangerous Man in Detroit: Walter Reuther and the Fate of American Labor.* 1995.

Reuther, Victor G. *The Brothers Reuther and the Story of the UAW: A Memoir.* 1976.

DANIEL CLARK

RFC. *See* RECONSTRUCTION FINANCE CORPORATION.

RICHBERG, DONALD

Donald Randall Richberg (July 10, 1881–November 27, 1960) was a labor attorney prominent in drafting the National Industrial Recovery Act and administering the National Recovery Administration (NRA). Richberg was raised in comfortable circumstances in Chicago, receiving his B.A. from the University of Chicago and his LL. B. from Harvard Law School. He embraced progressivism early in his career, fighting against utility monopolies and for the 1912 Progressive Party candidacy of Theodore Roosevelt.

Richberg came to national prominence in the field of labor law. He did not advocate direct government intervention in collective bargaining, but believed that unions needed legal protection if they were to effectively protect their members' interests. He was particularly concerned with the use of injunctions to undermine strikes. Richberg worked closely with railway unions to remedy this problem, helping to draft the 1926 Railway Labor Act and the more broadly cast Norris-La Guardia Anti-Injunction Act in 1932.

Franklin D. Roosevelt's first years in office marked the height of Richberg's national influence. He helped to write section 7a of the National Industrial Recovery Act, which appeared to secure the right of workers' to organize. Richberg subsequently became general counsel of the NRA and served on a number of New Deal agencies, most notably as executive director of the National Emergency Council. Richberg took over as head of the NRA in its last months and unsuccessfully defended its constitutionality before the U.S. Supreme Court.

During his service in the First New Deal Richberg steadily moved away from his early support of organized labor. He made a key decision that undermined the usefulness of section 7a and increasingly became identified with business opinion on industrial relations. Richberg left government service for private law practice after the NRA was struck down.

After leaving office Richberg continued his drift toward conservatism. He soon became a vocal opponent of the Wagner Act, believing that it allowed the government to intervene too much on the side of labor, and a critic of the power wielded by unions in politics and the economy. At the end of World War II, he played an important role in the 1947 passage of the Taft-Hartley Act, which sought to place limits on the power of organized labor. Richberg completed his journey away from the progressive ideals of his youth by becoming a vocal opponent of the government bureaucracies and social welfare programs advocated by liberals in the 1940s and 1950s.

See Also: NATIONAL INDUSTRIAL RECOVERY ACT (NIRA); NATIONAL RECOVERY ADMINISTRATION (NRA); NORRIS-LA GUARDIA ACT.

BIBLIOGRAPHY

Irons, Peter. *The New Deal Lawyers.* 1982

Richberg, Donald R. *Tents of the Mighty.* 1930

Richberg, Donald R. *My Hero: The Indiscreet Memoirs of an Eventful but Unheroic Life.* 1954.

Vadney, Thomas. *The Wayward Liberal: A Political Biography of Donald Richberg.* 1970.

ANDREW A. WORKMAN

Diego Rivera and Frida Kahlo in 1940. AP/WIDE WORLD PHOTOS

RIVERA, DIEGO

The artist Diego Rivera (December 13, 1886–November 24, 1957) is best known for the murals he completed in Mexico and in the United States during the 1920s and early 1930s. Rivera, along with the Mexican artists Jose Clemente Orozco and David Alfaro Siqueiros, was immensely popular among North American intellectuals and artists during the 1930s. His murals in large part provided the inspiration for the public art projects sponsored by New Deal agencies during the 1930s. Rivera served as a model of a socially committed artist whose work reflected the struggles of everyday people.

Born in Guanajuato, Mexico, and raised in Mexico City, Rivera started drawing at an early age. At age ten, he enrolled in the San Carlos Academy of Fine Arts, where he completed his studies in 1905. Upon graduation, Rivera spent several years in Spain and in Paris, where he encountered many of the modern masters, including Pablo Picasso. Influenced by Picasso, Rivera painted hundreds of cubist works between 1913 and 1917. Returning to Mexico in 1921, Rivera began work on several government-commissioned murals, including one at the Ministry of Education that encompassed three floors and spanned 17,000 square feet. Having been exposed to Marxism while in Europe, Rivera belonged to the Mexican Communist Party from 1922 to 1929, when he was expelled for his relationship with the Mexican government.

In 1930, Rivera traveled to the United States, where he prepared for major exhibitions of his work in San Francisco and in New York City. Rivera also painted murals at the San Francisco Stock Exchange, the California School of Fine Arts, and at the Detroit Institute of Arts. In the Detroit mural, Rivera explored the power of modern industrial technology and capitalism. In 1933, Rivera received a commission to paint a mural in the new Rockefeller Center in New York City. He was dismissed from the project when he insisted upon including the figure of Vladimir Lenin in the mural. He completed one more mural at the New Workers School before returning to Mexico in December 1933.

Rivera completed only one mural during the rest of the 1930s; instead, he focused on smaller works, such as landscapes. He was instrumental in arranging with the Mexican government Leon Trotsky's asylum. In 1937, Trotsky and his wife arrived in Mexico and stayed as guests of Rivera and his wife Frida Kahlo in Kahlo's family home in Coyoacán. For political and personal reasons, Trotsky and Rivera ended their affiliation in 1939. In 1940, Rivera returned to San Francisco to work in the Art-in-Action pavilion at the Golden Gate International Exposition, where visitors watched him as he painted the mural "Pan American Unity."

See Also: ART; COMMUNIST PARTY; POST OFFICE MURALS.

BIBLIOGRAPHY

Hamill, Pete. *Diego Rivera.* 1999.

Hurlburt, Laurance P. *The Mexican Muralists in the United States.* 1989.

Wolfe, Bertram D. *Diego Rivera: His Life and Times.* 1939.

Wolfe, Bertram D. *The Fabulous Life of Diego Rivera.* 1963.

LARISSA M. SMITH

ROAD TO PLENTY, THE

The Road to Plenty by William Trufant Foster and Waddill Catchings was a widely read book that challenged the assumption of classical economics that production and consumption were inherently in balance. It anticipated the ideas of John Maynard Keynes and the strategy of counter-cyclical government spending. Neither Foster nor Catchings were professional economists. Foster had been president of Reed College in Portland, Oregon, and Catchings was a manufacturer who became a partner in Goldman Sachs, an investment banking firm.

In *The Road to Plenty,* their fourth and most influential book, Foster and Catchings popularized and developed the ideas of the English economist John A. Hobson. They argued that consumption regulated production and that underconsumption could occur due to savings ("wasteful thrift"), artificially high prices, low wages, and other conditions that constrained purchasing power. The authors believed that the key to full employment and improved standards of living was public spending. The book became especially relevant after the onset of the Depression because it argued that the way to deal with unemployment was to stimulate consumption rather than production. Couched in terms of an instructional conversation, *The Road to Plenty* proposed the creation of a federal board that would gather data on economic conditions and make recommendations for public works to stimulate consumption during economic downturns. Foster and Catchings contended that reliance on fiscal policy would restrict the need for state intervention and would present no threat to American values and existing institutions. The book informed the congressional debate about public works expenditures during the early phase of the Depression, and it influenced Marriner S. Eccles, who became chairman of the Federal Reserve Board in 1934. However, it was not until the recession of 1937 to 1938 that the ideas of Foster and Catchings elicited significant support from New Dealers.

See Also: ECONOMY, AMERICAN; KEYNES, JOHN MAYNARD.

BIBLIOGRAPHY

Brinkley, Alan. "Origins of the 'Fiscal Revolution'." *Storia Nordamericana* 6, nos. 1–2 (1989): 35–56.

Dorfman, Joseph. *The Economic Mind in American Civilization,* Vols. 4–5: *1918–1933.* 1946–1959.

Gleason, Alan H. "Foster and Catchings: A Reappraisal." *Journal of Political Economy* 67 (1959): 156–172.

STUART KIDD

ROBESON, PAUL

Paul Leroy Robeson (April 9, 1898–January 23, 1976), a world-famous singer, actor, and political activist, was born in Princeton, New Jersey. The son of a runaway slave who became a Presbyterian minister, Robeson received a scholarship to Rutgers College in 1915. Only the third black student to be admitted, he starred in four sports, was twice named an all-America football end, and become valedictorian of his class and a member of Phi Beta Kappa, the national college honor society. To fulfill his class prophecy to be "the leader of the colored race in America," Robeson earned a law degree from Columbia University in 1923, supporting himself by playing professional football on the weekends.

At the urging of his wife, Eslanda Cardozo Goode, a fellow Columbia Law School student whom Robeson had married in 1921, he turned from the law to the stage. Beginning with the Provincetown Players in 1924, he eventually gained international acclaim for his performances in the title roles of Shakespeare's *Othello* and Eugene O'Neill's *The Emperor Jones,* and as Crown in DuBose Heyward's *Porgy.* Robeson also won praise for his moving interpretations of black spirituals and the folk music of many countries. Possessed of a magnificent bass voice, Robeson became known especially for his rendition of "Ol' Man River" in Jerome Kern's *Show Boat.* Despite his fame, Robeson could not escape the indignities of racism in the United States, and he was frequently denied service at hotels and restaurants, even in the North.

From 1928 to 1939 Robeson lived and worked primarily in London. There he became acquainted with leaders of the British Labor Party and with pan-Africanists such as Jomo Kenyatta and C. L. R. James. He came to see the connection between the struggles of the working class and those of oppressed colonial peoples, and he studied Marxist texts and the major ideas of communism. Increasingly, Robeson viewed his art as serving the fight for economic and racial justice.

In 1934 Robeson made the first of a series of visits to the Soviet Union. For the first time in his life, he would later claim of his time in Moscow, "I walk in full human dignity," entirely free from racial prejudice. This, and the Soviet Union's support of anti-fascist and anti-colonialist struggles, led to his close ties with American Communists, although he never formally joined the party. Having returned to

Paul Robeson, photographed by Gordon Parks in 1942. LIBRARY OF CONGRESS, PRINTS & PHOTOGRAPHS DIVISION, FSA/OWI COLLECTION

the United States in 1939, Robeson became a leading spokesperson for a variety of left-wing causes, especially equal rights for African Americans. The first major artist to refuse to perform before segregated audiences, he urged Congress to end of the color bar in major league baseball. Robeson also helped lead voter registration campaigns in the Deep South and the efforts to enlist black workers in the Congress of Industrial Organizations union-organizing drives in the 1940s.

Reacting to President Harry Truman's refusal in 1946 to sponsor legislation making lynching a federal crime, Robeson shocked many Americans by asserting that black Americans would exercise their right of self-defense. Then, attending a peace conference in Paris in 1949, Robeson expressed a widely publicized prediction that African Americans would not fight in a war against the Soviet Union.

Refusing on constitutional grounds to answer any questions from congressional committees concerning his Communist Party membership or affiliation, Robeson felt the full weight of McCarthy-era repression come crushingly down upon him. Branding him "one of the most dangerous men in the world," the State Department revoked his passport, and would not restore it until 1958. The Federal Bureau of Investigation and the Central Intelligence Agency hounded and harassed him until his death, and the entertainment industry blacklisted him, preventing Robeson from appearing in television, radio, and the concert stage until 1957. Most African-American organizations no longer wanted any association with him, and when his autobiography was published in 1958 most newspapers and magazines in the United States did not review, or even mention, the book.

The once eloquent and powerful performer and radical, depressed at the loss of audiences and friends, suffered a series of mental breakdowns and tried twice to commit suicide. Largely forgotten in the 1960s and 1970s, Robeson died after suffering a stroke in 1976.

See Also: AFRICAN AMERICANS, IMPACT OF THE GREAT DEPRESSION ON; CIVIL RIGHTS AND CIVIL LIBERTIES; DU BOIS, W. E. B.; RANDOLPH, A. PHILIP.

BIBLIOGRAPHY

Duberman, Martin B. *Paul Robeson.* 1989.

Foner, Philip S., ed. *Paul Robeson Speaks: Writings, Speeches, Interviews, 1918–1974.* 1978.

Robeson, Paul. *Here I Stand.* 1958.

Robeson, Susan. *The Whole World in His Hands: A Pictorial Biography of Paul Robeson.* 1981.

Stewart, Jeffrey C., ed. *Paul Robeson: Artist and Citizen.* 1998.

HARVARD SITKOFF

ROBINSON, EDWARD G.

Edward G. Robinson (December 12, 1893–January 26, 1973), actor noted for tough guy roles, was born Emmanual Goldenberg in Bucharest, Romania. He came to the United States in 1902 with his family and was educated in New York City's public schools. After winning a scholarship in 1911 to the American Academy of Dramatic Arts, he changed his name to Edward G. (for Goldenberg) Robinson. Between 1913 and 1930, with time out for a World War I navy stint, he appeared in over thirty plays, making a stab at the movies in 1923. He made some films at the end of the 1920s before moving to California and quickly becoming a star character actor.

His breakthrough role as an ambitious aggressive gangster in the 1931 film *Little Caesar,* released at the beginning of Hollywood's gangster cycle, helped define a particular image of Robinson. As he later said, "some people have youth, some have beauty—I have menace." Small of stature but blessed with a cutting voice, Robinson in his 1930s films (and well into the 1940s) was presented mainly as a guy who could "dish it out."

The gangster genre attracted Depression audiences because the protagonists, however sour their end, overcame adversity through most of the film. The initial gangster cycle petered out under pressure from various sources. A gangster cycle later in the decade took a different tack, downplaying the characters' heroic aspects. Robinson, whether or not on the right side of the law in his 1930s films, portrayed vigorously, convincingly, and with compassion a wide variety of characters: He played a gangster in *The Last Gangster* (1938), an Asian in *The Hatchet Man* (1932), a law enforcer in *Bullets or Ballots* (1936), and a self-made man in *Silver Dollar* (1932). He even spoofed his own image and the gangster genre in *A Slight Case of Larceny* (1938). Because of his passionate political convictions, he accepted a minor role as an FBI official in the controversial *Confessions of a Nazi Spy* (1939), an early entry in Hollywood's campaign against Hitler.

Star status notwithstanding, Robinson was blacklisted at the end of the 1940s. He strenuously campaigned to clear himself and his career revived in the mid-1950s but most of his subsequent roles were supporting ones. He did make a triumphal return to the stage and achieved a viable TV career. Robinson was awarded the Legion d'Honneur in 1952 and received posthumously a special Oscar for "lifetime achievement."

See Also: HOLLYWOOD AND THE FILM INDUSTRY.

BIBLIOGRAPHY

Beck, Robert. *The Edward G. Robinson Encyclopedia.* 2002.

Marill, Alvin. *The Complete Films of Edward G. Robinson.* 1990.

Robinson, Edward G. *All My Yesterdays.* 1973.

DANIEL J. LEAB

ROBINSON, JOSEPH

Joseph Taylor ("Joe T") Robinson (1872–1937) was the Democratic leader of the Senate from 1922 to 1937 (the majority leader from 1933 to 1937) and in 1928 was the Democratic candidate for vice president on the unsuccessful ticket headed by Al Smith.

Born August 26, 1872, in rural Lonoke County, Arkansas, Robinson, the ninth child of farmer and doctor James Madison Robinson and Matilda Swaim Robinson, attended the local elementary and secondary schools, one semester at the University of Arkansas and a summer law program at the University of Virginia. He became a successful lawyer after only a few months of study, partnering with local Democratic Party leader Tom Trimble.

In 1896 Robinson began a long, successful political career. Serving as a Democratic presidential elector, he gave up his position to form a fusion ticket for William Jennings Bryan with the Populist Party; in 1900 he received the same position, presidential elector. Two years later he won a seat in the U.S. Congress, where he supported progressive legislation during his five terms. In 1912 he won the governorship of Arkansas, but before he was inaugurated, Arkansas Senator Jeff Davis died suddenly, throwing the state's politics into turmoil. Days later, the legislature elected Robinson to fill the Senate vacancy.

In the Senate Robinson became a national figure. His staunch defense of President Woodrow Wilson and the Versailles peace treaty led Democrats to choose him to be chair of the 1920 party convention, a position he held again in 1928 and 1936. Just three years later he became minority leader of the Senate, leading Arkansans to back him in his failed bid for president in 1924. In 1928 Al Smith chose Robinson for the Democratic vice-presidential slot because of his fierce stand against religious bigotry. And in 1932 he delivered enough Democratic votes to pass Herbert Hoover's Reconstruction Finance Corporation; Hoover then named Robinson's friend, Harvey Couch, to the board.

After the 1932 election, Robinson became majority leader; in that capacity he guided much of the New Deal legislation through the Senate. In one instance, on March 8, 1933, the day before Franklin Delano Roosevelt introduced the Emergency Banking Act, Robinson shocked presidential advisers when he promised that the "bill will be passed tomorrow" (Weller, Jr., 1998, p. 137). Less than eight hours after its introduction, the measure passed the Senate. Robinson had only two major failures during the New Deal. In the first, he lost the battle for U.S. membership in the World Court, 52 to 36, seven votes short of the necessary two-thirds needed for victory. The Supreme Court "packing" plan was an even greater disappointment. Roosevelt promised Robinson that when the court-packing bill passed, he would appoint him to the Supreme Court. After bitter wrangling in the Senate, Robinson believed that he had enough votes to pass the bill in July 1937. But in the sweltering summer heat of Washington, Robinson pushed himself beyond his limits in fighting for the measure. On July 14, 1937, Robinson's death from a heart attack also killed the court-packing plan.

See Also: NEW DEAL; SUPREME COURT "PACKING" CONTROVERSY.

BIBLIOGRAPHY

Alsop, Joseph, and Turner Catledge. "Joe Robinson, the New Deal's Old Reliable." *Saturday Evening Post* (September 26, 1936): 5–7, 66–74.

Neal, Nevin Emil. "A Biography of Joseph Taylor Robinson." Ph.D. diss., University of Oklahoma, 1958.

Weller, Cecil E., Jr. *Joe T. Robinson: Always a Loyal Democrat.* 1998.

Weller, Cecil E., Jr. "Joseph Taylor Robinson: Keystone of President Franklin D. Roosevelt's Supreme Court 'Packing' Plan." *Southern Historian* 7 (1986): 23–30.

CECIL E. WELLER, JR.

Joseph Robinson (right) with Franklin and Eleanor Roosevelt in Washington, D.C., in March 1933. FRANKLIN DELANO ROOSEVELT LIBRARY

ROGERS, WILL

William Penn Adair Rogers (November 4, 1879–August 15, 1935) was known worldwide as a humorist, philosopher, writer, actor, and stage performer. Will Rogers was at the height of his popularity in 1935 when he died tragically in an airplane crash in Alaska.

Born in Indian Territory near present-day Oologah, Oklahoma, Rogers was the only son of well-to-do parents who were both part Cherokee. He attended schools in Indian Territory and Missouri, but never graduated from high school. After a brief time in Texas, he returned home, managed

the family ranch, and competed in roping contests. After traveling around the world, part of the time performing as a roper and rider, Rogers took his act to the Saint Louis World's Fair in 1904. Later that year, he appeared for the first time in vaudeville, launching a stage career that would include several seasons with the *Ziegfeld Follies*. An occasional contributor to newspapers by 1922, he started a syndicated weekly column that year and a daily column four years later, both eventually reaching millions of readers. He also starred in films—both silents and talkies—and on radio.

By 1929 Rogers had become one of the most visible, quoted, and recognizable figures in the country. He had taken advantage of almost every available media form and had succeeded at most. His commentary, although often pointed, rarely attacked. As a humorist he was both jokester and philosopher.

The Depression of the 1930s caused Rogers to turn more serious. He had long before gibed at the excesses he perceived in American society; therefore his initial reaction in the early months following the stock market crash reflected a hope for a return to normality. As the Depression deepened, however, Rogers criticized the refusal of the federal government to provide direct relief and in January 1931 he even proposed large-scale public works funded by increased taxation of the wealthy.

At the same time Rogers became directly involved in relief efforts. In early 1931 he voluntarily undertook a benefit tour of several agriculturally depressed states and raised significant funds for Red Cross relief programs. Rogers, a millionaire, donated to other organized appeals and to personal situations, and he urged the public to respond similarly.

Not surprisingly, he welcomed the presidency of Franklin Roosevelt and the promise of decisive action. He chose to interpret in the president's moves in the early days of his administration a return of confidence. Despite continued hardship in the country, Rogers's writings and public remarks took on a lighter, more positive tone from the beginning of Roosevelt's presidency in March 1933. From then until his death Rogers conveyed an optimistic message, even in his films, that good times would return, a point of view that critics on the left considered unrealistic. As evidenced by his rising popularity, however, the public seemed to agree with Rogers or, at least, to find comfort in his humor.

Rogers died with aviator Wiley Post in a plane crash at Point Barrow, Alaska, on August 15, 1935. He was survived by his wife, Betty, and three children.

See Also: HUMOR.

Will Rogers (left) with Eleanor Roosevelt in Los Angeles in June 1933. FRANKLIN DELANO ROOSEVELT LIBRARY

BIBLIOGRAPHY

Bergman, Andrew. *We're in the Money: Depression America and Its Films.* 1972.

Brown, William Richard. *Imagemaker: Will Rogers and the American Dream.* 1970.

Carter, Joseph H. *Never Met a Man I Didn't Like: The Life and Writings of Will Rogers.* 1991.

Collins, Reba. "Will Rogers: Writer and Journalist." Ed.D. diss., Oklahoma State University, 1967.

Croy, Homer. *Our Will Rogers.* 1953.

Gragert, Steven K., ed. *Will Rogers' Weekly Articles*, Vols. 4–6. 1981–1982.

Gragert, Steven K., ed. *Radio Broadcasts of Will Rogers.* 1983.

Rogers, Betty. *Will Rogers: His Wife's Story.* 1941. Reprint, 1979.

Rogers, Will. Papers. Will Rogers Memorial, Claremore, OK.

Rollins, Peter C., director. *Will Rogers' 1920s: A Cowboy's Guide to the Times.* 1976.

Rollins, Peter C. *Will Rogers: A Bio-Bibliography.* 1984.

Smallwood, James, and Steven K. Gragert, eds. *Will Rogers' Daily Telegrams*, 4 vols. 1978–1979.

Wertheim, Arthur F., and Barbara Bair, eds. *The Papers of Will Rogers*, 3 vols. 1996–2001.

Young Eleanor Roosevelt in 1887. FRANKLIN DELANO ROOSEVELT LIBRARY

Yagoda, Ben. *Will Rogers: A Biography.* 1993.

STEVEN K. GRAGERT

ROOSEVELT, ELEANOR

Eleanor Roosevelt (October 11, 1884–November 7, 1962), niece of President Theodore Roosevelt, wife of President Franklin Delano Roosevelt, first lady of New York State (1924–1932), and first lady of the United States (1933–1945), left the American people a great legacy. Considered by many to be the first lady of the world and a harbinger of human rights for all, she always said, governments exist for only one reason: to make life better for all people. But, she quickly added, you can never depend on governments to do anything about that: you have to organize, door to door, block by block, community by community, to make your wants and needs known.

EARLY LIFE AND REFORM EFFORTS

Activist, organizer, journalist, and devoted public citizen, Eleanor Roosevelt struggled to create and embolden communities of democratic might; to fight poverty, discrimination, homelessness, ignorance, and war. Born into a family of wealth, privilege, and power, she was the lonely orphaned daughter of an alcoholic who died at the age of thirty-four, when Eleanor was ten years old. Her father Elliott, Theodore Roosevelt's brother, was her hero, but he was embattled all his life. Her mother Anna, bitter and weary, died at the age of twenty-nine, when Eleanor was eight. After the deaths of her parents, Eleanor spent her life trying to make things better for people in want, in need, in trouble—people just like her own mother and father. Raised mostly by her grandmother, Eleanor was away at Allenswood School in England when her uncle Theodore became president. Headmistress Marie Souvestre appreciated and encouraged her leadership qualities and many skills. Eleanor flourished and returned to New York society with bold convictions: She believed personal involvement could improve conditions; individual action mattered; democracy was essential; politics was not an isolated individualist adventure. She never went anywhere without her gang.

Eleanor was eighteen when she joined her girlhood chums (Mary Harriman, Jean Reid, Gwendolyn Burden, and others) and helped build the Junior League for the Promotion of Settlement Movements. In 1903, she volunteered at the University Settlement on Rivington Street on the Lower East Side of Manhattan. She also joined the National Consumers' League and the Women's Trade Union League. Every day Eleanor sought to alleviate suffering, and she met and was inspired by her uncle's primary women advisers, Lillian Wald, Florence Kelley, and Jane Addams. Eleanor became ardent about public affairs, and she pursued a life of responsibility. To the end of her life, she believed that research and understanding, respect for people, and a politics of real concern would end mandated poverty, as well as racial and ethnic violence. From an early age, Eleanor was committed to a square deal and a new deal, for the United States and for the world.

Also in 1903, Eleanor became engaged to Franklin Delano Roosevelt, her fifth cousin once removed, then a student at Harvard University. She encouraged his career, while she sought to maintain her own activities. After their marriage on March 17, 1905, she had six children (one died in infancy) in ten years. She served as her husband's best advocate and volunteered her time mostly through the women's progressive movement. During World War I, Eleanor became aware of her own executive abilities, and after 1920 she plunged into a new level of activity, with new allies—most notably, Esther Lape and Elizabeth Read—with whom she rallied to get the United States into the World Court.

NEW DEAL LEADER

Eleanor Roosevelt's campaign for the World Court occupied many of her days between 1924 and 1935, when U.S. participation in the court failed to win approval in the Senate by six votes. With fascism on the rise and war looming, her public efforts during the 1930s were divided between the peace movement and the crying needs of the Great Depression. During her husband's presidency, she was notable as the most traveled public spirit behind the New Deal. Eleanor's work as leader, columnist, and broadcaster ensured specific victories concerning jobs, housing, and education. She put youth, race, and women's issues on the national agenda. In 1933, she protested the sex discrimination of her favorite New Deal agency, the Civilian Conservation Corps (CCC), and successfully demanded "She She She" camps as well as CCC camps. At the suggestion of her great friend Lorena Hickok, Eleanor held press conferences for women journalists only, and she lobbied for women's right to work with dignity and for equal wages. As early as 1934, she spoke out against lynching and school segregation. With new allies, including the great black educator Mary McLeod Bethune and Walter White, president of the National Association for the Advancement of Colored People, as well as several white radicals, notably Aubrey Williams, Virginia Foster Durr, and Lucy Randolph Mason, Eleanor Roosevelt championed an end to discrimination in New Deal agencies and programs, elimination of the poll tax, and racial justice. She helped create the

Eleanor Roosevelt in June 1911 in Hyde Park, New York, with her children (left to right) James, Elliott, and Anna. FRANKLIN DELANO ROOSEVELT LIBRARY

Southern Conference on Human Welfare (1938–1948), and championed unionism for all workers, including farm workers. She also became associated with the Southern Tenant Farmers' Union, and in 1936, when her *My Day* column was launched, she joined the Newspaper Guild, an affiliate of the Committee for Industrial Organization (later the Congress of Industrial Organizations, or CIO).

Eleanor and Franklin Roosevelt did not have a traditional, correct, or conventionally happy marriage, but it was one of Washington's most notably successful marriages. Together, they did more than either could have done alone. The first lady served her husband's interests and was his primary ambassador to neighborhood people, and to poor and hardworking and hidden communities in the mountains and deltas of the United States. Eleanor brought people who could not vote and, until the

Eleanor Roosevelt (right) and Nancy Cook nail a National Recovery Administration poster on a door at Roosevelt's Val-Kill home in 1933. AP/WIDE WORLD PHOTOS

New Deal, did not count, into the mainstream of American life.

Eleanor Roosevelt remains the only first lady to use her pen to disagree with her husband. In 1938 she wrote an entire book, *This Troubled World,* to illustrate alternatives to her husband's undistinguished international policies. Regarding housing and the creation of model communities, she made vital decisions and helped engineer policy. A particularly successful adventure was the building of Arthurdale in Preston County, West Virginia. On model communities and an end to suffering and homelessness, she worked closely with Will Alexander, head of the Resettlement Administration,

which presided over the fifty-seven New Deal communities. She also relied on her longtime friends and allies Clarence Pickett, head of the American Friends Service Committee (AFSC), and Senator Robert Wagner, architect of America's affordable housing efforts.

UNITED NATIONS DELEGATE

By 1939 the domestic New Deal was eclipsed by the needs of World War II. During the war, Eleanor continued her work for democracy, racial justice, and women's rights, and she traveled the globe on behalf of her husband's diplomatic needs. Franklin Roosevelt died before the war ended, on April 12,

Eleanor Roosevelt visits a WPA construction site in Des Moines, Iowa, in June 1936. FRANKLIN DELANO ROOSEVELT LIBRARY

1945, and the first lady announced to a group of journalists who sought to interview her: "The story is over." But for Eleanor Roosevelt a new story was about to begin. President Harry S. Truman appointed her to attend the United Nations' first general assembly in London in December 1945.

That declaration gave Eleanor an opportunity to fight for her vision of the future from an official position of leadership for over six years. She considered her appointment a great victory for women and a great opportunity. She wanted the United States to take the lead in a campaign for planetary decency and peace; to extend the best of Franklin Roosevelt's New Deal vision to the needs of the world. Her colleagues on the U.S. team included adversaries who initially resented her presence and generally opposed her views. But Eleanor took her

own advice: "If you have to compromise, be sure to compromise UP!" With hard work, a relentless schedule, and good advice from allies and State Department officials who kept her well briefed, Eleanor Roosevelt became an earnest, informed diplomat who usually achieved her goals against political conservatives within her own delegation and the disparate visions of a world that had shifted from world war to Cold War.

Eleanor's greatest victories involved Committee Three, the social, humanitarian, and cultural committee, where she was especially concerned about the plight of refugees and which quickly expanded to include all issues relating to human rights, fundamental freedoms, social progress, and world development. Eleanor's vigor at the first meetings impressed even U.S. delegate John Foster

Eleanor Roosevelt votes in Hyde Park, New York, in November 1936. FRANKLIN DELANO ROOSEVELT LIBRARY

Dulles, who had been appalled, he told her, by her appointment, but now acknowledged that her "work had been fine." Eleanor wrote in her diary: "So—against odds, the women move forward. . . ."

Eleanor left London optimistic. After all the disagreements were aired, "we still are a group of 51 nations working together." She was particularly pleased that the United Nations would be located in the United States because she felt that Americans had seen so little of the costs of war, the dislocation and human disasters, and she believed they needed to realize "that peace requires as much attention as war." Furthermore, public support for the United Nations was imperative because Eleanor felt that

the federation was "the last and best hope for our civilization."

As chair of the Human Rights Commission from 1946 to 1952, Eleanor Roosevelt's most significant diplomacy involved the passage of the Universal Declaration of Human Rights on December 10, 1948. Consisting of a preamble and thirty articles, the declaration was to serve as "a common standard of achievement for all peoples and all nations," and a yardstick to measure decency and human dignity, fundamental freedoms, and economic and social rights. At first, Truman instructed Eleanor to limit the principles to civil and political rights, and to ignore the Soviet-initiated social and economic rights. She refused and offered to resign: "You can not talk civil rights to people who are hungry." Moreover, Franklin Roosevelt's New Deal had promised freedom from want as well as freedom from fear. Truman acquiesced, and Eleanor agreed to divide the declaration and negotiate two enabling covenants.

The Universal Declaration of Human Rights was a compromise; every word was an agony of disagreement. The vote was forty-eight in favor, two absent, and eight abstentions, including Russia and its allies, Saudi Arabia, and South Africa. Eleanor Roosevelt understood that the declaration was a "first step," and she believed the United States would shortly ratify the binding covenants. But Roosevelt submitted her resignation in 1952 when Dwight David Eisenhower was elected president, and John Foster Dulles, who became Eisenhower's secretary of state, wanted nothing binding. In April 1953, Dulles told the Senate that the U.S. State Department no longer cared even to ratify the civil and political covenant. The matter did not come up again until President Jimmy Carter signed the covenant in 1977. Finally, at the Cold War's end in 1992, President George H. W. Bush called upon the Senate to ratify the covenant, which it did by acclamation. While most of the 191 member nations of the United Nations have ratified both covenants, the United States has still not brought up for discussion the Economic and Social covenant. With her work undone, Eleanor left the United Nations and joined the American Association for the United Nations, later called the United Nations Association, an activist lobby group she had founded in 1943 to bring United Nations issues to the public. From 1953 until her death, she traveled the United States and the world with messages of peace and human rights.

Eleanor Roosevelt was convinced that on the day the atomic bomb was dropped a new world situation had been created: "a world in which we had to learn to live in friendship with our neighbors of every race and creed and color, or face the fact that we might be wiped off the face of the earth." In *Tomorrow Is Now*, her last book, published posthumously in 1963, she wrote of America's responsibilities for the future, and its difficulties. She concluded that the United States needed to resurrect with conviction and daring the good American

word *liberal*, "which derives from the word *free*. . . . We must cherish and honor the word *free* or it will cease to apply to us."

By the beginning of the twenty-first century the domestic New Deal, from housing to jobs to Social Security, has been largely deboned. Every issue of Eleanor Roosevelt's struggle for decency and dignity for all Americans is once again on the national agenda. Internationally, peace and human rights are on the global agenda with ever more urgency and heartbreak. For hope, the American people have Eleanor Roosevelt's legacy of activist democracy—a timeless source of inspiration and faith in the global community.

See Also: RESETTLEMENT ADMINISTRATION (RA); ROOSEVELT, FRANKLIN D.; SOUTHERN CONFERENCE ON HUMAN WELFARE (SCHW); SOUTHERN TENANT FARMERS' UNION (STFU); WORLD COURT.

BIBLIOGRAPHY

Asbell, Bernard. *Mother and Daughter: The Letters of Eleanor and Anna Roosevelt.* 1988.

Beasley, Maurine H. *Eleanor Roosevelt and the Media.* 1987.

Beasley, Maurine H., et al., eds. *The Eleanor Roosevelt Encyclopedia.* 2001.

Black, Allida M. *Casting Her Own Shadow: Eleanor Roosevelt and the Shaping of Post-War Liberalism.* 1996.

Black, Allida M. ed. *Courage in a Dangerous World: The Political Writings of Eleanor Roosevelt.* 1999.

Black, Allida M. ed. *What I Hope to Leave Behind: The Essential Essays of Eleanor Roosevelt.* 1995.

Burns, James MacGregor, and Susan Dunn. *The Three Roosevelts.* 2001.

Cook, Blanche Wiesen. *Eleanor Roosevelt: 1884–1933.* 1992.

Cook, Blanche Wiesen. *Eleanor Roosevelt: Volume 2, The Defining Years.* 1999.

Cook, Blanche Wiesen. "Eleanor Roosevelt and Human Rights," In *Women and American Foreign Policy,* edited by Edward Crapol. 1987.

Flemion, Jess, and Colleen O'Connor, eds. *Eleanor Roosevelt: An American Journey.* 1987.

Glendon, Mary Ann. *A World Made New: Eleanor Roosevelt and the Universal Declaration of Human Rights.* 2001.

Goodwin, Doris Kearns. *No Ordinary Time.* 1994.

Hareven, Tamara K. *Eleanor Roosevelt: An American Conscience.* 1968.

Hickok, Lorena A. *Eleanor Roosevelt: Reluctant First Lady.* 1980.

Hoff-Wilson, Joan, and Marjorie Lightman, eds. *Without Precedent: The Life and Career of Eleanor Roosevelt.* 1984.

Lash, Joseph. *Eleanor and Franklin: The Story of their Relationship Based on Eleanor Roosevelt's Private Papers.* 1971.

Neal, Steve, ed. *Eleanor and Harry: The Correspondence of Eleanor Roosevelt and Harry S. Truman.* 2002.

Roosevelt, Eleanor. *This I Remember.* 1949.

Roosevelt, Eleanor. *This Is My Story.* 1937.

Roosevelt, Eleanor. *On My Own.* 1958.

BLANCHE WIESEN COOK

ROOSEVELT, FRANKLIN D.

Franklin Delano Roosevelt was born on January 30, 1882, in Hyde Park, New York. He was the only child of James and Sara (Delano) Roosevelt. Franklin had a half brother, James Roosevelt, Jr., nicknamed Rosy, whose mother was the first wife of James Roosevelt, Sr. Sara Delano was 26 years old when she married the 52-year-old widower. Of Dutch ancestry, James Roosevelt, Sr., was a wealthy landowner in Hyde Park, a small town along the Hudson River north of New York City. Roosevelt was a Harvard-educated lawyer who served as vice president of the Delaware and Hudson Railroad. He had been a Whig, but after the collapse of the Whig Party due to the slavery issue, he became a Democrat.

James Roosevelt's loyalty to the Democratic Party was weakened by his economic conservatism and his family ties to Theodore Roosevelt, a Republican and his distant cousin from Long Island. In the presidential election of 1896, James Roosevelt was a so-called Gold Democrat who voted for the victorious Republican presidential nominee, William McKinley. Roosevelt was repelled by William Jennings Bryan, the Democratic presidential nominee. He perceived Bryan as a rabble rouser and economic radical who threatened the gold standard. Roosevelt again voted for McKinley in 1900 when the president chose Theodore Roosevelt as his running mate. James Roosevelt died one month after the 1900 presidential election.

EARLY LIFE AND CAREER

As a boy tutored at home in Hyde Park and then as a prep school student at the Groton School in Massachusetts, Franklin Roosevelt demonstrated little interest in reading or learning about history and politics. He first expressed an interest in politics while eagerly following the career of Theodore Roosevelt as his cousin rapidly progressed from combat heroism in the Spanish-American War to the presidency. Nonetheless, Franklin Roosevelt's famous surname did not gain popularity and status for him among his classmates and teachers at the Groton School and Harvard University. Widely regarded by his peers and teachers as amiable yet superficial, Roosevelt did not distinguish himself in academics, athletics, student government, or social clubs.

Eleanor Roosevelt. Franklin Roosevelt's wife, (Anna) Eleanor Roosevelt, was another major influence in the development of his social conscience and political career. She was his distant cousin and the favorite niece of Theodore Roosevelt. She and Franklin were married in 1905. Her uncle, while president, gave away the bride. After completing one year of studies at Columbia University's law school, Franklin Roosevelt worked for a Wall Street law firm. He was often assigned minor clerical duties and soon became bored and frustrated with the practice of law.

During their courtship, Eleanor Roosevelt had volunteered in settlement houses in New York City. She showed her future husband the wretched living conditions of immigrants and their children. More so than Franklin, Eleanor earnestly and zealously identified with the ideals of the Progressive movement and its efforts to abolish child labor, improve public health and education, reduce poverty, and grant suffrage to women.

New York politics. As Roosevelt pondered his political future, it was still not clear if he would enter politics as a progressive Republican or a progressive Democrat. According to biographer Geoffrey C. Ward, Franklin Roosevelt decided to enter politics as a Democrat because Theodore Roosevelt had several sons who were expected to enter politics as Republicans. Also, since Franklin Roosevelt's home

Franklin D. Roosevelt greets a farmer while en route to Warm Springs, Georgia, during his campaign for the presidency in October 1932. FRANKLIN DELANO ROOSEVELT LIBRARY

county, Dutchess County, was heavily Republican, local Democratic politicians were often desperate to recruit patrician candidates who could finance their own campaigns and attract Republican votes.

Roosevelt was offered such an opportunity in 1910 when John E. Mack, the Democratic district attorney of Poughkeepsie, visited Roosevelt's law office and asked him to run for a seat from Dutchess County in the state senate. Roosevelt eagerly accepted the offer. In his campaign, Roosevelt asserted his political independence, especially by denouncing the machine politics and corruption of Tammany Hall and dissociating it from the progressive wing of New York's Democratic Party. Attract-

ing the votes of Democrats, concentrated in Poughkeepsie, as well as progressive Republicans and mostly Republican friends and neighbors in Hyde Park and other small towns, Roosevelt won the election. He also benefited from the national Democratic sweep of the 1910 midterm elections.

During his one term in the New York state senate, Roosevelt was disliked and dismissed by most Democrats in the state legislature, especially those from New York City. They perceived him as a political lightweight and a publicity-hungry dilettante, and they resented his self-righteous denunciations of Tammany Hall. Like progressives in both parties, Roosevelt supported the adoption of primaries to

Young Franklin Roosevelt in Hyde Park, New York, in 1889. FRANKLIN DELANO ROOSEVELT LIBRARY

determine party nominations and the direct election of U.S. senators.

The Wilson administration. Franklin Roosevelt first met Woodrow Wilson in November 1911 after Wilson had served less than a year as governor of New Jersey. Roosevelt was impressed by Wilson's intellect, ethics, inspiring rhetoric, and ability to break up the Democratic machine of Jim Smith and achieve progressive reforms in New Jersey. The young state senator now had a new mentor for his political career and ambition to distinguish himself as a progressive Democrat. Roosevelt subsequently supported Wilson's presidential nomination at the 1912 Democratic national convention. Tammany Hall Democrats backed Speaker of the House Champ Clark of Missouri for president. After Wilson became president, he rewarded Roosevelt's loyalty—which had continued through the general election despite the entry into the race of Theodore

Roosevelt as the candidate of the newly created Progressive Party—by appointing him assistant secretary of the navy.

To Roosevelt's dismay, Wilson continued to provide patronage to Democratic machines, including Tammany Hall. Until the American entry into World War I, Roosevelt had little control over the distribution of his department's patronage and contracts in New York. But he gained greater political influence in New York during the American war effort as he oversaw defense contracts and navy shipyards and bases there. Meanwhile, Louis Howe, a former newspaper reporter and close aide to Roosevelt, arranged for Roosevelt's control over post office patronage in upstate New York.

Roosevelt also used his position as assistant secretary of the navy to conduct a widely publicized inspection tour of war-torn Europe. He sought a political reconciliation with Tammany Hall, but he

Franklin Roosevelt (standing, center) with classmates in Groton, Massachusetts, in 1899. FRANKLIN DELANO ROOSEVELT LIBRARY

Franklin D. Roosevelt with Eleanor in Hyde Park, New York, in March 1905. FRANKLIN DELANO ROOSEVELT LIBRARY

politely declined its offer to nominate him for governor in 1918. Roosevelt wanted to remain in the Wilson administration and took a greater interest in foreign policy, especially in Wilson's effort to gain a leading role for the United States in the League of Nations after the war ended.

ROOSEVELT AND THE 1920s

With his service in the New York state legislature and as assistant secretary of the navy, Franklin Roosevelt's career had closely paralleled that of Theodore Roosevelt. Likewise, just as his Republican cousin accepted the Republican vice presidential nomination in 1900, Franklin Roosevelt readily accepted the Democratic vice presidential nomination in 1920. He had no illusions that James Cox, the Democratic presidential nominee, could win the election. Inflation, growing public disillusionment about American participation in World War I, and the unpopularity of the ailing Wilson and the

League of Nations indicated a Republican landslide in the 1920 elections. Instead, Roosevelt valued his vice presidential candidacy as an opportunity to meet Democratic politicians throughout the nation. He also earned their respect for his willingness to serve as the running mate in a doomed presidential campaign and to defend Wilson's unpopular position on the League of Nations.

Until he was elected governor of New York in 1928, Roosevelt remained a private citizen. Despite being stricken with infantile paralysis, commonly known as polio, in 1921, Roosevelt energetically tried to make the Democratic Party, both nationally and in New York, a more thoroughly progressive or liberal party that would provide voters with a clear, attractive alternative to the Republican Party in public policy and ideology. He persuaded Eleanor Roosevelt to join the women's division of the Democratic state committee and improve the participation of women in the New York Democratic Party, especially in upstate areas. Roosevelt also tried to reduce the divisive impact of the prohibition issue within the New York and national Democratic parties. After Calvin Coolidge's landslide election in 1924, Roosevelt noticed that Robert La Follette, the National Progressive Party's nominee for president, performed unusually well for a minor party candidate during the apparently prosperous, Republican-dominated era. La Follette's economic platform was similar to that of Theodore Roosevelt's 1912 "Bull Moose" platform. It was especially appealing to economically distressed farmers, miners, and factory workers. Nationally, La Follette received 16 percent of the popular votes compared to the 29 percent received by John Davis, the obscure, conservative Democratic nominee for president. In some states and congressional districts, La Follette ran ahead of Davis.

Roosevelt attributed La Follette's relatively impressive performance and Davis's comparatively poor showing to the ideological and programmatic fact that La Follette offered economically distressed voters an attractive alternative to the Republican Party's pro-big business, anti-labor, high tariff policies, while the Democratic Party did not. He was now convinced that the Democratic Party must become a distinctly liberal party in order to emerge as

President Roosevelt (second from right) and his advisors visit a farmer in Mandan, North Dakota, in 1936. The farmer was a recipient of a federal drought relief grant. LIBRARY OF CONGRESS, PRINTS & PHOTOGRAPHS DIVISION, FSA/OWI COLLECTION

the new majority in the two-party system and win future presidential elections and majorities in Congress. Meanwhile, Roosevelt wanted his party to avoid the divisive social issues, such as racial segregation, the Ku Klux Klan, Catholicism, and prohibition that plagued it at the 1924 and 1928 Democratic national conventions.

After New York governor Al Smith became the 1928 Democratic nominee for president, he asked Roosevelt to run for governor. Roosevelt reluctantly accepted Smith's offer, and was narrowly elected governor in an upset victory, while Smith lost the presidential election by a wide margin and failed to carry his home state. Even before the Great Depression began in late 1929, Roosevelt ambitiously pursued policies intended to serve as a harbinger of what he might do in the future if elected president. In order to make the New York Democratic Party and his governorship more attractive to mostly Republican, rural, upstate voters, he advocated state-sponsored, low-cost hydroelectric power for rural areas, farm-to-market paved roads and highways, property tax relief for farmers, and unemployment insurance. He communicated directly to New Yorkers through radio broadcasts as a way to circumvent the mostly Republican-owned newspapers.

PRESIDENTIAL AMBITION

Because the state legislature was controlled by Republicans, most of Roosevelt's legislation was either defeated or heavily compromised and diluted. Nevertheless, as Roosevelt prepared for his gubernatorial re-election campaign, he had succeeded in projecting the image of an effective, dynamic, innovative leader who addressed the immediate economic concerns of Depression-plagued New Yorkers, both urban and rural, agricultural and industrial, Catholic and Protestant, Republican and Democrat. Before the Great Depression began, Roosevelt had planned on running for president in 1936. But as the Great Depression worsened and President Herbert Hoover seemed unlikely to be re-elected, Roosevelt decided to run in 1932. With the help of political aides Louis Howe, Edward Flynn, and James Farley, Roosevelt wanted to be re-elected in 1930 by such an overwhelming margin, especially in staunchly Republican rural areas, that his victory would impress and persuade major Democratic politicians, especially those from the South and West, to commit their delegates to him before the 1932 Democratic national convention began its proceedings in Chicago.

Roosevelt was re-elected governor in 1930 with 62 percent of the popular votes. More significantly, the governor carried forty-one of the fifty-seven counties outside of New York City and received a plurality of more than 167,000 votes in mostly Republican upstate counties. Using these electoral statistics and Roosevelt's popular policy agenda, Farley and Flynn traveled throughout the United States promoting Roosevelt's presidential candida-

cy to powerful Democrats, such as Tom Pendergast, the machine boss of Kansas City, and Huey Long, a Louisiana senator and the virtual dictator of that state. Farley and Flynn generally avoided urban Catholic Democratic machine politicians from the Northeast and Midwest. They assumed that most Catholic Democrats would unite behind Al Smith, who was Roman Catholic, for the presidential nomination and understood that Roosevelt had alienated Catholic machine politicians since the governor had initiated a highly publicized investigation of Tammany Hall, the courts, and the police department of New York City.

After he had become afflicted with polio, Roosevelt regularly traveled to Warm Springs, Georgia, to soothe and refresh himself in its mineral waters. As he became more personally and politically familiar with the South during the 1920s and early 1930s, Roosevelt began to study and propose policy solutions to economic problems that were either peculiar to or especially severe in the South. He recognized the need for greater federal intervention in such policy areas as cotton growing, rural electrification, soil conservation, highway construction, and irrigation and flood control projects in order for the South to modernize and develop its economy. Unlike Smith, Roosevelt agreed with southern Democrats on the need to reduce tariffs significantly and revise the federal tax code in order to stimulate this chronically depressed region.

With overwhelming support from southern delegates and fairly solid backing from western delegates, Roosevelt won the 1932 Democratic presidential nomination on the fourth ballot. The Democratic national platform and Roosevelt's campaign speeches were ideologically and programmatically confusing and contradictory. The Democrats criticized Hoover and the Republican Party for excessive federal spending and regulations and a bloated federal bureaucracy that threatened states' rights and private enterprise. But they also promised more vigorous federal intervention to end the Great Depression, permanently reform the economy, reduce tariffs, balance the federal budget, and benefit farmers, laborers, business, and consumers. The Democrats also tried to appease both defenders and opponents of prohibition by promising to repeal national prohibition while giving states broad discretion to ban or regulate alcohol.

Roosevelt's only clear, consistent campaign proposal for economic recovery and reform was expressed in his Commonwealth Club address in San Francisco. In this speech, Roosevelt emphasized the need for government, business, labor, and agriculture to engage in economic cooperation and planning. He especially underscored the need for business to assume social responsibility for developing a more just, humane economic system.

Despite being paralyzed below his waist, Roosevelt energetically campaigned throughout the nation while Hoover rarely left the White House. Although there were more Republican than Democratic voters in 1932, Roosevelt won 57 percent of the popular votes and carried all but six states in the electoral college. His party also won large majorities in both houses of Congress. In his 1933 inaugural address, Roosevelt claimed that the underlying cause of the Great Depression was an unjust, irrational, ineffectively regulated economic system with a maldistribution of wealth. He also used biblical allusions to denounce the greed, callousness, and irresponsibility of big business. In the conclusion of this speech, the new president asked Congress to grant him "broad Executive power to wage a war against the emergency, as great as the power that would be given to me if we were in fact invaded by a foreign foe."

THE GREAT DEPRESSION AND THE NEW DEAL

Roosevelt frankly admitted that he had no clear, consistent economic philosophy or program to end the Great Depression because the nation had never previously experienced such a severe, complex, prolonged economic crisis. He sought to inspire the public's confidence about economic recovery, however, by asserting that he would boldly experiment with a variety of ideas and policies, and discard those that failed. Such tentative incrementalism was inevitable, though, since Roosevelt's top economic advisers and administration officials disagreed on how to analyze and eventually end the Great Depression. Raymond Moley, a leading member of Roosevelt's so-called Brains Trust, ad-

vocated a planned economy through cooperation between government and business. Negotiated yet government-enforced codes for prices, wages, working conditions, and agricultural and industrial production would stabilize and then improve the economy. They would also achieve social and economic reforms, such as minimum wages, maximum hours, the abolition of child labor, and legal rights for labor unions. Other administration officials, such as economist Robert Nathan, wanted to emphasize deficit spending on public works jobs and relief for the unemployed in order to increase mass consumption. Secretary of State Cordell Hull and Secretary of the Treasury Henry Morgenthau respectively wanted to concentrate on international trade agreements and monetary policy to stimulate the economy.

When Roosevelt and his speech writers first used the term *New Deal*, a reference from Mark Twain's 1889 novel *A Connecticut Yankee in King Arthur's Court*, during the 1932 campaign, they hoped to evoke favorable comparisons to Theodore Roosevelt's Square Deal and Woodrow Wilson's New Freedom progressivism. During Roosevelt's "First Hundred Days" as president, though, the most innovative of the administration's legislation that Congress passed mostly reflected the economic planning and cooperation of the Brains Trust. Distinct from the more conventional relief and public works programs, such as the Federal Emergency Relief Administration (FERA) and the Civil Works Administration (CWA), that Congress quickly passed, the National Recovery Administration (NRA) and the Agricultural Adjustment Administration (AAA) were the programmatic and intellectual foundation of the first New Deal's emphasis on federally enforced controls on prices, wages, trading practices, and production. In 1935 and 1936, the Republican-dominated Supreme Court struck down the NRA and AAA, the essence of the first New Deal.

Partially because of these Supreme Court decisions, the second New Deal emerged by the middle of 1935. The adoption of the National Labor Relations Act (or Wagner Act), the Social Security Act, and the Works Progress Administration (WPA) in 1935 signified the beginning of the second New

Deal. The second New Deal emphasized more "pump priming" to reduce poverty and unemployment and increase mass consumption through programs like the WPA, while adding new social welfare benefits, such as retirement pensions and unemployment insurance. It also pursued a more antagonistic approach to big business, major banks, and stock brokers through a more vigorous use of antitrust powers and a broader distribution of income and the tax burden through the Wealth Tax Act of 1935, although the latter accomplished little.

Roosevelt's pursuit of the second New Deal was also politically motivated by his desire to disperse and co-opt various economic protest movements and critics from the left and assure his own re-election in 1936 and the transformation of the Democratic Party as the new, enduring majority party in American politics and government. Politically, the Wealth Tax and the Social Security Act's pensions, unemployment insurance, and aid to dependent children were intended to reduce the political appeal of Huey Long and Francis Townsend, respectively. Townsend advocated federal retirement pensions for all elderly Americans, while Long's "Share Our Wealth" movement sought to heavily tax the wealthy and big business in order to redistribute income equitably and end poverty.

Likewise, Roosevelt eventually yet reluctantly signed the Wagner Act of 1935 in preparation for the 1936 election. John L. Lewis, president of the United Mine Workers (UMW) labor union, was a Republican who endorsed Hoover in 1932, but the Wagner Act and other New Deal measures led him to endorse Roosevelt for re-election. The UMW and other unions of the Committee for Industrial Organization (later the Congress of Industrial Organizations, CIO) were major sources of campaign funds, services, and votes for Roosevelt's campaign.

The 1936 presidential election. Despite a *Literary Digest* poll that projected Republican presidential nominee Alfred Landon's victory in the 1936 election, Roosevelt's re-election was assured by the summer of 1936. In addition to the electoral college votes of all southern and border states, Roosevelt could rely on the industrial states of the Northeast and Midwest, where the Democratic Party's voter appeal had rapidly grown since 1932. In the 1936

presidential election, Roosevelt received 61 percent of the popular votes and carried all but two states in the electoral college. Roosevelt's coattail effects increased the Democratic majorities in Congress to overwhelming ratios against the Republicans.

For the first time since 1856, most voters were now registered as Democrats. A realignment in the two-party system had occurred so that the Democratic Party dominated the voting behavior, presidential elections, control of Congress, and policymaking for the next generation. The Roosevelt-led Democratic Party's voter appeal proved to be especially strong in major cities throughout the nation. Catholics, Jews, blacks, labor union members, foreign-born Americans, and young adults provided Roosevelt with the highest percentages of votes. Southern whites, regardless of economic differences among them, were as monolithically loyal to Roosevelt in 1936 as they had been in 1932. Roosevelt, though, proved to be a less attractive candidate among non-southern, rural, white Protestants. Their voting behavior became even more Republican in the 1940 and 1944 elections.

Court-packing controversy. Roosevelt was confident that the 1936 election results gave him a mandate to continue and even extend the second New Deal into such policy areas as public housing, slum clearance, and executive reorganization. He also wanted Congress to pass labor and agricultural legislation similar to the National Industrial Recovery Act and the Agricultural Adjustment Act, which the Supreme Court had rejected. Consequently, Roosevelt submitted a court reorganization bill in early 1937. Its content included a provision that empowered the president and Senate to appoint additional justices to the Supreme Court, exceeding the traditional number of nine. Opponents of this bill soon denounced it as a "court-packing" plan that threatened the separation of powers and the political independence of the Supreme Court, and proved that Roosevelt was dangerously power hungry.

A bipartisan conservative coalition of southern Democrats and Republicans in Congress, especially in the Senate, soon formed to oppose this bill. In addition, the Supreme Court seemed to voluntarily develop a pro-New Deal majority in 1937 when it upheld the Wagner Act and the Social Security Act.

With little congressional or public support for his original legislation, Roosevelt reluctantly signed a weakened, heavily compromised court bill.

Despite this major legislative defeat and the invigoration of anti-New Deal forces in Congress, Roosevelt succeeded in securing passage of the Fair Labor Standards Act of 1938 and a second Agricultural Adjustment Act. After 1938, however, no new major New Deal legislation was passed. The New Deal and Roosevelt's presidency did not end the Great Depression and return the American economy to the prosperity of the 1920s. They succeeded, though, in reducing unemployment, poverty, and homelessness, and in reforming the economy in order to ensure a broader distribution of income, legal rights for labor unions, a more stable business cycle through federal regulations and subsidies, and a social safety net for the poor, unemployed, and elderly.

With Republicans and conservative Democrats frequently reminding the president and the public of his 1932 campaign promise to balance the federal budget, Roosevelt decided to begin reducing federal spending in 1937. His budget cuts, however, partially contributed to the recession of 1937 to 1938, which was characterized by higher unemployment, lower farm prices, and weaker stock market performance. Republicans labeled it the "Roosevelt recession" and cited it as proof of the failure of the New Deal as they prepared for the 1938 midterm elections. The Republicans gained eighty-two House seats and eight Senate seats in 1938. These Republican victories strengthened and emboldened the anti-New Deal, bipartisan, conservative coalition in congress, especially in the House committee system.

WORLD WAR II

In 1939, Roosevelt's attention turned from domestic to foreign policy. He signed all four major pieces of neutrality legislation that Congress sent him from 1935 to 1939. He relied on amendments to these laws and executive orders to provide the president with the discretion to determine such matters as whether a foreign nation was a belligerent and the imposition of trade sanctions on belligerents. Before the Japanese bombing of Pearl Har-

bor on December 7, 1941, Roosevelt recognized the degree to which Congress and public opinion were isolationist. Consequently, his public rhetoric cautiously combined denunciations of German, Japanese, and Italian aggression with assurances that the United States would maintain its neutrality after World War II began in Europe in 1939. Meanwhile, Roosevelt persuaded Congress to increase defense spending and pass the Selective Service Act of 1940, which began military conscription.

The growing prospect of American entry into World War II dominated the 1940 presidential election. This issue soon overshadowed Roosevelt's tradition-breaking decision to accept nomination for a third term. Determined to defeat Roosevelt, the Republicans nominated Wendell Willkie, a Wall Street lawyer and former Democrat, for president. Privately supportive of Roosevelt's military aid to Great Britain, Willkie vacillated in his campaign rhetoric between cautious internationalism and staunch isolationism.

Roosevelt defeated Willkie with 55 percent of the popular votes and carried thirty-eight states in the electoral college. Compared to the 1936 election, Roosevelt's electoral base had narrowed. Non-southern white Protestants, especially in the Midwest, accelerated their return to the Republican Party. Among the non-southern states that he carried, Roosevelt depended more on lower income voters in major cities for his popular vote margins.

Roosevelt preferred to avoid antagonizing southern Democrats on racial issues, but he began to take a modest, cautious step toward identifying his presidency, New Deal liberalism, and the Democratic Party with civil rights for blacks. During his first two terms as president, Roosevelt had limited his policy response to African Americans to minor patronage appointments, public works jobs, and relief. In 1941, however, he issued an executive order creating the Fair Employment Practices Commission, which investigated and prohibited job discrimination by defense contractors. Black labor leader A. Philip Randolph pressured Roosevelt into doing this by planning a march on Washington. Nonetheless, Roosevelt continued racial segregation in the military.

The 1944 presidential election. As the 1944 presidential election approached, Roosevelt's candidacy for a fourth term was less controversial than his 1940 candidacy. Roosevelt did little campaigning, and he defeated his Republican opponent, Governor Thomas E. Dewey of New York, with 53 percent of the popular votes and carried thirty-six states. Although Roosevelt carried all of the southern and border states, Dewey, as a moderately liberal northeastern Republican, performed relatively well in such border and southern states as Kentucky, Missouri, Tennessee, and North Carolina. More so than in the three previous presidential elections, Roosevelt relied on lower-income voters in the largest non-southern cities for his popular vote margins. The proportion of Roosevelt's plurality that was derived from the nation's twelve largest cities increased from 25 percent in 1932 to 65 percent in 1944.

With Roosevelt aging, ailing, and frail, many political insiders did not expect him to complete a fourth term. Democratic machine bosses, Democratic National Committee chairman Robert E. Hannegan, and several southern Democrats persuaded Roosevelt to replace Vice President Henry A. Wallace with Senator Harry S. Truman of Missouri as his running mate in 1944. Wallace was unpopular among these Democrats for his political ineptitude, outspoken liberalism on civil rights, and status as a former Republican. Truman was a loyal New Deal liberal on domestic issues, making him acceptable to labor unions, blacks, and big city mayors. He was also respected by southern Democrats and Republicans in the Senate for his competence, integrity, and bipartisan approach as the chairman of a Senate committee that investigated defense spending. Since the 1942 midterm elections resulted in a razor-thin Democratic majority in the Senate, Roosevelt realized that he needed a vice president like Truman to facilitate the Senate's passage of treaties and other postwar legislation.

ROOSEVELT'S PERSONALITY AND LEGACY

Throughout his life, Roosevelt exuded a charming, effervescent, engaging personality. His critics and political opponents often dismissed these traits as evidence of superficiality or duplicity. People who met Roosevelt individually or collectively often found him to be amiable and gregarious. His family and closest political associates, however, perceived him to be an intensely private, self-contained man who avoiding confiding in them. His wife and children often regarded him as remote and emotionally uninvolved in their lives.

Roosevelt, though, enjoyed flirtatious, bantering relationships with attractive, witty, self-assured women. Eleanor Roosevelt discovered evidence of her husband's affair with Lucy Mercer, her social secretary, during his tenure as assistant secretary of the navy. Although he promised to end this relationship, Roosevelt was with Lucy when he died. Marguerite "Missy" LeHand, Roosevelt's personal secretary, was widely rumored to be his mistress during his presidency. Thus, even before his presidency, Franklin and Eleanor Roosevelt's relationship resembled a political partnership rather than a conventional marriage.

Despite Franklin Roosevelt's shortcomings as a husband and parent, he was immensely effective in projecting his most positive, attractive personality traits in his radio broadcasts. For millions of Americans, Roosevelt exuded an infectious self-confidence and reassuring leadership during the grimmest days and events of the Great Depression and World War II. His affliction with polio enabled him to more genuinely express sensitivity and empathy to suffering Americans during these crises. In short, Roosevelt's skills as a communicator through radio and newsreels, combined with the connection that his own affliction gave him with less fortunate people, induced many Americans to develop a personal bond with Roosevelt, unlike any previous president.

Roosevelt died after serving less than three months of his fourth term on April 12, 1945, in Warm Springs, Georgia. During and after the 1944 presidential campaign, Roosevelt rarely conferred with Truman, so his vice president felt overwhelmed and unprepared in assuming the presidency. As Truman's presidency ensued, it became evident that the modern presidency that Roosevelt had established was not a temporary phenomenon that was a product of Roosevelt's unique combination of political skills and values or the successive crises of the Great Depression and World War II. Even with the end of World War II and the beginning of rapid economic growth, many Americans expected the president to behave in a Rooseveltian style as an articulate media figure who could influence public opinion and motivate Congress to pass legislation that improved their quality of life in such diverse policy areas as health care, education, inflation control, employment, economic development, and the public infrastructure. Roosevelt's wartime example as commander-in-chief and chief diplomat provided both a role model and high expectations for future presidents to be respected, powerful world leaders adept at forming American-led international coalitions through United Nations' decisions, treaties, and collective security organizations for the purposes of deterring or repelling antidemocratic aggression and spreading the American values of human rights, democratic government, and capitalism.

Much of the unattained policy agenda of New Deal liberalism and Roosevelt's presidency, such as health care for the poor and elderly, urban renewal, federal aid at all levels of education, civil rights protection for blacks and other minorities, and environmental and consumer protection, became the major domestic policy goals of Roosevelt's Democratic, and to some extent, his Republican, successors in the presidency, as well as most Democrats and some Republicans in Congress. Likewise, opponents and critics of Roosevelt's policies and his conduct as president devoted much time and effort after his death to stop the further advance of New Deal-based liberalism in domestic policy and to counter what they regarded as the "imperial presidency" that began with Franklin D. Roosevelt.

See Also: DEMOCRATIC PARTY; NEW DEAL; NEW DEAL, SECOND; NEW DEAL, THIRD; ROOSEVELT, ELEANOR.

BIBLIOGRAPHY

Burns, James MacGregor. *Roosevelt: The Lion and the Fox.* 1956.

Leuchtenburg, William E. *Franklin D. Roosevelt and the New Deal, 1932–1940.* 1963.

Maney, Patrick J. *The Roosevelt Presence: A Biography of Franklin Delano Roosevelt.* 1992.

McElvaine, Robert S. *Franklin Delano Roosevelt.* 2002.

Savage, Sean J. *Roosevelt: The Party Leader.* 1991.

Schlesinger, Arthur M., Jr. *Age of Roosevelt,* Vol. 3: *The Politics of Upheaval.* 1960.

Ward, Geoffrey C. *A First-Class Temperament.* 1989.

SEAN J. SAVAGE

ROSENMAN, SAMUEL I. *See* BRAIN(S) TRUST.

ROTHSTEIN, ARTHUR

Arthur Rothstein (July 17, 1915–November 11, 1985), a Farm Security Administration (FSA) photographer from 1935 to 1940, was born in New York City. Rothstein became interested in photography while in high school, and he pursued the medium as an undergraduate at Columbia University in New York City, where he was a student of Roy Stryker. In the summer of 1935 Stryker hired Rothstein to work in the Historical Section of the Resettlement Administration (RA). Rothstein continued with the agency after it became the Farm Security Administration in 1937. He left in 1940 to take a position with *Look.* During World War II, Rothstein worked for the Office of War Information, the Signal Corps, and the United Nations Relief and Rehabilitation Administration. With the end of the war, he returned to *Look,* remaining with the magazine until it ceased publication in 1971. The next year he went to work for *Parade,* where he held a position until his death.

The first photographer hired at the RA and the youngest member of Stryker's staff, Rothstein's initial duties were to set up the agency's lab. Lacking professional photographic experience, he was soon inspired by images taken by Walker Evans and Dorothea Lange, and he quickly gained confidence and technical expertise. Rothstein was sent on his first field assignment in October 1935, when he photographed rural farmers in the Blue Ridge Mountain region of Virginia. His two most famous series were executed the following spring. While in Cimarron County, Oklahoma, in April 1936 he shot

Arthur Rothstein on assignment for the Farm Security Administration in Pennsylvania in 1938. LIBRARY OF CONGRESS, PRINTS & PHOTOGRAPHS DIVISION, FSA/OWI COLLECTION

Fleeing a Dust Storm, an emblematic Dust Bowl image of a farmer and his two sons scurrying for cover in a bleak landscape.

More controversial was the work he did in May in the Badlands of Pennington County, South Dakota, when he used a sun-bleached steer's skull he had found in the parched riverbed as a moveable prop in several pictures. His purpose had been to create an image that would graphically convey to viewers the severity of the drought conditions. But anti-New Deal critics thought that in altering the scene, he had compromised his vantage as an objective documentary photographer in order to distort actual conditions for the political ends of the Washington politicians who employed him. Those opposed to Roosevelt's programs made charges of photographic fakery that generated a firestorm of criticism for the agency and administration.

In practice, many of the leading FSA photographers manipulated their scenes by posing their subjects, moving and removing objects, and using artificial light sources, or in the case of Pare Lorentz's film, *The Plow that Broke the Plains* (1936), even hiring actors. Lorentz, a skilled filmmaker and director, exerted a strong influence on Rothstein. As artists, both carefully thought out their work, and apparent spontaneity could be staged. Nevertheless, Rothstein regarded his images less as works of art than as instruments of social change.

Rothstein traveled widely for the FSA, passing through nearly every state and producing more than nine thousand images for the agency. These remain in the FSA/OWI collection of the Library of Congress. His career as a photojournalist spanned fifty years, and in addition to his studio work, he taught at the Columbia School of Journalism

(1961–1971) and published a series of books on photojournalism and documentary photography.

See Also: FARM SECURITY ADMINISTRATION (FSA); PHOTOGRAPHY; RESETTLEMENT ADMINISTRATION (RA).

BIBLIOGRAPHY

Curtis, James. "Flight from Reality: Arthur Rothstein and the Dust Bowl." In *Mind's Eye, Mind's Truth: FSA Photography Considered.* 1989.

Curtis, James. "Race, Realism, and the Documentation of the Rural Home during America's Great Depression." In *The American Home: Material Culture, Domestic Space, and Family Life,* edited by Eleanor McD. Thompson. 1998.

Dixon, Penelope. "Arthur Rothstein." In *Photographers of the Farm Security Administration: An Annotated Bibliography, 1930–1980.* 1983.

Fleischhauer, Carl, and Beverly W. Brannan, eds. "Tenant Farmers" and "FSA Migratory Labor Camp." In *Documenting America, 1935–1943.* 1988.

"Interview: Arthur Rothstein Talks with Richard Doud." *Archives of American Art Journal* 17 (1977): 19–23.

Rothstein, Arthur. *The Depression Years.* 1978.

BETSY FAHLMAN

ROUTE 66

Two of the myths most associated with the United States and the American way of life are westward expansion (the eternal frontier) and the open highway. Both these myths helped to turn Route 66 into a legend.

By 1910, there were around 180,000 registered automobiles in the United States. The decade from 1910 to 1920 saw that number increase to around seventeen million. The rising automobile culture in the United States was clear to see, and automobiles need good roads. The idea of Route 66 can be traced back to two entrepreneurs, Cyrus Avery and John Woodruff, who sometime in the early 1900s conceived the idea of a single continuous road linking Chicago and Los Angeles.

Congress enacted a bill in 1916 to create public highways. More comprehensive legislation that was passed in 1925 approved the construction of a road from Chicago to Los Angeles and designated it U.S. Highway 66. The new highway was to run approximately 2,400 miles and was to follow a meandering course in order to connect as many rural communities as possible. It was to be a modern all-weather road. The lanes were to be noticeably wider and the road less curvy than was standard at the time.

Even before paving was fully completed, Route 66 was widely used, mainly by truckers, who were taking advantage of the road's shortening of the distance between the Midwest and the West Coast, and by farmers, who were seeking a broader market for their goods and took advantage of how the road connected many disparate rural communities.

The onset of the Great Depression changed many things for Route 66. Before then its construction had mainly been a state responsibility, but during the Great Depression the massive public works projects of the New Deal included work on Route 66. Paving of the Route was completed in 1938, and the economic impact of the project was huge. In addition, the Route's use changed during the Depression. John Steinbeck's harrowing 1939 novel *The Grapes of Wrath* dramatized the real life predicaments of the approximately 210,000 people who traveled along Route 66 to escape the despair of the Dust Bowl. Most did not reach California, and most of those who did eventually returned, but Steinbeck's novel was based on fact, and his christening of Route 66 as the "mother road" continues to resonate. The escape from the Dust Bowl dovetailed nicely with America's emerging love affair with the open road and with the nation's frontier mythology.

As the Depression waned, Americans retained their romantic views of Route 66. The road spawned popular songs and a television series, and came to be associated more with pleasure and adventure than with escape. A kind of automobile culture sprang up along the Route, including motels, diners, and automobile repair shops.

As the Interstate Highway system was developed, Route 66 slowly fell into disuse. Eventually, it lost its designation, and its component stretches of highway were taken over by the various states it passed through. The road nevertheless retains a strong place in the American popular imagination.

See Also: DUST BOWL; *GRAPES OF WRATH, THE;* MIGRATION; OKIES.

BIBLIOGRAPHY

Cook, Sylvia Jenkins. *From Tobacco Road to Route 66: The Southern Poor White in Fiction.* 1976.

National Historic Route 66 Federation. Homepage at: www.national66.com

Route 66, the Mother Road: America's Most Famous Highway. Available at: www.hhjm.com/66/index.htm

Route 66 Patrol: Law Enforcement on the Mother Road. Available at: www.route66patrol.com/home2.htm

STEVEN KOCZAK

RPAA. *See* REGIONAL PLANNING ASSOCIATION OF AMERICA.

RUML, BEARDSLEY

Beardsley Ruml (November 5, 1894–April 18, 1960) was an important New Deal economic advisor on taxation issues. He was born in Cedar Rapids, Iowa, to a physician and a hospital superintendent, both Czech immigrants. Ruml graduated from Dartmouth College in New Hampshire in 1915 and received a Ph.D. in applied psychology from the University of Chicago in 1917 for work on mental testing. Ruml, along with other leading psychologists, participated in government mental testing for soldiers during World War I.

At an early age, Ruml demonstrated his supreme skills at mediating between the world of ideas and the nation's practical problems. Throughout the 1920s, Ruml served as the first and only director of the newly created Laura Spelman Rockefeller Memorial Fund. In that capacity, he was in touch with and offered substantial funding to other leading liberal social scientists. From 1931 to 1934, Ruml served as dean of the division of social sciences at the University of Chicago, an important center of social reform. In 1934, he accepted a job as treasurer of R. H. Macy and Company, the famous New York department store noted for offering the lowest prices possible. An acquaintance remarked that Ruml was trading ideas for notions, but as it turned out, he used his position in corporate America to play a formative role in crafting a liberal business response to the New Deal. He remained at Macy's for fifteen years, becoming chairman of the board in 1945. Dependent on consumer spending, that firm supported New Deal measures intended to increase mass income. On behalf of Macy's and other large retailers, Ruml drafted a report in support of federal unemployment insurance and social security pensions.

Within the New Deal, Ruml served as a leading voice favoring the use of deficit spending to bring about recovery. In 1937, President Roosevelt appointed him director of the New York Federal Reserve and he served as chairman from 1941 until 1946. Ruml joined Laughlin Currie, Aubrey Williams, and Harold Ickes in recommending the resumption of government spending in 1938 to end the "Roosevelt Recession." Ruml's major contribution came with his crafting of the idea of pay-as-you-go taxation during World War II as a way both to greatly expand the amount of revenue the government collected and to ease payment burdens, especially for those in military service, by spreading payments throughout the year. The Roosevelt administration implemented that withholding system in 1943 with the introduction of a mass tax that dramatically increased the number of taxpayers. To sell this mass tax, Ruml successfully advocated forgiving much of the previous year's taxes. As a member of the Committee of Economic Development in the postwar period, Ruml remained an advocate for the use of moderate Keynesian fiscal policies to stabilize the postwar economy.

See Also: FEDERAL RESERVE SYSTEM; KEYNESIAN ECONOMICS; TAXATION.

BIBLIOGRAPHY

Bulmer, Martin. "Philanthropy and Social Science in the 1920s: Beardsley Ruml and the Laura Spelman Rockefeller Memorial, 1922–29." *Minerva* 19 (1981): 347–407.

Collins, Robert M. *The Business Response to Keynes, 1929–1964.* 1981.

Stein, Herbert. *The Fiscal Revolution in America.* 1969.

MEG JACOBS

RUMSEY, MARY HARRIMAN

Mary Harriman Rumsey (November 17, 1881–December 18, 1934) was a reformer who believed in cooperation rather than competition as a vehicle for social and economic enterprise. Active in many civic, social, and philanthropic organizations, she co-founded the Junior League, a voluntary social service organization for debutantes, and during the Great Depression she served as chair of the Consumers' Advisory Board of the National Recovery Administration (NRA).

Born into a wealthy New York family (her father was railroad tycoon E. H. Harriman and her siblings included U.S. statesman W. Averell Harriman), Rumsey was expected to live a conventional privileged life. Instead, inspired by the work of settlement house reformers such as Jane Addams and the efforts of the College Settlement Association, Rumsey, her friend Nathalie Henderson Swan, and several other debutantes founded the Junior League for the Promotion of Settlement Movements in New York (later the Junior League) in 1901. Among the group's early members was Eleanor Roosevelt. Rumsey chaired the League until 1905, the year she graduated from Barnard College.

After her father's death in 1909, Rumsey helped manage the Harriman estate and promoted agricultural and livestock cooperatives. In 1910 she married sculptor Charles Cary Rumsey. The marriage, which resulted in three children, lasted until her husband's death in an auto accident in 1922.

In 1928 Rumsey and her brother, Averell, abandoned their family's Republican politics to support the Democratic presidential candidate Al Smith. The siblings also supported Franklin Roosevelt in 1932, although of the two, Mary Rumsey was closer to the Roosevelts and initially more involved with the New Deal. After Roosevelt's election, Rumsey became chair of the Consumers' Advisory Board of the NRA, which lobbied for consumers' interests when the agency's industrial fair practices codes were established. Rumsey also lobbied on behalf of consumers with the National Emergency Council, a coordinating group for New Deal agencies.

Although she lacked bureaucratic experience, Rumsey was influential because of her skill at working with academics and her strong ties with other New Dealers, and she was often mentioned as a possible candidate for a cabinet level position as secretary of consumer affairs. Her most significant achievement, however, may have been convincing Averell to take an administrative post with the NRA, thus beginning his long career in politics and public service.

An avid sportswoman, cattle breeder, and art patron, Rumsey's career ended abruptly when she died in 1934 from injuries suffered when she fell from a horse while fox hunting in Virginia. Her Washington funeral drew many prominent New Dealers, including her old friend, Eleanor Roosevelt.

See Also: NATIONAL RECOVERY ADMINISTRATION (NRA).

BIBLIOGRAPHY

Abramson, Rudy. *Spanning the Century: The Life of Averell Harriman, 1891–1986.* 1992.

Beasley, Maurine H.; Holly C. Shulman; and Henry R. Beasley; eds. *The Eleanor Roosevelt Encyclopedia.* 2001.

Cook, Blanche Wiesen. *Eleanor Roosevelt,* Vol. 1: *1884–1933.* 1992.

Cook, Blanche Wisen. *Eleanor Roosevelt,* Vol. 2: *1933–1938.* 1999.

MARY JO BINKER

RURAL ELECTRIFICATION ADMINISTRATION (REA)

By the end of World War I people recognized electricity as an important factor in the quality of life. Large and small cities and many towns were elec-

REA workers string transmission line in the Tennessee Valley region during the 1930s. Franklin Delano Roosevelt Library

An REA employee checks transformers at the REA cooperative headquarters in Hayti, Missouri, in 1942. LIBRARY OF CONGRESS, PRINTS & PHOTOGRAPHS DIVISION, FSA/OWI COLLECTION

trified at both the industrial and consumer level. Factories, homes, and recreational buildings had electric lights, appliances, indoor bathrooms, and other modern conveniences that depended on the availability of electricity. During the next decade the use of electricity would grow to such an extent that the 1920s came to be known as the "Electrical Age." American culture, the quality of health and education, and industrial productivity improved in urban areas because of the application of electrical energy. One exception, however, to this general development existed in the United States: Rural America did not have electrical service. In 1920 approximately half of the country's population lived on farms and unincorporated areas, which meant that

they did not enjoy the benefits of radio, lighting, refrigeration, and modern sanitation, all of which operated on electricity. By 1935 the situation had only improved slightly, with 10 percent of the rural inhabitants of the United States having electrical service in their homes and on their farms. The movement for public power, or the generation and sale of electrical energy by government means, emerged as a national issue during the period between the two world wars partly because of the national outcry for rural electrification.

During the 1920s the privately owned electrical companies recognized the importance of serving the countryside and created the Committee on the Relation of Electricity to Agriculture (CREA). This organization, an arm of the electrical industry, undertook research and educational programs to promote the use of electricity in country homes. Only limited progress occurred: The CREA touted its program at Red Wing, Minnesota, as an example of its efforts, but a more significant attempt came through the Alabama Power Company in Birmingham. A few power companies around the nation made a small effort to build distribution lines along rural highways and roads but made little progress in getting service to the inhabitants there, as demonstrated by the overwhelming lack of rural service in the United States by the mid 1930s. Cost was the drawback; farmers could not afford the rates to use enough electricity to warrant the construction of lines to them. An endless cycle of high costs and low usage for farmers and no profits for the power companies prevented a breakthrough. In 1935 President Franklin D. Roosevelt stated that he discovered the lack of electricity in rural America in 1923 when he first visited Warm Springs, Georgia, to bathe and swim in the soothing waters there to alleviate the pain of his polio. The demand for government action grew, so that by the early 1930s some states, such as North Carolina and South Carolina, attempted to start public rural electric programs on their own. For lack of funding and the inability to overcome the complex technical and distribution barriers of extending service to rural inhabitants, the few state efforts at the time made no progress either. Only a strong and well-organized and funded program could meet the challenge, and by the early 1930s public power proponents and the rural citizens of the United States looked to the federal government for help.

One of the commitments of Roosevelt's presidency was the development of public power, and the creation of the Tennessee Valley Authority (TVA) in December 1933 was the first example of such action. Soon after commencing operations, the TVA organized a farmer-owned rural electric cooperative to serve the area around Tupelo, Mississippi, on an experimental basis. There had always been doubts about the ability of farmers to organize and operate an electric cooperative, so through this experiment public power advocates in the Roosevelt administration sought an answer. To their delight, the cooperative progressed and suc-

ceeded well, greatly encouraging Morris L. Cooke, Roosevelt's chief advisor on public power, to push for the creation of a special agency dedicated solely to rural electrification. Using funds available from the Emergency Relief Appropriations Act, the president in 1935 created by executive order the Rural Electrification Administration (REA) and named Cooke as the administrator. Cooke had to develop a means by which REA funds could be used to build the electrical network for distributing electricity through rural areas. After some experimentation, he accepted the cooperative as the best method, partly because of the efforts of the American Farm Bureau Federation. Progress was too slow, however, to suit farmers and rural homeowners, and in 1936 Senator George Norris and Representative Sam Rayburn introduced legislation to make the REA a permanent agency with statutory authority. The legislation gave preference to public agencies in obtaining funds, but it did not exclude private power companies from using the funds.

After the Act passed in 1936, the REA got underway with a construction program relying mostly on farmer-owned cooperatives along the line of the TVA experiment in Mississippi. Rural families waited eagerly for the lines to reach their homes, and as electricity became available, they first bought small appliances such as irons and radios. Refrigerators and indoor bathrooms with running water typically came later, and many of the recipients of REA service regarded the agency as one of the New Deal's greatest achievements.

For the first time, the privately owned power companies showed an interest in the rural market. Some of them began "skimming the cream," meaning they built distribution lines into the most lucrative areas of local markets, thereby leaving the REA with the high-risk customers. Bitter court fights broke out between the REA and local power companies, and the differences were not entirely resolved until after World War II. During the war, however, REA construction slowed considerably, but in 1944 Congress passed the Pace Act that set the REA rate of interest on loans to cooperatives at two percent. With this advantage and the postwar boom in the United States, the REA began a massive construction program. So popular was the REA that Congress during some years after the war appropriated more funds than the agency requested. By 1955 the portion of farms and rural homes in the United States with electricity reached 90 percent. Rural electrification had been achieved.

Electrical service brought profound, and often unrecognized, changes in country living. Health vastly improved with indoor bathrooms. A sharp decline occurred in infant mortality and deaths of children under two years of age from infectious diseases dropped. In the South hookworm became a relic of the past with the disappearance of the outdoor "privy." The quality of diets and subsequent health benefits improved with the availability of refrigeration for storage of food. Country schools enjoyed modern lighting and heat, and teachers noted an improvement in the atmosphere of their rooms and performance of the students. Home life became more attractive as families joined their urban cousins in listening to their favorite radio shows, and women enjoyed the conveniences of electrical appliances and running water in their kitchens. The REA must be considered the instrument that brought rural America out of the preindustrial age.

See Also: PUBLIC POWER; TENNESSEE VALLEY AUTHORITY (TVA).

BIBLIOGRAPHY
Brigham, Jay. *Empowering the West: Electrical Politics before FDR.* 1998.

Brown, D. Clayton. *Electricity for Rural America: The Fight for the REA.* 1980.

Brown, D. Clayton. "Modernizing Rural Life: South Carolina's Push for Rural Electrification," *South Carolina Historical Magazine* 99 (1998): 66–85.

Fleming, Keith R. *Power at Cost: Ontario Hydro and Rural Electrification, 1911–1958.* 1992.

Kline, Ronald R. *Consumers in the Country: Technology and Social Change in Rural America.* 2000.

D. CLAYTON BROWN

RURAL LIFE

Rural Americans experienced much hardship and suffering during the Depression, but rural life also underwent changes. Farm prices had started dropping in the mid 1920s and only fell further when the crash of 1929 occurred. Low prices brought many foreclosures, insufficient tax revenues for schools, and depressed business in small towns. Like nearly all Americans, rural inhabitants had to make sacrifices and forego plans for the future. The plight of country folk went beyond low incomes, however, because their lifestyles had not kept pace with the more modern standard of living in the cities. Rural homes and farms generally had no running water, indoor bathrooms, electric lights, radios, or telephones. Small landowners, commonly known as "dirt farmers," and those farmers at the bottom of the social ladder, tenants and sharecroppers, lived under some of the most staggering conditions of poverty in the United States. In the most extreme cases, particularly in the Cotton Belt, it was not uncommon to find malnourished children and adults living in small houses or shacks with dirt floors and no window screens or coverings. By contrast, large and mid-level landowners often had nice homes with attractive features. A great deal of variation was evident in rural life, with large landowners and small business owners at the top of the social ladder, while a large number of small farmers and tenants lived in miserable conditions at the bottom.

Rural life during the Depression continued to differ from urban living. Farm families shared the common experience of working together for their livelihood. They shared the tasks, for example, of producing foodstuffs from gardens and orchards, or of tending livestock and poultry. Children had daily chores that gave them a place in the family hierarchy and made them participants in the family struggle for a livelihood. Boys cut firewood for the stove, drew water for the kitchen, and worked alongside their fathers in the fields. Girls helped their mothers in preparing meals, canning fruits and vegetables, tending gardens, and caring for younger siblings. Rural families were more self-sustaining and their lives required team effort compared with urban families, which often, though not always, depended on a sole breadwinner.

Rural education also lagged behind the national norm. The one-room schoolhouse could still be found, but consolidation of schools had moved for-

Although many rural American families abandoned their farms after recurrent crop failures during the 1930s, some, like this family in Bonner county, Idaho, in 1939, continued farming with the help of Farm Security Administration loans. LIBRARY OF CONGRESS, PRINTS & PHOTOGRAPHS DIVISION, FSA/OWI COLLECTION ward so that most of the schools for rural children were located in towns. These schools had fewer teachers and a narrower curriculum than their urban counterparts; many had no or ill-equipped laboratories for teaching science. Libraries in rural schools were nearly always smaller, with less reference material and fewer learning resources. Teachers not uncommonly taught more than one grade in the same room.

Transportation also varied. Automobiles and small trucks were common, but wagons drawn by horses and mules appeared often on roads. Unpaved roads, which turned into muddy quagmires during heavy rains, linked farms and homes with towns. Paved or graveled roads had become more numerous, however, since World War I, so that travel conditions were steadily, if slowly, getting better. Automobiles and roads ended much of the isolation of country life and stimulated the cultural growth of millions of rural inhabitants.

The Depression forced the United States to recognize that small family farms, particularly those engaged in self-sufficient operations, were becoming extinct. Small farmers in the past had managed to maintain homes and raise families with the use of home gardens, small flocks of poultry, and small herds of livestock. Home canning and butchering were common. For cash, farm families produced cotton, tobacco, some grains, and fruits and vegetables, but their cash flow was minimal. With the rising industrialization of the United States, agriculture became more commercialized, and to keep up with the rising standard of living in the United States, farmers needed cash for mechanized equipment, fuel and energy, home furnishings, clothing, the new improvements in medical care, and other features of modern life. No longer would small plots of land yield enough income for the farm family to remain a viable participant in American culture.

The Dust Bowl of the Depression expedited the decline of the small, self-sufficient farm in the southern plains. Forced to leave the land by this catastrophic event, farmers took their families to new lands, particularly the West Coast, or they moved into cities. In their wake they left dilapidated homes and barns, withering small towns, and fur-

Children in rural Alabama attend school in 1935. FRANKLIN DELANO ROOSEVELT LIBRARY

ther erosion of rural life. The infamous drought brought new respect for soil conservation and preventive measures for wind erosion, but the intensive small plot farming of the stricken area never returned. The steady decline of the family farm combined with the hardship of the Depression to produce a sense of unease and concern among rural inhabitants. So many of the values of rural life were falling by the wayside as the new order of industrialization took over. In 1920 the federal census had demonstrated that for the first time a majority of Americans lived in urban areas (defined as 2,500 or more inhabitants). Since then, young people had continued to flock to cities, abandoning the farm life prized by their ancestors. Concern had grown throughout the United States because the nation had always been predominantly rural and agricultural. Now, with the small family farm struggling to survive, small town residents and farmers worried about the future. Just as there was no parity of agricultural prices during the Depression, rural Americans were losing their social and cultural parity with urban America.

Despite these stressful conditions, rural Americans retained their sense of dignity and pride, a feeling of self-worth, and a strong work ethic. Their willingness to sacrifice and deny their own fulfillment were admirable qualities synonymous with the agrarian ideal. In this respect rural life was the embodiment of the American spirit. To watch their way of life change, however, to yield their individualism to the emerging commercialism, meant that rural people had to endure the pain that accompanied this significant period of America's transition to a highly industrialized country.

Toward the end of the Depression in 1941, the economy of the United States showed improvement, but not full recovery. Agricultural prices increased slightly, but were still below parity levels. Rural life began to show stirrings of improvement, however, owing to the impact of federal programs designed and operated to alleviate the substandard conditions on farms. The most effective agency was the Rural Electrification Administration (REA), which went into operation in 1935. It constructed electric transmission lines and enabled rural residents to have access to electrical service. At the end of the Depression in 1941, approximately 30 percent of rural homes and farms had electricity, and rural homeowners responded by installing lights and purchasing small appliances, such as radios and irons. Running water and indoor bathrooms quickly followed. Farmwives began using such kitchen conveniences as refrigerators and electric ranges. General health improved as indicated by drops in infant mortality, disease and illness rates among children, hookworm, and pellagra. Country schools with electric lighting offered a comfortable environment more conducive to learning. Merchants in small towns also took advantage of electrical service by modernizing their shops and making the premises more attractive. Electrification, which remained incomplete at the end of the Depression, brought a sense of renewal to rural life.

Beginning in 1933 the Agricultural Adjustment Administration (AAA) brought some relief to the producers of staple crops: cotton, wheat, corn, rice, tobacco, hogs, and dairy products. But the government price support program, which expanded in 1938 with a new AAA, could not lift farming out of the Depression. Price supports remained, however, and federal assistance became a regular feature of American agriculture.

The Farm Security Administration (FSA) also sought to better rural life. It went into operation in 1937, absorbing the Resettlement Administration.

The FSA had a broad program of rural rehabilitation aimed at small landowners, tenants, and sharecroppers. This agency also operated rural health cooperatives. But the FSA affected only a portion of residents. Migration into cities, which resumed in about 1940 after stalling during the Depression, reduced the surplus population on farms and helped resolve the plight of rural America.

When the United States entered World War II, which ended the Depression, rural life had changed, perhaps more than was apparent. Through its various support programs the federal government had become a new business partner in agriculture and had an impact on nearly every facet of farming. The result was much needed improvement in soil conservation, flood control, and reforestation, but price support was the most important change. Living conditions also improved because of the REA and the limited contribution of the FSA. Coupled with the advances underway in mechanization, particularly the growing use of tractors, rural life continued to modernize and farming became more commercial. More than anything, migration alleviated the plight of people living on small self-sufficient farms or working as tenants and sharecroppers. Such fundamental changes set rural life onto a course of change that lasted through the next generation. It was only appropriate that the U.S. Department of Agriculture entitled its 1940 yearbook, *Farmers in a Changing World.*

See Also: AGRICULTURE; AGRICULTURE ADJUST-
    MENT ADMINISTRATION (AAA); CITIES AND
    SUBURBS; FARM SECURITY ADMINISTRATION
    (FSA); RURAL ELECTRIFICATION
    ADMINISTRATION (REA).

BIBLIOGRAPHY

Brown, D. Clayton. *Electricity for Rural America: The Fight for the REA.* 1980.

Kline, Ronald R. *Consumers in the Country: Technology and Social Change in Rural America.* 2000.

Taylor, Carl C., et al. *Rural Life in the United States.* 1949.

D. CLAYTON BROWN

RYAN, FATHER JOHN A.

John Augustine Ryan (May 25,1869–September 16, 1945) was a Roman Catholic priest and a writer, educator, and social reformer. Reared in Minnesota, Ryan entered Saint Thomas Seminary in 1887 to study for the priesthood for the diocese of Saint Paul. Ordained in 1898, he was awarded his Ph.D. in sacred theology from Catholic University of America in Washington, D.C., in 1906. In his dissertation, *A Living Wage: Its Ethical and Economic Aspects,* Ryan argued that an employer was obligated to pay "a living wage," one sufficient to support a worker and his family in decent and comfortable surroundings. This concept, based on Catholic social teachings, was central to his socioeconomic worldview.

Ryan taught at Saint Thomas Seminary before returning to Catholic University, where, in 1916, he published *Distributive Justice: The Right and Wrong of Our Present Distribution of Wealth,* which elaborated on the obligations of workers and employers in an industrial society. Ryan's ideas concerning economic and social policy in post-World War I America became the basis for the Bishops' Program of Social Reconstruction in 1919. This program called for a legal minimum wage; labor laws to protect women and children; social insurance against old age, sickness, and unemployment; and labor's right to unionize. From 1920 until 1944, Ryan served as director of the social action department of the United States Bishops' National Catholic Welfare Council, a position that allowed him to present Catholic social teachings to a national audience. Catholic periodical publications such as *Commonweal, Catholic World, Catholic Charities Review,* and *Ecclesiastical Review* also provided Ryan with a forum for promoting social justice.

During the Great Depression, Ryan advocated government intervention to relieve economic hardship. Highly critical of Herbert Hoover's cautious policies, Ryan found in Franklin Roosevelt's New Deal—in particular the National Labor Relations Act of 1935 and the Fair Labor Standards Act of 1938—a near embodiment of Catholic social teachings. As a Roosevelt supporter, Ryan earned the nickname "Right Reverend New Dealer" from the Reverend Charles Coughlin, a critic of Roosevelt. During the Roosevelt years, Ryan served as chairman of the advisory council of the United States Employment Service, as a member of the President's Committee on Farm Tenancy, and as a member of the industrial appeals board of the National Recovery Administration. In general, Ryan played a greater role in presenting New Deal policies to his fellow Catholics than in influencing the formation of government policy.

See Also: NEW DEAL; RELIGION.

BIBLIOGRAPHY

Broderick, Francis L. *Right Reverend New Dealer: John A. Ryan.* 1963.

O'Brien, David. *American Catholics and Social Reform: The New Deal Years.* 1968.

Ryan, John A. *Social Doctrine in Action: A Personal History.* 1941.

BENTLEY ANDERSON

SAN FRANCISCO GENERAL STRIKE (1934)

What began as an isolated longshoremen's dispute developed in the spring and summer of 1934 into one of the most sweeping and violent industrial conflicts of the Great Depression. Over the course of eighty-two days, San Francisco's waterfront workers protested their mistreatment by ship owners. Employers organized as well, resulting in a bloody confrontation and a stalemate that brought a polarized San Francisco to standstill.

The roots of the general strike lay in the harsh working lives of San Francisco's longshoremen. Each morning, under what was called the "shape-up," workers lined up at the docks as private contractors chose whom they would employ that day, forcing men to beg for work and pay kickbacks to hiring agents. Represented only by an employer-controlled company union, longshoremen had few alternatives. With the passage of the National Industrial Recovery Act of 1933, and its promise of greater cooperation with unions, however, longshoremen started to organize. Workers formed Local 38-79 of the International Longshoremen's Association (ILA), a conservative union affiliated with the American Federation of Labor (AFL), and issued a set of demands: recognition, a six-hour workday, a thirty-hour workweek, and a pay in-crease. A radical faction of longshoremen led by Australian-born Harry Bridges raised the stakes further by demanding that the shape-up be replaced by a union hiring hall. When ILA officials negotiated an agreement that left out the hiring hall, rank-and-file members of Local 38-79 suspended their president.

Unable to win their broader demands, longshoremen throughout the Pacific Coast region went on strike on May 9, 1934. Workers rallied together in unprecedented solidarity, virtually closing down all West Coast ports. Responding to their members' pleas, the Teamsters and the seamen's unions supported the longshoremen by refusing to service the ports. Despite pressure from union and public officials, San Francisco's longshoremen, now led by Bridges, held firm. Responding in kind, business leaders coordinated their efforts to undermine the strike through the Industrial Association of San Francisco, an alliance of industrial, banking, shipping, railroad, and utility firms that was formed in 1921. The Association, with the help of a public relations firm, launched a campaign alleging that the strike was a Communist plot. Historians have since rejected that claim, though some strike leaders, including Bridges, were either members of or sympathetic to the Communist Party.

The violence between strikers, scabs, and police escalated on July 5, which would be remembered as

"Bloody Thursday." At midday, police and vigilantes fired on strikers who had retreated for a lunch break, killing two. By the day's end, another seventy strikers had been seriously injured. Over the next two weeks, California's governor mobilized the National Guard to restore order while the National Longshoremen's Board, appointed by President Franklin Roosevelt, struggled unsuccessfully to restart negotiations between strikers and employers. On July 16, sixty-three unions of the San Francisco Labor Council commenced a general strike that involved 130,000 workers, shut down the city, and took over basic services, such as the distribution of food. The Industrial Association of San Francisco, the mayor, and a consortium of the city's newspapers reacted with a hyperbolic campaign that depicted the general strike as a Communist insurrection. Although the campaign did not achieve its objective—a military crackdown by Roosevelt—the accusation of treason scared the more cautious labor leaders, who terminated the general strike after only three days. On July 30 the ILA membership overwhelmingly agreed to end their strike and to accept binding arbitration by the National Longshoremen's Board. The Board granted the ILA a collective bargaining agreement, a hiring hall virtually controlled by the union, and a significant pay increase.

The longshoremen and general strikes demonstrated the power and quickness with which ordinary workers could act if pushed too far. The latent radicalism and solidarity of the rank-and-file served as both a warning to employers, who slowly became receptive to mediated settlements, and a promise to aggressive labor leaders, who soon left the conservative AFL and formed the Congress of Industrial Organizations (CIO) to unionize workers across job categories. The strikes also demonstrated the impact of federal labor policy: The National Industrial Recovery Act and the federal labor board were vital to both the instigation and resolution of the conflict. Most of all, the general strike represented the fraying of social bonds that could only get worse if the economic crisis of the Depression continued.

See Also: AMERICAN FEDERATION OF LABOR (AFL); BRIDGES, HARRY; COLLECTIVE BARGAINING; CONGRESS OF INDUSTRIAL ORGANIZATIONS (CIO); INTERNATIONAL LONGSHOREMEN'S ASSOCIATION (ILA); ORGANIZED LABOR; STRIKES.

BIBLIOGRAPHY

Kimeldorf, Howard. *Reds or Rackets? The Making of Radical and Conservative Unions on the Waterfront.* 1988.

Larrowe, Charles P. *Harry Bridges: The Rise and Fall of Radical Labor in the United States.* 1972.

Nelson, Bruce. *Workers on the Waterfront: Seamen, Longshoremen, and Unionism in the 1930s.* 1988.

Selvin, David F. *A Terrible Anger: The 1934 Waterfront and General Strikes in San Francisco.* 1996.

Starr, Kevin. *Endangered Dreams: The Great Depression in California.* 1996.

EDUARDO F. CANEDO

SANGER, MARGARET

In an effort to protect the health of women, Margaret Higgins Sanger (September 14, 1879–September 6, 1966) began the birth control movement in the United States. One of eleven children of a Roman Catholic Irish-American family in Corning, New York, Margaret Higgins blamed her mother's early death on poverty and the rigors of bearing so many children. Determined to escape a similar fate, she enrolled in the White Plains Hospital School of Nursing in 1900. Margaret planned to become a registered nurse but her 1902 marriage to architect William Sanger ended her formal training. She bore two sons and one daughter who died at the age of four. The marriage proved troubled and the couple separated in 1914, finally divorcing in 1921 at a time when such actions were rare. Sanger would embark on a second marriage to wealthy oilman Noah Slee in 1922.

In an argument that she would repeat for the remainder of her life, Sanger maintained that women could not benefit from educational and political advances unless they also had the ability to control their own bodies. In 1914, she coined the term *birth control* in the pages of her magazine, *The Woman Rebel.* Days after opening the first U.S. birth control clinic in Brooklyn in 1916, Sanger was arrested. The subsequent court case gave physicians the right to prescribe contraception to women when medically indicated. The decision provided Sanger with the legal basis for the 1923 establishment of the Birth Control Clinical Research Bureau (later renamed the Margaret Sanger Research Bureau), a contraceptive distribution system of doctor-staffed clinics.

In the 1920s, Sanger joined other intellectuals in supporting eugenics. She challenged conservatives who worried that whites from the better classes would commit race suicide by using contraception. Sanger argued that all women, rich and poor, would limit childbearing if given the option to control their bodies because of the economic and health benefits of smaller families. She voiced support for negative eugenics that would weed out the physically and mentally disabled by mandating contraception but disdained positive eugenics that would promote the growth of the elite class.

Sanger spent most of the Depression trying to secure government funding for birth control as a benevolent social policy and a public health measure. She wheedled money from the rich for her clinics and political efforts by focusing on the impact of the economy on women. One form letter described a woman who, after her husband lost his job, resorted to an illegal abortion rather than raise another hungry child. Along with appealing to the sympathies of the rich, Sanger played on the anxieties of conservative donors over the potential costs of supporting an increasingly dependent population.

In 1932, a packet of contraceptives sent to Sanger by a Japanese physician was confiscated by U.S. Customs. The resulting court case led to a victory in 1936 when the U.S. Court of Appeals in *United States v. One Package of Japanese Pessaries* ruled that physicians were exempted from the ban on the importation of birth control materials. This decision effectively legalized the distribution of birth control for medical use.

With this victory, Sanger began to scale down her efforts. Her lobbying group, the National Committee on Federal Legislation for Birth Control, disbanded in 1937. In its place, Sanger helped estab-lish the Birth Control Federation of America. Deeming "birth control" too radical a concept, the organization changed its name to the Planned Parenthood Federation of America in 1942. Angry about the name change partly as a matter of sentiment but also because the term *family planning* seemed to lack the force and conviction of birth control, Sanger retired to Tucson, Arizona.

After World War II, Sanger resumed a public life. She sought to establish an international birth control movement to help foster economic development and social stability. In 1952, Sanger helped found the International Planned Parenthood Federation. Increasingly frail, she retired to Tucson for the last time in 1959.

See Also: GENDER ROLES AND SEXUAL RELATIONS, IMPACT OF THE GREAT DEPRESSION ON; WOMEN, IMPACT OF THE GREAT DEPRESSION ON.

BIBLIOGRAPHY

Chesler, Ellen. *Woman of Valor: Margaret Sanger and the Birth Control Movement in America.* 1992.

Gray, Madeline. *Margaret Sanger: A Biography of the Champion of Birth Control.* 1979.

Kennedy, David M. *Birth Control in America: The Career of Margaret Sanger.* 1970.

CARYN E. NEUMANN

SCHECHTER POULTRY CORP. V. U.S. See SUPREME COURT.

SCHW. *See* SOUTHERN CONFERENCE FOR HUMAN WELFARE.

SCIENCE AND TECHNOLOGY

Scholars of science and technology increasingly recognize the mutual influence between science and technology. Scientific understanding is often a prerequisite for technological advance. Technology in turn provides important inputs to science, in-

New farming technologies, like this automatic hay-loader in use in Jasper county, Iowa, in 1939, were a boon to farmers, but they also eliminated jobs and displaced farm laborers. LIBRARY OF CONGRESS, PRINTS & PHOTOGRAPHS DIVISION, FSA/OWI COLLECTION

cluding, most obviously, scientific instruments, but also research questions about why certain technologies work or do not work. Sometimes the links between science and technology are temporally close: In the development of nylon, radios, and airplanes, for example, scientific and technological advances were mutually reinforcing. In other cases science answers technological questions that have been around for decades, or science sets the stage for new products and processes that are not yet imagined.

TECHNOLOGY AND THE GREAT DEPRESSION

While economic analyses of the causes of the Great Depression have focused on a handful of aggregate economic variables, such as the money supply, there has always been a minority tradition that has argued that technology was largely respon-

sible for the Great Depression. Two broad types of technological innovation can be distinguished. *Product innovation* involves the development of a new or improved product. *Process innovation* involves the development of lower-cost ways of producing an existing product. The line between these is generally clear, but it can be blurred, as when the same innovation both reduces the cost and increases the quality of a particular product.

The course of technological innovation during the interwar period was highly unusual. In terms of product innovation, the decade between 1925 and 1935 is by far the worst in the entire twentieth century. The electric refrigerator was the only major new product. In terms of process innovation, however, there was rapid growth in worker productivity, due primarily to key technological advances. Worker productivity in industry grew by at least 50 percent in the 1920s and another 25 percent in the 1930s.

The development of new products will generally encourage investment, consumption, and employment. Factories and machines will be constructed to build the new products, and workers hired for this purpose. Consumers in turn will be encouraged to spend a greater proportion of their income in order to obtain the new product—though they may decrease purchases of existing goods that serve similar purposes (as the advent of radio and talking movies during the 1920s served to destroy vaudeville and decrease attendance at live theatre in the 1930s). Process innovation means that fewer workers, buildings, and machines will be needed to produce the same quantity of goods, though some initial investment may be required. Lower prices for existing goods will generally result in lower levels of consumer expenditure. There are exceptions when decreased cost leads to a more than proportional increase in the number of goods purchased.

In the long run, a market economy should be able to adjust to the uneven time path of technological innovation. Many economic models suggest, however, that over a period of a few years product innovation will cause a decrease in unemployment, and process innovation will cause an increase. The unemployment experience of the 1930s was likely exacerbated by market saturation in some of the new consumer durables of the 1920s, notably automobiles, radios, and various appliances: Consumers who had recently bought one did not need another.

CONSEQUENCES OF THE SECOND INDUSTRIAL REVOLUTION

To understand the technological experience of the Great Depression, it is useful to start with the second Industrial Revolution of the late nineteenth century. During the 1870s and 1880s, important innovations occurred in three broad areas: chemicals, internal combustion engines, and the generation, transmission, and use of electricity. With the singular exception of the zipper, all major twentieth century innovations, whether product or process, can be traced to one or more of these developments. All three of these strands of technological innovation

would generate new products in the early 1920s and late 1930s; they would also generate important process technologies that would have their major period of adoption during the interwar period. In each case the new products of the late 1930s were much more complex than those of the early 1920s; this may explain the paucity of new products in the decade after 1925.

The chemical industry developed continuous processing in place of the previous practice of producing one batch of chemicals at a time. This process technology was adopted by most factories producing a homogeneous output, whether paint or ketchup or oil, in the interwar period, and resulted in huge cost savings. In terms of new products, the major development of the early 1920s involved the semi-synthetic fiber rayon. The first fully synthetic fiber, nylon, would appear almost two decades later in 1939. Developments in plastics—including urea-formaldehyde, lucite, and vinyl—vitamins, and antihistamines are among other new products that would emerge in the late 1930s. The discovery of penicillin by Alexander Fleming in 1928 had a limited economic impact until methods for increasing the rate of natural production in mold were developed in 1940, and synthetic penicillin in 1944. These advances set the stage for the development of a range of antibiotics. Better photographic film and cameras would make the camera a mass market good in the 1930s as well.

While invented long before World War I, it was only with the development of the assembly line in Henry Ford's River Rouge plant in 1913 that the automobile became a potential mass market good. Sales would take off in the 1920s, and almost half of American families would own an automobile by 1929. The assembly line would be adapted to virtually every assembled good in the United States during the 1920s. While sales, and thus employment, in the automobile sector increased as a result, in other sectors the assembly line soon led to decreases in employment.

The automobile and truck generated cost savings in the distribution of goods. In particular, small local stores were replaced by larger and lower-cost enterprises. In agriculture, tractor use expanded throughout the interwar period, as costs decreased and quality improved: There were 80,000 tractors in 1918; 920,000 in 1930; and 1,545,000 in 1940. As tractor use and power expanded, a host of farm implements were developed.

The airplane also predated World War I, but it would only become a mass produced good, capable of generating significant economic activity in production and use, in the mid-1930s. The Douglas DC-3 of 1936 was the biggest single advance, causing costs per passenger mile to drop to a quarter of their level in 1929.

The bulk of American industry would switch to electric power in the 1920s. By the end of the 1930s the victory of electricity was almost complete. This switch reflected both the drop in the cost of electricity (by 50 percent in the 1920s alone) due to improvements in generation and transmission, and the development of ever-better electric motors. Electrification allowed great improvements in factory layout because machines powered by their own small motor, rather than connected by belts to an external power source, could be situated as needed. Electrification also made it much easier to run machines at different speeds. Many processes previously performed by hand were mechanized because of electrification.

In the home, the early twentieth century witnessed the electrification of simple goods like lightbulbs, toasters, and kettles. In the interwar period, a second stage of innovation, involving complex electronics, became evident. The technology of radio transmission and reception advanced to the point that the first commercial radio station was established by Westinghouse Corporation in Philadelphia in 1920. By 1929 virtually every American household owned at least one. The next major innovation in wireless communication would be the television. After a host of improvements in the 1920s and 1930s, the first regular broadcasts in the United States began in 1939.

The electric refrigerator only became a mass consumer good in 1931 after a series of improvements over the previous decades. Sales expanded until 1937, at which point half of wired homes possessed a refrigerator. The success of the only major new product innovation of the early 1930s suggests that consumption, investment, and employment

would all have been higher if other new products had emerged.

While productivity advance continued in the 1930s, this required little investment. The major new process innovation of the 1930s was tungsten carbide cutting tools. These cutting tools could generally be fitted to existing machines, but allowed much greater speed and accuracy. There were also improvements in management techniques. The rolling mill for producing sheet metal was one process innovation that did require significant investment. This only became technically superior to labor-intensive methods in 1930; twenty-eight rolling mills were built during the 1930s.

INDUSTRIAL RESEARCH LABORATORIES

Developed by German chemical firms in the late nineteenth century, the industrial research laboratory was adopted in the United States first in electrical products but eventually across a wide range of industries. Although innovations still often came from isolated tinkerers before the interwar period, after that time most new technologies were developed, at least in part, in formal industrial research settings. These laboratories have played an important scientific role. The invention of nylon depended on research by DuPont for a better understanding of the chemical composition of polymers. The airplane depended on advances in aerodynamic theory (in this case financed largely by the military).

The earliest industrial research laboratories, however, shied away from the expense and risk associated with pursuing projects in basic science. They instead tended to focus on process innovation and minor product innovation. The profits earned by companies pioneering such products as television or nylon in the late 1930s would encourage many industrial research laboratories to pursue major product innovation in the postwar years. If this change had occurred earlier, the technological, and thus economic, experience of the Great Depression might have been quite different.

SCIENTIFIC RESEARCH IN UNIVERSITIES

There were concerns during the 1930s that industrial research laboratories were not only absorbing those who might otherwise have been independent inventors, but attracting some of the best scientists away from universities. Yet industrial research laboratories also had a positive impact on university research: They provided direct funding to some researchers and also funded graduate fellowships.

The major source of funding of scientific research in the 1930s, though, was philanthropic foundations. Of these foundations, those tied to the Rockefeller or Carnegie names, and particularly the Rockefeller Foundation, provided some 90 percent of the funding. These foundations had, earlier in the century, tried to develop research facilities independent of universities. As the century unfolded universities came to see research as a key part of their mission. While professors now had the time and incentive to perform research, they also needed direct funding of research expenses. The foundations in the 1920s had provided funding to certain departments at key universities. In the 1930s the foundations moved toward supporting the research of individual professors. Determined to maximize the return on their funding, they insisted on evidence of publications before funding was renewed. This likely encouraged scientific effort, but raised concerns about scientific independence. Funding decisions were based on individual contacts between professors and foundation officers. Total foundation expenditures on research stagnated during the Depression; medical research was emphasized at the expense of basic science, and thus, for example, theoretical physicists seeking funding for particle accelerators spoke to the biological understanding that might result from these.

Governments, especially in the areas of military, health, and agricultural research, provided some limited funding in the 1930s. During World War II, expenditure on research would triple, with governments funding the increase. Postwar government funding of university research would soon eclipse foundation funding; governments would rely on a more bureaucratic process of official grant applications, and review by other experts in the area. Due largely to foundation encouragement the United States had become the most important country in the world of science by 1930; movement

of refugee scientists to the United States would enhance this dominance over the next decade.

Science was not only primarily identified with universities by the 1930s, but also with distinct disciplines such as physics and chemistry. Nevertheless, both foundations and scientists appreciated the value of interdisciplinary interaction. Many of the major scientific discoveries of the Depression era reflect cross-disciplinary communication. While physics loomed large in these conversations, advances in, for example, quantum chemistry, did not just involve the application of quantum theory, but the convergence of quantum theory with theoretical and empirical trends within chemistry itself. Scientific advances during this period also reflected the development of a host of new scientific instruments, such as the particle accelerator, electron microscope, and ultracentrifuge.

The discovery of the neutron in 1932 allowed physicists for the first time to understand the stability of nuclear structure in terms of quantum theory. The positron was also discovered in 1932, and physicists began to enumerate the various forces that operate between different particles. By the end of the decade, scientists in both Germany and the United States had achieved nuclear fission.

Improved instruments for studying distant parts of the universe, in combination with the theory of general relativity, led to widespread consensus among astronomers in the 1930s that the universe was expanding, though there was little consensus on how the process might have begun. At the same time, advances in nuclear physics allowed a theoretical understanding of how stars could generate energy over billions of years.

By understanding the internal working of molecules chemists were better able to predict and control chemical reactions. Polymer science in particular advanced rapidly. Only in the early 1930s had chemists come to accept the existence of large complex polymer molecules. An understanding of the internal working of molecules was also useful in the study of living organisms: Major advances occurred in the analysis of proteins that would set the stage for the postwar discovery of DNA.

The 1930s was also the period of the "modern synthesis" in biology. Theoretical and empirical discoveries in the area of genetics were shown to be consistent with "natural history." That is, the short-term genetic changes observed in the laboratory could be understood as generating the longer-term changes posited by evolutionary theories.

See Also: FORD, HENRY; RADIO.

BIBLIOGRAPHY

Beaudreau, Bernard C. *Mass Production, the Stock Market Crash, and the Great Depression: The Macroeconomics of Electrification.* 1996.

Bernstein, Michael A. *The Great Depression: Delayed Recovery and Economic Change in America, 1929–1939.* 1987.

Brock, William H. *The Norton History of Chemistry.* 1992.

Cross, Gary, and Rick Szostak. *Technology and American Society: A History.* 1995.

Freeman, Christopher, and Francisco Louca. *As Time Goes By: From the Industrial Revolutions to the Information Revolution.* 2001.

Fruton, Joseph S. *Proteins, Enzymes, Genes: The Interplay of Chemistry and Biology.* 1999.

Kohler, Robert E. *Partners in Science: Foundations and Natural Scientists, 1900–1945.* 1991.

Kragh, Helge. *Quantum Generations: A History of Physics in the Twentieth Century.* 1999.

Krige, John, and Dominique Pestre, eds. *Science in the Twentieth Century.* 1997.

North, John. *The Norton History of Astronomy and Cosmology.* 1995.

Nye, Mary Jo, ed. *The Cambridge History of Science,* Vol. 5: *The Modern Physical and Mathematical Sciences.* 2003.

Reich, Leonard S. *The Making of American Industrial Research: Science and Business at GE and Bell, 1876–1926.* 1985.

Schumpeter, Joseph A. *Business Cycles: A Theoretical, Historical, and Statistical Analysis of the Capitalist Process.* 1939.

Szostak, Rick. *Technological Innovation and the Great Depression.* 1995.

RICK SZOSTAK

SCOTTSBORO CASE

On March 25, 1931, nine young African-American men ranging in age from thirteen to twenty-one were arrested near Paint Rock, Alabama, for the alleged rape of two white women on a freight train, and were incarcerated in the town of Scottsboro. From these beginnings, the Scottsboro case would become the most celebrated legal battle of the 1930s and would focus the attention of the nation and the world on racial prejudice in America.

Dubbed the "Scottsboro Boys" by the media, Olen Montgomery, Clarence Norris, Haywood Patterson, Ozie Powell, Willie Roberson, Andy and Roy Wright, Charlie Weems, and Eugene Williams had all grown up in the rural South, and most were riding the rails in search of work. The nature of the defendants' accused crime made it unlikely they would receive a just trial. The charge of raping white women had been traditionally used to justify the lynching of African Americans in the South, with white men being cast in the role of protectors of southern white women. The nine defendants themselves narrowly escaped a lynching at the hands of an angry mob on the day after their arrest.

Subjected to speedy trials with a limited defense, eight of the nine defendants were sentenced to death. After the case was reported in the North, a Communist-led legal organization, the International Labor Defense (ILD), began to work on appeals for the defendants. Beginning in the late 1920s, the Communist Party had taken an increased interest in African-American issues, particularly anti-lynching efforts, and its role in supporting the Scottsboro defendants provided the party credibility within the African-American community. The ILD was soon drawn into conflict with the National Association for the Advancement of Colored People (NAACP), which viewed the ILD's Scottsboro campaign as little more than Communist propaganda aimed at gaining influence among African Americans. NAACP secretary Walter White later claimed that the ILD was looking to make martyrs of the defendants, and the two organizations battled for control of the defense over the next three years.

Along with securing legal counsel for the defendants, the ILD instigated a "mass action" campaign for the release of the defendants. Using extra-legal tactics to mobilize public opinion in favor of the defendants, the ILD's strategy turned the

The nine men accused of rape in what became known as the Scottsboro case in an Alabama prison shortly after their arrest in 1931: (left to right) Clarence Norris, Olen Montgomery, Andy Wright, Willie Roberson, Ozie Powell, Eugene William, Charlie Weems, Roy Wright, and Haywood Patterson. BETTMANN/CORBIS

Scottsboro Case into a cause célèbre of the 1930s. Slogans such as "Save the Scottsboro Boys" and "They Shall Not Die!" were commonly found in Communist meetings and rallies in the 1930s, and Communists across the country signed petitions and held marches in support of the ILD's legal efforts. Internationally, Communists, intellectuals, and human rights advocates in the Soviet Union, Europe, and Latin America attended demonstrations and petitioned American President Herbert Hoover to pardon the Scottsboro prisoners.

The African-American community also supported the ILD's mass action efforts. African Americans were outraged by the verdicts in Scottsboro, which many viewed to be the result of Jim Crow

justice in the South and representative of racial prejudice found throughout the entire nation. African Americans became an increasing part of the ILD's efforts, raising money for legal expenses and participating in demonstrations. African-American ministries and civic organizations allowed the ILD to hold rallies in their facilities, and even the NAACP was forced by community opinion to work with the ILD for a short time in 1933. Mothers of the Scottsboro defendants toured the country and went abroad, imploring crowds to support the ILD's efforts on behalf of their sons. Black celebrities and white celebrities attended fundraisers for the ILD, and the case inspired artists, such as poet Langston Hughes and bluesman Leadbelly, to compose works about the defendants.

While the Scottsboro case made national headlines, the defense team was stymied in its legal attempts to achieve the defendants' freedom. The Supreme Court granted the defendants a new trial due to inadequate counsel, and the ILD retained the services of a noted defense attorney, Samuel Leibowitz, to take up the case. A new trial for Haywood Patterson began on March 27, 1933, in Decatur, Alabama. During the trial, Leibowitz attacked the credibility of the two accusers, Ruby Bates and Victoria Price, by pointing out inconsistencies in their stories and intimating that the women had questionable sexual pasts. Ruby Bates also recanted her charges and testified for the defense, but an all-white jury returned a death sentence. In a surprising turn, Alabama Circuit Court judge James E. Horton set aside the verdict, but Patterson would again be tried and convicted in December of 1933.

On September 30, 1934, two ILD officials were arrested for trying to bribe Victoria Price. This action led Leibowitz to break with the group, and he formed the American Scottsboro Committee (ASC) with the support of African-American clergymen and anti-Communist leaders. Though the defense groups feuded, the Supreme Court overturned the convictions of Norris and Patterson on April 1, 1935, because African Americans had been systematically excluded from the jury rolls in Alabama. With the Communist Party's move to a Popular Front program, the ILD was willing to cooperate with the ASC, NAACP, and the American Civil Liberties Union to create the Scottsboro Defense Committee (SDC) in December 1935. The ILD agreed to limit its mass action campaign in favor of a more traditional legal campaign, and the Scottsboro case slowly lost importance in the Communist Party's agenda. After more legal failures, in July 1937 the SDC agreed to a plea bargain agreement, which released four of the defendants. Patterson escaped from prison in 1948, while the four other prisoners waited for parole. The last defendant was released in 1950, nineteen years after his initial arrest.

Though the Scottsboro defendants had limited success in Alabama courts, the Supreme Court decisions were an important legal legacy of the defense efforts. Perhaps more importantly, the case inspired legions of activists, both white and African

American, to challenge entrenched racial prejudice in America, and provided inspiration for the civil rights activism and mass protest of the 1950s and 1960s.

See Also: COMMUNIST PARTY; INTERNATIONAL LABOR DEFENSE (ILD); NATIONAL ASSOCIATION FOR THE ADVANCEMENT OF COLORED PEOPLE (NAACP); WHITE, WALTER;

BIBLIOGRAPHY

Carter, Dan T. *Scottsboro: A Tragedy of the American South,* 2nd edition. 1984.

Goodman, Barak, director. *Scottsboro: An American Tragedy.* 2000.

Goodman, James. *Stories of Scottsboro.* 1994.

Linder, Douglas O. *Famous American Trials*: "The Scottsboro Boys" Trials, 1931–1937. 1999. Available at: www.law.umkc.edu/faculty/projects/Ftrials/scottsboro/scottsb.htm

Martin, Charles H. "The International Labor Defense and Black America." *Labor History* 26, no. 2 (1985): 165–194.

Scottsboro: An American Tragedy. PBS and WGBH Boston. Available at: www.pbs.org/wgbh/amex/scottsboro/

ROBERT FRANCIS SAXE

SCS. *See* SOIL CONSERVATION SERVICE.

SEABURY, SAMUEL. *See* PROSTITUTION.

SEC. *See* PUBLIC UTILITIES HOLDING COMPANY ACT; SECURITIES REGULATION.

SECTION OF FINE ARTS. *See* POST OFFICE MURALS.

SECURITIES ACT. *See* SECURITIES REGULATION.

SECURITIES AND EXCHANGE COMMISSION (SEC). *See* PUBLIC UTILITIES HOLDING COMPANY ACT; SECURITIES REGULATION.

SECURITIES REGULATION

Appalled by the stock market crash of 1929 and the subsequent economic collapse, the federal government moved assertively during the 1930s to regulate both the issuance and sale of corporate securities. The federal government's traditional laissez-faire policy towards the stock markets had left the states to regulate stock sales through "blue sky" laws, which attempted to protect investors from unscrupulous stock sellers who promised everything, including the blue sky above. But the revelations of fraud and manipulation that followed the market crash revealed the inadequacy of state regulation. New Deal laws would separate commercial and securities banking; require full disclosure of financial information for all stock issues; limit margin purchases of stocks; and create an independent regulatory body, the Securities and Exchange Commission, to oversee stock exchange practices.

Of the fifty billion dollars in stock sold in the United States during the great bull market of the 1920s, the House Commerce Committee estimated that half had been undesirable or worthless. From 1932 to 1934 an intensive investigation by the Senate Banking Committee demonstrated how bankers and brokers had bilked investors and contributed to the financial catastrophe. Under examination by the committee's chief counsel, Ferdinand Pecora, prestigious financiers admitted that their banks' securities houses had unloaded dubious stocks onto unwary investors. The investigation exposed abuses ranging from speculative pools and insider deals to preferential distribution of stock. Generating months of headlines, the Pecora investigation swung public opinion behind efforts to reform and regulate the securities markets.

THE LEGISLATIVE BATTLES

Securities regulation became intertwined with banking reform. The Glass-Steagall Act of 1933 or-dered complete separation of commercial banks from their securities houses and provided federal insurance for bank deposits. In the previous congressional session, the bill sponsored by the two southern Democrats, Virginia Senator Carter Glass and Alabama Representative Henry Steagall, would not have divided banking and securities functions as rigidly, but the populist Senator Huey Long (Democrat-Louisiana) had killed the bill by filibuster. Glass and Steagall reintroduced the measure during the New Deal's "first hundred days" and tightened its provisions in response to the Pecora investigation's dramatic exposure of the abusive relationship between banks and their investment firms. Public opinion helped propel the bill to enactment in June.

Simultaneously, a bill to regulate the issuance of stocks was making its way through Congress. Samuel Untermyer, who had served as chief counsel of the Pujo investigation of the "Money Trust" in 1912, produced a plan by which the U.S. Post Office would supervise stock and bond sales. Former Federal Trade Commission (FTC) chairman Huston Thompson countered with a bill to empower the FTC to revoke the registration of stocks from any company it found to be "in unsound condition or insolvent." Dissatisfied with both approaches, President Franklin D. Roosevelt enlisted Harvard law professor Felix Frankfurter to prepare yet another bill. Frankfurter recruited a trio of young lawyers, James M. Landis, Benjamin V. Cohen, and Thomas G. Corcoran, who became known as Frankfurter's "happy hotdogs." The Frankfurter group reflected Supreme Court Justice Louis Brandeis's opposition to concentrations of economic power in either government or private finance. They considered it unwise to permit the government to judge the soundness of corporations and wrote a bill that instead required companies to publish complete and accurate financial information about their stock to allow investors to judge the risks for themselves. To insure truthfulness, the bill set criminal penalties for fraudulent stock registration. The Senate passed Thompson's bill, while the House adopted the Landis-Cohen-Corcoran version, as sponsored by Representative Sam Rayburn (Democrat-Texas). In conference committee, the House bill prevailed and became the Federal Securities Act of 1933. President Roosevelt appointed James Landis to the Federal Trade Commission, which would administer the new law.

The Pecora investigation and the Roosevelt administration next focused on stock exchange operations. Stock exchanges had operated as private trading grounds for brokers who bought and sold stocks for clients. Richard Whitney, president of the New York Stock Exchange, resisted efforts to oversee his operations. "You gentlemen are making a great mistake," he told Senate investigators. "The Exchange is a perfect institution." Once again several groups vied with conflicting legislative drafts. A task force headed by John Dickinson and composed of Treasury and Commerce department officials and Wall Street attorneys proposed creation of a "Federal Stock Exchange Authority" that would include representation from the stock markets. The authority would regulate the exchanges but would not specifically prohibit such controversial market practices as pools and short selling. Opposed to the Dickinson group, Cohen and Corcoran worked with Pecora's staff to draft a tougher measure that would empower the Federal Reserve Board to set margin requirements for stock purchases, separate broker and trader functions, outlaw all pools and short selling, and require all stock-issuing corporations to file quarterly reports with the FTC. President Roosevelt, although publicly neutral, privately favored the Cohen-Corcoran version, known as the Fletcher-Rayburn bill for its sponsors Senator Duncan Fletcher (Democrat-Florida) and Representative Rayburn.

Richard Whitney personally led the lobbying campaign against the Fletcher-Rayburn bill, warning corporations that the federal government could use the legislation to "dominate and actually control" their businesses. John Dickinson testified that the bill's high margin requirements would encourage widespread stock selling that would have a deflationary effect. Seeking to prevent the Federal Reserve Board from becoming "mixed up with stock market gambling," Senator Carter Glass proposed giving authority to police the stock exchanges to a new Securities and Exchange Commission (SEC). Unlike Dickinson's proposal, Glass made no provision for the stock exchanges to have representation on this independent regulatory commission. The final compromise, rather than specifically outlawing controversial trading practices, assigned the SEC to investigate them and set future policy. President Roosevelt signed the Securities Exchange Act into law on June 6, 1934.

SECURITIES AND EXCHANGE COMMISSION ENFORCEMENT

The SEC consisted of five commissioners appointed by the president and confirmed by the Senate, no more than three of whom could be members of the same political party. Initially, the commissioners chose their chairman (a later revision would give this right to the president). Roosevelt appointed James Landis and Ferdinand Pecora to the SEC, but encouraged them to elect a prominent stock trader, Joseph P. Kennedy, as the first chairman, to help ease Wall Street's fears.

Weighing the magnitude of the vast securities trading business against its small staff and limited budget, the SEC set out to guide and supervise the exchanges rather than to prohibit specific abuses. It demanded that all exchanges, and all corporations that listed their stocks on them, register with the commission. By registering, exchanges agreed to enforce SEC rules and to punish or expel members who violated them. Of the twenty-five exchanges that registered, the SEC shut down four and persuaded others, such as the New York Produce Exchange, to abandon their securities operations. Those that closed included the Boston Curb Exchange, for having listed illegal stocks, and the New York Mining Exchange, known as the "penny stock market," for fleecing the poorest investors.

Joseph Kennedy's resignation from the SEC after a year made James Landis chairman. Like Kennedy, Landis pursued a conciliatory policy that emphasized exchange self-regulation. Landis particularly worried that strict federal regulations would endanger economic diversity by falling harder on the smaller exchanges and driving some brokers out of business. Liberal detractors accused him of fostering self-control *by* Wall Street rather than government control *of* Wall Street. Despite this conciliatory policy, critics on Wall Street blamed the SEC for the market collapse and recession that occurred in 1937. That year, William O. Douglas became SEC chairman and challenged the giant New York Stock Exchange to reorganize or risk having the SEC step in to run the exchange. The exchange's board of governors endorsed the SEC's recommended rules revision, which provided for public representatives on the board and a paid president and technical staff for the exchange. The SEC's public disclosure requirements also brought to light the financial misconduct of former exchange president Richard Whitney, who admitted insolvency, was suspended from trading, and was imprisoned for embezzlement. Whitney's disgrace symbolized the new financial order.

While the SEC could supervise operations that were centralized on the floor of a few stock exchanges, it faced a more daunting problem with the thousands of brokers scattered across the nation, buying and selling stocks for investors. In 1938, Senator Francis Maloney (D. Conn.) sponsored legislation to encourage formation of a private National Association of Securities Dealers to supervise over-the-counter brokers and dealers. The SEC was given authority to review the association's rules, but the association took on the burden of regulation.

New Deal legislation transformed the nation's stock exchanges from private clubs into semipublic institutions with a federal commission to monitor their activities, police against manipulative and deceptive stock selling, and set standards for accounting procedures, in the interest of protecting investors. The SEC became widely acclaimed as one of the most successful experiments in federal regulation. During the latter half of the twentieth century American stock sales and values soared as millions of citizens invested in stocks with some confidence of protection from fraud. Although the SEC withstood the later trend toward deregulation, this enormous shift of personal savings from bank accounts to securities caused banks to protest the Glass-Steagall Act as a "New Deal dinosaur." Banks lobbied successfully for its repeal in 1996, when Congress permitted banks and securities firms to once again enter each other's business, with appropriate regulatory oversight.

See Also: GLASS-STEAGALL ACT OF 1933; KENNEDY, JOSEPH P.; PECORA, FERDINAND.

BIBLIOGRAPHY

Hawley, Ellis W. *The New Deal and the Problem of Monopoly: A Study in Economic Ambivalence.* 1966.

Lash, Joseph P. *Dealers and Dreamers: A New Look at the New Deal.* 1988.

Parrish, Michael E. *Securities Regulation and the New Deal.* 1970.

Pecora, Ferdinand. *Wall Street under Oath: The Story of Our Modern Money Changers.* 1939.

Ritchie, Donald A. *James M. Landis: Dean of the Regulators.* 1980.

Seligman, Joel. *The Transformation of Wall Street: A History of the Securities and Exchange Commission and Modern Corporate Finance.* 1982. Rev. edition, 1995.

DONALD A. RITCHIE

SELZNICK, DAVID O. *See GONE WITH THE WIND.*

SEX AND SEXUALITY. *See* GAYS AND LESBIANS, IMPACT OF THE GREAT DEPRESSION ON; GENDER ROLES AND SEXUAL RELATIONS, IMPACT OF THE GREAT DEPRESSION ON; PROSTITUTION.

SHAHN, BEN

The artist Benjamin Shahn (September 12, 1898–March 14, 1969) was born in Lithuania in the Pale of Settlement, the territory where Russian Jews were legally authorized to take up residence. His father was a furniture maker and craftsman. To escape pogroms (the officially-sanctioned massacres of Jews) the family fled Russia in 1906 and settled in Brooklyn, New York. Much of Shahn's later artistic work retained elements of his Jewish background: windows for a temple in Buffalo, illustrations for a Passover prayer book, a series of watercolors on the Dreyfus affair, the frequent appearance of stylized Hebrew lettering in his painting.

At fifteen, Shahn left school to become apprenticed to a New York City lithographer. In his late

This mural by Ben Shahn, painted as a WPA project and photographed in 1938, adorned the community building in Hightstown, New Jersey. LIBRARY OF CONGRESS, PRINTS & PHOTOGRAPHS DIVISION, FSA/OWI COLLECTION

teens and early twenties, however, he pursued his education doggedly. He went to night school for his high school diploma and attended classes at the Art Students League, New York University, and City College. He also received significant formal and informal education from two extended trips to Europe and North Africa (1924–1925 and 1927–1929).

By the time Shahn returned from Europe and began sharing a New York studio with the distinguished photographer Walker Evans, he was deeply committed to enlisting his artistic talent on behalf of liberal and radical social causes, portraying the travails of the poor and working classes, protesting corruption and injustice. In addition to his Dreyfus series (1930), he produced in 1932 a famous series of twenty-three gouache works depicting the trial and 1927 execution of the anarchists Nicola Sacco and Bartolomeo Vanzetti, and another fifteen works in 1933 illustrating the case of Tom Mooney, the labor leader who was languishing in San Quentin prison after a questionable trial for a 1916 bombing in San Francisco. Shahn's artistic talent and political views brought him to the attention of the Mexican muralist Diego Rivera and the two worked together on the Rockefeller Center mural that was eventually destroyed after Rivera's refusal to remove a portrait of Vladimir I. Lenin. Two subsequent murals by Shahn (one on prohibition, the other on the history of imprisonment) were rejected by New York's Municipal Art Commission.

During the New Deal, Shahn worked on several government projects, principally under the auspices of the Farm Security Administration. His work consisted of murals and thousands of photographs. The murals adorned post offices in the Bronx (1939) and Jamaica, New York (1939), the community center of a resettlement community in New Jersey (1938), and the Social Security Building in Washington, D.C. (1942). Shahn's photographs movingly depicted the poverty of rural life in the South and Midwest. During World War II Shahn undertook projects for the Office of War Information and was also hired by the Congress of Industrial Organizations to produce pro-Roosevelt campaign posters for the 1944 election. His painting during the war, as might have been expected, was filled with condemnation of Nazism and sympathy for its victims.

After the war he continued in various mediums his artistic advocacy of social causes. Shahn also taught at Boston's Museum of Fine Arts and at Harvard University. By the time he died, his work had been widely exhibited, and Shahn had gained numerous honors and an international reputation as a leading social realist and a talented artist who used his considerable and multifaceted skills on behalf of the poor and oppressed.

See Also: ART; POST OFFICE MURALS.

BIBLIOGRAPHY

Chevlowe, Susan. *Common Man, Mythic Vision: The Paintings of Ben Shahn.* 1998.

Greenfield, Howard. *Ben Shahn: An Artist's Life.* 1998.

Pohl, Frances. *Ben Shahn.* 1993.

DAVID W. LEVY

SHARECROPPERS

Sharecropping was the most impoverished level of the tenant farming that characterized cotton and tobacco production in the post-Civil War South. The almost 1.8 million tenant families reported by the 1930 census included about half the region's farmers. Tenants were classified according to their ability to farm and live independently and contribute supplies and equipment for making a crop. Relatively few were cash renters. Approximately 700,000 were share tenants, who might supply their own mules or equipment and who might receive from their landlords two-thirds or three-fourths of the year's profit. But sharecroppers, who lacked equipment, as well as cash or credit for self support, contributed only labor to production and usually received no more than a half share of the crop. In 1937 a special President's Committee on Farm Tenancy reported approximately 775,000 sharecroppers in the South, almost equally divided between whites and blacks.

SHARECROPPING AND SOUTHERN POVERTY

Cotton sharecroppers normally worked about twenty acres, with their tenure on farms at their

A sharecropper plows a sweet-potato field near Laurel, Mississippi, in 1938. LIBRARY OF CONGRESS, PRINTS & PHOTOGRAPHS DIVISION, FSA/OWI COLLECTION

landlords' discretion. To sustain themselves during the crop season, they received subsistence goods on credit. This "furnish" was provided, or arranged, by landlords at usurious interest rates. When landlords sold the crops and settled accounts, they subtracted all costs and interest from the sharecroppers' portions. Because landlords had liens on the crops and kept the books, such settlements left most sharecroppers still in debt, year by year. The system perpetuated intense poverty, along with poverty's related effects: dependence and lack of expectation, low farming skills, poor health, and illiteracy. Tenancy and sharecropping persisted in the South because of the region's dearth of cash and farm credit, its great surplus of unskilled rural workers, and the fact that cotton and tobacco remained hand labor crops before the mid-twentieth century.

SHARECROPPING AND THE AGRICULTURAL ADJUSTMENT ADMINISTRATION

As the agricultural depression bottomed out and rural living conditions became increasingly desperate in the early 1930s, sharecropping came under such economic stress that knowledgeable observers described the system as near collapse. Yet it still dominated newer plantation lands, such as those in eastern Arkansas. It was in that Delta region that sharecropping generated a political storm that embarrassed the New Deal, nearly wrecked the Agricultural Adjustment Administration (AAA), and focused national attention on landless farmers.

The objective of the AAA was to raise crop prices to certain target levels, known as *parity*, by eliminating surplus production. To accomplish this, the AAA offered landowners acreage reduction contracts. Under the first regular cotton contract, covering 1934 and 1935, the secretary of agriculture "rented" about three-eighths of the nation's cotton land from cooperating landowners. These farmers agreed to retire the rented acres from cotton, reserving them for food and feed crops. In return, they received a compensation (at 4.5 cents per pound) for the cotton they normally would have grown on those acres. Moreover, if acreage controls worked as planned, prices for a reduced crop would rise. Drafted by AAA officials closely connected to plantation interests, these favorable provisions gave landowners reliable profits for the first time in more than a decade. Critics charged that the contract was unfair on its face because it required landlords to give sharecroppers only about 11 percent of the benefit, far less than customary crop shares. Even more serious, any requirement to divide the AAA check would give landlords incentives to put sharecroppers off the land (switching to wage labor instead) in order to keep the whole payment for themselves. To prevent massive displacement of sharecroppers, the contract required landlords to retain their normal number of tenants, rent free, and with access to rented acres to grow their own food. But the AAA's legal staff warned that anti-eviction provisions were both vague and unenforceable. Just as they predicted, as soon as the contract went into effect, the AAA was flooded with complaints of cheating and eviction of tenants, especially in eastern Arkansas.

The formation of the Southern Tenant Farmers' Union in the summer of 1934 intensified sharecropper controversies. Centered in the Arkansas Delta and led by local Socialists, this biracial union protested evictions and contract abuses. In turn, it was subjected to violent repression by planters. Early in 1935 the AAA legal section, headed by Jerome Frank, resolved to take action against evictions. They held that retaining the normal number of tenants meant keeping the same individuals for the contract's duration. But AAA administrators insisted the contract gave landlords latitude to remove any tenants. The conflict was irreconcilable. In February 1935 AAA administrator Chester Davis demanded that Secretary of Agriculture Henry Wallace repudiate the legal section's interpretation and dismiss those responsible for it. Agonized by this dispute, but acutely aware of the AAA's constituen-

cy and congressional backing, Wallace allowed Davis to fire Frank and most of his staff. This "AAA purge" confirmed that an agency founded on price parity was politically unable to assure sharecroppers security on the land. As the number of sharecroppers declined steadily through the 1930s, New Deal cotton policy was partly responsible.

THE RESETTLEMENT AND FARM SECURITY ADMINISTRATIONS

The New Deal's most positive efforts against rural poverty were those of the Resettlement Administration (RA), organized in May 1935 under Rexford Tugwell. This eclectic agency pieced together such programs as land classification, relocation of people from submarginal lands, experimental cooperative communities, and planned "greenbelt" suburbs. But its largest component was rural rehabilitation, a program started by the Federal Emergency Relief Administration (FERA) in 1934. Hoping to stabilize poor farmers on the land, get them off relief, and improve their living standards, the FERA gave its clients a combination of credit and farming supervision. By the time it was transferred to the RA, the program had served more than 200,000 tenants, sharecroppers, and poor landowners, mostly in the South. To direct rehabilitation, Tugwell chose Will Alexander, a southern liberal who had led the Commission on Interracial Cooperation. Becoming head of the RA in November 1936, Alexander would make it one of the New Deal's most racially inclusive agencies.

Even before he joined the RA, Alexander and other liberals had developed tenancy legislation. Introduced by Senator John H. Bankhead of Alabama, their ambitious bill proposed a billion-dollar bond issue to finance federal purchase and resale of foreclosed land to supervised tenants on easy terms. Expecting it would help the ablest tenants, Alexander envisioned farm purchase lending as a capstone for the RA's array of programs. But after Senate approval in June 1935, the bill died in committee in the House. Not until July 1937 did Congress pass the Bankhead-Jones Farm Tenant Act, a token measure that ultimately provided only 44,300 loans by 1946. This modest credit program was added to the RA, then renamed the Farm Security Administration (FSA).

Under the leadership of Alexander (until 1940) and C. B. Baldwin (until 1943), the FSA grew into one of the New Deal's largest agencies, and the only one focused on chronic poverty. Many of its activities addressed the conditions of southern tenancy. Between 1935 and 1943 the RA/FSA served almost 400,000 rehabilitation clients in the region. It required these clients to keep farm and home budgets and grow food at home, and it promoted written leases between landlords and tenants. With uneven success the FSA organized some of its clients into innovative cooperatives for the purchase of feed and fertilizer, the marketing of produce, joint ownership of tractors or breeding stock, prepaid health insurance, and veterinary services. Nearly all these antipoverty programs attracted conservative opposition from the start, but as the New Deal waned and war began, the FSA came under heavy fire in Congress. Beginning in 1943, crippling budget cuts curtailed its effectiveness.

The New Deal never had the resources or political support to reach the majority of the poor or to reform southern tenancy. For a time, the RA/FSA alleviated poverty and stabilized some poor farmers on the land. But acreage reduction, the revolution of cotton mechanization beginning in the mid-1930s and accelerating after World War II, and outmigration during and after the war all contributed to the decline of sharecropping. By the last third of the twentieth century sharecropping had become rare in a region where it had once dominated so many lives.

See Also: AGRICULTURAL ADJUSTMENT ADMINISTRATION (AAA); BANKHEAD-JONES FARM TENANCY ACT OF 1937; FARM SECURITY ADMINISTRATION (FSA); RESETTLEMENT ADMINISTRATION (RA); SOUTHERN TENANT FARMERS' UNION (STFU).

BIBLIOGRAPHY

Baldwin, Sidney. *Poverty and Politics: The Rise and Decline of the Farm Security Administration.* 1968.

Cobb, James C. *The Most Southern Place on Earth: The Mississippi Delta and the Roots of Regional Identity.* 1992.

Conrad, David E. *The Forgotten Farmers: The Story of Sharecroppers in the New Deal.* 1965.

Daniel, Pete. *Breaking the Land: The Transformation of Cotton, Tobacco, and Rice Cultures Since 1880.* 1985.

Fite, Gilbert C. *Cotton Fields No More: Southern Agriculture, 1865–1980.* 1984.

Gray, L. C.; John D. Black; E. G. Nourse; et al. (U.S. National Resources Committee). *Farm Tenancy: Report of the President's Committee.* 1937.

Grubbs, Donald H. *Cry from the Cotton: The Southern Tenant Farmers' Union and the New Deal.* 1971.

Holley, Donald. *Uncle Sam's Farmers: The New Deal Communities in the Lower Mississippi Valley.* 1975.

Johnson, Charles S., Edwin Embree, and Will W. Alexander. *The Collapse of Cotton Tenancy.* 1935.

Mertz, Paul E. *New Deal Policy and Southern Rural Poverty.* 1978.

Mertz, Paul E. "Southern Liberals, the AAA, and the Memphis Cotton Hearings of 1935." In *Agricultural Legacies: Essays in Honor of Gilbert C. Fite,* edited by R. Alton Lee. 1986.

Nelson, Lawrence J. *King Cotton's Advocate: Oscar G. Johnston and the New Deal.* 1999.

Raper, Arthur F. *Preface to Peasantry: A Tale of Two Black Belt Counties.* 1936.

Whayne, Jeannie. *A New Plantation South: Land, Labor, and Federal Favor in Twentieth Century Arkansas.* 1996.

Woodruff, Nan Elizabeth. *As Rare as Rain: Federal Relief in the Great Southern Drought of 1930–31.* 1985.

PAUL E. MERTZ

SHELTERBELT PROJECT

Established by President Franklin D. Roosevelt under executive order on July 21, 1934, the Shelterbelt Project provided for a tree barrier one hundred miles wide extending twelve hundred miles north to south from the Canadian border through the Texas panhandle. It was designed to reduce wind velocity, which had occasioned severe soil erosion across the Midwest and dust storms to the eastern seaboard. When the comptroller general in September objected that Congress had not authorized the project, which would require financing for years into the future, the immediate funding was limited to a million dollars allotted under legislative appropriation for relief in the drought-stricken states. The value of the project as a relief program was to be one of its important accomplishments. Congress was reluctant to approve the work, and throughout its history the labor was carried out primarily through use of relief appropriations.

As originally conceived and as it was popularly viewed, the belt was to consist of north to south bands of woodland, each seven rods wide, one mile apart, over a zone one hundred miles wide and twelve hundred miles long. Newspapers and periodicals publicized these details with maps of a continuous zone. Although frequently characterized as a Plains project, it was, in fact, confined to the east of the fifteen-inch line of average annual precipitation. Average annual precipitation in the proposed zone varied from eighteen inches in the north to twenty-two inches in the south, where higher temperatures and higher rates of transpiration prevailed.

While enthusiasm for the proposal was reportedly widespread, there was also much skeptical criticism. Professional foresters realized that unsuitable terrain and soils would necessitate breaks in the belts. Some also deplored the expenditure for woodlands that might provide farm fence posts and woodlots but not commercial timber. Many commentators recalled the widespread failure that had characterized settlement under the Timber Culture Homestead Act of 1873. Others objected to diversion of prairie farmland, the so-called bread basket of the nation under normal weather. Not a few critics were merely opposed politically to President Roosevelt, who had been long identified with forest conservation.

The administration assigned direction of the project to the Lake States Forest Experiment Station of the Forest Service, which drew upon a wide range of research facilities and devoted the first year to thorough preparation. Analysts studied previous experiences under comparable conditions in Canada, Denmark, Russia, and Hungary, as well as at United States experiment stations in Montana, North Dakota, Kansas, and Nebraska. The Dryland Experiment Station at Mandan, North Dakota, somewhat west of the proposed shelterbelt, had been testing the use of windbreaks since 1914, and Canada had been planting trees in the Prairie Provinces since 1901. Surveys were made of the regional terrain, the effect of varying soil conditions, the most suitable tree varieties, the availability of acclimated forest stock, spacing of trees, the structure of planting for most effective wind lift, the requisite cultivation and protection of young trees, and the effect of windbreaks on adjacent land area. The need for adapted seedlings was so great that thirteen nurseries were established and seven others temporarily leased.

Approximately 6.5 million trees were planted in 1935, two-thirds of which survived. The work thus far had been carried out under authority of the Clarke-McNary Act of 1924, which had provided for distribution of tree-planting stock to farmers under a cooperative program with states nationwide. After extended debate in the spring of 1936, the 74th Congress approved only $70,579 for distribution of forest seeds and plants for shelterbelts and called for liquidation of the project. That year proved the driest of the prolonged drought period, yet the survival rate for the tree plantings remained over 50 percent. In May 1937 the 75th Congress adopted a Cooperative Farm Forestry Act that allotted up to $2.5 million annually for the program, with the proviso that cooperators must make the land available without charge.

Renamed the Prairie States Forestry Project, the program was continued with little change. Farmers donated the land, prepared it for planting, and agreed to fence the strips against damage by livestock and to provide cultivation as needed during the first two to four years. The Forest Service supplied the trees, arranged for their planting, and provided expertise on site and species selection, planting methods, and subsequent care.

As late as 1942, the Works Projects Administration (WPA) still provided $600,000 for tree planting, but wartime labor shortages led to termination of both the WPA and the Prairie States Forestry Project the following year. Over 190 million trees had been planted in nearly nineteen thousand miles of belts on thirty-three thousand farms. The survival rate had increased to 82 percent.

Surveying the results in 1944, forestry officials estimated that well-tended trees would survive for thirty to sixty years. In view of the benefits, they termed the Shelterbelt Project a success.

See Also: CONSERVATION MOVEMENT; DUST BOWL; WEST, THE GREAT DEPRESSION IN THE AMERICAN.

BIBLIOGRAPHY

Dahl, Jerome. "Progress and Development of the Prairie States Forest Project." *Journal of Forestry*. 38 (1940): 301–306.

Lake States Experiment Station, U. S. Forest Service. *Possibilities of Shelterbelt Planting in the Plains*. 1935.

Munns, E. N., and Joseph H. Stoeckeler. "How Are the Great Plains Shelterbelts?" *Journal of Forestry*. 44 (1946): 237–257.

Pates, C. G. "The Plains Shelterbelt Project." *Journal of Forestry*. 32 (1934): 978–991.

Tinker, E. N. "What's Happened to the Shelterbelt?" *American Forestry*. 44 (1938): 7–8, 48.

Work Projects Administration, Division of Information. "Shelterbelt Winning Battle of Wind and Dust." *Journal of Forestry* 40 (1942): 345–346.

Zon, Raphael. "Shelterbelts—Futile Dream or Workable Plan." *Science*. 81 (1935): 391–394.

MARY W. M. HARGREAVES

SINCLAIR, UPTON

Upton Sinclair (September 20, 1878–November 25, 1968) was a novelist and socialist whose challenge to President Franklin Roosevelt's cautious approach to recovery helped propel a second phase of New Deal reform after 1934. Sinclair was born in Baltimore, Maryland, the scion of a father who suffered from alcoholism and a mother who had descended from an affluent southern family. At age ten Sinclair, already exhibiting a keen intellect and a precocious interest in writing, moved with his family to New York. As the family struggled financially, the young Sinclair began to write dime novels and short fiction for various pulp magazines to finance his studies at City College in Manhattan, which he had entered at fourteen. Thus began a career as a prolific writer; by the time of his death Sinclair had published nearly a hundred books.

Following the first of three marriages in 1900, Sinclair began developing his interest in fiction grounded in or suggested by proletarian themes and social realism. In 1904 Sinclair was asked by the editor of the *Appeal to Reason*, the largest circulation socialist-populist newspaper in the country, to write a fictionalized series on the conditions facing immigrant workers in the packinghouses of Chicago. The result would become *The Jungle* (1906), undoubtedly the most significant and enduring product of Sinclair's body of work. President Theodore Roosevelt and a middle-class readership were thoroughly repulsed by the imagery of the contaminated meat that threatened to reach their tables. The result was the passage in 1906 of the federal Food and Drugs Act and the Meat Inspection Act.

In 1915 Sinclair moved to Pasadena, California, to enjoy a more temperate climate and indulge his affinity for tennis. In 1926 he rejoined the Socialist Party that he had left during World War I, and he became its candidate for governor with a less than impressive result. The Great Depression struck California with virulence and Sinclair, seeing no viable relief or recovery plan, penned a series of general propositions in August 1933 that he termed a "Plan to End Poverty in California" (EPIC). EPIC proposed to start up idle factories to benefit unemployed workers and make available untilled land to farmers, and then distribute goods and services through a system of statewide cooperatives. The EPIC plan would also provide $50 a month to those in need over sixty years old and a similar payment to the blind, disabled, and widowed mothers with dependent children. A steeply graduated state income tax and higher inheritance and stock transfer taxes would finance the social insurance programs. The proposals quickly caught the imagination of many Californians, who formed hundreds of EPIC clubs. Realizing a propitious political opportunity, Sinclair switched to the Democratic Party and declared his candidacy for the governorship.

The 1934 gubernatorial campaign in California became one of the most revealing and memorable in American history. Pitting Sinclair against a colorless business conservative in incumbent Frank Merriam, the campaign produced all of the hallmarks of a modern electoral event. Opinion and voter polling, the use of professional media experts, negative and distorted advertisements, and the infusion of large sums of money were used to defeat the left wing insurgency led by Sinclair. The troika of Metro-Goldwyn-Mayer, the Southern California Citrus Growers Association, and the *Los Angeles Times* organized the anti-Sinclair effort. The campaign culminated in an agreement by the Democratic establishment to swing the election to the Republican Merriam in exchange for bipartisan collaboration on a recovery program in the state. Although Sinclair continued to write, the EPIC campaign had clearly sapped his literary energies and for the remainder of the decade he involved himself largely in other interests, including the study of telepathy and an attempted collaboration with Russian filmmaker Sergei Eisenstein.

In 1940 Sinclair resumed writing with the publication of the first volume of his Lanny Budd historical novels, which totaled eleven volumes between 1940 and 1953. The third in the series, *Dragon's Teeth* (1942), based upon the rise of Nazism, won a Pulitzer Prize for fiction. Sinclair left Pasadena in 1953 and moved to Buckeye, Arizona, where he died on November 25, 1968.

See Also: END POVERTY IN CALIFORNIA (EPIC); LITERATURE.

BIBLIOGRAPHY
Dell, Floyd. *Upton Sinclair: A Study in Social Protest.* 1970.

Diedrick, James. *Upton Sinclair.* 1998.

Harris, Leon A. *Upton Sinclair, American Rebel.* 1975.

Mitchell, Greg. *The Campaign of the Century: Upton Sinclair's Race for Governor of California and the Birth of Media Politics.* 1992.

Sinclair, Upton. *The Epic Plan for California.* 1934.

Sinclair, Upton. *I, Candidate for Governor: And How I Got Licked* (1935), Reprint Edition, 1994.

Sinclair, Upton. Papers. Lilly Library, University of Indiana, Bloomington.

WILLIAM J. BILLINGSLEY

SIT-DOWN STRIKES

The National Labor Relations Act of 1935 buoyed the hopes of American workers. For the first time, the federal government officially encouraged the process of unionism and collective bargaining. By mid 1936, however, this optimism faded, as workers found themselves still vehemently fighting anti-union employers who refused to recognize the Act's constitutionality. In response, many workers adopted more aggressive and creative tactics to force their employers to the bargaining table. This new shop-floor militancy and ingenuity is best illustrated by the sit-down strike wave of 1936 to 1937, during which nearly 500,000 workers struck, not by erecting picket lines, but by laying down their tools and refusing to leave their employer's property.

The first wide-scale use of the sit-down strike occurred in January 1936 at Firestone's Akron, Ohio, tire plant. Worker-management relations in Akron had deteriorated through late 1935 and early 1936. The main points of contention concerned the lowering of piece rates, the length of the workday, and management's continued harassment of union members and activists. This frustration with management was further exacerbated by what many workers viewed as the American Federation of Labor's (AFL) conservative approach to labor relations. Tensions finally boiled over and in January 1936 a small group of militant workers peacefully occupied Firestone's main tire plant and brought production to a standstill.

The sit-down strike had many advantages over the traditional picket line. First, because workers physically held possession of company property, management was unlikely to do anything that might harm the expensive machinery. Second, occupying the factory made it much more difficult for the company to bring in replacement workers. Finally, and most importantly, this tactic permitted a militant minority of workers to force employers to the bargaining table. To succeed, strikers only needed enough workers to retain control of the plant. The success of a traditional strike, however, depended on near total participation. Though the Akron strike did not end with the signing of a formal contract, the workers did compel Firestone to bargain with their chosen representatives. Furthermore, the strike illuminated a growing militancy among American workers who were unwilling to wait for the government or the traditional labor movement to come to their rescue.

Employees of Woolworth's department store in New York City strike in 1937 for a forty-hour work week. LIBRARY OF CONGRESS, PRINTS & PHOTOGRAPHS DIVISION, NEW YORK WORLD-TELEGRAM AND SUN NEWSPAPER PHOTOGRAPH COLLECTION

Though the Akron rubber workers were among the first to successfully employ the sit-down strike, this tactic is most famously associated with the United Automobile Workers (UAW) efforts to organize General Motors (GM) during the winter of 1936 to 1937. Although autoworkers were relatively well paid, there was growing discontent over frequent seasonal layoffs, the speed-up of the assembly line, and the near dictatorial powers of foreman to hire, fire, and discriminate against union supporters. These grievances led to a series of strikes, conducted without official union approval, during the summer and early fall of 1936. Relations took a turn for the worse in December 1936, when GM turned down the request of Homer Martin, president of the UAW, to discuss worker grievances. In response, workers seized control of GM's Fisher

Body plant in Cleveland, Ohio, on December 28. Two days later workers at the company's Fisher Body No. 1 and No. 2 plants in Flint, Michigan, also sat down on the job and brought production to a complete halt. Within a few days, this core group of workers managed to idle nearly 120,000 of GM's 150,000 workers.

General Motors reacted by securing a court injunction requiring the sit-down strikers to vacate the company's plants. Confident the company would not rush the plant, the workers ignored the court order. The workers' hopes were further buoyed by the landslide reelection of President Franklin Roosevelt in November 1936. The same polling day witnessed the election of several pro-labor governors, including Frank Murphy of Michigan. While in the past employers could usually ex-

These employees of the Fisher body plant in Flint, Michigan, conducted a sit-down strike in early 1937. LIBRARY OF CONGRESS, PRINTS & PHOTOGRAPHS DIVISION, FSA/OWI COLLECTION

pect the governor or president to enforce judicial rulings against workers, the elections of 1936 temporarily altered the political balance of power. Governor Murphy refused to enforce the injunction, and instead of using troops to break up the strike, he deployed them to protect the workers from local authorities who sided with GM.

Realizing that neither Roosevelt nor Murphy would enforce the injunctions, and watching its competitors gain in market share, GM management finally decided to enter into negotiations in early February. The two sides signed a formal agreement on February 11, 1936. Though the agreement did not result in a complete victory for the workers in that the UAW did not achieve exclusive representation rights, it nevertheless did com-

pel GM to recognize the UAW as the bargaining representative for its members. Most importantly, though, the workers had successfully defeated the nation's largest employer and illuminated the power of the sit-down strike.

The impact of the Flint sit-down strike reverberated well beyond the auto industry. Workers inspired by the Flint strikers flocked to the labor movement, especially the new industrial unions associated with the Congress of Industrial Organizations (CIO). The most important post-Flint victory occurred on March 12, 1937, when, without a strike, U.S. Steel signed an agreement with John Lewis recognizing the Steel Workers' Organizing Committee as the bargaining representative for its members. Thus, by the spring of 1937, two of the nation's largest, most anti-union corporations were organized. The sit-down strike, however, quickly disappeared as a primary weapon in labor's arsenal. Workers first abandoned the tactic because of growing public resentment over what was deemed to be the lawless nature of the labor movement and its lack of respect for property rights. Political support for these actions also ebbed as public resentment began to rise. Furthermore sit down strikes became less necessary when the Supreme Court upheld, in April 1937, the constitutionality of the National Labor Relations Act. Now workers had a legal means for achieving unionization and no longer needed to occupy their employer's property—which, in *NLRB v. Fansteel Metallurgical Corp* (1939), the Supreme Court ruled constituted an illegal occupation of private property.

See Also: AMERICAN FEDERATION OF LABOR (AFL); COLLECTIVE BARGAINING; CONGRESS OF INDUSTRIAL ORGANIZATIONS (CIO); ORGANIZED LABOR; STRIKES; STEEL WORKERS' ORGANIZING COMMITTEE (SWOC); UNITED AUTOMOBILE WORKERS (UAW).

BIBLIOGRAPHY

Dubofsky, Melvyn. *The State and Labor in Modern America.* 1994.

Gray, Lorraine W. *With Babies and Banners. Story of the Women's Emergency Brigade.* New Day Films. 1978.

Lichtenstein, Nelson, ed. *Who Built America: Working People and the Nation's Economy, Politics, Culture, and Society,* Vol. 2: *From the Gilded Age to the Present,* 2nd edition. 2000.

Zieger, Robert H. *American Workers, American Unions: The Twentieth Century.* 1994.

Zieger, Robert H. *The CIO: 1935–1955.* 1995.

DOUGLAS J. FEENEY

SLAVE NARRATIVES

As part of the Works Progress Administration (WPA) work relief programs, the Federal Writers' Project (FWP) conducted interviews with former slaves that continue to have a major impact on the scholarly studies of slavery and on the portrayal of slavery in the popular culture. A group of ex-slave interviews submitted to the national FWP office by the Florida project in March of 1937 led to the establishment of a nationally directed interview program with former slaves. John Lomax, the first FWP folklore editor, encouraged field workers "to get the Negro talking about the days of slavery." Several months later, Henry Alsberg, national FWP director, added several new questions to Lomax's instructions. Alsberg asked interviewers to also focus on life since 1865—what the former slaves hoped freedom would mean and what they actually experienced. He wanted to ensure that the interviews were more than nostalgic tales of contented plantation slaves—a tradition that helped justify the southern caste system.

With the support of Sterling Brown, national FWP Negro Affairs editor, and B. A. Botkin, Lomax's successor as national folklore editor, the Washington, D.C., office worked to obtain a black perspective to help inform the study of slavery, emancipation, and Reconstruction. They hoped not only to obtain a better understanding of the past, but also to contribute to reopening the issue of race relations since the Civil War. They envisioned making these interviews available to general readers. They also saw these interviews as a new form of literature, folklore, and history in which the narrators, the former slaves, became their own historians, offering their own interpretation of the past, what Botkin called "folk history." Although the relationship between the civil rights movement, black nationalism, and the social upheavals of the 1960s and the new social history and revitalization of slavery studies in the 1970s is frequently recognized, much less attention has been given to connections between the study of slavery and the cultural programs of the New Deal and the ideological dimensions of World War II for New Dealers.

PUBLIC AND SCHOLARLY RECEPTION OF THE FWP EX-SLAVE NARRATIVES

Although the FWP ended before any of the interviews with former slaves could be published, historians have long been aware of these materials. Under Botkin's direction, the interviews were evaluated, inventoried, and deposited in the Library of Congress. In 1945, Botkin edited *Lay My Burden*

Josephine Hill, a former slave, photographed in Alabama in 1938 as part of the WPA slave narratives project. LIBRARY OF CONGRESS, PRINTS AND PHOTOGRAPHS DIVISION, WPA FEDERAL WRITERS PROJECT SLAVE NARRATIVES COLLECTION

Down: A Folk History of Slavery, an easily available collection of FWP interviews. Nevertheless, historians showed little interest in this material before the 1960s. In part this was because some historians did not question the plantation tradition, but even the increasing number of historians who did question it were slow to use the FWP interviews. They privileged written documents as objective and reliable over oral and folklore materials, which they regarded as subjective and untrustworthy. They thought of memory as individual and as only a matter of accurate recall, rather than as contested, communal, and socially constructed. Thus, although *Lay My Burden Down* was widely reviewed in the nation's newspapers and hailed by many, historians virtually ignored it.

In the opinion of many of these reviewers, the combination of folklore and oral history made the former slave narratives a contribution to American literature, as well as to American history. Like the FWP officials, the reviewers did not privilege one genre over the other or see them as mutually exclusive. They recognized that the narratives of former slaves could introduce readers to voices they had seldom heard or listened to. They understood that those voices associated with the romantic plantation tradition that had dominated public discussion regarding slavery were now being answered. Liberal reviewers interpreted the memories and lore they found in the narratives as a valuable part of an ongoing struggle to combat racism and segregation in the contemporary United States, especially in light of the end of a war for freedom and democracy and the results of the genocidal racism of Nazi Germany. They were working to make the black experience part of a more widely shared national memory of American history as a struggle for freedom. Most reviewers in southern newspapers saw the narratives as an attack on the plantation tradition, as an attempt to question contemporary race relations, and they reacted by denouncing the narratives as unreliable and folklore as irrelevant. It would be another generation before academic historians began to use these materials, and then with little knowledge or interest in the FWP's goals.

Despite the growing challenge to the authority of scholarly versions of the plantation tradition in the period since the end of World War II, influential studies using the FWP interviews with former slaves did not appear until the 1970s. Without a sense of the role oral tradition can play in a community, or of the usefulness of oral history interviews in studying the past, most historians dismissed the folklore in the FWP slave narratives as failing traditional tests of validity. Looking over the historiography of slavery in the period from World War II to 1970, historian Nathan Huggins argued that, given the problematic status historians assigned these FWP interviews, any historians who used them would have found the professional authority of their work compromised.

Only in the 1970s when scholars became interested in slave culture did they begin to carefully examine the FWP interviews and chart new directions in the history of American slavery. With the publication of *The American Slave: A Composite Autobiography* in 1972 (and subsequent supplemental volumes) under the editorship of George Rawick, these materials become easily accessible to historians. Historian David Brion Davis has called the publication of the entire FWP collection one of the major turning points in the post–World War II historiography of slavery. Along with this renewed interest there developed a scholarly literature on the validity and challenges of using this material. Initially this discussion focused on the representativeness and reliability of the interviews. In time the discussion broadened to include a debate over the role of oral tradition and folklore in these materials. Still, only a few historians have begun to treat the interviewees, interviewers, and FWP officials as historians contributing to the study of slavery, not merely the creators of a source for professional historians to mine.

SCHOLARLY AND PUBLIC USES OF THE EX-SLAVE NARRATIVES

Regarding the questions of representativeness and reliability, it must be noted that while the former slave narrative collection represented all types of slave occupations, the collection was not conducted on a scientifically random basis. Local fieldworkers chose interviewees on the basis of previous contact and geographical proximity. The slave experience in the upper South and the border states is underrepresented. Very few of the ex-slaves who were interviewed were more than fifteen years old when the Civil War began. It has been estimated that only two percent of the former slave population in the United States at the time was interviewed.

Historians have pointed out that the vast majority of the interviewers were white and worked in their local communities in the South in the 1930s during an era when economic depression, disfranchisement, and violent racial intimidation were a pervasive part of everyday life. The interviews, and FWP correspondence, provide ample evidence that most of these fieldworkers accepted the plantation tradition as fact and a segregated racial order as just. Drawn from the relief rolls, few interviewers had any experience relevant to interviewing. They often failed to pursue important topics and asked leading questions designed to confirm their preconceptions. In addition, former slaves interviewed by the FWP were frequently living in an abject poverty that in many areas of the South was demonstrably worse than what they had known in slavery. They often assumed their interviewers were government employees who could help them materially. Too often the interviewers did nothing to dispel these misconceptions. The interviews indicate that some interviewers were the direct descendants of individuals who had owned the interviewees. Given these factors, it has been argued that the interviews are biased toward a paternalistic view of slavery.

Comparing the small number of interviews conducted by blacks with those done by whites, scholars have discovered that interviewees talked more openly with black interviewers than they did with whites about attitudes toward slavery, their former masters, punishments, family customs, and other topics. Furthermore, white women interviewers received more open responses than did white men. Material dealing with kinship relations and slave culture appears to have been less affected by the race of the interviewer than other topics. Finally, the written transcripts of these interviews provide ample evidence that they are rarely verbatim accounts and have been heavily edited by either the interviewers or FWP officials. White editors tended

to find interviews that contained accounts of cruel treatment as untrustworthy and in at least several instances deleted such material. Although few historians would advocate disregarding the interviews for the above reasons, they have pointed out that the interviews need to be used with an awareness of their strengths and limitations, as is always the case with historical sources.

FWP officials understood that in the interviews with former slaves, they were challenging not only traditional scholarly authority, but also the role of scholarship in democratic public discourse and the role of those interviewed in interpreting the past. As historians drawing on oral history and folklore theory continue to analyze these interviews, they are increasingly focusing on issues that FWP officials first raised, such as the collaborative effort that goes on between interviewer and interviewee in creating an oral history, the value of the subjective perspective of historical actors, and the role of oral tradition and folklore in creating individual and group memory.

Remembering Slavery: African Americans Talk about Their Personal Experiences of Slavery and Emancipation marked a return to many of the concerns of FWP officials, and not only provided an introduction to these interviews in the light of modern scholarship on slavery but also recognized that in the aftermath of slavery former slaves kept alive memories that contested the once dominant romanticized plantation tradition. Berlin and his colleagues' commitment to public history was manifest not only in their book, but also in their collaboration with the Smithsonian production of a radio documentary based on the transcribed interviews and on previously unavailable audio recordings of former slaves in the American Folklife Center at the Library of Congress.

New caches of interviews with former slaves continue to be discovered and there is no end in sight because not all the interviews with former slaves were sent to the national office by the state FWP units and because interest in these materials shows no sign of declining. The number of published collections of FWP slave narratives organized by state or around specific topics continues to grow. Scholars continue to pose questions that these materials can help answer about the contested negotiations between slaves and masters about family, work, religion, the material culture of the plantation, growing up as a slave, disability among slaves, and slave expressive culture. Scholars have moved beyond using these materials to describe slave culture to examining these interviews as a way of understanding slaves as both the bearers of tradition and the creators of culture. These materials still await a thorough examination regarding what they can reveal about race relations in the 1930s. Scholars are learning that these interviews are important not only for what they reveal about slavery, but also for what they have to say about lives lived in slavery and freedom—a point FWP officials had made from the beginning.

See Also: AFRICAN AMERICANS, IMPACT OF THE GREAT DEPRESSION ON; FEDERAL WRITERS' PROJECT (FWP); RACE AND ETHNIC RELATIONS; WORKS PROGRESS ADMINISTRATION (WPA).

BIBLIOGRAPHY

Bailey, David T. "A Divided Prism: Two Sources of Black Testimony on Slavery." *Journal of Southern History* 46 (1980): 381–404.

Berlin, Ira; Marc Favreau; and Steven F. Miller; eds. *Remembering Slavery: African Americans Talk about Their Personal Experiences of Slavery and Emancipation.* 1998.

Blassingame, John W. "Using the Testimony of Ex-Slaves: Approaches and Problems." *Journal of Southern History* 41 (1975): 473–492.

Blassingame, John W. *The Slave Community: Plantation Life in the Antebellum South,* rev. edition. 1979.

Botkin, B. A. "The Slave as His Own Interpreter." *Library of Congress Quarterly Journal of Current Acquisitions* 2 (1944): 37–62.

Davis, Charles T., and Henry Louis Gates, Jr., eds. *The Slave's Narrative.* 1985.

Davis, David Brion. "Slavery and the Post World War II Historians." *Daedalus* 103 (1974): 1–16.

Genovese, Eugene. *Roll, Jordan, Roll: The World the Slaves Made.* 1974.

Hirsch, Jerrold. "Foreword." In *Lay My Burden Down: A Folk History of Slavery* (1945), edited by B. A. Botkin. Athens: University of Georgia Press, 1989.

Hirsch, Jerrold. *Portrait of America: A Cultural History of the Federal Writers' Project.* 2003.

Huggins, Nathan. *Black Odyssey: The African American Ordeal in Slavery* (1977). 1990.

Rawick, George P., et al., eds. *The American Slave: A Composite Autobiography,* 19 vols; Supplemental Series no. 1, 12 vols.; Supplemental Series no. 2, 10 vols. 1972, 1977, 1979.

Rawick, George P. *From Sundown to Sunup: The Making of the Black Community.* 1972.

Woodward, C. Vann. "History from Slave Sources: A Review Article." *American Historical Review* 79 (1974): 470–481.

Yetman, Norman R., ed. *Life Under the "Peculiar Institution": Selections from the Slave Narrative Collection.* 1970.

Yetman, Norman R. "Ex-Slave Interviews and the Historiography of Slavery." *American Quarterly* 36 (1984): 181–210.

JERROLD HIRSCH

SMITH, ALFRED E.

Alfred Emanuel Smith (December 30, 1873–October 4, 1944), who was known as the "Happy Warrior," won four terms as Democratic governor of New York from 1918 to 1928, became the first Catholic candidate nominated for president by a major party, and then opposed Franklin D. Roosevelt's New Deal and reelection in 1936.

In a career shot through with irony, Al Smith became the leading Democratic politician of the Republican 1920s, only to turn against his party just as it gained power during the Great Depression. Smith grew up on Manhattan's Lower East Side, lacking a high school education, but instilled with the virtues of hard work, strict morality, and loyalty to Tammany Hall, Manhattan's invincible Democratic machine. In 1903, Tammany's nomination gained Smith election to the State Assembly where he became the Democratic leader. He become known as a champion of the poor and working class, especially after the Triangle Shirtwaist Company fire of 1911 and service on the investigating commission. In 1918, Smith won his first of four two-year terms as governor of New York state, losing only in the Warren G. Harding landslide of 1920.

Governor Smith earned a solid reputation as a progressive reformer concerned with both social welfare and the efficiency of government. As his crowning achievement, Smith reorganized state government and overhauled its antiquated tax structure. Although the governor sought to restrain taxation and curb needless spending, he simultaneously expanded public projects and extended workmen's compensation and mothers' pensions.

After nearly capturing the Democratic presidential nomination in 1924, Smith succeeded in 1928, becoming the first Roman Catholic nominated by a major American party. Smith, who did not vigorously challenge Republican economics, lost in a near landslide to Secretary of Commerce Herbert Hoover, the legatee of Coolidge-era prosperity. The election was marked by an outbreak of anti-Catholicism, both scholarly and scurrilous, and a sharp division in the voting choices of Catholics and Protestants. In 1932, Smith joined a coalition of conservative Democrats in a failed effort to deny the Democratic nomination to his successor as governor, Franklin D. Roosevelt. Smith hoped to vindicate his 1928 defeat, but Democrats were not about to reignite religious conflict in what appeared to be the first winning year for their party since 1916.

Although Smith reluctantly campaigned for the Democratic ticket in 1932, he increasingly found himself at odds with New Deal policies. Pressed forward by the businessmen who were now Smith's closest associates, he became the prized recruit of the American Liberty League, formed in 1934 as an outlet for conservative criticism of Roosevelt's liberal solutions to the challenges of hard times. Smith's career came full circle in January 1936 when he addressed a Liberty League audience of millionaire couples at the Mayflower Hotel in Washington, D.C., replaying the same arguments that Republicans had used against him in 1928. Most inflammatory was his charge that Roosevelt had sold out to communism: "There can only be one capital, Washington or Moscow. There can only be the pure, fresh air of free America, or the foul breath of communistic Russia." Senator Joseph Robinson of Arkansas, Smith's running mate from 1928, lamented that his old friend was now "warring like one of the Janizaries of old against . . . the men and women with whom he fought shoulder to shoulder in the past." Smith supported Republican

Alfred E. Smith (right) with Franklin D. Roosevelt in 1930.

FRANKLIN DELANO ROOSEVELT LIBRARY

presidential candidates Alf Landon in 1936 and Wendell Willkie in 1940.

Smith's career illustrates the tensions within a progressivism that combined humanitarian impulse and commitment to efficient government with distrust of high taxes, redistributive spending, and government meddling in business. During the Great Depression, Franklin Roosevelt incorporated and moved beyond the progressivism of an earlier time: Al Smith did not.

See Also: AMERICAN LIBERTY LEAGUE; CONSERVATIVE COALITION; DEMOCRATIC PARTY; ELECTION OF 1928; ELECTION OF 1932; MOSKOWITZ, BELLE.

BIBLIOGRAPHY
Eldot, Paula. *Governor Alfred E. Smith: The Politician as Reformer.* 1983.

Finan, Christopher M. *Alfred E. Smith: The Happy Warrior.* 2002.

Lichtman, Allan. *Prejudice and the Old Politics: The Presidential Election of 1928,* rev. edition. 2000.

Schwarz, Jordan A. "Al Smith in the Thirties." *New York History* 45 (1964): 316–330.

Stayton, Robert A. *Empire Statesman: The Rise and Redemption of Al Smith.* 2001.

ALLAN J. LICHTMAN

SMITH, GERALD L. K.

Gerald L. K. Smith (February 27, 1888–April 15, 1976), a minister, publisher, orator, anti-Semite, and anticommunist, a hater of Franklin D. Roosevelt and the New Deal, was one of the most inflammatory speakers of the New Deal era.

Born in a Wisconsin village to a lower-middle-class family, Smith graduated from Viroqua High School in 1916, then completed a four-year B. A. program in biblical studies at Valparaiso University in two years, graduating in 1918. Nephritis, a kidney disease, kept him out of World War I. Smith started his career as a Disciples of Christ preacher in small villages in Wisconsin, where he converted hundreds and was an effective money raiser. He married Elna Sorenson, of Janesville.

Smith's career flourished and he moved to larger, richer churches in Illinois and Indiana. He accepted a call from the Kings Highway Christian Church in Shreveport, Louisiana, in 1929 because the warm climate offered the opportunity for Elna, who had contracted tuberculosis, to heal.

In Shreveport, Smith repeated his earlier successes and became an associate of U.S. Senator Huey P. Long. Smith quit his church, whose most influential and wealthy members opposed Long, then traveled the nation for Long promoting wealth-sharing. He might have been Long's campaign manager in his planned 1936 presidential campaign, but Long was killed by an assassin in 1935 and Smith, after preaching Huey's eulogy, lost a power struggle among Long's successors, and left Louisiana. For the rest of his life his career would mix religion and politics.

In 1936 Smith teamed with Father Charles E. Coughlin and Dr. Francis E. Townsend to sponsor the candidacy of North Dakota U.S. Representative William Lemke for president on the Union Party ticket. The party failed badly and its leaders split.

Smith increasingly demonized Jews, blacks, and communists, and was a leading figure on the far right through the Depression and long after. He moved his headquarters to New York in 1936, Cleveland in 1938, Detroit in 1939, St. Louis in 1947, Tulsa in 1948, and Los Angeles in 1953. His crusading included delivering speeches, publishing, seeking political office, and undertaking direct mail fundraising. Smith founded *The Cross and the Flag* in 1942, and published thousands of pamphlets. He became a near-millionaire from money sent to him through the mail by followers or left to him in bequests.

Smith used plot theories to blame Jews for World War I, the Bolshevik Revolution, the Great Depression, and World War II. He claimed FDR was a Jew yet Adolf Hitler was a good Christian.

See Also: COUGHLIN, CHARLES; LONG, HUEY P.; TOWNSEND PLAN; UNION PARTY.

BIBLIOGRAPHY

Bennett, David H. *Demagogues in the Depression: American Radicals and the Union Party, 1932–1936.* 1969.

Gerald L. K. Smith Papers, Bentley Historical Library, University of Michigan.

Jeansonne, Glen. *Gerald L. K. Smith: Minister of Hate.* 1988.

Jeansonne, Glen. "Preacher, Populist, Propagandist: The Early Career of Gerald L. K. Smith." *Biography* 2, no. 4 (Fall 1979): 303–327.

Ribuffo, Leo P. *The Old Christian Right: The Protestant Far Right from the Great Depression to the Cold War.* 1983.

GLEN JEANSONNE

SNOW WHITE AND THE SEVEN DWARFS

The December 21, 1937, release by Walt Disney of the animated feature film *Snow White and the Seven Dwarfs* (produced in 1937) was hailed by conservative newspaper columnist Westbrook Pegler as "the happiest thing that has happened in this world since the armistice" that had ended World War I in 1918. Surely he was correct in seeing the big screen adaptation of the Grimm Brothers' fairy tale as a pleasant diversion for many from the problems of the Depression, and specifically of the renewed economic collapse of 1937 to 1938. Yet this Disney cartoon held a significance far beyond its provision of an hour-and-a-half of escape from the harsh realities of the Great Depression.

Snow White was a milestone in filmmaking: the first feature-length animation in color. It was a huge commercial success that proved the economic possibilities for feature-length cartoons. The great Russian filmmaker Sergei Eisenstein rated *Snow White* as the greatest film ever made. But the deeper importance of the film lay in the powerful message it sent audiences about "proper" gender roles. In addition to its other meanings and interpretations, this film can readily be seen as a plea for a return to the "normalcy" in gender roles that had been so disrupted by the Depression—and as a foreshadowing of the rise of what Betty Freidan would term the "Feminine Mystique" in the post-World War II era.

The Depression severely undermined the traditional male role of provider. Many men who lost their jobs came to feel that they had lost their manhood. It was not unusual for women to hold jobs when their husbands did not. There was a palpable desire to restore male dominance and female dependence. *Snow White* embodied these fears and desires in two major ways. First, it portrayed a powerful woman as ultimately evil and a completely naïve woman who embodies the characteristics of the nineteenth-century vision of "true womanhood"—domesticity, submissiveness, purity, and piety—as the ideal female. Even more strikingly, *Snow White* reverses the actuality of many downcast, jobless, nearly helpless men who were dependent on women to make them feel alive in the 1930s. The film instead portrays a woman who falls into the complete helplessness of "sleeping death," from which she can only be revived by a man, who will carry her off so that they can live happily ever after. For many men in the Great Depression, this was indeed the state of affairs for which they were wishing.

See Also: DISNEY, WALT; GENDER ROLES AND SEXUAL RELATIONS, IMPACT OF GREAT DEPRESSION ON; HOLLYWOOD AND THE FLM INDUSTRY.

BIBLIOGRAPHY

Barrier, Michael. *Hollywood Cartoons: American Animation in Its Golden Age.* 1999.

Holliss, Richard, and Brian Sibley. *Walt Disney's Snow White and the Seven Dwarfs and the Making of the Classic Film.* 1987.

McElvaine, Robert S. *Eve's Seed: Biology, the Sexes, and the Course of History.* 2001.

Schickel, Richard. *The Disney Version: The Life, Times, Art and Commerce of Walt Disney,* 3rd edition. 1997.

ROBERT S. MCELVAINE

SNYC. *See* SOUTHERN NEGRO YOUTH CONGRESS.

SOCIALIST PARTY

The Socialist Party entered the Depression years with high hopes for revival, and exited in near collapse. The party's greatest weakness was internal disunity, but the ultimately debilitating conflicts reflected the dilemmas of a radical movement in the age of Franklin D. Roosevelt.

By the time of the stock market crash in 1929, the once-strong Socialist Party had reached internal collapse. Pockets of ethnic labor and local voting strength, notably German, Jewish, and Slovenian, had been greatly heartened by the emergence of Norman Thomas, a former minister, as perpetual candidate and replacement for the late figurehead Eugene V. Debs. But many younger radicals had defected to Communist circles, and the deep-set bureaucratic mentality of older, influential party figures sometimes proved as much of a liability as a benefit, offering a gloomy prospect for the near future.

Nonetheless, a fresh generation of socialists found themselves in the movement of the unemployed, leading the Workers Alliance and the

Young People's Socialist League, while older hands enjoyed a revival of municipal victories in heavily Germanic Milwaukee and Reading, Pennsylvania, and strong turnouts in scattered spots. The Student League for Industrial Democracy (SLID) prospered on some campuses amid the rise of antiwar sentiment. Presidential campaigner Thomas, winner of a straw poll among college students in 1932, expected to win millions of votes that year and actually received 800,000, a promising turnout.

Communist blunders contributed to a renewal of interest in the Socialists and to their hopes for a major revival, but those hopes were deeply disappointed within only a few years. Often sectarian and highly rhetorical during the early 1930s, Communists left open opportunities for organizing projects within existing unions and for the creation of a labor party. Novelist Upton Sinclair, who mobilized socialistic constituencies for his run for California governor—but within the Democratic Party—marked yet another promising way forward despite his defeat by a Republican candidate in 1934. For a moment it seemed that the Socialist Party membership of approximately thirty thousand might be multiplied by its influence within union locals, certain urban neighborhoods, and college or middle-class reform milieus.

Two key factors reversed these gains. The proclamation of a "Second New Deal" by the Roosevelt administration in 1935 killed the labor party initiative at the national level and drained off many important activists who were earlier involved in Socialist electoral campaigns. The announcement of a Popular Front by world Communist parties brought American Communists into the New Deal coalition just as the labor movement expanded rapidly into industrial unionism and cultural innovation flourished at every level. Communists benefited, absorbing the radicalized writers, artists, and musicians, as well as most militant unionists and African-American activists and intellectuals, while Socialists lost out decisively at almost every level.

The Socialist failure was presaged by their practical absence from three major strikes in 1934—in Minneapolis-St. Paul (led by followers of Leon Trotsky), in Toledo (led by members of the American Workers' Party under A. J. Muste), and in San Francisco (led by Communists). The Trotskyists and "Musteites" actually merged with the Socialist Party in 1936, after joining with each other, but this project of creating an alternative to the Communists occurred too late. A walk-out of older-generation Socialist conservatives, who took along the Rand School, radio station WEVD, and the weekly *New Leader,* left the party badly weakened.

The merger of unemployed groups and student groups into entities more influenced by the Communists better indicated the New Deal's magnetic attraction. Radicalism had become reformism, and pacifist rejection of war had evolved into anti-fascist support of armed resistance to Adolf Hitler and Benito Mussolini. The dramatic fall of Norman Thomas's presidential vote in 1936 to less than half his 1932 total suggested that little remained of the organization but a personal following of Thomas as "Mr. Socialism," America's voice of conscience.

This conclusion would, however, underestimate the ability of local Socialists to rebound within particular circumstances. Socialists held their own and gained new electoral ground in immigrant-heavy Milwaukee, Bridgeport, Connecticut, and Reading, Pennsylvania. Meanwhile, scattered sections of the party led autoworkers, coal miners, and various other groups. As the nation tilted increasingly toward war, a particularly pure strain of pacifism influenced liberal Christian pastors and the laity with a socialistic interpretation of approaching global trauma. Socialist support for the "Keep America out of War" Congress in 1938 marked a final high point.

This was the Indian summer of a movement that could not recover its momentum. Severe internal wrangling with the followers of Trotsky ended with the expulsion of the minority in 1938. The inevitability of war and the 1941 entry of the United States doomed pacifism to a moral outcry that was not supported in most of the ethnic milieus where Socialist sympathies had remained alive. Opposition to Communist ideology and tactics, once made from attacking compromises with the Roosevelt administration, now slipped toward the center, as influential Socialists, especially within the labor movement, poised to become cold warriors.

See Also: MUSTE, A. J.; THOMAS, NORMAN.

BIBLIOGRAPHY

Bell, Daniel. "The Background and Development of Marxian Socialism in the United States." In *Socialism and American Life,* Vol. 1, edited by Donald Drew Egbert and Stow Persons. 1952.

Socialist Party of America Papers. Duke University Libraries, Durham, NC.

Warren, Frank A. *An Alternative Vision: The Socialist Party in the 1930s.* 1974.

PAUL BUHLE

SOCIAL SCIENCE

Social science was established as a distinct field of study during the 1930s. When the Great Depression began, the debate over the proper purpose of social studies took on added importance, and experts in the various disciplines concerned with social studies—history, political science, economics, sociology, geography, and anthropology—agreed that the new challenges facing society mandated new approaches to research and teaching. History, as the branch concerned with synthesizing the various aspects of social studies, would take the lead in developing the discipline of social science.

Higher education had become more diverse in the 1920s, a process that continued during the next several decades. In an effort to be more scientific, scholars engaging in social science research began collecting original data that could be measured and rigorously tested; the days of armchair theorizing had ended. New subfields of study also began to take shape in the 1920s and 1930s. Historians continued to discover new directions. Political scientists moved beyond political theory in favor of a more behavioral approach and the new study of public administration. Influenced by John Maynard Keynes and his *The General Theory of Employment, Interest, and Money* (1936), economists abandoned many of their standard models for qualitative examinations. An assault on classical economics, Keynes's theory struck a particular chord in the Depression by challenging the popular notion that unemployment was voluntary and could be blamed on the refusal of a worker to work. Sociologists embraced a micro-level approach to social data and a more functional theoretical stance. Anthropology struggled to break free from its position as the field-work branch of sociology, aided by the foundational works of Franz Boas, Ruth Benedict, and Margaret Mead. Boas continued to challenge the system of race classification, while his student Benedict showed that the plasticity of human nature is such that culture can mold humans into a variety of forms, and Mead argued that masculine and feminine are cultural constructions rather than absolute categories. Geography stands out from the other social sciences for its shift from physical geography to a new kind of professional and research field of the sciences. Like anthropology, geography received little recognition as an academic discipline until the years following World War II.

The new scientific approach of social scientists required funds to support the collection and examination of data. The almost total absence of federal or state funding for such research meant that academics had to seek funding from foundations. This era also witnessed the emergence of the university system of social science research. The Institute for Social and Religious Research in New York provided money for studies of small towns and the countryside, including Robert Lynd's works on Middletown. The Laura Spelman Rockefeller Memorial Foundation, headed by Beardsley Ruml, was another major source of funding for social science research.

One of the projects funded by the Spelman Rockefeller Foundation proved enormously significant by setting a pattern for social science education that would last for the remainder of the century. With this undertaking (1929–1934), the American Historical Association Commission on the Social Studies established guidelines for the teaching of social science in the public schools. The membership of the board, dominated by historian and political scientist Charles A. Beard, consisted of various social scientists, including historian George Counts, geographer Isaiah Bowman, economist Leon Marshall, political scientist Charles E. Merriam, and sociologist Jesse Steiner. Historian A. C. Krey chaired the commission.

The problems facing the world in the 1930s dictated the need for such a commission. In 1932,

George Counts had enumerated these worries in his influential *Dare the School Build a New Social Order?* The book pointed to the failures of capitalism, the social costs of a government's laissez-faire approach to business, and the growing popularity of such right-wing extremists as Adolf Hitler. Like other social constructionists, Counts argued that the schools needed to mesh the needs of the individual with the needs of society. He believed that individualism had died and that schools should play a role in some sort of collectivist planning and control.

The American Historical Association commission reached conclusions that generally supported Counts's contentions. In reports and individual volumes issued throughout the mid-1930s, the commission tried to explain what social science should be. According to the commission, if educators continued to emphasize the traditional ideals and values of economic individualism, then American society would lose the ability to compete in the emerging world order. The commission argued that the main purpose of education must become that of building a well-rounded individual who could think critically and work with others to develop creative solutions. Accordingly, it suggested that the curriculum should include the history of the major peoples and cultures of the modern world; more attention to Latin America, Africa, and Asia to help promote international efforts to achieve peace; and the study of contemporary American life, including contradictions and tensions.

Several of the commission's many publications stand out. *A Charter for the Social Sciences* (1932) edited by Beard, articulated the philosophy of the liberal arts. Beard's *The Nature of the Social Sciences* (1934) analyzed the relationship of the social sciences to the natural sciences and promoted the scientific method of research. *Conclusions and Recommendations* (1934), written by the entire commission, argued that education should abandon methods of coercion and ignorance in order to shape the rising generation according to America's democratic ideals. Although educators relied on Beard's works to write textbooks and curriculum, the vagueness of the commission's conclusions meant that no specific guidelines grew out of its last volume.

See Also: HISTORY, INTERPRETATION, AND MEMORY OF THE GREAT DEPRESSION; KEYNESIAN ECONOMICS.

BIBLIOGRAPHY

Bulmer, Martin. "Knowledge for the Public Good: The Emergence of Social Science and Social Reform in the Late-Nineteenth and Early-Twentieth-Century America, 1880–1940." In *Social Science and Policy-Making: A Search for Relevance in the Twentieth Century,* edited by David L. Featherman and Maris A. Vinovskis. 2001.

Hertzberg, Hazel Whitman. *Social Studies Reform, 1880–1980.* 1981.

Jenness, David. *Making Sense of Social Studies.* 1990.

Lekachman, Robert. *The Age of Keynes.* 1966.

Smith, Mark C. *Social Science in the Crucible: The American Debate over Objectivity and Purpose, 1918–1941.* 1994.

CARYN E. NEUMANN

SOCIAL SECURITY ACT

When President Franklin D. Roosevelt signed the Social Security Act into law on August 14, 1935, he called it the "cornerstone" of a system of government-provided social protections that would take care of basic human needs while preventing the likelihood of crippling economic depression and mass poverty in the future. The several programs created by that historic legislation included Old Age Assistance (OAA) for the low-income elderly; Old Age Insurance (OAI) for retired workers; Unemployment Insurance (UI) for workers who lost their jobs; and Aid to Dependent Children (ADC) for single, principally widowed, women with children. Together, these programs would prove the mainstay of the social welfare system for decades to come. But only one of them, Old Age Insurance, would come to be associated with the favored term *social security,* a sign of its broader acceptance and growing popularity among the citizenry as the program that came closest to living up to President Roosevelt's ambitious aims.

OAI was initially created to protect individual workers in the paid labor force from the later loss of income due to old age or retirement. Later ex-

The Social Security Act offered much-needed benefits to elderly Americans, as this Depression-era poster testified. FRANKLIN DELANO ROOSEVELT LIBRARY

panded to include survivors and those with disabilities (becoming Old Age, Survivors', and Disability Insurance, or OASDI), the program popularly known as Social Security has become the single largest public income support program in the United States. Over 90 percent of all workers in the paid labor force are now covered by the program. As of 2003, the program paid monthly benefits to more than forty-five million Americans, including retirees and their surviving spouses, the long-term disabled, and the spouses and minor children of covered workers who die before retirement age. It is widely credited as the most important factor in reducing elderly poverty rates, from an estimated 50 percent at the height of the Great Depression, to less than 10 percent as officially measured at the beginning of the twenty-first century.

There are several features that distinguish OASDI from most other social welfare or "safety net" programs, and that help to explain both its comparative popularity and its claim to the mantle of "social security." One is that it operates on the principle of social insurance: Individuals draw benefits from a common fund to which they have contributed during their working years as a form of protection against a life-course risk—in this case, the risk of devastating income loss due to retirement or disability. Although benefit formulae favor lower-income retirees, the system is otherwise "needs-blind" and pays benefits automatically upon retirement or disability. This reflects Social Security's preventive approach, and distinguishes it from "means-tested" social welfare programs, which provide benefits only after recipients become eligible by offering proof that they are sufficiently impoverished and continue to abide by various program rules.

Social Security's reliance on worker contributions is a second feature that distinguishes it from more traditionally defined "welfare" or public assistance programs, and that has historically helped garner a broad base of political support. Its funding comes from automatic payroll taxes levied on employees and employers, which are put into a specially designated Social Security trust fund. As critics have pointed out, this is a relatively regressive form of financing since it imposes the same tax rate on all workers rather than taxing the affluent at a higher rate, and, since only income up to a certain level is subject to the tax, it actually takes a smaller percentage of the income of the most affluent than it does of low-income workers. And yet, much as the program's original architects predicted, this contributory element makes workers feel they have genuinely earned their benefits and have in interest in the program's success.

Third, unlike most other income support programs, Social Security is wholly administered by the federal government through the Social Security Administration, bringing a far greater degree of uniformity and efficiency in comparison to those administered at the state and local level. Of all government supported programs, it comes closest to embodying the idea of a social contract between the citizenry and national government.

Fourth, to a far greater degree than other programs, Social Security works as a family support system, offering protection against income loss to surviving spouses and children as well as to individual workers, while also relieving retirees from the prospect of financial dependence on their adult children in old age. Finally, Social Security's protection against post-retirement poverty is lasting, and not time-limited as most other income support programs are. Retired beneficiaries are guaranteed payments for the remainder of their lifetimes and, especially important, benefits are automatically adjusted each year to account for inflation.

Many of the features that have made Social Security a popular and effective program were strongly contested at the time of its creation and came about only through a process of political negotiation and programmatic reform. Indeed, in comparison to the more relief-oriented programs created by the Social Security Act, old-age insurance was highly controversial and remained so for much of its early history. Moreover, some of the very political compromises that made the initial passage of Social Security possible also created serious inequities within it that were only later addressed through hard-fought legislative reform.

PROGRESSIVE ERA ORIGINS

Although Social Security traces its legislative origins to 1935 and the Great Depression, the system was built on ideas and models for old-age provision that had been advocated within U.S. and European social reform circles throughout the late nineteenth- and early twentieth-century period known as the Progressive era. During a time marked by what one contemporary called a "reform spirit" and characterized by a great deal of cross-national "borrowing" in public policy, reformers sought new ways of coping with the growing inequities of an increasingly industrialized capitalist economy. Here, in the context of hotly contested debates over workers' rights and protections, unemployment, child labor, and access to health care, ideas such as compulsory social insurance, state-funded pensions, and subsidized private retirement funds began to get serious consideration as a way of dealing with the growing problem of economic need in old age.

These early reformers approached the issue that came to be referred to as old-age "insecurity" with an analysis and assumptions that later proved very influential in Social Security's design. Most significantly, they approached it as a problem of the growing industrial labor force, and with what they saw as the needs of the predominantly white, male breadwinner/wage earner in mind. As the economy became more industrialized, less agricultural, and less oriented to self-employment, they argued, workers relied more heavily on wages from outside employment as their chief source of income. This left older workers facing greater and greater insecurity as the prospect of retiring from, or being pushed out of, the paid labor force approached. At a time when union or employer-provided retirement benefits were virtually nonexistent, many of the elderly were being pushed to drain meager savings, to rely on their children, or to the humiliating recourse of poor relief or even institutionalization in an old-age home. In the eyes of reformers, this situation was inhumane and demeaning, especially at the end of a lifetime of productive work. In particular, the prospect of "dependency" in old age threatened to undermine an ideal of the wage-earning household in which men assumed the role of chief breadwinner and women remained economically subordinate, if not completely dependent.

Agree though they might on the outlines of the problem, reformers differed widely on the solution, and drew on different precedents for support. Early proponents of the social insurance approach looked abroad for inspiration, sending delegations to study and observe the comprehensive system of compulsory health, accident, and old-age insurance established in 1880s Germany, as well as the more limited approaches adopted by the British and other European countries in the early decades of the twentieth century. After World War I and throughout the 1920s, European social insurance continued to expand to cover new groups and new needs, starting from health and employment and eventually extending to old-age insurance. The momentum in the United States was far more halting and uncertain, however, reflecting controversy about the social insurance idea as well as ambivalence about how far it should extend. Thus, when an influential Progressive reform organization, the American Association for Labor Legislation, launched its campaigns for social insurance beginning in 1912, it focused on workmen's compensation, health, and unemployment but stopped short of endorsing old-age insurance. The American Association for Old Age Security (which later changed its name to the American Association for Social Security), established in 1927 by economist and leading social insurance advocate Abraham Epstein, also took the politically safer route of pushing for expanded old-age relief rather than insurance. By then operating in a more conservative political environment, old-age insurance advocates were mindful of the opposition they faced from private insurers, employers, and political leaders suspicious of its European roots, vaguely socialist undertones, and "un-American" collectivism.

But at least as important in the reluctance about old-age insurance was the comparative appeal of direct payments to the elderly in the form of government-funded pensions. Unlike social insurance, which was compulsory and based on the idea of shared risk, pensions involved outright grants to elderly recipients based on past service or established need. In addition to being more straightforward, this approach had the advantage of familiarity: Civil War pensions, originally intended for disabled Union army veterans, had grown into an enormous social welfare program for northern veterans, their families, and survivors—an expansion that drew disdain from some legislators but that nevertheless established an important precedent among the general public. Like other campaigns to establish public pensions for poor widowed mothers and their children, old-age pensions could be presented as aid to the "deserving" poor. Moreover, the pension movement had at least the appearance of being home-grown; old-age pension campaigns took place at the state level, sidestepping the charge of federal government expansionism and preserving local discretion over who among the elderly would receive aid. By the early 1930s old-age pensions had been proposed in a number of states but enacted in only six. That number quickly rose to thirty by mid-decade in response to the Great Depression.

Still another approach offered as an alternative to public old-age insurance envisioned relying on the private sector through expansion of company-sponsored retirement plans. For the most part, these "welfare capitalist" plans combined a percentage of withheld wages matched by employer contributions and invested in a retirement fund. Very few employer-sponsored programs existed by the late 1920s, however, and they offered workers no guarantee or protection against company default. Still, private retirement plans exerted a strong influence on public-sector planning, as influential business leaders organized to preserve a central role for employer benefits in any system of social provision.

THE GREAT DEPRESSION: GROWING
DEMAND FOR REFORM

Despite considerable groundwork on many fronts, in reality the system of old-age provision was threadbare on the eve of the Great Depression, and utterly inadequate once mass unemployment and destitution set in. With an estimated half of all elderly Americans living in poverty (a rate nearing 90 percent among non-whites), only about 3 percent were receiving public benefits from the state pension programs, and then only under the stringent conditions imposed by local administrators. As their presence in bread lines, among the homeless, and in harrowing letters to President and Mrs. Roo-

sevelt made evident, the plight of older Americans demanded action at the federal level. But what made federal action on old-age security a top priority was more than dire need. Equally important was the combination of political pressure and reform advocacy brought to bear on the Roosevelt administration by grassroots movements and social policy experts alike.

One important source of pressure was the growing segment of the population over age 65, which by the time the Roosevelt administration was facing the 1934 congressional elections had become an increasingly potent political force. Seeking to capitalize on that potential, Huey Long, the populist senator from Louisiana, made universal pensions for the elderly a prominent part of his "Share Our Wealth" campaign, promising generous monthly payments financed by taxes on millionaires. The Townsend movement was more singularly focused on the elderly, both as a constituency in need and a potential source of much-needed consumer spending. Named for Francis E. Townsend, a 66-year-old retired doctor from California, the Townsend Plan proposed to pay $200 monthly to people over 60, provided they were retired, American citizens, without criminal records, and prepared to spend the money within thirty days of receipt. Within months of its 1933 publication in a Long Beach, California, newspaper, the Townsend Plan had garnered millions of supporters across the country and thousands of local Townsend Clubs. The outcry for federal aid to the elderly, coming from a group the Democrats were eager to court, was a voice the Roosevelt administration could not afford to ignore.

Equally important in the momentum for change was the commitment to reform among a number of the social policy experts recruited for service by the Roosevelt administration, and ready to be mobilized as the New Deal shifted its focus from the immediate crisis of providing relief to the longer-range challenge of building a lasting system of protections against economic insecurity. While the demand for federal old-age pensions was mounting at the grass roots level, these policy experts were working behind the scenes on behalf of the more politically controversial social insurance approach. Dismissing the Townsend Plan and other popular pension schemes as far-fetched and prohibitively expensive, they used their expertise to present social insurance as the more fiscally responsible, long-term solution—one that they felt could be more easily insulated from the whims of politicians pandering to their constituencies.

Social insurance advocates also had two other important advantages in their efforts to influence the administration's approach to old-age security. One was Roosevelt's desire to avoid federal relief as a permanent policy, in line with his personal belief that "the dole" would undermine individual initiative and self-esteem. The other was that social insurance advocates found a strong institutional base within the administration. In the summer of 1934, President Roosevelt appointed the cabinet-level group known as the Committee on Economic Security (CES), and asked it to construct a comprehensive, stable, and permanent system of government social protections for consideration by the Congress. Secretary of Labor Frances Perkins, who chaired the committee, was a longtime advocate of social insurance for the unemployed. Edwin Witte, the University of Wisconsin professor brought in to head the CES staff, had played a central role in drafting the landmark unemployment insurance law in Wisconsin. And Roosevelt himself, while governor of New York and later as president, had expressed admiration for social insurance as a truly modern, forward-looking reform idea. While initially reluctant about extending the social insurance principle from unemployment to old age, the CES leadership eventually came to endorse the concept, thanks largely to the energies of the old-age security planners on its staff.

STRUCTURING SOCIAL SECURITY: THE CES PROPOSALS AND CONGRESSIONAL DEBATE

Chief responsibility for designing the old-age provisions was in the hands of a three-person committee headed by Berkeley law professor Barbara Nachtrieb Armstrong, a leading expert and fervent advocate of social insurance, along with Princeton economist J. Douglas Brown, and Murray Latimer, an economist with expertise in pension policy. It was their initial work, based on a combination of intensive study, careful actuarial calculation, and internal political negotiation, that gave Social Security some of its cardinal features. They were also animated by their own values and commitments to the New Deal, to a more socially responsible government, and to a principle of inclusion that did not always cross the boundaries of gender and race. Thus, in making federal retirement insurance rather than public pensions the centerpiece of their long-range proposal, they were not simply acting on research suggesting that this was the most fiscally sustainable approach. They were also embracing the New Deal spirit of revising and updating the social contract between government and the citizenry, with all the implications of a greater public responsibility for economic security it brought. Similarly, their decision to design a system that would be self-financing and based on worker contributions meshed with President Roosevelt's long-range political calculus, as well as their own concern for fiscal responsibility. Knowing that the payroll tax would initially prove unpopular, Roosevelt insisted that making the system contributory would eventually prove a political asset, avoiding the need to turn to general tax revenues while allowing workers to claim benefits as a right rather than on the basis of proven need.

Finally, their insistence on inclusiveness had both practical and principled elements. As a practical matter, universal coverage would help to ensure a large pool of contributors while helping to ease the unemployment problem by allowing older workers to retire at age 65. But the planners also saw inclusiveness as a matter of equity, and on this basis included the substantially nonwhite population of agricultural along with industrial wage earners in their original old-age insurance proposal. And yet, the spirit of inclusiveness only went so far. Domestic workers, sharecroppers, and temporarily or irregularly employed workers were all excluded from the original insurance proposals, along with the self-employed. Although couched as a practical decision, these exclusions effectively denied coverage for much of the female, non-white, and lower-class workforce. It would remain for Congress, and its powerful southern bloc, to instill even deeper racial divisions in the system, using the mechanism of occupational exclusion. Rightly perceiving the threat to their control over African-American labor, southern members of Congress insisted on excluding agricultural as well as domestic workers from coverage. It was a price the administration was willing to pay for the sake of passing the Social Security Act.

Two other aspects of the legislation's old-age security provisions reflect its careful balance of principle with practical and political considerations. The first was ensconced in Title I of the Social Security Act, providing federal aid to states for needs-based Old Age Assistance programs. Viewed by the CES planners as a necessary stopgap for those too old or otherwise unable to benefit from insurance, it was also a response to the political threat posed by the Townsendites and other sources of popular activism. Second was the legislation's implicit promise to keep public insurance benefits adequate but low, sending important reassurances to private employers that Social Security would complement, not replace, their own employee retirement plans. This unspoken bargain proved essential in garnering political support from liberal-leaning business leaders, who in turn helped to fight off congressional efforts to allow employers to opt out of Social Security altogether.

Significantly, the dynamics shaping the creation of the Social Security Act's old age provisions also played out in its other major provisions. Thus, the CES experts responsible for the unemployment insurance program were committed to using the social insurance model, based on a payroll tax imposed on employers, and designed to provide laid-off workers with temporary benefits. But, in efforts to reassure advocates of state control as well as business leaders wary of higher federal taxes, they adopted a proposal based on the approach developed in Wisconsin, which allowed states to devise their own plans and benefit levels, and to lower tax rates for employers with stable employment records. In this, they rejected an alternative, known as the Ohio Plan, which would have required uniform tax rates within states and minimum federal standards, thus assuring a more adequate level of benefits for unemployed workers. Meanwhile, capitulating to prevailing racial and gender norms, they also excluded agricultural, domestic, and irregularly employed workers from UI coverage.

The other major provision of the Social Security Act, Aid to Dependent Children, was based on the patchwork but widely accepted system of mothers' pension programs introduced during the progressive era and adopted in nearly every state by 1930. Advocated by a widespread and predominantly female network of "maternalist" reformers, the idea of providing relief for single—mostly widowed—mothers and their children proved appealing to Depression era legislators eager to discourage women from entering the full-time labor force. Although materinalists considered ADC an important achievement, their proposals to assure more adequate benefits, uniform standards, and to prevent discrimination were fought back in Congress. With states largely in control and due to weak federal oversight, the program remained riddled with inadequacies and racial inequities that would contribute to the stigma associated with welfare in future decades.

FROM RETIREMENT TO FAMILY SUPPORT SYSTEM: THE 1939 AMENDMENTS

No sooner had the Social Security Act won passage than its old-age insurance provisions came under fierce attack. Republican candidate Alfred Landon called for repealing old-age insurance in the 1936 presidential elections. With payroll deductions set to begin in 1937, some prominent employers simply refused to cooperate, and backed a constitutional challenge that came before the Supreme Court. The Court's 1937 decision ultimately upheld Social Security's constitutionality, but by then old-age insurance had once again come under congressional scrutiny. The Senate controversy hinged on the issue of financing, an increasingly volatile issue as the country receded into further economic downturn during the recession of 1937 to 1938. Under the original financing plan, the system would build up a large accumulation of funds before any benefits were paid out. Workers would start paying into the system in 1937, but no retirees would receive benefits before 1942. Besides draining income from already hard-pressed workers, critics charged, this represented an irresponsible build-up of funds that might otherwise be circulating in the economy. Meanwhile, Old Age Assistance was growing to unprecedented proportions, providing millions with immediate benefits that Social Security could only promise in the distant future.

With the entire system under threat, Congress and the Social Security Board agreed to appoint an advisory council, chaired by former CES staff economist J. Douglas Brown, to recommend changes. Their deliberations, which resulted in the 1939 amendments to the Social Security Act, sought to strengthen the program by transforming it in fundamental ways. The first was to broaden it from an individual retirement plan to a system of family support, by adding survivors' and spousal benefits; the second was to make benefit calculations more generous and favorable to lower-income workers, while making provisions to start benefit payments by 1940; and the third was to shift to a "pay as you go" financing formula to accommodate these more expansive benefits. Under this formula, worker contributions are not held in reserve for their own future retirement, but are used to finance benefits for the current generation of retirees. As the advisory council acknowledged, this method would provide ample funding for the Social Security trust fund created by the 1939 amendments for several decades, but would eventually require supplementation as the population aged and reached retirement age. Their shift to a "family concept" of Social Security also served to reinforce traditional gender roles, albeit in unacknowledged ways. Thus, the 1939 amendments made spousal and survivors' benefits available to wives and not to husbands, on the assumption that a wife was rightfully dependent on her husband and that her earnings were not essential to the overall well-being of the household. Most immediately important to the survival of Social Security, however, the 1939 changes would enable the program to deliver on its initial promise of a more dignified, and ultimately more generous, form of support than means-tested old-age relief.

SOCIAL SECURITY AND THE NEW DEAL LEGACY

Through these and other provisions, the 1939 amendments instituted a new, more expansive idea of Social Security that in turn set the stage for significant program expansions in the decades to come. Beginning in 1950 with amendments extending coverage to previously excluded agricultural, domestic, and self-employed workers, the program gradually came to realize the inclusive vision articulated by its original architects, and eventually to redress the racial, gender, and class inequities perpetuated by the occupational exclusions. The addition of disability insurance in 1954, along with more progressive benefit formulae, has also proved especially important to non-white and lower-wage workers. Major court decisions in the 1970s overruled the gender biases in survivors' and spousal benefits. Especially important to Social Security's anti-poverty objectives, the 1972 adoption of automatic cost of living allowances (COLAs) has provided crucial protection against inflation. Few of these major changes would have come about without the combination of political activism and policy advocacy that helped to shape the original program.

And yet, while these changes made it a more popular and effective program, since the 1980s Social Security has faced an ongoing series of "crises," stemming in part from concern about the program's ability to meet future benefit obligations in the wake of the "baby boom" retirement, but more fundamentally from an ideological challenge to the very principles of social insurance. Nevertheless, Social Security remains the most lasting legacy of Depression-era activism, New Deal policymaking, and above all of the public commitment to a broadly inclusive system of shared social protection against the insecurities of a market economy. Future debate will hinge on these values as well.

See Also: AID TO DEPENDENT CHILDREN (ADC); OLD-AGE INSURANCE; PERKINS, FRANCES; TOWNSEND PLAN; UNEMPLOYMENT INSURANCE.

BIBLIOGRAPHY

Abbott, Grace. *From Relief to Social Security: The Development of the New Public Welfare Services and Their Administration.* 1941.

Achenbaum, W. Andrew. *Social Security: Visions and Revisions.* 1986.

Advisory Council on Social Security. *Final Report.* 1938.

Altmeyer, Arthur J. *The Formative Years of Social Security.* 1966.

Armstrong, Barbara N. *Insuring the Essentials: Minimum Wage, Plus Social Insurance—a Living Wage Program.* 1932.

Berkowitz, Edward D. *America's Welfare State: From Roosevelt to Reagan.* 1991.

Berkowitz, Edward C. *Mr. Social Security: The Life of Wilbur J. Cohen.* 1995.

Cates, Jerry R. *Insuring Inequality: Administrative Leadership in Social Security, 1935–54.* 1983.

Committee on Economic Security. *Report of the Committee on Economic Security.* 1935.

Derthick, Martha. *Policymaking for Social Security.* 1979.

Epstein, Abraham. *Insecurity, a Challenge to America: A Study of Social Insurance in the United States and Abroad.* 1936.

Gordon, Linda. *Pitied but Not Entitled: Single Mothers and the History of Welfare, 1890–1935.* 1994.

Jacoby, Sanford M. "Employers and the Welfare State: The Role of Marion B. Folsom." *The Journal of American History* 80 (1993): 525–556.

Kessler-Harris, Alice. *In Pursuit of Equity: Women, Men, and the Quest for Economic Citizenship in 20th Century America.* 2001.

Lieberman, Robert C. *Shifting the Color Line: Race and the American Welfare State.* 1998.

Lubove, Roy. *The Struggle for Social Security, 1900–1935.* 1968.

Mettler, Suzanne. *Dividing Citizens: Gender and Federalism in New Deal Public Policy.* 1998.

Quadagno, Jill. *The Transformation of Old Age Security: Class and Politics in the American Welfare State.* 1988.

Rodgers, Daniel T. *Atlantic Crossings: Social Politics in a Progressive Age.* 1998.

Rubinow, I. M. *The Quest for Security.* 1934.

Witte, Edwin E. *The Development of the Social Security Act.* 1963.

ALICE O'CONNOR

SOCIAL WORKERS

The 1930s proved to be a transformative decade for the social work profession. The appointment of Frances Perkins as secretary of labor in 1933 and the passage of the Social Security Act in 1935 convinced many social workers that the Roosevelt administration would effectively address the major social woes of the Depression. Perkins, who was the first woman appointed to a presidential cabinet, was a noted social worker from New York, and many social workers anticipated that their concerns would receive national spotlighting as a result of her appointment. In addition, the Social Security Act convinced social workers that people in need could turn to the federal government for relief, and would no longer have to rely solely on local communities. Moreover, during the 1930s, the 1920s model of casework-related social work fell out of favor and there was a gradual move away from the community settlement house concept toward the establishment of government welfare agencies. John H. Ehrenreich contends that the 1920s model of social work professionalism became an anachronism with the advent of the Depression and its massive poverty, its newly energized social programs, its new social work institutions, and the transformation of the relationship between social workers and government. Social work elites could no longer claim that they worked solely in the interest of their clients, and division arose in the profession between the old guard and rank-and-file social workers who came of age during the 1930s.

The best known of the old guard reformers, Jane Addams, died in 1935, and according to historian Judith Trolander, no one came along in the settlement movement to replace her. Even the leaders of the settlement homes that remained by the mid-1930s began to realize that they had to make fundamental changes in order to keep up with trends in their profession. Perhaps the greatest failure of the settlement house movement was that it did not embrace integration during this period of Jim Crow segregation. Elisabeth Lasch-Quinn concludes that racial prejudice was the main cause of the decline of the settlement movement, and the reason the great promise of the movement remained unfulfilled.

There were some social workers, however, who addressed the concerns of racial injustice within the social work profession during the 1930s. These rank-and-file social workers also played a major role in left-wing agitation during the 1930s. Social workers who belonged to the leftist rank-and-file often focused their energy on linking the broad social objectives of their profession with the labor movement. The group's greatest success was the inauguration of the radical journal *Social Work Today* in 1934. The journal was edited by noted social work scholar Jacob Fisher of the Bureau of Jewish Social Research, and many of the era's major figures in social work were contributors, including Gordon Hamilton, Eduard C. Lindeman, Ira Reid, Roger Baldwin, and Mary Van Kleeck. By the 1930s, this leftist branch of the social work profession was cooperating with African-American reformers, such as Eugene Kinckle Jones of the National Urban League, Forrester B. Washington of Atlanta University school of social work, and Charles S. Johnson of the Fisk University department of sociology. Their goal was to eliminate discrimination within social work policies. *Social Work Today* stood in opposition to *Survey*, another professional journal that addressed more traditional and nonconfrontational issues within social work.

Jacob Fisher, chairman of the National Coordinating Committee of Social Service Employee Groups, was a leader of the rank-and-file radical social workers. Edith Abbott, president of the National Conference of Social Work during the 1930s and a faculty member at the University of Chicago, represented the more traditional social work core. Abbot and Fisher were particularly opposed on issues of race. Aside from concerns about racial discrimination within the profession, there were other forces that threatened peaceable relations. One conflict concerned new professional qualifications for the master of social work degree that was adopted in 1937 at the National Conference of Social Work. Since Atlanta University was the only black school of social work in 1937 that offered an advanced degree, the number of trained social workers serving the African-American community was limited. The ruling of the U.S. Supreme Court in *Missouri ex. rel. Gaines v. Canada* (1938), however, required many colleges that had previously been open only to whites to accept black students, a ruling that had a major impact on the social work profession.

Another important development in social work during the 1930s was its spread to the rural United States. Before the Depression, social work had mostly been accomplished in urban environments, but new government regulations facilitated social work in rural areas, and rural people were able to receive attention to their social needs for the first time during the 1930s.

See Also: PERKINS, FRANCES.

BIBLIOGRAPHY

Addams, Jane. *Twenty Years at Hull House.* 1910.

Brown, Josephine Chapin. *Public Relief, 1929–1939.* 1941.

Chambers, Clarke A. *Paul U. Kellogg and the Survey: Voices for Social Welfare and Social Justice.* 1971.

Ehrenreich, John H. *The Altruistic Imagination: A History of Social Work and Social Policy in the United States.* 1985.

Fisher, Jacob. *The Response of Social Work to the Depression.* 1980.

Lasch-Quinn, Elisabeth. *Black Neighbors: Race and the Limits of Reform in the American Settlement House Movement, 1890–1945.* 1993.

Simon, Barbara Levy. *The Empowerment Tradition in American Social Work: A History.* 1994.

Spano, Rick. *The Rank and File Movement in Social Work.* 1982.

Thyer, Bruce A., and Marilyn A. Biggerstaff. *Professional Social Work Credentialing and Legal Regulation: A Review of Critical Issues and an Annotated Bibliography.* 1989.

Trolander, Judith Ann. *Professionalism and Social Change: From the Settlement House Movement to Neighborhood Center, 1886 to the Present.* 1987.

FELIX L. ARMFIELD

SOIL CONSERVATION SERVICE (SCS)

In April 1935 the U.S. Congress passed the Soil Conservation Act, which created the Soil Conservation Service (SCS) within the Department of Agriculture (USDA) and declared that the federal government bore permanent responsibility for reducing water and wind erosion of the nation's soils. The SCS included more than ten thousand permanent and part-time employees, and utilized the labor of some 450 Civilian Conservation Corps units. The SCS also operated twenty-three research stations, where it studied the causes, extent, and prevention of soil erosion.

A farmer in Vernon County, Wisconsin, shows his fields to a representative from the Soil Conservation Service in 1942. This farmer was experimenting with strip cropping, a method used to prevent soil depletion. LIBRARY OF CONGRESS, PRINTS & PHOTOGRAPHS DIVISION, FSA/OWI COLLECTION

Before the creation of the SCS, soil conservation had not figured prominently in government policy and had been overseen variously by the Department of Agriculture's Bureau of Chemistry and Soils, by county agricultural extension agents, and from 1933 to 1935 by the Soil Erosion Service, a temporary agency in the Department of Interior. President Franklin Roosevelt transferred the Soil Erosion Service to the USDA in March 1935, only weeks before the SCS was created. The Great Depression, coupled with the massive dust storms that swept the country's southern Plains in the spring of 1935, compelled the federal government to address the urgent and related problems of the depressed

agricultural economy and the squandering and mismanagement of the nation's natural resources.

The Soil Conservation Service was headed by Hugh Hammond Bennett, who had directed the Soil Erosion Service. Bennett had been advocating soil conservation since the early twentieth century. In 1928, he warned that soil erosion posed a "menace" to the nation's food supply and prosperity. In 1934, experts from the Soil Erosion Service estimated that more than 260 million acres of American cropland had been severely damaged by water and erosion. The following year, Bennett estimated that more than 50 million acres had been so severely damaged that they were no longer arable.

Soil erosion during the 1930s ruined the fields of many farms, including this one near Dalhart, Texas, photographed in 1938.

The SCS addressed the problem of soil erosion by creating "demonstration projects" in which the Service cooperated with landowners to implement conservation measures. The SCS assisted farmers in devising and implementing soil conservation plans for their land. In exchange for the landowner's agreement to cooperate for a five-year period and to contribute his labor, the SCS supplied technical advice, materials, and additional labor. The Service urged farmers and ranchers voluntarily to plant ground cover vegetation to protect vulnerable soils, to rotate crops and allow fields to occasionally lie fallow, to build terraces and use contour plowing to retain soil moisture, and to refrain from planting crops on highly erodible land.

Although more than fifty thousand farmers participated in SCS demonstration projects, attacking the widespread problem of soil erosion one farm at a time was costly and inefficient. In 1936, therefore, the SCS published a model statute that would enable farmers to create a soil conservation district in their vicinity, which could stipulate land use practices within the district. Many state governments passed laws permitting farmers to form soil conservation districts, but many farmers and state legislators were reluctant to grant districts the power to require landowners to comply with district regulations, and soil conservation efforts remained largely voluntary.

See Also: DUST BOWL; SHELTERBELT PROJECT.

BIBLIOGRAPHY

Hardin, Charles M. *The Politics of Agriculture: Soil Conservation and the Struggle for Power in Rural America.* 1952.

Held, R. Burnell, and Marion Clawson. *Soil Conservation in Perspective.* 1965.

Nixon, Edgar, ed. *Franklin D. Roosevelt and Conservation, 1911–1945,* 2 vols. 1957.

Owen, A. L. Riesch. *Conservation under FDR.* 1983.

Simms, D. Harper. *The Soil Conservation Service.* 1970.

Steiner, Frederick R. *Soil Conservation in the United States: Policy and Planning.* 1990.

Worster, Donald. *Dust Bowl: The Southern Plains in the 1930s.* 1979.

CHRIS RASMUSSEN

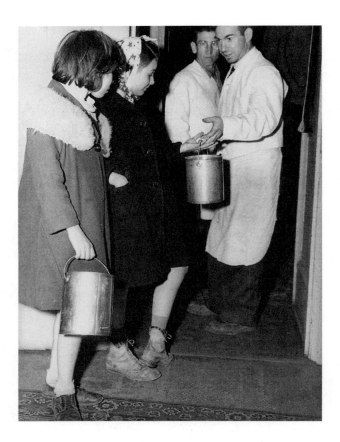

Young girls accept buckets of free soup for their families at a city mission in Dubuque, Iowa, in 1940. LIBRARY OF CONGRESS, PRINTS & PHOTOGRAPHS DIVISION, FSA/OWI COLLECTION

SOUP KITCHENS

Soup kitchens are establishments that prepare and dispense food to the needy on a regular basis, usually soup, sandwiches, bread, and other minimal dietary essentials. The soup kitchens of the Great Depression era were one small part of larger collective community-based efforts that included penny restaurants, welfare cafeterias, and milk lines that came into being to combat the negative impact of the Depression. Although soup kitchens existed in cities during the decades following the Civil War, and continue to exist at the beginning of the twenty-first century, the number swelled during the 1930s.

During the early years of the Depression, when Franklin Delano Roosevelt's predecessor, Herbert Hoover claimed that "No one has starved," soup kitchens provided food assistance when the federal government would not. In the absence of any substantial local or federal relief programs, Americans did as they had done in the past: They turned to churches and civic organizations for help. Despite the scarcity of government-sponsored support during the years that preceded the New Deal, the growth of these establishments was so extensive that virtually every town and city in America had a substantial number of private organizations offering food to those in need.

One charitable organization, the Ohio Fraternal Order of Eagles, opened a free cafeteria in 1930 serving soup, bread, milk, and cheese to an average of two hundred persons per day. Within a year, the number of people served quadrupled. In November 1929, a Franciscan order expanded its long-standing tradition of feeding the poor from the door of its monastery by opening a soup kitchen in Detroit to respond to the increasing number of unemployed. In the beginning, the Capuchin Soup Kitchen served only rolls and coffee. At its peak, the kitchen fed well over seven hundred people daily

Unemployed men line up for a meal at a soup kitchen in Washington, D.C., in 1936. FRANKLIN DELANO ROOSEVELT LIBRARY

using donations from local bakers, farmers, and merchants. So generous were the donations that the director of the kitchen boasted that the soup could be eaten with a fork. The infamous mobster Al Capone even joined this collective struggle against hunger by opening a popular soup kitchen in Chicago. Newspaper tycoon William Randolph Hearst did the same, opening soup kitchens at opposite ends of New York City's Times Square that served sandwiches from trucks plastered with posters advertising his paper's philanthropic efforts.

But the "good work" of feeding the indigent was not limited to established organizations and wealthy businessmen. Countless individuals supplemented those efforts, many volunteering in soup kitchens that were set up in abandoned or makeshift structures and horse-drawn carriages. In New York, samaritans like "Lady Bountiful" fed thousands of men daily in lower Manhattan. Urban Ledoux, known as Mr. Zero, handed out wagonloads of day-old doughnuts in Times Square, and a man called Mr. Glad not only gave out food, but also nickels and gloves. The beloved minister Father Divine opened his Long Island home to those in need and was convicted of disturbing the peace when his middle-class neighbors became appalled by the sight of busloads of hungry worshippers flocking to his doorstep.

Acquiring the food offered by soup kitchens was no simple task. Regardless of the weather, long lines (or breadlines) began to form outside soup kitchens at dawn. Many of the people waiting in breadlines did not have shoes or coats to protect them from rain or snow. To avoid public humiliation, women often sent children to collect the day's offering. Families could use the pail of soup (mostly broth) to supplement food acquired through their own efforts and the limited resources acquired from other relief agencies. Single persons and married couples without children in their households relied more heavily on soup kitchens than families did because they were not eligible for such relief as cash grants, food orders, food baskets, and commissary privileges. However humiliating the experience was for most Americans, soup kitchens provided a benevolent alternative for those reduced to begging for food, eating dandelions, or even worse, scavenging for discarded fruits and vegetables in the city dump.

See Also: BREADLINES; CHARITY; CHILDREN AND ADOLESCENTS, IMPACT OF THE GREAT DEPRESSION ON; FAMILY AND HOME, IMPACT OF THE GREAT DEPRESSION ON; FATHER DIVINE; HOMELESSNESS.

BIBLIOGRAPHY

Bendiner, Robert. *Just around the Corner: A Highly Selective History of the Thirties.* 1967.

Bicknell, Catherine. "Detroit's Capuchin Soup Kitchen." *Labor History* 21, no. 1 (1983): 112–124.

Glasser, Irene. *More Than Bread: Ethnography of a Soup Kitchen.* 1988.

Greenberg, Cheryl. *Or Does It Explode?: Black Harlem in the Great Depression.* 1991.

McElvaine, Robert S., ed. *Down and Out in the Great Depression: Letters from the Forgotten Man.* 1983.

McElvaine, Robert S. *The Great Depression: American, 1929–1941.* 1984, 1993.

"No One Has Starved." *Fortune* (September 1932): 18–29.

Poppendieck, Janet. *Breadlines Knee-Deep in Wheat: Food Assistance in the Great Depression.* 1986.

Terkel, Studs. *Hard Times: An Oral History of the Great Depression.* 1970.

Watkins, T. H. *The Great Depression: America in the 1930s.* 1993.

Watkins, T. H. *The Hungry Years: A Narrative History of the Great Depression in America.* 1999.

GREGORY BAGGETT

SOUTH, GREAT DEPRESSION IN THE

On the eve of the Great Depression the South was the poorest region in the United States, its per capita income scarcely 50 percent of the national figure. It was a poor rural one-crop society in which too many people chased too little farm income. It was the bastion of the open shop. It was rigidly segregated and African Americans were economically and politically powerless. The region's politics were dominated by a conservative alliance of county-seat elites, planters, and industrialists, largely immune to popular pressure because of their economic dominance and the restricted nature of the electorate. Planters and industrialists had a mutual interest in a surplus labor force, low wages, low taxes, and minimal government services.

POVERTY

The onset of the Depression merely confirmed the South's poverty. The collapse of world commodity prices and foreign markets devastated cotton and tobacco farmers. Overproduction meant that the cotton crop yielded $1.5 billion in 1929 but only $465 million in 1932. In Mississippi, times were described as "tough as jailhouse stew." On a single day in April 1932 one-quarter of the land in the state was sold at sheriff's sales. Total receipts for the cigarette tobacco crop in 1932 were one-third those of 1929. One tobacco county in North Carolina saw 3,500 foreclosures in one year on the county's 5,280 farms. In addition, in 1930 drought ravaged a number of states.

For the 8.5 million tenants and sharecroppers, 3 million of whom were black, the onset of the Depression reinforced their hopelessness and dependency. As one black Georgian wryly observed, "Most blacks did not even know the Great Depression had come. They had always been poor and only thought the whites were catching up." The cash incomes of black families rarely reached $100 a year.

Southern industries were just as vulnerable. Textiles firms had moved to the southern Piedmont region for lower labor costs in the 1920s, but too many small firms sought to grab a slice of a highly

A Farm Security Administration supervisor visits a client in Green County, Georgia, in 1939 to see how his crops are faring.

LIBRARY OF CONGRESS, PRINTS & PHOTOGRAPHS DIVISION, FSA/OWI COLLECTION

competitive market by expanding production at ever lower prices and lower wages. The same was true of coal in northern Alabama, the lumber industry, and oil. In Birmingham, where U.S. Steel paid its workers between ten and fifteen cents an hour, 25,000 of the city's workforce of 108,000 were out of work and most of the remainder were employed only part-time. The city had abolished its welfare department in the 1920s. Private charity, the community chest, could not meet Birmingham's welfare needs: It had helped eight hundred families in 1929; by 1932 it struggled to help nine thousand.

Revenue-starved state and local governments responded to the Depression with retrenchment: slashing government spending and services and turning to sales taxes to offset plunging income from property taxes. For the rural and industrial poor there was little to do other than endure. Sharecroppers, unable to move from the countryside to urban jobs, could only bargain by leaving one landlord and working for another, and 40 percent of Mississippi tenants did so in 1930. Occasionally desperation drove the poor to violence or radicalism: In Arkansas they threatened to loot food stores; in Alabama they joined a Communist-organized sharecroppers union; in the Piedmont they struck the textile mills in 1929 and 1931; in Atlanta they joined Unemployed Leagues. Violent repression met these efforts and simply emphasized

Flood refugees take shelter at a temporary camp in Forrest City, Arkansas, in 1937. LIBRARY OF CONGRESS, PRINTS & PHOTOGRAPHS DIVISION, FSA/OWI COLLECTION

the powerlessness of the "have-nots" in the segregated South.

PLANTER'S HEAVEN AND WELFARE REVOLUTION

What impact did the New Deal have on the region that Franklin Roosevelt described as the nation's number one economic problem? The New Deal rescued cotton and tobacco farmers. North Carolina senator Josiah Bailey wrote in December 1933, "Eastern North Carolina, a very large section devoted to agriculture has been prostrated for five years. This year the people are really prosperous . . . with one accord they give the credit to the President." A Mississippi banker told Turner Catledge in 1935 about his county's cotton farmers, "I can show you papers in our current portfolio that had been cancelled as uncollectable years ago. People come in here and ask to pay back interest on

notes we literally have to fish out of the waste basket." The Agricultural Adjustment Administration (AAA) established the mechanisms—production control, price-support loans, and ample credit that would enable farmers who managed to stay on the land to work in a relatively risk-free environment and to enjoy prosperity when it returned during World War II. The AAA also created the political processes whereby organized commodity groups could guarantee favorable government responses in the future. As William Faulkner observed, "Our economy is not agricultural any longer. Our economy is the federal government. We no longer farm now in Mississippi cotton fields. We farm now in Washington corridors and Congressional committee rooms."

The result was what Gavin Wright described as a "planter's heaven." Tenants and sharecroppers

An Alabama farmer surveys the eroded land surrounding his home in 1935. FRANKLIN DELANO ROOSEVELT LIBRARY

lost out both in the allocation of payments under the production control programs and in the operation of those programs by planter-dominated local committees. The worst abuses sparked the rise of the Southern Tenant Farmers' Union in the harsh Arkansas Delta and an abortive effort by New Deal radicals in Washington to interpret the cotton contract to protect the tenants. Ultimately the New Deal launched a tenant-purchase and resettlement program for poor southern farmers. But the harsh reality was that the New Deal was a step on the road to the mechanization of southern agriculture and the displacement of tenant farmers. The New Deal, through the rental and benefit payments of the AAA, gave the planters the capital to buy tractors and mechanize the pre-harvest cotton production. Acreage reduction gave them the excuse to

evict tenants. They could replace them with hired laborers. No longer did planters have to support tenants all year round to ensure that they had an adequate labor force for the still unmechanized harvesting. Now New Deal welfare programs could support the surplus labor force through the winter and early summer. Then, with the assistance of sympathetic relief administrators, the planters could simply hire that labor for the harvest. This process of mechanization was at an early stage in the 1930s. Few planters in 1940 in Mississippi owned tractors. More people left the land in the 1920s and after 1940 than during the 1930s. High prices and labor shortages during World War II were what gave planters the means and the incentive to bring in the cotton harvester. After World War II the revolution in agricultural chemistry en-

A Tennessee Valley Authority representative (sitting at left) interviews unemployed men for TVA jobs at a shop near Lead Mine Bend in Tennessee in 1933. Many unemployed Southerners found work with the TVA during the Depression. NATIONAL ARCHIVES AND RECORDS ADMINISTRATION

abled farmers to dispense with hired labor to eradicate weeds and defoliate cotton plants.

New Deal unemployment relief, works programs, and Social Security engineered a welfare revolution in the South. Aid from the Reconstruction Finance Corporation in 1932 had forced southern states, ensconced in the old Poor Law traditions of county responsibility, to adopt some form of welfare organization. But it was Harry Hopkins's Federal Emergency Relief Administration (FERA) that transformed relief provision in the South. Ninety percent of relief spending under FERA in the region was provided by federal money, compared to 62 percent in the rest of the country. To qualify for such aid, states had to professionalize their welfare

organizations. As Michael Holmes noted, "Many counties in Georgia that had never seen a social worker now had one permanently stationed within their borders." Later, to qualify for federal matching funds for categorical assistance to the old, the blind, and dependent children, southern states had to maintain that revolution in professionalism. Southern cities established departments of public welfare for the first time. Southern states were forced to develop unemployment compensation programs. Old-age insurance became a federal responsibility.

But local administration and joint federal-state responsibility lessened the impact of the welfare revolution. It was difficult to find qualified staff to run relief programs, especially as local politicians

Dilapidated quarters for migrant agricultural laborers in Homestead, Florida, in 1939. LIBRARY OF CONGRESS, PRINTS & PHOTOGRAPHS DIVISION, FSA/OWI COLLECTION

objected to women and nonpartisan appointments. Opposition from planters and employer elite to the whole idea of relief made state legislatures reluctant to make appropriations or to take over the burden of the able-unemployed, who did not get Works Progress Administration (WPA) jobs after 1935. Everywhere FERA and WPA operations were curtailed at harvest time to ensure the availability of as large a labor force as possible for cotton picking.

The federal-state operation of Social Security not only meant that states varied considerably in the generosity of the benefits they offered and the conditions they imposed on recipients, it also meant that many southern states could scarcely afford to participate in the system at all. Planters lob-

bied to keep benefits low: They feared that an alternative to their own paternalist but minimal in-kind benefits would loosen their control of their tenants. Poverty-stricken Mississippi was the last state in the union to enter the Aid to Dependent Children program. The principle of matching funds in general meant that poor southern states received less per capita from New Deal spending than any other region.

INDUSTRY AND WORKERS

New Deal industrial policy did little to solve the problems of southern industries in the short term. Cotton textile executives were so desperate to curb overproduction that they conceded the elimination of child labor and a $12-per-week minimum wage in return for the National Recovery Administration (NRA) code restricting the hours that mills could operate. When the Supreme Court ended the NRA in 1935 the industry lobbied, like the lumber industry, for legislation to perpetuate price and production controls, but failed. Southern coal operators, fearing wage rises and unionization, were less enthusiastic. Tobacco manufacturers, already operating as an oligopoly, resisted NRA codes until 1935, just before the NRA collapsed. The New Deal simply did not solve the problems of excessive production in southern industry. It would take dramatically rising demand and profits in World War II to absorb that production and to enable consolidation and integration in, for example, the textile industry, where larger firms could finally buy out smaller mills.

What the New Deal did do was to stimulate worker militancy. Inspired by section 7a of the National Industrial Recovery Act, twenty thousand Alabama coal miners joined the United Mine Workers in 1933 and 1934. In a massive explosion of frustration, Piedmont textile workers joined the moribund United Textile Workers, forcing their leaders into a premature strike in September 1934. In 1937 and 1938, the Textile Workers' Organizing Committee attempted to unionize the industry under the banner of the Congress of Industrial Organizations (CIO). Rubber workers in Gadsden, Alabama, made repeated efforts to unionize in the face of employer violence. Steelworkers in Birmingham unionized the Tennessee Coal and Iron subsidiary of U.S. Steel.

But determined protest was not enough. Nor could the new federal protections always help. The prospect of rapidly filling order books might persuade U.S. Steel to sign a union contract in 1937 and force their southern subsidiaries to do likewise, but other steel employees in Birmingham saw no need to follow. The final employer there to sign a union contract did so in 1974. In textiles, employers had no incentive to concede to union demands in 1934 when they already had excess capacity in stock, or in 1937 and 1938 when recession once again gripped the industry. As before, where employers were determined to resist they could utilize

local sentiment to defeat the unions, using the local press, vigilante strikebreakers, and sympathetic law enforcement officers. In the South, labor was too politically powerless to impose its will on local sheriffs, state legislatures, and state governors. Despite the 1935 Wagner Act (National Labor Relations Act), traditional anti-union tactics by employers would go unchecked, and neither rank and file militancy nor federal law could break down the longstanding patterns of worker dependency in labor relations.

Nevertheless, Gavin Wright has argued that "the economic underpinnings and social glue that had kept the regional economy isolated were no longer present in 1940." The Fair Labor Standards Act of 1938, despite its temporary provision of regional wage differentials, confirmed the trends of the NRA and meant that employers at the end of the 1930s and in World War II could no longer quarantine the low-wage economy of the South from national economic forces.

New Deal programs did modernize the infrastructure of the South. They rescued southern education: Relief programs, the National Youth Administration, and works programs paid teachers and students, and built and repaired schools and colleges at a time when southern governments had to slash school spending. The New Deal built and resurfaced thousands of miles of roads, and built and improved port facilities and airports. In the southern cities, New Deal programs built the capital projects that private enterprise had built in the northern cities a generation earlier. Above all, the New Deal provided cheap power and easy credit: The Tennessee Valley Authority (TVA) and the Rural Electrification Administration started the electrification of southern farms and provided abundant power and water for southern industry. The Reconstruction Finance Corporation made credit available to a new generation of regional entrepreneurs anxious to capture government contracts and to attract outside investment.

THE POLITICAL RESPONSE

Nevertheless, in 1940 the South was still a poor, rural, one-crop region, wedded to low wages and the open shop, in which African Americans were rigidly segregated and disfranchised. But a new generation of southerners had ambitious plans to reform and modernize the region from the bottom up. Southerners, such as Aubrey Williams, Clark Foreman, and Clifford Durr, who served in Washington in New Deal agencies, were radicalized on racial and economic issues: They saw full-scale rural poverty programs, unionization, and the extension of Social Security and political democracy to African Americans as the key to the development of mass purchasing power in the South. Newly elected congressman, such as John Sparkman and Albert Gore, Sr., saw the TVA as the model of what the federal government could do to transform not merely a river valley but a whole region through infrastructure investment and aid for education and health. African Americans were segregated in New Deal programs, discriminated against in the distribution of benefits and jobs, and, as farm laborers and domestic servants, disproportionately excluded from Social Security. But they received more than they had ever had before from the federal government and more than they would have received from white state governments. Black leaders saw how the federal government had intervened in the region's economy and, rightly, as it turned out, believed that the federal government could in the future intervene in the region's race relations.

There emerged, therefore, a loose pro-New Deal coalition of liberal politicians, union organizers, students, Communist Party members, and black leaders committed to the extension of political and economic democracy in the South. This alliance manifested itself in the Southern Conference for Human Welfare, the election of TVA liberals to Congress, the campaign to abolish the poll-tax, and membership campaigns and legal struggles by the NAACP.

Conservatives had an alternative top-down vision for modernizing the South. They believed that a low tax and anti-union environment would attract outside investment. Southern political leaders had been enthusiastic for the New Deal in the emergency of 1933, immensely grateful for the relief that Roosevelt brought to their desperate constituents. They remained fervent supporters of farm programs and measures to offset the power of northeastern financial interests. Many were personally loyal to Roosevelt and strong supporters of pro-British intervention in World War II. But the non-emergency direction of the New Deal after 1936 troubled them. More New Deal benefits seemed to be going to northern urban states. In addition, New Deal rural credit and labor policies seemed to undermine the traditional power of county seat elites: They disturbed the traditional patterns of deference and dependence between landlord and tenant, and employer and worker. Above all, conservatives feared that the New Deal, catering to newly Democratic black voters in the North, would threaten traditional patterns of white supremacy in the South.

Southern Democrats therefore joined Republicans after 1938 to form a bipartisan conservative coalition to thwart any significant expansion of the New Deal for the next quarter of a century. A casualty of this process in the short run were the ambitious plans of southern New Dealers to tackle rural poverty, unionize southern workers, and enfranchise African Americans. Instead, southern political leaders ensured that when the region modernized, kick-started into self-sustaining economic growth by federal defense spending during the war and after, the modernization strategy was a conservative one sustaining low-wage, open shop industries and traditional patterns of race relations.

See Also: AGRICULTURAL ADJUSTMENT ADMINISTRATION (AAA); SHARECROPPERS; SOUTHERN AGRARIANS; TENNESSEE VALLEY AUTHORITY (TVA).

BIBLIOGRAPHY

Biles, Roger. *The South and the New Deal.* 1994.

Daniel, Pete. *Breaking the Land: The Transformation of Cotton, Tobacco, and Rice Cultures since 1880.* 1985.

Kirby, Jack Temple. *Rural Worlds Lost: The American South, 1920–1960.* 1982.

Smith, Douglas L. *The New Deal and the Urban South: The Advancement of a Southern Urban Consciousness During the Depression Decade.* 1988.

Wright, Gavin. *Old South, New South: Revolution in the Southern Economy since the Civil War.* 1984.

TONY BADGER

SOUTHERN AGRARIANS

Meeting fortnightly at the apartment of a Nashville eccentric named Sydney Mttron Hirsch, John Crowe Ransom and Walter Clyde Curry, both of whom taught English at Vanderbilt University, launched the fugitive movement in 1914. Although American entry into the first world war temporarily dispersed the group, by 1921 the gatherings had resumed at the home of James M. Frank, a Nashville businessman and Hirsch's brother-in-law. Besides Ransom, Curry, and Hirsch, the original fugitives included Donald Davidson, William Yandell Elliott, Stanley Johnson, and Alec B. Stevenson. After the war, a number of younger poets also participated, among them Merrill Moore, Alfred Starr, Jesse Wills, Allen Tate, and Robert Penn Warren.

Initially confining themselves to the discussion of literature, the Fugitive poets, by 1925, had begun to examine the culture and history of the South and to voice their growing opposition to science, industrialism, capitalism, and the other forces shaping the modern world. During the next several years Ransom, Davidson, Tate, and Warren conferred with thinkers outside the Fugitive circle, including psychologist Lyle H. Lanier, political economist Herman Clarence Nixon, historian Frank Lawrence Owsley, and literary scholar John Donald Wade, all of whom, like Ransom and Davidson, were then members of the faculty at Vanderbilt. Andrew Nelson Lytle, a former Vanderbilt undergraduate and a future novelist, and Henry Blue Kline, who completed a master's degree in English at Vanderbilt in 1929, also joined the deliberations. The most celebrated figures of the 1920s associated with Southern Agrarianism were John Gould Fletcher, who enjoyed an international reputation as an Imagist poet, and Stark Young, already renowned as a playwright, journalist, and theater critic.

Believing the "American industrial ideal" inimical to the humane traditions of the South, the Agrarians sought to develop political, economic, social, and moral alternatives. In *I'll Take My Stand: The South and the Agrarian Tradition,* published by Harper and Brothers in 1930, and in dozens of essays written over the next decade, the Agrarians argued that industrialism had enslaved human beings, rendering modern life hurried, brutal, servile, and mercenary. To rescue society from the rigors of the assembly line, the blast furnace, and the bookkeeper's ledger, the Agrarians championed an "imaginatively balanced life lived out in a definite social tradition." For them, the historic South offered ideal terrain from which to mount a defense of family, community, manners, art, and religion against the destructive and dehumanizing onslaught of unbridled industrial capitalism.

The onset of the Great Depression made the Agrarian critique of modern America seem even more credible and prophetic. Although their proposals to resolve the economic crisis of the 1930s often lacked specificity, most of the Agrarians remained ambivalent about New Deal policies and programs. Fearful that the rise of bureaucracy and the emphasis on planning characteristic of the New Deal would result in the establishment of a collectivist regime, the Agrarians suggested that Americans preserve their independence by returning to the land. Only the abandonment of commercial farming and the adoption of production for use, sustained through the widespread ownership of property, could restore economic health and safeguard political liberty.

In practical terms, the Southern Agrarians failed. They never organized an Agrarian political party, secured control of a wing of the Democratic Party, or cultivated a mass following among fellow southerners. Even the appearance in 1937 of *Who Owns America?: A New Declaration of Independence,* which brought the Agrarians together with Hilaire Belloc's and G. K. Chesterton's English Distributists, who also advocated political decentralization and broad property ownership, could not prevent their movement from languishing. Yet, whatever their political weaknesses and philosophical defects, the Agrarians did raise fundamental questions about the beneficence of American national development and the impact of industrial capitalismon the spiritual welfare of the American people.

See Also: BACK-TO-THE-LAND MOVEMENT; SOUTH, GREAT DEPRESSION IN THE.

BIBLIOGRAPHY

Carlson, Allan. *The New Agrarian Mind: The Movement Toward Decentralist Thought in Twentieth-Century America.* 2000.

Conkin, Paul K. *The Southern Agrarians.* 1988.

Davidson, Donald. *Southern Writers in the Modern World.* 1957.

Lubick, George M. "Restoring the American Dream: The Agrarian-Decentralist Movement, 1930–1946." *South Atlantic Quarterly* 74 (1985): 63–80.

Malvasi, Mark G. *The Unregenerate South: The Agrarian Thought of John Crowe Ransom, Allen Tate, and Donald Davidson.* 1997.

Murphy, Paul V. *The Rebuke of History: The Southern Agrarians and American Conservative Thought.* 2001.

Rubin, Louis D., Jr. "Trouble on the Land: Southern Literature and the Great Depression." *Canadian Review of American Studies* 10 (1979): 153–174.

Shapiro, Edward S. "Decentralist Intellectuals and the New Deal." *Journal of American History* 68 (1972): 938–957.

MARK G. MALVASI

SOUTHERN CONFERENCE FOR HUMAN WELFARE (SCHW)

The Southern Conference for Human Welfare (SCHW), formed in 1938, was the product of an alliance of southern liberals and radicals, black and white, who sought to bring the full force of New Deal reforms and Popular Front ideals to the South.

In its original incarnation, the SCHW was an extremely diverse collection of men and women united by the common goal of revitalizing the southern economy. The founders sought to create an organization that could take advantage of the Roosevelt administration's increased interest in improving the stagnant southern economy. With the support of the president, who had recently classified the South as "the nation's no. 1 economic problem," in November 1938 the SCHW held its inaugural meeting in Birmingham, Alabama. Attendees included business-leaders, labor organizers, politicians, sharecroppers, and newspaper editors; of the 1,200 in attendance, approximately 20 percent was African American.

The SCHW sought to create broad-based support through advocating economic reforms, with a focus on improving the lives of the southern workers and farmers. While deeply committed to creating an interracial movement, the SCHW leaders also worked to prevent the race issue from dividing their fragile coalition. This approach lasted less than two days. On the second day of the convention, Birmingham police commissioner Eugene "Bull" Connor forced the group to adopt segregated seating in the meeting hall. In response, First Lady Eleanor Roosevelt, a featured speaker at the convention, famously placed her chair on the line dividing the races. The SCHW pledged not to hold any future meetings where segregation would be required, although the leadership steered clear of more sweeping denunciations of segregation. Even this attempt at moderation, however, alienated some early supporters, particularly after critics used the controversy to label the SCHW an advocate of racial equality. Throughout its ten-year history, the organization's ambivalent position toward the increasingly pressing question of racial segregation would prove a major point of division.

The SCHW's most significant policy initiative was its attack on the poll tax, an issue that perfectly encapsulated the organization's approach to reform. The poll tax was used as a tool of both economic and racial oppression. The anti-poll-tax campaign thus became a centerpiece of the SCHW's effort to create a labor and farmer coalition, to address civil rights concerns, and also to minimize the potential backlash of white southerners uncomfortable with the idea of racial equality. Although the campaign failed to achieve its ultimate goal of pressuring Congress to pass an anti-poll-tax bill, the SCHW brought much-needed attention to the voting rights issue in the South.

In 1948 the SCHW disbanded, the result of a chronic lack of funds, increased attacks on the organization for its connections with Communists, and internal rifts over its wavering position on racial segregation. Its auxiliary, the Southern Conference Educational Fund, continued to function with a more limited agenda, focusing predominantly on the civil rights issues that, by the late 1940s, had largely supplanted the movement for a working-class alliance envisioned by the founders of the SCHW in 1938.

During its ten-year life, the SCHW had two primary accomplishments. First, it successfully highlighted the benefits of an interracial working-class movement, even as this approach to social and economic reform lost momentum in the years following the Depression. Second, and more importantly, it did this in the South, the part of the country where such reform was not only most needed, but also where it faced the largest obstacles.

See Also: HIGHLANDER FOLK SCHOOL.

BIBLIOGRAPHY

Krueger, Thomas A. *And Promises to Keep: The Southern Conference for Human Welfare, 1938–1948.* 1967.

Reed, Linda. *Simple Decency & Common Sense: The Southern Conference Movement, 1939–1963.* 1991.

Sullivan, Patricia. *Days of Hope: Race and Democracy in the New Deal Era.* 1996.

CHRISTOPHER W. SCHMIDT

SOUTHERN NEGRO YOUTH CONGRESS (SNYC)

Founded in 1937, the Southern Negro Youth Congress (SNYC) was a civil rights organization that worked to empower southern black people to fight for their rights and looked with hope to interracial working-class coalitions as the key to undermining the southern caste system.

The SNYC had its roots in both the National Negro Congress (NNC) and the leftist student movement of the 1930s. In 1936, the NNC convened to address the economic problems and discrimination faced by African Americans, particularly in New Deal programs. Although the vast majority of NNC delegates were from northern communities, younger delegates acknowledged that the problems facing southern black people were especially acute and inseparable from the problems northern African Americans faced. Many of these younger delegates were also active in leftist student organizations, such as the American Student Union and the American Youth Congress. In fact, the student movement was an important training ground for SNYC leaders like Edward Strong, James E. Jackson, Jr., and Louis Burnham. These student activists resolved that the battle against discrimination and segregation had to be waged by a black-led southern organization, and they spearheaded a conference of young black southerners.

Over five hundred delegates attended the founding conference of the SNYC, held in Richmond, Virginia, in February 1937. The conference delegates issued a broad proclamation, demanding equal educational and employment opportunities, the right to organize unions, the right to vote, and an end to lynching and segregation. The delegates also reached out to southern white youth and to workers, especially those in the Congress of Industrial Organizations (CIO), which advocated organizing workers on an interracial basis. At the close of the conference, the delegates created a permanent organization, headquartered in Richmond. The SNYC initiated its work in April 1937, when it organized black workers on strike at the Carrington and Michaux tobacco factory. Their efforts resulted in an independent union, called the Tobacco Stemmers' and Laborers' Union (TSLU); the TSLU succeeded in gaining an eight-hour day and forty-hour workweek, along with a wage increase. The SNYC went on to organize other TSLU locals among black workers in other tobacco factories.

The SNYC exemplified the inclusiveness of Popular Front politics during the Great Depression by reaching out to all members of the black community and to political radicals, as well as to the white working class. SNYC moved its headquarters to Birmingham, Alabama, in 1940 and was active until 1949.

See Also: AFRICAN AMERICANS, IMPACT OF THE GREAT DEPRESSION ON; NATIONAL NEGRO CONGRESS.

BIBLIOGRAPHY

Cohen, Robert. *When the Old Left Was Young: Student Radicals and America's First Mass Student Movement, 1929–1941.* 1993.

Hughes, C. Alvin. "We Demand Our Rights: The Southern Negro Youth Congress, 1937–1949." *Phylon* 48, no. 1 (1987): 38–60.

These Arkansas sharecroppers were evicted from the Dibble Plantation in January 1936 because of their membership in the Southern Tenant Farmers' Union. They later found shelter in a tent colony. LIBRARY OF CONGRESS, PRINTS & PHOTOGRAPHS DIVISION, FSA/OWI COLLECTION

Richards, Johnetta. "The Southern Negro Youth Congress: A History." Ph.D. diss., University of Cincinnati, 1987.

Sullivan, Patricia A. *Days of Hope: Race and Democracy in the New Deal Era.* 1996.

LARISSA M. SMITH

SOUTHERN TENANT FARMERS' UNION (STFU)

As the Great Depression intensified by 1933, the plight of southern tenant farmers and sharecroppers worsened. Barely eking out a living for their families, tenant farmers and sharecroppers looked to Franklin D. Roosevelt and the New Deal for relief. Initially, the New Deal addressed the agricultural crisis by implementing the 1933 Agricultural Adjustment Act, which was designed to limit farm production by paying farmers not to plant certain crops, such as cotton. Although the intent of the law was to help all farmers, landowners took the Agricultural Adjustment Administration (AAA) subsidies and used them however they wanted, often without consideration for the needs of their tenants or sharecroppers. Even when Jerome Frank and other AAA legal administrators tried to force southern landowners to at least retain their tenants for more than one year, the situation did not change. Instead, AAA director Chester Davis fired the "Frank group" and sustained the landowners' practices.

An evicted Arkansas sharecropper, an active member of the Southern Tenant Farmers Union, builds a new home near Hill House, Mississippi, in 1936. LIBRARY OF CONGRESS, PRINTS & PHOTOGRAPHS DIVISION, FSA/OWI COLLECTION

Facing increasing economic pressures, a group of black and white tenant farmers met in the delta town of Tyronza, Arkansas, and organized the Southern Tenant Farmers' Union (STFU) in July 1934, under the leadership of H. L. Mitchell, a socialist and former sharecropper, and H. Clay East. Committed to helping tenant farmers, the STFU faced numerous problems, the most serious of which was the southern landowner. Although landowners initially did not take the STFU seriously, their attitudes changed when significant numbers of southern tenant farmers began to join the union. Landowners quickly implemented policies designed to intimidate and frighten the member-

ship. Violence was used to break up STFU meetings, members were beaten, and meeting places were burned down. Despite the threats and violence, the union grew and spread to other states, including Mississippi, Alabama, Oklahoma, North Carolina, and Texas. The STFU called strikes in 1935 and 1936 over such issues as cotton pickers' wages. In Earle, Arkansas, landowner violence against the union caught the nation's attention as local police opened fire in a church where STFU members were meeting. Further violence occurred as mobs organized to attack union members. In 1939, the STFU became involved in the famous Missouri roadside demonstration, designed to protest the AAA's refusal to help sharecroppers and led by Reverend Owen Whitfield, former sharecropper and STFU vice president.

By January 1937 the STFU claimed over thirty thousand members. In spring 1936, the La Follette congressional committee had begun investigating violations of basic rights guaranteed by the Constitution, certainly apropos of what the tenant farmers faced in the South. The leadership of the union, amid tensions and debate, decided to became a subsidiary of the Congress of Industrial Organizations' United Cannery, Agricultural, Packing, and Allied Workers of America in July 1937. This move, along with the union's identification with socialism (given its leadership and Socialist Party leader Norman Thomas's open support for the group) and some activities that were seen as sympathetic to Communists, eventually contributed to the union's decline. Remnants of the STFU were absorbed by the American Federation of Labor in the 1940s.

In spite of its decline, the STFU did accomplish more than it is given credit for. The union coalesced national attention on the plight of southern tenant farmers and sharecroppers, while exposing the violence southern landowners often used in dealing with their tenants. If nothing else, the STFU demonstrated the growing need for the federal government to step in and protect the rights of its poorest citizens.

See Also: SHARECROPPERS; SOUTH, GREAT DEPRESSION IN THE; THOMAS, NORMAN.

BIBLIOGRAPHY

Grubb, Donald. *Cry From the Cotton: The Southern Tenant Farmers' Union and the New Deal.* 1971.

Mitchell, H. L. "The Founding and Early History of the Southern Tenant Farmers Union." *Arkansas Historical Quarterly* 32, no. 4 (1973): 342–369.

Tinall, George B. *The Emergence of the New South.* 1967.

MICHAEL V. NAMORATO

SPANISH CIVIL WAR

The Spanish Civil War of 1936 to 1939 was the culmination of a prolonged period of national political unrest in a country that was increasingly polarized and unable to ameliorate the poverty in which millions of its citizens lived. In Spain at the time, landless peasants cobbled together a bare subsistence as migrant laborers, following the harvests on vast agricultural estates. The hierarchy of the Catholic Church, identifying with wealthy landowners, was in full control of secondary education; education for women seemed to the Church unnecessary, and universal literacy a danger rather than a goal. The military, meanwhile, had come to see itself, rather melodramatically, as the only bulwark against civil disorder and as the ultimate guarantor of the core values of Spanish society.

When a progressive Popular Front government was elected in February 1936 with the promise of realistic land reform as one of its key planks, conservative forces immediately gathered to plan resistance. The Spanish left, meanwhile, celebrated the elections in a way that made conservative capitalists, military officers, and churchmen worried that broader reform might begin. Rumors of a military coup led leaders of the Spanish Republic (the elected government) to transfer several high-ranking military officers to remote postings, with the aim of making communication and coordination between them more difficult. But the planning for a military uprising continued.

The military rebellion began on July 18, 1936, with the officers who organized it expecting a quick victory and a rapid takeover of the entire country. What the military did not anticipate was the determination of the Spanish people, who broke into barracks, took up arms, and crushed the rebellion in such key areas as Madrid and Barcelona. At that point, the character of the struggle changed, for the military realized that it was not going to win by fiat. Military leaders faced a prolonged struggle against their own people and an uncertain outcome. They appealed to fascist dictatorships in Italy, Germany, and Portugal for assistance, and they soon began receiving both men and supplies from Benito Mussolini, Adolf Hitler, and Antonio Salazar.

The 1936 election in Spain had been widely celebrated in progressive publications in Great Britain, France, and the United States. In the midst of the worldwide Depression, the military uprising was thus seen as an assault against the interests of working people everywhere. Moreover, the rapid intervention of German and Italian troops gave what might otherwise have remained a civil war a dramatic international character. Almost from the outset, the Spanish Civil War became a literal and symbolic instance of the growing worldwide struggle between fascism and democracy. Indeed, the Republic perceived the country as being under invasion by foreign troops. By the time the pilots of Hitler's Condor Legion reduced the Basque holy city of Guernica to rubble in April 1937, many in the rest of the world had come to share that opinion.

Yet the Spanish Republic faced the difficult task of defending itself against a substantial portion of its own military. Local militias worked well in inner city skirmishes but were of little use against mechanized battalions in the field. The Republic needed to raise an army, having lost most of its own to the rebel generals. After General Francisco Franco took command of the rebel army, he mounted an assault on the capital city of Madrid, hoping to end the war with one bold stroke. The situation looked desperate enough that the government fled to Valencia. Yet the capital held, with the small Spanish Communist Party playing a key role in the city's defense. Other Western powers signed a pact agreeing to abstain from arming either side, a pact that Hitler immediately violated. Only the Soviet Union was willing to sell quantities of arms to the Republic, a decision that helped gain the Communists increasing influence in the Spanish government. In addition, the Comintern, the international coalition of Communist parties, organized the International Brigades, with forty thousand people from fifty countries volunteering to fight on the side of the Republic. Among the International Brigades was the Abraham Lincoln Brigade, made up of volunteers from the United States.

Yet neither Soviet arms nor the international volunteers ever matched the arms supplied by Hitler and Mussolini. And the Spanish Left was deeply divided, with anarchists and anti-Soviet Marxists seeking a fundamental social revolution, while the Spanish Communist Party urged only moderate reform and cooperation with liberal parties as a way of winning the war. Despite winning occasional

battles, the Republic steadily lost territory until it fell to Franco's forces in the spring of 1939.

See Also: ABRAHAM LINCOLN BRIGADE; EUROPE, GREAT DEPRESSION IN; POPULAR FRONT.

BIBLIOGRAPHY

Jackson, Gabriel. *A Concise History of the Spanish Civil War.* 1974.

Nelson, Cary. *The Wound and the Dream: Sixty Years of American Poems about the Spanish Civil War.* 2002.

Thomas, Hugh. *The Spanish Civil War* (1961), 3rd rev. edition. 1986.

CARY NELSON

SPORTS

American athletics, especially commercial sports, were more heavily damaged by the Great Depression than was the rest of the entertainment industry. Still, American sports survived and managed to rebound after the middle of the 1930s.

THE IMPACT OF THE DEPRESSION ON MAJOR PROFESSIONAL SPORTS

Baseball. Major league baseball attendance dropped from 10.2 million in 1930 to 6.1 million by 1933. The Saint Louis Browns, for example, drew a paltry 88,113 fans in 1933. Major League gate receipts dropped from $17 million in 1929 to $10.8 million in 1933. Total payrolls dropped from $4 million in 1930 to $3 million in 1933, when the average salary was $4,500. Even Babe Ruth's $80,000 salary was cut by half. Professional baseball did not cut ticket prices or initiate rule changes. But low attendance caused Connie Mack, owner of the Philadelphia Athletics, World Series champions from 1929–31, to sell off star players Al Simmons, Mickey Cochrane, Lefty Grove, and Jimmy Foxx.

Baseball teams were leery of radio broadcasting, which they felt hurt attendance. New York's teams banned radio from 1934 until 1939. Night baseball was introduced following the model of the Kansas City Monarchs of the Negro National League (NNL), which had started using a portable

The Works Progress Administration promoted sports by building hundreds of swimming pools and athletic fields around the country. This swimming class was conducted by a National Youth Administration instructor in Boise, Idaho, in 1936. FRANKLIN DELANO ROOSEVELT LIBRARY

light system in 1929. In 1930, minor league teams in Des Moines, Iowa, and Wichita, Kansas, began playing night ball to encourage attendance of people who worked during the day. In 1935, the Cincinnati Reds became the first major league team to play night games, but no other team put in lights until 1938. Another Depression-era innovation was the creation of the All-Star Game in 1933. A further promotional effort was the founding in 1936 of the Baseball Hall of Fame, which opened in Cooperstown, New York, in 1939.

The NNL folded in 1931, but was reorganized two years later by Gus Greenlee and other African-American numbers racketeers, who instituted the East-West All-Star Game in Chicago before the first major league all-star game. A rival midwestern and southern association, the Negro American League, was founded in 1937. Top black players barnstormed extensively in the off-season, often playing major league all-star teams. Many players, especially star pitcher Satchel Paige, jumped teams with frequency.

Horse racing. Horse racing was badly damaged by the onset of the Depression. Stakes and purses, at near peak values in 1930, dropped from $13.7 million that year to $8.5 million in 1933, an average decline of $672 per race. The typical stakes event dropped from $8,309 to $4,741. The Belmont Stakes dropped from $66,040 in 1930 to $35,480 in 1935. The average price of yearlings fell from $1,966 in

Although professional football suffered during the Depression, the sport remained popular. These high school boys in Wildrose, North Dakota, played six-man football in the fall of 1937. High school enrollments were too low to field eleven-man teams.

1930 to $569 in 1932. Earnings did not return to 1930 levels until 1937, but by 1939 they were up to $15.9 million. Despite the sport's financial problems, the number of tracks increased 70 percent to fifty-eight. Ten states authorized pari-mutuel betting in 1933 as a new source of revenue. New tracks built during the 1930s included Sportsman's Park in Cicero, Illinois (the former site of Al Capone's dog track), Tropical Park and a rebuilt Hialeah in Florida, and Santa Anita and Hollywood Park in Los Angeles.

Football. Like horse racing, college football was hurt by the onset of the Depression. Although ticket prices were cut, attendance by the fall of 1932 dropped about 20 percent in the East and 15 percent in the Midwest, and many institutions considered dropping their football programs to save expenses. However, the sport recovered and spectatorship reached its pre-Depression level by 1935. In addition, the economic downturn encouraged several cities in warm climates to organize post-season bowl games to promote tourism: Miami inaugurated the Orange Bowl in 1933, followed by New Orleans with the Sugar Bowl in 1935, El Paso with the Sun Bowl in 1936, and Dallas with the Cotton Bowl in 1937.

By 1932, the National Football League (NFL), a struggling enterprise to begin with, was down to eight teams. By the late 1930s, however, spectatorship was growing. A championship game was initiated in 1933 to promote fan interest, and in 1934, the college football all-star game was established. In 1936, the NFL initiated a draft of college seniors to equalize competition. Pro football became more successful in attracting collegiate stars by helping players secure off-season employment.

Basketball. Basketball became much more popular in the 1930s than ever before. In 1931, Madison

Square Garden in New York City staged intercollegiate tripleheaders to raise funds for unemployment relief. This practice encouraged sportswriter Ned Irish to promote intersectional college doubleheaders in 1934. In 1938 the first national tournament, the National Invitational Tournament, was established. The National Collegiate Athletic Association tournament began one year later.

Professional basketball was a minor sport at the time. There were only two professional leagues, the predominantly Jewish American Basketball League, which became defunct in 1931 but was reorganized in 1934, and the mostly industrial Midwestern National Basketball League, founded in 1937. These leagues were mainly weekend organizations, and players held full-time jobs. Eastern basketball teams were often ethnically based, like the renowned SPHAs (South Philadelphia Hebrew All-Stars) and the Irish Brooklyn Visitations. Games were often played before dances at ballrooms. In 1939, the Harlem Globetrotters won the first Chicago World Professional Basketball Tournament.

Boxing. Boxing was one sport that benefited from the hard times of the Depression as tough inner-city Jewish, Italian, Irish, and African-American youths tried to escape poverty through prize fighting. There were some eight thousand professional boxers during the 1930s, and competition was fierce in nearly all weight classes. Contenders were commonly controlled by underworld figures, including gangster Frankie Carbo, who established a virtual monopoly over the middleweight division. The greatest fighter of the period was Joe Louis, the first African American to get a shot at the heavyweight title since champion Jack Johnson was defeated in 1915. Louis won the championship in 1937 by knocking out James Braddock. In 1938, Louis fought in a much anticipated rematch with Max Schmeling, a German former world champion who had beaten Louis in 1936. The fight at Yankee Stadium in New York drew over 70,000 spectators. The match had heavy political overtones because it symbolized the conflict between German Nazism and American democracy. Louis represented the hopes of all Americans regardless of race, and his first-round knockout of Schmeling was regarded as a vindication of the American way of life.

THE 1932 AND 1936 OLYMPIC GAMES

The United States hosted the 1932 Olympics. Winter sports were not popular then, but the winter Olympic games in Lake Placid, New York, spurred interest. American speed skaters Jack Shea and Irving Jaffee became stars after each of them won two gold medals. Los Angeles hosted the 1932 summer Olympic games. Organizers feared that the world-wide Depression would cause the games' cancellation, and, in fact, only about 1,400 athletes competed, less than half the number at the 1928 Amsterdam games. Still, the event was a great success, and boasted such innovations as the first Olympic village and many outstanding athletic performances. American athlete Babe Didrikson won two gold medals and one silver medal in women's track and field. The 1932 summer Olympics was also the first to make a profit; the games earned $214,000 for the city and county.

The next Olympic games, held in Berlin in 1936, were almost boycotted by the Americans to protest Nazi oppression of political opponents and ethnic minorities. The United States opted in the end to participate and sent a powerful track-and-field squad, led by Jesse Owens of the Ohio State University, who won an unprecedented four gold medals.

PARTICIPATORY SPORTS

Participation in recreational sports dwindled at the beginning of the Depression due, in part, to rising costs. After 1935 however, the need for diversion, coupled with increased governmental support for recreational activities, significantly improved opportunities for sports in America. The economic downturn did impact the preferred sports of the wealthy. Country club memberships dropped, many clubs closed, golf tournaments were cancelled, and prizes were drastically cut. The United States Golf Association, for example, included 1134 affiliated clubs in 1930; by 1936, there were only 763.

Participation in sports among working-class men and women declined during the early 1930s after one-fourth of company sponsored industrial sports programs were eliminated to save money, with the rest struggling to survive. But interest and

Boxing was one sport that benefited from the hard times of the Depression as tough inner-city youths tried to escape poverty through prize fighting. These two young men engaged in a boxing match in 1941 at the Farm Security Administration migratory labor camp in Athena, Oregon. LIBRARY OF CONGRESS, PRINTS & PHOTOGRAPHS DIVISION, FSA/OWI COLLECTION

participation reemerged later in the decade. Male industrial sports programs stressed bowling, softball, and basketball, while women engaged in bowling, softball, and tennis. Softball, in particular, grew in popularity. It required less skill or space than baseball and was often played at night at lighted parks. In the crowded inner city, neighborhood pool halls and bowling alleys remained important hangouts, but the number of facilities and bowling teams declined at the beginning of the Depression. Bowling rebounded in the late 1930s, as the number of registered teams tripled. Chicago alone had over nine hundred leagues. By 1939, there were 4,600 bowling alleys with receipts of nearly $49 million, and the purse for the American Bowling Congress tournament reached $170,000.

Second-generation immigrants relied on ethnic and religious organizations to facilitate sporting and social events. Ethnic basketball championships in Chicago drew huge crowds. In 1930, Bishop Bernard Sheil founded the Catholic Youth Organization in Chicago to promote sports and to shield young Catholics from Protestant influences.

During the Depression years, the public became increasingly dependent on community recreational facilities, which were heavily financed with $750 million in New Deal money. The Works Progress Administration (WPA) promoted sports by building 770 swimming pools and 5898 athletic fields. The Civilian Conservation Corps built ski runs, camp grounds, and boating facilities. The number of cities sponsoring public recreation programs between 1934 and 1936 doubled to 2,190. Expenditures on recreation programs in the United States rose from $27 to $42 million during those years, and reached $57 million in 1940.

See Also: LEISURE; LOUIS, JOE; OLYMPICS, BERLIN (1936); OWENS, JESSE.

BIBLIOGRAPHY

Betts, John R. *America's Sporting Heritage: 1850–1950.* 1974.

Davidson, Judith Anne. "The Federal Government and the Democratization of Public Recreational Sport, New York City, 1933–43." Ph.D diss., University of Massachusetts, 1983.

Noverr, Douglas A., and Lawrence E. Ziewacz. *The Games They Played: Sports in American History, 1865–1980.* 1983.

Rader, Benjamin G. *American Sports: From Folk Games to the Age of Television,* 4th edition. 1999.

Riess, Steven A. *City Games: The Evolution of American Urban Society and the Rise of Sports.* 1989.

STEVEN A. RIESS

STALIN, JOSEPH

Throughout the 1930s Joseph Stalin (December 21, 1879–March 5, 1953) was the leader of the Union of Soviet Socialist Republics (USSR) and the world Communist movement. Born Joseph Djugashvili, son of a Georgian cobbler, he studied at the Tiflis Orthodox Theological Seminary in his youth but was expelled in 1899. He was soon active in the Russian Social Democratic Labor Party, and by 1903 was drawn to its more militant and centralized faction, the Bolsheviks, led by Vladimir Ilyich Lenin. In the revolutionary underground, he assumed the name Stalin (man of steel) and rose in the ranks of the Bolshevik Party due to organizational and administrative skills.

With the working-class overthrow of the Russian monarchy in 1917, followed by a socialist revolution led by Lenin's Bolsheviks, Stalin assumed the important role of commissar of nationalities in the Bolshevik organization (renamed the Communist Party in 1918) and in the new Soviet Republic. In 1919 he became part of the Politburo, the central leadership of the Communist Party. Between 1919 and 1922 Stalin accumulated additional positions of authority, culminating in the newly created position of Communist Party general secretary, in which capacity he was nominally subordinate to the Politburo, but in fact increasingly able to "guide" its decisions. Stalin's power was greatly enhanced because during the brutalizing Russian Civil War of 1918 to 1921 "emergency measures" were established that gave the Communist Party a dictatorship over the country's political life.

During his fatal illness in 1922 and 1923, Lenin waged a struggle from his sickbed against Stalin's authoritarian policies and excessive power, enlisting the support of the brilliant revolutionary Leon Trotsky. But other key Communist leaders, including Gregory Zinoviev and Lev Kamenev, initially distrusted Trotsky and preferred the seemingly more easygoing Stalin. After Lenin's death, they discovered that Stalin's control of the bureaucratic apparatus of the party and the government allowed him to reject their perspectives. They joined with Trotsky to struggle against bureaucratic corruption and maintain a revolutionary-internationalist orientation for the Communist International, but they were no match for the powerful apparatus under Stalin's control, and Trotsky was even expelled from the country. Other veteran Bolshevik leaders aligned themselves with Stalin to defeat this opposition, the most prominent being Nikolai Bukharin, who was soon swept aside for opposing some of Stalin's most brutal policies.

From 1928 to 1930, Stalin's "revolution from above" through the forced collectivization of land and rapid industrialization employed extreme repression and violence against masses of peasants and workers who resisted the exploitative effects of

Joseph Stalin (left) with President Roosevelt and British Prime Minister Winston Churchill during the Teheran Conference in Iran in 1943. FRANKLIN DELANO ROOSEVELT LIBRARY

his new policies. Many were killed, with many more arrested and sent to forced-labor camps. Much of the USSR's agriculture was wrecked, resulting in famine that cost the lives of perhaps five million people. While the Communist apparatus under Stalin tightened its control over the intellectual and cultural life of the country, many seasoned Communist Party members nonetheless began to question Stalin's policies. In several sensational "purge trials" from 1936 through 1939, the Stalin regime claimed that a traitorous conspiracy against the USSR had been hatched by Trotsky, Zinoviev, Kamenev, Bukharin, and a majority of those who had led the 1917 revolution. Tens of thousands of Communists were arrested and shot, and many

more were sent to forced-labor camps. Millions of lives were destroyed.

At the same time, an immense propaganda campaign orchestrated a personality cult glorifying Stalin and proclaimed that socialism was now being established in the USSR. The mobilization of millions of people animated by the idealistic goals of socialism contributed to impressive economic development. Employment, the necessities of life, and an increasing number of social improvements were guaranteed to ever-broader sectors of the population. Much of the increase in industrial output was made at the expense of quality (half of all tractors produced in the USSR during the 1930s are said to have been defective), and government figures indicating that overall industrial production increased by about 400 percent between 1928 and 1941 are undoubtedly inflated. The fact remains, however, that the USSR became a major industrial power in that period.

Stalin's grand claim about creating "socialism in a single country" had a powerful appeal beyond the USSR. Especially with the onset of the Great Depression, idealistic workers and intellectuals throughout the world looked to the Communist revolutionary process in the USSR as an alternative to capitalism and a bulwark against the rising tide of fascism. In the early 1930s, Communist parties in many countries were denouncing other socialist parties as "social-fascists," but the failure of German Communists to unite with German Social-Democrats to stop the rise of Adolf Hitler led not to a workers' revolution but to the Nazi regime.

By 1934 the USSR was calling on the League of Nations for a "collective security" alliance of Western capitalist democracies with the USSR against the militaristic expansionism of Germany, Italy, and Japan. In 1935 the Communist International declared that all Communists should work to create a "Popular Front" of Communist and Socialist parties with liberal pro-capitalist parties to establish governments that would maintain both capitalism and political democracy, implement social reforms, and follow a foreign policy friendly to the USSR. After most of the Popular Front efforts collapsed, and major Western capitalist powers proved unwilling to make common cause with the USSR against Hitler, Stalin shifted toward an accommodation with Hitler. The consequent German-Soviet Non-Aggression Pact of 1939 enabled Hitler to launch World War II.

Stalin's regime and the Communist International proclaimed neutrality in this "imperialist conflict," but the German assault on the USSR in June 1941 belatedly helped to create the sort of "collective security" alliance that Stalin had advocated in the latter half of the 1930s. At the conclusion of World War II, however, tensions emerged between the USSR and its war-time capitalist allies, leading to the Cold War confrontation that would last for more than four decades. While millions sincerely mourned Stalin's death in 1953, within three years his successors denounced him for some of his worst crimes, and his system proved incapable of surviving the twentieth century.

See Also: DICTATORSHIP; EUROPE, GREAT DEPRESSION IN; POPULAR FRONT.

BIBLIOGRAPHY

Carr, E. H. *Twilight of the Comintern, 1930–1935.* 1982.

Deutscher, Isaac. *Stalin: A Political Biography,* 2nd edition. 1967.

Medvedev, Roy. *Let History Judge: The Origins and Consequences of Stalinism,* rev. edition, edited and translated by George Shriver, 1989.

Tucker, Robert C. *Stalin as Revolutionary, 1879–1929: A Study in History and Personality.* 1973.

Tucker, Robert C. *Stalin in Power: The Revolution From Above, 1928–1941.* 1992.

PAUL LE BLANC

STEEL WORKERS' ORGANIZING COMMITTEE (SWOC)

The Steel Workers' Organizing Committee (SWOC) was founded in June 1936 at a Washington, D.C., meeting marked by the absence of steelworkers. The reigning assumption was that because the nation's steel companies were rigidly hierarchical and ruthlessly autocratic, the union that developed in the industry would have to mimic its adversary. Thus, throughout its six-year history, SWOC was led by a cadre of trade union "executives" who spoke the language of "centralized" and "responsible" unionism and had little or no regard for rank-and-file democracy. But during those six years the industry witnessed a succession of militant strikes, most notably the bloody "Little Steel" strike of 1937, that challenged the prevailing image of a union characterized by "stability, strength, and unity."

SWOC was an arm of the Committee for Industrial Organization (later called the Congress of Industrial Organizations, or CIO) and was essentially the brainchild of John L. Lewis, the charismatic but dictatorial president of the United Mine

Workers of America (UMW) and the CIO. Lewis placed UMW vice president Philip Murray in charge of SWOC and staffed it mainly with organizers on loan from the miners' union. Murray had begun working in the mines of his native Scotland at age ten and had become the president of a UMW local in Pennsylvania's Westmoreland County at age eighteen. A long-time Lewis ally and loyalist, one of Murray's first acts as SWOC chairman was to establish the organization's national headquarters on the thirty-sixth floor of Pittsburgh's tallest office building, where he could, literally, look down on the steel barons.

The ties between coal and steel had always run deep. Many steelworkers were the sons of coal miners; some had begun their own working lives "underground." Moreover, Lewis and Murray saw to it that their "union of steel" would bear the mark of the UMW. Four of the top five officials in SWOC were also UMW officials, and as late as 1940 two-thirds of the organization's district directors continued to draw their salaries from the miners' union.

Speaking the language of the UMW and the CIO, Murray announced a policy of "absolute racial equality in Union membership." But in the idiom of the day, the word *racial* could refer to ethnicity and nationality, as well as color. Murray's priority in this regard was not the substantial concentrations of black workers in the industry but the fraternal organizations of the foreign-born, notably the International Workers Order, a Communist-controlled benefit society with more than sixty thousand members, many of them in the steel towns and other industrial communities of Pennsylvania and Ohio. In October 1936, Murray gave the keynote address at a Fraternal Orders Conference in Pittsburgh, where organizations such as the Croatian Fraternal Union, the National Slovak Society, the Lodge of Lithuanians of America, and the United Ukrainian Toilers came together to endorse the steel campaign.

Another key to SWOC's development was the steel industry's company unions, or Employee Representation Plans (ERPs), which the employers had formed after the passage of the National Industrial Recovery Act in June 1933. By the end of 1934, more than 90 percent of the industry's workers were en-

rolled in ERPs, and SWOC decided to capture them from within. Already, the leadership of these unions had demonstrated a remarkable degree of independence, especially in the plants of U.S. Steel's Carnegie-Illinois division, where ERP representatives, such as John J. Mullen and Elmer Maloy from Western Pennsylvania and George Patterson from Chicago, were destined to become important grassroots leaders in the steelworkers' union. By January 1937, many of the ERPs had voted to cast their lot with SWOC, which was claiming a membership of 125,000.

In fact, SWOC was hardly the juggernaut it claimed to be. In early 1937, its leadership had no reason to believe that it could win a representation election at any of the major steel companies. But on March 2, U.S. Steel, the giant corporation that accounted for nearly forty percent of the industry's steel-making capacity, signed a collective bargaining agreement with SWOC. Franklin Roosevelt's overwhelming electoral victory in November 1936, combined with the election of New Deal Democratic governors and mayors in states and municipalities that had long been loyal Republican strongholds, made it appear that government, at all levels, would be more likely to support than to suppress unions. Then, in February 1937, a militant minority of autoworkers, led by defiant sit-down strikers in Flint, Michigan, compelled mighty General Motors to come to terms with the CIO. In these radically new circumstances, it must have seemed to U.S. Steel board chairman Myron Taylor that cautious accommodation was a more appropriate response to SWOC than stubborn, and costly, resistance.

With "Big Steel" under contract, SWOC's next great test came with the Little Steel strike that began on May 26. The Little Steel companies—American Rolling Mill, Bethlehem, Inland, National, Republic, and Youngstown Sheet and Tube—were "little" only in comparison to U.S. Steel. In reality, they were major corporations, with abundant resources, and their leaders were rabidly anti-union. U.S. Steel's willingness to recognize SWOC only strengthened their determination to resist any further encroachment on the industry's open-shop tradition. On Memorial Day, at Republic Steel in Chicago, ten strikers and their supporters were gunned down by a vast phalanx of uniformed policemen in what became known as the Memorial Day Massacre. Overall, eighteen men died in the course of the strike, which ended in a crushing defeat for the union.

The Little Steel strike was a major setback for SWOC and the CIO, but the devastating impact of the Roosevelt recession created even greater problems. The nationwide economic downturn of 1937 and 1938 caused a 70 percent drop in steel production and massive layoffs among steelworkers. Even among workers who remained on the job, the number of paid-up union members fell sharply. Often, in giant plants with thousands of workers, only a few hundred continued to pay dues, and SWOC resorted to "dues picket lines," where staffers and loyal union members surrounded the plants and refused to let hourly employees go to work until they paid their monthly dollar.

Recession and employer intransigence caused the steel drive to falter; sympathetic government intervention and a booming war economy allowed it to triumph decisively. Bethlehem Steel fell to SWOC after a strike in the spring of 1941. Republic, the most intransigent symbol of the open shop, capitulated without a strike soon thereafter. With the American Federation of Labor still claiming jurisdiction at U.S. Steel, SWOC called for a representation election at "the Corporation" and defeated its rival by a margin of better than eleven to one. At this juncture, even the paternalistic Murray recognized that the time had come to transform SWOC into an international union. In May 1942 at Cleveland's Public Music Hall, 1,700 delegates gave birth to the United Steelworkers of America. In less than six full years, SWOC had organized the vast majority of the nation' steelworkers—often, they had organized themselves—into one big industrial union, thus breaking an employer stranglehold that had prevailed since the 1890s.

See Also: AMERICAN FEDERATION OF LABOR (AFL); COLLECTIVE BARGAINING; CONGRESS OF INDUSTRIAL ORGANIZATIONS (CIO); LEWIS, JOHN L.; MURRAY, PHILIP; ORGANIZED LABOR; STRIKES; UNITED MINE WORKERS OF AMERICA (UMWA).

BIBLIOGRAPHY

Bernstein, Irving. *Turbulent Years: A History of the American Worker, 1933–1941.* 1970.

Brody, David. *Steelworkers in America: The Nonunion Era.* 1960.

Brooks, Robert R. R. *As Steel Goes, . . . Unionism in a Basic Industry.* 1940.

Cayton, Horace R., and George S. Mitchell. *Black Workers and the New Unions.* 1939.

Clark. Paul F.; Peter Gottlieb; and Donald Kennedy; eds. *Forging a Union of Steel: Philip Murray, SWOC, and the United Steelworkers.* 1987.

Cohen, Lizabeth. *Making a New Deal: Industrial Workers in Chicago, 1919–1939.* 1991.

Lynd, Staughton, and Alice Lynd. *Rank and File: Personal Histories by Working-Class Organizers.* 1973.

Needleman, Ruth. *Black Freedom Fighters in Steel: The Struggle for Democratic Unionism.* 2003.

Nelson, Bruce. *Divided We Stand: American Workers and the Struggle for Black Equality.* 2001.

Rose, James D. *Duquesne and the Rise of Steel Unionism.* 2001.

Zieger, Robert H. *The CIO, 1935–1955.* 1995.

BRUCE NELSON

STEINBECK, JOHN

John Ernst Steinbeck, Jr., (February 27, 1902–December 20, 1968) was an American writer and winner of the 1962 Nobel Prize for literature. His 1939 novel *The Grapes of Wrath* is the single most important literary work dealing with the Great Depression.

Steinbeck was born in Salinas, California, and the area around Salinas became the setting of his best books. He graduated from Salinas High School in 1919 and attended Stanford University off and on without completing a degree. His first novel, *Cup of Gold* (1929), about the seventeenth-century pirate Henry Morgan, and his next two books, *Pastures of Heaven* (1932) and *To a God Unknown* (1933), received little attention. Carol Henning, who became his first wife in 1930, helped him focus his fiction on the suffering resulting from the Depression, and Ed Ricketts, a marine biologist he met shortly after his marriage, helped crystallize Steinbeck's vague notions about group behavior, individualism, and ecology. Ricketts's scientific outlook tempered Steinbeck's inveterate sentimentality. *Tortilla Flat* (1935), Steinbeck's first financially successful book, was the first to treat marginalized characters he had observed first hand. *In Dubious Battle* (1936) concerned a strike among migrant fruit pickers. *Of Mice and Men* (1937) is the tragic story of a pair of itinerant ranch hands. Steinbeck's greatest achievement, the crucial literary text of the Depression, *The Grapes of Wrath* (1939), is the story of an Oklahoma family who leaves the Dust Bowl and heads for California in search of the American dream. *The Grapes of Wrath,* a huge best-seller and Pulitzer Prize winner in 1940, assured Steinbeck's place in American literature.

Although Steinbeck published eighteen more books in his lifetime, nothing afterwards ever matched the critical success of *The Grapes of Wrath.* His writing after the 1930s lacks the power of his Depression novels. Perhaps what critics have regarded as Steinbeck's "decline" can be attributed to the prosperity after the war and his own financial success, which may have cost Steinbeck his affinity with those who are down and out. The divorce from his first wife in 1943 and the death of Ed Ricketts in 1948 contributed to his turning away from the concerns of the Depression-era novels. His moving to New York from California cut him off from the region so central to his best works. His return to that setting in *Cannery Row* (1945) and *East of Eden* (1952) resulted in books that were thematically incoherent and sentimental. Despite the critics' views about his later work, his books remained popular with the reading public. *Travels with Charley* (1962), an account of driving across the United States with his pet poodle to get a sense of the mood of the country in the 1960s, sold well but did not enhance his standing with literary critics. The Nobel Prize for literature that he was awarded in 1962 was clearly for his work more than two decades earlier. He died in New York in 1968. His ashes, taken across the country by his third wife and one of his sons from his second marriage, were interred in the Salinas cemetery.

See Also: GRAPES OF WRATH, THE; LITERATURE; OKIES.

BIBLIOGRAPHY

Benson, Jackson J. *The True Adventures of John Steinbeck, Writer.* 1984.

French, Warren G. *John Steinbeck's Fiction Revisited.* 1994.

Kiernan, Thomas. *The Intricate Music: A Biography of John Steinbeck,* 1979.

Parini, Jay. *John Steinbeck: A Biography.* 1995.

Steinbeck, Elaine, and Robert Wallsten, eds. *Steinbeck: A Life in Letters.* 1975.

AUSTIN WILSON

STFU. *See* SOUTHERN TENANT FARMERS' UNION.

STIEGLITZ, ALFRED. *See* PHOTOGRAPHY.

STIMSON, HENRY

Stimson, Henry Lewis (The Colonel, September 21, 1867–October 20, 1950), a Wall Street lawyer and Republican, served twice as United States secretary of war under presidents William Howard Taft, Franklin D. Roosevelt, and Harry S. Truman. Stimson also served as secretary of state for President Herbert Hoover. Born to privilege, Stimson attended Phillips Academy (Andover), Yale University, and Harvard Law School. He began his public service as the U.S. attorney for the Southern District of New York under Theodore Roosevelt, and later served as governor-general of the Philippines. Conservative on domestic politics, Stimson was an internationalist who advocated an increasing American involvement in world affairs.

As Hoover's secretary of state, Stimson pursued greater cooperation with the powers of Europe, modification of the financial burdens imposed by the Treaty of Versailles, and further disarmament as the keys to maintaining peace. With the coming of the Great Depression and the economic collapse of Europe in 1931, the Colonel, as Stimson liked to be called after his rank during World War I, pushed with limited success for further debt reduction and cancellation of reparations payments. Stimson could only convince President Hoover to agree to a one-year moratorium on debts and a temporary standstill agreement of private debts. Neither action, however, provided a long-term solution to the international economic crisis.

Japan's invasion of Manchuria in 1931 led to the establishment of the *Stimson Doctrine,* the principle of nonrecognition of territory seized by force. Stimson believed that the Japanese had to be made to realize that no matter what their success in Manchuria, they still had to contend with the opinion and power of the rest of the world. The Stimson Doctrine served as a clarion call for the United States to act against aggression during the 1930s and made Stimson the leading advocate of American opposition to first Japan's and then Germany's expansion. Throughout the decade Stimson served as the loyal opposition to Franklin Roosevelt, supporting the president's efforts to increase American awareness of international events and preparedness for the coming war.

When war erupted in Europe in 1939, Roosevelt needed someone capable of managing the War Department who would also make foreign policy a less divisive issue. In June 1940 the president turned to Stimson for this task, knowing he would approach it in a bipartisan manner while maintaining his loyalty to the administration's policies. As secretary of war, Stimson successfully oversaw the mobilization of the American economy, the military strategies of fighting in both Europe and Asia, and the development of the atomic bomb.

See Also: HULL, CORDELL; ISOLATIONISM;
MILITARY: UNITED STATES ARMY; MILITARY:
UNITED STATES NAVY.

BIBLIOGRAPHY

Hodgson, Godfrey. *The Colonel: The Life and Wars of Henry Stimson, 1867–1950.* 1990.

Schmitz, David F. *Henry L. Stimson: The First Wise Man.* 2001.

Stimson, Henry L., and McGeorge Bundy. *On Active Service in Peace and War.* 1948.

Stimson, Henry L. Papers and Diaries. Sterling Library, Yale University, New Haven, Conn.

DAVID F. SCHMITZ

STOCK MARKET CRASH (1929)

The great bull market of the 1920s and the spectacular collapse of the New York Stock Exchange (NYSE) in late 1929 occupy a pivotal position in popular explanations of the cause of the Great Depression. Professional historians, however, are more circumspect in assessing the impact of the Wall Street crash.

MARKET GROWTH DURING THE 1920s

The U.S. economy staged a rapid recovery from the postwar Depression of 1920 and 1921, and between 1922 and 1929 real gross national product (GNP) grew by 22 percent. This period was an era of stable prices, full employment, high levels of investment and high company profits. The United States exuded great confidence in the economy. The nation seemed blessed with business talent, which could skilfully employ the riches at its disposal. Big business in particular flourished, building on the technological advances that had been adopted during World War I. National prosperity encouraged stock market growth. Securities had been relatively undervalued at the start of the expansion but soon began to rise as corporate profits grew.

Everyone involved in the market seemed to benefit. Investors could look forward to a dividend and also to a rise in the value of their stock, which could easily be converted into cash if necessary. The small investor who could not afford to develop a diversified portfolio found especially attractive investment trusts, which grew spectacularly in the twenties. Business looked first to retained profits to fund investment on which future profits were based but did so in the clear knowledge that any shortfall could easily be addressed by approaching the market. Commercial banks, no longer approached by companies anxious to borrow, reacted to the loss of business lending opportunities by moving into the investment banking and brokerage business themselves. In doing so they encouraged greater participation in the market.

THE BOOM GATHERS PACE

It is difficult to be certain when the market was transformed from vigorous expansion to unsustain-

The trading floor of the New York Stock Exchange just after the October 1929 stock market crash. HERBERT HOOVER LIBRARY

able growth, but this change probably occurred in early 1928. Between early 1928 and the middle of 1929 the economy grew very rapidly, and the confidence that many investors had in the market increased also. Indeed, some scholars believe that those who bought stock at progressively higher prices were acting rationally as they would expect earning on their investments to justify the price paid. However, during this period stock prices were rising far more rapidly than dividends, and it is reasonable to assume that the judgement of a number of investors was clouded by the prospect of an inexorable increase in stock prices.

As Eugene White (1990) notes, when the market was at its most vigorous some of the stock which investors found most attractive was in companies that paid no dividends and did not expect to pay any in the near future. In other words the advantage of owning such stock was solely that its price would continue to rise. For example, investors were attracted to stock in public utilities, which had come to the fore in the 1920s with the expansion of electricity, and also in companies employing the latest technology, for example the movie-making industry. Both groups contained large numbers of firms that paid no dividends.

Moreover, many share deals were financed by credit. The investor made a deposit and borrowed the remainder of the purchase price from the broker using the stock as collateral. This transaction was called "buying on the margin" and seemed a sensible option, as the capital gain from the stock would easily cover the cost, including the interest charge on the broker's loan. The brokers, who supported

Nervous investors and curious onlookers crowd Wall Street in lower Manhattan after the stock market crashed in October 1929.
BETTMANN/CORBIS

this system of trading as more stock could be sold and more commission earned, borrowed from banks to advance loans to their clients. As long as stock prices continued to improve, the relationship between borrowers and lenders was relatively risk free. However, if securities failed to appreciate as expected, some purchasers would have difficulty in repaying their brokers' loans. If the price falls were very steep, the broker would be in difficulty as the shares accepted as collateral would have to be sold on a declining market. The majority of investors, however, did not consider the prospect of a collapse in prices as a realistic possibility.

Nevertheless, there was some unease as prices soared. A few major investors began to withdraw from the market, and some leading executives even volunteered that their own company stock was overvalued. Most significant, the Federal Reserve (Fed) became concerned that the mounting speculation was potentially destabilizing. The Fed decided to gently deflate the speculative bubble instead of running the risk that it might eventually burst and result in an economic collapse.

The Fed exhorted its member banks not to lend for speculative purposes. More positively, in early 1928 it began to pursue a tight money policy by raising interest rates and selling government bonds. The Fed believed that its action would make borrowing for speculation more expensive and that gradually it would cease and the market would return to normal. The monetary authorities were confident that their actions would only affect the stock market and would not impair the performance of the economy.

To the chagrin of the Fed, the funding of brokers' loans increased by 50 percent between June 1928 and June 1929. The source of the money flowing into the market was not member banks, but foreign banking houses and U.S. businesses and private individuals attracted by the high rate of interest which borrowers were prepared to pay. Idle balances and funds that had been earmarked for foreign investment were switched to the home market, causing consternation in those countries that had come to rely on U.S. international capital flows. Indeed, there was a plentiful supply of credit for brokers' loans even though the Fed had pursued a

restrictive monetary policy. Investors were prepared to pay higher rates to lenders because they believed that the rising market made it worthwhile. But the availability of credit was not the cause of continuing speculation. Speculators were not forced to borrow.

THE GREAT CRASH

The New York Stock Exchange (NYSE) hit its peak in early September 1929 and then declined, even though that month saw a record volume on new issues. During the first three weeks of October the market performed erratically, but on October 23 prices fell sharply to levels reached at the beginning of the year. On the following day, "Black Thursday," panic set in and 12.9 million shares were traded. The urge to sell became so overwhelming that the tickertape on which stockholders relied for the most up-to-date information ran several hours late, thus adding to the confusion. Brokerage firms were inundated. Good stock was liquidated along with the indifferent. A group of prominent bankers made a public move to rally the market by purchasing $125 million worth of stock, which for a while had a positive effect. However, on October 29, 16.4 million securities, a record volume, were traded on the NYSE. That day became known as "'Black Tuesday," and it symbolized the panic, helplessness, confusion, and fear that had taken a firm grip on the market. Confident statements from leading financiers, such as the Rockefellers, were seized upon by the few remaining optimists who attacked the gloomy for "talking down the market." However, nothing could arrest the fall, and the market continued to decline until November 14. The collapse had lasted three weeks during which time the average value of stocks had declined by over 50 percent. The market then seemed to revive coincident with the decision of the Fed to reduce interest rates, but those who thought the worst was now over were sadly mistaken.

Why did the stock market crash? There is no doubt that the price of some stocks had reached levels that could not be justified by a rational assessment of future earnings. Elements of the market were therefore potentially unstable. But the collapse embraced virtually all stock, not just the outrageously overpriced. Why did panic replace confidence so comprehensively?

The stock market crash followed the peak of economic activity, which was reached in the middle of 1929. As the prospects for the economy declined sharply, it was increasingly clear to investors that they would have to revise downward their estimates of future business profitability and do so quickly. Once the certainty of high company profits evaporated, so did confidence in rising stock prices. Buying "on the margin" had boosted sales in prosperous times, but the system worked sharply in reverse when conditions changed.

One significant factor acting as a brake on economic activity was the tight money policy pursued by the Fed to erase speculation. High interest rates and a slowdown in the growth of the money supply were sufficient to tilt the economy into a steep recession. The Fed's monetary initiative failed to halt stock market speculation, but unfortunately it did affect the economy. However, the Wall Street crash did not cause the Great Depression. It was an early and violent reaction to changing economic circumstances.

The crash did have some adverse effects. It markedly reduced the wealth of investors and adversely affected their ability and willingness to purchase goods and services. Public confidence was shaken as one of the most potent symbols of national prosperity tumbled. However, in early 1930 there was a note of optimism. The fortunes of the economy and the market were in the ascendant. Perhaps the speculative boil had been lanced, and the worst was over.

WALL STREET 1930–1933

Confidence in the market evident in early 1930 proved sadly misplaced, and in the second half of the year a steep decline in stock prices commenced. During 1931 the economy continued to deteriorate, and problems were compounded by domestic bank failures and by the international financial crisis that culminated in the devaluation of sterling in September. The consumer durable sector, which had been so vigorous during the boom, now faced declining sales. Few consumers purchased automobiles or other goods whose purchase was not con-

sidered essential. All these factors helped to increase unemployment, lower confidence, and erode corporate profits. The stock of some food manufacturers, some retailers, and most tobacco companies was relatively sound, but stock in heavy industry and investment trusts fell precipitously. The year 1932, during which aggregate business profits were negative, was the worst year of the Depression for most stocks. On average prices had fallen to a mere 12 percent of their 1929 levels and only five stocks exceeded by one-third their 1929 prices. The worst affected stock could be found in the automobile, steel, railroad, and farm equipment sectors.

Amid the gloom some individual companies performed relatively well. Wigmore identifies J. C. Penney, General Electric, IBM, and Woolworth as examples, in which cases exceptional management resulted in a financial performance far ahead of their rivals. Gold mining and tobacco companies had the best stock results between 1929 and 1933. The worst performances were in the financial sector and the entertainment industry where many major movie companies flirted with ruin. The downward slide of the market mirrored that of the depressed economy, though some stocks, which had been driven high by the unrestrained enthusiasm of the pre-Depression boom, fell a long way and became worthless. It is important to remember that this was a time of massive general deflation when all prices declined, so it is not surprising that the market also shared this phenomenon. It is also clear that the decline in stock prices after mid-1930 was even more dramatic than the falls during the Wall Street crash. However, at this time the falling market was just one of a number of shocks forcing public and business confidence to ever lower levels.

THE STOCK MARKET AND THE NEW DEAL

During the first few months of the Roosevelt presidency the economy began a vigorous recovery and dragged the securities market along in its wake. However, even in 1937, the best year for the economy during the 1930s, an index of total stock prices, using 1929 = 100 as its base, had only reached 59. A disaggregation of this index shows that the figure for railroad stock was 34 while public utilities stock, which had played such a vigorous role in the boom of the 1920s, had reached 44. The performance of industrial stock was relatively good but, at 69, was still a long way below the level achieved in 1929. The depressed stock market as a whole was substantially below even 1928 price levels. Since both business profits and investment were very depressed during the 1930s compared to the levels that had been achieved during the booming 1920s, it is not surprising that the market as a whole failed to stage a more vigorous recovery.

Many investors who had directly experienced the market at its most capricious called for some level of state regulation, especially as there was a lingering suspicion that unfair practices may have been responsible for the debacle. Early in the Depression President Herbert Hoover had asked the Senate Banking and Currency Committee to investigate trading practices on Wall Street. When Ferdinand Pecora was appointed counsel to the committee, he attracted public attention by exposing wrongdoing by senior financiers previously thought to be men of the highest probity. Pecora was a highly effective publicist, and newspapers were able to carry vivid stories of dishonesty or practices so close to it that the people were unable to make the subtle distinction to which the minds of several bankers were carefully attuned. Respect for financiers, which had been high in the 1920s, was eroded. The public expected something to be done, and bankers were in a very weak position to fight any congressional attempts at regulation. Although scandal caught the public attention and provided desirable scapegoats, it would be wrong, nonetheless, to see financial malpractice as other than a very minor contribution to stock market misfortune. Still, it is easy to appreciate the strong view emanating from Congress that investors, especially the small investors, needed strong protection, even if only to prevent them being misled.

The Securities Act (May 1933) and the Securities and Exchange Act (June 1934) provided investors with more accurate information so that they could feel more confident when purchasing stock. Investors were also given a breathing space, time to change their minds over stock purchase rather than having to regret an instant decision. As a result the

hard-sell tactics that had been used successfully to boost sales in the 1920s, and which were highly popular while the market boomed, were curtailed. The Fed was given the power to set margin requirements for the purchase of securities, which was seen as an additional tool in any future fight against speculation. An independent agency, the Securities and Stock Exchange Commission (SEC), was established to oversee the implementation of the new legislation. The first chairman of the SEC was Joseph P. Kennedy, in his day a formidable Wall Street operator and the father of President John F. Kennedy.

A separate piece of legislation, the Banking Act (1933), separated commercial from investment banking. This legislation compelled commercial banks to quit securities markets and restricted their authority to underwrite securities to those issued by states and local governments. During the 1920s the growth of commercial bank securities affiliates had led to increased competition in the sales of securities. In the frenzied atmosphere of the time, mass marketing techniques, aggressive advertising, and mail shots had drawn many small investors into the market. We see here a typical piece of New Deal regulation where restrictions on competition were seen as essential for the provision of stability. The Banking Act was an attempt, among other things, to curb activities that were considered contributory factors to the great bull market. Speculative excesses were, indeed, absent from the market for the rest of the 1930s, but neither the performance of the economy nor the mood of investors was likely to create the conditions for a return of them.

The securities market expanded, as did the rest of the economy during the 1950s, and in 1954 the Dow Jones Index exceeded its 1929 peak. During this period the Eisenhower administration reduced the SEC's staffing. The volume of trading on the NYSE reached and overtook its the pre-Depression high in 1963. By the 1960s it was becoming clear that the restrictions on competition that had seemed so sensible thirty years previously were contributing to a growing inefficiency in securities markets. Moreover, the increasing globalization of capital markets, and the growing use of computers that led to a rapid diffusion of knowledge as well as the speedy clearance and settlement of accounts, totally transformed the manner in which business was transacted. Indeed, in 1975 Congress urged the SEC to encourage competition rather than help curb it.

On October 19, 1987, the financial world was shaken by a dramatic stock market collapse when the Dow Jones Index fell 508 points, the largest single day drop in U.S. history. Immediately commentators drew parallels between the booming 1980s and the 1920s. They noted that both collapses followed attempts by the Fed to counter speculation by the use of restrictive monetary policy and wondered if the latest crash would be followed by a new Great Depression. In 1987 the Fed moved promptly and provided ample liquidity for the system by engaging in open market operations. Within a few months it was apparent that the economy had been unaffected by the crash, and as confidence in the market returned the Fed was able to reimpose a restraining monetary influence. The 1987 crash showed that regulation cannot prevent stock market crises, but rapid reaction by the Fed can minimize the effect. It was a pity that this was not part of the received wisdom in 1929.

See Also: CAUSES OF THE GREAT DEPRESSION; FEDERAL RESERVE SYSTEM; GLASS-STEAGALL ACT OF 1933; SECURITIES REGULATION.

BIBLIOGRAPHY

Bierman, Harold. *The Great Myths of 1929 and the Lessons to be Learned.* 1991.

Galbraith, John Kenneth. *The Great Crash: 1929.* 1954.

Kindleberger, Charles P. *Manias, Panics and Crashes: A History of Financial Crises.* 1978.

Parrish, Michael E. *Securities Regulation and the New Deal.* 1970.

Temin, Peter. *Did Monetary Forces Cause the Great Depression?* 1976.

Thomas, Gordon. *The Day the Bubble Burst: A Social History of the Wall Street Crash of 1929.* 1979.

Wigmore, Barrie. *The Crash and Its Aftermath.* 1985.

White, Eugene N. "The Stock Market Boom and Crash of 1929 Revisited." *Journal of Economic Perspectives* 4 (1990): 67–83.

White, Eugene N. "Banking and Finance in the Twentieth Century." In *The Cambridge Economic History of the United States,* Vol.111: *The Twentieth Century,* edited by Stanley L. Engerman and Robert E. Gallman. 2000.

PETER FEARON

Year	Number of Workers Involved in Work Stoppages
1929	289,000
1930	183,000
1931	342,000
1932	324,000
1933	1,170,000
1934	1,470,000
1935	1,120,000
1936	789,000
1937	1,860,000
1938	688,000
1939	1,170,000
1940	577,000
1941	2,360,000

SOURCE: United States Bureau of the Census. *Historical Statistics of the United States, Colonial Times to 1970.* 1975. Series D-971.

STRIKES

Between 1930 and 1941, 172 million days of labor were lost over the course of 27,000 work stoppages. Strikes, however, interrupted more than just the flow of business. Their failure to resolve the economic crisis early in the Great Depression led to growing desperation on the part of workers, union leadership, and government officials. The New Deal sought to contain popular protest but its effect was to encourage further labor militancy. Organized labor initially discouraged strikes but slowly realized the opportunities they offered. Rank-and-file workers, who started the majority of stoppages by either walking out or sitting down, also understood their costs and benefits. During the summer of 1937 alone approximately ninety workers lost their lives to employer violence and state repression, while countless more were wounded, evicted from their homes, or jailed because of their involvement in strikes. Still, organized labor could not have achieved its unprecedented victories in the

Year	Number of Work Stoppages
1929	921
1930	637
1931	810
1932	841
1933	1,695
1934	1,856
1935	2,014
1936	2,172
1937	4,740
1938	2,772
1939	2,613
1940	2,508
1941	4,288

SOURCE: United States Bureau of the Census. *Historical Statistics of the United States, Colonial Times to 1970.* 1975. Series D-970.

1930s without workers' willingness to employ their ultimate weapon.

The Great Depression began with a surprisingly passive labor movement. In the first three years of the 1930s, workers engaged in fewer strikes than at almost any moment in the twentieth century. Those that did occur mostly dealt with immediate bread-and-butter issues relating to wages and hours rather than with efforts to establish new independent unions. Indeed many were wildcat strikes—unplanned, spontaneous eruptions in which workers walked off the job without consulting their unions in reaction to conflicts with their supervisors. With little administrative and financial support from mainstream organized labor, these strikes were destined to be ineffective, short-lived, and have little impact.

Many of the major strikes that erupted in the early years of the Great Depression occurred in rural regions rather than in the urban centers of manufacturing that later proved more receptive to labor protest. Due to overproduction and falling prices, the agricultural and textiles industries had fallen on hard times well before much of the country. In Gastonia, North Carolina, for example, textile mills had begun laying off employees, lowering wages, and increasing workloads in the mid-1920s. In response, mill hands staged a walkout followed by a massive strike in April 1929. Although they called for modest reforms and quickly won the sup-

port of local residents, who joined in the pickets, the poor workers were no match for the desperate textile mills. Evictions from company-owned homes and a campaign to discredit the Communist Party organizers succeeded in derailing the strike after less than two weeks.

The prominence of the Communist Party in labor protest partly reflected the inaction of the American Federation of Labor (AFL), the nation's largest body of organized labor, which sought to resolve the economic crisis through closer cooperation with employers. Some labor leaders preferred confrontation but could not win the support of the AFL's Executive council. Rising unemployment also constrained workers, who felt fortunate to have a job and knew that they could easily be replaced by strikebreakers. Left without options, workers were forced to rely on company unions, which were controlled by employers and resolutely opposed to strikes.

The power of employers gradually weakened as the federal government increasingly became involved in labor disputes. Under growing pressure from trade unionists, Congress passed the Norris-La Guardia Act in 1932. The law limited the use of federal injunctions to forestall strikes and prevented federal courts from enforcing yellow-dog contracts in which workers agreed to not join unions as a condition of employment. Section 7(a) of the National Industrial Recovery Act of 1933 (NIRA) gave workers the right to "organize unions of their own choosing" and bargain collectively with their employers. The new legislation had an immediate impact. Twice as many strikes broke out in 1933 as the year before, involving three and a half times the number of workers.

The strike wave culminated in 1934, with one and a half million workers going on strike—more than eight times the number that had gone out in 1930. For the first time in thirty years, the principal issue in most strikes was long-term union recognition rather than immediate concerns involving wages or hours. The most severe unrest began on the docks of San Francisco. After years of abuse, longshoremen abandoned the company union to form a local of the International Longshoremen's Association (ILA) in the summer of 1933. When the

Striking workers picket the King Farm near Morrisville, Pennsylvania, in 1938. LIBRARY OF CONGRESS, PRINTS & PHOTOGRAPHS DIVISION, FSA/OWI COLLECTION

ILA failed to address the concerns of its members, longshoremen issued their own demands and went on strike in May 1934. The shipping companies responded violently, hiring vigilantes to beat strikers. The day after Independence Day, police opened fire on a crowd of unarmed strikers, killing two and wounding dozens more. Workers across the city responded by rallying together with a short-lived general strike. By the end of July, rank-and-file dockworkers had won their main demand, a union-controlled hiring hall, without any major outside support.

Employees at Electric Auto-Lite, a supplier of automobile parts in Toledo, Ohio, also exercised their NIRA-protected rights by organizing a federal

union under an AFL charter in 1933. When the company refused to negotiate, workers walked out in early 1934. Thousands of unemployed workers affiliated with A. J. Muste's American Workers Party joined the strike in solidarity, turning it into a wider popular protest. As in San Francisco, police provoked riots in which two strikers were killed. A general strike was averted, however, when the federal government successfully pressured the company to recognize the union. Community was also essential in the Teamster's strike in Minneapolis that same month. Trucking employers there had rejected their drivers efforts to organize an independent union. After a strike was declared, building trades workers and taxi drivers walked out in sympathy. In

Union strikers picket a Manhattan department store in 1934. FRANKLIN DELANO ROOSEVELT LIBRARY

short order, the city was polarized between workers and employers. After much tension a street fight broke out between police and twenty thousand workers that resulted in the death of two strikers. Fruitless negotiations led to another mass strike in July in which several more strikers were killed. Finally, President Franklin Roosevelt interceded directly and helped push through an arbitration in which employers agreed to bargain collectively with the Teamsters.

Although many strikes were successful, the failure of the nationwide textile strike—at that time the largest labor protest in American history—deeply worried many in the labor movement. Spontaneous walkouts had spread throughout the southern states and engulfed much of the East Coast in the summer and fall of 1934 when an industrial code was issued that neglected to increase wages or improve working conditions. In all, more than 400,000 strikers had crippled the industry. However, with victory in sight the United Textile Workers (UTW) called off the strike on what proved to be empty promises by the Roosevelt administration. Labor statesman John L. Lewis blamed the failure of the textile strike on the AFL's lack of support and demanded that the body encourage new forms of industrial unionism that would respond to workers' solidarity and militancy. Other labor leaders recognized that by 1935 many workers had dropped out of unions because the AFL could not maintain their enthusiasm. The UTW's membership, for instance, had dropped from several hundred thousand to only eighty thousand in a matter of months.

The Roosevelt administration, on the other hand, feared that popular unrest would continue to escalate unless the federal government established a stable balance between industry and labor. After the NRA was declared unconstitutional, it embraced Senator Robert Wagner's National Labor Relations Act of 1935 (NLRA) to strengthen labor's bargaining power. By establishing the National Labor Relations Board to oversee votes for union representation, the administration hoped that the law would remove the impetus for the recent burst of strikes.

Over the next few years, strikes would more than double in number, reaching a peak of 4,720 in 1937. The establishment of the Committee for Industrial Organization (CIO) by Lewis and his associates in 1935 gave industrial workers the financial and administrative support they needed to carry out effective unionization drives. The Supreme Court's decision on April 12, 1939, upholding the NLRA prompted a flood of efforts to take advantage of the newfound federal protection. But the CIO and the NLRA only gave structure and sustenance to what

was primarily a movement of ordinary workers enforcing their right to bargain collectively with employers.

One of the sources for the revitalization of the grassroots effort was the strike by United Rubber Workers (URW) in 1936. Rubber workers in Akron, Ohio, had broken from the company union the previous year and obtained an AFL charter establishing the URW. Among the union's earliest supporters were Lewis and the CIO, who demanded that the city's firms negotiate. At the end of January and through February spontaneous protests broke out at Firestone and Goodyear plants. Emulating a tactic conceived by rubber workers in 1934, tire builders sat down at their workplaces, refusing to move unless the firms negotiated with the union. Confounded URW officials, who did not authorize these unconventional actions, had no choice but to follow the course of action laid out by their aggressive members. The Akron community soon sided with the nonviolent rubber workers, donating to the strike relief fund and threatening a general strike if the municipal government interfered with the strike. On March 22, Goodyear signed an agreement that recognized the union, reinstated workers, and granted significant concessions.

The CIO rapidly built on its initial success. The United Automobile Workers (UAW), originally established by the AFL, broke away in 1936 and affiliated itself solely with the CIO. When the UAW president was unable to pressure the major car manufacturers to bargain collectively, militant workers closed down a General Motors plant in Flint, Michigan, on December 30, 1936. As it spread to other factories, the Great Sit-down Strike brought the entire company's production to halt. Unsure of how to contend with the occupying force, the company cut off the heat, attempted an invasion by police that was repulsed, and unsuccessfully lobbied for the National Guard to intervene. Finally, on February 11, 1937, under pressure from Roosevelt, General Motors recognized the union and agreed to negotiations.

The CIO's victory over the powerful company had an immediate effect. Over the next year, 400,000 workers in mass-production industries participated in similar sit-down strikes. The threat of such crippling strikes convinced companies that had never tolerated unions to negotiate settlements. On March 2, 1937, the CIO's Steel Workers' Organizing Committee (SWOC) and U.S. Steel, the nation's largest corporation with an unbroken history of resistance to organized labor, signed a contract that recognized the union and gave its members a 10 percent wage increase. Within two months, SWOC membership had tripled to 300,000 and it embarked on a campaign to unionize the remaining steel firms known as "Little Steel." By the end of 1937, the CIO represented over two million workers; even the turgid AFL experienced a significant growth in membership.

Yet, at its peak, the CIO began to suffer a backlash. It was unable to properly fund the Little Steel Strike, though 75,000 workers had walked out. The steel firms also fought more aggressively than had been expected. Rather than sign a gentleman's agreement as U.S. Steel had done, they organized citizens committees, won the assistance of municipal governments, and hired vigilantes to attack picket lines. On May 30, 1937, Chicago police fired on unarmed strikers, killing ten, injuring more than a hundred, and ushering in a summer of deadly violence that sapped labor's commitment to protest. An economic recession, beginning that same month and lasting for over a year, increased the ranks of unemployed by another two million. The number of workers participating in work stoppage fell by more than 60 percent in 1938.

The momentum would not shift again until the nation's economy recovered as it began its rearmament for war. By 1941, new records were set as workers surpassed the strike wave of 1937. But even then, the major unions soon issued no-strike pledges to demonstrate their patriotism and avoid the anti-labor crackdown that had followed World War I. Walkouts would remain numerous but the institutional base that had supported strikers would dramatically weaken. Again, strikes turned on immediate concerns of wage, hours, and working conditions. The AFL and the CIO would not regain effective control of rank-and-file militancy until after the war.

See Also: AMERICAN FEDERATION OF LABOR (AFL); COLLECTIVE BARGAINING; CONGRESS OF INDUSTRIAL ORGANIZATIONS (CIO); INTERNATIONAL LONGSHOREMEN'S ASSOCIATION (ILA); ORGANIZED LABOR; SAN FRANCISCO GENERAL STRIKE (1934); SIT-DOWN STRIKES.

BIBLIOGRAPHY

Bernstein, Irving. *The Lean Years: A History of the American Worker, 1920–1933.* 1960.

Bernstein, Irving. *Turbulent Years: A History of the American Worker, 1933–1941.* 1969.

Brecher, Jeremy. *Strike!,* rev. edition. 1997.

Daniel, Cletus E. *Bitter Harvest: A History of California Farmworkers, 1870–1941.* 1981.

Dubofsky, Melvyn. *The State and Labor in Modern America.* 1994.

Dubofsky, Melvyn, and Foster Rhea Dulles. *Labor in America: A History,* 6th edition. 1999.

Faue, Elizabeth. *Community of Suffering and Struggle: Women, Men, and the Labor Movement in Minneapolis, 1915–1945.* 1991.

Filippelli, Ronald L., ed. *Labor Conflict in the United States: An Encyclopedia.* 1990.

Fine, Sidney. *Sit-Down: The General Motors Strike of 1936–1937.* 1969.

Green, James R. *The World of the Worker: Labor in Twentieth-Century America.* 1980.

Hall, Jacqueline Dowd; James Leloudis; Robert Korstad; Mary Murphy; Lu Ann Jones; and Christopher B. Daly. *Like a Family: The Making of a Southern Cotton Mill World.* 1987.

Kessler-Harris, Alice. *Out to Work: A History of Wage-Earning Women in the United States.* 1982.

Lynd, Alice, and Staughton Lynd, eds. *Rank and File: Personal Histories by Working-Class Organizers.* 1973.

Nelson, Bruce. *Divided We Stand: American Workers and the Struggle for Black Equality.* 2001.

Nelson, Bruce. *Workers on the Waterfront: Seamen, Longshoremen, and Unionism in the 1930s.* 1988.

Nelson, Daniel. *American Rubber Workers and Organized Labor, 1900–1941.* 1988.

Norwood, Stephen H. *Strikebreaking & Intimidation: Mercenaries and Masculinity in Twentieth-Century America.* 2002.

Plotke, David. "The Wagner Act, Again—Politics and Labor, 1935–1937." *Studies in American Political Development* 3 (1989): 105–156.

Taft, Philip, and Philip Ross. "American Labor Violence: Its Causes, Character, and Consequences." In *Violence in America, Historical and Comparative Perspectives: A Report to the National Commission on the Causes and Prevention of Violence,* edited by Hugh Davis Graham and Ted Robert Gurr. 1970.

Members of a family of eight work in their garden at the El Monte federal subsistence homesteads in California in 1936. The father, a streetcar conductor whose monthly pay was one hundred dollars, paid sixteen dollars and twenty cents per month toward purchase of the four-bedroom house seen in the background. LIBRARY OF CONGRESS, PRINTS & PHOTOGRAPHS DIVISION, FSA/OWI COLLECTION

Zieger, Robert H. *The CIO, 1935–1955.* 1995.

EDUARDO F. CANEDO

SUBSISTENCE HOMESTEADS DIVISION

One of the smallest New Deal programs was the Subsistence Homesteads Division. The Division was created by Section 208, Title II of the 1933 Na-

tional Industrial Recovery Act. The Subsistence Homesteads Division was given $25 million and granted the task of addressing both urban concentration and unemployment by creating new rural communities where underemployed and unemployed industrial workers could combine part-time farming with work in nearby industrial establishments. President Franklin Roosevelt placed the division in the Department of the Interior, which was run by Harold L. Ickes. Ickes appointed agricultural economist M. L. Wilson as director of the program, a post that he held until 1934. In 1935 the Subsistence Homesteads Division was absorbed into the Resettlement Administration, which itself was replaced by the Farm Security Administration in 1937.

As director of the Subsistence Homesteads Division, Wilson stamped his own views on the program. He was idealistic and optimistic that the division would not only help to solve the economic problems of the nation but that it would spur the creation of a new type of community. Historian Paul Conkin describes Wilson as a relativist and pragmatist who hoped that the communities would be both democratic and locally controlled. Wilson believed that this would inspire communal, anti-materialistic, familial, agrarian, and democratic values to counter the dominant trends in modern society.

Initially Wilson and his associates decided that the Subsistence Homesteads Division would fund four types of communities, including colonies for stranded rural workers (most importantly unemployed coal miners), industrial communities for unemployed urban workers, experimental farm colonies, and subsistence gardens for city workers. Ideally, twenty-five to one hundred families were to live in each community and cultivate anywhere from one to five acres of fruits and vegetables. Of the thirty-four communities actually funded by the division, twenty-four were industrial communities, four were stranded communities (rural areas where the laborers lost their jobs when the main employers left town), three were farm communities for submarginal farmers, and one was a cooperative industrial community. The number of units in each community varied from 20 to 287, and the average cost per unit was $9,114.

In spite of the optimistic aspirations of Wilson and others, the Subsistence Homesteads Division became a victim of poor planning, administrative bungling, and political divisions. The stranded communities proved the least successful. The division found that it could not attract new industry to these areas and Congress refused to give the division federal funds to build its own factories. In 1934, the stranded communities were deemed illegal by the solicitor of the Department of the Interior because Section 208 did not authorize the resettle-

ment of farmers. The industrial communities were certainly the most successful of the entire program. More specifically, the Duluth (MN), El Monte (CA), San Fernando (CA), Granger (IA), and Longview (WA) homesteads were the most successful because of their close proximity to industrial employment and their siting on fertile soils for subsistence farming. However, if judged in terms of absolute numbers, the Subsistence Homesteads Division must be viewed as an interesting social experiment but ultimately an unsuccessful attempt to bridge the rural/agricultural and urban/industrial boundaries in modern America.

See Also: APPALACHIA, IMPACT OF THE GREAT DEPRESSION ON; ARTHURDALE, WEST VIRGINIA; FARM SECURITY ADMINISTRATION (FSA); NATIONAL INDUSTRIAL RECOVERY ACT (NIRA); RESETTLEMENT ADMINISTRATION (RA).

BIBLIOGRAPHY

Conkin, Paul K. *Tomorrow a New World: The New Deal Community Program.* 1959.

Garvey, Timothy J. "The Duluth Homesteads: A Successful Experiment in Community Housing." *Minnesota History* 46 (1978): 2–16.

Lord, Russell, and Paul H. Johnstone. *A Place on Earth: A Critical Appraisal of Subsistence Homesteads.* 1942.

Schwieder, Dorothy. "The Granger Homestead Project." *Palimpsest* 58 (1977): 149–161.

Wilson, M. L. "The Place of Subsistence Homesteads in our National Economy." *Journal of Farm Economics* 16 (1934): 73–87.

KATHY MAPES

SUICIDE

It is probably a myth that the stock market crash in October 1929 caused an epidemic of dramatic suicides by distraught investors after they lost their fortunes. Suicide rates in the United States had been steadily increasing each year since 1925, and only a slightly greater increase in 1930 and 1931 may be attributed to the effects of the Great Depression (see table).

Even for New York City, which is thought to have been particularly affected by the crash, the changes in suicide rates during this period are not dramatic and the rates were already increasing before 1930. Since the crash occurred in late October 1929, can a causal effect be seen by reviewing the suicide rate for the entire year? In fact, the number of suicides in the United States for October and November of 1929 was lower than in all the other months of that year except January, February, and September. Most suicides in 1929 occurred during the summer months when the stock market was doing well. Brad Edmondson found that the Manhattan suicide rate for October 15 to November 13, 1929, was lower than it had been the previous year. From October 24, 1929, to the end of the year, only eight people jumped to their death in Manhattan, and only two of these suicides occurred on Wall Street.

Although there was only a slight increase in suicide deaths during the Great Depression, there were certainly a few well-publicized suicides that may have fueled the myth of a suicide epidemic. Steven Stack has examined the possibility that media publicity on suicide influenced suicide rates during the Depression. When Stack looked for suicide stories that were printed on the first pages of seven American newspapers during the Depression, he found 105 such stories printed on the first page of the *New York Times* from 1933 to 1939. At that time, the *New York Times* served as a source paper from which other newspapers throughout the country picked up "important" stories, but only twenty of the page-one suicide stories received national coverage. The majority of suicide stories were not directly related to the Depression or the stock market crash, but involved sensational cases, including those of Kathy Schoch, who dressed up as Santa Claus and murdered six of her relatives while they slept before killing herself; an unemployed restaurant worker who killed himself by allowing his pet spider to bite him; and a chauffeur who jumped to his death while thousands watched after eleven hours of efforts to talk him out of it failed.

One of the most publicized Depression-era suicides was that of J. J. Reordan, who killed himself on Friday, November 8, 1929. Reordan was a well-known and important supporter of the Democratic Party in New York; he was treasurer of Mayor

Number of Suicides per 100,000 Population in the USA and the City of New York

Year	USA	New York City
1925	12.1	14.4
1926	12.8	13.7
1927	13.3	15.7
1928	13.6	15.7
1929	14.0	17.0
1930	15.7	18.7
1931	16.8	19.7
1932	17.4	21.3
1933	15.9	18.5
1934	14.9	17.0

SOURCE: Vital Statistics, Special Reports 1-45, US Department of Commerce, Bureau of the Census, 1937.

Jimmy Walker's election campaign and of Al Smith's campaign for president. Walker was president and Smith served on the board of directors of a bank called the County Trust Company. On November 8 Reordan walked into the bank, took a pistol from a cashier, returned home, and shot himself. The medical examiner withheld announcing Reordan's death until after noon the next day, just after the bank had closed for the weekend. Despite rumors (later proved to be true) that Reordan lost a fortune in the stock market, his colleagues announced that Reordan never invested in stocks and that the bank was financially sound. In addition, the City of New York announced that it would maintain all its deposits in the County Trust Company, and, in the end, Reordan's suicide did not cause a run on the bank. The Catholic Church concluded that Reordan was "temporarily insane" and thus had a right to a religious burial. His funeral was widely publicized and was attended by the political and banking elite of New York.

In his study of media effects, Stack concluded that, contrary to his expectations, publicity about suicides did not have a significant impact on the suicide rate during the Great Depression. Stack had hypothesized that people would be more vulnerable to media reports on suicide because of the effects of the economic collapse. He suggested that the lack of media impact (which has been shown to have occurred later in the twentieth century) may have been averted because "while mass unemployment may have put many members of the suicide audience in a suicidal mood, it also created many movements for social and economic change." Stack continued, "possibly a considerable portion of the frustration generated by the Great Depression did not get channelled into a suicidal mood, but, instead was channelled into other-directed aggression in such form as social movements."

Several studies of the relationship between suicide and unemployment cover the period of the Great Depression. Stephen Platt's extensive literature review of unemployment and suicidal behavior found that there is a consistent relationship between levels of unemployment and suicide rates during all periods. The twelve studies he reviewed that included the period of the Great Depression generally supported a relationship between unemployment and suicide. However, Platt's interpretation of the data was that there may not be a direct causal link; rather he concluded that both unemployment and an increased suicide risk may be due to mental health problems. Persons who are mentally ill are at greater risk of suicide and are also more likely to be unemployed. Stack's interpretation is, of course, subject to debate.

Thomas Cook compared different methods of time series analysis to examine the relationship between suicide and unemployment in the United States between 1900 and 1970. Unlike Stack, Thomas concluded that no matter which method is chosen, there is a significant link between unemployment and suicide. Since increases in unemployment rates precede increases in suicide rates, he suggests that the relationship may be interpreted as causal, with unemployment influencing suicide.

The relationship between marital disruption and suicide during this period has also been analyzed. During the Great Depression there was an increase in divorce and many couples postponed marriage because of financial difficulties. However, studies by Gideon Vigderhous and Gideon Fishman on the relationship between unemployment, family integration, and suicide rates in the United States between 1920 and 1969 found that unemployment rates tended to be the most important

and stable predictor of variations in suicide rates over time. Family disintegration as measured by the ratio of divorce to marriage was not found to be a significant predictor of suicide rates after controlling for unemployment.

This brief review of suicide during the Great Depression leads to the conclusion that if suicide rates did increase as a result of the distress caused by the Great Depression, the increase was not dramatic. The most likely explanation for increased suicide during this period is the well-documented link between unemployment and suicide, although the interpretation of this relationship is subject to debate. Unemployment may lead to greater social vulnerability and less social integration by decreasing the possibility of marriage and increasing divorce rates. However, both unemployment and suicide may result from other factors, such as stress-induced mental health problems. An alternative interpretation is that the presence of protective factors during the Depression, such as the development of social solidarity among vulnerable persons, may have compensated for any increased risk that resulted from economic factors. Another interpretation, which has not been subjected to empirical verification, is that people in a desperate situation tend to focus upon the needs of their family and loved ones. Such a focus upon the needs of others may protect against suicide, since most suicides involve a primary focus on one's own suffering.

BIBLIOGRAPHY

Cook, Thomas D.; Dintze Leonard; and Mark Melvin M. "The Causal Analysis of Concomitant Time Series." *Applied Social Psychology Annual* 1 (1980): 93–135.

Edmondson, Brad. "Dying for Dollars." *American Demographics* 9, no. 10 (1987): 14–15.

Galbraith, John Kenneth. *The Great Crash, 1929.* 1954.

Platt, Stephen D. "Unemployment and Suicidal Behaviour: A Review of the Literature." *Social Science and Medicine* 19, no. 2 (1984): 93–115.

Stack, Steven. "The Effect of the Media on Suicide: The Great Depression." *Suicide and Life-Threatening Behavior* 22, no. 2 (1992): 255–267.

Vigderhous, Gideon, and Gideon Fishman. "The Impact of Unemployment and Familial Integration on Changing Suicide Rates in the U.S.A., 1920–1969." *Social Psychiatry* 13, no. 4 (1978): 239–248.

BRIAN L. MISHARA
BOGDAN BALAN

SUPERMAN

Superman is the most important character to come out of American comic books and one of the most popular icons that American culture has ever produced. First conceived in 1933 by high school students Jerry Siegel and Joe Shuster, Superman debuted in the June 1938 issue of National Periodicals' (later called DC Comics) *Action Comics*. Emerging from a nexus of immigrant culture, New Deal sensibilities, and male adolescent insecurities, Superman found phenomenal success, helped to launch the fledgling comic book industry, and heralded a new era in the marketing of youth fantasies as consumer culture.

Superman was a science-fiction character whose origin mirrored the immigrant heritage of his young Jewish creators. Fleeing from a doomed planet, an infant arrives in the American heartland, is adopted by an elderly couple, demonstrates amazing physical strength and invulnerability, and grows up to take his place in the urban middle class as newspaper reporter Clark Kent. Shy, bespectacled, and unpopular in school, Siegel and Shuster created a two-sided character representing both how the world saw them and how they imagined themselves. The mild-mannered and, in the terminology of a later generation, nerdy Clark Kent was only a façade to disguise the heroic Superman. It was a compelling fantasy for a generation of powerless and insecure young males.

With his impossible abilities and colorful costume, Superman was so deeply rooted in a young imagination that Siegel and Shuster failed to sell their idea to the middle-aged businessmen who managed the newspaper syndicates. After years of frustration and rejection, they finally sold the publishing rights for the sum of $130 to a tiny comic book company soon to be known as DC Comics. Within a few years, Superman comic books were selling over a million copies per month.

Cast as a "champion of the oppressed," Superman was a wise-cracking hero for common Americans menaced by the forces of greed and corruption. Pitted against crooked stockbrokers, heartless businessmen, and "merchants of death" who plotted to embroil the nation in foreign wars, Superman struck a heroic balance somewhere between the righteous violence of hard-boiled detectives like Sam Spade and the benevolent interventionism of Franklin Roosevelt. Within a few years, spectacular commercial success and the demands of a world war would tame Superman into a much more conservative icon of stability. But in his formative period, no other hero in American culture spoke more directly and colorfully to the economic, social, and personal dislocations of a generation coming of age during the Great Depression.

See Also: COMICS; HEROES.

BIBLIOGRAPHY

Daniels, Les. *Superman, the Complete History: The Life and Times of the Man of Steel*. 1998.

Fleischer, Max, and Dave Fleischer, directors. *The Complete Superman Cartoons*. Image Entertainment, 2002.

Siegel, Jerry, and Joe Shuster. *Superman: The Action Comics Archives*, vol. 1. 1998.

Wright, Bradford W. *Comic Book Nation: The Transformation of Youth Culture in America*. 2001.

BRADFORD W. WRIGHT

SUPREME COURT

The 1930s was a period of transition and transformation for the United States Supreme Court. In 1930 the Court was comprised by the conservative "Four Horsemen": Willis Van Devanter, James Clark McReynolds, George Sutherland, and Pierce Butler; three constitutional liberals: Louis D. Brandeis, Harlan Fiske Stone, and Oliver Wendell Holmes (replaced in 1932 by the like-minded Benjamin Cardozo); and two constitutional moderates: Owen Roberts and Chief Justice Charles Evans Hughes. Of these, only Stone and Roberts would still be on the Court when the United States entered World War II in December 1941. Though Franklin Roosevelt would be frustrated by his lack of appointments to the Court during his first term, and by his inability to "pack" it early in his second, he would appoint seven New Dealers to the Court between 1937 and 1941: Hugo Black, Stanley Reed, Felix Frankfurter, William O. Douglas, Frank Murphy, James Byrnes, and Robert Jackson. Just as Roosevelt changed the face of the Court, his Court changed the face of American constitutional law.

This transformation took a variety of forms. By the end of the decade the Court had recognized significantly greater executive branch authority over domestic and foreign affairs, had upheld the massive regional power initiative embodied in the Tennessee Valley Authority, and had dramatically enhanced protections of civil rights and civil liberties, particularly concerning free speech and the rights of the accused. At the center of the Hughes Court's docket, however, were cases involving the constitutionality of the New Deal and related state attempts to confront the economic crisis that engulfed the nation. The key issues concerned the scope of the congressional powers to spend for the general welfare and to regulate interstate commerce, and the extent to which the provisions of the Fifth and Fourteenth amendments, most notably the due process clauses, limited state and federal regulatory authority. Many initiatives, particularly those involving spending, were comfortably accommodated by existing constitutional doctrine. Other programs were invalidated in their first incarnations, but survived challenge when reformulated to comply with constitutional requirements. Still others withstood challenge only due to transformations in constitutional doctrine brought about by changes in Court personnel. (Contentions that these doctrinal transformations and decisions sustaining New Deal legislation were caused by the pressure of Roosevelt's "court-packing plan" are more problematic.)

THE SPENDING POWER

The Roosevelt administration created the modern American welfare state, dramatically increasing both the number of federal programs designed to alleviate conditions of want and the amount of federal revenue devoted to that purpose. Yet no significant transformation of constitutional doctrine was necessary to accommodate this development. The Court did definitively settle a longstanding dispute in American constitutional discourse concerning the scope of the power to spend for the general welfare. Advocates of the Madisonian position had long maintained that the power to spend was con-

fined to carrying into effect exercises of other powers enumerated in Article I, Section 8 of the Constitution, while advocates of the Hamiltonian position treated the power to spend as an independent grant of power not so limited. In *United States v. Butler* (1936) and the *Social Security Cases* (1937), the Court confirmed that the Hamiltonian interpretation was the correct one. Indeed, most of the justices do not appear to have regarded this conclusion as open to serious doubt: The old-age pension provisions of the Social Security Act, for instance, were upheld in *Helvering v. Davis* (1937) by a vote of seven to two. Moreover, it had long been recognized that congressional exercises of the spending power could be immunized from judicial review by designing them in light of the taxpayer standing doctrine. *Frothingham v. Mellon* (1923) had confirmed that so long as Congress appropriated the funds to be spent from general revenue rather than from a specified or "earmarked" tax, no one would have the right to question the constitutionality of the expenditure. The Supreme Court and the lower federal courts repeatedly invoked this doctrine, for example, in upholding grants and loans made by the Public Works Administration, one of the New Deal's most important and popular agencies. Furthermore, the formidable obstacle raised by the taxpayer standing doctrine appears to have successfully deterred any constitutional challenge to a wide variety of New Deal spending programs financed from general revenue. These included the Civilian Conservation Corps, the Farm Credit Act, the Reconstruction Finance Corporation, the Rural Electrification Administration, and the Emergency Relief Appropriation Act of 1936. Established constitutional doctrine assured the safety of the safety net.

CONSTITUTIONAL CONSULTATION AND CONGRESSIONAL ADAPTATION

The justices were less receptive to a number of federal regulatory programs of the early New Deal. Yet it would be a mistake to conclude that the decisions invalidating these congressional statutes were motivated simply by hostility to their objectives. The opinions in a number of these cases offered implicit or explicit suggestions on how the statute might be reformulated so as to achieve its aim in a constitutional manner. In several instances Congress took the hint and redrafted the statute, this time paying greater attention to the constraints imposed by contemporary constitutional doctrine. The justices uniformly upheld this second generation of statutes, just as the earlier opinions had suggested they would.

So, for example, in May 1935 Justice Brandeis wrote the unanimous opinion in *Louisville Joint Stock Land Bank v. Radford* invalidating the Frazier-Lemke Farm Debt Relief Act of 1934 on the ground that it took the property of creditors without due process of law in violation of the Fifth Amendment. His opinion painstakingly identified the statute's constitutional deficiencies, enabling Congress quickly to eliminate those flaws in a reformulated statute enacted that summer. The Court upheld the revised statute in *Wright v. Vinton Branch Bank* in 1937. The decision was again unanimous—even the Four Horsemen agreed that Congress had rectified the earlier statute's shortcomings.

In early 1935 the Court also heard a challenge to the New Deal's program to stabilize oil prices in the face of frenetic wildcat drilling in the East Texas oil fields. Section 9(c) of the National Industrial Recovery Act authorized the president to prohibit interstate shipments of so-called contraband or hot oil—oil produced in excess of that allowed by the law of the state of production. The Court invalidated Section 9(c) by a vote of eight to one, holding that Congress had not provided any standard to guide the president's implementation of congressional policy, and that this omission constituted an unlawful delegation of legislative authority to the executive. Hughes's opinion left little doubt that Congress could achieve its policy objective—it needed only to remedy the delegation problem. Congress promptly did so with the Connally Act, which was uniformly upheld in the lower courts and unanimously sustained by the Supreme Court in 1939.

The Guffey Coal Act of 1935 sought to bring order to cutthroat competition in the coal industry in two ways: first, by regulating the price at which coal moved in interstate commerce, and second, by regulating wages, hours, and labor relations at the mines. In *Carter v. Carter Coal Co.* (1936), the Court

struck down the labor provisions of the Act on the ground that they regulated local production, a matter reserved to the states. The Court held that the price regulation provisions were inseparable from the labor provisions, and thus must fall with them. The majority did not, however, hold the price regulation provisions independently unconstitutional. Chief Justice Hughes wrote a concurring opinion explicitly stating his view that the price regulation provisions were constitutional. Justice Cardozo's dissent agreed with Hughes on this point, and suggested moreover that a statute regulating only the price of coal might nevertheless indirectly stabilize labor relations by enabling employers to pay higher wages. Observers in Congress construed the *Carter* opinions to indicate that a new statute containing only the price regulation provisions would be upheld by the Court. In 1937 Congress enacted such a statute, the Bituminous Coal Conservation Act of 1937. When the Act was upheld by the Court in *Sunshine Anthracite Coal Co. v. Adkins* (1940), only Justice McReynolds dissented.

In 1935 the Court held by a vote of five to four that the Railroad Retirement Act of 1934 was unconstitutional, on two grounds: because a number of its provisions violated the due process clause of the Fifth Amendment, and because creating a pension system for railroad workers lay beyond the power of Congress to regulate interstate commerce. Many observers, including Chief Justice Hughes, believed that this latter objection meant that no comparable pension legislation, even if revised to rectify the due process problems, could be sustained. Yet some in Congress recognized that a pension system financed out of general revenue rather than from a specific source would be insulated from constitutional challenge under the taxpayer standing doctrine. The revenue necessary to finance the payments could be raised by a separate tax on interstate carriers, with the proceeds of the tax paid into the treasury rather than earmarked for pension payments. At the urging of President Roosevelt, representatives of the major railroads and railway unions negotiated the terms of such a system, and by the summer of 1937 it had been embodied in the Carrier Taxing Act and the Railroad Retirement Act. Representatives of the railroads and the unions, moreover, honored their pledges not to contest the constitutionality of the legislation, and the pension system they negotiated survives in modified form today.

A similar story of congressional adaptation unfolded in the domain of agricultural policy. The Agricultural Adjustment Act of 1933 sought to lift farm commodity prices by reducing output. The mechanism for doing so was the acreage reduction contract, under which a farmer would agree to reduce production in exchange for a payment from the secretary of agriculture. These payments were to be financed by a special excise tax on food processors rather than from general revenue, which enabled a taxpayer challenging the validity of the excise to question the constitutionality of expenditures underwritten by his tax payments. In *United States v. Butler* (1936), the Court invalidated the tax, holding that it was a step in a plan to regulate agricultural production in violation of the Tenth Amendment.

Though *Butler* held that the excise tax could no longer be collected, the administration continued to pay farmers holding acreage reduction contracts out of general revenue. Congress effectively reenacted the program two months after the *Butler* decision with the Soil Conservation and Domestic Allotment Act of 1936, which paid farmers to shift acreage from "soil-depleting" to "soil-conserving" crops. This time the payments were to be made from general revenue, effectively immunizing them from constitutional challenge. In 1938 Congress enacted a second Agricultural Adjustment Act, which sought not to regulate the production of farm commodities, but instead authorized the secretary of agriculture to establish marketing quotas for such crops. The Act's congressional sponsors read a passage from Roberts's opinion in *Butler* to suggest that such a regulation of interstate commerce in agricultural produce might pass muster where the earlier Agricultural Adjustment Act had fallen short. This judgment was vindicated the following year by Roberts's opinion upholding the Act in *Mulford v. Smith.*

The unemployment compensation provisions of the Social Security Act provide a final illustration of this phenomenon. Justice Brandeis was himself intimately involved in conceptualizing, drafting, and even lobbying for the program. Brandeis's advice on framing the statute to withstand constitutional challenge was vindicated when the Court upheld the Act's provisions in *Steward Machine Co. v. Davis* (1937). And while two of the dissenting justices believed that certain provisions of the statute as ultimately enacted were unconstitutional, their opinion made it clear how Congress could easily remedy those deficiencies, thereby bringing the statute into conformity with constitutional requirements. At the same time, the Court upheld Alabama's state unemployment compensation statute by a vote of five to four. Yet three of the four dissenting justices indicated that, while the statute under review was plagued by constitutional defects, the relief of unemployment was an objective within the constitutional power of the states. The dissent identified the deficiencies in the statute and suggested the manner in which they might be rectified, specifically holding up as an exemplary constitutional statute the unemployment compensation act of Wisconsin. That Wisconsin statute had been drafted by Paul Raushenbush, Justice Brandeis's son-in-law, based on a memorandum written by the justice himself.

SUBSTANTIVE DUE PROCESS

Yet the fact that many of the objectives of the New Deal could be and ultimately were accommodated within the framework of existing constitutional doctrine should not obscure the real and significant changes in constitutional law that occurred between the onset of the Depression and the early years of World War II. Among the most important of these was a weakening of the constraints imposed upon federal and state economic regulation by the Fifth and Fourteenth amendments. The extent to which the Court deployed those amendments to obstruct regulatory reform in the decades preceding the Depression has often been significantly overstated. Nevertheless, there can be no disputing the fact that those constitutional constraints were far more substantial in 1930 than they were in 1940. Between 1921 and 1927, the Court had invalidated approximately 28 percent of the economic regulations alleged to violate the due process clause, often because the entity regulated was not a business "affected with a public interest." By the end of the 1930s, that percentage would drop to zero, and that legal category would have disappeared from the constitutional lexicon. It became clear early in the decade that President Herbert Hoover's appointments of Hughes and Roberts in 1930 had made a significant difference. In 1931, a narrowly divided Court issued an opinion upholding state regulation of commissions paid to fire insurance agents, in language indicating considerable deference to legislative judgment. That signal would be amplified in dramatic fashion in 1934, when the Court upheld a New York statute regulating the price of milk in *Nebbia v. New York.* "There is no closed class or category of business affected with a public interest," wrote Justice Roberts for a five to four majority. The guarantee of due process required only that the regulation be reasonable. Earlier that year the Court had surprised many observers by upholding the Minnesota Mortgage Moratorium in *Home Building & Loan Association v. Blaisdell* (1934). After *Nebbia* was decided, Justice McReynolds wrote despairingly to a friend that these two cases marked "the end of the constitution as you and I regarded it. An alien influence has prevailed." (McReynolds would similarly announce in open court that "The Constitution is gone" when, in early 1935, the Court upheld the administration's historic reorientation of monetary policy in the *Gold Clause Cases*). Meanwhile, New Dealers saw *Nebbia*'s sweeping approval of price regulation as a signal that the justices were prepared to sustain a variety of regulatory reforms, first among them the minimum wage. The Court did uphold the Washington minimum wage statute in *West Coast Hotel v. Parrish* (1937), though only after invalidating a similar New York statute the preceding year for what appear to have been technical reasons.

Yet neither *Nebbia* nor *Parrish* constituted a total repudiation of substantive due process. Hughes and Roberts had struck down a regulation designed to exclude new entrants to the ice business in Oklahoma in *New State Ice v. Liebmann* (1932); they would similarly join the majority invalidating provisions of a New York regulation raising a barrier to entry in *Mayflower v. Ten Eyck* (1936), and would dissent from the decision upholding a federal regulation disadvantaging small milk handlers in *United States v. Rock Royal Cooperative* (1939). Roberts would vote to invalidate a discrimi-

natory state tax under the privileges or immunities clause in *Colgate v. Harvey* (1935), and would dissent from the opinion upholding a comparable tax in *Madden v. Kentucky* (1940). And when the Court effectively overruled Roberts's 1935 railway pension decision in *United States v. Lowden* (1939), Roberts suppressed the dissent he had voiced in conference. "Regulatory legislation affecting ordinary commercial transactions," as the Court put it in *United States v. Carolene Products* (1938), would come to enjoy a virtually irrebuttable presumption of constitutionality, but only once Roosevelt appointments had begun to replace the retiring Four Horsemen, thereby depriving Hughes and Roberts of control over the Court's center.

THE COMMERCE POWER

Nebbia did, however, enable Congress to regulate the price at which such items as coal and agricultural produce moved in interstate commerce. The *Shreveport Rate Cases* (1914) permitted federal regulation of intrastate railroad rates where it was shown that such regulation was necessary to effective control of interstate rates. The *Shreveport* doctrine had always been confined to businesses affected with a public interest, because only such businesses were amenable to rate regulation. But with *Nebbia*'s abolition of that limitation, Congress could draw upon *Shreveport* in regulating intrastate sales of a broad range of commodities. The Court relied on *Shreveport* in sustaining congressional regulation of intrastate sales of tobacco in *Currin v. Wallace* (1939) and *Mulford v. Smith* (1939), and of milk in *United States v. Wrightwood Dairy Co.* (1942).

Nebbia also enlarged the category of local activities that could be regulated by Congress because they occurred in a "stream" of interstate commerce. Application of the stream of commerce doctrine had always been limited to businesses affected with a public interest, such as public stockyards and grain exchanges. After *Nebbia*, however, virtually any business located in such a flow was arguably subject to federal regulation. This development was of no consequence in the "Sick Chicken Case," *United States v. Schechter Poultry Co.* (1935), which struck down a conviction under the Live Poultry Code of the National Industrial Recovery Act on the ground that the code regulated a "local" activity (butchering) that affected interstate commerce only "indirectly." (The decision prompted Roosevelt to accuse the justices of having a "horse and buggy" conception of interstate commerce.) Schechter's slaughterhouse was not in a stream of commerce because interstate transportation had come to an end—the butchered chickens were sold locally rather than in interstate trade. The Guffey Coal Act invalidated in *Carter Coal* suffered from the same problem, but at the other end: The coal mine lay at the source of the stream rather than amidst its interstate flow. When defending the collective bargaining provisions of the National Labor Relations Act, therefore, attorneys for the government carefully selected test cases involving factories that brought in raw materials from outside the state of production and then shipped their products for sale across state lines. They argued that these businesses were located in a stream of interstate commerce, and that a strike at the plants could disrupt the interstate flow of that stream. The Court upheld application of the Act to those business in the *Labor Board Cases* (1937). Throughout the late 1930s, decisions in which the Court upheld application of the Wagner Act hesitated to suggest that the commerce power had been significantly enlarged. Uncertainty about the scope of the commerce power would not be resolved until the early 1940s, long after the court-packing plan was dead and buried, when Roosevelt appointees dominated the Court.

In *United States v. Darby* (1941), the Court upheld the Fair Labor Standards Act, which banned child labor and prescribed maximum hours and minimum ages for businesses selling goods in interstate commerce. And in *Wickard v. Filburn* (1942), the Court upheld a penalty imposed on a farmer for planting more wheat than he was allotted under the terms of the Agricultural Adjustment Act. Roscoe Filburn argued that he did not intend to sell the wheat, but only to keep it for use and consumption on his farm. Justice Jackson's opinion responded that if many farmers emulated Filburn, they would reduce the overall demand for those crops and thus the price at which those crops moved in interstate commerce. Congress could therefore reach Filburn's activity as a means of regulating the interstate price of wheat. Internal Court

records show that not all of the justices were comfortable with such expansive interpretations of the commerce power. By the end of the Depression, however, no one could doubt that there had been a dramatic increase in the federal government's power to regulate the nation's economy.

See Also: LEGAL PROFESSION; SUPREME COURT "PACKING" CONTROVERSY.

BIBLIOGRAPHY

Cushman, Barry. "The Secret Lives of the Four Horsemen." *Virginia Law Review* 83 (1997): 559-645.

Cushman, Barry. "The Hughes Court and Constitutional Consultation." *Journal of Supreme Court History* 1998 (1998): 79-111.

Cushman, Barry. *Rethinking the New Deal Court: The Structure of a Constitutional Revolution.* 1998.

Cushman, Barry. "Lost Fidelities." *William & Mary Law Review* 41 (1999): 95-145.

Cushman, Barry. "Formalism and Realism in Commerce Clause Jurisprudence." 67 *University of Chicago Law Review* 67 (2000): 1089-1150.

Cushman, Barry. "Mr. Dooley and Mr. Gallup: Public Opinion and Constitutional Change in the 1930s." *Buffalo Law Review* 50 (2002): 7-101.

Friedman, Richard D. "Switching Time and Other Thought Experiments: The Hughes Court and Constitutional Transformation." *University of Pennsylvania Law Review* 142 (1994): 1891-1984.

Irons, Peter H. *The New Deal Lawyers.* 1982.

Leuchtenburg, William E. *The Supreme Court Reborn: The Constitutional Revolution in the Age of Roosevelt.* 1995.

Mason, Alpheus Thomas. *Harlan Fiske Stone: Pillar of the Law.* 1956.

Parrish, Michael E. "The Hughes Court, the Great Depression, and the Historians." *The Historian* 40 (1978): 286-308.

Parrish, Michael E. "The Great Depression, the New Deal, and the American Legal Order." *Washington Law Review* 59 (1984): 723-50.

Pusey, Merlo J. *Charles Evans Hughes.* 1951.

White, G. Edward. *The Constitution and the New Deal.* 2000.

BARRY CUSHMAN

SUPREME COURT "PACKING" CONTROVERSY

After seeing important measures of the First New Deal repeatedly invalidated by the Supreme Court, President Franklin D. Roosevelt charged a small group of his advisors to devise a proposal that would increase the chances of future success. The result was the proposed Judicial Reorganization Act, which the president sent to Congress on February 5, 1937. One of the bill's provisions would have empowered the president to appoint to the Supreme Court an additional justice for each sitting justice who had not retired within six months after reaching the age of seventy. Six of the sitting justices were then over seventy, which would have enabled Roosevelt immediately to expand the Court from nine to fifteen justices. Though Roosevelt explained that the current justices were too aged to stay abreast of their work, it was widely recognized that the bill's true aim was to secure for the Roosevelt administration a sympathetic majority on the Court.

Such an effort to influence the Court's decisions was not novel. Comparable bills had made regular appearances in the legislative hopper since the 1890s, and a number of proposals to control the Court had been introduced in the wake of decisions invalidating New Deal initiatives in 1935 and 1936. None of these bills had gotten anywhere in Congress, and the support of an extremely popular president would not prove sufficient to secure for this proposal a different fate. Powerful opposition to the bill emerged almost immediately after its announcement. The press, leaders in higher education, and a variety of prominent civic organizations, including the American Bar Association, each denounced it. Eminent liberal spokesmen and former members of the administration also criticized the proposal. At the same time, crucial members of the New Deal coalition refused to rally to the president's cause. Organized labor issued official endorsements but otherwise sat on its hands, while key farm organizations actively campaigned in opposition. Meanwhile, the electorate that had so resoundingly returned Roosevelt to office the preceding November deluged Congress and the Court with letters and telegrams running nine to one against the proposal. Public opinion polls, while more closely divided, showed both consistent opposition to any proposal to enlarge the Court's membership and a steady decline in the president's popularity.

THE COURT PLAN IN CONGRESS

Roosevelt's more immediate concern, however, lay in shepherding the bill through Congress. He and his advisors had prepared the bill in secret, without consulting congressional leaders, and this left many of those leaders feeling alienated. So, for example, Vice President John Nance Garner was seen outside the Senate chamber shortly after the plan's announcement giving it the thumbs-down sign and holding his nose in distaste. Similarly disaffected was Hatton Sumners, the Democratic chairman of the House Judiciary Committee, who was provoked to take two steps. The first was to hustle a judicial retirement bill through Congress in hopes that he might persuade his colleagues to solve the problem of judicial obstruction simply by creating a financial incentive for the elderly conservative justices to leave the bench. The second was to assemble a comfortable majority of his committee in opposition to the president's proposal. Sumners's defection meant that the bill's opponents would control the committee hearings, and that the proposal might be bottled up in committee for an indefinite period. These circumstances persuaded the administration to take the unusual step of introducing the bill not in the typically compliant House, but instead in the Senate. But here, too, the obstacles were considerable. Unsurprisingly, every Republican senator quickly announced his opposition to the plan, as did a number of conservative Democrats. The opposition scored a coup when it secured the allegiance of Senator Burton Wheeler, a liberal Democrat from Montana. Wheeler became the opposition's leader, and recruited several fellow liberals to its standard, while a number of other key senators remained noncommittal or offered only nominal support. Within ten days of the plan's announcement, Roosevelt's secretary of the treasury, Henry Morgenthau, gave it at best a fifty-fifty chance of passage. Roosevelt's defense of the bill in a March 9 fireside chat did little to alter the dynamic. When the Judiciary Committee opened its hearings on March 10, its members were evenly divided, with two members undecided.

The opposition used the hearings to filibuster the bill, grilling administration witnesses at length while leisurely putting on a parade of opposing witnesses. The most dramatic moment came on March 22, when Senator Wheeler read a letter from Chief Justice Charles Evans Hughes. Wheeler and two colleagues had initially approached Hughes on March 18 to testify before the committee, but after consulting with two of his fellow justices, Hughes had declined. At the suggestion of Justice Louis Brandeis, however, Wheeler persuaded Hughes on March 20 to write a letter demonstrating that the Court was not behind in its work, that it was hearing all meritorious appeals, and that the president's proposal would impair rather than enhance the Court's efficiency. Hughes reported that he had been able to discuss the letter's contents with only two of his colleagues, the liberal Justice Brandeis and the conservative Willis Van Devanter, each of whom had approved it. He was confident, however, that its contents accorded with the views of his other colleagues as well. This statement left the impression that the justices endorsed Hughes's letter unanimously. When Wheeler had finished reading the letter, Garner telephoned Roosevelt and told him, "We're licked."

At least two weeks earlier, it had become clear that the opposition was planning to filibuster the bill on the Senate floor, and appeared to have the votes to do so successfully. Over the course of the ensuing weeks, the bill's fortunes only deteriorated further. By the end of April it was apparent the Judiciary Committee would issue an adverse report; by early May the opposition commanded an absolute majority in the Senate. A mid-May Gallup poll showed only 31 percent of the public supporting the bill. On May 18, the committee delivered its negative recommendation; on the same day, the conservative Van Devanter's announcement of his retirement seemed to deprive the bill of its very reason for being. Roosevelt could now fill the vacancy with a New Dealer.

Yet the president faced a difficulty: He had promised the next seat to Senator Joseph Robinson of Arkansas. Robinson was a loyal lieutenant in the Senate, but Roosevelt feared that, once on the Court, he would vote as a conservative. Roosevelt therefore withheld the appointment, urging Robinson to lead the fight for a compromise bill that would permit the president to appoint a smaller number of additional justices over a longer period of time. The obstacles to enactment of the compromise bill remained formidable, but the promise that its enactment would lead to a place on the Court for the popular senator breathed a measure of new life into a seemingly moribund initiative. That new life was brief, however. Robinson was found dead in his Washington apartment on July 14, and hopes for the bill's passage died with him. The Senate quickly voted to recommit the bill, instructing the committee to remove its court-packing provisions. The battle was over.

CONSEQUENCES OF THE COURT-PACKING CONTROVERSY

During the Court fight, the justices handed down a series of important decisions that further compromised the bill's chances. All of these decisions favored government regulation, and have been called collectively "the switch in time that saved the Nine." On March 29, the justices upheld a state minimum wage law similar to one they had invalidated only the preceding term. The cause of Justice Owen Roberts's "switch" on this issue is still debated, but it is clear that his change was not attributable to the Court plan. The vote in *West Coast Hotel v. Parrish* was actually taken in conference on December 19, more than six weeks before the justices knew about the president's scheme. Similarly, on May 24, the Court upheld the old-age pension and unemployment compensation provisions of the Social Security Act. Here again, the Court plan does not appear to have played a significant role. It had been known for nearly a month that the Senate committee would report the bill unfavorably and that the opposition had the votes to defeat the bill in the Senate. Moreover, two of the conservatives, who had dissented in the minimum wage case, actually voted to uphold the act's old-age provisions. There is perhaps a stronger case to be made that the April 12 decisions upholding the application of the National Labor Relations Act to three manufacturing enterprises may have been influenced by the plan. Those advancing this hypothesis take the view, disputed by others, that the Court would not have upheld the act without such external pressure. This claim similarly dismisses the possibility that the obstacles posed by the Senate filibuster and Sumners and company's opposition in the House may have given the justices reason to doubt the likelihood of the bill's ultimate enactment. It is generally agreed, however, that the Court-packing episode dealt a blow to Roosevelt's reputation for political infallibility, and opened a rift in the Democratic Party, contributing to the breakdown of the New Deal coalition and what one scholar has called the "End of Reform."

See Also: LEGAL PROFESSION; ROOSEVELT, FRANKLIN D.; SUPREME COURT.

BIBLIOGRAPHY

Alsop, Joseph, and Turner Catledge. *The 168 Days.* 1938.

Baker, Leonard. *Back to Back: The Duel Between FDR and the Supreme Court.* 1967.

Brinkley, Alan. *The End of Reform: New Deal Liberalism in Recession and War.* 1995.

Burns, James McGregor. *Roosevelt: The Lion and the Fox.* 1956.

Cushman, Barry. *Rethinking the New Deal Court: The Structure of a Constitutional Revolution.* 1998.

Cushman, Barry. "Mr. Dooley and Mr. Gallup: Public Opinion and Constitutional Change in the 1930s." *Buffalo Law Review* 50 (2002): 7.

Feinman, Ronald. *Twilight of Progressivism: The Western Republican Senators and the New Deal.* 1981.

Friedman, Richard D. "Switching Time and Other Thought Experiments: The Hughes Court and Constitutional Transformation." *University of Pennsylvania Law Review* 142 (1994): 1891.

Leuchtenburg, William E. *The Supreme Court Reborn: The Constitutional Revolution in the Age of Roosevelt.* 1995.

Parrish, Michael E. "The Great Depression, the New Deal, and the American Legal Order." *Washington Law Review* 59 (1984): 723.

Patenaude, Lionel V. "Garner, Sumners, and Connally: The Defeat of the Roosevelt Court Bill in 1937." *Southwestern Historical Quarterly* 74 (1970): 36.

Patterson, James T. *Congressional Conservatism and the New Deal: The Growth of the Conservative Coalition in Congress, 1933–1939.* 1967.

Ross, William G. *A Muted Fury: Populists, Progressives, and Labor Unions Confront the Courts, 1890–1937.* 1994.

Wheeler, Burton. *Yankee from the West: The Candid, Turbulent Life Story of the Yankee-Born U.S. Senator from Montana.* 1962.

White, G. Edward. *The Constitution and the New Deal.* 2000.

BARRY CUSHMAN

SWOC. *See* STEEL WORKERS' ORGANIZING COMMITTEE.

TALMADGE, EUGENE

Eugene Talmadge (September 23, 1884–December 21, 1946), a demagogic governor of Georgia, became a major opponent of the New Deal. Born in Forsyth, Georgia, to a prosperous farmer and cotton gin operator, Talmadge tasted farm work but had more aptitude for schoolwork. A superb debater, he graduated from the University of Georgia in 1904. After a short stint teaching at a rural school, Talmadge returned to his alma mater for a law degree and began practicing in Atlanta in 1907.

Talmadge soon moved to the greener pastures of small-town Georgia but tired of being paid in produce by his poor clients. After briefly farming, he entered politics and won a statewide election in 1926 as agricultural commissioner. A conservative who sought to maintain the Old South, Talmadge constantly urged farmers to keep doing what they had been doing despite the collapse of farm prices. Using a populist approach, he built a substantial power base among poor whites that propelled him into the governor's mansion in 1932 and kept him there in the 1934 election. Profane, quick-tempered, arrogant, and in possession of a mean streak, Talmadge preferred confrontation to compromise and government by executive decree. Not surprisingly, he had enormous trouble putting his programs into effect.

Once a supporter of Roosevelt, Talmadge soured on the president's policies by 1934. The emerging social activism and growing federal involvement of the New Deal offended his governmental and social philosophies. Privately critical of Roosevelt's programs, he came out publicly in opposition in 1935. Complaining that work relief programs benefited loafers and made it impossible for farmers to find anyone willing to accept low pay for menial tasks like plowing, he denounced the popular Civilian Conservation Corps. The Agricultural Adjustment Act came under similar attack.

Talmadge did not grasp that the Great Depression had forced an attitudinal change among Georgians. Unable to practice self-sufficiency, they regarded government relief programs as a godsend. Talmadge consequently lost the 1936 Georgia Senate race to Richard Russell in one of the biggest landslides in Georgia history.

Returned to the governor's mansion in 1940, Talmadge toned down his anti-Roosevelt rhetoric but increased his racial baiting. After insisting upon the termination of University of Georgia professors who advocated racial equality, the university lost accreditation and Talmadge lost the 1942 election. He formed the Vigilantes, a Ku Klux Klan-like group, to intimidate opponents and won the 1946 gubernatorial election but died a month before assuming office.

See Also: CONSERVATIVE COALITION; ELECTION OF 1936.

BIBLIOGRAPHY

Anderson, William. *The Wild Man from Sugar Creek: The Political Career of Eugene Talmadge.* 1975.

Logue, Cal M. *Eugene Talmadge: Rhetoric and Response.* 1989.

CARYN E. NEUMANN

TAMMANY HALL

Tammany Hall (or, the Executive Committee of the New York County Democratic Party) in the 1920s was the nation's most powerful political machine. It controlled New York City government, as it had with only brief interruptions since the days of the Tweed Ring (a group of corrupt politicians who dominated the Hall and New York City government in the 1860s.) It also dominated state politics, electing one of its own, Alfred E. Smith, as governor in 1918, 1922, 1924, and 1926. It even played a significant role in national Democratic Party politics: Smith captured the party's presidential nomination in 1928, and another Tammany graduate, Robert F. Wagner, sat in the U.S. Senate. However, after the death of its most able leader, Charles F. Murphy, in 1924, Tammany began a long decline. It was rent by internal squabbles, and population shifts to the other boroughs allowed the Bronx, Brooklyn, and Queens County Democratic organizations increasingly to assert their independence at Tammany's expense.

Tammany and the other party organizations did cooperate to elect James J. Walker mayor in 1925 and again in 1929. It was a disastrous choice. While "Gentleman Jimmy" played, his Tammany appointees looted the city. The electorate, which had been willing to overlook corruption and mismanagement in the booming 1920s, became more critical in the Depression. In response to mounting criticism, Governor Franklin D. Roosevelt and the Republican-controlled state senate launched three investigations of the Walker administration, all headed by Samuel Seabury. The inquiries uncovered sales of judgeships and extortion in the magistrates' courts, a district attorney's office that protected racketeers, and a pattern of citywide corruption that Walker knew of and tolerated. On the basis of these findings, Seabury recommended that Roosevelt remove the mayor from office in 1932.

At the 1932 national convention, angry Tammany chief John Curry led a delegation committed to Al Smith's presidential nomination and irreconcilably against Roosevelt's. Once Roosevelt triumphed, Tammany loyalists blocked a move to make the nomination unanimous. Later, candidate Roosevelt, eager to disassociate himself from Tammany's scandals, forced Walker's resignation. Even after Roosevelt's inauguration, Tammany did not follow the lead of most other urban Democratic machines and line up behind the president.

The Hall soon paid the price of its folly. The Roosevelt administration cut off all federal patronage, funneling it instead to Tammany's rivals, Bronx County Democratic Chairman Edward J. Flynn and Brooklyn County leader Frank Kelly. In 1933, a coalition of Republicans, anti-Tammany Democrats, and other reformers, disgusted by the Seabury revelations and Tammany's inability to handle the Depression-spawned fiscal and relief crises, organized the Fusion Party and elected Fiorello H. La Guardia mayor of New York City. La Guardia relentlessly cleared Tammany appointees from municipal posts, replacing them with people who were both Fusion backers and well qualified. By 1939, 74 percent of all city jobs were under civil service. Roosevelt wrote off Tammany and recognized in La Guardia an honest and progressive politician with whom he could work. Washington made it possible for La Guardia to build more public works and offer more services and jobs than the old political bosses ever could. The Works Progress Administration alone employed 700,000 city residents. To attract the votes of progressive Republicans, anti-Tammany Democrats, and independents for his own reelection in 1936, 1940, and 1944, and for La Guardia's in 1937 and 1941, Roosevelt gave his blessing to the establishment of the American Labor Party. In 1937 and 1941, the President endorsed La Guardia over his Democratic opponents.

Deprived of patronage, jobs, and money, the machine languished. By 1936, membership in Tammany clubs had declined by 70 percent. Its treasury was so empty by 1943 that it had to sell its headquarters to the International Ladies' Garment Workers' Union. While it did help elect a string of Democratic mayors after La Guardia and briefly revived under the leadership of its first Italian boss, Carmine DeSapio, it never returned to its 1920s glory.

See Also: FLYNN, EDWARD J.; LA GUARDIA, FIORELLO H.; ROOSEVELT, FRANKLIN D.; SMITH, ALFRED E.

BIBLIOGRAPHY

Blumberg, Barbara. *The New Deal and the Unemployed: The View from New York City.* 1979.

Connable, Alfred, and Edward Silberfarb. *Tigers of Tammany: Nine Men Who Ran New York.* 1967.

Eisenstein, Louis, and Elliot M. Rosenberg. *A Stripe of Tammany's Tiger.* 1966.

Flynn, Edward. *You're the Boss: The Practice of American Politics.* 1962.

Lankevich, George. *American Metropolis: A History of New York City.* 1998.

Savage, Sean J. *Roosevelt: The Party Leader, 1932–1945.* 1991.

Vos, Frank. "Tammany Hall." In The *Encyclopedia of New York City*, edited by Kenneth T. Jackson. 1991.

BARBARA BLUMBERG

TAXATION

Taxation during the Great Depression is confusing enough without the two competing narratives that historians have imposed on it. The more familiar, accessible narrative follows the storyline Franklin D. Roosevelt himself sought to project: noble democratic efforts to lift up the "forgotten man at the bottom of the economic pyramid" through whatever progressively redistributional tax reform could overcome the constraints of congressional special interests, corrupt "economic royalists," and financial exigencies. Like most myths, this first narrative reveals a great deal, but unfortunately obscures the second narrative on the fundamental ways in which the tax system evolved during the Depression.

The root of misunderstanding lies in certain peculiarities of the U.S. tax system. At the center of the standard twentieth-century tax reform story is the personal income tax. Today, that tax is an accoutrement—albeit an often-resented one—of citizenship. But, in the United States far more than anywhere else in the world, this tax emerged from a populist/progressive "soak-the-rich" tradition that exempted "the people" and specially targeted "surplus" incomes of privileged outlanders and plutocratic "malefactors of great wealth." Thus, between 1929 and 1939, upwards of 95 percent of Americans did not pay a dime of federal income tax, until World War II transformed it from a "class tax" to a "mass tax" through a 1,500 percent jump in the number of citizens covered by taxable returns. This narrowly-based "class tax" extracted most of its revenue in the 1930s from the tiniest fraction of 1 percent of Americans, the fewer than 20,000 tax returns reporting over $50,000. With so few shouldering this tax, the New Deal income tax collected only about 1 percent of the nation's total personal income, as opposed, for example, to over 12 percent today. New Deal revenue yields relied far less on politically and historically celebrated "progressive" rate hikes on upper incomes than on "regressive" levies, which claimed larger shares of incomes from the bottom of the economic pyramid than from those nearer the pyramid's top.

The economic collapse of 1929 to 1933 was bad enough, but fiscal collapse made it worse. With upper tax brackets decimated by the stock market crash and vanishing profits, federal government tax collections halved. This fiscal crunch came at the worst possible time, amidst desperate citizen needs and demands, New Deal commitments, state and local government debt limits, and reigning dictates of fiscal orthodoxy.

The government's response to this crisis went through three phases: economic heavy lifting between 1932 and the spring of 1935, a tax reform thrust between June 1935 and 1937, and an antitax reform parry in 1938 and 1939. The first phase opened during the Herbert Hoover administration with the Revenue Act of 1932, the nation's largest peacetime tax increase and the dominant tax legislation of the Great Depression. Though an insur-

A highway billboard in southern Alabama, photographed in 1939, promotes lower taxes to stimulate job growth. LIBRARY OF

CONGRESS, PRINTS & PHOTOGRAPHS DIVISION, FSA/OWI COLLECTION

gent congressional revolt blocked its most regressive sales tax formulation, the legislation still targeted consumers with new federal manufacturer's excise taxes on such widely-used items as cars, tires, gasoline, and electricity, while slicing exemptions and more than doubling most income and estate tax rates, restoring a gift tax, and hiking taxes on corporate profits.

Depression program costs, however, made it impossible simply to coast on these new revenues. At least until Roosevelt acquiesced to what came to be seen as a Keynesian policy of economic stimulation through deliberate deficits in the wake of the 1937 recession, Roosevelt was in principle a budget balancer, pledging fealty to fiscal responsibility by excluding what he labeled "emergency" expendi-

tures while "balancing" the "regular" budget. But as total federal spending doubled in his first term, even creative accounting could not erase the rising federal debt, as deficits at times exceeded tax collections. Seeking to minimize controversy and to pursue a "concert of interests" with corporate leaders positioned to spearhead economic recovery, the administration took a path of least resistance. Instead of offering a tax reform program between 1933 and the spring of 1935, it used a financial Trojan horse, bringing in regressive taxes as subordinate financial provisions of popular programs. It celebrated its reimposition of alcohol taxes as part of prohibition repeal in 1933. Redirecting grateful imbibers' money from bootleggers to the government was easy pickings. Its agricultural recovery program, the 1933

Agricultural Adjustment Act (AAA), was funded by processing taxes (e.g., imposed on millers of wheat, but then passed along to consumers of bread). And most important to the future of the U.S. tax system, at the insistence of Roosevelt and Secretary of the Treasury Henry Morgenthau in January 1935, its old-age insurance program was financed entirely by a tax (1 percent each for employees and—nominally—employers) on the first $3,000 paid annually to workers qualifying for the program. Casting Social Security taxes in private insurance terms—as "premiums" that established an "earned right" to future pensions—made them a comparatively painless way to narrow New Deal deficits and to assure the program's permanence. Decision makers and economists widely recognized that these taxes would ultimately either be subtracted from wages or added to prices. Yet a more progressive scheme—even general revenue subsidies used in social insurance programs elsewhere in the world—might have incurred unwelcome political costs.

In Roosevelt's first two terms, collections from manufacturer's excise taxes, alcohol taxes, the AAA processing tax, and Social Security taxes each separately peaked at over 12 percent of annual federal revenues—a regressive influence at odds with New Deal images of democratically redistributional taxation. State and local tax shifts only heightened this tilt toward taxes that exacted proportionately more from lower-income Americans. Local governments, primarily reliant on property taxes that squeezed farmers, home owners, and landlords whose Depression-wracked incomes could no longer cover their property tax bills, faced tax defaults, popular tax revolts, and reduced revenues that forced contraction at the very time when needs were most dire. State government spending rose substantially despite debt ceilings, partly in order to participate in shared federal/state welfare, public works, and unemployment insurance programs. But new regressive state retail sales taxes, along with the nonprogressive state unemployment insurance payroll taxes generated by the Social Security Act, carried a much greater portion of this new load than the personal or corporate state income tax.

Not all Americans took the regressive elements of this first phase of Depression taxation policy lying down. The Treasury, flexing its growing economic and legal expertise, relayed the broader conclusion of the economics profession and a few progressive political leaders, such as Senator Robert La Follette, Jr., that the New Deal tax system too heavily burdened the "forgotten man" while undertaxing—especially in comparison with European rates—lower and middle income tax brackets, where the real money was. Noting the New Deal's failure to rectify "our fundamental malady, the maldistribution of wealth and income," left-wing critics declared taxation to be "the weakest link in the Roosevelt program." Millions scapegoated wealth concentration as "the greatest menace this country faces," and gravitated toward plans such as those of Senator Huey Long's share-the-wealth movement, formed in 1934 to confiscate or heavily tax the fortunes of multimillionaires. Pressures from congressional progressives, with measured support from the Roosevelt administration, resulted in minor antiplutocratic initiatives in the Revenue Act of 1934, which boosted estate taxes and tightened several upper-income and corporate tax loopholes, such as preferential rates on capital gains. Congressional pressure only increased with the 1934 elections, as extraordinary gains by liberal Democrats and left-wing third parties left Republicans outnumbered by three-to-one in Congress. Some conservatives now cast Roosevelt as "the bulwark between the country and the 'wild men' of Congress."

Just as the thunder on Roosevelt's left made problematic any strategy of business conciliation, conservative opposition erupted. Earlier in the New Deal, with economic survival and political stability hanging in the balance, businessmen had reason to go along with the New Deal's "concert of interests" theme. But rising economic indicators quelled their desperation. In May 1935, the U.S. Chamber of Commerce stingingly condemned the New Deal, and the Supreme Court found unconstitutional the National Industrial Recovery Act, the New Deal's main institutional vehicle for partnership with business interests.

Roosevelt responded to this new balance with a political masterstroke. His June 19, 1935, message to Congress spearheaded a strategy that durably cast the New Deal on the side of the common people against "entrenched greed," "economic tyranny," and other evil "forces of selfishness and of lust for power" that his upcoming reelection campaign famously portrayed as "unanimous in their hate for me—and I welcome their hatred." Noting that the tax system had "done little to prevent an unjust concentration of wealth and economic power," he called for "very high taxes" on "vast fortunes" and "inherited economic power." This was a message very much in the "anti-bigness" mold of Roosevelt adviser Felix Frankfurter and his patron Louis Brandeis: scaling down the over-concentrated power of big business and the bloated super-rich to safeguard democratic institutions and foster economic opportunity.

The mere reading of this speech, confessed one corporate lawyer, practically left him "frothing at the mouth." But at first no draft legislation accompanied it. Would the speech itself suffice as a campaign document to preempt such critics as the flamboyant Huey Long, a likely third-party presidential candidate? Roosevelt was ambivalent, but a revolt of progressive senators forced his hand. By summer's end, the Revenue Act of 1935, popularly known as the wealth tax, entered the statute books. More a "hell-raiser" than a "revenue raiser," it institutionalized Roosevelt's oratory by strafing mammoth incomes, estates, and corporations, while only augmenting tax collections by $250 million. Contrary to conventional historical wisdom, this paltry yield—a fraction of collections from New Deal taxes disproportionately shouldered by ordinary Americans—cannot be attributed to congressional foot-dragging. Congress did reshuffle rates to dilute certain anti-bigness features of Roosevelt's proposed inheritance tax on legatees (replaced by a reduced exemption and higher rates for existing estate and gift taxes), graduated corporate income tax (which now favored small companies instead of specially penalizing giant ones), intercorporate dividend tax, and personal income tax. Yet that original incarnation would have collected even less than the final law. Even in the revenue-enhanced but "diluted" final income tax schedule, increases only kicked in at $50,000. Net incomes over five million dollars faced a 79 percent rate (up from 63 per-

cent)—an onerous-sounding top bracket, though it applied only to John D. Rockefeller, Jr.

The Wealth Tax established Roosevelt's tax credentials for the 1936 presidential campaign. But early in 1936 the Supreme Court invalidated the AAA processing tax and Congress overrode Roosevelt's veto of a budget-busting "bonus" for veterans of World War I. Into the breach came the undistributed profits tax. The Roosevelt administration dusted off a boldly innovative tax proposal to replace existing corporate taxes with a graduated levy on corporate profits not distributed to stockholders. Roosevelt, as was his wont (particularly in circumstances of high political visibility), joined the Department of the Treasury in casting the tax as a moral question of "fundamental equity" and "ability to pay." Undistributed corporate profits, he said, were a haven for what would otherwise have been the taxable dividends of wealthy stockholders. Others, such as Brain Truster Rexford Tugwell, conceived of the tax as a tool of economic planning, transforming idle surpluses into needed consumer buying power, while reducing the use of retained earnings for redundant expansion by diverting them into more competitive investment markets.

Thanks in part to the Treasury's inept defense of the tax (including a meltdown of its claim that the undistributed profits tax would reduce corporate concentration and empower smaller stockholders) and in part to corporate outrage over the government's intrusion into investment decisions, the Revenue Act of 1936 retained existing corporate taxes while introducing a supplementary 7 percent to 27 percent tax on undistributed corporate profits. Still, this tax promised to yield far more added revenue from corporations and the wealthy than the more symbolic assault upon the super-rich in the 1935 wealth tax or in the upcoming Revenue Act of 1937, which penalized tax dodges of the super-rich, especially "personal holding companies." The 1937 law—passed after genuinely indignant presidential denunciations of tax lawyers' "clever little schemes" to help millionaires avoid their "fair share" of taxes—followed Roosevelt's lead in targeting smaller, flagrantly sensational loopholes as opposed to more financially significant ones, such as oil depletion allowances.

Symbolic or not, New Deal tax reform of 1935 to 1937 infuriated congressional conservatives and business leaders, who bristled at New Deal campaigns that vilified them and denigrated their economic contributions. Rocked both politically and economically by the precipitous "Roosevelt Recession" of 1937 to 1938, the New Deal could not fend off these attacks. In 1938 and 1939, Congress one-sidedly gutted and then eliminated the undistributed profits tax, while slashing capital gains tax rates on the wealthy. This victory, however, came at a price to the resurgent congressional conservative coalition. Forced to recoup these cuts by raising the standard corporate income tax rate several points above its previous high, it left unscathed more fundamental New Deal transformations, such as in employment and labor policy. New Deal taxation, arguably a bane of the "forgotten man" in the 1930s, was a political masterpiece.

See Also: AGRICULTURAL ADJUSTMENT
   ADMINISTRATION (AAA); NEW DEAL;
   TAXPAYERS LEAGUES.

BIBLIOGRAPHY

Blum, John Morton. *From the Morgenthau Diaries,* Vol 1: *Years of Crisis, 1928–1938.* 1959.

Brownlee, W. Elliot. *Federal Taxation in America: A Short History.* 1996.

Jansson, Bruce S. *The Sixteen-Trillion Dollar Mistake: How the U.S. Bungled its National Priorities from the New Deal to the Present.* 2001.

Leff, Mark H. *The Limits of Symbolic Reform: The New Deal and Taxation, 1933–1939.* 1984.

Ratner, Sidney. *Taxation and Democracy in America.* 1967.

Tax History Project. Available at: www.taxhistory.org

MARK H. LEFF

TAXPAYERS LEAGUES

The Great Depression introduced unprecedented tax burdens to Americans. While real-estate values plummeted and unemployment skyrocketed, the cost of government remained high. As a result, taxes as a percentage of the national income nearly doubled from 11.6 percent in 1921 to 21.1 in 1932.

Most of the increase occurred at the local level and especially squeezed the resources of real-estate taxpayers. Local tax delinquency rose steadily from a median of 10.1 percent in 1930 to 26.3 percent in 1933.

Many Americans reacted to these conditions by forming taxpayers leagues to call for lower taxes and cuts in government spending. These organizations were relatively rare before the Depression but soon became commonplace. By some estimates, there were three thousand of them by 1933. Thomas Reed, a leading political scientist, lamented that taxpayers groups "spring up like mushrooms, every time you go out in the morning, you find more of them," while the American Library Association *Bulletin* observed that the "taxpayer is indeed in revolt. Local and state taxpayers leagues multiply." The banner year for such organizations was 1933, with several hundred formed in the spring alone, according to an estimate by Howard P. Jones of the National Municipal League.

Taxpayers leagues endorsed such measures as laws to limit and roll back taxes, lowered penalties on tax delinquents, and cuts in government spending. Partly as a result of their efforts, sixteen states and numerous localities adopted property tax limitations, while three states instituted homestead exemptions. The National Association of Real Estate Boards provided a limited degree of interstate coordination by establishing property owners associations.

Although taxpayers leagues usually favored traditional legal and political strategies, a few were more radical. Probably the best known of these was the Association of Real Estate Taxpayers in Chicago. From 1930 to 1933, it led one of the largest tax strikes in American history. At its height, it had 30,000 paid members, a budget of $600,000, and a weekly radio show.

By late 1933, the taxpayers leagues had entered a period of decline. The circumstances that had nurtured revolt were undermined as economic conditions gradually improved, the federal government extended aid to homeowners, and local governments reduced their reliance on real-estate taxes. To some extent, the tax revolt also fell victim to an effective counterattack by municipal reformers, government officials, and the holders of municipal debt, such as bondholders and bankers. In Newark, New Jersey, and other cities, groups ranging from the Bankers Trust to various teachers unions organized Pay Your Taxes campaigns that used a combination of door-to-door solicitation, threats of coercion, and inducements, such as installment payment plans, to collect back taxes. Members from the same groups formed the basis of the Citizens Councils for Constructive Economy. One strategy of the Citizens Councils was to co-opt more radical forms of tax resistance and budget cutting by emphasizing reforms, such as centralized purchasing, which would make government more efficient rather than reduce its size.

See Also: TAXATION.

BIBLIOGRAPHY

Beito, David T. *Taxpayers in Revolt: Tax Resistance during the Great Depression.* 1989.

Thornton, Mark, and Chetley Wise. "The Great Depression Tax Revolts Revisited." *Journal of Libertarian Studies* 15, no. 3 (2001): 95–105.

DAVID T. BEITO

TAYLOR GRAZING ACT

When railroads were built across the American West after the Civil War, livestock producers found it profitable to turn cattle and sheep onto the unfenced plains, where they grazed without fee on public lands. For decades overcrowding and the consequent denuding of grasses generated tension between cattle and sheep producers and between stockmen and homesteaders. In the early 1930s declining livestock prices increased reliance upon free grazing. At the same time, drought caused water holes to dry up, vegetation to shrivel, and the region's deteriorated soils to drift eastward in the form of dust storms.

In 1928 a group of stockmen had collaborated on a proposal to merge public and private holdings with state and railway grant lands in a project for range improvement in southeastern Montana. They obtained congressional legislation authorizing withdrawal of the public lands from further settlement and directing the secretary of the interior to lease tracts to stock producers who owned adjacent lands and who would agree to meet prescribed management regulations. The resulting range improvement there and in several similar ventures set a precedent for extending the program to public lands generally. As the drought conditions worsened, Representative Edward T. Taylor of Colorado assumed sponsorship of such a proposal, and the Taylor Grazing Act was passed by Congress. President Franklin D. Roosevelt signed the measure on June 28, 1934.

A landmark in the history of American public land policy, the Taylor Grazing Act virtually terminated the free homestead program initiated in 1862. The secretary of the interior was authorized to establish grazing districts over no more than 80 million, later amended to142 million, acres of "vacant, unappropriated, and unreserved lands from any part of the public domain (exclusive of Alaska) . . . chiefly valuable for grazing and forage crops." A few other exclusions were enumerated, together with reservation of areas needed for owners of adjacent land to drive their stock to market or to other properties, tracts lying within watersheds forming part of the national forests, and areas within grazing districts that the secretary might classify as "more valuable and suitable for the production of agricultural crops than native grasses and forage plants." As a consequence, the number of homestead entries declined from 7,741 in 1934, to 609 in 1937, and to less than 500 any year during the following decade.

The secretary was further authorized to issue permits for running livestock in grazing districts upon payment of "reasonable fees," with preference to those within or near a district who were "landowners engaged in the livestock business, bona fide occupants or settlers, or owners of water or water rights." Permits were to run for ten years, renewable at the discretion of the secretary. Fees were low, far less than the rates for privately rented grazing property or for grazing leases in public forest reserves. Congressional opposition withheld adequate funding for administrative regulation or range improvements. Some increase of water facilities by the Civilian Conservation Corps of the 1930s and the introduction of crested-wheatgrass seeding in 1940 were the most notable early achievements. In response to a Senate inquiry the secretary of the interior reported in 1962 that conditions over the past seven years showed only 1.6 percent of the ranges excellent, 15 percent good, but 53.1 percent fair, 25.8 percent poor, and 4.5 percent bad.

As interpreted and applied until the mid-1960s, the Taylor Act was focused almost solely upon conservation for grazing. With the development of environmental concerns, however, a series of measures for safeguarding public water supplies, protecting endangered species, and limiting use of pesticides for weed control had to be implemented. A requirement for environmental impact statements necessitated greatly increased administrative appropriations and led to higher grazing fees. Litigation ensued, particularly over determination of fees and interpretation of grazing preference. Although the U.S. Supreme Court generally upheld the administration of the Taylor Act, opposition increased. Disgruntled stockmen complained of government control and rising fees, and in 2000 a symposium of environmentalists declared a National Campaign to End Public Lands Grazing.

See Also: CONSERVATION MOVEMENT; WEST, GREAT DEPRESSION IN THE AMERICAN.

BIBLIOGRAPHY

Gates, Paul W. *History of Public Land Law Development.* 1968.

Mackey, Mike. "Wyoming Stock Growers and the Taylor Grazing Act." *Journal of the West* 35, no. 3 (1996): 18–25.

"Save Our Public Lands—End Public Lands Grazing." A Declaration from the RangeNet 2000 Symposium. Available at http://rangenet.org/rn2k/declaration.html

Whitlock, Clair M., and Larry L. Woodard, eds. *Taylor Grazing Act, 1934–1984: 50 Years of Progress.* 1984.

MARY W. M. HARGREAVES

TECHNOCRACY. *See* BLACK THIRTY-HOUR BILL.

TEMPORARY EMERGENCY RELIEF ADMINISTRATION, NEW YORK (TERA)

Because of the devastating effects of the economic Depression that hit the nation in 1930, New York State Governor Franklin Delano Roosevelt called for immediate state aid to be given to the unemployed, declaring that the purpose of the state is the protection and well-being of its citizens. In January 1931 newly reelected Governor Roosevelt declared that the national economic emergency demanded new solutions for new problems. Under authority granted to him by the New York State Legislature in Extraordinary Session, the governor created the Temporary Emergency Relief Administration (TERA) in October 1931, with an appropriation of $20 million for emergency relief of the unemployed. Roosevelt set a precedent by creating a new agency to meet a new problem, one he relied on during the New Deal years.

Roosevelt appointed Jesse Straus, president of R. H. Macy department stores, as chairman of the new agency and offered the job as executive director to New York City social worker Harry L. Hopkins, who took over the following August as chairman when Straus resigned. The TERA provided direct relief for approximately 160,000 New Yorkers in immediate need. Both Roosevelt and Hopkins were committed to jobs as a solution to the state's economic problems. The state legislature, prodded by Roosevelt, allocated an additional $5 million for work relief programs. Hopkins concentrated on creating an efficient and effective work-relief program for unemployed industrial workers in New York, one that could set an example for other states. In directing TERA projects, Hopkins made sure that they were consonant with economic needs as well as prevailing cultural attitudes. He insisted on socially useful projects that would neither replace or duplicate normal municipal functions nor interfere with private industry. The wages would be paid in cash and be set at the prevailing rate for the type of work performed. Because of limited funds, Hopkins required a means test for applicants and limited jobs to one person per household.

As the Depression deepened, relief in New York State became increasingly inadequate, due largely to lack of state funds. While Hopkins always insisted that the states participate in relief programs by providing the lion's share of the funding, he also believed that relief administered at the federal level was essential. Soon after Roosevelt was inaugurated president in March 1933, Hopkins proposed that the TERA be replicated on a federal level and that a federal relief administrator be appointed to head the new agency. Federal responsibility for relief, Hopkins believed, would also convince the public that the unemployed were not at fault. Two months after Roosevelt's inauguration both houses of Congress passed the Federal Emergency Relief Act (FERA) with an initial appropriation of $500 million. Roosevelt, relying on his experience with the TERA, immediately signed the legislation that would for the first time provide federal aid in the form of grants to the states to help them meet their relief needs. The president offered the job to Hopkins who used his experience with the TERA to direct his work as FDR's federal relief administrator and as director of the FERA.

See Also: HOPKINS, HARRY.

BIBLIOGRAPHY

Davis, Kenneth S. *FDR: The New York Years.* 1994.

Hopkins, June. *Harry Hopkins: Sudden Hero, Brash Reformer.* 1999.

McJimsey, George. *Harry Hopkins: Ally of the Poor, Defender of Democracy.* 1987.

Sherwood, Robert. *Roosevelt and Hopkins: An Intimate History.* 1948.

JUNE HOPKINS

TEMPORARY NATIONAL ECONOMIC COMMITTEE (TNEC)

Congress established the Temporary National Economic Committee (TNEC) in June 1938 to analyze the performance of the American economy. Created on the recommendation of President Franklin D. Roosevelt as part of the policy re-evaluation provoked by the recession of 1937 and 1938 and the persistence of the Great Depression, the TNEC initially was intended by the administration to focus on economic concentration and monopoly power. But the committee ultimately had a much wider scope and unexpectedly provided a more important forum for Keynesian fiscal policy than for anti-monopoly efforts. The TNEC conducted extensive hearings for more than two years, from December 1938 to March 1941, and published dozens of volumes of the testimony it received and the detailed economic studies it commissioned. Its final report and recommendations in 1941, coming in the much different atmosphere of defense mobilization and economic recovery, had little impact or influence.

The creation of the TNEC reflected long-term and short-term worries about business concentration and monopoly power as well as concern about the performance of the U.S. economy in the 1930s. A belief that excessive business concentration harmed the economy and gave big business too much political power was an important issue for many Progressive-era reformers, especially Louis Brandeis. With the Great Depression and the election of FDR, Brandeis and his followers argued for a renewal of anti-trust policy. Instead, the "First New Deal" of 1933 turned to the National Recovery Administration (NRA) and the suspension of anti-trust laws in an effort to achieve recovery by means of planning and controls worked out with business. But the NRA was unsuccessful and was declared unconstitutional in 1935. Anti-monopoly advocates inveighed against the NRA for permitting cartel-like arrangements that kept prices high and fixed production limits to the detriment of expansion and recovery.

Proponents of anti-trust policy had more influence in the mid-1930s, beginning with the "Second New Deal" of 1935. The Public Utilities Holding Company Act was designed to eliminate or reduce the sprawling conglomerates that dominated the electrical power industry. New Deal tax proposals, though watered down by Congress, had anti-trust dimensions, including the graduated corporate income tax in the 1935 Revenue Act and the undistributed profits tax in the 1936 Revenue Act. Legislation in 1936 and 1937 sought to protect small retailers from the economic power of chain stores.

Anti-trust policy did not, however, become central to New Deal efforts, even though some liberals continued to blame the ongoing economic troubles on the deleterious effects of economic concentration.

Then in the late summer and fall of 1937, the recession of 1937 and 1938 struck. Sending economic indexes down more sharply, though not more deeply, than at the onset of the Great Depression, the "Roosevelt Recession" set off a policy debate in the administration. Although there were proponents of balancing the federal budget and of moderating tax, regulatory, and other policies that upset businessmen, the principal debate involved spending and anti-trust factions. Led by Leon Henderson, the anti-monopoly position held that business concentration and monopoly behavior had constricted production and pegged prices too high; the result was diminished investment, production, employment, and income that had prolonged the Depression and triggered the 1937 and 1938 recession. Spending advocates, led by Marriner Eccles and Harry Hopkins, maintained that federal deficits had underwritten the moderate expansion between 1933 and 1936 and that when FDR had turned to more restrictive fiscal policy the economy had tumbled again. In their view, a return to spending could fire the economy.

But the anti-trust and spending approaches were not mutually exclusive. Indeed, Leon Henderson was a leading proponent of both positions. In April 1938, Roosevelt announced two new policy initiatives. In the middle of the month, he said that he would embark upon a renewed spending policy, especially on relief. Then on April 29, he sent Congress a message recommending a "thorough study of the concentration of economic power in American industry."

Anti-monopoly policy had important supporters in Congress, among progressive Republicans as well as among Democrats. On June 14, 1938, Congress passed legislation creating the Temporary National Economic Committee (TNEC), and Roosevelt signed it on June 16. But where Roosevelt had anticipated that an administration committee would carry out the study, Congress stipulated that half of the committee would come from the executive branch, with the other half from Congress. Six members of the TNEC represented the administration, among them Thurman Arnold, who in 1938 also began his service as the activist new head of the Justice Department's Anti-Trust Division. From Congress, the TNEC included three senators, with Wyoming Democratic senator Joseph O'Mahoney serving as committee chairman, and three congressmen, with Texas representative Hatton Summers the committee vice-chairman. Two Republicans, one from the Senate and one from the House, were named to the committee. Leon Henderson served as executive secretary. Congress also gave the TNEC a broad charge going beyond studying economic concentration, to include "the effect of the existing tax, patent, and other government policies upon competition, price levels, unemployment, profits, and consumption."

The TNEC began its hearings in late 1938. The committee heard testimony from 552 witnesses, who provided a variety of information and recommendations. Some of the witnesses argued for stepping up anti-trust policy, in order to break up the monopolies that they thought kept the economy from expanding to full production and full employment. Others called for accepting economic concentration, on the grounds that it was inevitable and had its positive aspects, but said that more stringent and effective regulatory policy should be implemented in order to reduce the harmful impact of concentrated economic power.

The most noted and influential testimony came in the spring of 1939 when proponents of compensatory deficit spending, led by Harvard economist Alvin H. Hansen, came before the TNEC. By that time, Keynesian ideas as adapted and disseminated by Hansen and others, had become more widely accepted, and more economists and New Deal officials had become persuaded of the potential of compensatory fiscal policy. And the better performance of the economy following the 1938 spending decision seemed to corroborate the potential of a spending policy to stimulate the economy. The testimony on behalf of fiscal policy as the path toward recovery thus came at an especially opportune time—all the more as the economy continued to turn upward as defense spending increased in 1939 and 1940.

The TNEC worked on, hearing from more witnesses and conducting studies of the U.S. economy. Ultimately dozens of volumes of testimony and economic analysis were published, providing important information and insights. But increasingly the TNEC became peripheral. The economy was recovering, the advocates of Keynesian fiscal policy grew in numbers and influence, and anti-trust efforts seemed divisive and an impediment to economic mobilization as big business began to convert to war production. After expanding the Justice Department's anti-trust efforts, Thurman Arnold encountered increasing opposition by 1941.

When the TNEC issued its final reports and recommendations in 1941, they attracted little attention. Except for helping to focus attention on Keynesian fiscal policy, the hearings had changed few minds. Reflecting the wide-ranging nature of the testimony and investigation, the recommendations lacked consistency and often clarity and seemed irrelevant to the new priorities of defense mobilization. The hearings and reports did provide an extraordinary array of viewpoints and information, but ultimately that had nothing like the impact envisioned in the spring of 1938. And the economic recovery of the war years, produced by the spending that underwrote mobilization, confirmed the triumph of Keynesianism over anti-monopoly policy.

See Also: KEYNESIAN ECONOMICS; NATIONAL RECOVERY ADMINISTRATION (NRA); PUBLIC UTILITIES HOLDING COMPANY ACT.

BIBLIOGRAPHY

Brinkley, Alan. *The End of Reform: New Deal Liberalism in Recession and War.* 1995.

Hawley, Ellis W. *The New Deal and the Problem of Monopoly.* 1966.

Lynch, David. *The Concentration of Economic Power.* 1946.

May, Dean L. *From New Deal to New Economics: The American Liberal Response to the Recession of 1937.* 1981.

JOHN W. JEFFRIES

TENNESSEE VALLEY AUTHORITY (TVA)

The Tennessee Valley Authority (TVA) arose as a World War I footnote. In 1916, as part of war preparedness, Congress authorized President Woodrow Wilson to build munitions-grade nitrate plants and a hydroelectric support facility on the Tennessee River at Muscle Shoals, Alabama. After the war the project sparked a furious national debate over public ownership of productive capacity. The Republican administrations of the 1920s were adamantly opposed to government-run power and nitrate production, now being used for fertilizer instead of explosives. However, two factors kept the project in the public domain: no entity made an acceptable offer to take the facilities private, and progressive legislators, led by the venerable Nebraska senator, George Norris, felt the project was an important symbol of government responsibility. For years, Norris and other members of Congress kept Muscle Shoals from being dismantled while the facilities continued producing fertilizers and electricity for the area surrounding the renamed Wilson Dam.

By the early 1930s the debate began to tilt in favor of public ownership, or at least strong public regulation. During the 1920s, private utilities poisoned their own wells by establishing distant holding companies that drained profits from local companies whose stock they owned. Moreover, the holding companies kept gas, electric, and telephone rates steady or increased them when millions could barely pay the pre-Depression rates. Meanwhile, progressive politicians, including governors Franklin D. Roosevelt in New York and Philip La Follette in Wisconsin, established powerful state utility regulatory commissions. In other areas, especially the northwestern United States and Canada, public power companies were proving that government could produce electricity as efficiently as private companies—and almost always more cheaply.

BEGINNINGS

The 1932 Democratic platform was silent on public ownership, but the party's candidate was not. In September, in Portland, Oregon, Roosevelt

The Hiawassee Dam in North Carolina, under construction by the TVA in the late 1930s. FRANKLIN DELANO ROOSEVELT LIBRARY

insisted that the government was justified in going into the power business when private utilities were inefficient or practiced exorbitant pricing. Furthermore, government utilities could provide a "yardstick," a competitive price comparison, for the private utilities. In Montgomery, Alabama, right before inauguration, the president-elect suggested that Muscle Shoals could provide such a yardstick and serve as an instrument of planning and social development for the economically devastated region.

With little hesitation, Congress approved the Tennessee Valley Authority (TVA) on May 18, 1933. The act established an agency whose purpose was to build hydroelectric dams on the Tennessee River to achieve the unified development of industry, agriculture, flood control, and conservation throughout the entire watershed. As important, at least for President Roosevelt, was the production of low-cost electricity to act as a "yardstick" by which electricity rates could be judged throughout the nation. The president immediately deemed it "a corpora-

tion clothed with the power of government, but possessed of the flexibility and initiative of a private enterprise." He set about appointing three men to the governing board, each with special talents related to TVA's multiple mission. First, he asked Arthur E. Morgan, president of Antioch College in Ohio and an experienced dam builder, to assume the chair. At Morgan's suggestion Roosevelt appointed Harcourt Morgan (no relation), president of the University of Tennessee and distinguished agriculturist, and David E. Lilienthal, utilities lawyer and charismatic leader of the Wisconsin Public Service Commission.

In spite of Roosevelt's support and the caliber of his appointments, TVA immediately faced serious problems that threatened its existence. First, the directors had no clearly specified goals—the TVA Act was basically hortatory and thematic, calling for such vague objectives as planning, conservation, and natural resource development. And Roosevelt, typically, issued no clear directives. In late 1933, presidential advisor Rexford Tugwell told the

A young couple in Lauderdale county, Alabama, prepares dinner on an electric stove in 1942 after the TVA provided electricity to the area. LIBRARY OF CONGRESS, PRINTS & PHOTOGRAPHS DIVISION, FSA/OWI COLLECTION

three directors that he had no idea what the president wanted. Roosevelt told a delighted but puzzled Senator Norris that the TVA was "neither fish nor fowl, but, whatever it is, it will taste awfully good to the people of the Tennessee Valley." Second, the act was silent on administrative structure except for a three-person board with a chair nominated by the president. The act said nothing about the chair's powers, which meant that all three directors had equal authority. In other circumstances, a multiple executive might have been feasible. This board, however, had three directors of strong character and very different visions. The third challenge was the hostility of the private utilities. Days after the directors settled in, the powerful Commonwealth & Southern (C&S) holding company, with extensive interests in Tennessee, Georgia, Missis-

sippi, and Alabama, began an assault on TVA's then modest power program.

INITIAL STRUGGLES AND TRAVAILS

Wendell Willkie, the energetic president of C&S, suggested that TVA should limit its power program to selling its production to private companies at the source (initially, and until 1936 only at Wilson Dam). Chairman Morgan thought this a reasonable compromise—the utilities would continue to transmit, market their product, and make their profits. Meanwhile, TVA could peacefully proceed with its other programs. Lilienthal saw it very differently, and thus began an acrimonious feud between the two directors until Roosevelt fired Morgan in March 1938.

Unemployed laborers hoping to become TVA employees take the TVA examination at a high school in Clinton, Tennessee, in 1933. NATIONAL ARCHIVES AND RECORDS ADMINISTRATION

Fresh from three bruising years on the Wisconsin Public Service Commission, Lilienthal was in no mood to compromise with the utilities. In the first place, selling power at the source would deny TVA the ability to provide a "yardstick" that could force private utilities to lower their prices in the face of lower TVA rates. And much like Roosevelt, Lilienthal felt that each community should be free to choose its own power provider. For six years, the battle raged. Three federal suits challenged TVA's constitutional right to produce and distribute electricity. At points, lower courts enjoined TVA from building facilities and distributing power. In each case, however, the U.S. Supreme Court ruled that TVA had a right not only to produce power but also to distribute and market it. In August 1939, in the face of the last Supreme Court decision and over-

whelming demand for TVA power, the weary Willkie sold all C&S valley holdings to TVA.

The Morgan-Lilienthal feud was fueled by more than power policies, however. Arthur Morgan was a rigid crusader who disdained political intrigue. He was also a bona fide utopian who believed that TVA could make the Tennessee Valley into a new Jerusalem, a model of social and moral betterment. In his zealotry, he alienated powerful political figures, including the third board member, Harcourt Morgan. Lilienthal, on the other hand, was a consummate pragmatist. For him public power was the key to success, as was the careful accommodation of valley interests. To that end Harcourt Morgan and Lilienthal decided that all TVA agriculture programs—test demonstration farms, erosion control, fertilizer development and distri-

Laborers weed seedlings at a TVA tree nursery near Alabama's Muscle Shoals region in 1942. FRANKLIN DELANO ROOSEVELT LIBRARY

bution—should cooperate with the region's land grant colleges and that Harcourt Morgan should control these programs. Thus, Lilienthal and Harcourt Morgan formed an unshakable alliance; for five years Chairman Morgan was constantly frustrated by two-to-one votes against him. The feud ultimately took a fierce psychological toll: both Arthur Morgan and Lilienthal suffered crushing periods of depression and paranoia. The impact on Morgan was more severe, however, and by 1938, his irrational behavior forced the president to remove him from the board.

THE TVA IDEA—REALITY AND MYTH

It was obvious that TVA was a unique creation, harnessing human and natural resources in search of unified social and economic development. The brilliant rhetoric of Roosevelt, Norris, and especially Lilienthal, only enhanced its aura. As Norman Wengert observed, "TVA differs considerably from most federal agencies in that an explicit body of doctrine—ideology if you will—has developed around its purpose." Historically, this ideology has embraced five principles: unified development, decentralized administration, citizen participation in TVA decisions, social responsibility, and policy making free of political considerations. To be sure, as in all ideologies, reality and rhetoric are part and parcel of each of these tenets.

With its innovative dams combining flood control, navigation, and power production, TVA exemplified unified and coordinated development. Also, dam building and agricultural reform were integrally related: Without containing endemic soil erosion, the reservoirs would silt up and become useless for any purpose. The idea of freeing TVA from Washington political intrigue, allowing authorities in the Tennessee Valley to make fundamental policy, was the heart of decentralized administration. Historically, TVA boards have been highly sensitive to regional concerns. TVA has always affirmed the mantra of citizen participation. Typically, participation has manifested itself in programs like the early demonstration test farm experiments, whereby farmers passed on progressive farming practices to each other. Other examples include citizen involvement in home energy conservation projects or in the development of local utility boards. Rarely, however, has participation manifested itself literally, with citizens actually deciding important policy decisions.

No doubt, the notion of social responsibility has been more than rhetorical. In the 1930s, TVA was staffed by thousands of men and women who believed they could make a profound difference in the midst of the Depression. In a region where labor unions were rare, the first board insisted that the blue-collar work force organize into an independent union. In addition, TVA is well known for its job training, education, and community and economic development efforts. Finally, political neutrality has been a strong tradition. TVA's peerless merit system more than once crossed swords with local politicians who were accustomed to patronage systems of public employment. Moreover, there is nary an instance where dams or other facilities were built because of political pressures.

On the other hand, these principles mask other aspects of TVA reality. Lilienthal's success in expanding the power program and the insatiable demand for power during World War II resulted in a significant erosion of the rest of TVA's programs and the goal of multiple purpose development. One critic noted that after the war, TVA became nothing more than the largest public utility in the country. Moreover, the authority's later massive expansion into nuclear power and the construction of environmentally questionable coal plants and dams was disastrous. These power decisions nearly bankrupted TVA and led to widespread accusations of pollution and environmental abuses.

There was also many a slip twixt cup and lip in the commitment to decentralized administration and citizen participation, the grassroots administration and democracy articulated by Lilienthal in his rhetorical masterpiece, *TVA: Democracy on the March* (1944). Without a doubt, TVA enjoyed an independence unmatched by other agencies; its merit and auditing systems, for example, were autonomous from Washington, as were the labor relations programs. Nevertheless, it was still bound to congressional purse strings, and often obligated to play partisan political games. Furthermore, there is no intrinsic virtue in decentralized authority—one only has to look at what decentralized authority meant for African-American citizens in the South before the 1960s. Likewise, grassroots participation never meant that valley citizens actually shaped public policy. Indeed, TVA's comprehensive power and flood control system belied meaningful citizen participation. Dams had to be built according to system requirements regardless of the feelings of individual communities along the river. Likewise, thousands of valley citizens had little chance to participate in decisions that resulted in the flooding of their rich river bottom farms and their relocation to less desirable sites. In the 1970s the decision to build the Tellico Dam on the Little Tennessee River drew enormous public opposition, but to no avail.

TVA's reputation for social responsibility has also been suspect. The early policy of hiring black workers in proportion to their numbers in the population was overshadowed by the fact that only one African American was appointed to a managerial-technical position in the 1930s. Likewise, the agriculture programs favored medium and large farmers and ignored small or tenant farmers and black agriculturists. Finally, by the 1970s TVA had a well-deserved reputation for environmental arrogance as it threatened endangered species and created serious air pollution. It is ironic that these lapses are functions of TVA's peculiar conceptualization of political neutrality as the avoidance of partisan influence in the form of, for example, patronage hiring or dam building because of political pressure. What TVA has failed to acknowledge is that acceding to the racial biases of the valley or serving only the more powerful elements of the agricultural community were just as political as bending to party influences. So, too, was proceeding with projects justified by intra-authority rationale but bereft of public approval.

ASSESSMENT

TVA's history has been marred by questionable and wrongheaded policies and programs of the sort discussed above. Too often, the rhetoric of the TVA idea masked the reality of actions taken by the authority in spite of constituent interests. Furthermore, William Chandler in *The Myth of TVA* (1983) makes a strong case that TVA's economic impact has been less than the rhetoric suggests. Certainly TVA was very different in later decades from what was envisioned in 1933; the multipurpose vision had given way to a clear central focus on power.

Nevertheless, on the whole TVA has had a positive impact in American life. It was an important symbol of constructive government action and of the idea that the public weal should vigorously challenge a negligent private will. TVA quickly provided universal electrification to the least electrified region of the country. It sold electricity as cheaply as anywhere in the United States and provided an effective "yardstick" for utilities across the nation. Taming the Tennessee River stopped the devastating floods that hindered economic development and provided the means for eliminating the scourge of malaria in the valley. Also, the dams, and later the coal-fired plants, were significant in enabling the development of one of the largest aluminum production facilities in the world in Alcoa, Tennessee, and for providing crucial power needs both during and after World War II for the atomic energy industry in and around Oak Ridge, Tennessee. Finally, TVA reservoirs stimulated the development of a strong recreational industry throughout the region.

TVA's other great legacy was the example it set for others. True, no other showcase authorities arose in the United States. Lilienthal argued for a Colombia River Authority, but the Department of the Interior controlled most of the power production in the Northwest and resisted the establishment of a new agency. Other efforts to establish authorities in the Arkansas and Missouri river basins were thwarted by President Roosevelt's waning support because of war concerns, private utility resistance, and fear in the states that independent authorities would reduce state power. Nevertheless, TVA provided other inspirations. TVA's success in rural electrification was a model for the Rural Electrification Administration, which had a national mandate. In addition, the TVA model was important in the development of smaller authorities, such as the Lower Colorado River Authority, which provides power, flood control, and agricultural support for hundreds of thousands of people in central Texas.

Perhaps as important, TVA has been a worldwide inspiration. In *TVA: Democracy on the March*, Lilienthal quotes the late U.S. Supreme Court justice, William O. Douglas, who reported after travels abroad, "Everywhere I went, people asked, 'Why can't we have a TVA?'" For more than seventy years, thousands of foreign visitors have come to the Tennessee Valley to learn about river development. And over the years, TVA has inspired unified river development in several nations including the Cauca River Valley in Columbia, the Papaloapan Basin in Mexico, the Khuzistan region in Iran, and the Damodar Valley in India.

For all the controversy and for all the times TVA's policies seemed to run counter to its high flown principles, it has remained a great example of public service for the Tennessee Valley, the nation, and the world. George Will perhaps expressed it best in *Newsweek* (April 25, 1988) where he talked about the value of public works: "The Tennessee Valley Authority and the Interstate Highway System were not just good in themselves. They were good for the morale of government, which periodically needs some inspiring successes."

See Also: NORRIS, GEORGE; SOUTH, GREAT DEPRESSION IN THE.

BIBLIOGRAPHY

Callahan, North. *TVA: Bridge over Troubled Waters.* 1980.

Chandler, William U. *The Myth of TVA: Conservation and Development in the Tennessee Valley, 1933–1983.* 1983

Cole, William; Steven M. Neuse; and Richard Sanders. "TVA: An International Administrative Example." *Public Administration Quarterly* 8 (1984): 166–183.

Colignon, Richard A. *Power Plays: Critical Events in the Institutionalization of the Tennessee Valley Authority.* 1997.

Davidson, Donald. *The Tennessee,* Vol. 2: *The New River, Civil War to TVA.* 1948.

Hargrove, Erwin C., and Paul K. Conkin, eds. *TVA: Fifty Years of Grass Roots Bureaucracy.* 1983.

Kazan, Elia, director. *Wild River.* 1960.

Lilienthal, David E. *The Journals of David E. Lilienthal,* Vol. 1: *The TVA Years, 1939–1945.* 1966.

McCraw, Thomas K. *Morgan vs. Lilienthal: The Feud within the TVA.* 1970.

McCraw, Thomas K. *TVA and the Power Fight: 1933–1939.* 1971.

Morgan, Arthur E. *The Making of TVA.* 1974.

Neuse, Steven M. "TVA at Age Fifty—Reflections and Retrospect." *Public Administration Review* 43, no. 6 (1983): 491–499.

Neuse, Steven M. *David E. Lilienthal: The Journey of an American Liberal.* 1996.

Owen, Marguerite. *The Tennessee Valley Authority.* 1973.

Pritchitt, C. Herman. *The Tennessee Valley Authority: A Study in Public Administration.* 1943.

Selznick, Philip. *TVA and the Grass Roots: A Study in the Sociology of Formal Organization.* 1949.

Talbert, Roy, Jr. *FDR's Utopian: Arthur Morgan of the TVA.* 1987.

Tugwell, Rexford G., and E. C. Banfield. "Grass Roots Democracy—Myth or Reality?" *The Public Administration Review* 10 (Winter 1950): 47–49.

TVA Heritage. Archive. Availiable at www.tva.gov/heritage/index.htm

Wengert, Norman. "The Politics of Water Resource Development as Exemplified by TVA." In *The Economic Impact of TVA,* edited by John R. Moore. 1967.

STEVEN M. NEUSE

TERA. *See* TEMPORARY EMERGENCY RELIEF ADMINISTRATION, NEW YORK.

THOMAS, NORMAN

Socialist Party leader Norman Mattoon Thomas (November 20, 1884–December 19, 1968) was born in Marion, Ohio, to a family of Presbyterian ministers. Thomas was educated at Princeton University in New Jersey and Union Theological Seminary in New York. An adherent to Social Gospel theology, Thomas worked in a settlement house in New York City and in 1911 he received a pastorate in East Harlem. World War I turned Thomas into a pacifist. In 1918, endorsing the political left's opposition to business profiteering and government repression, Thomas resigned his church and joined the Socialist Party, quickly becoming one of its leading spokesmen. Thomas emerged as the heir to Eugene V. Debs's "American" brand of socialism, somewhat distant from its European immigrant roots, espousing gradual democratic change and rejecting the absolutist and revolutionary dogma of the American Communist Party and others.

In the 1920s Thomas produced numerous books, articles, and speeches attacking that decade's alliance of business and government and recommending central economic planning and the nationalization of industries and utilities. He ran for the mayoralty of New York and for other offices, and in 1926 he succeeded Debs as leader of the U.S. Socialist Party. In 1928 he mounted the first of six consecutive campaigns as the party's candidate for the presidency.

As the Great Depression began, Thomas advocated national, state, and municipal reform. Condemning the limited relief efforts of Herbert Hoover and New York Governor Franklin Roosevelt, he called for labor legislation, complete rights for unions, full social security, and government-sponsored worker retraining. Thomas's City Affairs Committee attacked Tammany Hall, whose mismanagement of New York City had created financial near-ruin and ineffective relief programs. Although his articulate criticism helped to topple Tammany mayor Jimmy Walker, Thomas gained few political advantages. In 1932 he won only 884,781 votes for president, finishing a distant third behind Roosevelt and Hoover. This, however, was also by far his best nationwide showing; in 1944 he would receive less than one-tenth as much support.

This statistic underscores the drastic decline of socialism under Thomas's leadership, paradoxically occurring during capitalism's darkest years. A diffident political manager, he allowed his party to dissolve into bitterly opposed factions and to lose much support in New York to the antiradical new American Labor Party. Thomas's cerebral style won little mass support for his cause, although he vigorously supported labor organizing and even suffered a beating in Arkansas while helping to organize the Southern Tenant Farmers' Union. He criticized the New Deal but grudgingly admired its "socialistic" aspects. Thomas deplored Roosevelt's political opportunism but could not counter his popular rhetoric (or that of more demagogic New Deal critics such as Huey Long).

The Socialist Party dwindled even further in the late 1930s when Thomas, still a pacifist, passionately opposed U.S. war preparedness measures. Labeled an isolationist, Thomas and his party became further relegated to the political fringe. Throughout the 1930s—and for decades beyond—Norman Thomas was the genteel, articulate tribune of the doomed cause of American socialism, at a time when ideological passions overtook the political left and Roosevelt's centrism proved far more decisive.

See Also: SOCIALIST PARTY.

BIBLIOGRAPHY

Fleischman, Harry. *Norman Thomas: A Biography.* 1964.

Swanberg, W. A. *Norman Thomas: The Last Idealist.* 1976.

Thomas, Norman. *After the New Deal, What?* 1936.

Thomas, Norman. *America's Way Out: A Program For Democracy.* 1931.

Thomas, Norman, and Paul Blanshard. *What's the Matter with New York: A National Problem.* 1932.

BURTON W. PERETTI

THOMAS AMENDMENT

The Thomas Amendment, named for its sponsor, Oklahoma Democrat Elmer Thomas, was signed into law by President Franklin Delano Roosevelt on May 12, 1933, and included as a compromise amendment to the Farm Bill of 1933 (the Agricultural Adjustment Act). The amendment joined monetary inflation to complement the less familiar policy of crop reduction under the Agricultural Adjustment Act.

The omnibus amendment included all of the principal features of other inflation proposals was the brainchild of Senator Thomas, leader of the inflationary bloc in Congress. By exploiting monetary inflation, long touted as a economic remedy since the days of nineteenth-century Populism, Thomas could mobilize a clear majority by bringing inflationists (politicians who zealously sought to stimulate an economic boom by devaluing the dollar) into a powerful coalition with natural allies in the farm belt and political allies in the mining industry (namely, silver) of the West. The silver bloc would use their leverage as an "entering wedge," a tactic that eventually led to the Silver Purchase Act of 1934.

In its final form the Thomas Amendment (also called the Inflation Act) gave the president unprecedented discretionary power over monetary policy. It permitted the president to authorize the Federal Reserve to unleash the full power of capitalism on the Treasury by placing U.S. securities on the open market and allowing Federal Reserve banks to hold up to $3 billion in U.S. Treasury bills and other government bonds acquired directly from the Treasury. The president could even authorize the secretary of the Treasury to put up to $3 billion into circulation to retire government bonds. Roosevelt never used his power to increase the amount of money in circulation, nor did he ever exploit the power to sell government securities directly to Federal Reserve banks. One provision allowed the president to alter the gold value of the dollar by not more than 50 percent, thereby decreasing debt by devaluing the dollar. Roosevelt eventually used this measure to fix the value of gold at $35—$15 below the value permitted by the legislation. Other provisions empowered the president to remonetize silver, to reestablish bimetallism (the practice of using gold and silver jointly as a monetary standard), and to accept a maximum of $200 million in silver from foreign governments in payment of debts.

There has been considerable debate whether Thomas's original construction included mandatory inflationary measures that were "thoroughly amended" to permissive inflationary measures by the White House. As one specialist has shown, neither Thomas's version nor the White House version contained any language calling for mandatory inflation. It was, however, mandatory for the president to accept the inflation rider or risk congressional passage of radical monetary policy that sidestepped White House involvement altogether. The president had no choice but to surrender to pressure politics. Responding to the mounting inflationary trend, he persuaded Thomas to introduce a version of the bill in which the legislative body delegated authority over monetary policy to the executive branch, giving Roosevelt the "broad executive power," for which he had asked Congress, in his inaugural address, to combat the national crisis.

See Also: AGRICULTURAL ADJUSTMENT ACT; MONETARY POLICY.

BIBLIOGRAPHY

Brennan, John A. *Silver and the First New Deal.* 1969.

Byrnes, James F. *All in One Lifetime.* 1958.

Chandler, Lester V. *American Monetary Policy, 1928–1941.* 1971.

Everest, Allan Seymour. *Morgenthau, the New Deal and Silver: A Story of Pressure Politics.* 1950.

Moley, Raymond. *After Seven Years.* 1939.

Moley, Raymond. *The First New Deal.* 1966.

Patterson, James T. *Congressional Conservatism and the New Deal: The Growth of the Conservative Coalition in Congress, 1933–1939.* 1967.

Perkins, Van L. *Crisis in Agriculture: The Agricultural Adjustment Administration and the New Deal, 1933.* 1969.

Phillips, Ronnie J. *The Chicago Plan and New Deal Banking Reform.* 1995.

Schlesinger, Arthur M., Jr. *The Age of Roosevelt,* Vol. 2: *The Coming of the New Deal.* 1959.

Shover, John L. "Populism in the Nineteen-Thirties: The Battle for the AAA." *Agricultural History* 38 (October 1965): 17–24.

GREGORY BAGGETT

THOMPSON, DOROTHY

Dorothy Thompson (July 9, 1893-January 30, 1961) was one of the most influential female journalists of her time. Her work reached wide audiences through radio broadcasts, her column "For the Record" in the *New York Herald Tribune,* which appeared for twenty-one straight years, and her work as a bureau chief in Berlin for the *Philadelphia Public Ledger.*

After her graduation from Syracuse University in 1914, Thompson was unable to find a job in journalism. She turned her energies to the Women's State Suffrage Party in New York, conducting public relations work. In 1919, she traveled to Europe, and through her interviews of prominent Zionist leaders secured a reporter's position with the Jewish Correspondence Bureau. This began her lifelong commitment to writing stories relevant to social justice issues and her striking track record of interviewing some of the most newsworthy people of the 1920s and 1930s, including Sigmund Freud, Gustav Stresemann, Leon Trotsky, Mustafa Kemal, and Adolf Hitler.

In 1931, when Thompson was the Philadelphia Public Ledger's bureau chief in Berlin, she interviewed Hitler. She became an outspoken critic of Hitler and his policies, and in 1934, following the publication of her book, *I Saw Hitler!,* the Gestapo gave her twenty-four hours to leave Germany. Her expulsion brought her to American public attention, and she used this fame to continue to critique and warn about Hitler's regime. In 1938, she organized a nationwide campaign to raise awareness and funds for the defense of Herschel Grynszpan, the Polish youth whose assassination of a German diplomat played a role in a massive pogrom in Germany known as Kristallnacht.

Throughout the Third Reich (1933-1945), Thompson remained a vocal critic of Germany's government and consistently called attention to the problems faced by Jewish refugees fleeing Nazi persecution. In 1939, *Time* magazine named her and Eleanor Roosevelt as America's most influential women. Thompson was the inspiration for Katherine Hepburn's character, Tess Harding, in the 1942 film *Woman of the Year.*

See Also: ANTI-SEMITISM; KRISTALLNACHT.

BIBLIOGRAPHY

Kurth, Peter. *American Cassandra: The Life of Dorothy Thompson.* 1990.

Thompson, Dorothy. *I Saw Hitler!* 1932.

Thompson, Dorothy. *Refugees: Anarchy or Organization?* 1938.

LAURA J. HILTON

TNEC. *See* TEMPORARY NATIONAL ECONOMIC COMMITTEE.

TOWNSEND, FRANCIS. *See* TOWNSEND PLAN.

TOWNSEND PLAN

The Townsend Plan was a scheme of old-age pensions devised by Dr. Francis E. Townsend in an effort to alleviate the desperate economic circumstances of the elderly in America and to stimulate a general economic recovery during the Great Depression. The Townsend Plan was one of many utopian social panaceas that emerged during the early 1930s, and it played a major role in third party politics during the election of 1936. Although the plan never had a serious chance of being written into law, it did focus people's attention on the pension problem facing the nation and helped generate momentum for the passage of the Roosevelt administration's Social Security Act of 1935.

Townsend frequently recounted the story of how one evening late in 1933 as he was looking out the rear window of his home in Long Beach, California, he saw three old women picking through garbage for food. That incident compelled the 66-year-old doctor to devote the remaining years of his life to working for adequate pensions for the aged. Apocryphal or not, the story embodied the profound concern Townsend harbored for the elderly, with whom he had been working as assistant director of the city health office, where he observed the distress inflicted on old people by the economic crisis. Only twenty-eight states had any kind of pension plan in operation by the early 1930s, and all of them were woefully inadequate. Three had already gone bankrupt, and the others ranged from Montana's monthly allowance of $7.28 to Maryland's

payment of less than $30. Approximately 7.5 million Americans (6 percent of the population) were sixty-five or older, many of them destitute and on government relief.

Francis Townsend was born on January 13, 1867, and grew up in a family of seven on a farm near Fairbury, Illinois. His parents, George and Sarah Ann Townsend, were poor but deeply religious. Seeking more fertile soil to farm, they moved to Nebraska, where Francis completed his secondary schooling. After a brief, unsuccessful effort to take advantage of the southern California land boom, he attempted homesteading in Kansas, worked as an itinerant laborer in Colorado, and tried his luck as a salesman back in Kansas. In 1899, he enrolled in Omaha Medical College, graduating four years later and starting a medical practice in the Black Hills of South Dakota. When the United States entered World War I, Townsend, at the age of fifty, joined the Army medical corps. An attack of acute peritonitis after the war led him to move his family in 1919 to Long Beach in search of more healthful conditions. For the next fourteen years his practice languished, and with the onset of the Depression, most of his savings disappeared. The plight of the elderly that became his crusade was thus one with which he could deeply identify on a personal level.

After losing his political post in the Long Beach health service, Townsend conceived a plan that would provide adequate pensions for elderly people like himself. It called for a $150 monthly benefit (later raised to $200) paid by the federal government to every citizen over the age of sixty. The money to pay for the plan would be raised by a 2 percent tax on all wholesale and retail transactions. In order to receive the pension, people over sixty who held jobs would be required to quit them to open up opportunities for the unemployed. Townsend decided that recipients would also have to spend their stipends within thirty days as a means of stimulating the economy. Thus, he spoke about the velocity of money as it circulated from hand to hand and began emphasizing the revolving aspect of the plan.

After proposing his idea in the People's Forum column of the local Long Beach newspaper in Sep-

A driver in Columbus, Kansas, expresses support for the Townsend Plan prior to the 1936 election. LIBRARY OF CONGRESS, PRINTS & PHOTOGRAPHS DIVISION, FSA/OWI COLLECTION

tember 1933 and advertising for canvassers to obtain endorsements, the doctor was inundated with volunteers. Robert Earl Clements, a young real estate broker, signed on as promoter and fund-raiser, and on New Year's Day 1934 the two opened the first headquarters for their new Old Age Revolving Pensions, Ltd. In short order, the Townsend movement emerged as a political force to be reckoned with. By September, their office in Long Beach was averaging two thousand letters a day from interested people, and within a year more than a thousand

Townsend clubs were functioning. By 1936, a presidential election year, the organization claimed to have more than three and a half million members, and it obtained more than twenty million signatures on petitions calling for congressional approval of the Townsend Plan. Clements proved to be a genius at organization, utilizing everything from card parties and quilting bees to box suppers and raffles to draw people out to meetings. Revenues from Townsend license plates, tire covers, buttons, badges, banners, and other novelties stoked the organization's national treasury. A weekly newspaper kept members up to date with news of the organization's activities. The movement was more than a lobbying group; it was a social movement that welded its membership into a unit much like a church or a political ideology.

Americans, who during the previous half century had experienced the transition from a rural-agrarian economy to an urban-industrial one, found comfort in the Townsend movement's insistence that they deserved appreciation and financial reward for the contribution they had made to the national welfare. Townsend appealed to the hurt pride of people who felt they had been cast aside by a system that did not value the sacrifice and hard work they had exhibited over a lifetime of labor. His program, while expensive and radical in its reliance upon governmental expenditures to solve a social problem, was not anticapitalist but rather fundamentally conservative in its approach. Club meetings featured patriotic songs, flag saluting, religious trappings, and traditional symbols. The leader of the movement was a gaunt, white-haired, soft-spoken man in his sixties whose appearance and demeanor oozed traditional values and ways of living. Most of the people who joined the movement were old stock Americans. It was especially strong among Protestants of British origin, and middle-class people dominated its ranks. Few wealthy businessmen joined, nor were there many professional men or unskilled factory workers. At the outset, the organization was especially strong in California and the West, many of whose residents were displaced Midwesterners. Later, the movement gained strength in the Northwest and the Midwest.

The Roosevelt administration was quick to take note of the movement's growth, and work on a Social Security bill in 1934 and 1935 accelerated as a result. Final passage of the act in August of 1935 did nothing to slow the Townsend movement, however, since its followers considered the pensions contemplated under the new law to be totally inadequate. Conversely, academic economists who scrutinized the Townsend Plan's details judged its assumptions to be fatally flawed and warned that its implementation would have disastrous effects on the economy. Calculating that the plan would cost one and a half times all local, state, and federal governmental expenditures in 1932, economists deemed it a cruel economic joke on the populace. Paul Douglas estimated that obtaining the necessary revenues to finance the plan would require as much as a 75 percent increase in retail prices and that workers' real income might be cut by as much as half. Administration officials, including relief director Harry Hopkins and Secretary of Labor Frances Perkins, turned their guns on weaknesses in both the pension and tax provisions of the plan. Oklahoma Representative Phillip Ferguson called it a racket, and Senator Kenneth McKellar of Tennessee termed it a wild-eyed scheme for looting the federal treasury. In response, Dr. Townsend turned against the New Deal, likening some of its actions to Mussolini's fascism. In hearings before a House subcommittee chaired by Missouri Democrat C. Jasper Bell in the spring of 1936, Townsend was made to look foolish and walked out of the proceedings before they finished.

The stage was set for a move into third party politics by the summer, and Townsend joined with Father Charles E. Couglin, the Detroit radio priest, in the establishment of the Union Party in June 1936. Although participating at the national convention forming the party in Cleveland and in the campaign of the party's presidential nominee, Congressman William Lemke of North Dakota, Townsend remained lukewarm toward the enterprise, even calling on followers to vote for Republican candidate Alf Landon in the fourteen states where the Union Party failed to get its name on the ballot.

After the dismal showing of the Lemke candidacy in November 1936, and the dismantling of the Union Party afterwards, Townsend continued to push for more adequate pensions for the elderly. In the 1938 off-year elections, he rallied his followers against the New Deal, calling it a snare and a delusion. Two years later he worked for Republican presidential nominee Wendell Willkie. In 1948, Townsend backed the quixotic candidacy of former Vice President Henry Wallace. Townsend continued to demand more adequate old-age pensions until his death in Los Angeles on September 1, 1960.

See Also: ELDERLY, IMPACT OF THE GREAT DEPRESSION ON THE; ELECTION OF 1936; SOCIAL SECURITY ACT; UNION PARTY.

BIBLIOGRAPHY

Bennett. David H. "The Year of the Old Folks' Revolt." *American Heritage* 16 (1964): 48–51, 99–107.

Bennett, David H. *Demagogues in the Depression: American Radicals and the Union Party, 1932–1936.* 1969.

Holtzman, Abraham. *The Townsend Movement: A Political Study.* 1963.

JOHN E. MILLER

TRANSIENTS

Americans became accustomed to seeing transients during the Depression. They were cut from different molds—some young, some old, many male, some female, some with families, many without, some African American, many white from varied ethnic backgrounds. Transients were the unemployed who knocked at backdoors and asked for handouts in return for doing odd jobs, the teenagers who jumped on boxcars and rode the rails, the hollow-faced families who tried to exchange beloved dogs or cats for gasoline so they could keep on going in worn-out cars held together by baling wire. All were hoping for better lives elsewhere.

With an estimated ten million individuals jobless in 1932, it is not surprising that hundreds of thousands moved from place to place in search of work or simply struck out on their own to keep from being extra burdens on already overburdened families. Adolescents sought adventure as they hopped freight trains to get away from home, but they soon confronted the realities of begging for their next meals and being run out of towns by local officials. Although the kindhearted sometimes helped them on their way with coffee and sandwiches, transients typically received little welcome even in communities that operated public or private shelters for the homeless. In many areas law enforcement officials claimed transients violated local laws against vagrancy and refused to let them stay within city limits.

This transient twenty-year-old man, photographed on a freight car between Bakersfield and Fresno, California, in 1940, claimed to have been riding the rails for two years. NATIONAL ARCHIVES AND RECORDS ADMINISTRATION

Some transients ended up in "jungles," camps populated by the destitute on the fringes of incorporated areas. There the unemployed came in contact with hobos, tramps, and derelicts who had lived for years on the fringes of society. Hobos were long-term wanderers willing to work in exchange for food and shelter, while tramps simply sought handouts, and derelicts were alcoholics unfit to work even if they wanted to. Unlike the hobos, who preferred temporary labor and life on the road, transients wanted to settle down, but Depression conditions conspired to blur the distinctions between them and social outcasts who lived marginal existences.

Communities hard-pressed to take care of their own residents had no enthusiasm for newcomers. Indeed, the very word *transient* came to have an un-

This transient laborer was photographed in 1939 in a camp near Harlingen, Texas, where he lived with two other men. LIBRARY OF CONGRESS, PRINTS & PHOTOGRAPHS DIVISION, FSA/OWI COLLECTION

favorable connotation synonymous with *undesirable*. Animosity against transients came to a head in California, a magnet for the Okies, farmers unable to scratch livings from the drought-stricken southwestern Plains states. In 1936 the police chief of Los Angeles ordered 125 policemen to patrol the state's borders with Arizona and Oregon to deter transients from entering. Previously, in an effort to hold down welfare costs, the city had deported trainloads of Mexican-Americans, totaling nearly thirteen thousand, to Mexico (although many later returned).

In the case of the Okies, the Los Angeles police chief's efforts, which led to a suit by the American Civil Liberties Union in defense of migration, proved futile. By 1938 some 300,000 families, mainly from Oklahoma and neighboring Dust Bowl states, had entered California in three years in spite

of resentment from native residents. Many of the transients, although they dreamed of acquiring their own farmlands, become part of California's force of migrant workers, following the crops to eke out a seasonal living on a few dollars a day.

EXTENT OF THE PROBLEM

The relatively new profession of social work, which attempted to ameliorate the plight of the transients and other Depression victims, produced one of the first credible estimates of the number of transients. The National Committee on Care of Transient and Homeless (NCCTH), a private group composed of social workers, sociologists, and citizens, surveyed persons in shelters in January 1933 and counted 370,000. Since many other individuals were sleeping in alleyways and other places, the total number of homeless was estimated to be

By January 1934 a total of forty states and the District of Columbia had established a network of camps, centers, and rooming houses to take care of transients. These men dined in a transient camp, formerly a lumber camp, at Hagerman Lake, Michigan, in 1937. LIBRARY OF CONGRESS, PRINTS & PHOTOGRAPHS DIVISION, FSA/OWI COLLECTION

1,225,000, of whom about half were thought to be transients.

NCCTH pushed hard for federal help for transients, which Congress authorized in 1933 as part of a relief fund of $500,000,000 to be given out by the newly created Federal Emergency Relief Administration (FERA). States, which were required to allocate matching funds, acted quickly to submit plans for transient relief to FERA. By January 1934 a total of forty states and the District of Columbia had established a network of camps, centers, and rooming houses to take care of transients, many of whom received a cash benefit of one dollar per week. Free medical care also was provided, in part because some transients were carriers of tuberculosis and other diseases.

Federal transient relief was phased out in 1935 when the New Deal changed its approach from direct assistance to work relief. At its peak the price tag for the transient program, which aided some 300,000 persons, was $5,000,000 per month. In subsequent years transients tended to be a neglected group in terms of government aid. Some federally-funded camps for migrant workers, however, were set up.

At the instigation of Representative John H. Tolan of California, in 1940 the U.S. House Select Committee to Investigate the Interstate Migration of Destitute Citizens held a series of lengthy hearings around the country. Bertha McCall, executive director of Travelers Aid, which had absorbed the NCCTH, testified to the lack of accurate statistics on the number of actual transients, which was due in part to the difficulty of distinguishing them from hobos and bums. McCall gave a figure of about 400,000 transients known to her organization.

Many of the five hundred witnesses who came before the committee, whose hearings generated 4,245 pages of printed testimony, pleaded for federal help for transients. Yet they also argued that transients should not be set apart from the rest of the population, contending that general relief should be available throughout the nation for all needy persons, whether settled or not. First Lady Eleanor Roosevelt appeared as a witness, reporting on deplorable living conditions that she had seen while visiting migrant camps in California, Texas, and Florida. She said society benefited from some movement by persons seeking employment, but that steps should be taken so that people could live decently.

Before the committee had finished its work, the approach of World War II changed the picture. Defense plants opened their doors, drawing in the unemployed. Congress extended the term of the committee but changed its name to the House Committee Investigating National Defense Migration. A new set of issues confronted those traveling to seek employment, but the days of countless numbers of unemployed transients were over. They left in their wake many touching stories of individuals who managed to survive painful circumstances.

TEENAGE TRANSIENTS

Sociologist Thomas Minehan, who spent two years on the road studying rootless juveniles in the early 1930s, estimated that 10 percent of the adolescents he encountered were girls, usually dressed in male clothing and often traveling with a group of boys. Frequently, the women exchanged sexual favors for food, protection, and transportation in railroad boxcars. Riding the rails offered a dangerous

form of adventure, with transients facing the possibility of being injured or killed in accidents while trying to elude railroad police looking for trespassers.

Lack of sanitation coupled with exposure and a poor diet led to weakness and disease for transients, regardless of their mode of transportation. Women and African Americans faced extra perils. Their sex and their race made them particularly vulnerable to harassment.

When another sociologist, Herman Schubert, surveyed transients in 1935 in New York state, he found African Americans from fifteen to twenty-four years old likely to be on the road longer than whites. In interviews with nearly three thousand youths, about one-fourth of whom were African American, he discovered that the median time for the whites to have traveled was three months, while the comparable figure for the African Americans was six months. The difference reflected prejudice that made it more difficult for African Americans than for whites to either settle down or return to their homes.

For some, however, riding the rails and other manifestations of the transient life remained life-long memories of bittersweet excitement. Among the juvenile transients of the 1930s was Eric Sevareid, later to become a noted broadcast journalist. As quoted in T. H. Watkins's *The Hungry Years* (1999), Sevareid remembered with some fondness years later how he had joined a polyglot substratum of all races. He described Americans of varied ages who roamed restlessly, eating out of cans, sleeping in "jungles," eager to leave one place for another, content only to be on the move, lulled to momentary comfort by the clicking of the rails and the sight of telephone poles going by.

In spite of its hardships, life as a transient served as a way of growing up for a generation of American youth, who had little option except to become part of a vast army of the homeless. Forced to shift for themselves, they developed strategies of coping that testified to spiritual resiliency in the midst of desperation. Another transient adolescent told Minehan that he was eating better than he had been at home and was free of friction with his father who was out of work. The transient's life, hard as it was, offered one way of living through the Depression.

See Also: BOY AND GIRL TRAMPS OF AMERICA; HOMELESSNESS; MIGRATION; MIGRATORY WORKERS.

BIBLIOGRAPHY

Anderson, Nels. *Men on the Move.* 1940.

Crouse, Joan M. *The Homeless Transient in the Great Depression: New York State 1929–1941.* 1986.

Federal Emergency Relief Administration. Records of the Transient Division. Record Group 69, National Archives II, College Park, MD.

Frederickson, Kari. Review of *Riding the Rails* (1997), produced and directed by Michael Uys and Lexy Lovell. *Journal for MultiMedia History* 2 (1999). Available at: *http://www.albany.edu/jmmh/.*

Gregory, James N. *American Exodus: The Dust Bowl Migration and Okie Culture in California.* 1989.

Hopkins, Harry L. *Spending to Save: The Complete Story of Relief.* 1936.

McWilliams, Carey. *Ill Fares the Land: Migrants and Migratory Labor in the United States.* 1942.

Minehan, Thomas. *Boy and Girl Tramps of America.* 1934.

National Association of Travelers Aid Societies. Records. Social Welfare History Archives, University of Minnesota, Minneapolis.

National Committee on Care of Transient and Homeless. Records. Social Welfare History Archives, University of Minnesota, Minneapolis.

Reitman, Ben L. *Sister of the Road: The Autobiography of Box-Car Bertha.* 1937.

Schubert, Herman. J. P. *Twenty Thousand Transients: A One Year's Sample of Those Who Apply for Aid in a Northern City.* 1935.

U.S. House of Representatives, 76th Congress, 3rd session. Hearings before Select Committee to Investigate the Interstate Migration of Destitute Citizens. 1940–1944.

Uys, Michael, and Lexy Lovell, writers and producers. *Riding the Rails.* The American History Project/Out of the Blue Productions, Inc. 1997.

Watkins, T. H. *The Great Depression: America in the 1930s.* 1993.

Watkins, T. H. *The Hungry Years: A Narrative History of the Great Depression in America.* 1999.

MAURINE H. BEASLEY

TRANSPORTATION

A comprehensive transportation system is necessary to any developed country because it allows for the efficient movement of people and goods from one location to another. A nation's economic strength and military power are directly related to the efficiency of the nation's transportation system because it promotes domestic and international trade and provides access to valuable natural resources. Thus, when the United States slumped economically because of the Great Depression, the construction and improvement of its transportation systems were important for the country's eventual recovery. The spending and work relief programs initiated by the New Deal to help alleviate the Depression had among their targeted benefits a significant improvement in the nation's transportation system.

From 1933 to 1939, the Public Works Administration (PWA), administered by Harold Ickes, provided the money and supervision for federal agencies and local governments to construct roads, dams, airports, bridges, subways, tunnels, and harbors. The PWA also lent money to states and municipalities for similar projects. About one-third of all PWA funds were allotted for transportation projects, with the greatest amount—over $750 million—going for highways and roads. For example, the PWA lent $80 million to the Pennsylvania Railroad so it could electrify its New York to Washington route. The state of Oregon used PWA funds to build the Oregon Coastal Highway. Some of the PWA's other major projects included the Lincoln Tunnel under the Hudson River, the Skyline Drive in Virginia, and the Overseas Highway from Miami to Key West in Florida. In addition, the PWA helped to install streetlights, traffic signals, and other transportation-related equipment throughout the country.

From 1935 to 1943 the Works Progress Administration (in 1939 it was renamed the Work Projects Administration, WPA), headed by Harry Hopkins, was one of the primary New Deal programs that addressed the nation's transportation needs. According to writer Edward Robb Ellis, quoted in T. H. Watkins's *The Great Depression,* the WPA, "built

651,087 miles of highways, roads and streets; constructed, repaired or improved 124,031 bridges; erected 125,110 public buildings; created 8,192 parks; built or improved 853 airports." Some of its more notable projects were New York City's La-Guardia Airport and Chicago's Lake Shore Drive.

Transportation projects during the Great Depression provided much-needed jobs for unemployed workers across the country. In the process, New Deal construction made major contributions toward significantly improving the nation's infrastructure for a modern system of transportation. The roads, bridges, airports, and other transportation-related facilities that were built by the PWA, the WPA, and other New Deal agencies during the Depression helped prepare the country for World War II and for its role as the world's leading industrialized nation.

See Also: PUBLIC WORKS ADMINISTRATION (PWA); WORKS PROGRESS ADMINISTRATION (WPA).

BIBLIOGRAPHY

Bernstein, Irving. *A Caring Society: The New Deal, the Worker, and the Great Depression—A History of the American Worker, 1933–1941.* 1985.

Biles, Roger. *A New Deal for the American People.* 1991.

Biles, Roger. *The South and the New Deal.* 1994.

Braeman, John; Robert H. Bremner; and David Brody, eds. *The New Deal,* Vol. 2: *The State and Local Levels.* 1975.

Nash, Gerald D. *The Crucial Era: The Great Depression and World War II: 1929–1945,* 2nd edition. 1992.

Patterson, James T. *The New Deal and the States: Federalism in Transition.* 1969.

Public Works Administration Division of Information. *America Builds: The Record of PWA.* 1939.

Watkins, T. H. *The Great Depression: America in the 1930s.* 1993.

WILLIAM ARTHUR ATKINS

TUGWELL, REXFORD G.

Rexford Guy Tugwell (July 10, 1891–July 21, 1979) was a professional economist who joined Franklin D. Roosevelt's Brains Trust in 1932. Tugwell re-mained with the New Deal in the U.S. Department of Agriculture (USDA) as assistant and undersecretary, and as director of the Resettlement Administration. He left the administration in 1936 to become vice president of the American Molasses Company. Thereafter, Tugwell served as chairman of the New York City Planning Commission (1938–1941) and governor of Puerto Rico (1941–1946). He returned to academe in 1947, finishing his career at the Center for the Study of Democratic Institutions in Santa Barbara, California.

The son of Charles Tugwell, a successful businessman and banker, and Dessie Rexford, Tugwell was born in Sinclairville, New York, and grew up in Wilson, New York. He received his bachelor's degree in economics in 1915, his master's degree in 1916, and his Ph.D. in 1922 at the University of Pennsylvania. In 1914 Tugwell married Florence Arnold and they had two girls. Later, in the 1930s, he married Grace Falke, with whom he had two sons. Although he tried farming, Tugwell was too much of an academic to stay in that occupation. In the 1920s, he taught at Columbia University, where he quickly ascended the academic ladder as a professor of economics. In 1928 Tugwell made his first foray into politics when he advised Governor Alfred E. Smith during Smith's presidential campaign. In 1927, Tugwell made a trip to the Soviet Union as a member of a trade delegation, a trip that would haunt him throughout his academic and New Deal career. As a result of this trip, Tugwell became identified with radical ideas, socialist/communist solutions, and the political far left. Some reporters even referred to him as "Rex the Red."

During the 1920s, Tugwell wrote prolifically. Teaching a relatively light schedule, he devoted his energies to research and writing on a wide variety of topics including the growing problems in the American economy, planned obsolescence, the American agricultural system, and Herbert Hoover's failed attempts at economic recovery after the Great Depression began. Tugwell consistently argued that American business had to do more in dispersing America's abundance, that the U.S. economy needed to adopt a more rational approach to economic affairs through planning, and that Amer-

Rexford Tugwell (right) discusses land conditions with a farmer in the Texas Panhandle in 1936. LIBRARY OF CONGRESS, PRINTS & PHOTOGRAPHS DIVISION, FSA/OWI COLLECTION

ican agriculture needed to address the issue of overproduction through such measures as domestic allotment. Tugwell's two most important works, which crystallize his ideas in the 1920s, were *Industry's Coming of Age* (1927) and *The Industrial Discipline and the Governmental Arts* (1933). Another Columbia professor, Raymond Moley, introduced Tugwell to Franklin Roosevelt, and, thereupon, assured Tugwell's entrance into the Brains Trust.

Designed to help educate Roosevelt for the 1932 campaign, the Brains Trust, consisting of Raymond Moley, Rexford Tugwell, and Adolf Berle, worked closely with the presidential candidate, informing him of the intricacies of economic issues, updating him on the most current solutions being

offered on the Great Depression, and writing speeches for him. Although often frustrated with Roosevelt's inclination to politic, Tugwell did work with the presidential Democratic hopeful, especially in the area of agricultural relief and domestic allotment. Once Roosevelt received the Democratic nomination, Tugwell's role in the inner circle continued in a more limited fashion until Roosevelt's victory in November 1932.

During the interregnum, Tugwell worked on a number of problems, particularly the upcoming London Economic Conference. After inauguration day, Tugwell decided to stay with Roosevelt in the Department of Agriculture as assistant and later under-secretary of agriculture, helping Henry Wal-

Rexford Tugwell (standing) inspects the foundations of houses under construction at the Greenbelt project in Maryland in 1936. LIBRARY OF CONGRESS, PRINTS & PHOTOGRAPHS DIVISION, FSA/OWI COLLECTION

lace with the day-to-day administrative details. Very much devoted to the president, Tugwell also served in a number of other capacities during his New Deal tenure: coordinating USDA reorganization, conservation, relief efforts; implementing Puerto Rican sugar quotas; and serving as general apologist for the New Deal. It was, however, Tugwell's involvement in the Agricultural Adjustment Administration (AAA) that not only most interested Tugwell, but also got him into serious trouble. Not a firm supporter of AAA director George Peek, Tugwell was active in blocking Peek's marketing efforts and eventually contributed to Peek's resignation. Although Tugwell saw Peek's resignation as somewhat of a victory, it proved to be a hollow one. With the succession of Chester Davis, the AAA became more committed to domestic allotment. Davis, moreover, was not fond of anyone who dis-

agreed with him, and he acted to dismiss Jerome Frank and other so-called liberals in the AAA Legal Division who overstepped their authority in dealing with southern landlords. The famous AAA purge was a direct affront to Tugwell, who immediately offered to resign. Roosevelt refused his resignation and put Tugwell in charge of the newly-formed Resettlement Administration (RA). Although Tugwell only served one year as director of the RA, his accomplishments were extensive as he worked to resettle farmers to better lands while implementing such visionary programs as the famous "greenbelt" towns. By 1936, however, "Tugwell, Rex" or "Rex the Red," as he was not so affectionately known to his critics, became too much of a burden for Roosevelt. At the instigation of James Farley, Roosevelt accepted Tugwell's resignation.

Receiving a cold shoulder from Columbia and other academic institutions, Tugwell entered the business world as a vice-president for the American Molasses Company, owned and operated by his friend Charles Taussig. Shortly thereafter, Tugwell left the company and accepted the chairmanship of the New York City Planning Commission under Mayor Fiorello LaGuardia. By the 1939 to 1940 period, Tugwell had become so committed to the concept of planning in the American economy that he believed a "fourth power" or branch of the American government needed to be created to implement planning. Although Tugwell actually did a fine job in New York, he ran head-on into New York's Robert Moses, who eventually was able to limit Tugwell's effectiveness. Harold Ickes, the secretary of the Department of the Interior in Roosevelt's cabinet and a friend of Tugwell, intervened and offered Tugwell the opportunity to study Puerto Rican land holdings in 1940. Tugwell's study was so impressive that Ickes recommended to the president that Tugwell be appointed governor of the island. Roosevelt agreed and Tugwell served as governor from 1941 to 1946. Working closely with Luis Munoz Marin and the Populares Party, Tugwell helped sustain a political makeover in the island republic.

After 1946, Tugwell was much more in demand in academics. Initially moving from university to university, he eventually settled at the Center for the Study of Democratic Institutions in Santa Barbara. From then until his death in 1979, Tugwell wrote a remarkable number of books, articles, book reviews, and seminar papers. He focused his attention on four specific themes: the atomic bomb, Franklin D. Roosevelt, a new American constitution, and planning. Writing almost compulsively throughout his life, Tugwell longed for a future when another Franklin D. Roosevelt would appear and the United States would achieve its potential to alleviate poverty and suffering and become the land of abundance that Tugwell always envisioned. In the end, despite all the attacks made on him, Rexford G. Tugwell remained an individual who deeply believed in America's potential.

See Also: AGRICULTURAL ADJUSTMENT ADMINISTRATION (AAA); BRAIN(S) TRUST; GREENBELT TOWNS; RESETTLEMENT ADMINISTRATION (RA).

BIBLIOGRAPHY

Namorato, Michael V. *Rexford G. Tugwell: A Biography.* 1988.

Namorato, Michael V. *The Diary of Rexford G. Tugwell: The New Deal Years.* 1992.

Tugwell, Rexford. *The Brains Trust.* 1968.

Tugwell, Rexford. *A Chronicle of Jeopardy: 1945–55.* 1955.

Tugwell, Rexford. *The Light of Other Days.* 1962.

Tugwell, Rexford. *To The Lesser Heights of Morningside: A Memoir.* 1982.

Tugwell, Rexford. *Roosevelt's Revolution: The First Year, A Personal Perspective.* 1977.

MICHAEL V. NAMORATO

TULLY, GRACE

Grace Tully (August 9, 1900–June 15, 1984) served Franklin Delano Roosevelt as one of his closest personal secretaries from 1928 until his death in 1944. Throughout this period, Tully shared the workload of the president's primary secretary, Marguerite (Missy) LeHand, until LeHand suffered a stroke in 1941, and Tully was elevated to the preeminent secretarial position.

A native of New Jersey, Tully worked as a secretary for the Archdiocese of New York until the Democratic National Committee hired her to assist Eleanor Roosevelt, who was busily preparing for the 1928 presidential campaign. That same year Franklin D. Roosevelt was elected to the New York governorship, and Tully accepted an offer to work for him in Albany. By 1932 Tully had established herself as a devoted employee and an important member of the Roosevelt inner circle, but health problems prevented her from moving to Washington, D.C., and joining the rest of "the team" until early 1934.

Once she moved to Washington, Tully had virtually unfettered access to Roosevelt that few others in Depression-era Washington enjoyed. Tommy Corcoran, an influential presidential adviser, once remarked that anyone who wanted to see the president, "except Missy and Grace," had to clear it with the White House appointments secretary (Caro, p. 670). Tully's entrée to the Oval Office made her an important figure at a time when the president had been granted immense authority to dispense patronage as the result of New Deal legislation. Securing time with Roosevelt to discuss the direction of that patronage was nearly impossible, but for many Washington operatives a quick word with the president could be arranged through Tully's intervention.

In addition to her secretarial duties, Tully frequently participated in White House social events, including Roosevelt's late-afternoon cocktail parties, and she often accompanied him on trips to Hyde Park and Camp David (then called Shangri-La), where one of the outbuildings came to be called the Grace Tully Cabin. She was present in Warm Springs, Georgia, the day that Roosevelt died in April 1945, and she was one of the first people to rush into the room upon hearing of the president's collapse.

Roosevelt's death did not bring an end to Tully's time in Washington, and she went on to work for senators Lyndon Johnson and Mike Mansfield before retiring.

See Also: LEHAND, MARGUERITE (MISSY).

BIBLIOGRAPHY

Caro, Robert A. *The Path to Power, Vol. 1: The Years of Lyndon Johnson.* 1982.

Grace Tully with Franklin D. Roosevelt in 1942. FRANKLIN DELANO ROOSEVELT LIBRARY

Freidel, Frank. *Franklin D. Roosevelt: A Rendezvous with Destiny.* 1990.

Goodwin, Doris Kearns. *No Ordinary Time: Franklin and Eleanor Roosevelt, The Home Front in World War II.* 1994.

Graham, Otis L., and Meghan Robinson Wander. *Franklin D. Roosevelt: His Life and Times, An Encyclopedic View.* 1985.

CHRISTOPHER BRICK

TUSKEGEE SYPHILIS PROJECT

The Tuskegee syphilis study of "untreated syphilis in the male Negro" became the longest-running nontherapeutic and racist research study in American history. Approximately 399 African-American men with syphilis and 201 without the disease who served as controls were followed, but deliberately not treated for their illness, in several counties surrounding Tuskegee, Alabama, between 1932 and 1972. The men, however, did not know they were participating in a study being run by the United States Public Health Service (PHS). They were told they were being treated for "bad blood," a local term used to cover venereal diseases, as well as anemia and other ailments.

In 1932, syphilis was only one of many problems that plagued the black population in Tuskegee and the surrounding Macon County. "Cash money" was often hard to come by, and many families were sharecroppers who were in perpetual debt. One survivor of the Tuskegee study who lived about twenty miles outside of town recalled, for example, that during the 1930s he could not drive his car because he did not have cash to pay for licensing tags.

In the heart of Alabama's "black belt," serious malnutrition, inadequate housing, illness, and illiteracy were widespread, especially as the Depression deepened. Illnesses were borne or cured with the help of local folk healers. People occasionally sought treatment from doctors, but physician visits to rural homes were uncommon and expensive. In a 1932 survey of 612 black families, only 258 of the families had seen a physician during the year. Despite the existence of both a black-run U.S. Veteran's Administration hospital and the John A. Andrew Hospital at Tuskegee Institute, the historically black college founded by Booker T. Washington, it was difficult for people living in the country to come to town or pay for clinic visits.

The syphilis study started as part of the Rosenwald Foundation's work to improve educational and health conditions for black southerners. The foundation, in conjunction with the PHS, began a survey and treatment program on syphilis in six southern counties in 1929. The highest rates of syphilis were found in Macon County, where few people had been treated.

When the funds for the surveys and treatment program ran out, several of the PHS researchers realized that the area around Macon County would serve as a "perfect" laboratory to study untreated syphilis. In 1932 there were medicines available, but they required a long period of treatment. Medical wisdom at the time also assumed that patients who had survived to the disease's latent or tertiary stage probably could not be helped by the then known treatments. It was also thought that African Americans were more prone to cardiovascular complications from the disease and that whites were more likely to develop neurological symptoms. The researchers hoped to show whether racial differences existed.

The study of untreated syphilis began in 1932. It was only supposed to last six to twelve months. Physicians and nurses from the PHS, the local health department, and Tuskegee Institute selected and followed the men. They were given aspirin, iron pills, and tonics, and were told that they were being treated. Spinal taps were ordered to monitor the progress of their disease; the men were told these were "back shots." Autopsies were needed to examine syphilis's effect on the body more definitively. In order to obtain permission for autopsy the families were promised money for burials. In 1936, the first of what would become the pattern for twelve other reports on the study was published in a respected and widely read medical journal. The findings made clear that the lack of treatment had shortened many of the men's lives.

As the study progressed during the 1940s, penicillin became recognized as a certain cure for syphilis, although it would probably not have helped the men with advanced cases of the disease. The study continued throughout the 1960s, through the civil rights era, and even after more formal ethical canons were promulgated that would have made such a study unthinkable.

In 1972 a horrified investigator revealed the story of the Tuskegee syphilis study to a reporter. When newspapers reported the story, a huge public outcry erupted, followed by congressional hearings, a federal investigation, and a lawsuit that provided some compensation to the men and their families. No one was ever prosecuted for their role in the study. In 1997, President Bill Clinton apologized to the six remaining survivors, their families, and the entire African-American community. The Tuskegee syphilis study remains a monument to racialized assumptions about disease and to unethical behavior in research.

See Also: AFRICAN AMERICANS, IMPACT OF THE GREAT DEPRESSION ON; HEALTH AND NUTRITION; RACE AND ETHNIC RELATIONS.

BIBLIOGRAPHY

Gray, Fred D. *The Tuskegee Syphilis Study: The Real Story and Beyond.* 1998.

Johnson, Charles S. *Shadow of the Plantation.* 1934.

Jones, James H. *Bad Blood: The Tuskegee Syphilis Experiment.* 1981. Rev. edition, 1992.

Reverby, Susan M., ed. *Tuskegee's Truths: Rethinking the Tuskegee Syphilis Study.* 2000.

Vonderlehr, R. A., et al., "Untreated Syphilis in the Male Negro: A Comparative Study of Treated and Untreated Cases," *Venereal Disease Information* 17 (1936): 260–65.

Susan M. Reverby

TVA. *See* TENNESSEE VALLEY AUTHORITY.

UAW. *See* UNITED AUTOMOBILE WORKERS.

UFL. *See* UNITED FARMERS' LEAGUE.

UMWA. *See* UNITED MINE WORKERS OF AMERICA.

UNEMPLOYED COUNCILS

Unemployed Councils were grassroots organizations of unemployed workers created in the early 1930s to protest mass unemployment and inadequate relief. The first councils were established by the American Communist Party's Trade Union Unity League, an organization created in the 1920s to promote radical unionism. In March 1930 the Trade Union Unity League organized highly successful mass demonstrations to protest unemployment and demand government relief. In July of that year a national conference sponsored by the Trade Union Unity League declared the formation of the "unemployed councils of the USA."

From 1930 to 1935 the councils organized numerous conferences, demonstrations, and national "hunger marches." These actions often combined demands for aid ("work for wages") with calls for an end to the capitalist system. In late 1931 the councils were separated from the Trade Union Unity League and placed under the direction of Herbert Benjamin, a veteran Communist Party functionary.

The frequent national protests and conventions sponsored by the councils during these years were small, but they spawned local organizations that had an important impact on relief policy. By mid 1931 thousands of Americans were receiving aid from large relief organizations with local offices in urban neighborhoods. Relief aid was inadequate, and workers were often subjected to degrading investigations by social workers. Taking advantage of these conditions, local unemployed councils helped clients apply for aid, demonstrated at relief offices, and sent delegations to demand more adequate relief from local officials.

The unemployed councils' most successful tactics were eviction protests. These were a response to the fact that local relief agencies were too financially strapped to provide rent until a recipient was faced with eviction. Relief recipients were often awakened by landlords, accompanied by police, moving their furniture out of apartments when the rent had not been paid. Local councils of the unemployed would mobilize neighbors to forcibly stop

A group of unemployed miners from the Scott's Run area of West Virginia attend a meeting of the local unemployed council in 1937. NATIONAL ARCHIVES AND RECORDS ADMINISTRATION

the evictions and even move furniture back into the apartments when the police had left the scene. Violent rent protests generated a good deal of publicity (and support) for the councils.

The success of the councils in 1931 attracted more moderate socialists less inclined to demand that recruits follow the "party line." A Chicago-based Workers Committee on Unemployment, led by the socialist Karl Borders, recruited twice as many local workers as the Communist leagues by the end of 1932. In Seattle, the Unemployed Citizens League played an important role in local relief administration. Radicals led by the independent socialist A. J. Muste organized Leagues of the Unemployed in the cities and small towns of Ohio, Pennsylvania, and West Virginia.

The advent of the New Deal in 1933 transformed the grassroots movement of the unemployed. Local relief agencies were more willing to negotiate with organizations of the unemployed, and Socialist and Communist organizations focused more of their attention on national campaigns for unemployment insurance. The work relief programs of the New Deal stimulated new protests and organization efforts that resembled the growing union movement.

In early 1935 the various Socialist organizations and the Communist-dominated councils united to create the Workers Alliance of America. Most councils of the unemployed were disbanded and absorbed by the alliance. This development was, in part, consistent with the new Communist Party line, which stressed a "united front" (or Popular

Front) of all leftists against the "fascist threat." This development also reflected the fact that the organized unemployed, now focusing on Works Progress Administration projects, had become an influential interest group in the New Deal "broker state."

See Also: COMMUNIST PARTY; HUNGER MARCHES.

BIBLIOGRAPHY

Klehr, Harvey. *The Heyday of American Communism: The Depression Decade.* 1984.

Leab, Daniel. "United We Eat: The Creation and Organization of the Unemployed Councils in 1930." *Labor History* 8 (1967): 300–315.

Nelson, Steve; James Burrett; and Rob Ruck. *Steve Nelson: American Radical.* 1981.

Piven, Frances Fox, and Richard A. Cloward. *Poor People's Movements: Why The Succeed and How they Fail.* 1977.

Rosenzweig, Roy. "Radicals and the Jobless: The Musteites and the Unemployed Leagues, 1932–1936." *Labor History* 16 (1975): 52–77.

Seymour, Helen. "The Organized Unemployed." Ph.D. diss., University of Chicago, 1937.

JEFF SINGLETON

UNEMPLOYMENT, LEVELS OF

The Great Depression was an economic catastrophe without comparison in American history. Within a few years, between 1929 and 1933, an economy that had appeared functional and highly dynamic collapsed, throwing millions out of work. Although wage cuts, underemployment, and economic instability were common experiences, unemployment was the paradigmatic crisis of the Depression, with effects that spread through the entire economy. The fact that many of the people who lost their jobs and were unable to get new ones were, by and large, highly productive people in the middle of their working lives, more often than not the sole breadwinner for a family, created an acute sense of desperation in the country at large.

Unemployment levels reached their height in 1933, when one-quarter of the nation's work force—thirteen million people—was unemployed. To give a sense of the rapidity of the change, unemployment rates had been remarkably low throughout the 1920s, falling to 1.6 percent in 1926 and up to only 3.2 percent in 1929. For unemployment to climb so rapidly to 25 percent in only a few years was an unprecedented and shocking experience. Even more dramatic was the fact that high levels of unemployment persisted throughout the decade, never falling below 14.3 percent (1937). The high rates of unemployment also reduced wages for workers who were lucky enough to keep their jobs, and many workers worked on part-time, reduced schedules. No region of the country was immune to the crisis. The coal fields of Kentucky and West Virginia, the rural towns of the South, the cities of Los Angeles, San Francisco, New York, and Philadelphia—all were affected by the disappearance of work.

The expansion of the 1920s had hidden a deep layer of poverty in the United States, and many people worked in substandard jobs for substandard wages throughout the boom. Studies done in the early 1940s showed that among people on unemployment relief in the late 1930s, about 14 percent had actually lost their jobs at their usual occupation prior to the crash of 1929. Of the men on relief in nine cities, including Detroit, 20 percent had been unemployed prior to the Depression. In addition, much of the deepest poverty in the United States was not a product of unemployment but of the depression in farming areas, for example among sharecroppers and tenant farmers in the Deep South. Nonetheless, there is no question that the conditions of people who were poor during the boom only worsened during the 1930s, and unemployment was a major part of the crisis.

Unemployment did not affect every demographic group equally. It fell most cruelly on young, old, uneducated, unskilled, and rural workers, especially blacks, Mexican-Americans, and immigrants. Workers under twenty and over sixty were more than twice as likely to be out of work. One-fifth of the people on unemployment rolls was black, twice their proportion in the overall popula-

Unemployed men wait in line outside the State Employment Service office in Memphis, Tennessee, in June 1938. LIBRARY OF CONGRESS, PRINTS & PHOTOGRAPHS DIVISION, FSA/OWI COLLECTION

tion. Thousands of immigrants, finding that the United States was no longer paved with bricks of gold, returned to their home countries, and in 1931, 100,000 Americans set off to find work in the Soviet Union. (Not all immigrants were eager to leave the United States; about 400,000 Mexican immigrants were deported to their home country over the decade.)

But in some ways what is most striking about the Depression is that the people affected by it were not only the marginal workers, or workers who labored under the stresses of racism and sexism in good economic times and who were usually the last hired and first fired. Instead, the "typical" unem-ployed worker, according to studies of the day, was a white male in his late thirties, the head of a family and the sole breadwinner, who had never completed elementary school and typically worked as an unskilled laborer in the manufacturing or mechanical industries. He was out of a job for an average of two years. Heavy industry was hit especially hard throughout the Depression, with such companies as Ford laying off two-thirds of their workers by 1933 and General Electric and Westinghouse each laying off more than half. The Depression had an acute impact upon people in the mainstream of the labor market, men and women who had likely never expected or anticipated that their adult lives would be marked by such a crisis.

Unemployed single women hold a job-demand parade in New York City in 1933. LIBRARY OF CONGRESS, PRINTS & PHOTOGRAPHS DIVISION, FSA/OWI COLLECTION

For working women, who were concentrated in the service sector, the Depression, though traumatic, was different than for men. Women were more likely to lose their jobs early in the Depression, but they were also more likely to find employment again later in the decade because they benefited from the long-term trend towards greater employment in services over the course of the twentieth century. In many families, women became the primary breadwinners, a development that transformed relationships within the home.

Much of the social policy of the New Deal was aimed at alleviating the crisis of unemployment in the Great Depression. The Federal Emergency Relief Administration provided direct cash relief to families in dire need. The Civil Works Administration was the first major work-relief program, along with the Civilian Conservation Corps. By February 1934 these programs employed 22.2 percent of the population, a high for any point in American history. Beginning in 1935, the Roosevelt administration cut back on general relief in favor of work-relief programs, especially the Works Progress Administration. In some ways, this reflected the fact that the crisis of the Depression was not simply one of unemployment and poverty for individuals. It was one of a lost decade of social investment and productive capacity, and while federal investments in public works could help to make up for this somewhat, to a great extent the decade was simply lost forever.

Men wait in line to apply for unemployment compensation at the State Employment Service office in San Francisco in this 1938 photograph by Dorothea Lange. If eligible, these men could receive six to fifteen dollars per week for up to sixteen weeks. LIBRARY OF CONGRESS, PRINTS & PHOTOGRAPHS DIVISION, FSA/OWI COLLECTION

See Also: CIVILIAN CONSERVATION CORPS (CCC); CIVIL WORKS ADMINISTRATION (CWA); UNEMPLOYMENT INSURANCE.

BIBLIOGRAPHY

Bernstein, Michael A. *The Great Depression: Delayed Recovery and Economic Change in America, 1929–1939.* 1987.

Bordo, Michael D.; Claudia Goldin; and Eugene N. White. *The Defining Moment: The Great Depression and the American Economy in the Twentieth Century.* 1998.

Chandler, Lester V. *America's Greatest Depression: 1929–1941.* 1970.

Kennedy, David. *Freedom From Fear: The American People in Depression and War, 1929–1945.* 1999.

Leuchtenburg, William E. *Franklin D. Roosevelt and the New Deal, 1932–1940.* 1963.

Lowitt, Richard, and Maurine Beasley, eds. *One-Third of a Nation: Lorena Hickok Reports on the Great Depression.* 1981.

Patterson, James T. *America's Struggle Against Poverty, 1900–1994.* 1994.

KIM PHILLIPS-FEIN

UNEMPLOYMENT INSURANCE

The Social Security Act of 1935, commonly associated with the nation's old-age pension system, also created a national system of unemployment compensation—a guarantee of income for temporarily unemployed workers. At the time of the act's passage, this provision seemed more of a historic milestone than did the old-age insurance provision, which is now synonymous with the term *Social Security.*

To most Americans on the eve of the Depression, the idea of unemployment insurance was an unwelcome European import—a "dole" that undermined the work ethic and the fiscal stability of the nation. This view reflected the fact that policies to assist unemployed workers were a European invention. In the early decades of the twentieth century a number of countries in continental Europe began to augment union-sponsored out-of-work plans with tax funds. But when the Depression struck, it was England's pioneering program that was the most closely associated with the term *unemployment insurance.*

The British unemployment system, passed in 1911, created a large central fund financed initially by "contributions" from employees and employers, although the government also subsidized the program with general tax revenues. Thus the policy looked more like "insurance" than traditional relief, a fact that was constantly emphasized by its proponents. Between 1911 and 1930, ten other countries in Europe adopted compulsory unemployment insurance programs.

The British precedent generated much enthusiasm among American reformers. A key center of support for unemployment insurance was the University of Wisconsin in Madison, where economics professor John R. Commons developed a uniquely "American" version of unemployment insurance. Commons's "Wisconsin plan" focused more on preventing unemployment than on creating funds to assist the jobless. Commons proposed an unemployment tax on employers, with the rates adjusted for "experience" and the funds channeled into individual "reserves." Employers with healthy employment records would pay less than those who tend-

Unemployed miners, photographed by Arthur Rothstein in 1939, pass the day loitering near a bank in Herrin, Illinois.
LIBRARY OF CONGRESS, PRINTS & PHOTOGRAPHS DIVISION, FSA/OWI COLLECTION

ed constantly to lay off and then rehire workers at various points in the business cycle. The goal was to encourage stable employment and avoid what were perceived as European-style doles from large central funds.

Commons's plan was, in part, a response to the strong opposition in the United States to European-style social insurance in the 1920s. The British system, which experienced a constant financing crisis throughout the 1920s, seemed to prove that government-mandated insurance proposals would quickly evolve into doles. Although numerous commissions were organized to study the problem, no state had established unemployment insurance prior to the 1930s.

The Great Depression turned the tide in favor of unemployment insurance. Insurance plans organized by private enterprises collapsed, and local private charity and public relief were inadequate substitutes for a national unemployment policy. The federal government was soon forced to take up the unemployment relief burden. By the time Franklin D. Roosevelt was inaugurated, Washington was financing the bulk of aid to the unemployed through local welfare agencies. There now seemed to exist a national "dole" more insidious than any European import.

Roosevelt voiced his support for state-level unemployment insurance in 1931, and the policy was endorsed by the Democratic platform for the 1932 presidential elections. In the early months of the New Deal several proposals for unemployment insurance surfaced, but none received sustained congressional attention. Then, in early 1934, Senator Robert F. Wagner and Representative David J. Lewis of Maryland introduced a bill that would profoundly shape the Social Security Act of 1935.

The Wagner-Lewis bill proposed a policy that became known as a *tax-offset plan*. A federal tax of 5 percent on employers' payrolls would be levied to finance benefits for the unemployed. If states passed their own unemployment insurance laws, employers would receive a credit against the federal tax. In short, the federal tax was a mechanism to encourage state-operated unemployment insurance systems. This formula was introduced, in part, out of fear that the Supreme Court would find a strictly federal program unconstitutional.

Roosevelt, however, disliked certain aspects of the Wagner-Lewis plan. He believed that employees, as well as employers, should pay into this "insurance" system. Furthermore, the New Deal was considering other related social reforms, such as an old-age pension plan and a public employment policy to replace relief. Thus, in June 1934 Roosevelt proposed a broad Committee on Economic Security to study the "great task of furthering the security of the citizen and his family though social insurance."

Although the Committee on Economic Security was designed, in part, to resolve conflicts over un-

employment insurance, it temporarily intensified them. The Depression had increased support for reform but also generated sharp divisions among reformers themselves. While many supported the Wisconsin plan, which focused on individual employer reserves, others believed that this approach would provide inadequate benefits. They supported what became known as the "Ohio plan," which advocated state-wide "pooled funds." Still other members of the Committee on Economic Security advocated a national system operated by the federal government.

The debates over the unemployment provisions of the social security legislation dominated the committee's work in late 1934. In the end, these conflicts were resolved by adopting a version of the Wagner-Lewis tax-offset approach. The Committee on Economic Security proposed a federal tax (3 percent of payroll by 1938) to be reduced by up to 90 percent if a state system was established. The proposal mandated that one-third of the tax would finance a state "pooled" fund (Ohio plan), but also that federal credits would be given to state plans that created employer reserves based on experience (Wisconsin plan).

National unemployment insurance became federal law with the passage of the Social Security Act in 1935. In the final legislation, Congress stuck to the basic tax-offset formula, but modified the Committee on Economic Security proposal on significant points. For example, the requirement that one percent of payroll be earmarked for "pooled funds" was eliminated, a defeat for the proponents of the Ohio plan. Congress also weakened the ability of federal officials to influence procedures for the selection of personnel. Finally, the federal law excluded employers of agricultural workers from the tax.

Over the years, the system has been expanded to include workers not originally covered. The "American plan" of individual reserves, championed by the Wisconsin reformers, proved impractical. All states adopted the approach of creating pooled funds along with an "experience rating" of employer contributions, in which employers with good employment records were rewarded with lower payments into the system.

Numerous policy experts have criticized the state-level unemployment compensation system as inefficient, but such critiques have not generated significant political debate. Ironically, unemployment insurance, one of the most controversial policy issues in the years that preceded the Social Security Act, has generally avoided the public controversies that have marked other provisions of the 1935 law.

See Also: SOCIAL SECURITY ACT; UNEMPLOYMENT, LEVELS OF.

BIBLIOGRAPHY

Altmeyer, Arthur J. *The Formative Years of Social Security.* 1966.

Berkowitz, Edward D. *America's Welfare State: From Roosevelt to Reagan.* 1991.

Haber, William, and Murray, Merrill G. *Unemployment Insurance in the American Economy.* 1966.

Lubove, Roy. *The Struggle For Social Security, 1900–1935.* 1968.

Nelson, Daniel. *Unemployment Insurance: The American Experience, 1915–1935.* 1969.

JEFF SINGLETON

UNION PARTY

The Union Party was an incongruous and short-lived alliance of left-leaning opponents of the Roosevelt administration whose presidential candidate, Congressman William Lemke of North Dakota, received less than 2 percent of the vote in the 1936 election, leading to the swift demise of the party. Its futility in the wake of President Franklin D. Roosevelt's huge landslide victory that year demonstrated the continuing popularity of the president after one term in office and underscored the weakness of the leaders and organizations that had voiced criticisms of him and his administration's policies.

Lemke, a graduate of Yale law school and no country hick, nevertheless projected something of a rough image as an outspoken champion of agrarian dissidents through his advocacy of farm mortgage relief, better lending conditions for farmers, and currency inflation. Disappointed with the president's failure to back him firmly on these issues, he readily accepted the opportunity to make a presidential run on a third party ticket when it was offered to him in June 1936. The prime mover in the establishment of the Union Party was Father Charles E. Coughlin, the Detroit radio priest whose National Union for Social Justice (NUSJ), established soon after the 1934 election, focused its attention on money and banking issues. In addition, a shaky alliance was formed with followers of Shreveport minister Gerald L. K. Smith, who had inherited some of Senator Huey Long's following after the latter fell victim to an assassin's bullet in September 1935, and Dr. Francis E. Townsend, an advocate of old-age pensions. Coughlin's support was concentrated among Irish and German Catholic workers in urban areas of the Northeast and Midwest, Smith's greatest strength was in the deep South and southern Midwest, and Townsend's following—probably the largest of the three—was heaviest initially in the far West.

The national convention that officially founded the Union Party in Cleveland in mid-July was anything but the "love feast" it was billed as. Coughlin, Smith, and Townsend were more interested in promoting the interests of themselves and their own organizations than in advancing the candidacies of Lemke and his running mate, Thomas O'Brien, a Boston Irish Catholic lawyer and Harvard law school graduate. The new party's platform endorsed neither the Townsend old-age pension plan nor Long's proposals for sharing the wealth, and half of the principles of Coughlin's NUSJ were omitted too. It general, the Union Party was a strange combination of progressive and conservative ideas.

Lemke hoped to capture 6 percent of the popular vote and enough electoral votes to throw the election into the House of Representatives. He was the first presidential candidate to travel extensively by plane, but he could not overcome the internal divisions and bickering within the hastily-formed party and failed to attract much press coverage for his campaign. In November, the party mustered only 892,000 votes, registering its strongest showing in Lemke's home state, where it captured 13 percent of the vote, and doing no better than 7 percent in any other states. After North Dakota, the Union Party received its greatest support in Massachusetts, Rhode Island, Pennsylvania, Ohio, Michigan, Illinois, Wisconsin, Minnesota, and Oregon.

See Also: COUGHLIN, CHARLES; ELECTION OF 1936; SMITH, GERALD L. K.; TOWNSEND PLAN.

BIBLIOGRAPHY

Bennett, David H. *Demagogues in the Depression: American Radicals and the Union Party, 1932–1936.* 1969.

Brinkley, Alan. *Voices of Protest: Huey Long, Father Coughlin, and the Great Depression.* 1982.

Leuchtenburg, William E. "Election of 1936" In *History of American Presidential Elections, 1789–1968,* Vol. 3, edited by Arthur M. Schlesinger, Jr. 1971.

JOHN E. MILLER

UNITED AUTOMOBILE WORKERS (UAW)

The United Automobile Workers of America (UAW) was the largest and most politically important trade union that emerged out of the labor insurgency of the 1930s. Between the spring of 1933 and the summer of 1935 an episodic series of plant specific strikes demonstrated that automobile workers sought some form of collective organization. Under sponsorship of the American Federation of Labor, the UAW held its first convention in 1935. But the union's real founding took place the next year when it elected its own officers and linked together key local unions at Studebaker and Bendix in South Bend, Toledo Auto-Lite, White Motor in Cleveland, Chrysler in Detroit, and a skilled-trades group centered in the same city. The UAW was an industrial union, seeking to represent all workers in a single factory or firm. It therefore affiliated with the new Committee for Industrial Organization (CIO).

After a dramatic, six-week sit-down strike that shut down the heart of General Motors production in Flint, Michigan, the UAW won union recognition at GM, then the nation's largest corporation. This February 1937 victory paved the way for U.S. Steel's equally important recognition of the CIO's Steel Workers Organizing Committee in March. In addition, the GM victory inaugurated a wave of strikes in Detroit and other Midwestern cities. Autoworkers occupied Chrysler's huge production complex at Dodge Main and briefly shut down scores of auto industry supplier plants in March and April 1937. When Detroit police began to arrest pickets and sit-downers, the UAW stanched the tactic by putting more than 100,000 workers in Cadillac Square. But the sharp recession that began in the fall of 1937 put an end to this initial burst of shop-floor militancy. It would therefore take almost four difficult years to organize the Ford Motor Company, an intransigent union foe. By 1943 the UAW had organized more than a million workers in the auto, aircraft, and agricultural equipment industries. It would remain the nation's largest union for the next two decades.

The UAW was a uniquely democratic and militant union for three reasons. First, under conditions of mass production, supervisors and unionists fought bitterly and continuously over the pace of production, the distribution of work, and the extent to which seniority would govern job security. An alert, aggressive cadre of shop stewards and committeemen enforced the contract and contested managerial authority, especially at companies like Studebaker, Packard, Briggs, Chrysler, and Ford, after it was finally organized in 1941. Second, the UAW enrolled hundreds of thousands of Poles, Hungarians, Slavs, Italians, African Americans, and white Appalachian migrants for whom unionism represented a doorway to an engaged sense of American citizenship. At Ford's gigantic River Rouge complex, for example, the foundry building became a cockpit of racial militancy for thousands of black workers and the incubator for a generation of Michigan civil rights leaders. Finally, the founders and officers of the UAW were a notably factional and ideological cohort, among which Socialists, Communists, Catholic corporatists, and Roosevelt liberals fought for power and office.

Homer Martin, who served as union president from 1936 until 1939, was a former Protestant minister whose maladroit leadership nearly wrecked the union after the 1937–1938 recession gave man-

UAW officials (left to right) Walter Reuther, R. J. Thomas, Richard Frankensteen, and George Addes in Detroit, Michigan, in 1942. LIBRARY OF CONGRESS, PRINTS & PHOTOGRAPHS DIVISION, FSA/OWI COLLECTION

agers the upper hand. Although once a socialist, Martin mistrusted shop militancy and the urban, ethnic radicals who now formed the union cadre. He was opposed by a fractious coalition that briefly united a "right-wing" Socialist-Catholic grouping led by Walter Reuther with a Communist-backed caucus that looked to Secretary-Treasurer George Addes and Vice-President Richard Frankensteen for leadership. Martin was eliminated in early 1939, but to avoid another factional bloodbath, CIO officials imposed Chrysler unionist R. J. Thomas as the new UAW president. He straddled a complex set of internal union rivalries for six tumultuous years until Reuther won the UAW presidency in 1946 and his anti-Communist caucus, which nevertheless embodied the radicalism of many shop militants

and progressive unionists, took full control of the UAW the next year. Reuther served as president until 1970, when he died in an airplane crash.

During the late 1930s and 1940s the UAW established the template that defined much of modern U.S. unionism. In bargaining with the big three auto corporations, the union raised and equalized wages between plants, regions, and occupations. It established a grievance arbitration system that limited the foreman's right to hire, fire, and discipline, and it won for its members a wide array of health and pension "fringe benefits" when it became clear that the unions and their liberal allies could not expand the U.S. welfare state. The real income of automobile workers more than doubled between 1937 and 1973.

Auto workers guard window entrances in Fisher body plant number three during a six-week sit-down strike that shut down the heart of General Motors production in Flint, Michigan, in January and February 1937. LIBRARY OF CONGRESS, PRINTS & PHOTOGRAPHS DIVISION, FSA/OWI COLLECTION

Politically, the UAW was a liberal presence in national Democratic politics and in those states, such as Michigan, Missouri, Ohio, Illinois, New York, Iowa, California, and Indiana, where it had a large membership. In 1937 the UAW sought to put a labor slate in Detroit's city hall, and until 1948 many in the UAW leadership had supported formation of a labor-based third party. But after Harry Truman's unexpected reelection, the UAW sought a liberal "realignment" of the Democrats. The union pushed for aggressive Keynesian fiscal policies to lower unemployment, it fought for an expanded welfare state, and favored détente with the Soviets.

See Also: AMERICAN FEDERATION OF LABOR (AFL); COLLECTIVE BARGAINING; CONGRESS OF INDUSTRIAL ORGANIZATIONS (CIO); ORGANIZED LABOR; REUTHER, WALTER; SIT-DOWN STRIKES; STRIKES.

BIBLIOGRAPHY

Babson, Steve. *Building the Union: Skilled Workers and Anglo-Gaelic Immigrants in the Rise of the UAW.* 1991.

Halpern, Martin. *UAW Politics in the Cold War Era.* 1988.

Jefferys, Steve. *Management and Managed: Fifty Years of Crisis at Chrysler.* 1986.

Keeran, Roger. *The Communist Party and the Auto Workers Unions.* 1980.

Lichtenstein, Nelson. *The Most Dangerous Man in Detroit: Walter Reuther and the Fate of American Labor.* 1995.

NELSON LICHTENSTEIN

UNITED FARMERS' LEAGUE (UFL)

The United Farmers' League (UFL) was a radical farmers' group that first sprang up in the Dakotas during the 1920s. It was one of several such groups, some of which came to eclipse the UFL in history.

The UFL was the brainchild of a Norway native named Alfred Knuston. Born in 1880, Knuston entered the United States at age nineteen. He was a carpenter by trade and a radical by political orientation. By 1915, he was affiliated with the Non-Partisan League, an agrarian radical group. A wave of anti-left sentiments during the 1920s basically destroyed the League, but a similar group called the Farm Labor Party emerged from its ashes during the early to mid 1920s. The name change appears to indicate that Knuston was attempting to link agrarian and industrial interests. Such a linkage and its viability or lack thereof has always been something of a contentious point in radical political theory. Indeed, the attempt to make such a link was the goal of a Soviet program known as the Red Peasant International.

Knuston reformed the Farm Labor Party into the United Farmers' Educational League(UFEL), which was established in Bismarck, North Dakota, in 1925. The organization began publishing a periodical, *United Farmer,* in March 1926. In 1929, the UFEL became the UFL. The UFL/UFEL was radical, but not explicitly Communist. For example, as the UFEL, the organization praised the Red Peasant International, but did not formally ally itself with it.

In a handful of places, the UFL served as an alternative to the radical and better known Farm Holiday Association. Members of the UFL engaged in activities similar to those of the Farm Holiday Association. They interfered in foreclosure auctions, for example, either through outright riots or the use of "penny auctions," wherein members of the League or friends of the farmer would crowd an auction and bid only a pittance. Sometimes, the mere threat or possibility of UFL action was known to forestall foreclosure and force the bank to renegotiate with the farmer. That the UFL and the organizations that spawned it could have achieved even the modest political and economic successes that they did in relatively conservative territory is a testimony to

how bad the situation was, and to the political skills of Knutson and the UFL membership.

The UFL supported Franklin Roosevelt in the 1932 presidential election. Ironically, Roosevelt's activities, particularly the enactment of massive public works projects and the Agricultural Adjustment Act (AAA), made the UFL irrelevant, and first its influence and then the organization itself slowly faded out of existence. In the end, farmers mainly wanted a better deal than they had been getting. They were not radicals at heart; radicalism was merely a means to an end. By 1938, the Dakotas had so returned to their conservative ways that they were ready to elect Republicans again.

See Also: AGRICULTURE; FARMERS' HOLIDAY ASSOCIATION (FHA).

BIBLIOGRAPHY

Choate, Jean. "Debt, Drought, and Depression: South Dakota in the 1930s." *Journal of the West* 31 (October 1992): 33–45.

Dyson, Lowell K. "The Red Peasant International in America." *Journal of American History* 58 (1972): 958–973.

Matthews, Allan. "Agrarian Radicals: The UFL of South Dakota." *South Dakota History* 3 (1973): 408–421.

O'Connell, Thomas Gerald. *Toward the Cooperative Commonwealth: An Introductory History of the Farmer-Labor Movement in Minnesota (1917–1948).* Ph.D. diss., Union Graduate School (Union Institute), 1979.

Remele, Larry. "The North Dakota Farmers Union and the Non-Partisan League: Breakdown of a Coalition." *North Dakota Quarterly* 46 (1978): 40–50.

Shover, John L. "The Communist Party and the Midwest Farm Crisis of 1933." *Journal of American History* 51 (1964): 248–266.

STEVEN KOCZAK

UNITED MINE WORKERS OF AMERICA (UMWA)

Once the largest union in both the nation and the American Federation of Labor (AFL), the United Mine Workers of America (UMWA) fell on hard times during the 1920s and in the early years of the

Great Depression. Claiming nearly 500,000 members in 1920, the union consisted of barely 100,000 dues-paying members by 1929 and even fewer by 1932, most of whom were concentrated in the last remaining unionized field, southern Illinois, itself wracked by internal union conflict. Elsewhere in Pennsylvania, Ohio, Indiana, and the West, coal operators broke the union. In southern Appalachian coal fields the UMWA had rarely enjoyed success. All this changed with the election of Franklin D. Roosevelt in 1932 and the coming of the New Deal. Almost overnight the coal miners seemed to organize themselves, as one union organizer reported from West Virginia. In every coal field miners seemed to believe that their "president" wanted them to unionize; whether they took that president to be Roosevelt or John L. Lewis, their union leader, remained unclear.

By mid-summer 1933 the nation's coal fields had been largely re-unionized, with even the antilabor bastions in the South crumbling before the UMWA offensive. Coal operators and UMWA officials were among the first group to develop an approved industrial code under the New Deal National Recovery Administration (NRA). Employers saw the UMWA as a means to limit destructive competition in the market for coal by equalizing wages and operating costs, a goal consonant with the aims of the early New Deal. In the case of coal, then, public officials, employers, and union leaders all read from the same text. Once again the UMWA, as it had been before and during World War I, became a power in the labor movement and the land, and its president, John L. Lewis, the most prominent and powerful of labor leaders.

The success of his union, one that he ran almost as a tyrant, and the pro-labor policies of many in the Roosevelt administration, led Lewis to grow even more ambitious. Not satisfied with having won a union shop in all the coal mines, save those owned and operated by the steel industry (the so-called captive mines), Lewis sought to expand the power of the labor movement by organizing workers in the non-union mass-production industries. When his fellow labor barons in the AFL refused to follow Lewis's lead, he joined with several other union leaders in 1935 to form the Committee for Industrial Organization (CIO). Using the ample financial resources of the UMWA, Lewis hired staff for the new committee, as well as organizers to recruit among workers in the automobile, rubber, steel, and other mass-production industries. For nearly six years after its founding in 1935 through its incarnation as the independent Congress of Industrial Organizations in 1938, the CIO survived largely on donations of cash from the UMWA. The UMWA also provided the bulk of the funds labor generated through Labor's Non-Partisan League, which Lewis established to back Roosevelt's bid for reelection in 1936. Hence, it would be no exaggeration to suggest that the UMWA deserved credit for the unionization of the mass-production industries in the 1930s; without its resources and its president, there would have been no CIO, no CIO alliance with Roosevelt, and likely no union victories over General Motors and U.S. Steel in 1937.

The UMWA did more than benefit other unions and their members during the 1930s. It also had enormous success in improving the material circumstances of its own members. Not only did the union organize nearly all the nation's employed coal miners; by the end of the 1930s it had also eliminated the wage differential between northern and southern mines and between white workers and black workers in the South. Few other institutions did as much to raise the standards of southern workers, black and white. Along with higher and more equal wages came the union shop and seniority principles that combined to generate greater job security for miners. On the eve of World War II—indeed on December 6, 1941—the UMWA won the union shop for miners in the captive coal mines, making the industry the most thoroughly unionized in the nation.

If, at first, the coal miners had unionized themselves, they nevertheless remained deferential and obedient to a leadership that ran the union in autocratic fashion. As president of the union, Lewis brooked neither criticism nor opposition. Critics and opponents he ridiculed or repressed. Not even Roosevelt could escape Lewis's wrath in 1940 when the labor leader endorsed Wendell Willkie, the Republican candidate for president, instead of the Democrat who had refused to defer sufficiently to

Lewis. Yet, however much UMWA members disagreed with their leader's choice in 1940, they continued to shower Lewis with respect, plaudits, and exceptional loyalty. For a time, at least from 1941 to 1950, such loyalty paid off in higher wages, a generous retirement program, and an excellent union-built, company-financed health and welfare system. Thereafter, however, the UMWA experienced a cycle of stagnation and rapid decline reminiscent of the 1920s and the early Great Depression years.

See Also: AMERICAN FEDERATION OF LABOR (AFL); COLLECTIVE BARGAINING; CONGRESS OF INDUSTRIAL ORGANIZATIONS (CIO); ORGANIZED LABOR; STRIKES.

BIBLIOGRAPHY

Bernstein, Irving. *Turbulent Years: A History of the American Worker, 1933–1941.* 1969.

Dubofsky, Melvyn, and Warren Van Tine. *John L. Lewis: A Biography.* 1977.

Fox, Maier B. *United We Stand: The United Mine Workers of America.* 1990.

Galenson, Walter. *The CIO Challenge to the AFL, A History of the American Labor Movement, 1935–1941.* 1960.

Hevener, John W. *Which Side Are You On? The Harlan County Coal Miners, 1931–39.* 1978.

Laslett, John H. M., ed. *The United Mine Workers of America: A Model of Industrial Solidarity.* 1996.

Taylor, Paul F. *Bloody Harlan: The United Mine Workers of America in Harlan County, Kentucky, 1931–1941.* 1989.

Zieger, Robert. *John L. Lewis: Labor Leader.* 1988.

MELVYN DUBOFSKY

UNITED STATES HOUSING AUTHORITY (USHA)

On February 24, 1942, President Franklin D. Roosevelt ordered the consolidation of more than a dozen federal housing agencies into the National Housing Agency. The United States Housing Authority (USHA), the agency that had overseen the nation's controversial, federally subsidized, low-income public housing program since the passage of the United States Housing Act in 1937, was abolished and its activities were transferred to the National Housing Agency's Federal Public Housing Authority.

The USHA was the second agency to administer the public housing program started under the Federal Emergency Administration of Public Works in 1933 with the primary goal of aiding the economic recovery of the construction industry. Under the terms of the United States Housing Act, popularly known as the Wagner-Steagall Act, the USHA loaned funds to public housing authorities formed by local governments for the construction and operation of public housing developments. Local public housing authorities were required to meet the USHA's design and construction standards, resident selection policies, and management procedures. Ownership of USHA-aided public housing developments rested with the sponsoring local public housing authorities, not the federal government.

The USHA and the public housing program were supported by representatives of secular and nonsecular social work and civic organizations, architectural and planning agencies, and labor unions who believed that the private housing market had failed to provide an adequate supply of housing for persons of low to moderate income. Under the leadership of Administrator Nathan Straus, a former New York City social worker, the USHA offered down-on-their-luck, wage-earning families a temporary escape from the slums so they could recover both their finances and dignity. The Wilmington, North Carolina Housing Authority, for example, demonstrated that public housing worked as intended by publicizing the case of Benjamin Jenkins, a fertilizer factory worker. After living in the city's (racially segregated) USHA-subsidized New Brooklyn Homes for a brief time, Jenkins and his wife purchased a home in a nearby neighborhood.

The most outspoken opponents of public housing were home-building, real estate, and banking interests who saw the USHA as a threat to the private residential construction industry and the cherished ideal of home ownership. Homeowners from neighborhoods or areas targeted for public housing who were convinced that real estate values would decline frequently joined campaigns to stop public housing.

Louisiana Site 1-1 in New Orleans during the 1930s before the U.S. Housing Authority razed the old buildings and began a housing construction project. FRANKLIN DELANO ROOSEVELT LIBRARY

The USHA staff worked with officials from local public housing authorities to create the local support necessary to build public housing and raze the equivalent number of substandard housing units. Their task was aided by the policy whereby existing racial patterns determined whether the housing would be designated as "white," "Negro" or "mixed occupancy." The USHA furthered racial segregation and at the same time, worked to empower residents in small ways. Classes, health clinics, childcare centers, and newly created resident councils were intended to combine with architecture and planning to foster community identity. The severe construction cost restrictions added to the Wagner-Steagall Act by the opponents of public housing had their desired effect: The USHA and local housing authorities were forced to decrease

the size of dwelling units and eliminate nonessentials such as closet doors; increase overall project density; and trim community facilities that were supposed to help integrate the developments into the larger urban fabric.

In the months prior to the implementation of the 1942 housing reorganization plan, the USHA was the subject of bitter partisan attacks that ultimately led to the resignation of Administrator Straus. At the heart of these political battles was the future of public housing. Congressional opponents were determined that the public housing program would not benefit from the appropriation of funds for the construction of housing for civilians employed by the armed forces or defense contractors under the National Defense Housing Act of October 1940. Straus unsuccessfully maintained that the

Louisiana Site 1-1 in New Orleans in 1940 after completion of the U.S. Housing Authority project. Franklin Delano Roosevelt Library

United States should continue building housing for impoverished families and at the same time, erect housing for defense workers.

During the five brief years of its existence, the USHA helped thousands of families escape the slums—at least temporarily. Attitudes and beliefs concerning public housing and the men, women, and children who reside there hardened during this time, and continue to influence legislation and public policy regarding housing, urban development, poverty, and homelessness today.

See Also: BAUER, CATHERINE; HOUSING; WAGNER, ROBERT F.

BIBLIOGRAPHY

Biles, Roger "Nathan Straus and the Failure of U.S. Public Housing, 1937–1942." *The Historian* 53 (Autumn 1990): 33–46.

Daly, Gerald. "The British Roots of American Public Housing." *Journal of Urban History* 15, no. 4 (1989): 399–434.

McDonnell, Timothy. *The Wagner Housing Act: A Case of the Legislative Process.* 1957.

Straus, Nathan. *Seven Myths of Housing.* 1944.

Vale, Lawrence. *From the Puritans to the Projects: Public Housing and Public Neighbors.* 2000.

Wright, Gwendolyn. *Building the Dream: A Social History of Housing in the United States.* 1981.

Kristin M. Szylvian

VALUES, EFFECTS OF THE GREAT DEPRESSION ON

The Great Depression precipitated a significant, albeit not lasting, change in the predominant values in the United States. To understand the nature of this shift in values, it is first necessary to examine what "traditional American values" had been and what had happened to them earlier in the twentieth century, particularly in the 1920s.

TRADITIONAL VALUES AND THE MODERN ECONOMY

It is a commonplace that Americans are a very individualistic people. This is certainly true in many respects, but leaving it at that is misleading. There had always been a strong strain of community operating alongside American individualism. From John Winthrop's shipboard sermon, "A Modell of Christian Charity," to his fellow Puritans before their arrival in Massachusetts in 1630 ("Wee must beare one anothers burthens. We must not looke onely on our owne things, but allsoe on the things of our brethren") to Herbert Hoover's 1922 book *American Individualism*, which stressed the idea of voluntary cooperation rather than "rugged individualism," Americans had been urged to think of others as well as themselves. The American ideal—though certainly not always the practice—had been

what might be termed "cooperative individualism." The insightful French observer of American practices, Alexis de Tocqueville, had seen in the 1830s that American democracy tended to produce an emphasis on conformity that counteracted the self-centered acquisitive individualism that other aspects of the American experience, such as the abundance of resources, encouraged.

The values that Winthrop had called for in 1630 and Tocqueville had observed in the 1830s enjoyed a revival under the impact of the Depression in the 1930s. Such cooperative values had to be resuscitated, rather than continued, because changes in the economy had gone a long way toward undermining them. This was true not only of the value placed on community, but also of such other long-established American values as frugality and deferred gratification. Americans had traditionally been future-oriented, confident in the progressive view that today's sacrifices would be rewarded by a better future for their children and grandchildren.

Such values were fine for the first three hundred or so years after the initial English settlement in North America, but during the twentieth century the demand for mass consumption to soak up the products of mass production necessitated a reversal of many time-honored values. Most traditional values had to be jettisoned if people were to be persuaded to buy more and more, indulge themselves, go into debt to consume, and stop thinking about tomorrow. The ironic subversives who directed the attack on traditional values were the putatively conservative leaders of business and industry. Their agents were advertisers, who, beginning at an extraordinary level in the 1920s, used their considerable persuasive skills to woo Americans away from the values preached by Benjamin Franklin into a self-centered, highly individualistic, live-for-the-moment life oriented toward the consumption of products purchased in the marketplace.

THE AMORAL MARKETPLACE VERSUS REVIVED TRADITIONAL VALUES

Having been beguiled by the sirens of the good life as measured by the accumulation of things, large numbers of Americans in the 1920s went into debt to purchase such consumer goods as automobiles, radios, and household appliances. A debtor tends to move away from a future orientation and concentrate on the present. Yet most of the Americans who were won over to the consumption ethic in the 1920s had been brought up on the traditional values, to which much lip service was still being paid, even as the reality was that they were being abandoned. Many Americans were, therefore, not entirely comfortable with the new practices.

The Depression caused Americans who had bought into the radical new values based on consumption to step back and reconsider them. The collapse of an economy based on consumption and hyper-individualism was seen by many as chastisement for having allowed themselves to be enticed away from the older ways that, deep down, they still believed were right. Tennessee Williams nicely captured this feeling when he had the narrator of his 1945 play, *The Glass Menagerie*, refer to the 1930s as a time when middle-class Americans, whose "eyes had failed them, or they had failed their eyes," in the 1920s "were having their fingers pressed forcibly down on the fiery Braille alphabet of a dissolving economy."

A major aspect of the modern view of the world as a marketplace that had been gaining so much ground in the 1920s is that morality has and should have no bearing on the operation of the economy, which is viewed as a constant struggle among un-

connected individuals pursuing their own self-interest. This outlook was quite different from the traditional one, in which the common good was seen as the foremost goal and economic decisions were supposed to be made in light of moral considerations. (Of course this ideal often had failed to be matched by reality, but it had remained the ideal.) After the marketplace economy fell apart in 1929 and the years following, growing numbers of Americans appear to have abandoned their flirtation with the idea of an amoral economy and turned back to the traditional values that took account of the social consequences of individual actions.

Viewed from the perspective of the next century, what is most striking about the shift in values in the 1930s is that the decade stands out as the only time in the twentieth century during which the seemingly inexorable thrust of the modern world toward the acquisitive individualism and present-mindedness—and concomitant social disintegration—dictated by the consumption-based economy was temporarily reversed. In reaction to the disaster into which the abandonment of older values seemed to have led them, large numbers of Americans turned against greed and excessive individualism and returned more to such ideals as prudence, deferred gratification, future-orientation, cooperation, and community—ideals that had fallen into disuse in the prosperous 1920s.

CHANGING VIEWS OF SMALL-TOWN LIFE AND COMMUNITY

Among the more striking changes in values evident during the Depression was a turnaround in the viewpoint on small communities expressed in the culture. Small towns had often been castigated in the 1920s, for example, in the novels of Sinclair Lewis. After the collapse, however, there was a growing trend toward appreciation of the sense of place and belonging associated with such communities (although usually not in a completely uncritical way). This movement in attitudes is evident in the films of Frank Capra and John Ford, in Thornton Wilder's play *Our Town* (1938), the 1939 film classics *The Wizard of Oz* and *Gone with the Wind*, and Norman Rockwell's paintings of scenes of small-town life that appeared in the *Saturday Eve-*

ning Post, among many other cultural products of the era.

Others of the decade's altered values were also reflected in the popular culture of the Depression years. The gangster film genre that became so popular often (as in the 1930 film *Little Caesar*) linked greedy gangsters with businessmen and suggested in ways subtle and not-so-subtle that the latter—men who had often been revered in the twenties—were little more than greedy criminals themselves. And the whole range of social values and cooperation can be seen in John Steinbeck's novel *The Grapes of Wrath* (1939). "Use' ta be the fambly was fust," Ma Joad says of those people who feel obliged to help. "It ain't so now. It's anybody. Worse off we get, the more we got to do."

A RENEWED RESPECT FOR VALUES ASSOCIATED WITH WOMEN

One of the paradoxes of the Depression era is that at the same time that many men felt that their manhood was threatened by unemployment and their inability to fulfill the traditional male role of provider, there was a decided move away from the highly competitive, every-man-for-himself economic system, which was generally perceived as being essentially masculine. The emphasis on community, sharing, cooperation, interdependence, and compassion that was evident in so many quarters during the Depression has generally been seen as a more female approach to the world.

A possible explanation for the willingness of men during the Depression to accept values associated with women is that their loss of position put them in the accustomed place of women in society: dominated, powerless—on the bottom. While the feeling that he was in this position was likely to threaten a man's self image as a "real man," it was also likely to produce a general outlook more suited to such a diminished status in society. In any case, the putatively more male approach that had held sway in the twenties had been discredited, so another set of values would seem to be worth a try.

CHANGING VALUES AND THE NEW DEAL

One of the major reasons for the popularity of Franklin D. Roosevelt and the New Deal was that their outlook and policies seemed to match the resurgent values of cooperative individualism that were so widely re-embraced by Americans during the Depression years.

Having bought into the promises that a free market from which government restraints were lifted would produce the common good and having experienced instead what might be termed the "common bad" of the Depression, many Americans were ready to accept the re-imposition of limits. The New Deal did just that. In his first inaugural address in March 1933, Franklin Roosevelt castigated "a generation of self-seekers" and pledged to restore "ancient truths" by applying "social values more noble than mere monetary profit." The American people, the new president declared, "now realize as we have never realized before our interdependence with each other."

On all these counts and many more, Roosevelt was giving voice to the values that had made a comeback among the American people. In his speech accepting the 1936 Democratic presidential nomination, Roosevelt captured the resurgent values of the Depression years and his government's embrace of them in a single sentence: "Better the occasional faults of a Government that lives in a spirit of charity than the consistent omissions of a Government caught in the ice of its own indifference."

VALUES AFTER THE DEPRESSION

The revived values of a more cooperative individualism that took hold under the impact of the Great Depression and the accompanying rejection of consumption-based acquisitive individualism did not long survive a return to prosperity. The modern world's—and especially modern America's—rush toward the social disintegration demanded by the consumption-based marketplace economy accelerated in the post–World War II years. In those years, little has stood in the way of the rapid advance of the present-minded, self-indulgent consumerism that characterized most of the twentieth century. Remnants of the values of the Great Depression and the government programs and policies that reflected them have provided most of the few checks that still exist on the all-conquering marketplace values of the modern world.

See Also: CONSUMERISM; INDIVIDUALISM.

BIBLIOGRAPHY

McElvaine, Robert S. *The Great Depression: America, 1929–1941.* 1984, 1993.

McElvaine, Robert S. *Eve's Seed: Biology, the Sexes, and the Course of History.* 2001.

Pells, Richard H. *Radical Visions and American Dreams: Culture and Social Thought in the Depression Years.* 1973.

Steinbeck, John. *The Grapes of Wrath.* 1939.

Terkel, Studs. *Hard Times: An Oral History of the Great Depression.* 1970.

ROBERT S. MCELVAINE

VANN, ROBERT

Pittsburgh Courier publisher Robert Lee Vann (August 27, 1879–October 24, 1940) served as special assistant attorney general to Franklin D. Roosevelt from 1933 to 1936. Vann was born in rural Ahoskie, North Carolina. After graduating as valedictorian from Walters Training School in 1901, he attended Virginia Union University's Wayland Academy, graduating in 1903. He then received a scholarship to Western University of Pennsylvania at Pittsburgh (now the University of Pittsburgh), where he served as the editor-in-chief of the campus newspaper. Vann graduated in 1906 and entered the university's law school. He was admitted to the Pennsylvania bar and opened a small firm, specializing in criminal law, in 1909.

In 1910 Vann became legal counsel, treasurer, and editor for the *Pittsburgh Courier,* a newspaper founded three years earlier by Edwin Harelston. Vann's ingenuity in advertising, distribution, reporting, and coverage attracted a devoted readership and increased the paper's circulation from 3,000 in 1910 to 150,000 by the mid 1930s, and 250,000 by the end of the Depression.

Vann's growing stature as *Courier* editor invigorated his struggling law practice, and enhanced his reputation as a successful criminal attorney, compassionate civic leader, and savvy businessman. Vann's reputation also boosted his standing within the white-dominated Pennsylvania Republican Party. After his 1917 election as mayor of Pittsburgh, E. V. Babcock appointed Vann as assistant city solicitor, a position that whetted Vann's appetite for future political appointments. However, a series of political disappointments in the 1920s and early 1930s—his dismissal as city solicitor, two failed county judgeship election attempts, an unappreciative Republican Party, and white Republicans' refusal to address issues facing black America—soured Vann's commitment to the Republican Party. In 1932, he abandoned the party, denounced its blatant racism, campaigned for Roosevelt, and used his newspaper as a vehicle for cultural consciousness, political change, and social protest. Vann's hard work paid off when a small yet significant shift in African-American votes helped elect Roosevelt in November 1932.

The Roosevelt administration appointed Vann as special assistant attorney general on Negro affairs in 1933. A confident Vann immediately recommended African Americans for federal posts. His suggested appointees included: the National Urban League's Eugene Kinkcle Jones as advisor of Negro affairs in the Department of Commerce; social worker Lawrence A. Oxley, as head of Negro labor for the Department of Labor; and economist Robert Weaver as associate advisor on the status of African-Americans in the Department of the Interior.

Regrettably, Vann's enthusiasm soon waned as he realized his limitations inside the Justice Department. He routinely met hostility from office staffers, and received mundane tasks that hardly challenged his intellect. He mainly worked in the Land Division, examining titles for the Resettlement Administration and reforestation program. Only on rare occasions did Vann receive purposeful reprieves from his duties. He chaired two committees during his short stay in Washington: The Negro Advisory Committee of the Advisory and Planning Council for the Department of Commerce, and the Interdepartmental Group Concerned with the Special Problems of Negroes. While both committees attempted to eradicate racism from government agencies and other institutions, discrimination, in the end, prevailed. Vann was especially troubled by the nonchalant attitude of New Dealers regarding African-American issues. He felt that the Democrats, the administration, and Roosevelt were uncommitted and unconcerned about improving the status of African Americans.

To make matters worse, many Washingtonians considered Vann an anachronism in the Roosevelt administration. Most Washington insiders separated Vann from the up-and-coming intellectuals generally referred to as the Black Cabinet. New dealers considered Vann an outdated career politician or a political patronage appointee rewarded for his loyalty to the Democratic Party. Robert Weaver, Charles Hamilton Houston, Ralph Bunche, William H. Hastie, and Mary McLeod Bethune, however, were prominent government advisors brought into the fold for their potential ability to influence social policy, and for their expertise and academic training in education, the social sciences, and law. These men and women were intellectuals, not politicians with direct ties to the Democratic Party. Vann, on

the other hand, had little or no influence in the Justice Department. He found himself in Washington because of patronage politics, and his loyalty to the National Democratic Party. A frustrated and humiliated Vann left his post in 1936.

In his final years, Vann continued to enhance the reputation and quality of the *Courier*. He also endorsed Democrats in local, state, and national elections. But he realized that neither political party cared much about improving the quality of life for African Americans. A disillusioned Vann died in 1940 of complications from abdominal cancer.

See Also: AFRICAN AMERICANS, IMPACT OF THE GREAT DEPRESSION ON; BETHUNE, MARY MCLEOD.

BIBLIOGRAPHY

Buni, Andrew. *Robert L. Vann of the Pittsburgh Courier: Politics and Black Journalism.* 1974.

"Pittsburgh Courier." In *Africana: The Encyclopedia of the African and African American Experience,* edited by Kwame Anthony Appiah and Henry Louis Gates, Jr. 2000.

BERNADETTE PRUITT

WAGNER, ROBERT F.

Robert F. Wagner (June 8, 1877–May 4, 1953), the United States senator widely regarded as the "legislative pilot of the New Deal" and the "architect of social justice in America," was born in Nastatten, Germany, the youngest of seven children. Immigrating with his parents to the highly Teutonic Yorkville section of New York City at the age of nine, he worked his way through the City College of New York and New York Law School, graduating from the latter with honors in 1900. While practicing law among the people of his neighborhood, Wagner became increasingly involved in ward-level politics, where he soon drew favorable attention from the Tammany Hall leadership of the local Democratic Party. Elected to the state assembly in 1904 and to the state senate in 1908, he became the latter body's youngest ever president pro tempore in 1911, teaming with his assembly counterpart, Alfred E. Smith, to head the commission investigating the horrific Triangle Shirtwaist Factory fire that year. Based upon that experience, Wagner and Smith sponsored fifty-six factory health and safety laws, as well as numerous other progressive measures. Widowed with a young son (future New York City mayor Robert F. Wagner, Jr.) in 1919, he accepted an appointment to the state supreme court, where he gained an impressive reputation as a champion of labor unions, consumers, renters, and government regulation of the economy.

Elected to the United States Senate in 1926, Wagner soon established himself as an outspoken critic of the Republican administrations of Calvin Coolidge and Herbert Hoover. In March 1928, he gained national attention through the introduction of his "Three Bills," which provided for more accurate government gathering of unemployment statistics, the establishment of an effective system of public employment agencies, and the creation of a federal employment stabilization board that would oversee counter-cyclical government spending on public works projects. Although the Three Bills were tabled by the Republican Congress, they provided a preview of the greatly revised role that the federal government would come to play during the New Deal. Wagner also pushed for the abolition of "yellow-dog" contracts (by which employees were required to pledge they would not join a union), national unemployment insurance, and federal farm relief. When the Great Depression struck in 1929, Wagner joined with such progressive lawmakers as Robert M. La Follette, Jr., George W. Norris, David I. Walsh, Edward P. Costigan, and Fiorello La Guardia in advocating numerous measures to combat unemployment and to aid workers and farmers. In 1933, philosopher John Dewey, head of the People's Lobby and the Joint Committee on Unemployment, identified Wagner as "the key man in Congress."

With the advent of the New Deal, Wagner consistently pressured Congress and the Franklin D. Roosevelt administration to intervene more directly into the socioeconomic order on behalf of those most disadvantaged by the Depression. He was instrumental in adding Section 7a to the National Industrial Recovery Act, giving workers a voice in formulating and implementing the law's "codes of fair competition." Two years later, he succeeded in enacting the National Labor Relations Act that still bears his name, guaranteeing "the exercise by workers of full freedom of association, self-organization, and designation of representatives of their choosing, for the purpose of negotiating the terms and conditions of their employment or other mutual aid or protection." He also was a major force behind the eventual passage of the Social Security Act of 1935, and he crusaded for public housing, national healthcare, veteran's benefits, and federal anti-lynching legislation. Forced to resign from the Senate in 1949 due to deteriorating health, he lived in relative seclusion until his death. In his obituary, the *New York Times* lauded Wagner's "deep-seated humanitarianism" and "sympathy for those handicapped in the race for life." Pick any law designed to help the common people, the *Times* proclaimed, "and the chances are that Bob Wagner's name is attached to it."

See Also: COLLECTIVE BARGAINING; LABOR'S NON-PARTISAN LEAGUE; NATIONAL LABOR RELATIONS ACT OF 1935 (WAGNER ACT); NATIONAL LABOR RELATIONS BOARD (NLRB).

BIBLIOGRAPHY

Gross, James A. *The Making of the National Labor Relations Board: A Study in Economics, Politics, and the Law,* 2 vols. 1974–1981.

Huthmacher, J. Joseph. *Senator Robert F. Wagner and the Rise of Urban Liberalism.* 1968.

Schlesinger, Arthur M., Jr. *The Age of Roosevelt,* 3 vols. 1957–1960.

JOHN D. BUENKER

WALLACE, HENRY A.

Henry Agard Wallace (October 7, 1888–November 18, 1965) served as the nation's secretary of agriculture throughout much of the Great Depression. He used his office to promote change in the country's agricultural system with the goal of restoring profitability to the farm business and holding the large American farm population on the land.

Born on an Iowa farm, Wallace came from a well-known family in agricultural circles. His grandfather Henry (Uncle Henry) Wallace, his father Henry C. (Harry) Wallace, and his uncle John Wallace founded a successful farm journal, *Wallaces' Farmer*, in 1895. Uncle Henry served on President Theodore Roosevelt's Country Life Commission in 1908 and 1909, and Harry became the U.S. secretary of agriculture in 1921. Hoping to modernize farming, improve the lives of farm people, and encourage them to remain farmers, the Wallaces contributed in large ways to the development of the U.S. Department of Agriculture (USDA) and the country's agricultural colleges.

After graduating from Iowa State College in 1910, Henry A. Wallace had gone to work for *Wallaces' Farmer*. When his father moved to Washington, Henry replaced him as editor and carried forward the family's program on behalf of farming and farmers. He championed the further development of the USDA and of agricultural colleges as research and educational agencies, and he joined his father in an ultimately unsuccessful fight for "Equality for Agriculture." This initiative proposed the establishment of a government corporation that would market farm products, raise farm prices, and thereby convince farmers that they need not move to the city. In 1926, the editor also founded a private corporation, the Hi-Bred Corn Company, designed to develop hybrid corn seed and persuade farmers to use it.

In the 1928 presidential contest, Wallace actively opposed Herbert Hoover. To Wallace, Hoover appeared determined to make the United States an industrial nation. The process, Wallace feared, would drastically shrink the farm population, deprive the United States of its capacity to feed itself,

Henry A. Wallace, in his garden in 1942. LIBRARY OF CONGRESS, PRINTS & PHOTOGRAPHS DIVISION, FSA/OWI COLLECTION

and rob it of other contributions that, Wallace assumed, only farm people could make.

DEPRESSION-ERA SECRETARY OF AGRICULTURE

After the Great Depression changed American politics, Wallace moved to a higher post, becoming President Franklin D. Roosevelt's secretary of agriculture. Wallace was a logical choice because he had great prestige in farm circles, was one of Hoover's prominent critics, and had helped to persuade Iowa farmers to desert the Republican Party. Having become restless in the job he had held for many years, Wallace welcomed the new opportunity.

Roosevelt's first term. When he moved to Washington in March 1933, Wallace confronted grim conditions in rural America, for the Depression had hit

farmers extremely hard. The producers of grain and cotton had not participated in the economic boom of the 1920s, and after 1929 farm prices had dropped even more than the prices of goods farmers needed to buy. Some farm owners lost their farms, and many renters, sharecroppers, and wage laborers lost their places on the land. Farm people demanded change; some even employed violent means to express their discontent, and moderates warned of a revolutionary upheaval.

The new secretary brought the leaders of farm organizations to Washington and persuaded them to back legislation that would give him the power to experiment with a variety of proposed solutions to the farm crisis. He favored one of them: the Voluntary Domestic Allotment Plan, which would pay farmers to cut back on the acreage devoted to raising several crops, including wheat and cotton. The argument was one Wallace had made since the early 1920s, that industrial corporations managed their production levels in ways that made their operations profitable, and farmers should do the same. Farmers, however, were only small operators; they were not corporate giants, and thus they needed help from a government agency if they were to manage their production successfully. The agency should not merely try to convince farmers to curtail production, as the Hoover administration had done, quite unsuccessfully. Instead, it should use the federal government's taxing and spending powers to persuade farmers to change. Roosevelt accepted the idea, Congress responded with a broad Agricultural Adjustment Act, and Wallace established the Agricultural Adjustment Administration (AAA) in May 1933 to implement the legislation.

Wallace promoted other ideas for the protection and improvement of American agriculture, most of which served to enlarge the federal government. Two of his efforts focused on soil conservation. In 1935, he took over a soil erosion program from the Interior Department and established the Soil Conservation Service to develop and administer the program. Because he promoted long-range agricultural planning, he was prepared when the U.S. Supreme Court ruled in 1936 that the Agricultural Adjustment Act violated the U.S. Constitution. In response, Wallace championed passage of legislation that empowered the AAA to pay farmers to shift acres from soil-depleting crops, like wheat and cotton, to soil-building ones, such as clover.

Wallace also successfully resisted a proposal championed by the National Farmers Union, which called upon the federal government to guarantee farmers a price for their products that would more than cover their production costs. The aim was to hold all farmers on the land, but Wallace regarded it as unrealistic. His aim was to protect farmers who could succeed if they received fair prices. In response, the Farmers Union demanded Wallace's removal from office, but failed to get it.

Roosevelt's second term. By 1936, most farmers approved of Wallace's efforts on their behalf. At least they liked the money that came from Washington and the higher prices they obtained in the market.

Thus, they rewarded the president with their votes in the election that year. Support for Roosevelt came from farmers in the Midwest, who had customarily voted Republican, as well as farmers in the South, who had traditionally supported Democrats.

During Roosevelt's second term, Wallace continued his efforts to make farming more profitable and to hold commercial farmers on the land. He also moved in a direction new to him when he championed programs that focused on the poorest people in farm communities. As recently as 1935 Wallace had ousted lawyers from the AAA after they pushed a scheme to make southern sharecroppers more secure, but beginning in 1937 he supported a new agency, the Farm Security Administration (FSA), that had a similar aim. The FSA tried to help tenant farmers become farm owners and to improve conditions for sharecroppers and migratory farm workers.

Although many Americans at the time were concerned about such people, Wallace concluded before the end of the 1930s that Congress would not appropriate the funds required to make a meaningful difference in the lives of the poorest folks in the land. Thus, he turned to industrialization and a high-wage economy as solutions to their problems and as a means of improving the lot of more prosperous farm people at the same time. Industrial development and high wages, Wallace now believed, could draw people out of depressed rural conditions and enlarge markets for those who continued to farm.

VICE PRESIDENT DURING ROOSEVELT'S THIRD TERM

Wallace's success as secretary and the broadening of his point of view enabled him to move higher in American politics and government. By the late 1930s, his admirers favored him as Roosevelt's successor, seeing him as the leader who could maintain the New Deal's momentum. However, the leaders of the American Farm Bureau Federation had become unhappy with Wallace; to them, Wallace seemed to have become more interested in the rural poor and in urban workers than in substantial commercial farmers. The Farmers Union, on the other hand, which had new leadership and advocated a political alliance between farmers and wage earners, had moved to Wallace's side. Roosevelt's decision to run for a third term ended Wallace's bid for the White House, but the president insisted that Democrats nominate this former Republican for the vice presidency, and they did.

Wallace's service as vice president shifted his focus away from agriculture but did not lead him to the presidency. Pressured by Robert Hannegan, the chair of the Democratic National Committee, and other prominent democrats, Roosevelt deserted him in 1944; the Democrats nominated Harry Truman for the vice presidency, and he, not Wallace, succeeded Roosevelt. After a year and a half as secretary of commerce in the Roosevelt-Truman administration, Wallace broke with Truman over foreign policy and was forced to resign. Running on a third-party ticket, he challenged Truman in 1948 and finished fourth in a field of four. The outcome destroyed his political career.

Living his last years on a farm in Westchester County, New York, Wallace devoted much of his attention to his lifetime passion for plant breeding. The corporation he had founded in 1926 had become a huge success, while other developments he had promoted in agriculture, including the enlarged role of the federal government, continued to have his support. Although the now enormous productivity of American farmers pleased him, one feature of rural life troubled him: The American farm population had become alarmingly small.

See Also: AGRICULTURAL ADJUSTMENT ADMINISTRATION (AAA); AGRICULTURE; ELECTION OF 1940; FARM POLICY.

BIBLIOGRAPHY

Culver, John C., and John Hyde. *American Dreamer: A Life of Henry A. Wallace.* 2000.

Hamilton, David E. *From New Day to New Deal: American Farm Policy from Hoover to Roosevelt, 1928–1933.* 1991.

Kirkendall, Richard S. "The New Deal and Agriculture." In *The New Deal*, edited by John Braeman, Robert H. Bremner, and David Brody. 1975.

Kirkendall, Richard S. *Social Scientists and Farm Politics in the Age of Roosevelt.* 1966. Reprint edition, 1982.

Kirkendall, Richard S. "The Second Secretary Wallace." *Agricultural History* 64 (1990): 199–206.

Kirkendall, Richard S. *Uncle Henry: A Documentary Profile of the First Henry Wallace.* 1993.

Kleinman, Mark L. *A World of Hope, A World of Fear: Henry A. Wallace, Reinhold Niebuhr, and American Liberalism.* 2000.

Lord, Russell. *The Wallaces of Iowa.* 1947.

Rogers, Earl M., ed. *The Wallace Papers: An Index to the Microfilm Editions of the Henry A. Wallace Papers in the University of Iowa Libraries, the Library of Congress, and the Franklin D. Roosevelt Library.* 1975.

Saloutos, Theodore. *The American Farmer and the New Deal.* 1982.

Schapsmeier, Edward L., and Frederick H. Schapsmeier. *Henry A. Wallace of Iowa: The Agrarian Years, 1910–1940.* 1968.

Schapsmeier, Edward L. *Prophet in Politics: Henry A. Wallace and the War Years, 1940–1965.* 1970.

Walker, J. Samuel. *Henry A. Wallace and American Foreign Policy.* 1976.

Wallace, Henry A. Papers. University of Iowa Libraries, Iowa City, Iowa.

Wallace, Henry A. Papers. Franklin D. Roosevelt Library, Hyde Park, New York.

Wallace, Henry A. Papers. Library of Congress, Washington, D. C.

Wallace, Henry A. Reminiscences. Columbia University Oral History Collection, New York.

White, Graham, and John Maze. *Henry A. Wallace: His Search for a New World Order.* 1995.

Winters, Donald L. *Henry Cantwell Wallace as Secretary of Agriculture, 1921–1924.* 1970.

RICHARD S. KIRKENDALL

WASHINGTON COMMONWEALTH FEDERATION (WCF)

The Washington Commonwealth Federation (WCF) was established in Seattle, Washington, on June 8, 1935, to improve economic and political conditions in the city and the state. In addition to its public service functions, the WCF served as a liberal Seattle wing of the Democratic Party.

In response to the Great Depression, in August 1931 Seattle liberals, radicals, reformers, socialists, unionists, and unemployed workers organized into a self-help group, which they called the Unemployed Citizens' League (UCL). Members began to organize relief measures for unemployed workers, such as harvesting crops, cutting fuel wood, and fishing. One of the UCL's first political activities was to support the campaign of John F. Dore, who was elected Seattle's mayor in 1932. However, Communist Party members began to gain influence in the UCL, damaging the group's credibility.

In 1934, the UCL's non-Communist members broadened the organization's goals in order to attract new members and distance it from Communist Party. It changed its name to Commonwealth Builders, Inc. (CBI), and began working with state and federal Democratic Party members. In 1935 CBI reorganized in order to develop a statewide employment campaign based on the notion of "production for use" instead of "production for profit." The plan was to reopen abandoned factories and farms, and distribute products through publicly owned stores, where workers could exchange scrip for goods. The new organization—the Washington Commonwealth Federation—began with Cyrus Woodward as president and Howard Costigan as executive secretary. Its goals included labor rights, farm policies, consumer protection, social security, and public health and housing. Over the next ten years the WCF was instrumental in the passage of important social policy for Washington residents.

In 1936, WCF members gained control of the state Democratic Party. Critics, however, charged that the WCF was affiliated with the Communist Party because some WCF members were also Communist Party members, and the organization's influence waned as a consequence. WCF membership dwindled when fuller employment developed as the buildup for World War II brought contracts and money into Seattle and the Puget Sound region for the construction of ships, airplanes, and tanks. The WCF disbanded in 1945, with its leaders claiming the organization had fulfilled "its historical and anti-Fascist role."

See Also: COMMUNIST PARTY.

BIBLIOGRAPHY

Acena, Albert A. *The Washington Commonwealth Federation.* Ph.D. diss., University of Washington, 1975.

Berner, Richard C. *Seattle 1921–1940: From Boom to Bust.* 1992.

Phipps, Jennifer. *The Washington Commonwealth Federation & Washington Pension Union.* Available at: http://faculty.washington.edu/gregoryj/cpproject/phipps.htm

Reese, Michael. *The Cold War and Red Scare in Washington State: A Curriculum Project for Washington Schools Developed by the Center for the Study of the Pacific Northwest.* Available at: www.washington.edu/uwired/outreach/cspn/curcan/main.html

WILLIAM ARTHUR ATKINS

WCF. *See* WASHINGTON COMMONWEALTH FEDERATION.

WEAVER, ROBERT CLIFTON

Robert Clifton Weaver (December 29, 1907–July 17, 1997), New Deal race relations adviser, was born and raised in the black middle class of Washington, D.C. Weaver attended Harvard University on a scholarship, where he came to know fellow African-American students Ralph Bunche, John P. Davis, and William H. Hastie. In 1933, during the New Deal's first "100 Days," Weaver and Davis formed the Joint Committee on National Recovery to represent the needs of black people at congressional hearings. In November 1933 Weaver was chosen to assist Clark H. Foreman, then race relations adviser to Secretary of Interior Harold L. Ickes. Two years later, Weaver succeeded Foreman as Ickes's adviser in both the Department of the Interior and the Public Works Administration (PWA). In 1938, Weaver joined the newly created United States Housing Authority and from 1940 to 1944 he served in a number of capacities with federal agencies.

With Mary McLeod Bethune, Weaver was one of the most influential members of the Black Cabinet, an informal group of African Americans appointed in the Roosevelt era as racial advisers to federal departments and newly established agencies. Weaver's importance as an advocate for African Americans derived from his expertise in black housing and labor issues, his academic and personal qualities, and his belief in the New Deal's significance as an agency for change. Although he helped force integration of the Interior Department's lunchroom facilities in the 1930s, he was not a political or civil rights activist like Bethune or Davis. Focusing on jobs and housing, Weaver used statistics and analysis to influence federal policy and to expand public awareness of the "Negro problem."

Weaver saw New Deal reform as instrumental in transforming the condition of African Americans. The integration of blacks into the American economic system, through expanded federally financed employment and housing opportunities, would not only create necessary skills for blacks and facilitate their entry into a growing industrial society, it would also improve the climate for race relations. For Weaver, economic segregation reinforced the social and political separation of the races. The Depression had illuminated the depth of black destitution and the urgency for immediate black assistance. Only the federal government possessed the power necessary to modify social institutions and provide blacks and other minorities with the material and spiritual aid necessary to secure their ultimate integration into American life. At Weaver's urging, racial discrimination was not only prohibited in PWA labor contracts, but in 1934 Harold Ickes supported a quota system to assure black worker participation. Weaver had an equally important impact in gaining black inclusion in public housing programs begun in the late 1930s. He left the government in 1944 believing that his influence was limited but he never lost faith in the New Deal or in the government's critical role in improving the quality of black life. In 1966, when Lyndon Johnson appointed Weaver secretary of the Department of Housing and Urban Development, he became the first African American to head a federal cabinet post.

See Also: AFRICAN AMERICANS, IMPACT OF THE GREAT DEPRESSION ON; BETHUNE, MARY MCLEOD; BLACK CABINET.

BIBLIOGRAPHY

Kirby, John B. *Black Americans in the Roosevelt Era: Liberalism and Race.* 1980.

Weiss, Nancy J. *Farewell to the Party of Lincoln: Black Politics in the Age of FDR.* 1983.

Williams, Alma Rene. "Robert C. Weaver: From the Black Cabinet to the President's Cabinet." Ph.D. diss., Kent State University, 1982.

Wolters, Raymond. *Negroes and the Great Depression: The Problem of Economic Recovery.* 1970.

JOHN B. KIRBY

WELFARE CAPITALISM

Welfare capitalism encompassed a wide range of private, firm-level social policies, including innovations in personnel management, employee representation, recreation, stock ownership, and cash benefits for retirement and unemployment and sickness. Benefits were most common and most expansive for "white collar" employees whose occupational status rested on loyalty to the corporation and mobility within it. In a limited fashion, benefits spread to small family-owned firms and company towns and then to large industrial concerns facing new challenges in labor and community relations. At the core of both the benefits provided and the often-onerous service provisions attached to them was the urgency of creating or recreating workers' dependence upon, and loyalty to, their employers. Employment benefits, and wages deferred to pensions, savings, or company stock, encouraged workers to equate their own economic future with the prosperity and good favor of their employers. "Many of you are now real 'partners' . . . because you have your share of the 'surplus profits,'" a 1920 circular of the Endicott-Johnson Shoe Company reminded employees, "your own selfish interest, now, demands that you protect this business" (Zahavi, 1988).

Welfare capitalism marked an important transition in labor relations. Many firm-level welfare policies (recreation, company housing, health and hygiene programs) reached back to late-nineteenth century or Progressive Era efforts to protect workers from the ravages of industrialization. Many policies (employee representation plans, stock ownership plans) tried to replicate or recapture the paternal relationship between employer and employee common in older family firms. Moreover, many policies (private pensions, sickness insurance, unemployment insurance) anticipated the private and public social insurance programs that would become commonplace after the mid-1930s. In most cases, a given firm's welfare program reflected all of these diverse motives and methods.

It is easy to exaggerate the scope and impact of welfare capitalism. While employers dispensed platitudes about "industrial democracy" or "employee loyalty" quite liberally, few devoted substantial resources to such programs, and most abandoned them when deferred wages could not meet their costs. The most promising and important private welfare plans, in this respect, also proved the most fickle. Industrial pensions, for example, were found primarily in larger Northern non-union firms. Yet while nearly 80 percent of workers in these settings belonged to a private pension plan, barely 4 percent of male workers and 3 percent of female workers ever met the underlying service requirements. Through the 1920s and 1930s, employers used pension plans with some success to avert strikes and moderate labor turnover. Private pensions were, like most welfare capitalist plans, noncontributory and discretionary: Workers had no "vested" rights in company pension funds, and employers could change plan rules or terms at their whim. Employers also proceeded with little appreciation of the actuarial demands or real costs of their pension plans and began to abandon them in the late 1920s. Similarly, private unemployment plans were widely trumpeted but adopted by only a few maverick firms (including General Electric) and a few industries (including the garment trades in Rochester, New York, Chicago, and Cleveland) that hoped that they might regulate competition by compelling continuous employment and curtailing the freedom of "fly-by-night" contractors.

Welfare capitalism also drew clear distinctions according to the gender or race of its beneficiaries. This discrimination was especially pronounced in white collar work, in which the managerial ranks remained a white (even Anglo-Saxon) enclave and in which fringe benefits helped to distinguish manly careers from the "pink collar" rank-and-file.

In the industrial economy, programs for male workers focussed on masculine diversions (sports) or "breadwinner" wage-based benefits. By contrast, programs for women (mostly safety and personnel policies) were concerned largely with ameliorating the burden of work in such a way as to challenge the social and political assumption that women needed to be protected from wage labor. Black workers also had little claim on welfare capitalism—in part because such programs were rare in the agricultural and industrial labor markets in which black labor was concentrated and in part because employers routinely excluded or segregated black employees.

For its part, organized labor understood employers' motives and the conditional and limited nature of benefits. Through the 1920s, unions consistently opposed the introduction of employer-initiated welfare plans and, when plans were introduced in union firms, fought to ensure that they would be administered equitably. Workers and their unions, for the most part, understood welfare capitalism to be part and parcel of the "open shop" offensive against organized labor. The American Federation of Labor (AFL) dismissed welfare capitalism as both an alternative to higher wages and an aspersion on the masculine independence of its members. The position taken by AFL unions, and CIO unions after 1935, was that employment benefits were bargainable rights; in the contest over worker loyalty, such benefits should be won by the union and not conferred by management.

Welfare capitalism was truncated and transformed by the Depression and the New Deal. Many firms, already retreating from their welfare commitments, abandoned them entirely after 1929. Some firms, seeking to retain the benefits of welfare capitalism, encouraged the state to socialize their costs, and many workers turned to the state as private benefits evaporated. These pressures contributed to the passage of the Social Security Act in 1935. While federal social insurance programs and the emergence of the CIO after 1935 displaced many of the older welfare capitalist plans, important elements persisted. Non-union firms and sectors continued to use private benefits to maintain the loyalty of employees. Employers continued to offer benefits that supplemented either social security or collectively bargained benefits. Management continued to toy with New Era innovations in labor management, such as the company union. Yet many programs, most notably employment-based group insurance, remained at the core of the "private welfare state" (employment-based private health insurance and pensions) that emerged after the 1940s.

See Also: ORGANIZED LABOR.

BIBLIOGRAPHY

Brandes, Stuart. *American Welfare Capitalism.* 1976.

Brody, David. "The Rise and Decline of Welfare Capitalism." In *Workers in Industrial America: Essays in the 20th Century Struggle.* 1980.

Cohen, Lizbeth. *Making a New Deal: Industrial Workers in Chicago, 1919–939.* 1990.

Davis, Clark. *Company Men: White-Collar Life and Corporate Cultures in Los Angeles, 1892–1941.* 2000.

Gordon, Colin. *New Deals: Business, Labor, and Politics, 1920–1935.* 1994.

Halpern, Rick. "The Iron Fist and the Silk Glove: Welfare Capitalism in Chicago's Packinghouses, 1921–1933." *Journal of American Studies* 26 (1992): 159–183.

Jacoby, Sanford. *Modern Manors: Welfare Capitalism since the New Deal.* 1997.

Klein, Jennifer. "The Business of Health Security: Employee Benefits, Commercial Insurers, and the Reconstruction of Welfare Capitalism." *International Labor and Working Class History* 58 (2000): 293–313.

Tone, Andrea. *The Business of Benevolence: Industrial Paternalism in Progressive America.* 1997.

Zahavi, Gerald. *Workers, Managers, and Welfare Capitalism: The Shoeworkers and Tanners of Endicott Johnson, 1890–1950.* 1988.

COLIN GORDON

WELLES, ORSON

George Orson Welles (May 6, 1915–October 9, 1985) was an American director and actor in film, theater, and radio. Born in Kenosha, Wisconsin, Welles was a precocious child, whose mother began reading Shakespeare to him when Orson was two. At sixteen, traveling in Ireland, Welles was hired as an actor at the renowned Gate and Abbey theatres. When he returned to the United States, he acted on Broadway and soon began to direct plays. Welles's uniquely modern productions gained acclaim, and he led his theater company into the new field of radio drama. His famously deep, melodic voice became the incarnation of *The Shadow,* and his version of H. G. Wells's *The War of the Worlds,* broadcast in October 1938 and intended as a Halloween entertainment, was so realistic that it caused a panic—and brought Welles to the attention of Hollywood. RKO invited the then 25-year-old to direct a picture; the result was *Citizen Kane* (1941), considered one of the finest films ever made.

The New Deal's Works Progress Administration (WPA) sought to provide appropriate work for artists, as well as laborers; the WPA's theatrical arm was the Federal Theatre Project. Welles, then in his twenties, became the creative force behind New York's Negro Theatre Project, and selected *Macbeth* as its first production. To deal with the issue of black dialect and black actors playing Shakespeare, he changed the play's setting from Scotland to Haiti. The resulting "Voodoo Macbeth" combined *Macbeth*'s tragic elements with voodoo chants, dramatic lighting, and music scored by composer Virgil Thomson. Welles then headed the Federal Theatre Project's classical wing, Project 891, for which he directed a variety of plays, from *Horse Eats Hat,* an eighteenth-century farce, to Christopher Marlowe's *Doctor Faustus,* in which he also starred. Welles continued to evolve a dramatic use of lighting, sometimes on an empty stage.

Although Project 891 was funded by the federal government, Welles mounted Marc Blitzstein's controversial *The Cradle Will Rock,* a "sociological light opera" that condemned big industry corruption and championed the gallantry of struggling labor unions. When the government reduced funding to programs in 1937, WPA members went on strike and closed all federal theatres. Blitzstein and the opera's cast stood in front of the theater, handing out leaflets protesting the government's imminent action, which was a parallel to the opera itself. On the day of the sold-out first performance of *The*

Cradle Will Rock, the front doors of the theater were padlocked and federal guards were placed outside. Welles stood on a box and shouted to the waiting audience that the play would go on in the Venice Theatre, twenty blocks uptown, at no charge. Cheering, the crowd made its way north, doubling by the time it reached the Venice. Without funding to pay for an orchestra, they rented a battered upright piano. The Federal Theatre Project actors were not allowed to appear onstage at another theater, so they sat in the audience, standing when appropriate to sing their parts. The review in *Stage* magazine claimed "a great art became a living crusade."

Time magazine featured the 23-year-old Orson Welles on its May 9, 1938, cover for simultaneously directing plays, acting in his own and other productions, and being host, director and star of weekly radio dramas. With his direction of *Citizen Kane,* he added film to his repertoire. The parallels of *Citizen Kane* to the life of newspaper magnate William Randolph Hearst caused Hollywood to turn against Welles, and he spent the next decade working in Europe. Only years later was *Citizen Kane* acknowledged as one of the most innovative, cinematically original films ever made. Despite his struggles in Hollywood, Welles managed to direct thirteen feature films, including *The Magnificent Ambersons, Macbeth,* and *Touch of Evil.* He also acted in dozens of films, including his small but memorable role as Harry Lime in *The Third Man,* in which he wrote much of his own dialogue.

See Also: CRADLE WILL ROCK, THE; FEDERAL THEATRE PROJECT (FTP); HOLLYWOOD AND THE FILM INDUSTRY.

BIBLIOGRAPHY

Bessy, Maurice. *Orson Welles* (1963), translated by Ciba Vaughan. 1971.

Brady, Frank. *Citizen Welles: A Biography of Orson Welles.* 1989.

Cantril, Hadley. *Invasion from Mars: A Study in the Psychology of Panic.* 1940.

Cowie, Peter. *A Ribbon of Dreams: The Cinema of Orson Welles.* 1973.

Flanagan, Hallie. *Arena.* 1940.

McBride, Joseph. *Orson Welles.* 1972.

FRANK BRADY

WEST, GREAT DEPRESSION IN THE AMERICAN

Commentators in the region claimed that the Depression came late to the West, the area extending from North Dakota to Texas, and west to the Pacific Coast. But the western economy, heavily dependent on agriculture and the production of a variety of natural resources, probably deteriorated as rapidly as the rest of the nation. By the end of 1930, the Depression was at hand. Agriculture had been in the doldrums throughout the 1920s, and the western Plains was suffering from a Dust Bowl preview. Oil prices collapsed as the East Texas field came into production. In 1930 Oregon's lumber production was off 60 percent from 1929, western mining had dropped by half, and construction had declined significantly in Los Angeles, San Francisco, and Portland. By the winter of 1932 to 1933, urban unemployment in the West was between 30 and 40 percent. Hoovervilles sprouted in most cities; homeless families lived in caves along the Canadian River in Oklahoma City, and the squalor of the Hispanic barrio in Phoenix was described as appalling. Farmers were pushed into tenancy (60 percent of farmers in Oklahoma and 45 percent in North Dakota were tenants by the end of the 1930s), or they left the land for the city or better opportunities farther west.

HOOVER YEARS: RESPONSES

In their first responses to the Depression, westerners opted for cooperative individualism over rugged individualism, the ideal generally thought typical of the western outlook. Cooperative individualism, a tenet the West shared with President Herbert Hoover and much of the rest of the nation in the early 1930s, links the ideal of self-reliance with an assumption that those better off will offer charitable assistance to the truly needy. In the first years of the Depression, private institutions, especially the Community Chest, the Red Cross, and church-related groups, raised record amounts to meet the needs. In Los Angeles, Seattle, and Denver, self-help groups bartered work for food and other needs. Local governments responded reluctantly, first creating an employment committee to ponder

This camp for migrant agricultural and seasonal cannery workers (photographed in 1940) near Sacramento, California, was typical of migrant camps that appeared across the state during the Depression. Families at this camp paid approximately one dollar per month to rent space. NATIONAL ARCHIVES AND RECORDS ADMINISTRATION

the situation, then, after forcing contributions from municipal employees, making limited relief appropriations. Officials, especially in Denver and Oklahoma City, expressed concern that generous relief would only attract transients. Starting as early as spring 1931 in San Francisco and Los Angeles, voters in most large western cities endorsed bond issues to aid the unemployed. Once the cities and counties began dispensing relief they often blurred the lines between private and public responsibilities, funneling public relief funds through charitable agencies. Seattle made its self-help organization, the Unemployed Citizens' League, the basis

for city-administered relief, with politically tumultuous results.

By the end of the Hoover years, local efforts had collapsed. Municipal treasuries were depleted and tax relief organizations pressured officials to reduce spending. In the countryside, rabbit hunts provided for the needy in several western states; Texas farmers burned corn for heat; and throughout the Plains farm women tended larger gardens, raised more chicken and egg money, cooked Sunday dinners for others, and made their own soap to get by. Most states did accelerate public works projects to absorb a small portion of the jobless, though governors

This sign, photographed in 1941 on a ranch in Canyon County, Idaho, declared faith in federal land reclamation initiatives.

Water for this ranch was to be furnished by the Black Canyon irrigation project. LIBRARY OF CONGRESS, PRINTS & PHOTOGRAPHS

DIVISION, FSA/OWI COLLECTION

Roland Hartley of Washington and Edwin Johnson of Colorado perceived virtually no state responsibility for the needy. Minorities were either short-changed on relief (Mexicans in Los Angeles), or tended to their own without outside help (the Friendly House in the Phoenix barrio and Asians all along the Pacific Coast).

Some found self-help and charity insufficient from the beginning. The Farm Holiday movement, active in the Plains states, Colorado, and New Mexico, demonstrated for suspension of foreclosures and tax relief. Governors William Langer of North Dakota and William Murray of Oklahoma declared foreclosure moratoriums. Marches of the unemployed occurred in the larger cities, but violence

was rare. The Bonus Expeditionary Force that went to Washington in 1932 seeking early payment of a bonus for veterans of World War I originated in Portland, and one of the largest contingents came from Los Angeles. By the end of 1932 cooperative individualism had collapsed. Property owners clamored for tax relief even as the need for unemployment relief funds was growing. Westerners welcomed the chance to vote for a New Deal. Every western state switched from Republican in 1928 to Democratic in the 1932 presidential election.

THE NEW DEAL AND RELIEF

The Federal Emergency Relief Administration (FERA), as it provided direct relief (stipends with-

Thousands of migrant laborers traveled west in search of work during the 1930s. These carrot pullers in Coachella Valley, California, in 1937, were from Texas, Oklahoma, Missouri, Arkansas, and Mexico. LIBRARY OF CONGRESS, PRINTS & PHOTOGRAPHS DIVISION, FSA/OWI COLLECTION

out work in return), revived the severely under-funded relief effort, but stimulated controversy. Under FERA guidelines, states were to provide three dollars in relief for every federal dollar, but no western state came close to doing so; for example, FERA provided 87 percent of relief in Nebraska and 85 percent in Colorado. Ultimately, FERA director Harry Hopkins relented; if a state made a good-faith effort to match federal contributions, funding continued. Idaho, Wyoming, and Utah passed sales taxes; Colorado passed a gasoline excise tax; and other states similarly improvised or scrounged to find at least token matching funds. Still, problems

arose. In several states, FERA money seemed to be dispensed as patronage. Hopkins deprived the governors of North Dakota, Oklahoma, and Colorado of their control of relief due to non-cooperation with the agency. The Mormon Church in Utah was not comfortable with federal relief, although it did not prohibit its members from taking aid. Eventually, the church created a Church Security Program, in part to help its members avoid the dole.

The Franklin D. Roosevelt administration exit-ed the direct relief business in 1935 by creating the Works Progress Administration (WPA). This too proved both a boon and a problem. The WPA be-

Former farmers and sharecroppers from the South and Midwest wait in line for semimonthly relief checks at Calipatria in Imperial Valley, California, in 1937. LIBRARY OF CONGRESS, PRINTS & PHOTOGRAPHS DIVISION, FSA/OWI COLLECTION

came the largest employer in Nevada and funded millions of dollars of work in other states, but the agency was tinged by patronage accusations in New Mexico. In California, Arizona, and Colorado, growers criticized the WPA for not ousting Hispanic migrant laborers from the program so they would work in the fields at lower pay.

The Civilian Conservation Corps (CCC) had a doubly beneficial impact on the West. Not only did it put the region's unemployed young men to work, it also brought thousands of new workers to the West, where many CCC projects were based. CCC workers planted trees on the Plains, helped construct Boulder Dam (Hoover Dam), and did forestry work throughout the Rockies and Cascades.

Hard-pressed cities gladly turned over relief responsibilities to these agencies and rejoiced at fed-

erally funded civic improvements: a bridge over the Missouri River in Omaha, dredging of the ship channel in Houston, a three-way underpass in downtown Dallas, as well as extensive road paving and sewer building throughout the major cities. Buoyed by the rising price of oil and the developing defense industry, the largest western cities by 1939 had emerged from Depression gloom and had devolved the major responsibility for their citizens' social welfare onto the federal government.

New Deal agencies that targeted farmers played crucial roles in the West. The Rural Electrification Administration began hooking up farms, the Farm Credit Administration refinanced mortgages, and the Bankhead-Jones Act of 1937 provided loans to tenant farmers trying to purchase land.

Minorities in the West were not forgotten, but they were not served especially well; still, many who obtained relief saw their standard of living rise. African Americans comprised less than 5 percent of the population in the West and tended to be segregated and ignored, but they were not barred from relief roles. The Tydings-McDuffie Act of 1934 classified Filipinos as aliens, making it difficult for them to obtain government aid. Both Filipinos and Mexican citizens in the United States were invited, and often compelled, to leave. Between 30 percent and 40 percent of the Mexican population was repatriated.

Few state officials shared the Roosevelt administration's penchant for planning or urgency for providing relief. Even "Little New Deals" under governors Culbert Olson in California and Ernest Marland in Oklahoma were less than dynamic. More typical were budget balancers like Alfred Landon in Kansas and Edwin Johnson in Colorado. Even though few states cooperated with Roosevelt, per capita federal expenditures were highest in the West. This was due, in part, to the region's small population, but it was also because the New Deal provided generous relief and recovery and funded several large region-transforming projects. The average expenditure for every citizen in the West was $306, compared to $224 in the Midwest, $196 in the Northeast, and $189 in the Southeast. The top fourteen states in per capita expenditure during the New Deal were western states.

AGRICULTURE

The New Deal probably made its greatest impact on the West in the area of agriculture. Farming, the backbone of the region's economy, was in desperate shape during the 1930s. Plummeting farm prices were to blame. Moreover, the Plains were parched by drought. From 1929 to 1939 the area suffered nine years of below-average rainfall, and by mid-decade it was afflicted with debilitating dust storms that lifted tons of dirt from the land. Heat, aridity, grasshopper plagues, and poor farming methods produced misery for farmers. In some counties as much as 80 percent of the population was on relief. The Roosevelt administration formed the Great Plains Drought Area Committee in 1936 to study the problem. Many of the Committee's recommendations were enacted: Some submarginal land was taken out of production, the Soil Conservation Service taught proper techniques, and various agencies worked at conserving or developing water supplies. Another of the more imaginative responses was the shelterbelt program, a pet idea of the president. The Forest Service, with WPA assistance, planted thousands of strips of trees in a zone stretching from Bismarck, North Dakota, to Amarillo, Texas, to moderate wind velocity on the farms they protected.

The two Agricultural Adjustment Administrations (AAA) took land out of production throughout the West. Because the drought was widespread, few of these plots would have been highly productive, but independent-minded western farmers initially balked at the idea of restrictions. Nonetheless, needing the money, they cooperated with the government. The New Deal aided ranchers as well. Both the AAA and the Federal Surplus Relief Corporation purchased livestock from farmers throughout the West. The Drought Relief Service subsidized farmers in almost every Dust Bowl county by buying cattle that would have died anyway.

Perhaps the closest the West came to embracing public planning for agriculture was the Taylor Grazing Act of 1934, which effectively ended the Homestead Act by virtually closing the public domain to entry and reclassifying it as grazing land available on a fee basis. Though cattlemen from Wyoming and other grazing states opposed it, they soon acknowledged the utility of land management and low fees.

INTERNAL MIGRATION: OKIES

Perhaps the best known story of the Depression-era West is the saga of internal migration. Beginning in the mid-1930s and peaking in 1937 and 1938, hundreds of thousands of Plains residents emigrated to California. The majority came from Oklahoma, Texas, and Arkansas, but they were known collectively as *Okies*. Others moved from the northern Plains to Oregon and Washington. Most were fleeing unworkable land both within and around the Dust Bowl of the western Great Plains. The most noticeable contingents became itinerant field workers, replacing Filipinos and Mexicans, in part because the Okies were more resistant to unionization. Nonetheless, the Associated Farmers, a powerful California growers' group, and the United Cannery, Agricultural, Packing, and Allied Workers of America, a Congress of Industrial Organizations (CIO) union, clashed often in the late 1930s.

California welcomed the Okies as cheap labor, but rejected them as residents. Los Angeles briefly set up a "Bum Blockade" in 1936, and the state denied relief money to newly arrived migrants. Most of the migrants lived in squalor in California and Arizona, although the Resettlement Administration and its successor, the Farm Security Administration, created a few model camps. These two administrations also purchased submarginal lands from families, and relocated them on settlements throughout the western states, including Alaska. The program was only partially successful because most of the resettlement land was itself of inferior quality.

If Depression-era western residents contributed anything exceptional to the national culture it was stimulated by the Okies' experience. John Steinbeck's novel *The Grapes of Wrath* (1939), Dorothea Lange's photographs, Woody Guthrie's ballads, and Carey McWilliams's *Factories in the Fields* (1939) all indicted California agriculture and vividly portrayed the migrants' travails.

THE NEW DEAL AND WATER

Some members of the Department of Agriculture, including Rexford Tugwell, had sought thorough planning coupled with federal management for land use in the West, but the policies actually formulated by Secretary of Agriculture Henry Wallace were mainly responses to critical conditions. The Department of Interior, under Harold Ickes, came closer to creating a major decision-making role for the federal government in the West. Not only in grazing, but in water policy and Indian affairs, Ickes's Department of Interior, sometimes successfully and other times problematically, drew up grand and comprehensive plans for often reluctant westerners.

The Bureau of Reclamation and the Public Works Administration (PWA) designed or assisted on a number of critical water projects during and immediately after the Depression that transformed several sections of the region. The projects, which created jobs in the short run, provided flood control, irrigation to reclaim arid lands, recreational sites, and, above all, hydroelectric power for the West Coast and intermountain regions. As the Bureau of Reclamation and the PWA completed the Boulder Dam project, actually authorized in 1928, Ickes and his staff realized the myriad effects of such an enormous project. Out of this understanding came Parker Dam in California to provide electricity to Los Angeles and the All-American Canal to irrigate the Imperial and Coachella valleys. On the Columbia River, the Bonneville Dam enhanced navigation and the 450-foot-high Grand Coulee Dam furnished irrigation for the dry eastern half of Washington. Above all, the dams created megawatts of public hydroelectric power (administered by a federal agency, the Bonneville Power Administration) that contributed to the defense industry, as well as to post-World War II diversification in the Northwest. In Montana the multipurpose earthen Fort Peck Dam regulated the flow of the Missouri River. At the end of the Depression era, the ambitious Colorado-Big Thompson project got underway in Colorado. And despite real questions about whether the project was more for the benefit of small farmers (which the Bureau of Reclamation served) or agribusinesses, the Central Valley Project in California, designed to supply more water to the San Joaquin Valley, got under way.

NATIVE AMERICANS

The Department of Interior's ideal of central planning surely affected Native Americans, who benefited from a variety of New Deal programs, especially the Indian Emergency Conservation Works Program—a separate CCC that allowed Native Americans to stay near their homes. The keystone to Indian policy was the Indian Reorganization Act of 1934 (Wheeler-Howard Act). Commissioner of Indian Affairs John Collier believed Indian communalism could be an antidote for an exceedingly individualistic American society. In tune with this ideal, the act repealed allotment in severalty, restored surplus lands to the tribes, and encouraged purchase of already allotted lands to be added to tribal lands. Tribal bodies could be created and tribal corporations formed to obtain federal loans.

Despite the fact that this legislation restored tribal autonomy, not all Indian groups approved. Full-blooded Native Americans tended to oppose the measure, fearing they would lose their allotments. Others had accepted assimilation and saw no reason for change. Many felt the commissioner and his staff were trying to manipulate them, especially after local agents seemed to control the writing of the tribal constitutions. Ultimately, ninety-three tribes voted for incorporation, but, significantly, the Navajos declined, perhaps upset by an overly aggressive Indian Bureau livestock purchasing program. It appears the Indian Reorganization Act was a partial success, mainly limited by government planners too zealous in instructing Native Americans on how to preserve their own heritage.

NATURAL RESOURCES

The New Deal record was modest in the area of natural resources. Wallace and Ickes vied for control of the forests. Futilely dreaming of transforming the Department of Interior into the Department of Conservation, Secretary Ickes sought to capture the Department of Agriculture's Forest Service by showing Interior's skill in multiple use planning and sustained yield forestry in the O and C Lands, an expanse of forest in western Oregon revested by the Oregon and California Railroad in 1916 and placed under Interior's control. Though he ultimately failed to expand his bureaucratic turf, Ickes was moderately successful expanding the forestland under his control through the Grazing Service and an enlargement of Olympic National Park in Washington.

The oil industry worked through much of the decade to prop up prices in the face of a petroleum glut. Ickes was again at the center of activity, advocating comprehensive federal regulation rather than the proration of production sought by the oil industry. After the Supreme Court abolished the National Recovery Administration and its regulations on production, several oil producing states negotiated the Interstate Oil and Gas Compact in 1935. This, along with the Connally Act to eliminate the transport of hot oil (oil produced in excess of the proration limits on each oil field), brought stability, and the oil industry became substantially self-regulating. The Silver Purchase Act of 1934, compelling the federal government to buy quantities of silver for possible monetization, was the most significant New Deal contribution to the mining industry. Though Roosevelt and, especially, Ickes saw the West as a land of resources to be carefully looked after and preserved, political realities in the end transformed this preservationist notion into, at best, more careful stewardship to produce later economic advantage for westerners.

DEPRESSION-ERA POLITICS IN THE WEST

Politics in the West largely followed national trends. Roosevelt swept the West in 1932 and 1936, then lost five states in 1940 (the Dakotas, Nebraska, Kansas, and Colorado). Many Democrats whom Roosevelt had helped sweep into office were loyal to him. Other Democrats proved to be prickly opponents. Governors Johnson of Colorado, Murray of Oklahoma, and Charles Martin of Oregon were particularly hostile. Senator Burton K. Wheeler of Montana, a one-time Roosevelt supporter, broke with the president over the issue of adding justices to the Supreme Court. Part of the reason for intra-party opposition was that Democrats in the West were often conservative. Republicans, particularly those infused with a Progressive tradition, were more liberal. Bronson Cutting of New Mexico, Edward Costigan of Colorado, and Nebraska's George Norris, all Republicans, were New Deal supporters.

The Washington and Oregon Commonwealth associations and North Dakota's Non-Partisan League generally shunned party affiliation, but seemed to find common cause with more progressive New Deal policies. With such a topsy-turvy political situation, it is no surprise that the Roosevelt coalition did not hold up well in the West, even though Roosevelt's programs found philosophical support among some opinion makers in the region. As the need for federal assistance lessened, traditional independent-mindedness reasserted itself, and westerners went back to voting for candidates rather than parties and to voting Republican more often.

Though not numerous, there were some who sought to go beyond the New Deal. In 1934, socialist Upton Sinclair waged a successful primary campaign to win the Democratic nomination for governor of California, but he lost the race to a conservative Republican when leading Democrats, including Roosevelt, sat out his End Poverty in California (EPIC) campaign. Dr. Francis Townsend's old age pension plan started in Long Beach, California. Even before organized labor benefited from the Wagner Act, union leader Harry Bridges organized one of the most significant Depression-era strikes among Pacific Coast dockworkers. Marked by violence, the action evolved into a four-day general strike in San Francisco in 1934. In the end, Bridges's International Longshoremen's Association gained recognition.

EVALUATIONS

The Great Depression in the West may have sapped cooperative individualism in the early years, but by World War II it was clear that some variety of individualism was active in the region. Westerners accepted the federal government as an agent of relief, whether it was outright relief, work relief, subsidies for farmers, or livestock purchases. But when New Dealers sought to plan or merely guide the western economy, the federal government was still seen as interfering. Federal planning affected the West in varying degrees: Some marginal land was taken out of production; agronomy methods improved; grazing on federal land was fairly closely controlled; land allotments for Native Americans were halted; and forests were managed, perhaps better than before. But individual westerners, especially the more powerful ones, still had a good deal of autonomy in agriculture, lumber, oil, and mining. The greatest impact of central planning in the West occurred in water management, where only the federal government could afford to undertake the huge projects that changed the western half of the region. The hydroelectricity these projects produced prepared the West for diversification during the war years and beyond. Politically, the story was the same. Westerners demonstrated their gratefulness to President Roosevelt for his assistance, but they clung to their independent, mainly Republican, ways. The Depression in the West produced significant change, but could not be accurately described as a watershed.

See Also: BOULDER DAM; DUST BOWL; GRAND COULEE PROJECT; INDIAN NEW DEAL; MIDWEST, GREAT DEPRESSION IN THE; NORTHEAST, GREAT DEPRESSION IN THE; OKIES; SHELTERBELT PROJECT; SOUTH, GREAT DEPRESSION IN THE; TAYLOR GRAZING ACT.

BIBLIOGRAPHY

Arrington, Leonard. "The New Deal in the West: A Preliminary Statistical Inquiry." *Pacific Historical Review* 38 (1969): 311–316.

Balderrama, Francisco, and Raymond Rodriguez. *Decade of Betrayal: Mexican Repatriation in the 1930s.* 1995

Braeman, John; Robert H. Bremner; and David Brody, eds. *The New Deal,* Vol. 2: *The State and Local Levels.* 1975.

Cannon, Brian Q. *Remaking the Agrarian Dream: New Deal Rural Resettlement in the Mountain West.* 1996.

Droze, Wilmon. *Trees, Prairies, and People: A History of Tree Planting in the Plains States.* 1977.

Ford, John, director. *The Grapes of Wrath.* 1940.

Gregory, James N. *American Exodus: The Dust Bowl Migration and Okie Culture in California.* 1989.

Hendrickson, Kenneth D., Jr., ed., *Hard Times in Oklahoma: The Depression Years.* 1983.

Hoffman, Charles. "Drought and Depression: Migration into Oregon, 1930–1936." *Monthly Labor Review* 46, no. 1 (1938): 27–35.

Hurt, Douglas R. *The Dust Bowl: An Agricultural and Social History.* 1981.

Loftis, Anne. *Witness to the Struggle: Imaging the 1930s California Labor Movement.* 1998.

Lorentz, Pare, director. *The Plow That Broke the Plains.* 1936.

Lowitt, Richard. *The New Deal and the West.* 1984.

Luckingham, Bradford. *Minorities in Phoenix: A Profile of Mexican American, Chinese American, and African American Communities, 1860–1992.* 1994.

Mullins, William H. *The Depression and the Urban West Coast: Los Angeles, San Francisco, Seattle, and Portland.* 1991.

Nash, Gerald D. *The American West in the Twentieth Century: A Short History of an Urban Oasis.* 1973.

Nash, Gerald D. *The Federal Landscape: An Economic History of the Twentieth Century West.* 1999.

Nugent, Walter. *Into the West: The Story of its People.* 1999.

Parman, Donald. *Indians and the American West in the Twentieth Century.* 1994.

Patterson, James T. *The New Deal and the States: Federalism in Transition.* 1969.

Patterson, James T. "The New Deal in the West." *Pacific Historical Review* 38 (1969): 317–327.

Philp, Kenneth R. *John Collier's Crusade for Indian Reform, 1920–1954.* 1977.

Pomeroy, Earl S. *The Pacific Slope: A History of California, Oregon, Washington, Idaho, Utah, and Nevada.* 1965.

de Roos, Robert. *The Thirsty Land: The Story of the Central Valley Project.* 1948.

Sheridan, Thomas E. *Arizona: A History.* 1995.

Steinbeck, John. *The Grapes of Wrath.* 1939.

Stock, Catherine. *Main Street in Crisis: The Great Depression and the Old Middle Class on the Northern Plains.* 1992.

Taylor, Graham. *The New Deal and American Indian Tribalism: The Administration of the Indian Re-organization Act, 1934–1935.* 1980.

Whisenhunt, Donald W. *The Depression in Texas: The Hoover Years.* 1983.

White, Richard. *"It's Your Misfortune and None of My Own": A History of the American West.* 1991.

Worster, Donald. *Dust Bowl: The Southern Plains in the 1930s.* 1979.

WILLIAM H. MULLINS

WEST, MAE

Mae West (August 17, 1893–November 22, 1980) reigned during the 1930s as one of Hollywood's most popular and controversial actresses. Born Mary Jane West in Brooklyn, New York, on August 17, 1893, West was raised in a poor family. A precocious child, she began performing with local stock companies. By 1910, she embarked on a professional career and for years bounced between vaudeville and burlesque with occasional Broadway engagements in between.

By the 1920s, West had developed a unique and bold performance style rooted in vaudeville, melodrama, drag performance, and African-American culture. In 1927, her fame grew with her appearance in *SEX*, a play she had authored. *SEX*'s frankness, combined with her attempt to stage another play about homosexuality, landed West a ten-day jail sentence. In 1928, she wrote and starred in the hit, *Diamond Lil*, the story of a former prostitute with a heart of gold. The image of the swaggering, hand on her hip, wise-cracking Lil became enmeshed with West's public persona.

West's film break came in 1932 when Paramount Studios, despite movie censors' ban on the actress, slipped her into a small part in *Night after Night*. Critics agreed: West was brilliant. Realizing her earning potential, the nearly bankrupt studio gave West complete creative control and proceeded with filming *Diamond Lil*. The result, *She Done Him Wrong* (1933), broke all box office records and revived Paramount. West's follow-up, *I'm No Angel* (1933) was equally successful. The actress became a national phenomenon. Her clever sayings, including "Come up and see me sometime" and "When I'm good, I'm very good, but when I'm bad I'm better," and Mae West look-alike contests swept the country.

Although Hollywood's most powerful woman, Mae West could not outsmart censors for long. They drastically sheared her fourth film, *Belle of the Nineties* (1934). West made only five more films during the decade, and with each one her character became blander and her audience dwindled. Nonetheless, she remained a presence and even found herself banished from radio after a saucy performance in an Adam and Eve skit in 1937.

Much of West's appeal rested in her ability to empower people struggling through the Great Depression. West played the underdog who tri-

Mae West, circa 1930s. LIBRARY OF CONGRESS, PRINTS & PHOTOGRAPHS DIVISION, NEW YORK WORLD-TELEGRAM AND THE SUN NEWSPAPER PHOTOGRAPH COLLECTION

umphed through wit and guile. Her bold celebration of female sexuality empowered women. But her rags-to-riches story also spoke to Americans from all walks of life, giving them hope that they too could overcome adversity.

See Also: GENDER ROLES AND SEXUAL RELATIONS, IMPACT OF THE GREAT DEPRESSION ON; HOLLYWOOD AND THE FILM INDUSTRY.

BIBLIOGRAPHY

Curry, Ramona. *Too Much of a Good Thing: Mae West as Cultural Icon.* 1996.

Hamilton, Mary Beth. *When I'm Bad I'm Better: Mae West, Sex, and American Popular Entertainment.* 1995.

Leider, Emily Wortis. *Becoming Mae West.* 1997.

Robertson, Pamela. *Guilty Pleasures: Feminist Camp from Mae West to Madonna.* 1996.

Watts, Jill. *Mae West: An Icon in Black and White.* 2001.

JILL WATTS

WEST, NATHANAEL

Nathanael West (October 17, 1903–December 22, 1940) may well have been the quintessential Depression-decade novelist. He published all four of his depressive short novels in the 1930s and then died, quickly and tragically. He was born Nathan Wallenstein Weinstein in New York City. A voracious reader, he was a surprisingly poor student and dropped out of high school. Using faked transcripts, he gained admission to two colleges, and, after some chicanery, managed to graduate from Brown University in Rhode Island. While at Brown, West wrote an early draft of his first novel, *The Dream Life of Balso Snell.* After graduation, he worked at a number of small Manhattan hotels as an assistant or night manager.

Working nights, he was able to spend his time reading and observing the seedier aspects of urban American life. He also spent time rewriting his earlier drafts of *The Dream Life of Balso Snell.* He told a friend that he considered this novel "a protest against the writing of books." He then follows, he explains, the meanderings of "an American Babbitt. . . . through the anus of the Trojan horse, and [describes] his encounters there with various forms of deception, pretense, and illusion." In 1931 West had five hundred copies of *The Dream Life of Balso Snell* privately printed by the avant-garde firm of Contact Editions. The author was listed as Nathanael West, marking Nathan Weinstein's official name change. The novel received only two reviews, both written by friends.

In 1929, the writer S. J. Perelman, who had been a close college friend and was to become his brother-in-law, showed West a group of letters written to the lovelorn columnist of a Brooklyn newspaper. West saw immediately that the letters were cries for help. Deeply moved, he started transmuting his reactions to the letters into fiction. He worked on this second novel for four years, completing the final draft of *Miss Lonelyhearts* only in November 1932. In it, a young newspaperman, known only by his byline, Miss Lonelyhearts, devises replies to "Desperate," "Brokenhearted," "Sick-of-it-all," and others of the lovelorn who write to him for advice. Despite a smattering of generally favorable reviews, *Miss Lonelyhearts* garnered few readers and was quickly remaindered. West spent a few months in Hollywood in 1933, working as a junior writer at Columbia Pictures. About this time he conceived the idea of writing a novel about the dream capital's "subterranean life." He soon returned to New York, bitter and disenchanted with Hollywood. Other favorable reviews to *Miss Lonelyhearts* continued to appear, and to cash in on these positive reactions to his second novel, West quickly wrote *A Cool Million.* It was a savage attack on the Horatio Alger, rags-to-riches myth of capitalist America's rugged individualism. But the manuscript was rejected by his previous publisher, Harcourt, Brace. Its editors considered it a disappointing fall from the level of *Miss Lonelyhearts.* Published instead by Covici-Friede in 1934, *A Cool Million* was savaged by most of the reviewers and, like its predecessor, was almost immediately remaindered.

West now found himself without viable options for making a living. So, despite his distaste for Hollywood, he returned there to be a scriptwriter at Republic Studios. Hollywood was now his real home, whether or not he wished to recognize it as such. But whereas novelists like F. Scott Fitzgerald, William Faulkner, and Aldous Huxley were working for studios such as MGM and Twentieth Century-Fox, West worked mostly at "Poverty Row" film factories like Republic. Only near the end of his life did he make it even to RKO and Universal. By then West had finally found his niche. In the end he derived more from his schlock Hollywood experiences than did those writers who were better situated. After all, he was researching and writing *The Day of the Locust* on a daily basis, so he was quite content and amused to grind "out the rather stupefying plots" his Republic, Universal, and RKO bosses demanded. Yet despite his professed negativism and his bitter disappointment over his new novel's poor sales, West continued to work steadily and live comfortably. In 1939 he published *The Day of the Locust,* which he had finished between studio assignments. In this novel West's Yale man observer-hero, Tod Hackett, finds himself involved with an array of the movie town's castoffs. West hoped the novel would prove successful enough for him to leave Hollywood. It was not; in fact, it sold only

1,480 copies. However, the reviews were generally positive, even enthusiastic at times.

The decade of the 1930s had not proved especially kind to West, despite his having published four novels that established his literary reputation. But the 1940s seemed to hold promise of both greater personal happiness and literary success, for in 1939 he had met and fallen in love with a young widow with a sunny disposition and a son from her previous marriage. She was Eileen McKenney, the heroine of Ruth McKenney's *My Sister Eileen,* widely popular as a book and a movie. They married in April 1940, and West adopted her son. The newlyweds spent three happy months in Oregon hunting and fishing, but this blissful period was to be short-lived. On December 22, he and his wife were returning from a hunting trip in Mexico, when West, a notoriously poor driver, ran a stop sign near El Centro, California, and crashed their station wagon into another automobile. Eileen died on the spot, and West died an hour later on the way to the hospital. He was 37. Very likely West would find dark humor in his posthumous fame.

See Also: LITERATURE.

BIBLIOGRAPHY

Comerchero, Victor. *Nathanael West: The Ironic Prophet.* 1964.

Hyman, Stanley Edgar. *Nathanael West.* 1962.

Light, James F. *Nathanael West: An Interpretive Study.* 1961.

Madden, David, ed. *Nathanael West: The Cheaters and the Cheated.* 1973.

Martin, Jay. *Nathanael West: The Art of His Life.* 1970.

Reid, Randall. *The Fiction of Nathanael West: No Redeemer, No Promised Land.* 1967.

Siegel, Ben, ed. *Critical Essays on Nathanael West.* 1994.

West, Nathanael. *The Complete Works of Nathanael West.* 1957.

BEN SIEGEL

WHEELER, BURTON K.

Burton Kendall Wheeler (February 27, 1882–January 7, 1975) was a United States senator from Montana (1923–1947) best known for opposing U.S. entry into World War II. The youngest of ten children of Asa Wheeler, a Quaker shoemaker, and Mary Tyler, Wheeler was born in Hudson, Massachusetts and graduated from the University of Michigan Law School in 1905. He practiced law in Butte, Montana, and served one term as a Democrat in the Montana House of Representatives. President Woodrow Wilson in 1913 appointed him United States district attorney general for Montana.

In 1922, Wheeler was elected as a Democrat to the United States Senate. In 1924 he charged Attorney General Harry Daugherty with failing to prosecute those involved in the Teapot Dome scandal and directed a Senate inquiry into the scandal, causing President Calvin Coolidge to force Daugherty's resignation. In 1924, he ran unsuccessfully for vice president on the Progressive Party ticket headed by Senator Robert LaFollette of Wisconsin.

During President Franklin Roosevelt's first term, Wheeler backed most New Deal legislation. As Interstate Commerce Committee chairman, he led the successful floor battle in 1935 for the Public Utilities Holding Company Act. Wheeler considered the measure his toughest Senate battle because of resistance by the powerful utilities lobby.

In 1937 Wheeler protested Roosevelt's "court-packing" plan to enlarge the U.S. Supreme Court as an unconstitutional attempt to seize power. Roosevelt, hoping to give the Supreme Court a New Deal majority, personally sought to dissuade Wheeler, who rallied conservative Democrats to bury the president's proposal by fifty votes. The setback marked Roosevelt's worst legislative defeat to that point and sparked a resurgence of congressional power.

Wheeler helped lead isolationist resistance to Roosevelt's internationalist policies until the Japanese attacked Pearl Harbor. The powerful, sharp-tongued orator spoke at numerous America First Committee rallies in 1941 opposing U.S. aid to the Allies. In January 1941 he infuriated Roosevelt by denouncing the lend-lease bill aiding Great Britain as "the New Deal's triple-A foreign policy" and warning "it will plow under every fourth American boy." Wheeler ultimately supported the U.S. military effort during World War II, but his influence declined dramatically. He lost his re-election bid in 1946 and spent the rest of his career practicing corporate law in Washington, D.C., in support of right-wing causes.

An adept legislative infighter, Wheeler usually criticized government programs rather than initiating or building them. The independent, fiesty politician seemed happiest in the opposition or on the offensive. His legislative skills, deal-making, arm-twisting abilities, and proficiency at stroking egos made him a leading Senate figure.

See Also: ISOLATIONISM; PUBLIC UTILITIES HOLDING COMPANY ACT; SUPREME COURT "PACKING" CONTROVERSY.

BIBLIOGRAPHY

Cole, Wayne S. *Roosevelt and the Isolationists, 1932–1945.* 1983.

Leuchtenburg, William E. *The Supreme Court Reborn.* 1995.

Ruetten, Richard T. "Burton K. Wheeler of Montana: A Progressive between the Wars." Ph.D.diss., University of Oregon, 1961.

Wheeler, Burton K., with Paul F. Healy. *Yankee from the West.* 1962.

DAVID L. PORTER

"WHICH SIDE ARE YOU ON?"

Of the many songs born out of labor strife in America's coal camps, Florence Reece's classic 1931 union song "Which Side Are You On?" is one of the best known. The struggle in Harlan County emerged from the depths of the economic crisis in the coal fields in the early 1930s, which produced successive wage cuts and layoffs for miners. In the battle of Evarts, strikers and mine guards fought a violent battle, leading to mass arrests and prosecutions of striking miners on criminal charges. The struggle in Harlan aroused people across the country in support of the right to organize, leading ultimately to the enactment of the Wagner Act's protections for union rights.

In the spring of 1931, citing the dangerous conditions in the mines and their low pay, the coal miners of Harlan County, Kentucky, began a strike that was stridently opposed by the local Coal Operators' Association (COA). On one side of the conflict stood the forces of the COA and local law enforcement, led by the high sheriff of Harlan County, J. H. Blair. (In an interview with the writer John Dos Passos, Blair admitted that most of his deputies were mine guards who were still being paid by mine owners.) On the other side were the striking miners, who organized themselves under the tutelege of the National Miners' Union (NMU) and armed themselves against Blair's forces of so-called law and order.

Florence Reece became involved in the conflict when Sheriff Blair and his men broke into her family's cabin, ransacking it in their search for union literature, terrorizing her and her children, and lying in wait for her husband, Sam Reece, an NMU organizer. Luckily, Sam did not fall into Blair's trap, but Florence was moved to action. She tore a sheet from a wall calendar and, using the old Baptist tune "Lay the Lily Low," she wrote "Which Side Are You On?" The song opens by asking "all you poor workers" to listen to the good news that the union "has come in here to dwell." The chorus asks the dividing question: "Which side are you on?" Then the third verse lays out the two sides: "If you go to Harlan County / There is no neutral there / You'll either be a union man / Or a thug for J. H. Blair."

"Which Side Are You On" became an anthem of labor struggle, as the folk process transformed it in different ways. Pete Seeger and various workers organizing unions as part of the Congress of Industrial Organizations picked up the song as their own, changing lyrics to fit the situation at hand. Song leader Zilphia Horton and others at Highlander Folk School transmitted the song to new groups of southern workers who came there to learn about organizing. The song eventually passed over from the union movement to the black freedom movement. In 1961, Congress of Racial Equality leader James Farmer revised the words to fit the circumstances in the south during the Freedom Rides: Whenever members felt that other African Americans were betraying the cause of equality and freedom, CORE members sang, "Oh people can you stand it, / Tell me how you can. / Will you be an

Uncle Tom / Or will you be a man?" Reece's song moved from Harlan County to Mississippi, and then to Alabama, where Len Chandler created new verses for the voting rights march from Selma to Montgomery in 1965, satirizing people who feared to take a stand as well as the state's bigoted governor George Wallace and the Ku Klux Klan.

"Which Side Are You On?" has long outlasted Reece, who died at her home in Knoxville in 1986. It remains her lasting legacy to the world and a reminder of how the culture of struggle created during the Depression era continues to influence protest and social movements.

See Also: HARLAN COUNTY; MUSIC; ORGANIZED LABOR.

BIBLIOGRAPHY

Carawan, Guy, and Candie Carawan, eds. *We Shall Overcome: Songs of the Southern Freedom Movement.* 1963.

Florence Reece interview with Ron Stanford, "Which Side Are You On?" in *Sing Out!* 20, no. 6 (July/August 1971): 13–15.

Reece, Florence. *Against the Current: Poems and Stories.* 1981.

MARK JACKSON
MICHAEL HONEY

Walter White, 1942. LIBRARY OF CONGRESS, PRINTS & PHOTOGRAPHS DIVISION, FSA/OWI COLLECTION

WHITE, WALTER

Walter White (1893–1955), secretary of the National Association for the Advancement of Colored People (NAACP) between 1930 and 1955, was born in Atlanta, Georgia. According to his *New York Times* obituary (March 22, 1955), "Mr. White, the nearest approach to a national leader of American Negroes since Booker T. Washington, was a Negro by choice." The blonde-haired and blue-eyed White could "pass" for white, yet he chose not to do so. Central to his decision to identify himself as African American was his witnessing of the Atlanta race riot of 1906. After graduating from Atlanta University in 1916, White helped to found that city's branch of the NAACP; two years later, he moved to New York City to be the association's assistant secretary. Because of his complexion, his first assignments were incognito investigations of lynchings and race riots; between 1918 and 1926 he investigated more than forty acts of mob violence.

Lynching increased dramatically with the onset of the Depression, rising from an average of ten recorded in the nation each year during the late 1920s to thirty in the first nine months of 1930 alone. Reacting to this steady growth, in January 1934 White and the NAACP decided to make passage of a federal antilynching law a priority. For the next five years, White led this effort by persistently lobbying senators and representatives to pass such legislation sponsored variously by Senators Edward Costigan, Robert Wagner, and Frederick Van Nuys, and Representative Joseph Gavagan. Working out of congressional sponsors' offices, White directed the legislative strategy and publicity campaign. Three times he marshaled majorities in the Senate, only to have the bill defeated by a filibuster—or the threat of one—by southern senators.

White also made his presence felt in the White House. He and Eleanor Roosevelt became close friends, and she joined the NAACP board of directors after her husband's death in 1945. With her aid, White secured meetings with the president to plead the Negroes' case for antilynching legislation and equity in New Deal programs. Though White did persuade the president to denounce lynching, Roosevelt would not actively back an antilynching bill, and the Congress never passed one.

Under White's leadership, the NAACP developed a strategy to attack segregation in education. Beginning in 1934, association lawyers won important legal victories mandating that public universities admit black applicants on an equal basis to their professional programs and compelling public school systems to equalize black and white teachers' salaries. These were precedents for the Supreme Court's 1954 *Brown* v. *Board of Education* decision declaring segregation in education unconstitutional.

Responding to rampant employment discrimination in defense industries and the labor movement's unwillingness to eliminate discrimination in its own ranks, White and A. Philip Randolph pressed the president to take corrective action. Threats of a mass march on Washington in June 1941 compelled Roosevelt to issue executive order 8802, which banned defense contractors from practicing racial discrimination.

See Also: NATIONAL ASSOCIATION FOR THE ADVANCEMENT OF COLORED PEOPLE (NAACP); RACE RELATIONS.

BIBLIOGRAPHY

Papers of the NAACP. Parts 7 and 10. Microfilm. 1981–.

Janken, Kenneth R. *White: The Biography of Walter White, Mr. Naacp.* 2003.

White, Walter. *A Man Called White.* 1948.

Zangrando, Robert L. *The NAACP Crusade against Lynching, 1909–1950.* 1980.

KENNETH R. JANKEN

WHITE, WILLIAM ALLEN

William Allen White (February, 10 1868–January 29, 1944), over a long career as a journalist, author, and political commentator, came to be widely respected as the embodiment, in the words of a *Life* profile, of "small-town simplicity and kindliness and common sense." Born in Emporia, Kansas, he attended the College of Emporia and the University of Kansas. In 1895 he purchased a daily newspaper, the *Emporia Gazette,* which he continued to publish even as he won a national audience for his many books and magazine articles. With Theodore Roosevelt and other reform-minded Republicans, White founded the Progressive Party in 1912. Though White returned to the Republican Party in 1916, he remained a pillar of its progressive-to-moderate wing.

White's reputation as spokesman for middle-class middle America deepened over the next decades, prompting H. L. Mencken to dub him the "Sage of Emporia." He criticized presidents Warren Harding and Calvin Coolidge for bowing to the interests of "benevolent plutocracy," and supported fellow progressive Herbert Hoover in 1928. His support of the liberal values of free speech and opposition to the influence of the Ku Klux Klan in Kansas won the respect of big-city liberals. But they were mystified by his support of prohibition and loyalty to the Republican Party in the 1930s, after Franklin D. Roosevelt seized the banner of reform for the Democrats. White gave a mixed reception to the New Deal, supporting measures to regulate the economy and improve the lot of common Americans while repeatedly expressing reservations about concentration of power in the federal government. Yet White was largely consistent to the small-town values that had shaped his ideology. Like many former progressives, he warned that New Deal programs imposed a wasteful and distant bureaucracy upon everyday life. He also expressed misgivings that Roosevelt's charisma and appeals to class interests smacked of the totalitarianism sweeping much of the rest of the world. In 1936 he supported Kansas governor Alfred Landon for president, leading Roosevelt to thank him for his "support for three and a half years out of every four."

White supported Roosevelt's efforts to counter American isolationism in the 1930s. In 1940 White headed the bipartisan Committee to Defend America by Aiding the Allies, which argued that military assistance to Britain would help stop German aggression without requiring outright American involvement. The committee's work helped secure the Lend-Lease Act in March 1941. During the last years before his death in 1944, White wrote his autobiography, which was posthumously awarded the Pulitzer Prize.

See Also: COMMUNICATIONS AND THE PRESS.

BIBLIOGRAPHY

Agran, Edward Gale. *Too Good a Town: William Allen White, Community, and the Emerging Rhetoric of Middle America.* 1999.

Griffith, Sally Foreman. *Home Town News: William Allen White and the Emporia Gazette.* 1989.

Jernigan, E. Jay. *William Allen White.* 1983.

Johnson, Walter. *William Allen White's America.* 1947.

White, William Allen. *The Autobiography of William Allen White,* 2nd edition, revised and abridged, edited by Sally Foreman Griffith. 1990.

"William Allen White of Emporia: An American Institution is 70." *Life,* February 28, 1938, 9–13.

SALLY F. GRIFFITH

WHITNEY, RICHARD. *See* SECURITIES REGULATION.

WILLIAMS, AUBREY

Aubrey Willis Williams (August 1890–March 1965) was deputy administrator of the Federal Emergency Relief Administration (FERA) and deputy administrator of the Works Progress Administration (WPA) under Harry Hopkins, and also head of the National Youth Administration (NYA) throughout its existence. Born in Springville, Alabama, into a family impoverished by the Civil War, his formal education was minimal. At twenty-one he enrolled at Maryville College in Tennessee as a student for the ministry, before serving in World War I, first in the French Foreign Legion and later, after U.S. intervention, with the U.S. Army. Already a committed social activist, he qualified as a social worker at the University of Cincinnati, then worked for a decade in Wisconsin before joining Harry Hopkins's team in the first days of the New Deal.

Williams was responsible for the day-to-day operations of both the FERA and WPA, as well as being in effective control of the NYA. He was tough, resourceful and outspoken, firmly located in the New Deal's left wing, determined to use his position to attack the United States's social and economic imbalances, and especially to further the cause of civil rights for black Americans. In particular he used the NYA to provide employment and training for the nation's disadvantaged young people. He made powerful enemies among the forces opposed to New Deal liberalism, and in 1943 they engineered the dismantling of the NYA in spite of its importance to the war effort.

With that, Williams left public office, never to return. In 1945 he returned to Montgomery, Alabama, where he edited a small newspaper, and for the rest of his life, worked as a courageous and increasingly isolated regional spokesperson for the coming civil rights revolution. As such, he was frequently investigated by Senator Joseph McCarthy's lieutenants in the1950s. He lived long enough to take part in Martin Luther King, Jr.'s March on Washington in 1963.

See Also: BETHUNE, MARY MCLEOD; HOPKINS, HARRY; NATIONAL YOUTH ADMINISTRATION (NYA).

BIBLIOGRAPHY

Lindley, Ernest K., and Betty Lindley. *A New Deal for Youth: The Story of the National Youth Administration.* 1938.

Rawick, George P. "The New Deal and Youth." Ph.D. diss., University of Wisconsin, 1957.

Salmond, John A. *A Southern Rebel. The Life and Times of Aubrey Willis Williams.*

JOHN A. SALMOND

WILLKIE, WENDELL

Wendell Lewis Willkie (February 8, 1892–October 8, 1944), whose grandparents came to America after the failure of the German democratic revolution of 1848, was the unsuccessful Republican candidate for president in 1940. Willkie was born and raised in rural Indiana, and before undertaking the study of law, he reflected on the progressive intellectual background of his upbringing in Elwood.

As a young attorney with the Firestone Tire and Rubber Company in Akron, Ohio, and then as a junior partner in a prestigious local law firm with a specialty in utilities matters, he engaged in political affairs, speaking out for Woodrow Wilson and the League of Nations and leading a fight against surging Ku Klux Klan power. At the Democratic Party's 1924 national convention, Willkie participated in a futile floor battle to condemn the Klan. His leadership of the local bar association and experience in the utilities field led to an invitation to move to New York as a legal representative of Commonwealth and Southern, a newly formed holding company. Later, at the age of forty-one, and at the depth of the Great Depression, he took over as its president.

Willkie's corporate position clashed with the New Deal's Tennessee Valley Administration, bringing him into conflict with the federal government's efforts to provide cheap power to a vast backward area. Willkie's fight against such federal ownership ended when the Supreme Court upheld TVA. Commonwealth and Southern was paid an impressive $78,600,000 for its facilities, a process that gave Willkie prominence that endeared him to anti-New Deal businessmen as the administration's most engaging critic.

Even before Willkie became a Republican in the fall of 1939, the concept of him as United States president was promoted by an alliance that included businessmen, bankers, electrical power interests, and influential editors and publishers. Hastily organized Willkie Clubs tried to prevent Franklin D. Roosevelt from winning an unprecedented third term. Such corporate and grassroots Republicanism aimed at sparing the party from entering the election as indifferent to European victims of Nazi Germany. While other GOP presidential candidates held to a strong Midwestern sense of isolationism, Willkie feared that England was in imminent danger of invasion. With the announcement in January 1940 that Willkie had become a Republican and the news that spring that the Nazi blitzkrieg had rolled through France and the Low Countries and reached the English Channel, Willkie's popularity made quick gains. His promoters comprised a loosely organized so-called Eastern Establishment that came to dominate Republican presidential politics for the next twenty years.

At the Republican national convention, amid tumultuous nominating sessions energized by spectator galleries filled with Willkie boosters, "the darkest horse in the stable" won the nomination on the sixth ballot. His ranking in the Gallup poll had shot ahead of New York District Attorney Tom Dewey, a fact confirmed only after his victory at that enthusiastic Philadelphia convention. The candidate chose Senator Charles McNary of Oregon as his running-mate.

Leading a party dominated by anti-interventionists, Willkie wavered between backing aid for Great Britain and warning that Roosevelt's reelection would surely lead to young Americans dying in a European war, rhetoric he later dismissed as "a bit of campaign oratory." His key contribution to preparedness was the muting of political conflicts threatening to slow Roosevelt's efforts. In August, he offered a forthright endorsement of a selective service bill, which Congress approved the following month by a single vote. In early 1941, after the election, he testified in support of Roosevelt's efforts to help Great Britain via the Lend-Lease program, which fellow Republicans denounced as "the war dictatorship bill."

Failing to block a third term, losing by 449 to 82 in the electoral college (while picking up a Republican record of 22,321,000 popular votes to Roosevelt's 27,308,000), Willkie returned to New York City for a partnership in a law firm that gave him enough time to remain active politically. He undertook two overseas trips, the second on Roosevelt's behalf after Pearl Harbor was attacked in 1941, which resulted in a very popular book, *One World*, an anticolonialist view of the future. Willkie also fought in the courts for civil liberties and worked for racial justice. Deserted by GOP conservatives, especially after losing a primary in Wisconsin during the spring of 1944, he received invitations to team up with Roosevelt, possibly to form a more liberal third party. Wary of being manipulated for political purposes by a shrewd president, Willkie decided to postpone his response until after the election, but he died on October 8, 1944, after a series of heart attacks at the age of 52.

See Also: ELECTION OF 1940; REPUBLICAN PARTY.

BIBLIOGRAPHY

Barnard, Ellsworth. *Wendell Willkie: Fighter for Freedom.* 1966.

Burns, James MacGregor. *Roosevelt: The Soldier of Freedom, 1940–1945.* 1970.

Goodwin, Doris Kearns. *No Ordinary Time: Franklin and Eleanor Roosevelt, The Home Front in World War II.* 1994.

Johnson, Donald Bruce. *The Republican Party and Wendell Willkie.* 1960.

Moscow, Warren. *Roosevelt and Willkie.* 1968.

Neal, Steve. *Dark Horse: A Biography of Wendell Willkie.* 1984.

Parmet, Herbert S., and Marie B. Hecht. *Never Again: A President Runs for a Third Term.* 1968.

Persico, Joseph E. *Roosevelt's Secret War: FDR and World War II Espionage.* 2001.

HERBERT S. PARMET

WILSON, EDMUND

Edmund Wilson (May 8, 1895–June 12, 1972), journalist, critic, novelist, and historian, vigorously commented on American culture and society for five decades. He was born in Red Bank, New Jersey, and graduated from Princeton University in 1916. In World War I, he served in France with an army medical unit and in Germany on occupation duty. On his return to the United States in 1919, he became a magazine writer and editor, first at the monthly *Vanity Fair*, then at the liberal weekly *The New Republic*. In 1927, he completed his first novel, *I Thought of Daisy*, and in 1930 his first major book of criticism, *Axel's Castle*.

As the United States's economic crisis worsened after the 1929 crash, Wilson went on the road to report what he saw as the breakdown of U.S. capitalism and the onset of class war. With such contemporaries as John dos Passos and Sherwood Anderson, he used vivid literary journalism to counter indifference or ignorance about the country's growing distress. His articles on Communist demonstrations in New York, Detroit's automobile factories, West Virginia coal mines, workers at the Hoover (Boulder) Dam, and suicides at "The Jumping-Off Place," San Diego, were collected in *The American Jitters: A Year of the Slump* (1932). Alfred Kazin wrote that the book caught "perfectly the revolutionary and unsettling impact of the 1930s" (*Kazin* 1962, p. 408). Wilson's subsequent Depression-era reporting—notably "Hull-House in 1932," a dark portrait of Chicago in the pit of the Depression—was republished in *Travels in Two Democracies* (1936).

In the early 1930s Wilson called himself a communist, but he avoided contact with the Communist Party. In 1935 he won a Guggenheim Fellowship for travel in the Soviet Union—the other "democracy" in *Two Democracies*. By the time he published his major historical work on the roots of *Marxism, To the Finland Station*, in 1940, he had become more skeptical of the Soviet system.

Wilson continued to produce scholarship, polemic, and criticism for the remainder of his life. Among the notable works of his later career were the novel *Memoirs of Hecate County* (1946), which censors declared obscene; *Apologies to the Iroquois* (1960), on Native American culture; *Patriotic Gore* (1962), analyzing the literature of the U.S. Civil War (1962); and, finally, the melancholy *Upstate* (1971). He considered himself primarily a journalist, and his Depression writings remained the most enduring example of that aspect of his work. As the critic Robert Cantwell commented, "The body of writing that . . . Wilson produced in the period of his pilgrimage is one of the major accomplishments of the American imagination" (Cantwell 1958).

See Also: LITERATURE.

BIBLIOGRAPHY

Cantwell, Robert. "Wilson as Journalist." *The Nation* (February 22, 1958): p. 166–170.

Castronovo, David. *Edmund Wilson.* 1985.

Kazin, Alfred. *Contemporaries.* 1962.

Wilson, Edmund. *The American Earthquake.* 1958.

Wilson, Edmund. *Letters on Literature and Politics 1912–1972.* Edited by Elena Wilson. 1977.

Wilson, Edmund. "The Literary Consequences of the Crash," in *The Shores of Light: A Literary Chronicle of the Twenties and Thirties.* 1952.

Wilson, Edmund. *The Thirties: From Notebooks and Diaries of the Period.* Edited by Leon Edel. 1980.

JAMES BOYLAN

WISCONSIN PROGRESSIVE PARTY

The Wisconsin Progressive Party provided a political vehicle for La Follette Progressives and their political allies between 1934 and 1946. The party emerged out of the peculiar political dynamics prevailing in the state after the 1932 election. Progressive Republicans in Wisconsin had frequently talked about starting a new party, and Senator Robert M. La Follette, Sr., had run for the presidency on a third party ticket in 1924. When his son Philip lost the governorship to conservative Democrat Albert Schmedeman in 1932, the state faction faced a difficult decision. Remaining in the party of Herbert Hoover was distasteful to many, but trying to operate within the Wisconsin Democratic Party, which was at least as conservative in orientation, held little appeal. Despite its inherent riskiness, launching a new party seemed to many to offer a better chance for winning elections while allowing the Progressives to remain doctrinally pure.

Senator Robert M. La Follette, Jr., remained hesitant, but when more radical movement spokesmen, such as former Congressman Thomas R. Amlie, threatened to go ahead without the La Follettes, Philip La Follette, more open to the idea from the beginning, became an active proponent of a new party. Taking the traditional name *Progressive*, rather than the *Farmer-Labor* label favored by the radicals, the new party succeeded spectacularly in the fall elections. Along with putting the La Follette brothers back in the Senate and the governorship, the Progressives elected seven of Wisconsin's ten congressmen and won healthy proportions in both houses of the state legislature. Factionalism continued to split the Wisconsin Progressive Party during its brief existence. In November 1935 a group of advanced Progressives led by Amlie, State Federation of Labor leaders, and radical farm group spokesmen established a Farmer-Labor Progressive Federation, intended to promote the interests of their memberships and to move the party in a leftward direction. While cooperating with the new organization, Governor La Follette, who continued to be the real leader of the party as long as he remained in office, sought to deflect its influence and retain his freedom of action.

The election of 1936 witnessed the apex of party success. With the active cooperation of the Roosevelt administration, Phil La Follette won a third gubernatorial term and Progressives captured enough legislative seats to forge a working majority in that body. They legislated a "Little New Deal" for the state in 1937, and in April 1938 the governor attempted to expand his influence by launching a new national party, the National Progressives of America. It flopped and he lost his bid for re-election that fall, along with dozens of other progressives and liberals across the nation. The party rapidly declined. Its last spark of hope came with the election of Governor Orland Loomis in 1942, but he died before being inaugurated. With the disbanding of the party in 1946, most of its members went back into the Republican Party, but a group of its more advanced adherents became the core of a new liberalized state Democratic Party during the late 1940s and 1950s.

See Also: ELECTION OF 1936; LA FOLLETTE, PHILIP; LA FOLLETTE, ROBERT M., JR.

BIBLIOGRAPHY

Backstrom, Charles H. "The Progressive Party of Wisconsin, 1934–1936." Ph.D. diss., University of Wisconsin. 1956.

Johnson, Roger T. *Robert M. La Follette, Jr., and the Decline of the Progressive Party in Wisconsin.* 1964.

Maney, Patrick J. *"Young Bob" La Follette: A Biography of Robert M. La Follette, Jr., 1895–1953.* 1978.

Miller, John E. *Governor Philip F. La Follette, the Wisconsin Progressives, and the New Deal.* 1982.

Schmidt, Lester. "The Farmer-Labor Progressive Federation: The Study of a 'United Front' Movement

Judy Garland as Dorothy Gale and Billie Burke as Glinda, the Good Witch of the North, in the 1939 film The Wizard of Oz.
THE KOBAL COLLECTION / MGM

among Wisconsin Liberals, 1934–1941." Ph.D. diss., University of Wisconsin. 1954.

JOHN E. MILLER

WIZARD OF OZ, THE

MGM's 1939 film adaptation of L. Frank Baum's 1899 book, *The Wonderful Wizard of Oz,* was to become perhaps Hollywood's best-loved product, although it was not a huge box office success when it came out. The year 1939 is considered by many critics to have been the greatest in the studio era, with such classics as *Gone With the Wind, Stagecoach, Mr. Smith Goes to Washington,* and *Wuthering Heights,* along with a gaggle of near-greats, joining

Dorothy and her companions on the big screen that year. It was, however, the two color extravaganzas, *Oz* and *Gone with the Wind,* that became the most enduring movies in history.

The film has a much greater connection with the issues of the Depression era than is at first apparent. Harold Arlen and E. Y. "Yip" Harburg's song "Over the Rainbow" perfectly captured the continuing and long-deferred hopes of a people about to enter their second decade of depression. Dorothy Gale (a 12-year-old played by Judy Garland at sixteen), along with her family, is mistreated by Almira Gulch, the evil woman who owns most of her Kansas county and plainly represents the greedy bankers and capitalists who were widely seen as oppressing ordinary Americans during the Depression. Dorothy yearns to escape the dreary sepia world where such injustice prevails, to find "some place where there isn't any trouble." When a tornado carries Dorothy and her dog, Toto, to a magical land of blazing color, she finds herself seemingly in the land of every Depression victim's dreams, over the rainbow.

The conflicting American values during the Great Depression are evident in the messages contained in *The Wizard of Oz*. For all the populism of the original story from the 1890s and the meshing of the emphasis on cooperative effort to defeat the Wicked Witch of the West, the take-away messages of *The Wizard of Oz* are largely conservative. First, the Wizard who promises everything (seen by some observers as representing Roosevelt and his big government programs) is in fact just the man behind the curtain creating illusions with smoke and mirrors. Second, the idea that people must look inside themselves to find the courage, brains, and heart to succeed was a clear reference to the need for self-reliance. Third, the hope that one's problems will be solved and one's "troubles melt like lemon drops" somewhere over the rainbow is an empty promise because, in truth, "there's no place like home." That closing line reflects the Depression era's renewed emphasis on small town community values, evident in much of the decade's popular culture. Those values will prevail, viewers are told, if they will look within themselves, cooperate voluntarily, and defeat the greed and evil represented by Margaret Hamilton in the dual role of Miss Gulch and the Wicked Witch.

See Also: HOLLYWOOD AND THE FILM INDUSTRY; VALUES, EFFECTS OF THE GREAT DEPRESSION ON.

BIBLIOGRAPHY

Harmetz, Aljean. *The Making of the Wizard of Oz.* 1977. Rev. edition, 1998.

McElvaine, Robert S. *The Depression and New Deal: A History in Documents.* 2000.

Nathanson, Paul. *Over the Rainbow: The Wizard of Oz as a Secular Myth of America.* 1991.

ROBERT S. MCELVAINE

WOMEN, IMPACT OF THE GREAT DEPRESSION ON

The Great Depression affected women and men in quite different ways. The economy of the period relied heavily on so-called "sex-typed" work, or work that employers typically assigned to one sex or the other. And the work most directly associated with males, especially manufacturing in heavy industries like steel production, faced the deepest levels of lay-offs during the Great Depression. Women primarily worked in service industries, and these jobs tended to continue during the 1930s. Clerical workers, teachers, nurses, telephone operators, and domestics largely found work. In many instances, employers lowered pay scales for women workers, or even, in the case of teachers, failed to pay their workers on time. But women's wages remained a necessary component in family survival. In many Great Depression families, women were the only breadwinners.

An important corrective to a male-centered vision of the Great Depression is to note that while men's employment rates declined during the period, women's employment rates actually rose. In 1930, approximately 10.5 million women worked outside the home. By 1940, approximately 13 million women worked for wages outside the home. Even so, women's work continued to be less than well regarded by American society. Critics, overlooking the sex-typing of most work opportunities for women, lambasted laboring women for robbing men of much-needed jobs. Even women's colleges formally charged women not to pursue careers after graduation so that their places could be filled by men.

Federal law stood consistently with this conservative position regarding women workers. Laws in effect between 1932 and 1937 made it illegal for more than one person per family to find employment within the federal civil service. Despite the protestations of Eleanor Roosevelt, the New Deal program the Civilian Conservation Corps, developed in 1933, had a formal policy against hiring women. Many New Deal job programs cast women in traditional housekeeping roles. Camps operated by the Federal Emergency Relief Administration

Many poor women from the South and Midwest took refuge in California during the Dust Bowl years. This destitute Oklahoma mother and her baby lived in a migrant tent camp in Imperial Valley, California, in 1937. LIBRARY OF CONGRESS, PRINTS & PHOTOGRAPHS DIVISION, FSA/OWI COLLECTION

(FERA) specifically for young women taught household skills. FERA work relief projects employed women in producing such goods as canned foods, clothes, and mattresses for distribution to needy families. Women were employed as housekeeping aides to families in need of household help. The housekeeping aides project kept to traditional racial stereotypes as well as gendered ones, as most of its employees were African-American women. Other federal agencies paid women much less than men or gave preferences to male job seekers over female ones.

Women of minority groups faced particular difficulties. Employers preferred white men, and then white women, over black or Hispanic women in most instances. Relegated to domestic work and farm work through centuries of racism and misogyny in the job market, most African-American women found themselves left out of new laws passed to ensure worker safety. The Fair Labor Standards Act of 1938, with its minimum wage and maximum hour provisions, did not apply to domestic or farm workers. Given the pressures of the economy, many women—white and black—were willing to work in domestic positions, but fewer households had the extra income to hire help. Many cities developed specific locations where prospective domestic workers would stand outside and

During the early 1940s thousands of American women began working in factories in support of the war effort. The swing shift of drill press operators at this West Coast airplane factory was composed entirely of women when this photograph was taken in 1942. FRANKLIN DELANO ROOSEVELT LIBRARY

wait for wealthier women to hire them for a day's work. Given that those seeking employment were most often black and given the low wages one would earn in such arrangements, the process and the area of town associated with it became known colloquially as a "slave market." The casual nature of the oral contract between employer and employee in this hiring system meant that many women were inadequately paid for their labors.

Women in professional careers lost gains made in earlier, more stable periods. Fewer women found positions in business in the Great Depression than in the 1920s. Losing ground in the traditional male

sphere, some men also entered into jobs heretofore relegated to women. This trend occurred even in the very female bastion of teaching. The teaching profession grew slightly less female during the Great Depression; women had constituted 85 percent of teachers in 1920, but by 1940 they constituted only 78 percent.

The federal law's refusal to champion women workers occurred even with the unprecedented presence of women of considerable power in Washington, D.C. Frances Perkins became the first female member of a presidential cabinet when she assumed the post of Secretary of Labor in 1933.

Residents gather for dinner at a FERA camp for unemployed women in Atlanta, Georgia, in 1934. FRANKLIN DELANO ROOSEVELT LIBRARY

Mary McLeod Bethune, head of the Division of Negro Affairs of the National Youth Administration and acting head of Roosevelt's informal group of black advisors or "black cabinet," became the highest-ranking African-American woman in government. Eleanor Roosevelt, first lady from 1933 to 1945, fought the public policies when it came to women on several fronts and led Franklin D. Roosevelt's presidency more to the political left than it would have otherwise been. The New Deal did not outwardly target women's issues. Eleanor Roosevelt did, however, provide some moral support to American women in the troubled 1930s. Her newspaper column, "My Day," in national periodicals reached an eager audience. Although Eleanor Roosevelt was the mother of five children, the first lady was nonetheless not known for her housewifery skills initially. As a young mother Roosevelt had even once hung her daughter Anna outside her bedroom window in a box with wire sides so that the child could nap in fresh air; the child's cries had significantly scared the neighbors. Yet during the Depression Eleanor Roosevelt inspired less-famous Americans with her earnest example, as when she served Franklin Roosevelt seven-cent meals in the White House.

American women found the task of homemaking increasingly challenging in the face of the sharp cuts in the family budget due to the nation's economic crisis. Women continued to supervise the feeding and clothing of their families during the period but needed increased creativity to complete these tasks. A common saying of the time explained how to stretch one's household dollar: "Use it up, wear it out, make it do, or do without." Although the 1920s had introduced more convenience goods into the mainstream kitchen, housewives in the

Many southern sharecropper families were beset by poverty in the 1930s, leaving mothers like this one, photographed in Washington County, Arkansas, in 1935, barely able to feed or clothe their children. FRANKLIN DELANO ROOSEVELT LIBRARY

Great Depression returned to money-saving techniques like canning fruits and vegetables. Women sewed more of the family's clothes. "Outwork," or performing labor for wages at home, became a popular way to add to the family income. For instance, many women opted to take in the laundry of others for a fee. Even with these creative choices, malnutrition and disease became the results of extended poverty for some families.

Relations between husbands and wives grew strained because of financial insecurity. The financial downturn disrupted the husband's traditional role as breadwinner added space for the family, leading to increasingly rancorous marriages. Tight budgets in families led to the end of simple pleasures like leisure-time activities and further added to stress. The rate of husbands deserting their families rose during the period. Couples delayed marriages or even decided not to marry at all given the financial constraints of setting up new households. Childbearing rates decreased, and more couples utilized contraception to limit family size. Extended families, including multiple generations, also decided to share housing to cut costs.

In the face of a collective mood that championed women's domestic ties and disparaged working women, the feminist ideals that had grown during earlier periods lost momentum. Already waning during the 1920s, feminist sentiments faltered further during the Great Depression due to the pressing economic concerns. Groups that had supported women's rights, including the radical National Women's Party and the educational body, the League of Women Voters (formed out of the former National American Woman Suffrage Association in 1920), remained in the political background during the 1930s. The momentum of feminism would not be rediscovered until the late 1960s. Women did, however, take part in labor's struggle to take advantage of the legal changes that made organizing workers more possible. Women become a vital part of the labor movement during the era of the Great Depression. For example, a particularly spirited group of women took part in the Women's Emergency Brigade of the United Autoworkers and helped support the lengthy sit-down strike in Flint, Michigan, that brought the General Motors Company to sign a contract with the union in 1937.

Delving into women's experiences in the Great Depression period leads us to a much broader understanding of the time. While men faced major unemployment, and the disruption of typical bread-winner roles, women maintained employment or even took on new paid labor in order to support their families. While feminism as a concept was not nourished during the economically tumultuous period, women around the nation did become politically and economically active because of the pressures of the time. The societal role of women came under increasing examination during the period, out of the impetus of such factors as the increased numbers of national female leaders, and the absence of substantial places for women in new deal legislation.

See Also: GENDER ROLES AND SEXUAL RELATIONS, IMPACT OF THE GREAT DEPRESSION ON; MEN, IMPACT OF THE GREAT DEPRESSION ON.

BIBLIOGRAPHY

Cook, Blanche Wiesen. *Eleanor Roosevelt: 1884-1933.* 1992.

Cook, Blanche Wiesen. *Eleanor Roosevelt: Volume 2, The Defining Years.* 1999.

Dubofsky, Melvyn and Stephen Burwood, eds. *Women and Minorities during the Great Depression.* 1990.

Evans, Sara M. *Born for Liberty: A History of Women in America.* 1997.

Hapke, Laura. *Daughters of the Great Depression: Women, Work, and Fiction in the American 1930s.* 1995.

Melosh, Barbara. *Engendering Culture: Manhood and Womanhood in New Deal Public Art and Theater.* 1991.

Palmer, Phyllis. *Dirt and Domesticity: Housewives and Domestic Servants in the United States, 1920-1945.* 1989.

Scharf, Lois. *To Work and to Wed: Female Employment, Feminism, and the Great Depression.* 1980.

Sternsher, Bernard and Judith Sealander, eds. *Women of Valor: The Struggle against the Great Depression as Told in Their Own Life Stories.* 1990.

Woloch, Nancy. *Women and the American Experience: A Concise History.* 1996.

Youngs, J. William T. *Eleanor Roosevelt: A Personal and Public Life.* 1985.

LISA KRISSOFF BOEHM

WOMEN'S EMERGENCY BRIGADE

The Flint Women's Emergency Brigade, formed on January 20, 1937, was a militant expression of the United Auto Workers (UAW) Women's Auxiliary movement. Reporting on the formation of the Brigade, the Associated Press quoted Brigade founder Genora Johnson: "We will form a line around the men, and if the police want to fire then they'll just have to fire into us." Starting with fifty members who were wives, mothers, and sisters of strikers, the Flint Brigade grew to 350. Brigades were also formed in Lansing and Detroit. The Brigade used military titles to show its readiness for combat. They wore colored berets and armbands with "EB" inscribed on them; the Flint Brigade's berets were red, Detroit's green, and Lansing's white. On February 1, 1937, the Flint Women's Emergency Brigade played a crucial role in a battle that enabled UAW members to seize control of the plant that produced all General Motors engines. The *New York Times* headline read "Women's Brigade Uses Heavy Clubs," and it accompanied a photograph of Brigade members with the long clubs they used to break factory windows to counter the teargassing of workers.

The first UAW Women's Auxiliary had been established in December 1936 during the sit-down strike at Detroit's Midland Steel Company. Its focus was the preparation of food for the strikers. The Flint Women's Auxiliary was formed after a New Year's Eve dance in front of Fisher Body Plant 2. It fed the strikers, staffed picket lines, and ran a first aid station, a speaker's bureau, and a daycare center.

Hundreds of members of the women's auxiliaries and women's brigades from several cities paraded in Flint on February 3, 1937, a day the UAW designated Women's Day. The women's militancy and support activities helped the strikers to victory. The UAW incorporated support for the women's auxiliaries into its formal structure at its convention in August 1937. Although the brigades received significant attention in the daily press and journalist Mary Heaton Vorse highlighted their story, they proved to be a temporary formation.

Although the UAW's male leadership appreciated women's support, it neglected women autoworkers. UAW Local 155 had established the Midland Women's Auxiliary as a vehicle to involve women workers whom it had neglected to consult prior to the strike. The pattern of neglecting women workers and suggesting they work with the auxiliary occurred frequently. Discrimination and the problems of women workers on the job went unchallenged. Although women workers organized at plants where they were numerous, they were not promoted into union leadership positions. The women's auxiliaries proved to be one of the few voices within the union that spoke out for the needs of women workers. As support organizations, however, they did not offer a challenge to the union's gender hierarchy. But the militancy and advocacy of female independence and strength that was articulated by participants in the women's brigades provided a germ of a radical feminism that would flower in a later period.

See Also: ORGANIZED LABOR; SIT-DOWN STRIKES; STRIKES; UNITED AUTOMOBILE WORKERS (UAW).

BIBLIOGRAPHY

Fine, Sidney. *Sit-down: The General Motors Strike of 1936–1937.* 1969.

Foner, Philip. *Women and the American Labor Movement,* Vol. 2: *From World War I to the Present.* 1980.

Gabin, Nancy F. *Feminism in the Labor Movement: Women and the United Auto Workers, 1935–1975.* 1990.

Gray, Lorraine, director; Lorraine Gray, Lynn Goldfarb, and Anne Bohlen, producers. *With Babies and Banners: The Story of the Women's Emergency Brigade.* Women's Labor History Film Project, 1978.

Zimmelman, Nancy A. "The UAW Women's Auxiliaries: Activities of Ford Workers' Families in Detroit, 1937–1949." M.A. thesis, Wayne State University, 1987.

MARTIN HALPERN

WOOD, GRANT. *See* AMERICAN SCENE, THE.

WOODWARD, ELLEN

Woodward, Ellen Sullivan (July 11, 1887–September 23, 1971), Works Progress Administration (WPA) administrator and Social Security Board member, was born in Oxford, Mississippi, to William Van Amberg Sullivan, later a U.S. congressman and senator, and Belle Murray Sullivan. She was educated in Oxford and Washington, D.C., and briefly attended Sans Souci, a South Carolina academy. In 1906 she married Albert Y. Woodward and became a community activist in Louisville, Mississippi, where she developed the humane and egalitarian outlook that characterized her work.

Her public career began in 1925 when Woodward succeeded her deceased husband in the Mississippi House of Representatives. At the term's end (1926), she became an official with the new Mississippi State Board of Development, where she became known in 1930 and 1932 to social work officials who were close to Harry Hopkins, soon to become the New Deal relief "czar." As a result, Hopkins named her late in 1933 the director of women's relief work in the Federal Emergency Relief Administration. She retained that post in the short-lived Civil Works Administration and then became an assistant administrator of the WPA in 1935, directing the new Women's and Professional Projects division.

Supported by first lady Eleanor Roosevelt, Woodward succeeded in placing 300,000 women household heads on work relief projects by the end of 1933. At the peak in February 1936, almost 500,000 women were at work, although Woodward never succeeded in achieving work for women on a basis equal to that afforded men on construction projects. More than half of women were on projects that produced goods, principally food and clothing, and provided community services, such as libraries, recreation, school lunchrooms, and health care never before available in many areas. In 1936 Woodward assumed direction of the Four Arts projects—Music, Art, Theatre, and Writers—that gave work to the white collar unemployed. It was congressional disenchantment with the Theatre and Writers' projects that led to investigation and Woodward's decision to resign in December 1938.

She then became one of the three members of the Social Security Board, where she was a strong advocate of stiff merit systems to thwart exploitation of Social Security programs by state politicians. When the Social Security Board was abolished in 1946, she became a director within the new Federal Security Agency and worked to expand United States influence in international welfare. She retired at the end of 1953 but remained in Washington where she died.

See Also: FEDERAL EMERGENCY RELIEF ADMINISTRATION (FERA); WOMEN, IMPACT OF THE GREAT DEPRESSION ON; WORKS PROGRESS ADMINISTRATION (WPA).

BIBLIOGRAPHY

Swain, Martha. "'The Forgotten Woman': Ellen Woodward and Women's Relief Work," *Prologue* 15 (1983): 201–213.

Swain, Martha. *Ellen S. Woodward: New Deal Advocate for Women.* 1995.

Ware, Susan. *Beyond Suffrage: Women in the New Deal.* 1981.

Woodward Papers, Mississippi Department of Archives and History, Jackson.

MARTHA H. SWAIN

WORKERS EDUCATION PROJECT

Practically speaking, workers' education accounted for a tiny part of the federal government's New Deal emergency education programs—and was, because it yoked together the interests of American capitalism with those of left-oriented trade unions, a controversial enterprise at that. But these workers education programs played a key role in the development of a "labor culture" in the Popular Front movement in the United States.

Schools set up for the purpose of training working-class activists and intellectuals had been pioneered by the Communist Party, the Socialist Party, and leftist labor unions, such as the International Ladies' Garment Workers' Union, the United Electrical Workers, and others. These education pro-

This poster announced a WPA Workers Education Project study group to be held at the Henry Street Settlement in New York City. LIBRARY OF CONGRESS, PRINTS & PHOTOGRAPHS DIVISION, WPA POSTER COLLECTION

grams included both urban night schools and residential labor colleges, most famously the Highlander Folk School in Tennessee, co-founded by Myles Horton and Don West. In particular, the growth of the labor movement during the 1930s had created a pressing need for trained leadership. From 1933 to 1942, these schools were able to receive some federal funding, and became what was called the Workers Education Project (the name changed in 1939 to the Workers Service Program). When the Work Projects Administration ended in 1942, labor unions attempted to continue the schools without government funding.

Hilda Smith, an education specialist who founded and directed Bryn Mawr's Summer School for Women Workers, was program director. The first funds went to hire unemployed teachers, working through relief agencies, to lead classes in adult literacy. As the number and variety of classes grew, local unions and community groups could request classes or speakers through a government sponsor, such as a state university or a state department of labor or education. The classes met in labor halls and in public schools. At its peak enrollment, 65,000 workers participated in approximately 3,000 classes. Classes in the social sciences, economics, and labor history were the most popular.

An early memo among Workers Education Project administrators, which would come to be widely circulated and quoted, differentiated the mandates of workers' education from adult education more generally: "Workers' education offers men and women workers in industry, business, domestic service and other occupations an opportunity to train themselves in clear thinking through the study of those questions closely related to their daily lives as workers and as citizens."

See Also: HIGHLANDER FOLK SCHOOL; ORGANIZED LABOR.

BIBLIOGRAPHY

Bloom, Jon. "Workers Education." *Encyclopedia of the American Left,* 2nd edition, edited by Mari Jo Buhle, Paul Buhle, and Dan Georgakas. 1998.

Denning, Michael. *The Cultural Front: The Laboring of American Culture in the Twentieth Century.* 1996.

Kornbluh, Joyce. *A New Deal for Workers' Education: The Workers' Service Program, 1933–1942.* 1987.

RACHEL RUBIN

WORK ETHIC

The term *work ethic* refers to efforts to apply oneself diligently to the task at hand. The application of the work ethic became important during the industrial revolution when a majority of people gradually began to work for wages. The work ethic contained

This billboard, photographed by Dorothea Lange in California in 1937, promoted a work ethic endorsed by the National Association of Manufacturers. LIBRARY OF CONGRESS, PRINTS & PHOTOGRAPHS DIVISION, FSA/OWI COLLECTION

a strong moral dimension by promoting the spiritual idea of "living to work" rather than "working to live." According to historian Daniel T. Rodgers, the work ethic placed work at the center of moral life—work made people useful in a world of economic scarcity. In fact, the work ethic, while still an icon of lip service, had already been substantially undermined before the Depression began. The needs of the mass production economy that came into its own in the 1920s required an emphasis on consumption that severely weakened the work ethic.

Nonetheless, during the Great Depression, many politicians and business leaders feared that the traditional work ethic was being undermined by

the economic situation that many people found themselves in, and it was threatened even more by many of the proposed solutions to that situation. For this reason, most of the New Deal programs that aimed to assist individuals economically, including the Civilian Conservation Corps (CCC) and the Works Progress Administration (WPA), required that recipients work for the assistance that they received. Even Social Security, a pay-as-you-go program, was sold to the American public as a program for which people "earned" credit, even though the money that an individual paid into the system was immediately dispersed to someone else.

Although the United States was an advanced industrial nation at the onset of the Great Depression, it had one of the most rudimentary social welfare systems. The unemployed and underprivileged had to rely on private charity or local (city or county) welfare systems. The severity of the economic malaise during the early years of the Great Depression quickly taxed this system beyond its capacity to respond; many industrial cities found that they had to reduce essential services, like fire and police departments, in order to simply feed their citizens. President Herbert Hoover's insistence on a program of "voluntarism" meant that he discouraged any legislation that would provide additional funds to supplement these programs. When Franklin D. Roosevelt assumed office in 1933, one of the earliest agencies established was the Federal Emergency Relief Administration (FERA), headed by Harry Hopkins. FERA's purpose was to provide funds to states so that they could supplement the funds being dispersed locally. Much of the money was to be augmented by state and local governments, particularly those in the north, since southern states provided little or no support or social welfare.

Concern both inside and outside the administration that this program would undermine the work ethic, and demean those receiving such assistance "for nothing," quickly led to the creation of programs like the CCC. The purpose of the CCC was, in part, to rescue young men from "dangerous" influences in the city, such as criminal gangs and Communists, and relocate them to the countryside, where the work ethic could be instilled in them through projects such as building roads, digging ditches, and planting trees. Similar programs, such as the Civil Works Administration (CWA) and the WPA, eventually put millions of men and women to work on a variety of public works projects, ranging from road-building to writing travel guides to the states.

Franklin Roosevelt envisioned Social Security as a "cradle to grave" social welfare system, but the political realities of the time, as well as Roosevelt's need to use his political capital judiciously to coax recalcitrant southern congressmen to support the New Deal, prevented Roosevelt's vision from becoming a reality. The need to retain as many southern votes as possible for Social Security legislation meant that in exchange for those votes Congress excluded farm and domestic workers, a part of the labor force that in the 1930s largely consisted of women and African-American men. The old-age pension system was funded exclusively by contributors through a new tax levied by the federal government, while unemployment and aid to families with dependent children were funded by matching contributions from the federal government to state governments. This led to widely varying levels of aid from state to state, with the greatest disparity being between northern states (supplying greater amounts of aid) and southern states (supplying lesser amounts).

Some critics of these New Deal initiatives have argued that the Roosevelt administration undertook them in a cynical attempt to undermine more radical political possibilities; defenders of the New Deal argue that these limitations were imposed on the administration by the political realities of the time. On the contrary, until this point in the history of the United States, the federal government had largely left individual citizens of the nation to shift for themselves during times of economic distress, and it was the expectation of a large number of people that the poor would have to continue to rely on their work ethic to see them through this latest crisis.

See Also: COLLECTIVE BARGAINING; INDIVIDUALISM.

BIBLIOGRAPHY

Badger, Anthony J. *The New Deal: The Depression Years, 1933–1940.* 1989.

McElvaine, Robert S. *The Great Depression: America, 1929–1941,* rev. edition. 1994.

Piven, Frances Fox, and Richard A. Cloward. *Regulating the Poor: The Functions of Public Welfare.* 1971. Updated edition, 1993.

Rodgers, Daniel T. *The Work Ethic in Industrial America, 1850–1920.* 1978.

Schlesinger, Arthur M., Jr. *The Coming of the New Deal.* 1958.

GREGORY MILLER

The dance unit of the WPA Federal Theatre Project opened this production of Candide *in New York City in 1935.* FRANKLIN DELANO ROOSEVELT LIBRARY

WORKS PROGRESS ADMINISTRATION (WPA)

When Franklin D. Roosevelt assumed the presidency on March 4, 1933, he focused much of his inaugural address on the approximately thirteen million unemployed Americans constituting roughly 25 percent of the workforce. "Our greatest primary task," Roosevelt advised, "is to put people to work." Characterizing President Herbert Hoover's approach to poverty as "scattered, uneconomical, and unequal," Roosevelt called for a massive attack on the Depression. On May 12, 1933, Congress responded with a law creating the Federal Emergency Relief Administration (FERA). FERA became the first stage in an evolutionary process during which the New Deal shifted its Depression-fighting strategy from the dole to public employment by way of the Civil Works Administration and the Works Progress Administration.

HISTORICAL BACKGROUND OF RELIEF

Depressions, recessions, and financial panics have plagued the United States since its colonial period. Early Americans relied on British methods, mainly the dole, to relieve the persistent problem of poverty. Although outright grants and indentured servitude constituted the primary methods, America's attitude toward poverty soon became obvious with the emergence of poor houses, also known as

The Melrose Art Center in New Mexico, shown here in 1935, was one of many art centers the WPA established across the country. FRANKLIN DELANO ROOSEVELT LIBRARY

"pest houses," which became common. These isolation structures, provided by churches and wealthy humanitarians, reflected a national belief that privatism, the private solution to public problems, was the most efficient means of aiding the needy. From 1929 to 1932, President Hoover insisted that if Americans relied upon private initiative, "prosperity was just around the corner." Having served as food administrator and relief commissioner during World War I, Hoover claimed early in his administration to have found a "final solution to poverty." However, after three years of depression, it became obvious that the old methods were not working in a country where more than 50 percent of the people lived in what the Census Bureau de-

fined as urban areas (populations of 2,500 or more). Hoover, who feared that government relief payments would undermine people's self-reliance, became a national scapegoat and lost his 1932 reelection bid by a landslide to Governor Franklin D. Roosevelt of New York.

Roosevelt's philosophy of dealing with the Depression was apparent during his New York governorship when he created the Temporary Emergency Relief Administration (TERA), headed by Harry L. Hopkins, in October 1931. Roosevelt clearly stated his belief that cities and counties should control relief and local funds should supplement state money. He steadfastly warned against deficit spending. However, as the Depression deepened,

Roosevelt placed New York in debt by supporting an emergency $30 million bond issue.

When Roosevelt assumed the presidency in March 1933, he faced a Congress representing a public that demanded action on the problem of widespread poverty and unemployment. However, during the first "Hundred Days" of his presidency (March to June 1933), even the political opposition agreed that he had made a good start at handling the problem. Republican floor leader Bertrand Snell, indicating bipartisan congressional support, said, "the house is burning down and the president of the United States says this is the way to put out the fire."

RELIEF DURING THE FIRST NEW DEAL (1933–1935)

During the First New Deal, Roosevelt's approach to relief closely resembled that taken by his predecessor, with one major difference. Whereas Hoover felt that public employment that competed with private enterprise was un-American, Roosevelt followed Hopkins's advice to incorporate public works into his relief programs. With urban bread and soup lines lengthening and farmers destroying their crops and livestock, Roosevelt placed Hopkins in charge of the $500 million Federal Emergency Relief Administration (FERA).

One New Dealer stated that Hopkins combined "the purity of St. Francis of Assissi with the sharp shrewdness of a race track tout." A social worker, bureaucrat, and politician from Iowa who ran relief programs in New Orleans and New York, Hopkins was an unusual Washington power broker. Unlike most of the Washington establishment in 1933, he had been divorced and had undergone psychoanalysis. By 1936, Hopkins had become Roosevelt's closest advisor and remained in that position until the president died in 1945. Roosevelt ordered Hopkins to provide quick relief and keep politics out of relief. He achieved the first goal. The second proved an impossible task.

Political intuition, empathy for the poor, and speed with the dispensation of relief were Hopkins's greatest assets. The FERA administrator spent millions even before workers installed a desk in his office. His goal was to provide assistance to poor people and he did not care about the political fallout. "I'm not going to last six months here," he noted, "so I'll do as I please." To the surprise of many, he lasted twelve years.

Hopkins's chief aide in the business of dispensing relief was Aubrey Williams of Alabama. Starting as a regional administrator with FERA, Williams moved up the bureaucratic ladder and eventually controlled the WPA during Hopkins's prolonged medical absences. A liberal idealist, Williams had a relationship to Hopkins that resembled Hopkins's role in Roosevelt's cabinet. They made a formidable team, relieving misery and enabling millions of Americans to survive the crisis.

FERA established a practice that was followed by the Civil Works Administration (CWA) and the Works Progress Administration (WPA). Late in the fall of 1933, President Roosevelt expressed concern that economic recovery was proceeding too slowly. The slow-moving Public Works Administration (PWA) under Secretary of the Interior Harold L. Ickes left millions of unemployed workers and their families facing a harsh winter. Hopkins seized the initiative and persuaded Roosevelt to adopt a plan that became the CWA, which paid the jobless a minimum wage. Roosevelt, who agreed with Hopkins's argument that the dole demeaned and demoralized recipients, subsequently approved $400 million worth of work relief. Hopkins and his FERA staff ordered the CWA to construct more roads, buildings, and airports. Fifty thousand CWA teachers taught in rural schools built by the same organization. The program was a spectacular success, although cost overruns and Republican cries about waste and political corruption marred its image. On balance, however, public reaction was favorable and the CWA so impressed Roosevelt that he became amenable when Hopkins proposed the Works Progress Administration.

WORKS PROGRESS ADMINISTRATION (1933–1943)

Early in 1935, Roosevelt decided to emphasize public works over direct relief. The principal result was the WPA. Executive Order 7034 on May 6, 1935, created the WPA, which Congress had previously authorized by passing the Emergency Relief

Appropriation Act. The WPA probably constituted the most successful effort at public works ever conducted by the federal government. Certainly it spent the most money, finished the most projects and hired the most people, averaging 2,112,000 on its monthly payroll from 1935 to 1941.

The influence of Hopkins, who became the chief administrator, could be seen in Roosevelt's speech announcing that the intent of the massive program was to "preserve not only the bodies of the unemployed from destruction, but also their self-respect, their self-confidence, courage, and determination." The dole, Roosevelt warned, was "a narcotic, a subtle destroyer of the human spirit. . . . Work must be found for able-bodied but destitute workers."

Hopkins also persuaded Roosevelt to see that a greater percentage of the vast sums of WPA money would go into the workers' paychecks, not materials, based on the argument that increased revenue would come back to the treasury. Only "useful projects" should be funded and they should be staffed solely by workers taken directly off relief. State governments would be given the right to request projects, and hire and fire employees. Although Roosevelt and Hopkins strongly desired to keep local and state politicians out of the process, the WPA nonetheless opened the door to political coercion, interference, waste, and corruption.

This was the WPA's Achilles heel. The massive organization had the potential to provide tremendous support for Roosevelt's 1936 reelection campaign. Accordingly, the president, not Congress, controlled billions of WPA dollars. Republicans, such as minority leader Bertrand Snell, complained vociferously, warning that the WPA gave Roosevelt "greater spending power than any ancient or modern dictator ever wielded." Democrat Huey Long, who was planning to run for president himself, asked "why should Congress give Roosevelt a $5 billion blank check with an election coming on?" Others, however, such as columnist Walter Lippmann, congratulated Roosevelt for not allowing Congress to earmark pork barrel projects in their home towns, counties, and states. Stating that "everything is political," Hopkins concluded that the WPA staff should control the program. It was Roo-

sevelt, however, who determined the nature and direction of work relief.

Despite the best efforts of the president and his WPA administrator, state and local politicians did control and manipulate many of the projects. Occasionally, as with Governor Martin Davy of Ohio, Hopkins federalized state WPA programs. In other instances, where urban machines run by bosses like Edward Crump of Memphis, Frank Hague of Jersey City, and Edward J. Kelly of Chicago, controlled their states' electoral votes, Roosevelt did not attempt to keep politics out of relief.

When reformers complained, Roosevelt reminded them of his rule never to interfere in local Democratic politics. The principal exception to this rule occurred in Missouri when Roosevelt, over Senator Harry S. Truman's protests, allowed the Federal Bureau of Investigation to prosecute Truman's Kansas City mentor, Thomas J. Pendergast, and the Missouri WPA director, Matthew Murray. The prosecution of Pendergast and Murray proceeded because Roosevelt could rely on Governor Lloyd C. Stark to deliver Missouri's electoral vote in 1940. Roosevelt ignored similar charges against Hague and Kelly because he had no replacements to run the machines that controlled the electoral votes in New Jersey and Illinois.

Against this broiling political scenario, Hopkins determinedly proceeded to ensure that the WPA would employ as many as 3,500,000 people taken off the relief rolls. He hoped that WPA workers would perform jobs that suited their particular skills. The FERA staff, with Aubrey Williams assisting Hopkins, would run the program. Subordinates in Washington and throughout the country played a key role. They included Jacob Baker, who directed FERA and CWA public works; Corrington Gill, research and statistical director; Lawrence Westbrook, assistant administrator; David K. Niles, publicity and political advisor; Dallas Dort, chief investigator; and Ellen S. Woodward, head of the Women's Division.

Woodward, possibly the second most important woman in the New Deal after Secretary of Labor Frances Perkins, worked her way up the FERA into the WPA. She ensured that sufficient funding be provided to more than 500,000 women working on projects that focused on public health, sewing, and school lunch preparation. Later, Woodward expanded the program to include actresses, artists, and writers.

Below the Washington staff were the field investigators led by Lorena Hickok, Hopkins's personal representative, whose close friendship with Eleanor Roosevelt gave her sharply analytical reports great influence. Hickok identified the major problems throughout the country, such as drought and starvation. She attacked political greed and bureaucratic inefficiency. Her letters to the First Lady also became a source of pressure on Roosevelt and Hopkins to take action.

Other field representatives, such as Howard Hunter, Pierce Williams, and Alan Johnstone, supplied a wealth of information on such varied subjects as waste, inefficiency, corruption, and the coercion of WPA workers in election campaigns. State directors controlled by Democratic bosses and officeholders, however, maintained their jobs unless charges of corruption forced Hopkins to appoint civil engineers to direct those programs. Numerous complaints from Republicans and excluded Democrats charging waste and inefficiency reached the Washington staff. Although these accusations damaged the program's image, the WPA nonetheless succeeded in relieving poverty and unemployment for the millions who benefited from it.

At its peak, the WPA employed 3,300,000 persons working on projects as diverse as roads, sewers, theatre and art, football stadiums, courthouses, dams, historical and literary writing, and sewing circles. Although defenders of the private enterprise system saw waste, Roosevelt and Hopkins operated under the premise that, while they knew some of the money would be stolen, enough would reach the people who needed it, thus satisfying the WPA's chief goal.

Hopkins never wavered from his mission to aid that one-third of the nation Roosevelt described as "ill housed, ill clad, and ill nourished." WPA workers basically built (or rebuilt) America's infrastructure, including approximately 2,500 hospitals, 572,000 miles of road, 1,000 airports, 5,900 schools, and 85,000 courthouses, police stations, firehouses, and arenas. The projects varied widely, ranging

from the multimillion dollar Lake of Ozarks Project in Missouri, through shelterbelts in Kansas, to a children's hospital in Brooklyn, New York.

WPA instructions required that the government hire unemployed workers from the relief rolls who passed a "means test." WPA workers were encouraged to accept employment opportunities in private enterprise since fear of competition with the private sector was deeply embedded in the New Deal's public works philosophy. WPA projects were aimed at filling local needs and paying people quickly so that their wages would translate into purchasing power to stimulate the economy and ultimately into tax revenue. Monetary expenditures and project selection required approval from New Dealers working in tandem with Democratic National Committee Chairman James A. Farley, but patronage sometimes went to Republicans, causing complaints from Roosevelt's party.

Federal One. Although most of the WPA men worked on construction sites and women taught, sewed, or learned home economics, thousands of actors, artists, writers, and musicians benefited from Federal One, the WPA arts program that included the Federal Art Project, the Federal Music Project, the Federal Theatre Project, and the Federal Writers' Project. Federal One reflected Roosevelt's willingness to experiment. Its controversial plays and paintings prompted criticism from Roosevelt's political opposition, especially since many of its projects reflected the New Deal's liberal political philosophy. Hopkins counterattacked, asserting that the recipients of the New Deal arts program needed "to eat just like other people."

Perhaps the most famous of Roosevelt's artistic work relief programs was the Federal Writers' Project, whose employees were free to write in their specialties. Historians, as well as many nonhistorians, for example, traveled from town to town, and state to state, writing guides that described the history and culture of their subjects. Urban and state histories, biographies of former slaves, sharp analyses of conditions in areas as diverse as New York's Bowery, Missouri's Bootheel, and San Francisco's Cannery Row contributed much to the national literature.

Struggling directors and actors received employment opportunities in the Federal Theatre Project. Plays, puppet shows, vaudeville presentations, and even circuses became part of the New Deal's effort to keep the culture alive. Hallie Flanagan, Hopkins's classmate at Grinnell College in Iowa, ran the theatrical program with assistance from such famous actors as Charles Coburn and playwrights such as Elmer Wright. *It Can't Happen Here,* a play based on Sinclair Lewis's novel by the same title, opened on twenty-one stages simultaneously throughout the country. Lewis, who had previously become the first American to receive the Nobel Prize for literature, played the leading role in the New York production.

Criticism of the WPA. The WPA's Federal Theatre Project added to a growing political controversy swirling about the basic nature of President Roosevelt's approach to poverty and unemployment. Conservative Republicans ridiculed the agency, stating that WPA stood for "we piddle around," and remarking that "you can always identify the federal government's road builders by they way they lean on their shovels." Such Republicans as Representative Hamilton Fish, who ironically represented Roosevelt's New York congressional district, branded the WPA as a huge political machine whose purpose was to achieve the election of 100 percent Roosevelt Democrats. Comparing "the whole rotten mess. . .[to] a dead mackerel," Fish exclaimed that it "stinks and shines and shines and stinks."

Southern conservatives also became increasingly disgruntled with the WPA. Walter George and Eugene Talmadge of Georgia, Josiah Bailey of North Carolina and "Cotton Ed" Smith of South Carolina railed against the New Deal's interference with southern states' rights. In particular, Eleanor Roosevelt's excursions south of the Mason-Dixon line to promote the WPA's employment of African Americans infuriated southern politicians and embarrassed Roosevelt. Senator Joseph T. Robinson of Arkansas warned that the WPA would inflict damage on the national character by making a large percentage of the population permanently dependent on government aid. "I get very much discouraged," he warned, [that] it is going to be very diffi-

cult to ever get away from this habit of giving out federal favors." Even South Carolina Democratic Senator James Byrnes, who loyally supported Roosevelt on most issues, thought the WPA wasted millions of dollars. In response to the critics, the president admitted that waste existed.

A deepening recession in 1937 to 1938, however, caused Roosevelt to reverse his position and increase the WPA workforce. In 1938, Roosevelt's congressional opponents, concerned with the president's growing power as evidenced by his attempted court-packing scheme and campaign to purge conservatives from the Democratic Party, created a coalition dedicated to blocking New Deal measures. As these Republicans and southern Democrats gained strength in Congress, various committees began scrutinizing the WPA's political activities. The House Un-American Activities Committee (HUAC) condemned the Federal Theatre Project's employment of Communists and other "un-patriotic Americans," prompting Roosevelt to end the program on June 30, 1939. Mindful that Roosevelt had increased the WPA workforce in the months preceding the 1938 off-year elections, Congress further passed two Hatch acts in 1939. Aimed at eliminating political corruption and coercion in New Deal agencies, they attempted to prevent Roosevelt from using the WPA to produce votes for the 1940 presidential campaign, despite his claim that he was not a candidate.

On July 1, 1939, the Works Progress Administration became the Work Projects Administration, an effort by Roosevelt to shift the emphasis from welfare to more positive achievements, such as infrastructure construction. The new WPA focused on military projects after 1939, and Roosevelt ended it on June 30, 1943.

Legacy. Despite all the controversy generated by the criticisms, the WPA made important contributions to the American economy and culture. Many of the buildings constructed by WPA projects still functioned as the nation entered the twenty-first century. Millions of Americans received an education from teachers employed by the agency. Although politicians, including Roosevelt, used the WPA as a form of patronage, its $10 billion subsidized families of the unemployed and relieved their misery.

In the years that followed President Roosevelt's death in 1945, other politicians advocated philosophies similar to the one that produced the WPA. In 1965, President Lyndon B. Johnson secured the passage of several laws providing job training, federal employment, highway construction, and education as a part of his Great Society. In 1988, Senator Paul Simon made a revived WPA his campaign promise in his unsuccessful bid for the Democratic presidential nomination. For whatever reasons, these attempts did not succeed in continuing the practice of public employment in the way that the WPA had addressed America's economic woes. Such programs as the National Endowment for the Arts and the National Endowment for the Humanities, however, reflected one of the WPA's legacies to the nation as it entered the twenty-first century.

The Works Progress Administration succeeded in enabling millions of desperate Americans to survive the 1930s. Employment generated by World War II achieved the WPA's primary goals.

See Also: FEDERAL ART PROJECT (FAP); FEDERAL MUSIC PROJECT (FMP); FEDERAL ONE; FEDERAL THEATRE PROJECT (FTP); FEDERAL WRITERS' PROJECT (FWP); HOPKINS, HARRY.

BIBLIOGRAPHY

Adams, Grace K. *Workers on Relief.* 1939.

Adams, Henry H. *Harry Hopkins: A Biography.* 1977.

Bloxom, Marguerite D., ed. *Pickaxe and Pencil: References for the Study of the WPA.* 1982.

Bremer, William W. "Along the 'American Way': The New Deal's Work Relief Program for the Unemployed." *Journal of American History* 62 (1975): 636–652.

Blumberg, Barbara. *The New Deal and the Unemployed: The View From New York City.* 1979.

Daniels, Roger. *The Relevancy of Public Works History: The 1930s, a Case Study.* 1975.

Federal Works Agency. *Final Report of the WPA Program, 1935–1943.* 1946.

Hickok, Lorena. Papers. Franklin D. Roosevelt Library, Hyde Park, NY.

Hopkins, Harry L. Papers. Franklin D. Roosevelt Library, Hyde Park, NY.

Hopkins, Harry L. *Spending to Save: The Complete Story of Relief.* 1936.

Hopkins, June. *Harry Hopkins: Sudden Hero, Brash Reformer.* 1999.

Howard, Donald S. *The WPA and Federal Relief Policy.* 1943.

Macmahon, A. W.; J. D. Millett; and Gladys Ogden. *The Administration of Federal Work Relief.* 1941.

McDonald, William F. *Federal Relief Administration and the Arts: The Origins and Administrative History of the Arts Projects of the Works Progress Administration.* 1969.

McJimsey, George T. *Harry Hopkins: Ally of the Poor and Defender of Democracy.* 1987.

Millett, John D. *The Works Progress Administration in New York City.* 1938.

Roosevelt, Franklin D. President's Official File, President's Personal File, President's Secretary's File. Franklin D. Roosevelt Library, Hyde Park, NY.

Rose, Nancy E. *Put to Work: Relief Programs in the Great Depression.* 1994.

Rosen, Howard. "Public Works: The Legacy of the New Deal." *Social Education* 60 (1996): 277–279.

Salmond, John A. *A Southern Rebel: The Life and Times of Aubrey Willis Williams, 1890–1965.* 1983.

Schnell, J. Christopher. "Harry L. Hopkins and the Politics of Relief." *American Historical Association Proceedings.* 1981.

Swain, Martha H. "'The Forgotten Woman': Ellen S. Woodward and Women's Relief in the New Deal." *Prologue* 15 (1983): 201–214.

Works Progress Administration, Division of Information. Press Releases and Clippings; Investigations and Politics. National Archives, Washington, D.C.

J. CHRISTOPHER SCHNELL

WORLD COURT

The interwar World Court (officially called the Permanent Court of International Justice) was the judicial arm of the League of Nations, just as the present-day International Court of Justice is the "judicial arm" of the United Nations. The earlier Court was expected both to adjudicate disputes between member-states of the League of Nations and to maintain the treaty system established at the Paris Peace Conference that concluded World War I. But for many Americans, no less than foreigners, the World Court became a symbolic battle-ground, with American membership to the Court seen as a possible point of entry into the League of Nations.

The triumph of Warren Harding in the presidential election of 1920 had apparently decided

Woodrow Wilson's "solemn referendum" against U.S. involvement with the League of Nations. Article XIV of the League Covenant had called for the "establishment of a Permanent Court of International Justice," a provision that escaped serious opposition even from those who bitterly opposed U.S. membership in the League during the campaign. Indeed, in 1920 a committee of jurists from ten countries had drafted the statute (or constitution) of this embryonic World Court, and one of the most influential participants was Elihu Root, who was prominent in the Republican Party leadership outside Congress.

The World Court was inaugurated in 1922 at The Hague, with the preeminent American international lawyer, John Bassett Moore, one of the fifteen judges. In the United States, activists divided into three groups: those (like Moore) who opposed American membership in the League of Nations but favored adherence to the World Court; those who sought adherence to the Court as the first stage to full League membership; and those who opposed the Court precisely because they saw it as a "back door" to the League. In December 1925 the Senate began full debate on adherence to the Court—the delay due more to the cautious pro-League supporters than to their opponents. Indeed it was the proponents in the Senate who followed the Harding and Calvin Coolidge administrations in framing the eight conditions governing senatorial consent to ratification and thus U.S. membership in the World Court. The affirmative vote of seventy-six to seventeen in January 1926 reflected how uncontentious these conditions were: protection of the Monroe Doctrine, a senatorial veto over the president's submission of disputes to the Court; U.S. agreement to any changes in the court statute; and voting power equal to that of any of the major member-states (such as Britain, France, and Japan) in the League-based elections to the Court bench. Only one issue began contentiously but ended in unanimity: the requirement that the U.S. government have a veto over the Court's advisory jurisdiction. Such a technical matter of jurisdiction (or competence) to decide an international dispute was highly political, for only the League of Nations could request advisory opinions and thus insert itself quasi-judicially into interstate conflicts.

Although legal specialists appreciated the political importance of the Court's advisory jurisdiction, the arguments appeared abstract before the Senate vote and during the next three years when the League itself twice refused to accept this one American demand. Then in 1931, the League of Nations and World Court combined to justify the anxieties of those who supported U.S. adherence to the Court and vindicate the warnings of those who opposed membership in the League of Nations. In its advisory opinion on the "Austro-German Customs Union" the Court decided by a single vote that a proposed tariff agreement constituted the threat of an economic *Anschluss* (union) and was therefore subject to the veto of the League Council. With many predicting war in Europe before full-scale war broke out between Japan and China, on the eve of the 1932 presidential campaign, the Senate reaffirmed the 1926 conditions because of, rather than despite, the intervening double rejection by the League. Such was the international context in which Franklin Roosevelt famously repudiated his earlier support of U.S. membership in the League, mainly to appease the Hearst press.

Throughout the seventy-third Congress Roosevelt and his bipartisan supporters concentrated upon a New Deal whose orientation was unilateralist and nationalistic (isolationist) rather than multilateral (internationalist). Yet progressive Republicans, like Senators William Borah of Idaho and Hiram Johnson of California, on whose votes and influence Roosevelt relied, feared pro-League "Wilsonianism" in the State Department and hence dangerous foreign diversions from the domestic crisis. The midterm elections of 1934, a personal success for Roosevelt and an endorsement of the pro-New Deal ad hoc coalition, tempted Roosevelt to defer to the conservative Senate majority leader, Joseph Robinson of Arkansas, and cautiously back U.S. adherence to the Court.

Knowledgeable observers agreed that, at best, the Senate would repeat the terms of 1926; at worst, the recent Manchurian crisis and current Italian preparations for war with Ethiopia, both raising fears of League involvement, would deter the Senate altogether. Astonishingly, Roosevelt agreed with Robinson to alter the terms of adherence approved by the Senate a decade earlier, despite the objections of pro-Court Democrat Key Pittman, chair of the Foreign Relations Committee. This combination of executive arrogance and foreign anxieties prevented, after three weeks of animated debate, the two-thirds majority needed for approval, despite the virtual rewriting of the resolution by the proponents to conform to the language of 1926. Commentators then, and historians later, emphasized the last-minute impact of the anti-League "propaganda barrage" from Father Charles Coughlin and the Hearst press. Rather, roll calls showed that the decisive alignments against the rewritten conditions coalesced days before the final vote on January 29, 1935. The "triumph of isolationism" registered by the defeat of the World Court owed as much to Roosevelt's misguided leadership and the reality of dangerous events abroad as to the power of home-grown American isolationism.

See Also: COUGHLIN, CHARLES; ISOLATIONISM.

BIBLIOGRAPHY

Dunne, Michael. *The United States and the World Court, 1920–1935.* 1988.

Fachiri, Alexander P. *The Permanent Court of International Justice: Its Constitution, Procedure, and Work,* 2nd edition. 1932.

Fleming, Denna F. *The United States and the World Court, 1920–1966,* rev. edition. 1968.

Gill, George. *The League of Nations: from 1929 to 1946.* 1996.

Hudson, Manley O. *The Permanent Court of International Justice, 1920–1942: A Treatise.* 1943.

Kuehl, Warren F., and Lynne K. Dunn. *Keeping the Covenant: American Internationalists and the League of Nations, 1920–1939.* 1997.

Ostrower, Gary B. *The League of Nations: from 1919 to 1929.* 1996.

Rosenne, Shabtai. *The Law and Practice of the International Court, 1920–1996,* 4 vols., 3rd edition. 1997.

Walter, F. P. *A History of the League of Nations,* 2 vols. 1952.

MICHAEL DUNNE

WORLD WAR II AND THE ENDING OF THE DEPRESSION

World War II had a profound and multifaceted impact on the American economy. Most obviously, it lifted the nation out of the Great Depression of the 1930s. As late as 1940, unemployment stood at 14.6 percent; by 1944 it was down to a remarkable 1.2 percent, and the gross national product (GNP) had more than doubled. But the wartime economic mobilization did more than end the Depression. It greatly increased the size, power, and cost of the federal government. It corroborated the argument of the British economist John Maynard Keynes that deficit spending could stimulate economic growth, with consequences not only for government fiscal policy, but also for the agenda of New Deal liberalism. It virtually revolutionized the tax structure by vastly increasing the number of taxpayers, making personal income taxes a larger source of federal income than corporate taxes, and inaugurating the withholding system. It enlarged the economic and political power of big business, spurred the mechanization of agriculture and the further consolidation of big agribusiness, and increased the size and influence of organized labor. It catalyzed major breakthroughs in science and technology, including the development of the atomic bomb. It contributed to the resurgence of conservatism in Congress that had begun in the late 1930s. And among its other consequences, it made the United States overwhelmingly the dominant economic power in the world.

As the United States became the "arsenal of democracy" during World War II, economic mobilization brought a double victory for the American people by ending the decade-long Great Depression at home, as well as playing a pivotal role in defeating the Axis Powers abroad. President Franklin D. Roosevelt's New Deal of the 1930s had contributed to economic improvement after the calamitous collapse of the American economy that had led to unemployment of at least 25 percent by 1933. It had also provided essential assistance to the impoverished and unemployed. But the New Deal had not ended the Depression. Indeed, after some recovery from 1933 to 1937, the sharp recession of 1937 to

An anthracite miner in an eastern Pennsylvania mine shows an American soldier how to swing a pick under a low ceiling during a war production drive in 1942. LIBRARY OF CONGRESS, PRINTS & PHOTOGRAPHS DIVISION, FSA/OWI COLLECTION

1938 sent economic indexes plummeting again, with unemployment reaching 19 percent. The economy then headed up again, but in 1940 unemployment still stood at a Depression-level 14.6 percent.

By 1940, however, the war in Europe and the American national defense program provided economic stimulus, and in 1941 and 1942 defense spending and mobilization for war began to send the economy to new levels of prosperity. With the United States accounting for about 40 percent of all war goods produced worldwide by 1944, the GNP rose from $91 billion in 1939 to $126 billion in 1941, to $193 billion in 1943, and to $214 billion in 1945. Civilian employment increased by eight million

workers, to some fifty-four million, between 1939 and 1944, at the same time that the armed forces mushroomed from one-third of a million to 11.5 million. Unemployment virtually vanished, falling to just 1.2 percent in 1944. National income soared from $73 billion in 1939 to $183 billion in 1944. And as the United States prospered, the economies of the other major nations were distorted and damaged by the war. In 1947, the United States produced about half of the world's manufactured goods, three-fifths of the world's oil and steel, and four-fifths of the world's automobiles. Such newer industries as aviation, petrochemicals, and electronics also grew in size and importance because of the war—as did new technologies in those and

Dante Electrical Company in Connecticut, pictured in 1942, was one of many small factories around the country that joined the war production effort in the early 1940s. FRANKLIN DELANO ROOSEVELT LIBRARY

other areas, including computers. One leading economic historian has argued that such American economic dominance was perhaps "the most influential consequence of the Second World War for the postwar world."

World War II thus brought the return of good times for the American people and laid foundations for the unparalleled prosperity of the postwar era. Even allowing for wartime inflation and shortages, the new employment opportunities and higher incomes produced increased consumer spending and rising living standards. And while there was very little redistribution of income during the war, personal income increased so dramatically—it nearly

doubled among the lowest 40 percent of families—that it seemed to many that the war had worked a revolutionary change in their circumstances and aspirations. Wartime shortages of workers also led employers to hire women, African Americans, and other groups in larger numbers and better positions than before. In addition to their wartime training and experiences, armed forces personnel received important educational and economic benefits from the G.I. bill.

Economic mobilization not only produced widespread prosperity, rising living standards, and new opportunities, but also helped to enhance and institutionalize the economic and political power of

President Franklin D. Roosevelt signs the declaration of war against Japan on December 8, 1941. NATIONAL ARCHIVES AND RECORDS ADMINISTRATION

big business, big farming, and big labor. In manufacturing, defense contracts tended to go to corporate giants with a demonstrated capacity for high-volume, high-quality production. Just thirty-three firms won more than half of all prime war contracts awarded from 1940 to 1944. The proportion of workers employed by businesses with 10,000 workers or more rose from 13 to 30 percent of the total. Working with the military, in an early manifestation of what came to be called the "military-industrial complex," big business resisted spreading war contracts around more, lobbied successfully for curtailing antitrust efforts, and helped prevent early reconversion to peacetime production by smaller firms.

Mobilizing the economy was achieved more by government support and subsidy than by controls and coercion. Though federal power over materials, priorities, manpower, and production increased significantly during the war, expansion was facilitated by such assistance to business as tax breaks, subsidies, low-cost loans, and contracts that guaranteed the cost of production plus a profit. War contractors also received federal assistance in postwar demobilization. To bring needed experience and expertise to economic mobilization, moreover, executives from such business giants as General Motors, U.S. Steel, General Electric, and Sears, Roebuck were brought to Washington and played key roles in the war mobilization agencies. These "dollar-a-year men," who remained on their corporate payrolls while accepting a nominal salary from the government, further augmented the influence of big business. In all, big business emerged from the war with its reputation enhanced and with enlarged economic and political power.

Organized labor and big commercial farmers also experienced gains during the war. Membership in American Federation of Labor (AFL) and Congress of Industrial Organizations (CIO) unions rose by about 50 percent during the war, and AFL and CIO leaders played significant roles in wartime mobilization agencies, though without the same influence as business. Big commercial farmers represented by the "farm bloc" in Congress saw that farm prices received relatively high ceilings in the wartime price control efforts. To make up for the loss of farm labor, more farmers turned to mechanization, which contributed to the ongoing depopulation of parts of rural America and to the consolidation of large commercial farming. The growing size and influence of big business, big labor, and big farming gave clearer shape to the modern American political economy that had been emerging over the previous half century.

So also did the larger size, power, and cost of the federal government. To manage wartime economic mobilization and organize the material, manpower, and money needed to win the war, the number of civilian employees of the federal government quadrupled, to some four million. Such agencies as the War Production Board (WPB), the Office of Price Administration (OPA), the Office of Economic Stabilization (OES), the National War Labor Board (NWLB), the War Manpower Commission (WMC), the Office of Scientific Research and Development (OSRD), the Office of War Mobilization (OWM), and the Office of War Mobilization and Reconversion (OWMR) greatly increased the power of the federal government over virtually every aspect of the economy. The mobilization agencies got off to a slow and stumbling start, but by 1943 became far more efficient and expanded federal power over the economy well beyond what the New Deal had done. Wartime agencies and powers were curtailed in the postwar era—but in 1950, the federal government had two million civilian workers, twice the 1940 level. To finance war mobilization, annual federal expenditures rose from $9 billion to nearly $98 billion between 1939 and 1945. In all, the government spent some $300 billion during the war—twice as much as in all its previous history going back to 1789.

Less than half of federal spending was financed by taxation, but that required an enormous effort that profoundly and permanently changed the tax system. Wartime taxation, especially the Revenue Act of 1942, greatly expanded the reach of the tax system, as the number of taxable individual incomes rose from four million in 1939 to almost forty-three million by 1945. With so many more people paying taxes, the government introduced the withholding system. And for the first time, individual income taxes became a larger source of federal revenues than corporate taxes—another pattern that continued into the postwar era.

But the greater part of wartime spending was financed by borrowing, through war bonds and other devices. And by underwriting full-production, full-employment prosperity, the massive deficits—of some $50 billion in each of three years, a sum amount twelve times the highest deficit of the New Deal years of the 1930s—corroborated the arguments of John Maynard Keynes. Keynesian economic analysis had maintained that large-scale, purposeful deficit spending could stimulate economic growth and produce full-employment prosperity. Keynesian analysis became increasingly central to economic theory and government policy, and the new tax system of the war years enabled government fiscal policy—taxes and spending—to be implemented more quickly and easily.

Wartime prosperity had other political implications as well. For one thing, it helped reorient liberal policy. Partly because of some of the inefficiencies and the business domination of wartime mobilization agencies, liberals became less attracted to microeconomic planning and regulation, and, as deficit spending produced full-fledged prosperity, they become more attracted to macroeconomic policy to achieve full-production and full-employment prosperity by means of Keynesian fiscal policy. Liberals proposed expensive and expansive social programs that might produce both reform and prosperity. But the return of prosperity made Depression-era social welfare policies seem less necessary and less attractive to many Americans, and wartime prosperity and frustrations produced striking Republican gains in the 1942 elections that made a congressional conservative coalition of Republicans and conservative (mostly southern) Democrats more powerful. The conservative coalition stymied social reform—except for the enormously important G.I. Bill—and remained in control of the Congress in the postwar era.

See Also: EUROPE, GREAT DEPRESSION IN.

BIBLIOGRAPHY

Brinkley, Alan. *The End of Reform: New Deal Liberalism in Recession and War.* 1995.

Fearon, Peter. *War, Prosperity, and Depression: The U.S. Economy 1917–45.* 1987.

Janeway, Eliot. *The Struggle for Survival: A Chronicle of Economic Mobilization in World War II.* 1951.

Jeffries, John W. *Wartime America: The World War II Home Front.* 1996.

Koistinen, Paul A. C. *The Military Industrial Complex: A Historical Perspective.* 1980.

Milward, Alan S. *War, Economy, and Society: 1939–1945.* 1977.

Stein, Herbert. *The Fiscal Revolution in America.* 1969.

Vatter, Harold G. *The U.S. Economy in World War II.* 1985.

JOHN W. JEFFRIES

WPA. *See* WORKS PROGRESS ADMINISTRATION.

Richard Wright, 1943. LIBRARY OF CONGRESS, PRINTS & PHOTOGRAPHS DIVISION, FSA/OWI COLLECTION

WRIGHT, RICHARD

Born near Roxie, Mississippi, in 1908, Richard Nathaniel Wright (September 4, 1908–November 28, 1960) became one of America's foremost chroniclers of African-American life under segregation. The son of a sharecropper and a schoolteacher, Wright spent a grim childhood in Mississippi. He detailed his attempts to retain individual dignity in the face of poverty and racism in the autobiographical *Black Boy* (1945). Valedictorian of his ninth-grade class, Wright received little further formal education. A voracious reader, he was influenced by contemporary literary naturalists and modernists, such as Sinclair Lewis, Theodore Dreiser, and James T. Farrell, as well as the critic H. L. Mencken.

In 1927 Wright joined the great migration of black southerners to Chicago, where he worked as a delivery boy, dishwasher, and a post office clerk, a job he lost after the economy soured in 1930. Wright began to produce poetry and fiction, the bulk of which details the corrosive effects of southern racism. Conditions in Chicago acquainted Wright with the northern face of Jim Crow. While black Chicagoans did not face the threats of physical violence so common in the Deep South, they were segregated on Chicago's South Side, where they paid high rents for bleak ghetto housing. Wright attended meetings of the John Reed Club, read Marxist theory, and joined the Communist Party in 1932. He published poetry and short fiction in progressive magazines such as *Left Front, Anvil,* and *New Masses.* In 1935 Wright was hired by the WPA's Federal Writers' Project to help research the Illinois volume in the American Guide series. He also worked for the Negro Federal Theatre of Chicago, a division of the Federal Theatre Project. In 1937 he moved to New York, where he became editor of the Harlem-based *Daily Worker,* a Communist newspaper. Wright's work in the 1930s and 1940s revealed to white Americans the frustration that black Americans felt toward poverty and racism. One of his best-known essays, "The Ethics of Living Jim Crow," was published in *American Stuff: WPA Writers' Anthology* (1937).

In 1940 Wright published his first novel, *Native Son,* which gained critical and popular success. Set in Chicago, the novel traces the life of Bigger Thomas from his encounters with racism, both paternalistic and violent, through his flirtation with radical politics, to his accidental murder of his white employer's daughter. Wright's fiction was influenced by Marxian materialism and the work of contemporary sociologists. Wright portrayed a society riven by class tensions exacerbated by racism. Wright's characters, like most Americans of the Depression years, seem buffeted by economic, social, and political forces beyond their control.

During World War II, Wright broke with the Communist Party, but he continued to be critical of American racism. In 1947, Wright became an expatriate in France, where he was joined by other major black writers, including James Baldwin and Ralph Ellison. Wright's later works did not enjoy the critical or financial success he had met in the 1930s and

1940s, although his reputation as one of America's major twentieth-century writers is secure. He died in France in 1960.

See Also: AFRICAN AMERICANS, IMPACT OF THE GREAT DEPRESSION ON; HUGHES, LANGSTON; LITERATURE.

BIBLIOGRAPHY

Baldwin, James. "Everybody's Protest Novel." In *Notes of a Native Son.* 1955.

Barnes, Deborah. "'I'd Rather Be a Lamppost in Chicago': Richard Wright and the Chicago Renaissance of African American Literature." *The Langston Hughes Review* 14 (1996): 52–61.

Fabre, Michel. *The Unfinished Quest of Richard Wright,* rev. edition, translated by Isabel Barzun. 1993.

Gayle, Addison. *Richard Wright: Ordeal of a Native Son.* 1980.

Rowley, Hazel. *Richard Wright: The Life and Times.* 2001.

TRENT A. WATTS

ZANUCK, DARRYL F. *See* "GRAPES OF WRATH, THE."

BACKMATTER

TIMELINE

1893–1898: Panic of 1893, the worst economic collapse in American history prior to 1929.

1913: Henry Ford introduces the moving assembly line in production of his automobiles, pointing the way toward an economy of mass production that will require the stimulation of mass consumption.

1914–1918: World War I severely disrupts the international economy, distorts international trade, transforms the United States into the world's leading creditor nation, prompts overproduction in American agriculture, and leads to the development of techniques of mass persuasion that will be used in advertising in the 1920s.

1919: Versailles Peace Conference demands huge reparations from Germany.

1920–21: Severe postwar deflation and economic recession.

1923–24: Hyperinflation in Germany.

1925–26: Florida real estate bubble.

1928–29: Great Bull Market on Wall Street. Speculators push stock prices far above their realistic values.

November 6, 1928: Herbert Hoover is elected president of the United States.

October 24–29, 1928: Stock Market Crash, followed by continuing severe decline through mid-November.

1930: Grant Wood paints *American Gothic*.

1930: Repatriation programs begin to deport Mexican immigrants.

1930: Dashiell Hammett's *The Maltese Falcon* is published.

June 17, 1930: Hawley-Smoot Tariff is enacted, raising duties on products imported into the United States.

1931: Empire State Building in New York is completed.

January 1931: Gangster movie *Little Caesar* released.

March 25, 1931: Scottsboro Boys arrested. Nine black men are accused of raping two white women in Alabama, beginning a celebrated legal battle.

May 1931: Austrian Kreditanstalt collapses, precipitating a financial crisis in central Europe.

July 1931: Donatbank in Germany goes bankrupt, leading to closure of all German banks.

February 2, 1932: Reconstruction Finance Corporation established to provide loans to banks and other financial institutions.

March 23, 1932: Norris-LaGuardia Act prohibits injunctions against strikes and boycotts.

May–July 1932: "Bonus Army" of World War I veterans comes to Washington to demand immediate payment of a bonus Congress had enacted in 1924. Troops forcibly evict the group on July 28.

June 30, 1932: Franklin D. Roosevelt wins Democratic nomination for president.

July 2, 1932: Roosevelt accepts the Democratic nomination in a speech in which he pledges himself to a "new deal" for the American people.

October 1932: Recording of "Brother, Can You Spare a Dime?" The song became an anthem for Depression victims.

November 8, 1932: Franklin D. Roosevelt is elected president in a landslide over Herbert Hoover.

November 11, 1932: *I Am a Fugitive from a Chain Gang* released.

1933: Elaborate Busby Berkeley musicals score big at the box office.

January 30, 1933: Adolf Hitler becomes chancellor of Germany.

February–March 1933: Banking crisis in which runs on banks force bank failures and several states proclaim "bank holidays," closing the banks statewide. Almost all banks in the nation are closed by March 4.

March 4, 1933: Franklin D. Roosevelt inaugurated as president, asks for powers similar to those he would be given in a war.

March 9, 1933: Emergency Banking Act gives the government the power to reopen banks once they are declared secure.

March 12, 1933: Roosevelt addresses the nation by radio in his first "fireside chat."

March 31, 1933: Civilian Conservation Corps (CCC) established, providing reforestation and conservation work for unemployed young men.

April 19, 1933: United States officially abandons the gold standard.

May 12, 1933: Federal Emergency Relief Act (FERA) appropriates $500 million to aid states in providing relief payments.

May 12, 1933: Agricultural Adjustment Act enacted with the purpose of raising prices and farm income by cutting excess production.

May 18, 1933: Tennessee Valley Authority established to improve life in the impoverished region through planning, the provision of hydroelectric power, flood and erosion control, and other means.

May 27, 1933: Federal Securities Act requires full disclosures when new securities are issued.

June 12–July 27, 1933: London Economic Conference fails to agree on international approach to fighting the Depression.

June 13, 1933: Home Owners' Loan Act provides for federal refinancing of mortgages on homes.

June 16, 1933: National Industrial Recovery Act (NIRA) establishes the National Recovery Administration (NRA) to set up codes of fair competition in industries and establishes the Public Works Administration (PWA) to construct public buildings, roads, etc.

June 16, 1933: Glass-Steagall Banking Act separates investment banking from commercial banking and creates the Federal Deposit Insurance Corporation (FDIC) to guarantee bank deposits.

June 16, 1933: Farm Credit Act provides for the reorganization of credit for farmers.

September 30, 1933: Dr. Francis Townsend's letter outlining his proposal for an old-age pension system is published in the *Long Beach Press-Telegram*.

October 18, 1933: Commodity Credit Corporation (CCC) set up to make loans to farmers on their crops.

November 8, 1933: Civil Works Administration (CWA) established to provide work relief for millions of the unemployed.

January 1, 1934: Frank Capra's film *It Happened One Night* is released.

June 6, 1934: Securities Exchange Act establishes the Securities Exchange Commission (SEC) to regulate the operation of the stock market.

June 18, 1934: Wheeler-Howard (Indian Reorganization) Act is passed, starting the Indian New Deal.

June 19, 1934: Communications Act sets up the Federal Communications Commission (FCC) to regulate radio and other electronic communication.

June 19, 1934: National Labor Relations Board (NLRB) established.

June 28, 1934: National Housing Act creates the Federal Housing Administration (FHA) to insure loans for home building.

July 1934: Southern Tenant Farmers Union (STFU) formed.

July 16, 1934: San Francisco General Strike begins.

August 1934: American Liberty League formed to oppose the New Deal.

August 28, 1934: Upton Sinclair wins the Democratic nomination for governor of California on his socialist "End Poverty in California" platform.

November 6, 1934: Congressional elections give Democrats an additional nine seats in each house of Congress; Sinclair defeated in California.

March 19, 1935: Race riot is touched off in the Harlem area of New York City when false rumors spread that a policeman had killed an African-American boy.

April 8, 1935: Emergency Relief Appropriation Act provides $4.8 billion for relief, most of which goes to the new Works Progress Administration (WPA).

May 1, 1935: Resettlement Administration (RA) set up to assist impoverished families by resettling them on productive land.

May 11, 1935: Rural Electrification Administration (REA) established to provide electricity to rural areas on the nation.

May 27, 1935: In the case of *Schecter Poultry Corp. v. U.S.*, the Supreme Court unanimously invalidates the National Recovery Administration (NRA).

June 19, 1935: Roosevelt sends "Wealth Tax" message to Congress calling for changes to reverse the concentration of wealth and economic power.

June 26, 1935: National Youth Administration (NYA) set up to assist people aged 16–25.

July 5, 1935: National Labor Relations Act (Wagner Act) provides protections for workers seeking to organize unions.

August 14, 1935: Social Security Act establishes a system of old-age pensions, unemployment compensation, and aid to dependent children.

August 28, 1935: Public Utility Holding Company Act (Wheeler-Rayburn Act) restricts the use of holding companies in the ownership of utilities.

September 8, 1935: Senator Huey P. Long assassinated in Baton Rouge.

November 9, 1935: Committee for Industrial Organization (CIO, later Congress of Industrial Organizations) is formed to promote unionization of mass production industries.

February 1936: John Maynard Keynes's *General Theory of Employment, Interest, and Money* is published.

February 5, 1936: Charlie Chaplin's film *Modern Times* is released.

June 27, 1936: In a speech accepting his renomination, Roosevelt attacks "economic royalists."

June 30, 1936: Margaret Mitchell's novel *Gone with the Wind* is published.

July 17, 1936: Spanish Civil War begins.

August 1936: African-American athlete Jesse Owens wins four gold medals at The Olympic Games in Berlin, confounding Hitler's racial views.

November 3, 1936: Roosevelt defeats Republican Alfred Landon by an extraordinary margin, winning all but two states.

December 30, 1936: Sit-down strike against General Motors begins in Flint, Michigan.

January 20, 1937: Roosevelt gives second inaugural address, in which he speaks of "one-third of a nation ill-housed, ill-clad, ill-nourished."

February 5, 1937: Roosevelt submits to Congress his plan to reorganize the judiciary, beginning the fight over court-packing.

February 10, 1937: General Motors agrees to a contract with the United Auto Workers (UAW), ending the sit-down strike.

March 2, 1937: U. S. Steel Corporation recognizes and signs an agreement with the Steel Workers' Organizing Committee (SWOC) without a strike.

May 30, 1937: Memorial Day Massacre of union members outside the Republic Steel plant in South Chicago.

July 2, 1937: Aviator Amelia Earhart disappears over the Pacific during attempted around-the-world flight.

July 22, 1937: Bankhead-Jones Farm Tenancy Act establishes the Farm Security Administration (FSA).

August 1937: "Roosevelt Recession" of 1937–38 begins.

September 1, 1937: National Housing Act (Wagner-Steagall Act) creates the U.S. Housing Authority to assist in providing housing for low-income people.

December 1937: Publication of report by La Follette Civil Liberties Committee in the Senate details tactics used by anti-union employers.

December 21, 1937: Walt Disney's *Snow White* is released.

February 16, 1938: Agricultural Adjustment Act of 1938 revived the AAA of 1933 in a form that avoided the problems that had led to the earlier act being declared unconstitutional.

June 1938: *Superman* comics begin.

June 16, 1938: Temporary National Economic Committee (TNEC) is formed to investigate concentration and monopoly in business.

June 25, 1938: Fair Labor Standards Act provides for a minimum wage and a maximum number of working hours and outlaws child labor.

October 31, 1938: Orson Welles radio broadcast of *War of the Worlds* touches off a panic about Martians landing in New Jersey.

November 7, 1938: Kristallnacht, the "Night of Broken Glass" in which Nazi thugs, encouraged by the government, looted and vandalized Jewish homes, businesses and synagogues across Germany.

November 8, 1938: Congressional elections bring significant gains for Republicans, but maintain large majorities in both houses.

1939: Film versions of *Gone with the Wind* and *The Wizard of Oz* are released.

1939: Frank Capra's *Mr. Smith Goes to Washington* and John Ford's *Stagecoach* present moviegoers with pre-capitalist values.

February 6, 1939: Raymond Chandler's *The Big Sleep* is published.

February 18, 1939: Golden Gate Exposition in San Francisco opens.

April 3, 1939: Administrative Reorganization Act rearranged and reorganized the units within the executive branch of government.

April 9, 1939: Marian Anderson gives free concert for seventy-five thousand at the Lincoln Memorial after the Daughters of the American Revolution deny her use of Constitution Hall.

April 14, 1939: John Steinbeck's *The Grapes of Wrath* is published.

April 30, 1939: New York World's Fair opens.

August 2, 1939: The Hatch Act prohibits federal officials from participating in political campaigns.

August 24, 1939: Nazi-Soviet nonaggression pact opens the way for World War II.

September 1, 1939: German invasion of Poland starts World War II.

1940: Richard Wright's *Native Son* is published.

January 1940: Frank Capra's film version of *The Grapes of Wrath* is released.

July 18, 1940: Franklin Roosevelt is nominated for a third term as president.

November 5, 1940: Roosevelt defeats Republican Wendell Willkie to win an unprecedented third term as president.

1941: Military production in preparation for World War II brings the Great Depression to an end.

May 1, 1941: Orson Welles' film *Citizen Kane* is released.

INDEX

Page numbers are sequential from volume to volume. Volume 1 is comprised of pages 1–544; volume 2 pages 545–1075. Page numbers in boldface indicate the main article on the subject. Those in italics indicate illustrations, figures and tables.

Volume 1 pp: 1–544; Volume 2 pp: 545–1075.

Volume 1 pp: 1–544; Volume 2 pp: 545–1075.

Volume 1 pp: 1–544; Volume 2 pp: 545–1075.

Volume 1 pp: 1–544; Volume 2 pp: 545–1075.

Volume 1 pp: 1–544; Volume 2 pp: 545–1075.

Volume 1 pp: 1–544; Volume 2 pp: 545–1075.

Volume 1 pp: 1–544; Volume 2 pp: 545–1075.

Volume 1 pp: 1–544; Volume 2 pp: 545–1075.

Innovation, 866–868

Institute for Social and Religious Research, 895

Insull, Samuel, **510,** 780–781. *See also* Stock market crash (1929)

Insurance

crop, 337–339

mortgage, 344–345

Insurrection law, 435

Interdepartmental Group Concerned with the Special Problems of Negroes, 1018–1019

Interior, Department of the, 205, 783, 1036–1037

Interior, Secretary of the, 496–498, 499, 968–969

International Bank for Reconstruction and Development, 516

International Brigades, 1, 924

International finance, 151

International impact of the Great Depression, **510–516.** *See also specific countries and regions by name*

Internationalism, 752, 934–935

International Labor Defense (ILD), 198, 435, **516–517,** 683, 870–872. *See also* Communist Party

International Ladies' Garment Workers' Union (ILGWU), 199, 247, **517–520,** *518. See also* Organized labor

International lending, 512–513, 514–515

International Longshoremen's and Warehousemen's Union, 120, 520–521

International Longshoremen's Association (ILA), 120, **520–521,** 863–864, 942–943. *See also* Organized labor

International Match Company, 219

International Monetary Fund (IMF), 516, 539

International Olympic Committee, 733, 734

International Planned Parenthood Federation, 865

International Red Aid, 516

International Style (architecture), 61, 62

International Sugar Agreement (1937), 74

International trade, 155, 402

International Unemployment Day, 491

International Workers Order, 932

Interpretation of the Great Depression. *See* History, interpretation, and memory of the Great Depression

Interstate commerce, 525, 703, 955–956

Interstate Oil and Gas Compact (1935), 1037

Investment banking, 395–396

Iowa Farmers' Union, 318

I Saw Hitler! (Thompson), 981

Isolationism, **521–523.** *See also* World Court

Coughlin, Charles, 214, 215

Ethiopian War, 299, 522

Johnson, Hugh, 531

Lindbergh, Charles, 579

Roosevelt, Franklin D., 847

Wheeler, Burton K., 1041

World Court, 1068–1069

Italian Americans, 300, 329, 790

Italy. *See also* Europe, Great Depression in

dictatorship, 236

Ethiopian War, 299, 300

fascism, 329, *329*

gold standard, 667

World War II and the ending of the Depression, 667

It Happened One Night, 145, 145–146

Ivory Coast, 4–5

J

Jackson, Kenneth, 474

Jackson, Robert, **525–526,** 951–952, 956. *See also* Supreme Court

Jacobsson, Sten, *68*

Jahncke, Ernest Lee, 733

Jamieson, Stuart, 633

Japan, 73–74, 74–75, 329. *See also* Asia, Great Depression in

Japanese Americans, *76*, 790

Jarrett, Eleanor Holm, 734

Jazz, 63–64, 400–401, **526–529,** *527, 528,* 663–664. *See also* Big band music; Music; *specific musicians by name*

JCNR. *See* Joint Committee for National Recovery (JCNR)

Jeansonne, Glen, 589

Jemison, Alice Lee, 503

Jenkins, Benjamin, 1011

Jersey City, N.J., 419–420

Jewish Americans, 681, 790, 808–809, 811

Jews without Money (Gold), 580

Jitterbug dance, 526, 575

Jive talk, 528

Johnson, Charles S., 791–792

Johnson, Cornelius, 734

Johnson, Edwin, 1031–1032, 1034, 1037

Johnson, Genora, 1056

Johnson, Hiram, 521, 1068

Johnson, Hugh, **529–531.** *See also* National Recovery Administration (NRA)

and Baruch, Bernard, 93–94

National Industrial Recovery Act, 529–530, 677, 678

National Recovery Administration, 126, 530, 531, 684–687, 688

Johnson, James Weldon, 51

Johnson, Lyndon B., 213, **531–532,** 1067

Johnson, Rev. Mordecai, 480, 481

Johnson, Philip, 61, 62

Johnson, Reginald, 62

Johnson, Robert, 610, 662–663

Johnson Debt Default Act (1934), 521

Johnson-O'Malley Act (1934), 189

Johnson-Reed Immigration Act, 55–56

Johnson v. Zerbst (1938), 179–180

Johnston, Oscar G., 192

Johnstone, Alan, 1065

Joint Committee for National Recovery (JCNR), **532–533,** 671, 690

Joint WPA Folklore Committee, 368

Jolson, Al, 393

Jonah's Gourd Vine (Hurston), 493

Volume 1 pp: 1–544; Volume 2 pp: 545–1075.

Murray, Donald Gaines, 180, 640

Murray, Matthew, 1065

Murray, Philip, **656**, 932, 933. *See also* Congress of Industrial Organizations (CIO); Steel Workers' Organizing Committee (SWOC)

Murray, William, 1032, 1037

Muscle Shoals, Ala.

federal development of, 281–282, 972, 973, *976*

Norris, George, 719

public power, 780

Museum of Modern Art (MoMA)

Cahill, Holger, 133

documentary film, 240

Evans, Walker, 306, 757

federal art show, 68

museums, art, 657

photography, 757

Museums, art, **656–658**. *See also* Art

Museums and monuments, historic, **658–660**. *See also* American Guide series

Music, **660–665,** *661, 662, 663. See also* Jazz; *specific musicians by name*

African Americans in, 47–48

Anderson, Marian, 47–48, *48*

Armstrong, Louis, 63–64

blues and jazz, *662,* 662–664

classical music, 665

country music, 664

folk music and the WPA, *663,* 664

Music education, *346, 347, 350, 663*

Mussolini, Benito, **665–667,** *666. See also* Fascism

dictatorship, 236

Ethiopian War, 299, 300

fascism, 329, *329*

Spanish Civil War, 923, 924

Muste, A. J., **668**, 998. *See also* Peace movement

Musteites, 492, 668, 894

Mutual Broadcasting System, 793

Mutualistas, 568

MWAK Company, 409

My America: 1928–1938 (Adamic), 2, 581

"My Day" column, 833, 1053

Myers, William I., 317

My First Days in the White House (Long), 589

My Man Godfrey, 487

Myrdal, Gunnar, 124, 752, 799

The Myth of TVA (Chandler), 978

N

NAACP. *See* National Association for the Advancement of Colored People (NAACP)

Nabrit, James, 480

NAM. *See* National Association of Manufacturers (NAM)

Nanton, Sam, 294

Natchez, Miss., caste and class, 150

Nathan, Robert, 845

National American Woman Suffrage Association, 1055

National Association for the Advancement of Colored People (NAACP), **669–672**. *See also* African Americans, impact of the Great Depression on

anti-lynching legislation, 51–52, 180, 593, 594

Du Bois, W. E. B., 248, 249

Houston, Charles, 479

and Joint Committee for National Recovery, 532–533

Legal Defense Fund, 479

legal profession, 573

lynching, 45–46

Missouri ex rel. Gaines v. Canada (1938), 640

and National Negro Congress, 683

Scottsboro case, 870, 871, 872

White, Walter, 669–670, 671, 1043–1044

National Association of Manufacturers (NAM), **672,** *673, 1059. See also* Businessmen

National Association of Real Estate Boards, 967

National Association of Securities Dealers, 875

National Bituminous Coal Commission (NBCC), 414, 415

National Broadcasting Company (NBC), 793, 796, 811

National Bureau of Economic Research, 759

National Campaign to End Public Lands Grazing, 969

National City Bank (New York, N.Y.), 747

National Commission on Law Observance and Enforcement, 773

National Committee on Care of Transient and Homeless, 986–987, 988

National Committee on the Cause and Cure of War, 746

National Committee to Abolish the Poll Tax, **672–674**. *See also* Southern Conference for Human Welfare (SCHW)

National Consumers' League, 600–601

National Council for the Prevention of War, 746

National Council of Negro Women, 97

National Credit Corporation, 804

National Defense Act (1920), 633

National Defense Housing Act (1940), 1012–1013

National Education Association Joint Committee on the Emergency in Education, 269–270

National Emergency Council, 853

National Farmers Union (NFU), **674–675,** 1024–1025. *See also* Agriculture

National Federation for Constitutional Liberties, 683

National Federation of Business and Professional Women's Clubs, 691

National Firearms Act (1934), 570

National Football League, 926

National Frontier Defense Act, 634

National Gallery of Art, 60–61, 605

National Housing Act (1934), 348, 355, **675**. *See also* Federal Housing Administration (FHA); Housing

National Housing Agency, 1011

National Hunger March, 107

Volume 1 pp: 1–544; Volume 2 pp: 545–1075.

Oxley, Lawrence A., 1018

P

Pace Act (1944), 856

Pacifica (Stackpole), 398

Pact of Steel (1939), 667

Panay (ship), 636

Panics, banking. *See* Banking panics (1930–1933)

Paris Peace Conference, 538

Park, Robert E., 791

Parker, Bonnie. *See* Bonnie and Clyde (Bonnie Parker and Clyde Barrow)

Parker, George, 646

Parker, John J., 669–670

Parker Brothers, 645, *646*, 646–647

Parks, Gordon, *97, 485, 753, 827*

Parrish, West Coast Hotel v. (1937), 484, 955, 958

Partisan Review, 600, 716

Paterson, N.J., substandard housing, *171*

Patman, Wright, 107, 109, **745–746.** *See also* Bonus Army/Bonus March

Patterson, Haywood, *871, 872. See also* Scottsboro case

Patterson, James, 706

Paul, Alice Stokes, 690, 691

Pavy, Benjamin Henry, 589

Pay Your Taxes campaign, 968

Peace Mission movement, 14, 330–331

Peace movement, 41–42, 668, **746–747,** 894

Pearson, F. A., 643

PECE. *See* President's Emergency Committee for Employment (PECE)

Pecora, Ferdinand, 647, **747,** 873, 874, 940. *See also* Securities regulation

Pecora Committee, 125, 647

Peek, George N., 20, 93–94, 225, 529, 802–803, 992

Pegler, Westbrook, 892–893

Pelley, William, 53, 810

Pells, Richard, 506

Pendergast, Tom, **748,** 1065. *See also* Democratic Party

Pendleton Act (1883), 426

Penicillin, 867

Pennsylvania, 406

Penny auctions, 318–319, 321, 638, 1009

Pennypacker, Mrs. Percy, *749*

"Penny stock market," 874

Pension plans, 142, 982–984, 1028

Pentecostal church, 809, *809,* 812

The People's Front (Browder), 766

The People, Yes (Sandburg), 582

Pepper, Claude, 674, **748–749.** *See also* Democratic Party

Perelman, S. J., 1040

Perhaps Women (Anderson), 49

Perisphere, at New York World's Fair, 717

Perkins, Frances, *749,* **749–751.** *See also* Organized labor

    Black thirty-hour bill, 105

    National Industrial Recovery Act, 676, 677

    National Women's Party, 691

    old-age insurance, 731

    Social Security Act, 901

    and social workers, 904

Permanent Court of International Justice, 521–522, 833, 1067–1069

Perry, Clarence, 413

Petersen, Hjalmar, 638

Peterson, Harry, 639

Petroleum Administration, 499

Philadelphia, Pa., relief efforts, 160, 295–296, 722

Philadelphia Savings Fund Society Building, 61

Philanthropy, **751–752,** 869. *See also* Charity; *specific foundations by name*

Philippines, 74. *See also* Asia, Great Depression in

Photography, 327, **752–757,** *753, 754, 755, 756. See also specific photographers by name*

Picture essays, 755

Piece rates, 519

Pittman, Key, 1068–1069

Pittsburgh Courier, 1018, 1019

Planned Parenthood Federation of America, 865

Planning, 688–689, **757–762,** 992. *See also* National Resources Planning Board (NRPB); Regional Planning Association of America (RPAA)

Plan Orange, 636

"Plan to End Poverty in California." *See* End Poverty in California (EPIC)

Platt, Stephen, 950

Plessy v. Ferguson (1896), 640, 670

The Plow that Broke the Plains, 195, 241, 850

Poetry, 484, 485, **762–764.** *See also* Literature; Popular Front

Poland, and Nazi-Soviet Pact, 699, 700

"Policy Analysis: Alcohol Prohibition was a Failure" (Thornton), 570

Political cartoons. *See* Cartoons, political

Political realignment, **764–765.** *See also* Democratic Party; Republican Party

    Democratic Party, 231–232, 764–765

    election of 1934, 283–285, 765

    election of 1936, 289, 765, 846

    New Deal, 709

    Republican Party, 816

Poll tax

    Africa, 4–5, 6

    Asia, 74

    National Committee to Abolish the Poll Tax, 672–674

    Southern Conference for Human Welfare, 919

Polymer science, 869

Poor, "worthy" and "unworthy," 161, 164, 469

Pope, John Russell, 60–61, 660

Popular Front, **765–766.** *See also* Communist Party

    Browder, Earl, 123

    consumerism, 210

    Culture and the Crisis, 221

    Dos Passos, John, 245

    Guthrie, Woody, 416

    Hollywood and the film industry, 451

Volume 1 pp: 1–544; Volume 2 pp: 545–1075.

Report on the Economic Conditions of the South, 814

and Robinson, Joseph, *830*

and Roosevelt, Eleanor, 833–834, 838, 842, *842*

and Ryan, John A., 861

securities regulation, 873, 874

silver, 73

and Sinclair, Upton, 298

and Smith, Al, 843

and Smith, Alfred E., 891, *891*

Social Security Act, 900–901

and Stalin, Joseph, *930*

state utility regulatory commission, 972

and Stimson, Henry, 935

strikes, 944, 945

Supreme Court, 951–952

Supreme Court "packing" controversy, 846–847, 957–958, 959

Tammany Hall, 481, 482, 839, 840, 842, 844, 962

taxation, 964–966

Temporary Emergency Relief Administration, New York, 969–970

Temporary National Economic Committee, 971

Tennessee Valley Authority, 972–975, 976, 978

Thomas Amendment, 980–981

and Townsend, Francis, 846

and Truman, Harry S., 848–849

and Tugwell, Rexford G., 991, 992

and Tully, Grace, 993, *994*

unemployment insurance, 1004

United Mine Workers of America, 1010–1011

values, 1017

West, 1037

and White, Walter, 1044

and White, William Allen, 1044

and Willkie, Wendell, 1046–1047

and Wilson, Woodrow, 840, 842

work ethic, 1060

Works Progress Administration, 343, 1061, 1063–1066

World Court, 1068–1069

World War II and the ending of the Depression, 847, *1072*

Roosevelt, James (son of FDR), *833*

Roosevelt, James, Sr. (father of FDR), 838

Roosevelt, Theodore

and Costigan, Edward, 214

and Roosevelt, Eleanor, 832

and Roosevelt, Franklin D., 840, 842

and Roosevelt, James, Sr., 838

and Sinclair, Upton, 882

"Roosevelt recession." *See* Recession of 1937

Root, Elihu, 1068

Rosenman, Samuel I., 115–116. *See also* Brain(s) Trust

Rosenwald Foundation, 995

Rosenwald Fund, 752

Rothstein, Arthur, *92, 754, 775,* **849–851,** *850, 1003. See also* Photography

Rourke, Constance, 486–487

Route 66, **851–852**

RPAA. *See* Regional Planning Association of America (RPAA)

Rubber workers, 201

Rubinow, Isaac, 730, 731

Rukeyser, Muriel, 762

Ruml, Beardsley, 688, 758, 759–760, 801, **852–853.** *See also* Taxation

Rumsey, Mary Harriman, 208, **853.** *See also* National Recovery Administration (NRA)

Runaway shops, 519

Rupee, 72–73

Rural Electrification Administration (REA), **853–857,** *854, 855. See also* Electrification; Public power

agriculture, 24, 25

public power, 779–780

rural life, 860

Rural life, **857–860,** *858, 859. See also* Agriculture; Cities and suburbs

health and nutrition, 428–429, 430, *431*

and social workers, 905

Russell, Richard, 961

Russell Sage Foundation, 759

Ryan, John A., **861**

Ryan, Joseph P., 520, 521

S

Saarinen, Eero, 61

Saarinen, Eliel, 61

Sachs, Paul J., 657

Salvation Army, *159*

San, Saya, 74

Sandburg, Carl, 582

San Francisco, and Golden Gate International Exposition, 397–398

San Francisco Examiner, 194

San Francisco general strike (1934), *570,* **863–864,** 942–943

Bridges, Harry, 120

International Longshoremen's Association, 521

Perkins, Frances, 750

West, 1037

San Francisco-Oakland Bay Bridge, 397, 398

Sanger, Margaret, **864–865**

Sanitary Grocery, New Negro Alliance v. (1938), 181

San Joaquin Valley, Calif., and Okies, 728–730

Sarnoff, David, 237

Savings and loans, 354–356

Scarface, 384–385, 448

Schacht, Hjalmar, 446

Schatz, Thomas, 384

Schechter Poultry Corp. v. United States (1935)

Cardozo, Benjamin N., 147

civil rights and civil liberties, 180

Frankfurter, Felix, 377

Hughes, Charles Evans, 483

National Industrial Recovery Act, 126, 678, 687, 955–956

Schlesinger, Arthur, 489

Schlink, F. J., 207–208

Schmeling, Max, 15, 591, 927

Schneiderman, Rose, 776

Schoch, Kathy, 949

Schubert, Herman, 988

Schultz, Dutch, 234

Schutzstaffel, 543–544

SCHW. *See* Southern Conference for Human Welfare (SCHW)

Schwab, Charles M., 723–724

Silver Shirts, 53

Simon, Paul, 1067

Simple Simon (Rodgers and Hart), 487

Simpson, John, 674

Simpson, Russell, *372*

Sinatra, Frank, 662

Since Yesterday: The Nineteen-Thirties in America (Allen), 30

Sinclair, Upton, **882–883.** *See also* End Poverty in California (EPIC); Literature
    election of 1934, 284, 297–298, 882–883
    Hollywood and the film industry, 451
    Socialist Party, 894
    West, 1037

Single tax theory, 646

Sisal, 613–614

Sit-down strikes, **883–886,** *885. See also* General Motors sit-down strike (Flint, Mich.); Strikes
    Congress of Industrial Organizations, 201–202, 945–946
    Firestone, 883
    Midwest, 623
    Reuther, Walter, 823
    Supreme Court, 201, 886
    Woolworth, *884*

Six Companies consortium, 535

"The Skyline," 761

"Slave market," 8, 1051–1052

Slave narratives, **886–890,** *887. See also* Federal Writers' Project (FWP)

Slum clearance projects, 787, *1012, 1013*

Small-town community life, 1016–1017, 1050

Smart Set, 611

Smith, Alfred E., **890–892,** *891*
    election of 1928, 228, 276, 765, 891
    election of 1932, 891
    and Moskowitz, Belle, 651
    and Moskowitz, Henry, 652
    and Perkins, Frances, 750
    Prohibition, 772, 773
    and Raskob, John J., 800

    and Roosevelt, Franklin D., 229, 843, 891, *891*
    suicide of campaign treasurer, 949
    Tammany Hall, 890, 962

Smith, Elder Lucy, 812

Smith, Ellison "Cotton Ed," 291, 1066

Smith, Elna Sorenson, 892

Smith, Gerald L. K., 810, **892,** 1005. *See also* Union Party

Smith, Henry Ladd, 578

Smith, Hilda, 1058

Smith, Kate, 662

Smith, Mulford v. (1939), 954, 955

Smith-Connally Act, 578

Smithsonian Gallery design, 61, 62

Smith v. Allwright (1944), 180

"Smoke Gets in Your Eyes" (Kern), 661

Snell, Bertrand, 490, 1063, 1064

Snow White and the Seven Dwarfs, 238, 392–393, 451, **892–893.** *See also* Disney, Walt; Hollywood and the film industry

SNYC. *See* Southern Negro Youth Congress (SNYC)

Snyder, J. Buell, 414–415

Social Credit Party of Alberta, 141

Social engineering, 479, 480

Socialist Party, **893–895.** *See also* Communist Party
    and American Labor Party, 980
    Ameringer, Oscar, 44–45
    election of 1932, 283
    election of 1936, 288, 289
    hunger marches, 492
    Niebuhr, Reinhold, 718
    peace movement, 746
    Randolph, A. Philip, 797
    Thomas, Norman, 893, 894, 979–980

Social realist artists, 41

Social science, 727–728, 768–769, **895–896**

Social Science Research Council, 759, 768

Social Security Act (1935), **896–904,** *897. See also* Aid to Dependent Children (ADC); Old-age insurance
    amendments (1939), 902–903
    businessmen, 126

Byrd, Harry, 128

CES proposals and Congressional debate, 901–902

children, 163–165

critique, 712

demand for reform, 900–901

Emergency Relief Appropriation Act, 297

government, United States federal, 404–405

Hopkins, Harry, 471

and New Deal legacy, 903

Old Age, Survivors', and Disability Insurance, 898

Old Age Assistance, 896, 902–903

Old Age Insurance, *273, 273–274,* 730, 731, 896–903, 958

Perkins, Frances, 750, 901

Progressive era origins, 898–900

roots, 713

and social workers, 904

and Townsend Plan, 982, 984

Unemployment Insurance, 896, 954, 958, 1004, 1005

work ethic, 1059, 1060

Social Security Board
    Bureau of Public Assistance, 28
    changes to Social Security Act, 903
    migration, 626, 627
    posters, *273, 311, 897*
    Woodward, Ellen, 1057

Social Security Cases (1937), 952

Social workers, **904–905.** *See also* Perkins, Frances

Social Work Today, 905

Society for the Preservation of New England Antiquities, 658, 659

Softball, 928

Soil conservation, 204–205, 253–255

Soil Conservation and Domestic Allotment Act (1936)
    Agricultural Adjustment Administration, 21
    American Farm Bureau Federation, 33
    conservation movement, 205
    farm policy, 324
    government, United States federal, 404
    Supreme Court, 954